WRITING,
REPRESENTATION
AND CRITICISM
IN ARCHITECTURE

SEMI-DETACHED

EDITED BY NAOMI STEAD

4   **NAOMI STEAD** | A Semi-detached Introduction to Commentary on Architecture

CONFERENCE: Writing

19   **KATJA GRILLNER** | A Performative Mode of Writing Place: Out and about the Rosenlund Park, Stockholm, 2008–2010

32   **SALLY BREEN** | It's Not the End of the World But You Can See It From There

40   **LINDA CARROLI** | Placing: Writing place, place writing

49   **ERK GHENOIU** | Writing as Architecture: Theorist practitioners and DIY architecture 1917/1974

61   **DEIRDRE GILFEDDER** | The Invisible House: David Malouf's *12 Edmondstone Street* and a colonial rhetoric of space

68   **STEPHEN FRITH** | *Ekphrasis* and the Writing of Architecture

80   **ANDREW P. STEEN** | Kurilpa Bridge

CONFERENCE: Representation

87   **GAVIN HIPKINS** | I'm There Right Now: Occupying architectural spaces photographically

105   **MATHEW AITCHISON** | Dilettantes, Amateurs and Eccentrics: *The Architectural Review's* Townscape campaign

116   **ARI SELIGMANN** | Reading and Writing the Seattle Public Library, New regimes of architectural (re)presentation

129   **DANICA VAN DE VELDE** | Cinematic Architecture and Subversive Sites: Wong Kar-wai's Hong Kong cityscapes

139   **KATARINA WADSTEIN MACLEOD** | Remembering Home

152   **CATHY SMITH** | Remembering in Red: Architectural followings

CONTENTS

160 **DIANNE PEACOCK** | Ancient Modernists: Junction Dam

166 **JOAN BEDDOE** | Pillars of a Nation: A layperson's journey into photographing and writing architecture for the general public

CONFERENCE: Criticism

175 **NAOMI STEAD** | New Belle-Lettrism

182 **PHILIP GOAD** | Robin Boyd and the Art of Writing Architecture

197 **PAUL HOGBEN** | International Comparison as Critical Strategy

211 **DEBORAH VAN DER PLAAT** | Critical [Re]connections: Oscar Wilde's 'The Critic as Artist' (1891)

221 **JUSTINE CLARK and PAUL WALKER** | Interpretation, Intention and the Work of Architecture

229 **JOHN MACARTHUR** | Sense, Meaning and Taste in Architectural Criticism

PRACTICE

238 **NAOMI STEAD** | Words and Pictures: Communication in architectural practice

240 **SHANNON MCGRATH** | 'It may be that the image outlives the project itself'

244 **JUSTINE CLARK and ANDREW MACKENZIE** | In Conversation

250 **DIANNA SNAPE** | 'The architect's involvement must be considered as an influence'

255 **OLIVIA HYDE and MARCUS TRIMBLE** | In Conversation

260 **PETER BENNETTS** | 'Clarity, to distil a moment'

265 **PAUL OWEN and ELIZABETH WATSON-BROWN** | In Conversation

269 **CHRISTOPHER FREDERICK JONES** | 'The photographer applies a mask to the building'

273 **JILL GARNER and JAN VAN SCHAIK** | In Conversation

277 **BRETT BOARDMAN** | 'We shoot, stuff and exhibit the game'

WORKSHOP

285 **LINDA MARIE WALKER** | Messages of the Wind

290 **ISABEL D'AVILA WINTER** | They Told us They Would be Checking our Papers (Sic): A text under revision

293 **JASON HAIGH** | Horizontality

296 **ANDREW BLYTHE** | Picture Perfect: The home that wasn't

298 **JON HENZELL** | Kurilpa Reach and Northbank

304 **CLAIRE HUMPHREYS** | St Lucia House Film Stills

306 **CHRISTINE DAUBER** | Land Living and Spatiality: My home at The Gap

308 **AUDREY LAM** | Mechanics of Materials (or: Mechanics of Deformable Bodies)

314 **LYNETTE GURR** | The Queen's Land – 2010

317 **VIRGINIA RIGNEY and ALEX CHOMICZ** | Fantasy Island: Suburban dreams on the Isle of Capri

325 **GEORGINA RUSSELL** | Unfixed Collage

328 **SUSAN ROTHNIE** | The Effects of Time

330 Contributor Biographies

335 Acknowledgements

336 Colophon

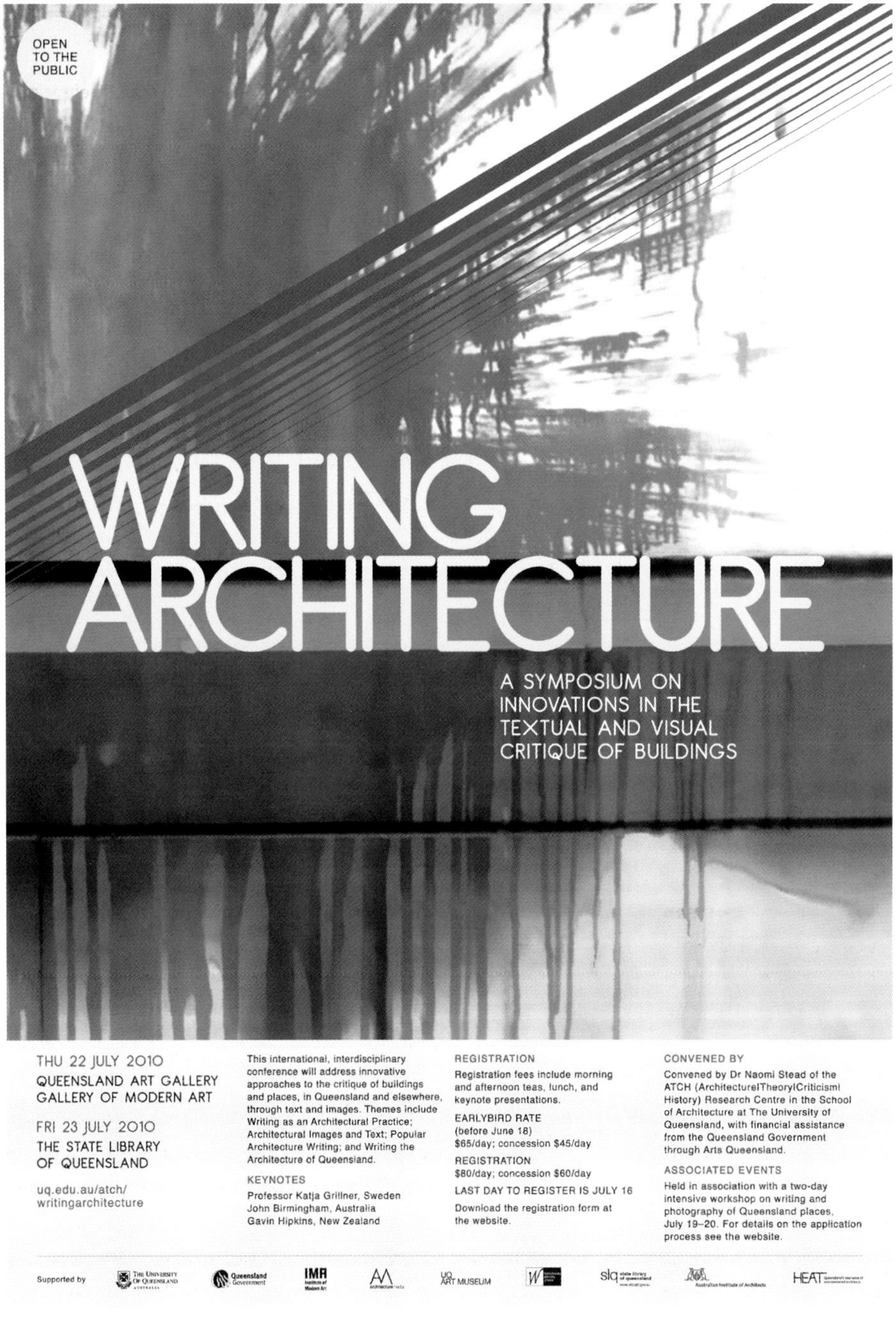

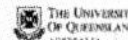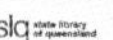

Poster for 'Writing Architecture: A symposium on innovations in the textual and visual critique of buildings', 2010. Design by Cheri Cunningham.

A Semi-detached Introduction to Commentary on Architecture

NAOMI STEAD

Semi-detached: the term refers first to a building type, a pair of dwellings built side by side and sharing a party wall; attached and yet separate, connected yet distinct, the inhabitants' twinned lives mirrored but never touching. But the idea of *being semi-detached*, as a state of mind, especially when contemplating architecture, offers something more. Traditionally, pure detachment was the valued term. It was thought that critical appraisal of any form of art or culture required a certain distance and disinterest – a certain detached persona, if not actual objectivity. Anyone who had an 'interest' in a work was seen to be too attached – with too much at stake to be a good judge of the work's absolute quality or worth, too close to represent it truthfully. Attachment was thus synonymous with relativity and bias. But in fact, there is a particular place for relativity and attachment in the appreciation of architecture, and it takes a unique form for each of architecture's distinct audiences. The architect's particular attachment to a building is very different, for example, from that of the occupants who inhabit it every day, which is different again from the engagements of the professional photographer, the architectural scholar and the specialist architecture critic. Each of these figures has their own specific expertise in architecture, and their own way of conceiving, describing and critiquing it. What is surprising then is that these diverse voices are so seldom heard in the same place, or in conversation.

So what of the idea of being *semi-detached* from architecture: attached and yet separate, connected yet distinct. The act of representing a building or built place, whether in words or pictures or some other medium, brings a certain intimacy and tactility of its own. Writing in, on, around and about architecture brings it close. Could this idea open other ways to consider buildings, other ways to write and represent them, other ways to evaluate and interpret their meanings? That is the project of this book: to examine the very different proximities that, architects, photographers, critics, scholars and members of the lay public, have in relation to buildings, and to encourage a shared space for imagining and describing these attachments, in words and pictures. *Semi-detached* thus refers to a proximity that also holds itself apart from its object; it refers to affective connections to buildings and places, and how we articulate these, just as it considers subjective modes of critical engagement.

In its ubiquity, architecture could be seen as the most 'popular' art of all, in that it surrounds most people for most of every day. Architecture thus finds itself in the paradoxical position of being used and apprehended by an enormous audience, but understood in many competing and divergent ways, including being thought to be irrelevant, elitist and out of touch. Such hierarchies are not unique to architecture, with parallels able to be seen in distinctions between 'high' and 'low' culture more broadly. But here again architecture runs into a conundrum, since 'low' culture is traditionally associated with the popular, in both the pejorative sense of that which is thought to be both intellectually and aesthetically facile, and in the positive sense of being appreciated by a large number of people. If architecture is by definition an elite culture, this condemns it also to perennial unpopularity – and this is a widespread perception, that architecture is reserved for the rich, and it is resented accordingly. These oppositions are strongly evident in perceptions of architecture and architects in the public domain, where they often play out in negative terms – the adage that 'architects make art with other people's money' well summarises the vision of the architect pursuing their own arcane aesthetic ideals at the expense of a building that 'works'.

The culture of architecture is thus sometimes out of sync with the social and cultural conditions in which buildings are occupied and understood, and is often thought to be so. Likewise, the professional culture of architecture tends to be self-enclosed, hermetic, with its own (exclusionary) language, and concerns that are separate from wider practices in popular culture and the arts. The taste of architects and that of the public are sharply out of alignment.

This mismatch was demonstrated for me very clearly in the week leading up to the conference[1] and workshop[2] upon which this book is largely based, in mid-July of 2010. I had been invited to do a short interview on a local Brisbane radio station to promote the events. I tried hard to prepare for the interview, which was for a general audience in a semi-talkback slot – that is, for an audience not accustomed to thinking about architecture in depth and, perhaps, not that interested or convinced of any need for such thought. It seemed to me that speaking to this audience was important, and so was trying to do that on a level that they could understand and that was engaging. After all, the purpose of the larger project that led to the conference and workshop in the first place was to create a space where architects, architecture critics, architecture scholars and the general public could find some middle ground to discuss their ideas and ideals about the built environment. So, in preparing for the interview I read back over my folder of clippings of where architecture had appeared in the popular press in Queensland in the previous few months. As we know, architecture usually appears in one of four places in the newspaper: either in the arts pages, in the real estate section, in an opinion column, or in the news, where it is reported as an event.

I re-read an article that had appeared in Brisbane's *The Courier Mail* newspaper in mid-January of that year.[3] The essay was an opinion piece from Robert MacDonald, the newspaper's 'Viewpoint Editor', arguing that Brisbane is becoming uglier every year, increasingly afflicted with hideous concrete buildings and infrastructure. The article actively solicited comments from readers ('What do you think of your city? Is it getting uglier? Tell us below'), and in the online version the readers had participated in droves – engaging in unruly debate about Brisbane's ugliest buildings, remonstrating with architects, bemoaning the appearance of their city, arguing ferociously amongst themselves about other comparably bad or good cities, and so on. Reading this response to the story I was struck by three things. First, the level of vitriol that people seemed to harbour towards the built environment of Brisbane, and also towards architects, who were seen as precisely the ones who should know better. Second, I was surprised that people were so impassioned at all – when there is generally so little public discussion about buildings and places, the response to this one article seemed to reveal hitherto unsuspected depths of opinion and passion about the built environment. But the third thing that surprised me was that this passion, all of these opinions and judgements, were overwhelmingly negative. It seemed that people were able to become exercised about architecture, but only if it was (seen to be) ugly. In fact, the terms of the debate were strikingly reductive: of beauty and ugliness, with nothing in between. For this reason it was clear that the conversation was circular: both because of the participants' unquestioned belief in the objectivity of beauty, its self-evidence to those equipped with the correct eyes to recognise it, and perhaps more importantly, because there was so little rapprochement between the vehement attackers and defenders of Brisbane's appearance.

So I was thinking of all this when the radio interview duly took place, by mobile phone, as I sat in the undercroft beneath the State Library of Queensland. But as the interview proceeded, I had a growing sense of unease. It seemed to me that the questions were just as blunt and polarising as that op-ed article had been, with its glib generalisations and easy sensationalism. In fact, as the conversation continued, the questions began to sound uncannily familiar – the references to the ugliness of the Roma Street transit centre, to pebblecrete, to the idea that practical buildings are necessarily hideous… I began to think that the announcer's background briefing to this interview had been that very same article I had read. It was, after all, the story that came up if you googled 'ugly Brisbane'. And so despite my best efforts, in my short radio interview I suspect I failed to inject much sophistication or nuance into the broader public debate, in the few short minutes in which I was called upon to 'explain why buildings look the way they do'.

Demoralising as it was at the time, this radio interview was actually the best indication I could have hoped for that my larger project was a valuable one: to open a space for discussion, between different audiences for architecture, and different critical voices on its meaning, value and significance to society more broadly. The premise was simple: that architectural commentary as it currently stands, written largely for architects and largely by specialist critics, has very little bearing on the reception, understanding, or role of architecture in the public domain more broadly. And so long as architectural commentary and public debate is marginal in this way, so will the practice of architecture be.

At present there is a widespread perception in the English-speaking world that architectural commentary and criticism is in a state of crisis. This is based on the idea that it is undervalued by or simply inaccessible to a lay audience, that it is marginalised in the popular press, and that its direct contribution to the architectural profession is obscure. There is also a question about *when* architectural critique is useful – how can it be productive when critics almost always write about buildings after they are already built and finished, whether well or badly. Commentary and criticism on the subject is also made complex by the long-held opposition between architecture and building. A building only qualifies as 'architecture', and therefore becomes open to serious critical evaluation, if it embodies a sufficient level of quality, and is thus elevated above 'mere' building. The act of architectural criticism carries a judgement of value and worth by definition.

The origins of this book thus lay in the idea that by improving the relevance and inclusiveness of architectural commentary, and by better understanding the purpose and role of architectural criticism, it would be possible to deepen the public conversation about architecture in Australia. This is an attempt to place architectural commentary within architectural theory and practice more broadly, and examine how architectural criticism, in particular, mediates between the production and reception of architecture. The reason for this emphasis on criticism is that it opens fundamental questions: not only of what is good architecture, but also what is architecture *per se*. Specialist criticism is a significant bellwether for the wider discipline of architecture because it manifests some of the fundamental tensions of the discipline – for instance the question of whether architecture is an art or a profession; thus whether architects should be seen as artists or service providers; and whether the products of architecture are pragmatic buildings or works of art. Naturally these oppositions are not necessarily polarised but exist on a scale, where contemporary architectural practice most often strikes a balance between the two extremes. But when an architecture critic addresses a building, such fundamental questions of definition rise again to the fore.

In lay terms, the pendulum between aesthetics and pragmatics in architecture is often framed in terms of a hierarchy of building uses, where an art gallery or theatre is seen to lend itself to more 'artful' or even 'conceptual' building than a school or hospital. This is crossed again by questions of building status, as famously articulated by Nikolaus Pevsner in his statement that, 'A bicycle shed is a building; Lincoln Cathedral is a piece of architecture. Nearly everything that encloses space on a scale sufficient for a human being to move in is a building; the term architecture applies only to buildings designed with a view to aesthetic appeal.'[4] This hierarchical distinction sets out architecture as a particular, reduced and elevated sub-category of generic buildings, where architecture is distinguished by its higher conceptual and aesthetic aspirations, its authorship, its cultural significance, its expense, its beauty, or its superior quality in design or construction. Such distinctions are entrenched by professional architectural criticism, which tends to ignore the generic category of 'buildings' altogether, and designate its own critical attention as itself proof that a particular artefact must be 'architecture', otherwise it would not be worthy of evaluation in the first place. Paradoxically, this is still the case even when the critique turns out to be negative – a 'bad' piece of architecture does not always or automatically drop back into the category of 'mere' building.

In light of all this, it is quite clear that the question of what is good architecture, and how to recognise it when you see it, has a very different answer depending on who asks the question and to whom it is asked. Critical evaluation by a building's actual occupants, based on direct experience, may be diametrically opposed to the opinion of an expert critic, and different again from that of a practicing architect. This is because the criteria that each of these groups employ are vastly different and sometimes mutually exclusive, and also because the most appropriate criteria for judgements of quality in the built environment remain conceptually unclear.

Martin Filler writes that '[t]here can be little question that architecture has a far more pervasive influence on the daily lives of people than any of the other arts, and yet the level of critical discourse on the subject lags far behind – in quality as well as quantity – that pertaining to painting, sculpture, music, theatre, dance, and film.'[5] Suzanne Stephens argues that 'the absence of well-thought-out standards for evaluation, a weak cultural context for debate, and the critic's need to write for several audiences with different needs and levels of knowledge are significant barriers'[6] to architectural criticism, while Paul Goldberger, former architecture critic at *The New York Times*, writes that 'I don't think criticism matters very much, at least not in the sense that a lot of people, including architects, want it to matter… Nobody tears down a building if the architecture critic doesn't like it.'[7]

So there we have a damning assessment of the state of architectural criticism. But is it really justified? The accounts of professional architects and architectural photographers collected in the 'Practice' section of this book offer a more nuanced, perhaps more subtle, and certainly more self-conscious account, of what happens in the day-to-day commercial practice of architecture and its visual representation. Nevertheless if the practice of architectural commentary and critique really is too narrowly defined, then there is a pressing need for other, more experimental, more expansive and more popular modes of visual and textual commentary and critique of buildings. This project has of course been underway for some years in the work of scholars such as Jane Rendell,[8] Katja Grillner,[9] Linda Marie Walker[10] and many others, with a recent major contribution by Alexandra Lange.[11] Likewise it can be seen in the photographic work of Gavin Hipkins, reframing buildings through images.[12] But there is still a need for other ways of thinking about buildings, of writing them, showing them, and judging them, and these are also the subjects of this book.

The aim of the larger project was thus to understand architectural commentary in the public domain in Australia, attempting to contribute to a more productive debate about the value and evaluation of buildings, leading ultimately, hopefully, to an improved built environment. This project was funded by Arts Queensland, with the specific objective to develop a stronger and more robust culture of critical discourse and debate around architecture in this state, directed both 'inward', to local architects and the local public, and 'outward' to the national and international community.[13] The project set out to develop this culture in four ways, firstly by opening architectural critique to a broader audience through new publishing initiatives and events; second by mentoring and training arts and other practitioners to

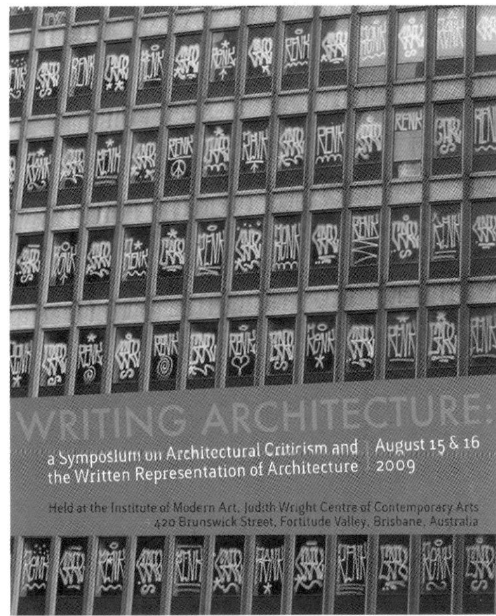

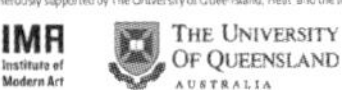

Convened by Dr Naomi Stead of the ATCH (Architecture Theory Criticism History) Research Group, in the School of Architecture at the University of Queensland

Generously supported by The University of Queensland, Heat and the Institute for Modern Art

IMA Institute of Modern Art   THE UNIVERSITY OF QUEENSLAND AUSTRALIA   AA

Held in association with AA Roundtable 02 'Media and Architecture: Building Communities'

a chaired public discussion convened by Justine Clark, editor of Architecture Australia.

6-8pm, 14 August →
University of Queensland Art Museum

Poster for 'Writing Architecture: A symposium on architectural criticism and the written representation of architecture', 2009. Design by Zoe Sadokierski.

architectural criticism; third by encouraging creative and innovative practice in criticism through the unconventional use of text and images; and finally, using scholarly enquiry to clarify the principles by which architecture is valued by distinct groups, leading to a more well-defined context for critical debate.

Attempting to fulfil such ambitions has been a long effort. It began in August of 2009 with 'Writing Architecture: A symposium on architectural criticism and the written representation of architecture', which was held at Brisbane's Institute of Modern Art. The proceedings of that event were collected and published in a special issue of *Architectural Theory Review*.[14] It included an opening night public discussion forum, 'Architecture and Media: Building Community', held at the University of Queensland Art Museum, and chaired by editor Justine Clark as part of the *AA Roundtable* series of events associated with the professional journal *Architecture Australia*. Later, two additional events in 2011 acted as postscripts to the conference that is anthologised in this book – a panel discussion at the Brisbane Writers Festival,[15] and another panel entitled 'Critical Alternatives: The counterculture of publishing in design and architecture' which was staged as part of Queensland's inaugural Asia Pacific Design Triennial.[16]

But the main events, the proceedings of which are gathered in this book, were a conference, which explicitly attempted to draw in members of the public, as well as practicing architects, academics and critics; and a two-day workshop inviting writers and photographers from other disciplinary backgrounds to turn their attention to writing and representation of buildings, places and the city. These two events duly came to pass as 'Writing Architecture: A symposium and workshop on innovations in the textual and visual critique of buildings'. The conference was held at the Queensland Art Gallery's Gallery of Modern Art, and the State Library of Queensland, on 22–23 July 2010. It was preceded by the workshop, which occurred over two days at the University of Queensland School of Architecture.

This book represents the expanded and extended proceedings from both workshop and conference, with an important additional section, including the voices and work of practicing architects and professional architectural photographers. The dialogues collected here, conversations between practicing architects who deal every day with words and pictures about buildings, emphasise the pivotal role of *communication* – whether textual or visual – in the design and materialisation of the built environment. Likewise the professional architectural photographers whose work is presented here, who make their daily living from the visual representation of buildings and places, are sophisticated mediators between the built environment and its *publication* – literally, its being made public.

The book is arranged to reflect its origins – in three sections representing the different events and voices from which each springs. There is an additional layer of structure in the 'Conference' section, with three sub-sections according to the three key themes of writing, representation and criticism. A keynote essay – the first by Katja Grillner, the second by Gavin Hipkins, and the third by myself – opens each of the sub-sections. The three categories in the book's subheading thus chart a tripartite approach to an attached, detached, and semi-detached engagement with architecture: through writing, representation, and criticism.

1   The conference was titled 'Writing Architecture: A symposium on innovations in the textual and visual critique of buildings,' and held on Thursday 22 and Friday 23 July 2010, at the Queensland Art Gallery Gallery of Modern Art, and the State Library of Queensland. The keynote speakers were Katja Grillner, Professor in Critical Studies in Architecture, KTH Stockholm, Sweden; Gavin Hipkins, photographer and Senior Lecturer at Elam School of Fine Arts, The University of Auckland; and John Birmingham, Brisbane-based novelist and essayist.

2   The workshop was held at the University of Queensland School of Architecture on July 19th and 20th, 2010. The workshop experimented with innovative approaches to writing and photography about places and buildings, in Queensland and elsewhere. It was led by Katja Grillner, Professor in Critical Studies in Architecture, KTH Stockholm, Sweden; also Dr Linda Marie Walker, artist and writer and senior lecturer in the Art Architecture School of the University of South Australia, Adelaide; and Peter Bennett, professional architectural photographer, Melbourne. Participants were selected from an open competitive call, which attracted a wide range of writers and photographers with a diversity of past experience – fiction writers, architecture critics, curators, heritage professionals, journalists, poets, novelists, non-fiction writers, and editors. The photographers were similarly diverse, including architectural as well as art and documentary photographers. No prior expertise in architecture was required, but some experience as a writer or photographer, as well as an interest in places and/or buildings, was essential.

3   Robert MacDonald, 'Brisbane: concrete examples of aesthetic failures,' *The Courier Mail*, January 13, 2010, retrieved www.couriermail.com.au/news/queensland/brisbane-concrete-examples-of-aesthetic-failures/story-e6freoof-1225818549610 July 15, 2010. The story was eventually to gather 350 comments from online readers.

4   Nikolaus Pevsner, *An Outline of European Architecture*, Harmondsworth: Penguin, 1957 [1942], 23.

5   Martin Filler, 'American Architecture and its Criticism: Reflections on the State of the Arts,' in Tod A. Marder (ed), *The Critical Edge: Controversy in Recent American Architecture*, Cambridge, Mass.: MIT Press, 1985, 27.

6   Suzanne Stephens, 'Assessing the State of Architectural Criticism in Today's Press', *Architectural Record*, vol. 186, March 1998, 68.

7   Paul Goldberger, 'Postscript', in András Szántó, Eric Fredricksen, and Ray Rinaldi (eds), *The Architecture Critic: A Survey of Newspaper Architecture Critics in America*, National Arts Journalism Program, Columbia University, New York, 2001, 27.

8   See for example Jane Rendell, Jonathan Hill, Murray Fraser and Mark Dorrian (eds.) *Critical Architecture*, London: Routledge, 2007; and Jane Rendell *Site-Writing: The Architecture of Art Criticism*, London: I. B. Tauris, 2011.

9   See for example the keynote essay in this book, as well as Katja Grillner, *Ramble, linger, and gaze: Dialogues from the landscape garden*, PhD Dissertation, Stockholm: Kungl Tekniska Högskolan, 2000; also Tim Anstey, Katja Grillner, Rolf Hughes (eds), *Architecture and Authorship*, London: Black Dog Publishing, 2007.

10   See for example the keynote essay in this book, as well as Linda Marie Walker, *International Corporation of Lost Structures, Department of Dislocated Memory*, available at http://www.icols.org/pages/MainFrame.html, and the *Electronic Writing Research Ensemble*, http://ensemble.va.com.au/.

11   Alexandra Lange, *Writing about Architecture: Mastering the Language of Buildings and Cities*, New York: Princeton Architectural Press, 2012.

12   See for example the keynote essay in this book.

13   The project was funded by a 'Development and Presentation Grant' under the terms of the Visual Arts, Craft and Design Focus Area of the Queensland Arts Industry Sector Development Plan. Interestingly, Arts Queensland includes and funds architecture initiatives as a sub-section of design, whereas architecture is specifically excluded from funding under the national arts funding body, the Australia Council for the Arts.

14   Naomi Stead and Lee Stickells eds., *Architectural Theory Review*, special issue on Writing Architecture, vol 15, no.3, December 2010.

15   The Brisbane Writers' Festival panel, 'Write the City' was chaired by author and essayist John Birmingham, and comprised Professor John Macarthur, Sydney architect and commentator Tone Wheeler, and Vanessa Mooney, who also took part in the Writing Architecture workshop. The session description argued, in part, that 'the imaginative potential of architecture is sometimes overlooked, and this panel discussion will explore the potentials of architecture in fiction, and equally how real buildings can encourage a rich and imaginative life for their occupants. Buildings provide the setting for literary narratives, just as the work of the architect is always imaginative, thinking new buildings into being. So how do writers see and understand buildings, and how is this different to how architects see them?' The panel took place on 4 September 2010.

16   The Asia Pacific Design Triennial session, 'CRITICAL ALTERNATIVES: The counterculture of publishing in design and architecture,' was chaired by Naomi Stead with guests Fleur Watson (co-director of the Asia Pacific Design Triennial), Jeremy Staples of the Papercuts Collective (http://papercutscollective.tumblr.com/) and Carl Lindgren of *Map Magazine* (http://mapmagazine.com.au/). It was held on 4 October 2010 at the Asia Pacific Design Library in the State Library of Queensland.

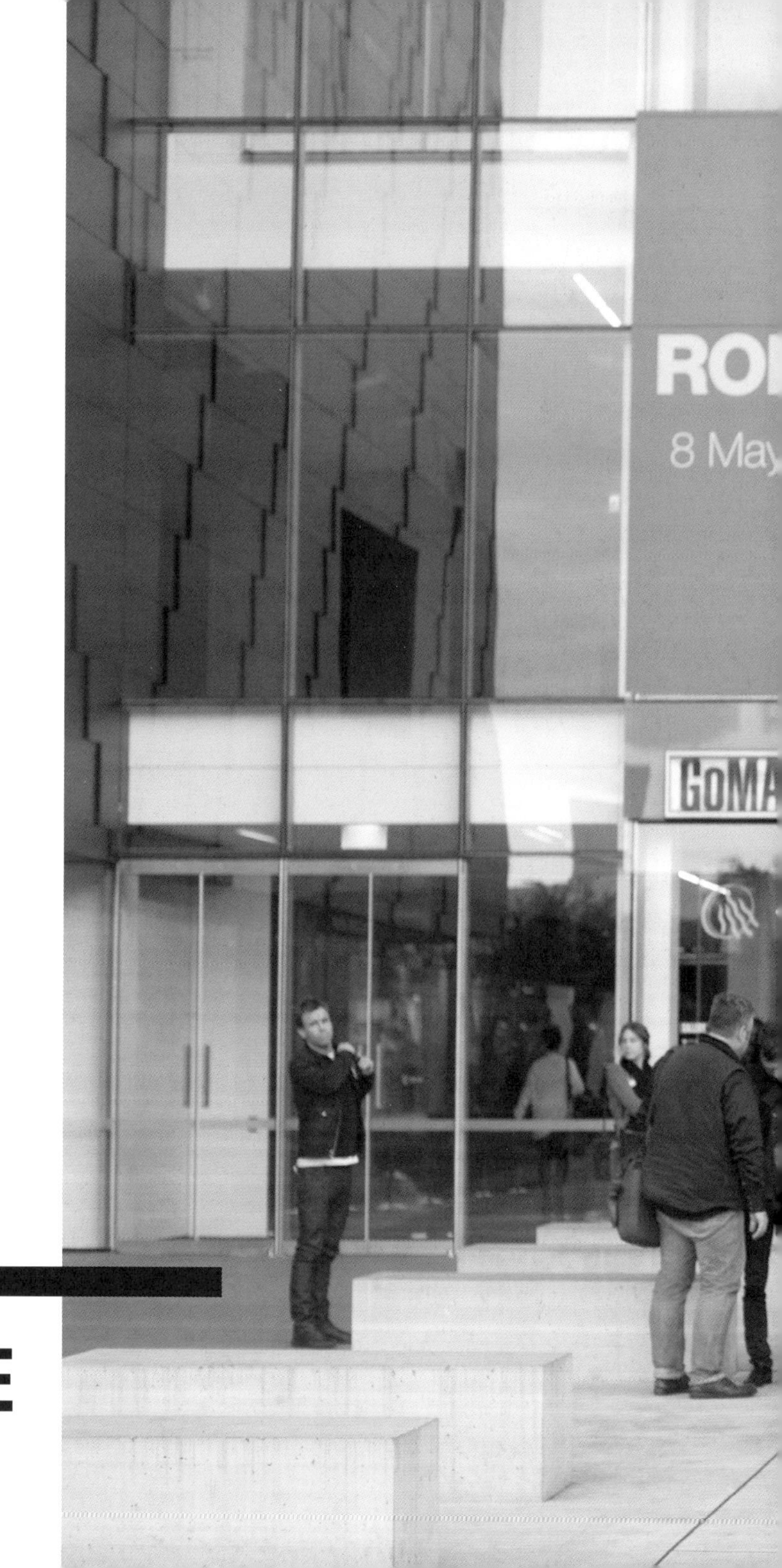

CONFERENCE

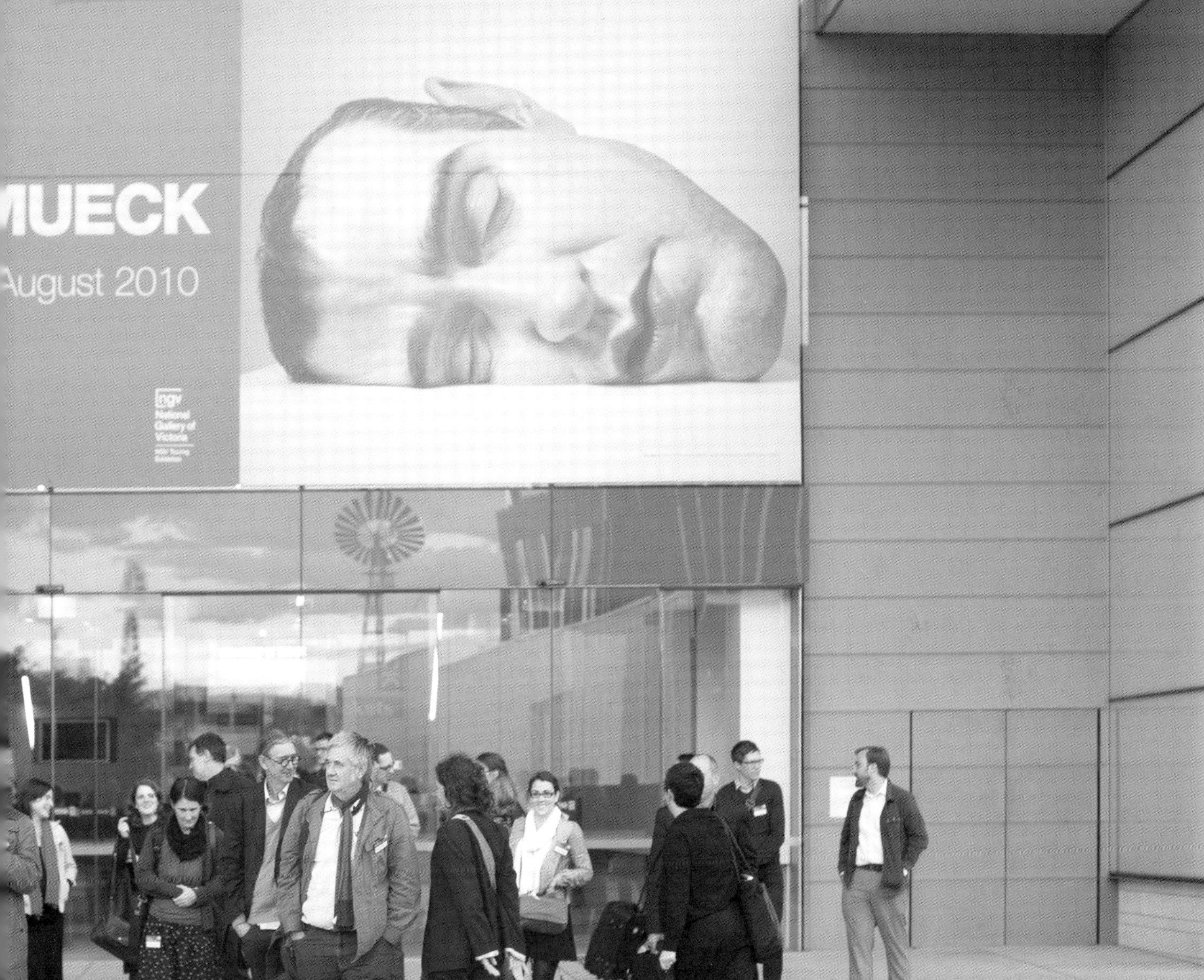

Conference and workshop photographs by Peter Bennetts.

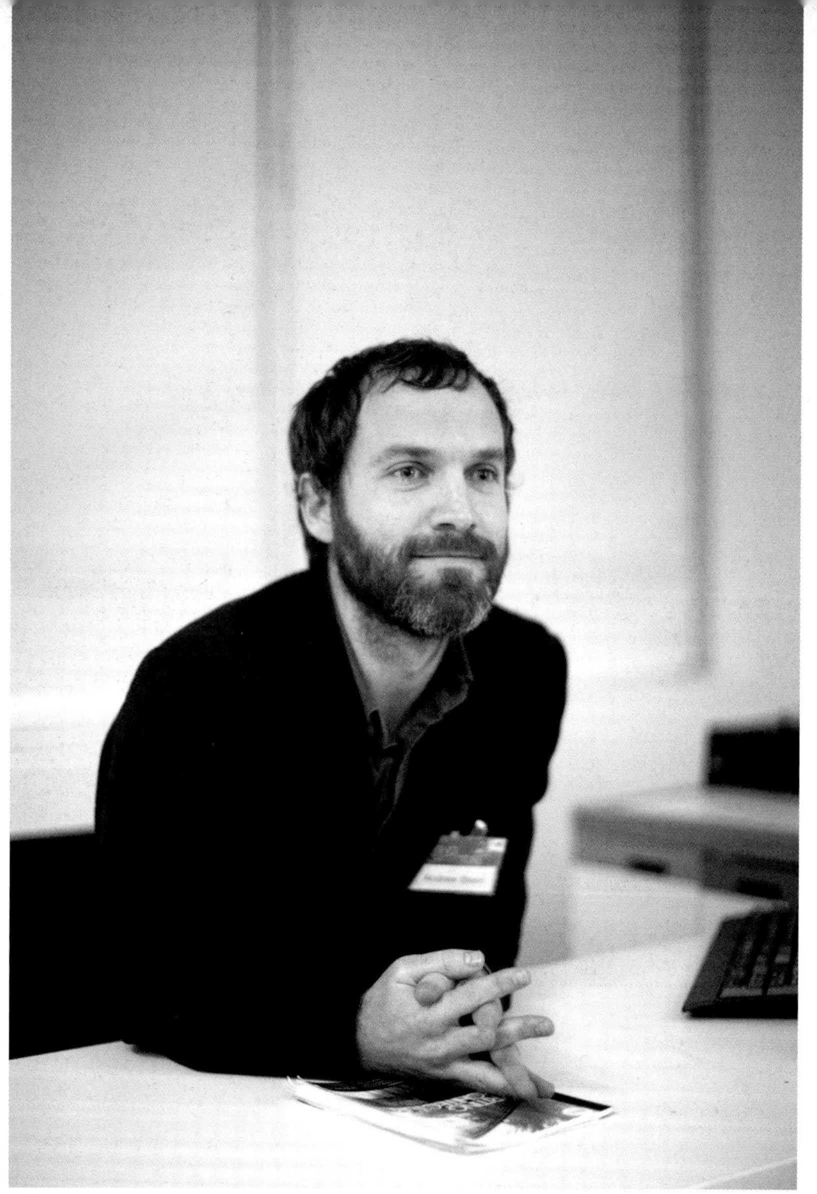

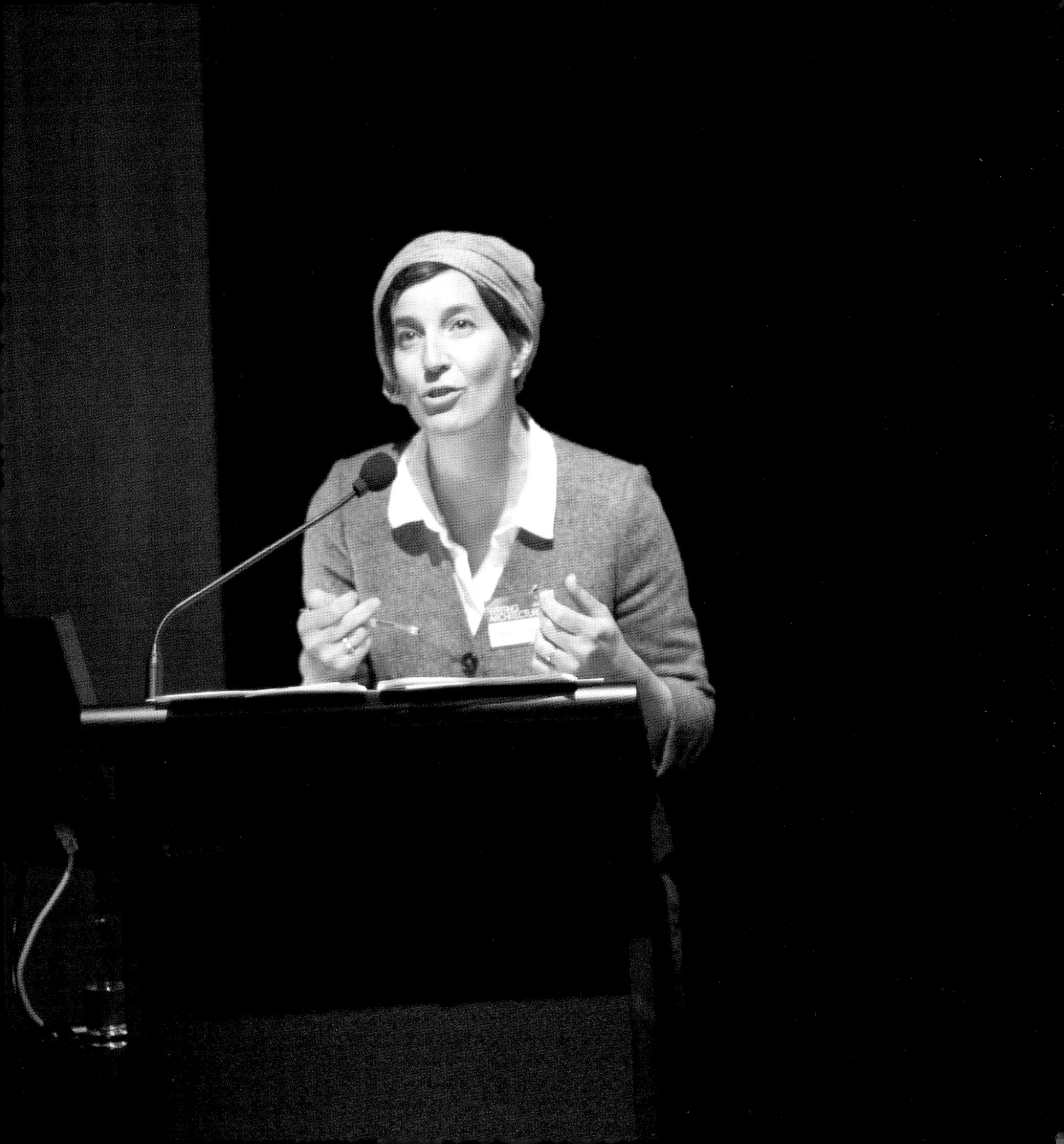

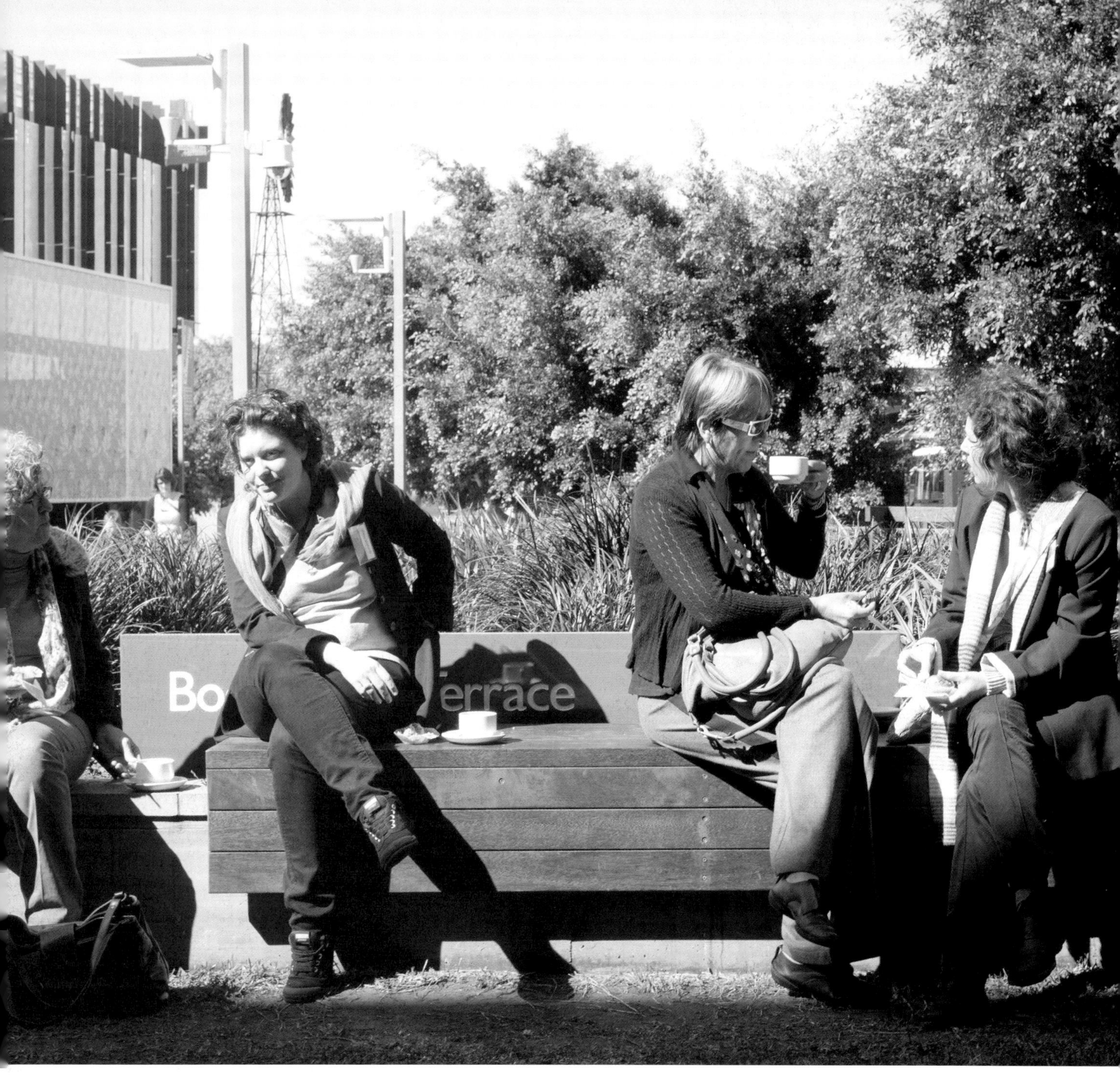

Bo
errace

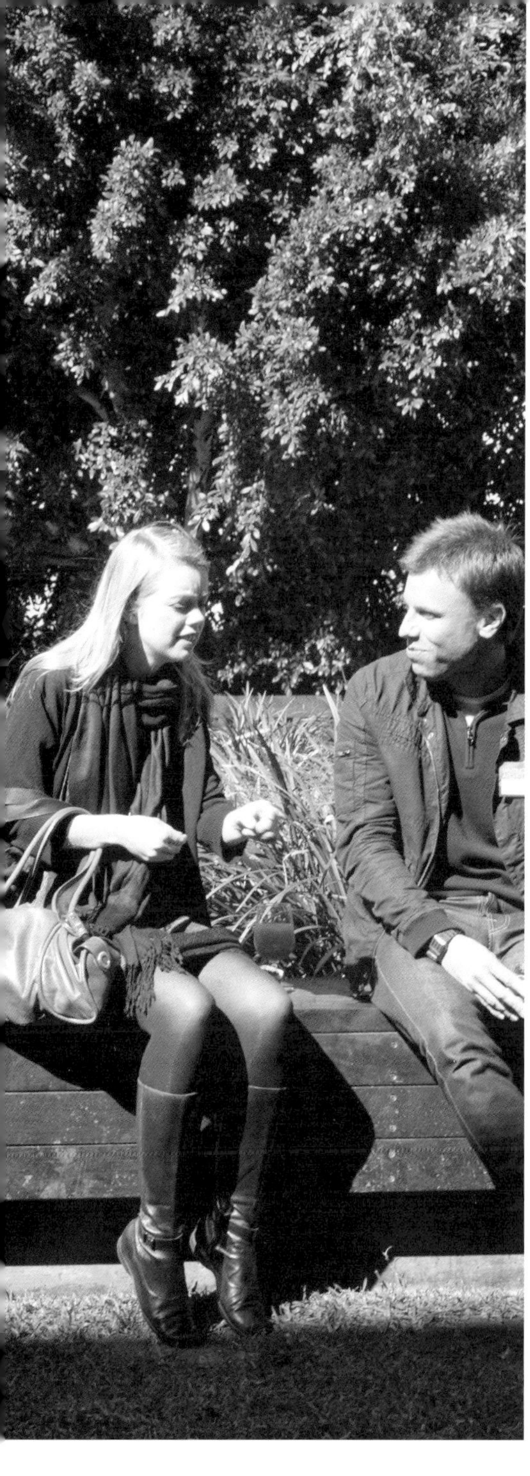

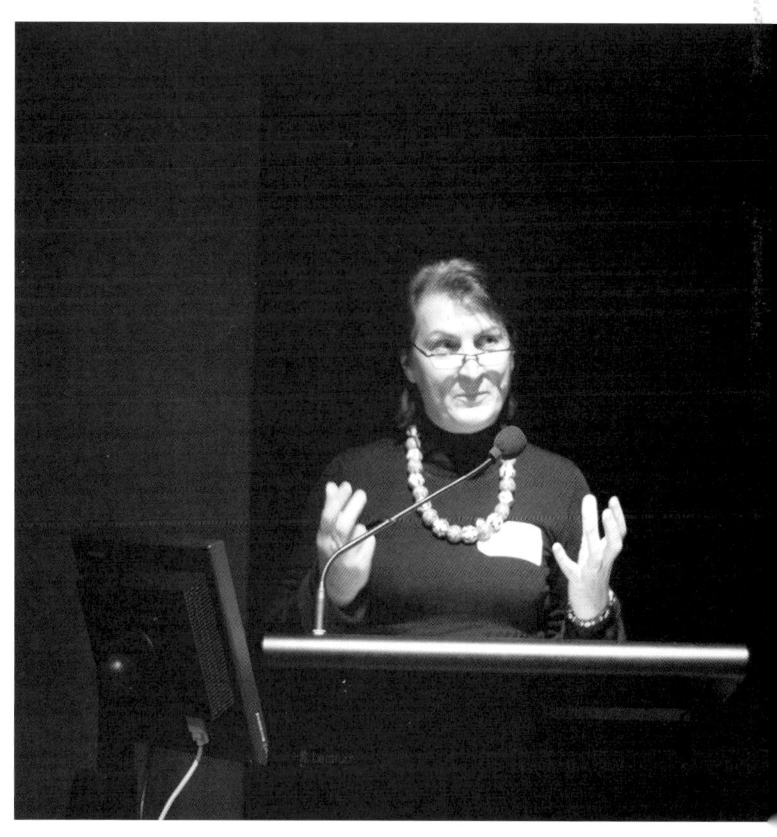

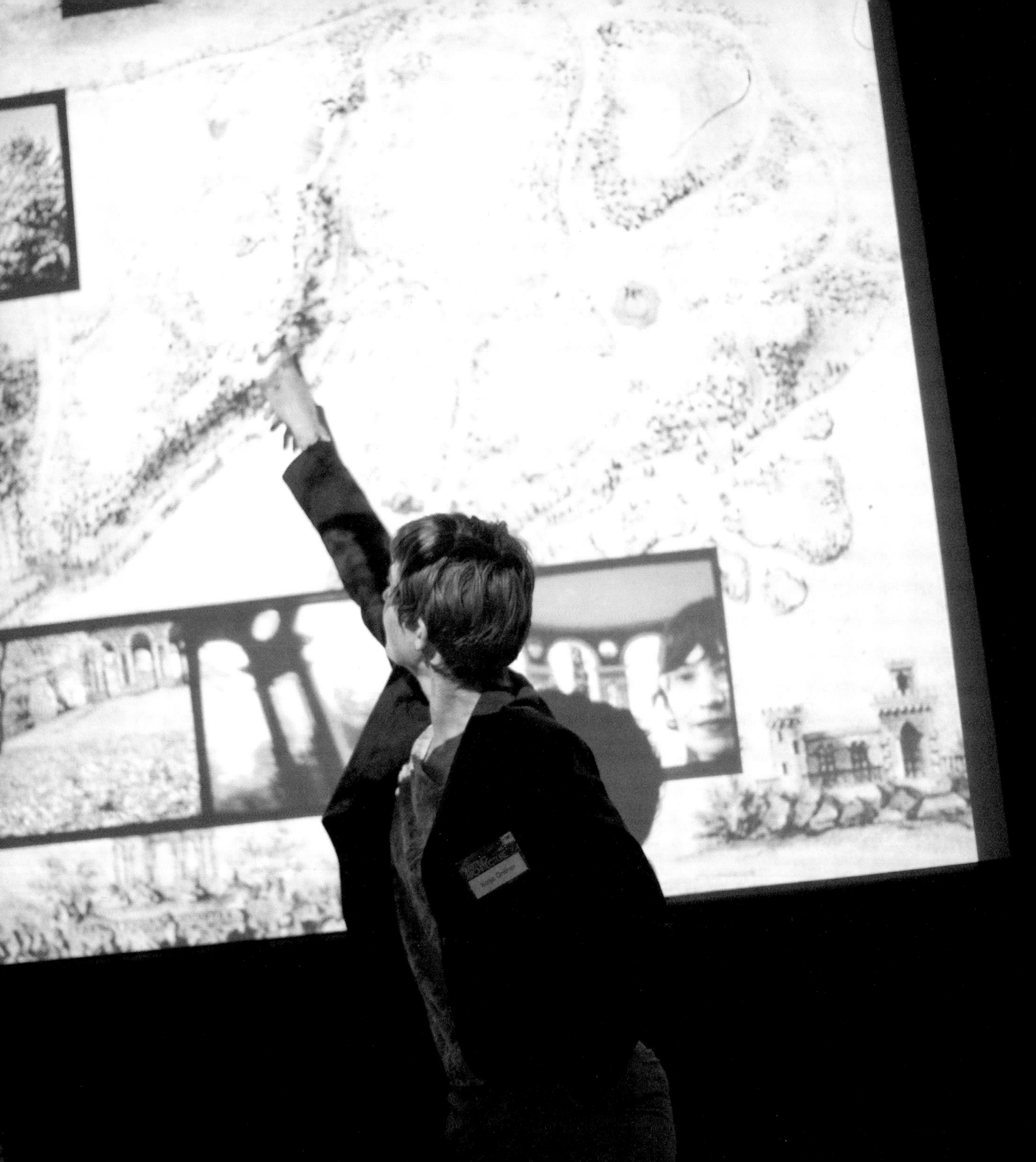

A Performative Mode of Writing Place: Out and about the Rosenlund Park, Stockholm, 2008–2010

KATJA GRILLNER

It might have been my first encounter.[1] Going for a walk together in a rather melancholic mood. Early spring, still cold, but a pale sun to warm you up just a little. Deciding, for some reason, to cross Götgatan, leaving behind the robust turn-of-the-19th-century urban fabric, five to six-storey buildings, moderately decorated, the streets and proper sidewalks. The space we walked into then, just five years ago, does not exist any more. Now we happen to live just across from that entrance point. We can imagine watching our historical selves from the window of our present home, passing by just 75 metres away.

A performative mode of writing place

This essay suggests a performative mode of writing that engages in and activates specific spaces, here a particular park, through different forms of self-reflexive engagement. As an author (critic, researcher) I am looking in particular at the role of memory and everyday appropriation in place perception, using my own experience as a primary source. I am attempting to capture an essentially distracted mode of spatial perception, arguing that in such a mode there lie important keys to understanding and knowing a particular place. This knowledge is often left aside in critical or historical accounts, where much effort goes into providing a distanced and as far as possible neutral and factual representation. The critical tools we have for representing spatial and artifactual physical realities in their immediate relation to use and experience in research are very limited. As soon as one stops to focus in, or climbs up to get an overview, one has stepped outside of practice or use. This is the principal challenge explored in this essay.

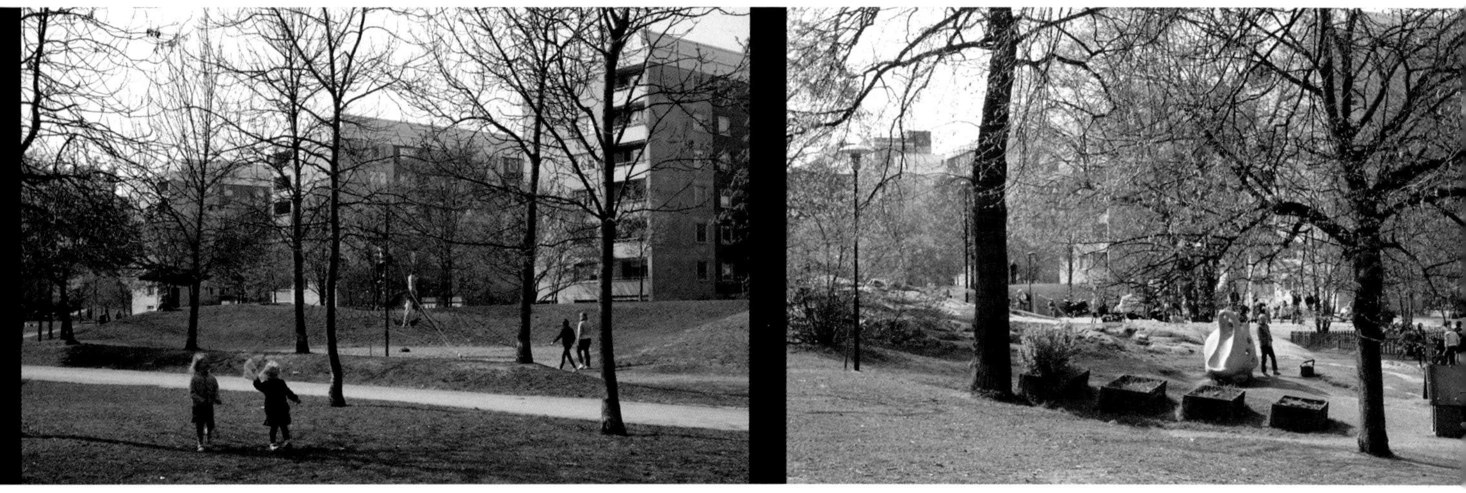

Rosenlund Park. Photographs Katja Grillner.

Performative modes of writing in academia have a long history with multiple lines of development and sources of inspiration.[2] For all disciplines dealing with relational research 'objects', objects that can by no means be ultimately fixed or exhaustively accounted for, and toward which the researcher has to take up a reflexive position, it is crucial to challenge the available formats of research representation.[3] In architectural theory, a contemporary lineage of feminist modes of experimental textual engagement in critical spatialities can be said to emanate from writers such as Jennifer Bloomer, Katherine Ingraham, Karen Burns, Meaghan Morris and, in the last decade, Jane Rendell, Naomi Stead, Katarina Bonnevier and several others.[4] The exploration of questions of critical representation and phenomenological challenges to architecture as a material and poetic practice calls for alternative forms of writing, as well as visualising architecture, a project which is urgent and ongoing, but which can also trace its history back to at least the 15th century.[5]

My own practice is tightly interwoven with both groups of architectural writers just mentioned, having taken this particular academic challenge so far as to present my PhD dissertation in fictional form, an experiment with situated dialogue and discourse that has since been followed up in Katarina Bonnevier's PhD dissertation, which I supervised.[6] In previous publications concerning criticality in distraction, I have in particular drawn on notions of distracted perception, hapticity and tactility developed from Walter Benjamin and by extension Riegl.[7] This essay focuses on the phenomenological implications of this account, specifically, and its mode of operation in relation to writing place from a more general epistemological perspective. Key references are Sara Ahmed's work on queer phenomenology, and Iris Marion Young's earlier work, which both help to loosen up, in productive ways, the stern intentionality of the phenomenological tradition.[8] Further, an epistemological critique will be developed in relation to Donna Haraway's notion of 'situated knowledges' and Rosi Braidotti's notion of 'nomadic subjects'.[9]

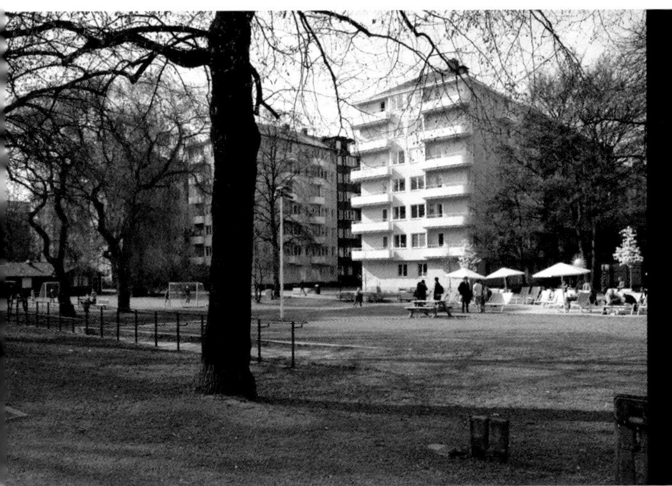

The specific site, Rosenlund Park, influences the structure of this text, its narrative and its lines of argument. Interwoven with that structure runs an associative line of critical discussion creating a rhythm of showing and telling. That is, this text does something, it performs, and for the reader this shows directly what is at stake, while at the same time the text engages in a self-reflexive mode, which also has its logic and structure determining the text. In previous essays I have engaged in similar studies in relation to places with which I have a long-term autobiographical relationship (another park, a summer house).[10] This time I am exploring my current immediate surroundings, toward which I have a shorter history. We have now lived in the vicinity of Rosenlund Park for three years. It is the everyday route to daycare and the closest playground.

A dazzling bright over-exposure

Back to that first encounter: I remember a dazzling bright over-exposure. It might in fact have been tax declaration day – that is why we had crossed the street. The tax authority building from 1959, designed by the architect Paul Hedquist, is 84 metres high. In 2007 this building was converted from tax authority offices to student housing. It still towers unchallenged over Södermalm. It is not a particularly beautiful building. Rather it is a typical but crude, international style, high-rise variation. Until recently it was framed on the ground by an extensive open space proportionate to its height. Åsötorget, the name of the square, was considered a cold and windy, unfriendly space. On this day in 2005, Åsötorget was still in place, and it was bright and hazy.

We entered a park, passed a series of gravelly playgrounds and found ourselves in a green picnic universe. Still it was not yet the right season. The surrounding buildings were light concrete slabs. I had never been here before. 1960s optimistic urbanism – children everywhere, no traffic nearby, artificial hillocks and a tall spidery climbing net. Little did we know that this would be our very own neighbourhood park in a couple of years. That the yellow building we passed on our way through was our future son's future daycare. But the memory of the place remained.

This memory is emotionally charged. In my mind, even the weather changed as we walked those 150 metres. An initial sense of deep sadness, gloom and aimlessness accompanied by the particular chill of an early spring day when you have dressed too lightly, transforms into a still melancholic, but rather nostalgic sense of happiness. The sun breaks through.

Remembering our first encounter with Rosenlund Park threw me back to early childhood. In his collection of essays, *The Remembered Film*, the artist and essayist, Victor Burgin, writes about the difficulties of distinguishing – in our memory – between places that we have actually experienced and images of places we have constructed out of impressions from films and other media. We imagine places we remember through filmic filters and perhaps mistake the memory of a place we have experienced for a scene in a film we have never seen.[11]

In Gothenburg we lived in a typical 1960s apartment block neighbourhood, Nordostpassagen. We had a balcony that was really a terrace. There I learned to bike. There was an expansive open courtyard between the long row of houses, no traffic. As I remember it very little greenery, but a pond into which one might venture out in a small inflatable boat. At least that is what we did one day. Some boys threw spiky chestnut shells at the boat, pricking a hole. (I thought the boat would sink.) My impression is that we were out there on our own, my sister and I. Possibly we were. The courtyard was huge, not enclosed, and we were just five and seven years old, but there was no traffic anywhere nearby. It might be that this happened just once, but my sense of happy, adventurous independence as a five-year-old left a strong impression.

Discovering Rosenlund Park on that gloomy day evoked this particular place in myself. At least I thought so – a remembered place that shapes and determines my dreams and actions. But it is also a place of a particular generic type and aesthetic dating from the late 1960s. Variations of this place are found in and around all the bigger cities in Sweden, but are quite rare in inner-city Stockholm, where I grew up. Considering Burgin's observation, that we cannot be certain that the places we remember are what we think they are, I hesitate for a second. I was hoping that my sense of nostalgic optimism had to do with actual memories, lived experiences. What if I am mixing them up? I do not really know. Places like these have not yet, in terms of their spatial characteristics and qualities, been exhausted by popular media representations. If anything, burning cars, graffiti covered walls and unsettling decay still feature in the media. But my architectural background provides me with alternative imagery: grand drawings of international housing schemes from the 1960s offering generous (but raw) pedestrian landscapes flicker by. Subtle traces

of these visions can be found in many Swedish housing areas from the 1960s and early 1970s.

Layers of time and lived experience

This essay moves between different layers of time and lived experience. At the outset we encounter the main site, Rosenlund Park, in 2005. The memories are my own: of the first encounter with this place. The perspective is that of a still childless couple on a walk in an unfamiliar neighbourhood, which is not yet their own. From here, we make a brief excursion back to 1975 and my early childhood neighbourhood in Gothenburg, Nordostpassagen. Then, in the near present (in 2008–2009), we encounter my then two to three-year-old child and myself in Rosenlund Park. A fourth layer is the current present, the writing subject now, and my now four-year-old child, biking independently around the park and kicking the football with strength and precision. Thus an autobiographically layered representation of Rosenlund Park is put into motion for a reading imagination, making this place another in rather specific terms (playing, caring, discovering, growing, everyday routine).

In her 1988 article, 'Situated Knowledges', Donna Haraway calls for a 'doctrine of embodied objectivity', where 'objectivity turns out to be about particular and specific embodiment … Feminist objectivity,' she continues, 'is about limited location and situated knowledge, not about transcendence and splitting of subject and object.'[12] Her call for a new 'doctrine' and engagement with notions of 'objectivity' is made in relation to the debate at the time about whether the postmodern radical epistemological critique in effect rendered feminist research useless in relation to political struggles for change. If feminist research could not make any significant claims about real conditions, of what value could that knowledge be? Haraway's response here is that we need to move beyond those simple dichotomies and understand that empirical knowledge is objective even though it is always situated and embodied. With this view, it is possible to build up objective knowledge on real conditions and to act on this information. In this essay our concern is primarily with place. What does it mean to know a place and who is expected to act on such knowledge? The autobiographical focus of this essay positions my child, myself, and our actions and interactions, as specific actors over time, at a site where radical urban transformations are currently taking place.

In 2006 the Stockholm Municipality presented a program for renovation and redevelopment of Rosenlund Park.[13] This was one year after my first encounter with that site. In 2006 I was still not aware of the particular developments in the area. As I lived in another part of Stockholm, I was not locally engaged. A major reason for redeveloping Rosenlund Park is argued in the program to be the eradication of the nearby Åsötorget (mentioned above). That is, what had been a large public square was at the time being turned into a regular housing block (public space privatised). This housing block (where we live) is now, in 2010, almost completed. In response to these developments, the program argues, the park will have to serve an additional purpose and provide the new inhabitants with a representative space (a town square?). Because of this, a large and popular climbing structure has been demolished.

This program provides an interesting example of what kind of site-specific knowledge the city planning office considers to be significant in relation to a specific set of proposed alterations. The primary user groups addressed are: parents of smaller children playing in the park, school children, the strolling citizen, and the daily passersby (on their way to work or school). Problematic uses discussed are drinking (by alcoholics), late night partying (by youth), and walking the dog (by dog-owners), which lead to a sense of insecurity in the evenings in certain areas of the park, and uncleanliness (dog poo on the lawns).

None of these latter groups of users have been called upon to participate in the process. The program was largely realised according to the proposals in the winter of 2007–2008. Other parts of the park remain unaltered, possibly waiting for new funding to be released.

Most attention was given to the new entrance to the park, which is the new representative space claimed to be needed 'for the new inhabitants'. Designed as an art installation, with permanent deckchairs and sunshading umbrellas, placed on a light concrete slab surrounded by a coarse gravel surface, it can be as bright and hazy a place as I remember Åsötorget to have been that one day, walking across it in spring 2005. But this new place is all about dreams of summer, leisure and vacation.[14] Before, the windy, modernist plaza was a mark of city life. Technocratic, bureaucratic, grey, grand? I never really knew that place; most probably it was a failure of sorts. But what is this 'new' thing that has come to replace it? That has stepped over the street and into the park. That takes its place from that of the giant climbing frame. What does it mean to the park and to the neighbourhood, to everyday life?

I reside in the middle of this transition. A new inhabitant, I am a co-producer of the situation, an intensive user, simply, with my family. But also in writing this essay, as a writer and researcher, engaging in an investigation of what this can be, from the limited perspective of my own experience and use, the place that is becoming? In *Nomadic Subjects*, Rosi Braidotti articulates the feminist figuration of the 'nomadic subject'. It shies away from the notion of a stable identity, and emphasises the political necessity for the feminine subject to make constant shifts and re-positioning moves. This is in subjective response to current conditions, as well as establishing new strategic positions in order to instigate change, to inhabit the fictional 'as if', which can envision a different world.[15] In her introduction to *Altering Practices*, Doina Petrescu cites Braidotti's notions of subjectivity and change, reminding us as well that all processes of becoming are in the end specific, material and corporeal. They take place somewhere and involve particular actors.[16] It is thus important to be precise in these accounts, even if only partial perspectives are provided.

At the lowest point in the park

Autumn 2008, another day at work has passed and it is time to leave to pick up my son from daycare, a yellow building at the lowest point in the park. Up on the hill behind, a giant housing block towers; on the other side, a muddy playground, and far in the background graffiti-covered concrete walls. We walk out the front. Rosenlund Park at Södermalm in Stockholm in its current appearance has a mixed 1930s and 1960s character. The hills in the latter section are perfectly shaped as artificial little bumps and ridges. The earlier parts are dominated by playgrounds and at the far end the posh gravel section for grown-up kids recently installed. Permanent deckchairs signal vacation all year round at this end. Here we are. Walking and stopping, running through the park, splashing in the puddle, we get home. We spend a lot of time in this park. I am thinking now, how will this park shape my son's future perceptions of place? Will it become a deeply rooted point of reference in spite of its banal everydayness? If so, what is it that lingers in the memory, what is it that makes up a remembered place?

Is it the muddy playground where, as a two-year-old, he chases the ball into either of the goals and imagines himself to be playing the same game as the deadly serious seven-year-old, who is out perfecting his goal shooting skills with his dad? If so, what in the playground? The deep puddles that are so much fun to run through? Its boundaries (the bushes, the pathway, the red shed and its stair, the backside of the park pavillion), the places where the ball tends to disappear, or where another child might take it? Or is it just the feet touching the ground, the

stumbling, hands down, face down, stand up again, and continue? The materiality of that mud, that damp cold, and that movement keeping you warm. The other day when we passed by, a team of seven-year-old boys were playing in thin cotton shirts, coats thrown aside on the ground. It was about zero degrees but they were warm.

Is it the flat granite slope behind the 1950s organic playing sculpture, which in itself is a cave, a slide, a climbing adventure all in one? I think back to the first picnic in springtime when we had just moved in. A small grassy spot just below the rock, keeping the hot coffee and the bread out of reach of my son, who had the longest arms and the quickest grip. At that point I would bend my back to hold his hands as, with quick but unstable feet, he explored the flat sloping rock surface, struggling upwards, letting go downwards, getting stuck in a minor cleft, stopping there to put down his hands. Standing still. A year later my main concern was to keep up with his pace, to be there before he got to the end of the rock from which there would be a two-metre fall, and to be prepared to catch a possible fall as he runs down.

Playing field. Damp, wet, mud. Photographs Katja Grillner.

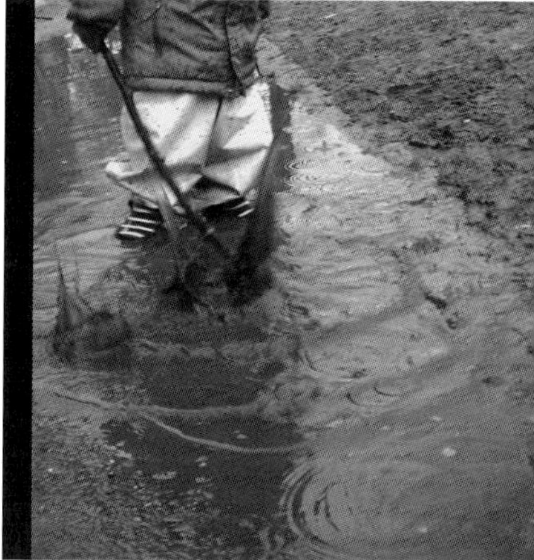

Especially after the rain. A slippery slope. Spring 2009, we have not yet gone there (until last week it was covered with snow), but the time has clearly come when, in spite of some anxiety, the boy must be trusted to explore the rock on his own. For myself, this rock could be a small island in the Swedish west coast archipelago where I spent my childhood summers. On sunny days it offers a place to comfortably lie back. Only here, there is no water around.

Is it the recently installed climbing frame (approximately four by four by four metres), which bears a sign telling us that it is only to be used by children over six? We help him pass all the difficult obstacles so he can reach the principal attraction, the steep slide. But the obstacles prove to be a real problem at the moment when his courage fails him and we have to bring him down through holes not fit for grown-up bodies. Before this moment, up on the platform, his sense of independence is great. Proud to be up there, us down below, hello, goodbye, hello, goodbye, peekaboo! Does he ever stop to look out further behind us? Our heads at his foot level.

The classicist facades of 1920s houses high up looking south; the grassy undulating landscape and the path toward daycare to the west; or the sand box and path toward home to the east. Or he looks downwards, closing in on the modern orange EU-standard rubber surface on the ground. It is less wet here, no puddles, but it hurts less when one falls. A plane passes by and we look up into the sky together.

Making the horizon shift

When I first began to write this essay, I was fascinated by the way in which, in my experience, place perception seems fundamentally affected by the everyday company of a small child. A matter of anxious safety concerns combined with playful interaction makes the horizon shift, not only closing in on the details, the ground, its challenging thresholds, street paving patterns, litter and dog poo, but at the same time expanding your self through the anticipation of the child's next move. Before he even moves, you want to know where he will be heading. It is

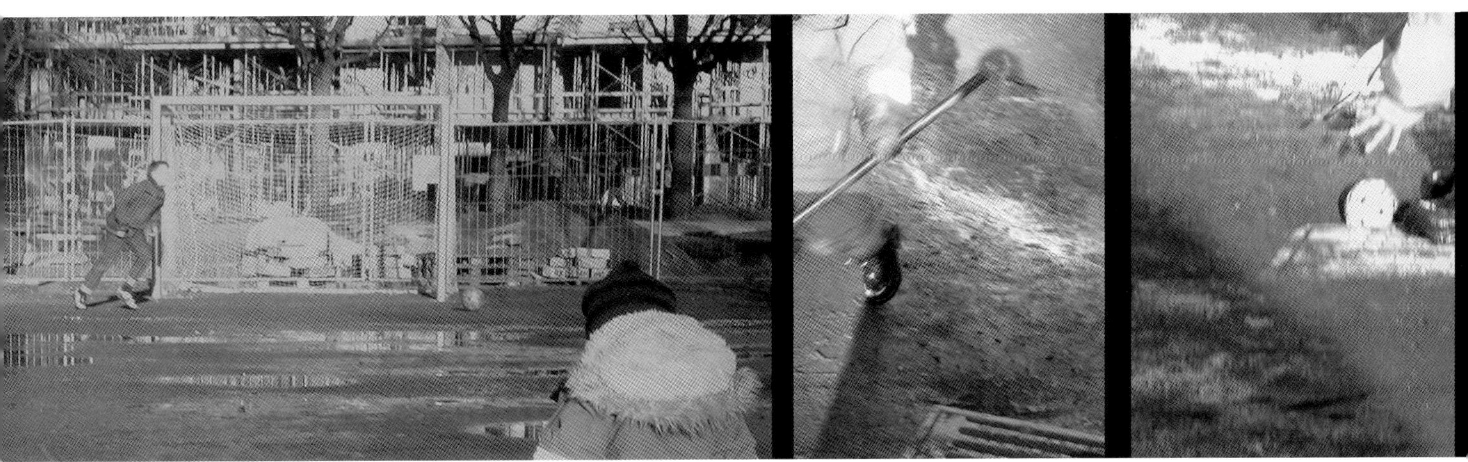

a technique and I am quite certain it affects you deeply. Walking along the street there is always this double perspective, keeping up the pace, being close enough to grab his arm quickly, and at the same time looking up to register all the potential dangers, bikes and cars as they approach. And in the midst of this I hear him say: 'A one.' We stop, I look around, and the number on the neon sign right above us is 51. A five and a one. Or he shouts: 'An ambulance!' We stop and I look, then I hear. In the very far distance, the sirens are calling.

In her seminal essay, 'Throwing like a girl' (1980), Iris Marion Young critiques the phenomenological model of a subjectivity characterised by its essential directionality – 'being oriented towards' the world. The phenomenological subject does not, she argues, throw like a girl, that is, hesitantly, insecurely, but projects the ball through his whole body along his arms to the throwing hand and out into the world in an elegant, clearly directional trajectory. The phenomenological subject, thus, is clearly gendered. Female subjectivity, Young provokingly argues, might rather be characterised by an oscillating directionality, knowing always that, while she acts on and toward the world, she is simultaneously gazed upon as an object in the world.[17]

With Sara Ahmed's introduction of queer phenomenology, Young's critique gains greater momentum.[18] Ahmed takes an early point of departure in Edmund Husserl's account of his writing table, how his intense focus on the writing paper and the pen is set against a distant recollection of a domestic background (children playing in the summer house). It tells the story of a philosopher's privilege to absent-mindedly co-perceive his children while, in order for his paper to remain the focus of his attention someone else is intensely taking care of that very background. A queer phenomenology, by contrast, accounts for alternative and multiple non-straight modes of being both oriented and disoriented toward the world and toward others.[19] Ahmed describes

how, for Merleau-Ponty, the loss of orientation, or grasp, in relation to the world, is seen to constitute a fundamental crisis, causing the body to 'collapse and become once more an object'. The making sense of the world (taking up a subject position) is ultimately conditioned by being able to *face* it straight on and close up.[20] The oblique angle and the blurriness of peripheral vision are thus, in his view, not only of little significance but rather detrimental to subject formation.

Rather than mourning (or striving for) the perfectly straight, upright and unconditional subject–position directed toward the world, Ahmed points instead to the thickness of the queer moment of disorientation. In between subject and object, it is a relational place for potential new beginnings and where alternative lines of orientation may be drawn or sought for.[21] Going back to Young, we don't need to be trapped in the image of the throwing girl who fails, but can instead make clever use of the expertise that ultimately develops from our oscillating subjectivity, constantly projecting out and being projected onto, knowing what that means and carefully tending to our moments of disorientation.

The intense intersubjective dynamic that is introduced when caring for and playing with a small child adds further complexity to the phenomenological model. Much as Merleau-Ponty at times experienced his car as becoming an extension of his body and perceptual apparatus, the child appears for fleeting moments to be an extension of your self, an extension that however, has its own subjectivity.[22] It is at once an oddly disconcerting and enriching sensation. The place that takes shape in such moments is particular and yet evasive. How does one write that place? Rosi Braidotti engages the reader in her own nomadic life experiences in order to write, and make herself accountable for, the performative image of the nomadic subject she envisions.[23] Making the queer moments of caring-grown-up-and-small-child-relational-place-experience appear through writing articulates a temporary yet intense and significant subject position. Since I began working on this essay time has passed, and it has become clear to me how rapidly the character of this intersubjective dynamic is changing ground with time. Those moments are soon gone. It was with some sadness that I discovered, while working on this text, that already in the spring of 2009 I could lean back and gradually retreat into my old self from time to time. From then on, visits to the playground have included more moments of detached observing, more or less engaged, chatting with other parents or on the phone. Just sitting, standing, letting the time go by. It can be boring too.

The moment of inevitable destruction

As a particular place changes, expands or shrinks, along with our own actions and relations within and toward it, its conditions within the larger context of urban redevelopment sets another framework that, as in the case of Rosenlund Park and Åsötorget, can be the objective of radical change. During the three years in which we have lived in our apartment, our view has been that of permanent construction work. They have almost finished building now. When we moved in, Åsötorget was already gone, a hole in the ground being filled in as an underground garage. What remained of the plaza was a fragmentary circular paving pattern on patches of ground, a displaced park bench, and a bush of red red roses. The roses survived almost two years of construction. I lamented the moment of their inevitable destruction, and regretted that I never sneaked in to save a sapling. I had thought of doing that so many times (overleaf).

On what kinds of information were the radical transformations of this particular city block based? Was it easy to make the plan, to decide on eradicating not only a little-loved plaza, but a modernist architectural composition, an historical urban type? To convert the block into its present hybrid character, a regular city block with a high-rise building and a shopping mall oddly squeezed in? What did they know? A wide array of methods is used for the purposes of site mapping within architecture and planning practice. Collecting composite knowledge of spatial, material, technical, legal and market conditions, potentials and limitations; historical background and traces; current uses and users; articulations of user needs and desires etc. In a regular commercial development project, heavy emphasis is placed on mapping out the necessary hard facts, i.e. what are the physical, legal and market conditions on the site, what is possible, and where might development meet resistance, etc. Some methods are dependent on general information systems, site-specific conditions as chartered by GIS and accessible from the city planning office, others on history writing and museum archives, and an important further layer of knowledge is gained from neighbourhood surveys, interviews, workshops or information meetings and program discussions with future users. The planning process in Sweden also always includes public presentations, hearings and a right for citizens and legal bodies to file an opinion.

Corporate commercial interests tend to play an explicit role as driving agents in most larger planning schemes in Stockholm today, that is, proposing what needs to be done and negotiating with the city planning office to run the proposal through the legal process, while individual citizens or citizens' groups are rarely understood to be significant actors or agents for change. User groups, if involved, are expected to give their views on current conditions or respond to ready propositions, not to work actively to make something new take place. This means that the principal agency for change is located with architects, planners and politicians (on the level of conception) and with commercial or public institutions (on the level of programming and funding). The citizen's role is reduced to that of informer rather than knowing subject or potential agent for change.[24]

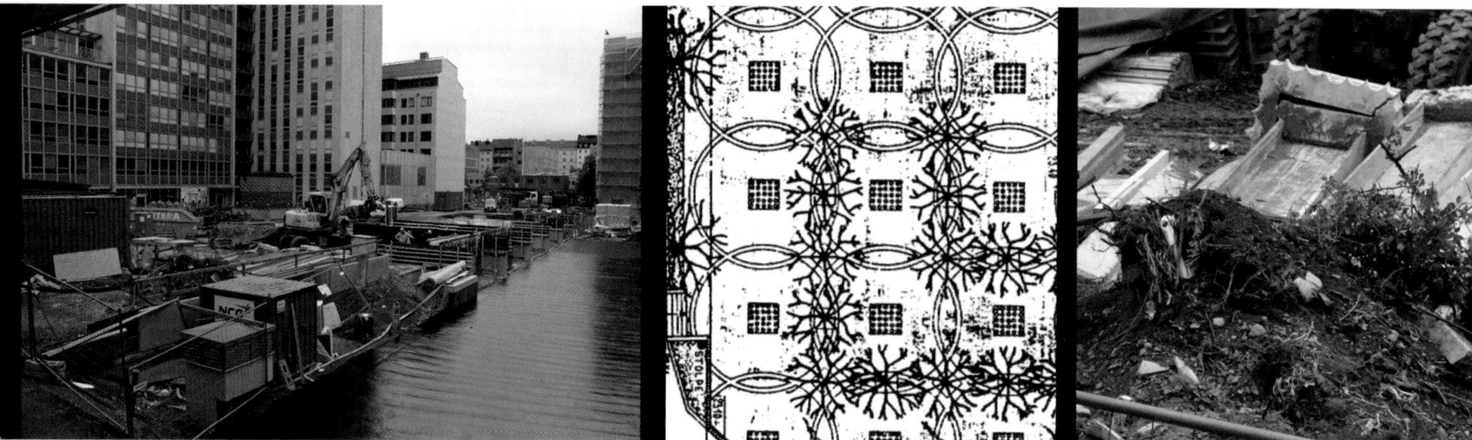

How more adaptive frameworks may be applied, which are sensitive to grassroots initiatives, can be observed in a city like Berlin or, closer to Stockholm, in Malmö.[25]

While specific to the site, the information accumulated and assimilated in these processes does not build up knowledge of a *situated* kind. By situated, Haraway understands the concept of embodied. That is, partial perspectives as articulated through human action and experience. This is a perspective clearly at odds with the more generalising and objectifying mechanisms at work in both architecture and planning. The highly partial perspective on Rosenlund Park presented (and produced) in this essay is one attempt to articulate what situated knowledge can be in direct relation to place perception and production. However it remains a largely theoretical project in its current implementation. That is, so far these writings have not been shared or discussed in their very local context. For them to take site-specific effect, a larger network of actors needs to be formed.[26] As a critic, scholar and architectural researcher, I have approached these questions experimentally in a very basic

and rather cautious sense – careful to keep abstractions and generalisations at bay, never to forget how specific experiences are, when they are in effect taking place. Writing is a practical tool for this investigation, retelling and restructuring site-specific memories, allowing the narrative to introduce layers of different times and sites that are then put into motion.

What then, if anything, might be generic in this tale, in terms of the site that it claims to write? What specific value may a few glimpses of a rather ordinary neighbourhood park in Stockholm, and of my own and my son's particular place relations, have for a broader readership, not familiar with, or having no particular interest in, this very place? The ambition, after all, has been to write this place, to write it in a way that will allow it to enter into your imagination, to make it a place of your own. It is a place that is intensely mine in the sense that it has been created from my own experiences, actions and associations. By writing, not *about* the place, but the place itself, writing it, the place can take on an independent existence for the reading imagination. An essay such as this may

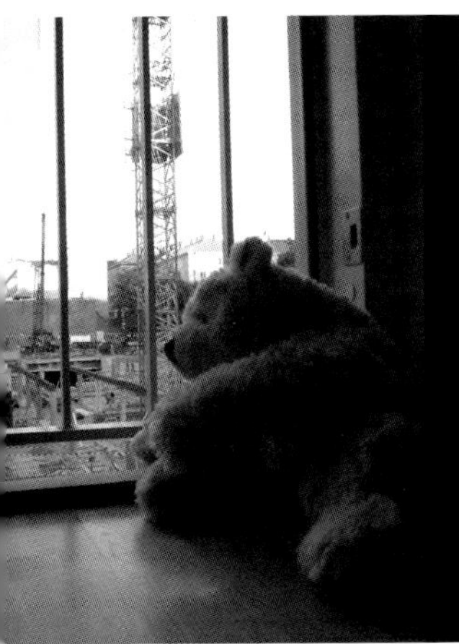

Åsötorget. Destruction, construction. The bush of roses turned upside down. The image includes a detail from the 1960 plan of the square. Photographs Katja Grillner.

offer multiple moments of knowing recognition and, related to those, moments of critical discovery, influencing the way in which you might understand and value a very different situation and location elsewhere. Thus, its criticality lies not primarily in what it represents, but in how it creates a new point of reference for understanding, use and action elsewhere.

Squinting at the low evening sun

Early summer 2010, sitting on the warm granite slope, squinting at the low evening sun and at my soon-to-be four-year-old son busy climbing. Every morning for the last few weeks we have biked together through the park; for him it is a new movement and sensation, for us both a new relationship and a new space (yet another park). The early days of biking (without support wheels) brought back momentarily the sense of intense co-perception described above: being nowhere but there, just there by the child, to avoid the fall, to avoid an accident. Only here was this rattly vehicle in between, with its spiky pedals

and handlebars. It hurt. Gradually that bodily attention (and tension) was released. Even if the passage through the park takes only a couple of minutes, to bike there, side by side, or myself after him, together, was then a great relief. This park will continue to change, I now understand, from season to season, over the years to come, depending on my relational ties and its various uses. I find myself returning again to that spring day, five years ago now, when I first encountered the park and passed that place, which has now disappeared. I still do not know why I miss it.

1   This essay was originally published in Mona Livholts *Emergent Writing Methodologies in Feminist Studies*, London, Routledge, 2011. Routledge has kindly granted due permission for republication. The research for this study was supported by the Swedish Research Council. I wish in particular to thank my architecture and writing research colleagues and collaborators, Rolf Hughes, Mona Livholts, Jane Rendell and Naomi Stead, for providing challenging and inspiring input to this research, and to fellow teachers in *FATALE*, Katarina Bonnevier, Brady Burroughs and Meike Schalk, as well as my architecture and writing students, for providing ample opportunities to discuss and articulate what this investigation might really concern. This aside, however, from the depths of my heart, I thank Leo, my lovely son. I wonder what you will think one day, if you read this essay. It is simply wonderful to make place together with you!

2   For its development in relation to feminist studies see in particular Mona Livholts (ed), *Emergent Writing Methodologies in Feminist Studies*, London, Routledge, 2011, the volume in which this essay was originally published. See further Annelie Bränström Öhman and Mona Livholts (eds), *Genus och det akademiska skrivandets former.* [Gender and Forms of Academic Writing] Lund: Studentlitteratur, 2007; Nina Lykke, *Feminist Studies: A Guide to Intersectional Theory, Methodology and Writing*. New York: Routledge, 2010.

3   Katja Grillner, 'Writing Architecture – Introduction' and 'The halt at the door of the bootshop' in Katja Grillner, Per Glembrandt and Sven-Olov Wallenstein (eds), *01.AKAD – Experimental Research in Architecture and Design – Beginnings*, Stockholm: AKAD/AxlBooks, 2005, 64-71; Rolf Hughes, 'The Poetics of practice-based research writing', *The Journal of Architecture* 11, no 3 (2006): 283-301; Katja Grillner and

Rolf Hughes. 'Den kritiska texten i arkitektur-, konst- och designforskning'. [The Critical Text in Architecture Art and Design Research] In *Vetenskapsrådets årsbok för Konstnärligt FoU.* [The Swedish Research Council Yearbook for Artictic Research] Stockholm: Vetenskapsrådet, 2009.

4   Karen Burns, 'EX LIBRIS: Archeologies of Feminism, Architecture, and Deconstruction'. *Architectural Theory Review,* 15, no 3 (2010): 242-265; Naomi Stead, ed, *Architectural Theory Review: Special Issue on Writing Architecture,* 15, no 3 (2010); Jane Rendell, *Site Writing: The Architecture of Art-Criticism.* London: I. B. Tauris, 2010.

5   Alberto Pérez-Gómez, *Polyphilo or The Dark Forest Revisited: An Erotic Epiphany of Architecture.* Boston: MIT Press, 1992; Tracey Winton, 'Footprints in Stone: A Psychogeography of Rome.' In *01.AKAD – Experimental Research in Architecture and Design – Beginnings,* Katja Grillner, Per Glembrandt and Sven-Olov Wallenstein (eds), Stockholm: AKAD/AxlBooks, 2005, 90-101; Marco Frascari, Jonathan Hale and Bradley Starkey, *From Models To Drawings: Imagination and Representation in Architecture.* London: Routledge, 2007.

6   Katja Grillner, *Ramble, Linger, and Gaze: Dialogues from the Landscape Garden,* Stockholm: KTH 2000; Katarina Bonnevier, *Behind Straight Curtains: Towards a Queer Feminist Theory of Architecture.* Stockholm: AxlBooks, 2007.

7   Katja Grillner, 'In the Corner of Perception – Spatial Experience in Distraction'. *Architectural Research Quarterly,* 9, no 3-4, (2005): 245-254. Also published in Frascari et al, *From Models to Drawings,* 2007; Katja Grillner, 'Fluttering butterflies, a dusty road, and a muddy stone: criticality in distraction (Haga Park, Stockholm, 2004)', in Jane Rendell, Jonathan Hill et.al. (eds), *Critical Architecture* London: Routledge, 2007, 135-142.

8   Sara Ahmed, *Queer Phenomenology.* Durham: Duke University Press, 2006; Iris Marion Young, 'Throwing like a girl'. In *On Female Body Experience: 'Throwing Like a Girl' and Other Essays,* Iris Marion Young. New York: Oxford University Press, 2005, 27-45. Originally published in 1980, *Human Studies,* 3: 137-156.

9   Donna Haraway, 'Situated Knowledges: The Science Question in Feminism and the Privilege of Partial Perspective'. *Feminist Studies* 14, no 3, (1988): 575-599; Rosi Braidotti, *Nomadic Subjects: Embodiment and Sexual Difference in Contemporary Feminist Theory.* New York: Columbia University Press, 1994.

10   Grillner, 'Fluttering butterflies', 2007; Katja Grillner, 'Housing the Swedish Summer (Utopia in Reverse?)' in Edward Whittaker, and Alex Landrum (eds), *Nonsite to Celebration Park,* Bath: Bath Spa University, 2008, 71-84.

11   Victor Burgin *The Remembered Film,* London: Reaktion Books, 2004, 22.

12   Haraway, 'Situated Knowledges', 1988, 581-583.

13   Stockholm City Planning Office, *Rosenlundsparken. Program för upprustning. April 2006.* [Rosenlund Park. Programme for Renewal and Care, April 2006] Stockholm: Stockholms Stad, Markkontoret, 2006.

14   Designed by Thomas Bernstrand (Bernstrand & Co.), the project, which was entitled 'The Beach', received the Siena Award for the best outdoor design in Sweden, 2008.

15   Braidotti, *Nomadic Subjects,* 1994.

16   Petrescu, Doina, *Altering Practices: Feminist Politics & Poetics of Space,* London: Routledge, 2007.

17   Young, 'Throwing like a girl', 2005/1980.

18   Ahmed, *Queer Phenomenology,* 2006.

19   Ahmed's use of queer addresses its double signification as, on the one hand, concerning more generally an oblique, or non-straight, angle, that is any diversion from norms or standards from a cultural or aesthetic perspective, and on the other hand a more specific use concerning non-straight sexual orientations (Ahmed, *Queer Phenomenology,* 2006, 131).

20   Maurice Merleau-Ponty, *The Phenomenology of Perception.* London: Routledge and Kegan Paul, 2002, 294-305. Originally published 1945.

21   Ahmed, *Queer Phenomenology,* 2006, 157-179.

22   Merleau-Ponty, *The Phenomenology of Perception,* 2002, 143.

23   Braidotti, *Nomadic Subjects,* 1994, 6-7.

24   For further critical discussion and research concerning issues and potentials of social agency and participatory processes in planning see further the following references to articles and book chapters by Carina Listerborn, Meike Schalk, Ernstson and Sörlin, and Erixon and Ernstson: Carina Listerborn, 'Who speaks? And who listens? The relationship between planners and women's participation in local planning in a multi-cultural urban environment'. *Geo Journal,* 1, no 70 (2008): 61-74; Meike Schalk, 'Taking care of public space'. Architectural Research Quarterly, 13, no 2: 141-150, 2009; Meike Schalk, 'Meike Schalk, Apolonia Sustersic'. Presentation in Urban/Act: A Handbook for Alternative Practices. Paris: aaa-peprav, 2007, 218-229; Meike Schalk, 'Urban Curating – A Practice of Greater Connectedness' in Doina Petrescu (ed) *Altering Practices: Feminist Politics & Poetics of Space,* London: Routledge, 2007, 153-165; Henrik Ernstson and Sverker Sörlin, 'Weaving

protective stories: Connective practices to articulate holistic values in Stockholm National Urban Park', Environment and Planning A 41 (2009): 1460-1479; Erixon, Hanna and Henrik Ernstson. MS in progress. Spatial Agency in Urban Green Space Conservation Processes: Exploring the Dynamics of Protective and Projective Stories.

25 *Urban Pioneers* presents different social and urban actions that have greatly influenced the development of Berlin after the Wall (Senatsverwaltung für Stadtentwicklung, *Urban Pioneers*. Berlin: Jovis Verlag, 2007). The book *Urban/Act Catalogues on a European Level: Alternative Urban Development Practices, Groups, and Networks* (Atelier d´Architecture Autogeree, eds, Paris, 2007) is a catalogue of alternative practices in the urban field. In the Swedish context, the city planning office in Malmö is testing alternative approaches to planning in specific projects, for example in Stapelbäddsparken (Malmö City, 'Stapelbäddsparken'. [Stapelbädd Park] Accessed 2011-02-10. http://www.malmo.se.).

26 For example, the London-based writing practice, Urban Words, developed by Sarah Butler, engages in site-specific writing projects in urban regeneration areas. Local engagement is sought and stories of the place, past and present, are collected and presented. The publication and website, *Home from Home*, portrays through photos and personal accounts the migrant neighbourhood Elephant and Castle in London, which is currently subject to radical regeneration (Eva Sajovic and Sarah Butler, *Home from Home*. London: Urban Words, 2010).

It's Not the End of the World But You Can See It From There

SALLY BREEN

'It's not the end of the world but you can see it from there.' My father used to say this phrase often. We'd pull up to a house that didn't quite meet his precise expectations, an aesthetic which leaned towards a kind of suburban outdoor perfection – bright green lawn edges done to within millimetres of life, garden beds rimmed with concrete delineations, everything clipped, hosed down and beaten back into control; or I'd hear that phrase as we rolled through a suburb at home or interstate, which dad would declare a mess, all the decay and abandonment evidence of a lack of control, of effort.

Not the end of the world. But you can see it from there. A declaration of disappointment; a phrase that comes to mind when I think of the relationship between architecture and literature. This might surprise – structurally, aesthetically and even philosophically, the

connections between the two vocations are tangible. Writers and architects are both inherent scholars of the city; they take the city's pulse, they are the wanderers and dreamers, whose visions manifest in works which, in some cases, can come to define that city, spatially, figuratively and imaginatively. How far for example is Dickensian London from Norman Foster's London, or Raymond Chandler's Los Angeles from Frank Gehry's, in the public imagination. All of these names conjure experiences, images, textures, vistas and public sites, whether they are real or imagined. What is curious then, is the exception to this sense of connection between the makers and the interpreters of cities flares up in the narrative content. It's a question of perspective.

Writers have often loved living in cities and been associated with them even if their locales were more often than not in the seedier fringes, the underground dens, warehouses, jazz bars and less officious facades of the cities they inhabited. When various urban cultural movements erupted in the 20th and 21st centuries the presence of writers and cohorts of artists and musicians could not be separated from the streets they played in. Surely the desire to be in these cities was often (and perhaps still is) generated by these associations. For many people Warhol's New York, for example, acted as a powerful counter brand to an increasingly consumerist American life in the 'burbs, but then became a brand itself, counter-appropriated by advertising, design and architecture into a 'New York loft lifestyle' replete with Edie Sedgwick prints. A cycle of capital in the city, many writers and artists continue to be wary of. As William S. Burroughs once suggested: 'A paranoid is someone who knows a little of what is going on.'

And in the bohemian, teeming San Francisco? Now synonymous with the beat generation, whose unwilling poster boys were Burroughs, Jack Kerouac and Allen Ginsberg – these writers came to represent a sense of freedom from and refusal of conservative life, whose one-time presence in that city now helps sell cheap beer and coasters in fake saloons. These were writers who sought to tear down the political and corporate structures that built the cities the broader culture decided they defined. When Jack Kerouac was interviewed on the *Steve Allen Show* in 1959 and was asked how he would describe 'beat', he shrugged and then replied, 'Well, sympathetic', suggesting that the American culture he was operating in largely wasn't. 'All our best men,' he said, 'are laughed at in this nightmarish land.' His wingman, Burroughs, agreed:

> There is simply no room left for freedom from 'the tyranny of government' since city dwellers depend on it for food, power, water, transportation, protection and welfare. Your right to live where you want, with companions of your choosing, under laws to which you agree, died in the eighteenth century

with Captain Mission. Only a miracle or a disaster could restore it.

Across the Atlantic a similar big city mythology had manifested and been played out. Woody Allen's recent film *Midnight In Paris* draws on the creative loop that happens when many of us conjure Paris in the early 20th century. Just like Allen's transported *flâneur* it is not hard to imagine Jean-Paul Sartre, Simone de Beauvoir, F. Scott Fitzgerald, Henry Miller and Ernest Hemingway drinking wine, dancing on tables and arguing in the now infamous Café de Flore. A romantic vision of Paris perhaps, one we can only access now in cinematic or literary dreams, but one that continues to roll out as a real and potent signifier in western culture (and if the popularity of the Café de Flore and the price list suggests, in tourism). You pay four times the price for a Caffé Americano just for the privilege of imaging where Hemingway might have nearly shot a guy.

The difference is a writer's *l'amour* for a city does not necessarily extend to literary depictions of it. Nietzsche once said, 'An artist has no home in Europe except for Paris', which is of course as much of a lament as it is a celebration. When writing and architecture meet on the page the mood is often uneasy because literary and philosophical writers like Burroughs, Miller and Nietzsche were often pitching against the spin – distrustful, circumspect, paranoid. Traditionally, many great cities have come under attack in literature more than they have been celebrated.

In Leo Tolstoy's St. Petersburg the tensions between the old Russia and the new are played out, critiqued, subverted – the idiocy of new statesmen pushing papers, and policy more than the plough, his real heroine not Anna Karenina who, disgraced, is unable to bear her isolation and confinement. 'What is the city', Shakespeare said, 'but the people'. Lonely and without a position in society, Anna turns inward and eventually throws herself under a train (the train being a symbol throughout *Anna Karenina* of encroaching and relentless progress). Lenin and Kitty are Tolstoy's real heroes; the relatively innocent couple who defy urban progress and seek a more earthly, spiritual connection to each other, in the country. And while Tolstoy does not romanticise the rural – the problems of farming are present in the book also – the city, Tolstoy seems to be saying, may be a place of heady amusement, great debate, art, but more often this noise results in a confusion of intent, between all the voices and all the things – enough to confound a man from a truer sense of himself and deny a woman like Anna Karenina altogether. A place where Lenin never feels comfortable.

Classically, writers and poets reserved poetic reverie for nature, or for the symbolism of the sensual, whether human or natural, they saw in the world. They yearned for sensory experiences. Classically writers have distrusted cities and therefore urban critique is built into the writer's poetic DNA. Henri Rousseau, the French philosopher and novelist whose works were said to have inspired the French revolution, saw 'Cities as the abyss of the human species'. Lord Byron wrote that 'High mountains are a feeling, but the hum of human cities torture'. Keats, in *Sonnet 14*, says:

> To one who has been long in city pent
> 'tis very sweet to look into the fair
> And open face of heaven – to breathe a prayer
> Full in the smile of the blue firmament.

And for Plato, 'Any city however small, is in fact divided into two, one the city of the poor, the other of the rich. These are at war with one another'. This sentiment is still in force in contemporary western fiction, perhaps not surprisingly, given our stretched times. In Australian and British fiction, in particular, we encounter a heady sense of suburban despair. Christos Tsiolkas's novel *The Slap*, set in Australian suburbia, reeks of mortgage stress, middle class guilt and a plain unapologetic disappointment at the

underside of the dream, the relentless pursuit of spoils and the breakdown of the flimsy veneer of families fracturing under the pressure of keeping up with the Joneses with their swimming pools, back decks, splashbacks and renovations. Dystopian visions and vacuous spectacles have driven urban representation from a literary point of view since industrialisation. The rise of speculative fiction gave voice to both our fascination with technology and our subsequent fears. Overall a critical tone dominates. We see characters in despair. Characters that, despite the fascinations they covet in and of the city (or indeed because of them), are people who are lost. The gap between how they have imagined life, or how they have been sold it and how they actually live is too far, too keen.

Who can forget Hunter S Thompson's description of Las Vegas as symbolising the point where the 1960s revolution rolled up and rolled back – the high watermark still visible in a certain light. I think here we can see the crux of the problem for writers. The city is a vehicle, a mirror, a message, a warning of other concerns, not an end in itself. Since the late 19th century literature has chronicled the mass exodus to cities, country to city migrations, the cool remove of modernist expression and the more recent dispersive effects of technological advancement and globalisation. Literature has attributed to that development, overall, a sense of alienation and anxiety. A dystopian vision attached poetically to the rise of the machine. To the lost promise of Paradise, of Arcadia, even if these utopias were only ever dreams in the first place. And of course this sense of loss is 'romantic', but more potent because of that yearning. That feeling of failing to grasp something we never really had. Again and again we read of urbanised cultures moving further and further away from the earth; literally in the development of the tall building, figuratively in the relentless desire for the American dream, ideologically via the lofty intellectual heights imposed by modernism and in the fragmentation and simulacra we see in the media-saturated landscapes of postmodernism. All of these visions have been represented in literature perhaps to the point of cliché, but they are nonetheless powerful messages, which question the ability of a city to save or protect anyone except perhaps the elite.

With more people living in cities than in the country for the first time in human history, the rapidity of this shift seems to have enhanced the poetic panic in an atmosphere of protest as writers try futilely to extract themselves from nature, the classic romantic sensibility, the call of the wild. It's not so much that the majority of 20th and 21st century writers have posited a return to a prelapsarian state; many have celebrated the joys and headiness of city life, but they have found it hard to shake off the idea of a 'wild', unregulated, uncontrolled nature altogether. And so the city and the moon, the skyscraper and the light, the drugstore and the brittle wind, the billboard and the sun hitting it at the shooting hour in Los Angeles cannot be separated. The city has not yet stood in for all forms of reverie. In beat generation narratives for example, the city was as Shakespeare suggested: only ever as wild as its people, people who were sometimes in revolt against the city state – the walls and the demarcations, which sought to contain them.

Perhaps the poet and the architect are not as enamoured as we'd like to think. They are in fact at loggerheads in a question of at cross-purposes. For just as architects are continually seeking to wrestle with ideas relating to form and function and at best (when the client allows) beauty, liveability, sustainability, perhaps even social and democratic space, the purpose of literature, at its best, is to reveal the gaps between how we like to see ourselves and how we really are; the space between intent and outcome; and so the city becomes a potent nexus, symbolising the fallout, the failed projects of politics, policy and ideology.

Juhani Pallasmaa in 'The Eyes of the Skin' attributes this lived disappointment in architecture to the dominance of the visual realm in today's technological and consumer culture at the expense of other sensorial experiences. The dominant eye. The world rendered flat, screen read and produced, something slick, something to be gazed at. An urban vision that looks better in the drawing, he says, than it actually works. He quotes Luis Barragan:

> In our time, light has turned into a mere quantitative matter and the window has lost its significance as a mediator between two worlds, between enclosed and open, interiority and exteriority, private and public, shadow and light. Having lost its ontological meaning, the window has turned into a mere absence of a wall. Take the use of enormous plate windows; they deprive our buildings of intimacy, the effect of shadow and atmosphere. Architects all over the world have been mistaken in the proportions which they have assigned to large plate windows or spaces opening to the outside. We have lost our sense of intimate life and have become forced to live public lives essentially away from home.

This sense of exposure or lack of gradience is expressed beautifully by American novelist Bret Easton Ellis in his recent release *Imperial Bedrooms,* once again focusing on the lives of the rich and famous, the disaffected in Los Angeles. Ellis's characters are at all turns exposed – watched, followed, pursued. In the following quote the narrator, Clay, has recently moved back to LA, taking what he believes is a kind of refuge in his condo.

> Minimally decorated in soft beiges and grays with hardwood floors and recessed lighting, it's only twelve hundred square feet – a master bedroom, an office, an immaculate living room opening onto a futuristic sterile kitchen – but the entire window wall that runs the length of the living room is actually a sliding glass door divided into five panels that I push open to air the condo out and where the

large white tiled balcony drops into an epic view – the view is impressive without becoming a study in isolation; it's more intimate than the one a friend had who lived on Appian Way which was so far above the city it seemed as if you were looking at a vast and abandoned world laid out in anonymous grids and quadrants, a view that confirmed you were much more alone than you actually thought you were, a view that inspired the flickering thoughts of suicide. The view from the Doheny Plaza is so tactile that you can almost touch the blues and greens of the design centre on Melrose. Because of how high I am above the city it's a good place to hide when working in LA. Tonight the sky is violet tinged and there's mist.

There are so many contradictions at play here. Initially Clay views his apartment as superior to that of his friend precisely because of the tactile proximity to the city. Ellis reminds us of the sensorial Barragan yearns for; through the plate glass, Clay gazes at the colours of other buildings, at the sky, the mist, but it is a false sense of intimacy. Clay is projecting onto the space rather than the other way around and words like 'sterile', 'futuristic' and 'suicide' ignite questions in the reader; with all this description of shiny hardwood floors and recessed lighting now so clichéd in terms of affluent domestic space is Clay reeling off a set of determinates of status, or understanding what he really needs? Reading the book is like watching a car crash and as the novel progresses Clay takes to sitting in his apartment in the dark after receiving text messages which describe what he is doing – 'Where did she go?' and 'I'm watching you'. He knows he can be seen from various vantage points, his apartment no longer the removed haven he once perceived it to be. The setting mimics the predatory emptiness of the Hollywood machine, permeating his reality to the point where there is nowhere to hide not even from himself. Like a curtain drawing back across a movie screen the walls don't close in around him, they fall away.

Of course Ellis, in his treatment of Los Angeles, is speaking to and drawing on a long history of rendering that city as a flawed dreamscape. Los Angeles is arguably the world's most mythologised contemporary city, precisely because its new frontier construction and dispersal has allowed for such imaginative treatment. Los Angeles was conjured, idealised and constructed before it existed. It operates quite differently from the Italian humanist ideal of a centrifugal organised system of urban formation focused on the place of worship. Perhaps the concept of Hollywood has in the last century replaced the traditional place of worship – a new shrine that is not solid but ephemeral. In *Imperial Bedrooms* and indeed in his whole oeuvre, Ellis joins hands with many American and European writers in exile who preceded him: Raymond Chandler, Nathanael West, Aldous Huxley, even Bertolt Brecht, who once famously described Los Angeles in similarly degrading terms in his poem, *Contemplating Hell*.

Contemplating Hell, as I once heard it
My brother Shelley found it to be a place
Much like the city of London. I,
Who do not live in London, but in Los Angeles,
Find, contemplating Hell, that it
Must be even more like Los Angeles

Also in Hell
I do not doubt it, there exists these opulent gardens
With flowers as large as trees, wilting, of course,
Very quickly, if they are not watered with very
    expensive water. And fruit markets
With great leaps of fruit, which nonetheless

Possess neither scent nor taste. And endless trains
    of autos
Lighter than their own shadows, swifter than
Foolish thoughts, shimmering vehicles, in which

Rosy people, coming from nowhere, go nowhere.
And houses, designed for happiness, standing empty,
Even when inhabited.

Even the houses in Hell are not all ugly.
But concern about being thrown into the street
Consumes the inhabitants of the villas no less
Than the inhabitants of the barracks.

This poem mourns the absence of what a poet like
Brecht and 'his brother Shelley' would consider a more
tactile, earthy experience. The power and tradition of the
European poetic sensibility is still present here; even in
a contemporary place of such sensory overload Brecht
seems to want to remind us that the natural cannot be
constructed, fabricated or replaced, though of course to
some extent it has been. Today we see a similar critique
accelerated by Ellis, who extends the idea toward a new
millennium sensibility where screens in all manner of
forms (signs, billboards, intercoms, mobile phones) and
flat planes (controlled surfaces, empty streets, still blue
pools) permeate the landscape to the point where, for his
characters, unreality and reality are no longer delineated.
The people who inhabit his narratives are often disorien-
tated, forgetful, confused and this suits his cool, detached,
existential style. Ellis's actual position is much more slippery
– he critiques the landscape of Los Angeles while celebrating
it. He derides the excess while glorifying it. He seduces
while he defiles and nothing is what it seems. In the
famous closing line from *American Psycho*, 'This is not an
exit', he suggests that whether we're in Los Angeles or New
York we're all stuck in a kind of urban no-end game – and
so the succession of urban mythologisation continues.

The Boulevard of Broken Dreams has long fuelled
the mythic power of Los Angeles and allowed writers to
evoke provocative images, moods and atmospheres. These
positions are not so much a criticism of the city itself but
of the machinations of late capitalism; the ubiquitous
presence of a saturated media culture, which the city by

default, comes to symbolise. But of course Los Angeles
is real. People actually live there. And in studying this
literature I began to see the pattern of approach; a kind
of literary erasure, which refused recognition of the real
in order to mourn its absence. Los Angeles was a city it
was better not to really know. 'Real people' and 'ordinary
lives' weren't useful in the development of such surreal,
ambitious narratives. The neon-soaked streets of Los
Angeles, its glass facades, its skyscrapers required fallen
angels, vampiric-style murderers, anti-heroes, surveillance
and counter-surveillance, meaningless sex, rogue asteroids
and Armageddon.

How then, I thought, could we write cities like Los
Angeles, Vegas and perhaps even Australia's Gold Coast
from a different point of view – cities that shared this
postmodern urbanism without tipping into the enormous
literary tide of what had come before, without siding in
terms of a line of enquiry with one of two camps: theorists
like Robert Venturi, Denise Scott Brown and Edward
Soja, who celebrated and valued what was interpreted as
garish, junk culture in Las Vegas and Los Angeles, and
those like Mike Davis, who critiqued the vacuous excess
and spectacle from a Marxist perspective. Each of these
positions has after all, been clearly represented by their
literary counterparts for many decades and in ways which
have become known, owned and perhaps even old.

As a one-time resident of all three cities I felt neither
position held definitive sway over the lived experience. At
times the dystopian visions resonated, at others I felt the
rush and thrill of the surreal dream but in the end, these
cities resisted absolute definition. We had grappled with
dramatic urban change and an 'either or' mentality, or a 'for
and against' dialogue did little to extrapolate on the curious
assemblage of sites, projections and experiences now alive
and continuous in these cities. I wanted to consider how
might we write them into a different imaginative future.

When potent mythologies wrap around cities like Los Angeles, Vegas and the Gold Coast the shroud of mystique can prevent more nuanced kinds of understanding about how they work and how writers might depict them. In cities seemingly made to expose the dark behind the light, the tarnish underneath the glitter, the horror of a place where the sun always shines it's hard to resist that noirish lure, to be true to the characteristic of a place but to develop a view from the inside. I wanted to find out. I wanted to write about the Gold Coast from the point of view of the inside – to try and resist the clichéd, almost automated responses to the landscape embedded in our culture – so pervasive that very few Australian writers have actually gone there. Matthew Condon in *A Night at the Pink Poodle* does well, Helen Garner in *Postcards from Surfers* less so, as her view is pinched tight – a Melbournian in exile scowling at the perceived vacancy of the city, while conversely taking respite from her old world history within it. A view not unlike Fran Lebowitz's description of Los Angeles as, 'A large city-like area surrounding the Beverley Hills Hotel'.

I thought perhaps I could do something different. The result was *Ante Up,* a novel to be released by Harper Collins in 2012. *Ante Up,* though it is certainly noir, is deliberately conscious of the influence of the gamut of noir literature, especially that written in and about Los Angeles and is an attempt to wrestle the Australian crime narrative from the historically reductionist treatment it receives in narratives like *Underbelly* which, I believe, mimic the American rather than progress the Australian noir strain. Based on a true story; the main character is a croupier, the heroine a scamster, who by the time she is 19 has been arrested on 48 counts of fraudulent activity. Moving against the tide of moody critique the story is set in what appears to be a California-esque sunny place for shady people but one in which the city gets to speak back.

In the novel the Gold Coast acts as a kind of character watching and observing its players – the glitter so easily dismissed or reviled becomes a potent reverie.

The challenge for writers, as it is for architects, is to develop ways of seeing and interpreting living, which are appropriate to the city or locale, which respond to the city on its own terms. The boulevards might be constructed on the Gold Coast, the canals might be man-made, but the water which fills them still rolls in from the sea and you can still be taken by a shark. The connection therefore between the real and the man-made, between the constructed and the tangible is not necessarily enacted in a binary but within a complex set of relationships – of exchanges, engagements and actions between different states of being. I thought there might be another way to write crime without sacrificing a closer, more open and therefore more interesting vision of the city.

Buoyed by the notion that it might be possible to reconfigure long-held, outmoded, perhaps even snobbish ideas of what a city should be and how it should read I became fascinated with the notion and spectacle of Dubai – here was a city I thought was the epitome of relentless acceleration, the collapse of boundaries, the sheer thrill of urban vision, an idea that had so excited me about Los Angeles and the Gold Coast. What I found though when travelling there to do a major essay for *The Griffith Review* in 2008 was that my theory evaporated in the dust and the heat as the imagined city began to bounce up against the real.

I had landed and I was snared, caught in a literary and architectural conundrum, in a pre-Global Financial Crisis Dubai, which seemed to know no limits.

If Los Angeles was the mother ship and the Gold Coast the sister city of postmodern urban life, then Dubai was the death star. I realised just as Plato had suggested so long ago that what a writer cannot do is ignore the gaps, the trespasses taken in the name of progress, even with so much titillating diversion. After spending 30 days in Dubai I saw the enormous folly in the project of trying to sublimate nature to our point of view. Dubai is unhealthy, an environmental travesty and actually murderous. The kilometres and kilometres of labour camps attesting to the slavery such unmitigated and unregulated progress requires. Men in blue overalls falling out of the tallest building in the world, the Burj Dubai, at 50 bodies a month – their hands still clutching the small packets of rice they are given to eat high in steel towers in horrific heat. An enormous global farce we were all complicit in.

In Dubai it became important, as Juhani Pallasmaa posited, to shut off my eyes, to write about what I couldn't see, what I wasn't allowed to see, what I was told was merely a mirage. One of the ultimate goals of literature is to critique the political and economic machines that disenfranchise people and I realised this position could not be erased by a detached worship of spectacle for its own sake or, at the other end of the scale, a romanticised version of urban decay.

I read Dubai on its own terms and realised that perhaps there was something in the position of all those romantic poets: Keats, Byron and later, Brecht, walking lonely and appalled by all the condoms washed up on a Californian beach, that while their sensibilities did not translate well to the 'new' cities of America, living is and always has been about the body. That even in the most unnatural of places a human being reads the world through the five senses, through the 'Eyes of the Skin' – the environment, the economics and the culture. As writers or architects we should not ignore the context in which a city is placed even if in many instances we are drawing on assumptions, the swirl of narratives spinning around places we think we know and the mythologies which come to define the people who inhabit them. All those reassuring stories we have told ourselves since we sat around the campfire. Every practice, whether it is written in the word or in stone, is an amalgam of what has gone before. And so, in considering the relationship between writing and architecture we come full circle. How do we wrestle the spirit of both vocations into the problematic textures of human experience as it morphs and progresses? It is not as easy an endeavour as we may like to think. Hard not to rest on laurels, on the assurances, even the entertainment value of an old tale. Hard not to appropriate and paraphrase because something has worked so well before. Perhaps we have forgotten that we need only to continually reach for the essence of corporeal experience in the tastes, textures and aural messages of contemporary life, in the scent of the real, the tangible, the recesses of nature and the body, even if it is through a plate glass, against a slick facade, over a flat screen or from a safer vantage point inside the tallest building in the world.

I do not want to be able to see the end of the world from here.

Placing: Writing place, place writing

LINDA CARROLI

The *Placing* project is an ongoing critical and cultural exploration of place, writing place and place writing in the face of mounting need for change in the way we design, plan, create and live.[1] I started work on the project in 2008 with funding from the Australia Council's Visual Arts Board. The project engages broad questions about city-making (*poiesis*) and dwelling (*oikos*), as well as ideas about 'care'.

In his TED lecture, James Howard Kunstler observed that many of America's public spaces are not worth 'caring' about and that the places that have been built have deprived us of the ability to live in a hopeful present.[2] We don't have to look very far in Australia, particularly our suburbs, to see environments afflicted by a lack of care (or carelessness). Caring, for me, is an important idea to carry into our thinking about dwelling and city-making, and into practices of writing place. In this respect, I am referring to care in the sense of cultivate and curate – 'care-taking'. In *Sprawltown: Looking for the City on its Edges*, Richard Ingersoll discusses *synoikismos* as an ancient process of city-making, which involves agreeing to live together in dialogue.[3] Writing and conversation are vital for establishing that process. In developing *Placing*, I started looking around and talking to people about options and alternatives for our cities and communities and this idea of *synoikismos* was a springboard for considering other ways of telling stories and of shaping narrative in and of the city.[4]

Placing considers both practices of place and practices of writing place – both those of my own and those of others. Place is both a noun and a verb. This prompts an enquiry of place as something we do; something that is beyond place-making, and beyond the confines of single professions or disciplines. If place is something we do, then it is realised in or as our practices of place, including those practices of writing place and place writing. Where and how we live is captured in our acts of representation – as John Rennie Short says, 'space is turned into place through acts of discursive representation'[5] – and place has particularity through our acts of description and evaluation. Short points out that regimes of representation can, sometimes, result in the foreclosure of alternatives. I note these can manifest in reductionist sloganeering rather than potent aphorism. Where do ideas of 'creative city' or 'sustainable city' sit for you? As Short says, who can argue with those powerful representations of urban renewal and revitalisation as life-saving surgery? Now, as the shifting geographies of globalisation overwrite our cities, imposing other images and imaginations, our private and collective acts of reading and writing the city seem more pressing – almost begging for those alternative stories and gestures to emerge.

This paper is comprised of several fragments extracted and rewritten from the Placing Project weblog, PlaceBlog.[6]

One: Relocation

Several years ago, my partner and I relocated to the outer northern suburbs of Brisbane to live closer to my ageing mother. I've found it to be a fraught environment and I have fought with it, struggled against it. I've tried to find and create ethical moments in what I consider to be an unethical environment. During this time, largely as a result of this experience, I was moved to commence postgraduate studies in urban planning and design. My local area bears all the hallmarks of outer suburban development characteristic of sprawl. During my studies, I had taken to reading course-related material on my bus journey to work. Between reading descriptions of unhealthy sprawling environments in my textbooks, I would catch glimpses of it out the bus window. Can I imagine or write a future beyond this, *other* than this? So in the face of this question, my work is increasingly concerned with and engaged with suburban communities and lives in a broader context of culture, sustainability and futuring.

This is the sort of environment that evokes, quite starkly, Tony Fry's ideas of ontological design – that is,

Gympie Road at the bottom of my street.

On the footpath next to Gympie Road. Photographs Linda Carroli.

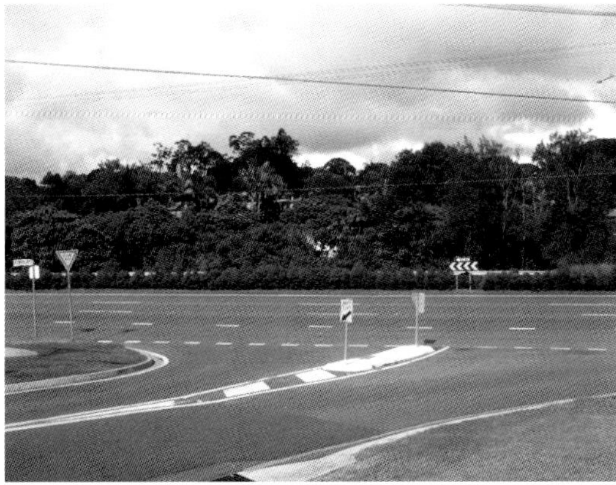

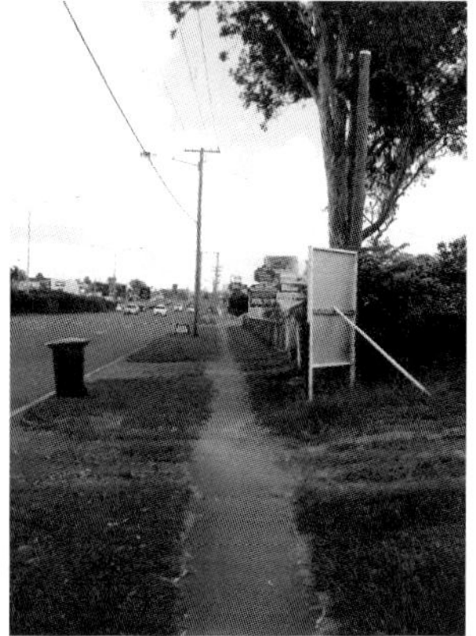

we design a place or a thing and that place or thing designs us. In suburban environments, we are designed as car-dependent consumers, fuelling a wasteful culture and economy of vapid consumption. In that circuit, we are ever more exploited and our resources are ever more exploited. In *The Three Ecologies*, Félix Guattari proposes that we need to pay attention to our mental and social ecologies.[7] In that work, he provides an example of a patient who spends all day walking around in circles, habitually reproducing their disorder until, one day, they do something else. That 'something else' isn't a distraction; it is compellingly another course, another pathway, a rupture in the reproduction of the disorder. This, of course, doesn't mean that the disorder no longer exists – there are other matters in the 'ecology of mind' to consider.

If we 'take care' about how we are to live, then we also need to 'take care' in how we design and build – how we make. This means being cognisant of the relationship between design (*designare*) and *designation*, which has some specific inferences in terms of land use and the making of the suburbs – and which, drawing on Paul Carter, alludes to ungroundedness and the application of moral hierarchies like suburban and urban. Carter states that we only appreciate the ground or the land 'only in so far as it bows down to our will'.[8]

Two: Writing

I've worked predominantly as a journalist or rather in a mode that is journalistic – concerned with the 'middle ground', the documentary or the report and the interrogation of circumstances. For me, journalists are gleaners – they map issues and current affairs in order to rearrange and tell various kinds of stories and elicit various kinds of responses. So I endeavour to bring an interdisciplinary mode of thought to my work and thinking in any of those fields. I am wary of evoking any particular professional identity, preferring instead to chart agency as a more trajectory relationship between identity and practice.

However, I have considered – and do consider – that writing, even journalism, can be a built environment practice, especially when engaged in solutions-based processes and advocacy. It creates environments by marking, drafting, designing, mapping and narrating.

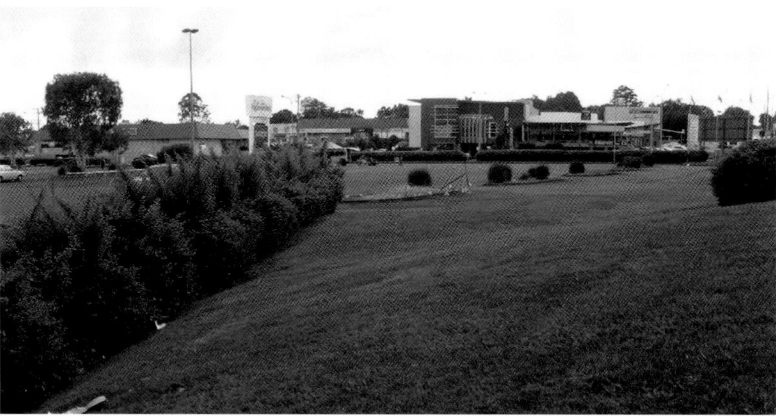

Aspley Hypermarket carpark looking towards town centre. Photograph Linda Carroli.

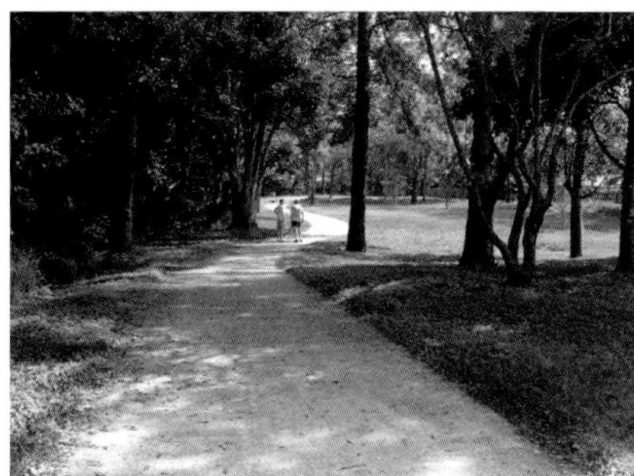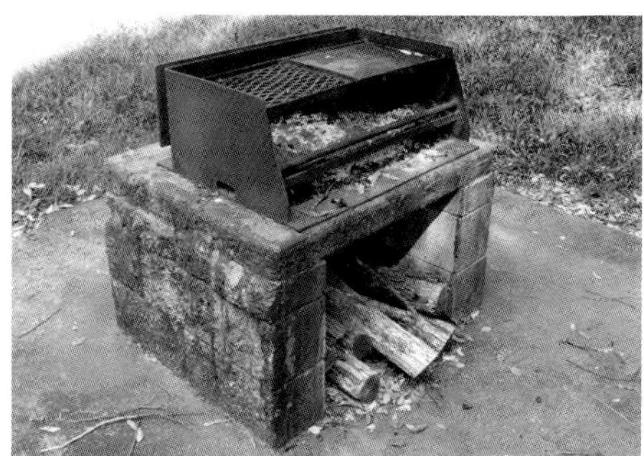

Walking and cycling path next to Little Cabbage Tree Creek.

Barbeque in local park.
Photographs Linda Carroli.

It can also be a type of caring; it can elicit caring. It is a kind of care-taking (perhaps more obviously recognisable in historic relationships between our newspapers and cities).

On reading an essay by Andrew Blum titled 'In Praise of Slowness: Thoughts on Writing About the Future of the City', I was struck by the following comment: 'what's obvious is that the city is slow and we write too fast.'[9] Our writing overtakes, possibly overwrites the city. Does fast writing force the city to move too quickly, causing it to blur in some Virilioan fantasy? Or does writing mask slowness and incrementality? Blum, an architecture journalist, notes 'how sharp the disconnect is between the immediacy required of journalism and the sheer evolutionary slowness of the city itself'. As I re-read this piece, I am acutely aware of its structure as threaded thoughts, where the writer self-consciously narrates an internal dialogue, drawing on other things he's read while trying to negotiate the possibilities of stories, buildings and cities. It's almost as if a journalism of the city is impossible: journalism is about today, while the meaning of building in the city is in the future. Stories perish daily.

In considering this and other points Blum raises, I'd become aware of some currents encircling the idea of 'slow journalism', a proposition that draws on the 'slow food' movement and means, according to Sasha Anawalt, that journalism is less mass-cultured and less celebrity-centred.[10] A practice of slow journalism may not be like any kind of journalism we've seen before – for example, the narrative feature, languid prose or the investigative expose – though these may certainly be part of it. We have new spaces and technologies to explore this idea and that, in part, is what the *Placing* project has set out to do through various social media platforms such as blogging. It may mean something more fractured, assembled publicly and collaboratively over time, like the city itself. Stories in this sense can be finely grained and populated, like place itself, and the story of the story is alive. It impels us into the future.

Three: Encounter

Encounter is a word or an idea that I often return to … and … begin from. It is chance and happening, meeting and discovery, desire and hope. Encounter is a commencement of experience and revelation, of learning and exploration, of relationship and interpellation. My deep respect for this idea has filtered through my journalism and writing on culture for a long time. It came of reading Roland Barthes's *A Lover's Discourse* and becoming entranced in the tremulous possibility of wonder: 'I am totally given over to this discovery (I tremble within it), to the point where any intense curiosity for someone encountered is more or less equivalent to love.'[11] The encounter is relational. It is a space – an event, often fleeting – a coming together of two or more 'things' or 'elements', generally not prefigured and with a generally indeterminate future. As if possessed by some strange aleatory conceit, I ordinarily write that which I experience in some way and that which I have had some cause to imagine beyond the encounter. It's not so much that I want to write myself into here, there or somewhere. The encounter becomes something other, something else. Rarely do I write of the encounter or the meeting itself, whether pleasurable or not. To encounter is to catalyse or to move, it is to conjure something anew or new. In the spaces of *synoikismos*, encounters abound and reverberate; through them 'taking care' is potent.

Recently, while walking along the main road, my partner and I were hassled by cars wanting to park on the footpath outside the big name franchise pizza shop. It's not the first time it has happened and it is common for pedestrians to have to negotiate cars as they walked along this stretch of foothpath. There could be six cars parked in this space rather than in the carparks at the rear of the building or next to the building. This particular evening, as we walked, we'd just had enough. The driver was particularly aggressive, a woman walking her dog had to walk on the main road (i.e. eight-lane highway) to pass the parked cars and we had to walk single file to squeeze between them. A wheelchair or a pram probably couldn't get through.

To walk in peace is a humble claim to make. So on returning home, I emailed the local councillor to ask if anything could be done about it. I had in my mind that a combination of footpath improvement measures were in order: bollards, plantings, grassing etc., perhaps a shady tree or two, perhaps even a collaboration with the property owner to improve the streetscape, perhaps something that drew the community into the streets to participate. Even though the space is on a main road, it could be used and walked more comfortably. The more bearable it is, the more likely it is that people will walk. I was pleased when the councillor's office responded with a commitment that something would be done.

In a matter of weeks, a forest of 16 bare galvanised steel bollards was installed and that was it. While I thought, at the time, that it was better than nothing, I did feel that this small win for pedestrian safety was indeed a loss for urban design and community benefit. I then asked the councillor if it was possible to paint the bollards, perhaps a community art project with local school children, just to have something happening at street level. It presented an opportunity to form some connections between the community and the physical/design of the space as a step, perhaps, to encouraging some kind of civic pride in our locality. However council's response was that it did not want the maintenance burden that painting the bollards would bring. It just goes to show how public works activity can degrade public and community spaces, particularly in suburban areas where council continually fails to invest in social and community life beyond the basics. [12] It reinscribes what Robin Boyd described in 1960 as the Australian ugliness[13] and what we have come to experience as suburban degeneration while the urban is expensively regenerated. For me, that is a prevailing example of not caring, not care-taking.

Recently installed bollards on Gympie Road. Photograph Linda Carroli.

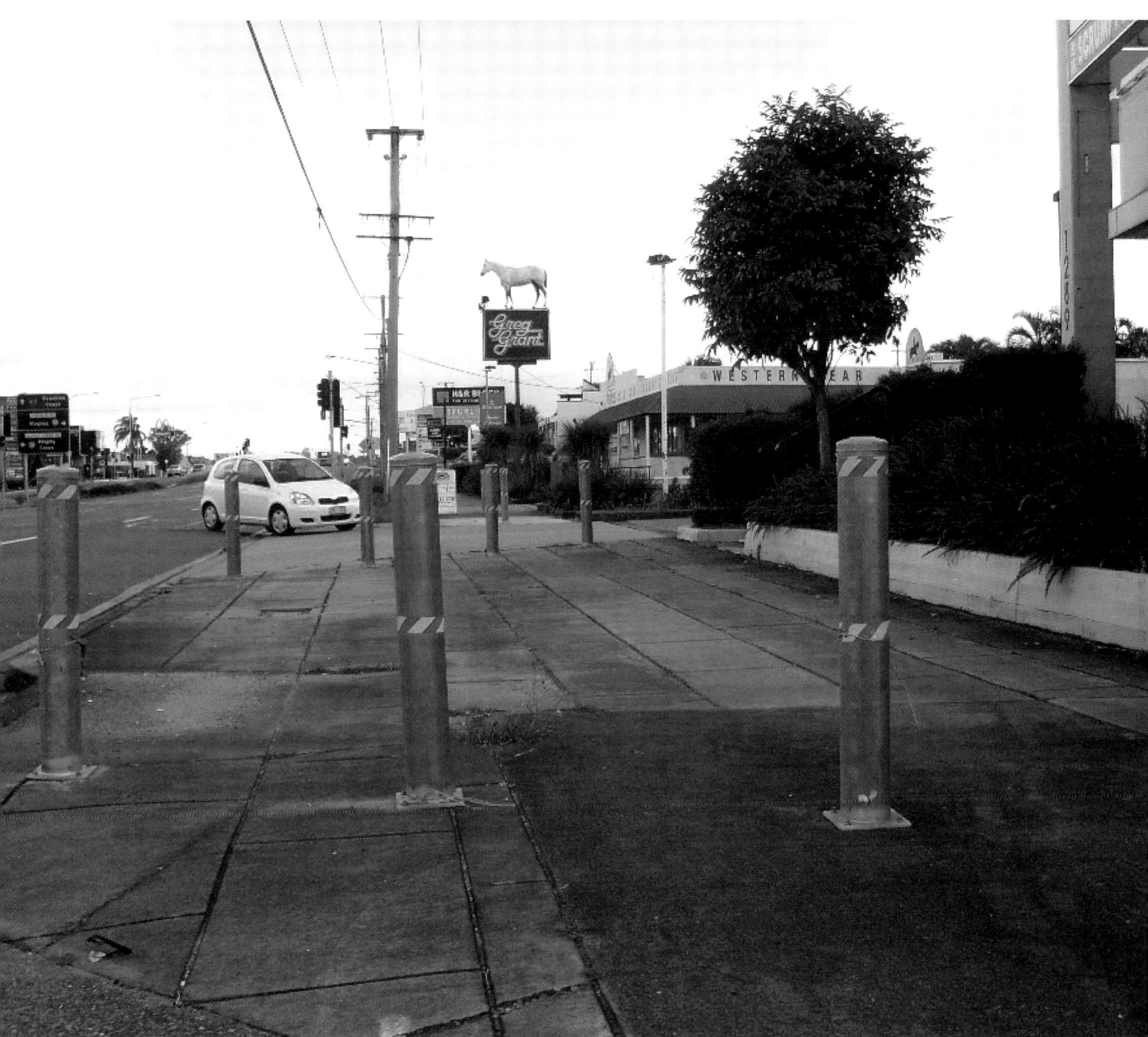
Greg Grant
WESTERN WEAR
H&R BLOCK

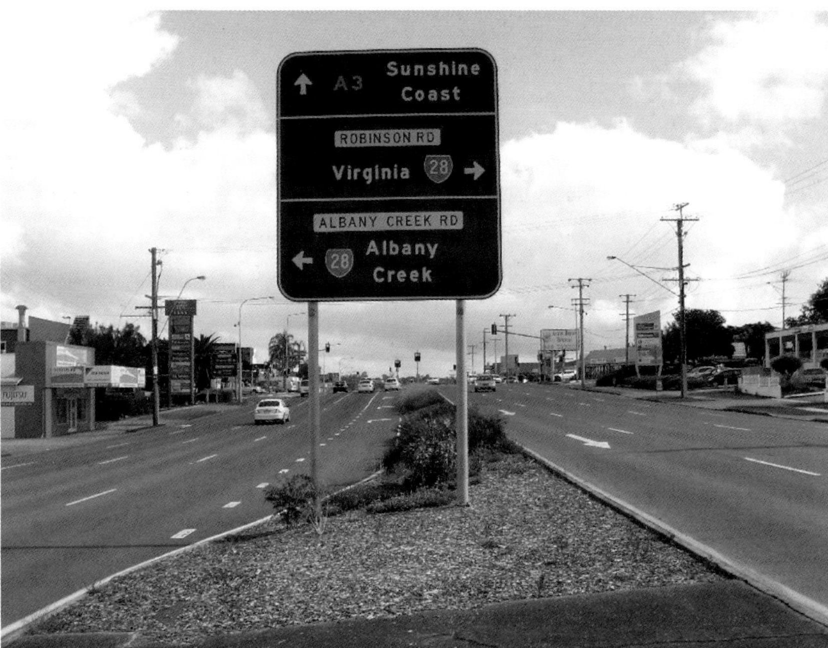

Gympie Road.

(Opposite) A family of ducks in Little Cabbage Tree Creek where it meets Albany Creek Road and the Aspley Hypermarket. Photographs Linda Carroli.

Four: Unsettlement

Imagine your grandmother and hold her image in your mind.

There are quite a few retirement villages in this outer suburban world, clustered around the Aspley Hypermarket, yet severed from the surrounding landscape. While walking home from the bus stop, waiting to cross the main road, which at eight lanes wide, can feel like a life and death undertaking, I've crossed on the walk sign many times as cars whizzed by, oblivious to traffic signals and to me. I'm not the only one: a white cross, adorned with fabric flowers, is staked into the traffic island, commemorating 15-year-old Joline.

Imagine your grandmother.

An elderly woman paused beside me as I waited, then asked if she could walk across the road with me because it's so wide. I was pleased to oblige and offered her my arm. So we chatted and she said that she had visited the doctor but wasn't sure of her way home. Where do you live I asked her, and she replied with the name of her retirement village. As we stepped onto the road, I told her that I was sure that she needed to be travelling in the opposite direction. No, no, she said, it's up there – and she pointed in the direction that we were facing. So I suggested we ask at the pet shop on the other side of the road. There, they confirmed that the retirement village is located in the other direction. She was embarrassed and agitated, saying that she usually came out in the car. As I escorted her, I tried to be reassuring. It can happen to anyone I told her as we returned across the road and headed to the next intersection, where I suspected she might sight her destination – unmissable next to the monolithic shopping centre set on its wide bitumen plane. After thanking me for my help, she turned away to walk safely home. Many elderly people are relocating or have relocated to my local area, with little or no connection to the place, harbouring in the compressed walled or gated estates, only to lose their way across the faceless terrain of roads and carparks, seeking refuge in cars because walking exposes frailty.

Because there is both hope and fear in our current situation, I used the *Placing* project to search for paths, utterances and moments of hope. If that hope means the way we live has to change – and so the way we plan, design and create – then the question is 'what are you/ we/I prepared to change?' The question was put during my participation in a series of seminars with Tony Fry on 'design futures'.[14] In a mix of poetry, philosophy, politics and performance, Fry situates alternative possibilities for design and the possibility of a 'future by design': he speaks of 'redirected practice' and 'designing unnecessary or unsustainable things away'. What I find most compelling about Fry's commentaries is his assertion that the prevailing human condition in the current epoch is one of 'unsettlement'. Increasingly, he says, individuals and communities will be – ontologically – insecure in the way and where they are. In large part, this 'unsettlement' will result from climate change and weather events.[15] If we are 'unsettled' what does that mean for our sense of place, our relationship with the world and our connections to each other? How do we write place, how do we write for place – how do we dwell, care and make? Is it another iterative experience of disengagement? In this seminar series, Fry asked, 'What will change you?'. In reflecting on the self, as practitioner or as someone who takes care, we begin to reflect on how things, more generally, are changed, where something different is brought into existence.

For Fry, there is a need to change design and to change our understanding of design and reconsider how we might think, act and design sustainment. He says, 'we dwell in our thinking' and I think we also dwell in

our writing, caring through it. I understand the idea of 'dwelling' through the Greek *oikos*, which is the root for words like ecology, economy and *ekistics*. It tends to be translated as house or habitat. In terms of developing a rhetoric of sustainment, this idea of dwelling is pivotal. In addressing the words, the sound and image of sustainment, Fry points out that there is the danger of collapsing into rhetoric, into empty language. And we see this already in the various proclamations for sustainability (another process that Fry says produces more of the same, that is, sustaining the unsustainable).

What are the statements we can make with and about art, architecture, urban design and planning that genuinely respond to social and ecological concerns and that genuinely create or design the future? For me, it means an emergent and disruptive rhetoric, an overwriting of criticisms and hegemonies that stubbornly resist change.

Stop

Planning and design are as much about narrative as they are about form, about writing stories or scripts for the future. This involves writing place. There is no greater joy

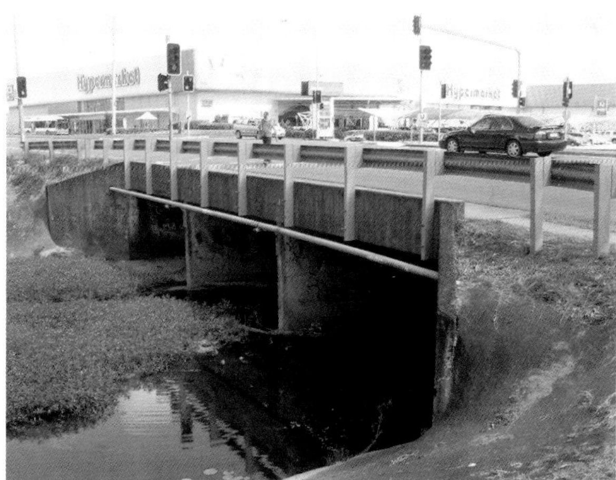

than being lost in the process of writing; to be immersed in every word and the spaces between them. So for me, if planning is one of those professions that tug at a range of disciplines, including design, and if it casts lines across the past and future, then the range of storytelling opportunities and conversations has the breadth and depth of the landscape itself. In terms of the *Placing* project, this means looking at new kinds of practice-based scenarios – a different kind of ethos that is related to *oikos* and *poiesis*: care and design. So I am considering what stories I can – or need to – cast into the future. How will or can you be part of them? That is what writing place does.

Images from a walk around my suburb

Most days I go for a walk. The route I have plotted and now habitually follow around my suburb of Aspley follows Gympie Road and then across to Albany Creek Road, through some newish housing estates and then along a walking and cycling path running through the park beside Little Cabbage Tree Creek. The photographs in this essay were taken during a walk on the morning of Saturday 5 February 2011.

1   The project has resulted in electronic writings and publications addressing the intersection of cultural and urban life. The objective of the project is to draw out emerging and changing ideas about urban environments with a particular emphasis on the role artists, designers, planners, architects and other urbanists can play as change-makers or change-scapers. This paper engages themes from the project through the presentation of fragments from writing to reflect on the relationship between writing, design and place.

2   James Howard Kunstler, 'James H Kunstler dissects suburbia'. TED. May 2007, http://www.ted.com/talks/james_howard_kunstler_dissects_suburbia.html (accessed 27 April 2010).

3   Richard Ingersoll, *Sprawltown: Looking for the city on its edges*, New York: Princeton Architectural Press, 2006.

4   The quality of our conversations is of concern to me as I work in private consulting and that much of my work is focused on community consultation and engagement about urban development. It's been pointed out to me that planners are often an early sign that a change is mooted for a locality: 'You know something is going down when the planners show up' is how it was expressed to me.

5   John Rennie Short, 'Urban Imagineers: Boosterism and the Representation of Cities', *The Urban Growth Machine: Critical Perspectives Two Decades Later*, New York: State University of New York Press, 1999, 38.

6   *Placing* is at http://placing.wordpress.com

7   Felix Guattari, *The Three Ecologies*, London: Continuum, 2008, fp 2000.

8   Paul Carter, *The Lie of the Land*, Melbourne: Faber & Faber, 1996, 2.

9   Andrew Blum, 'In Praise of Slowness', *Urban Omnibus*, 21 January 2009, http://urbanomnibus.net/2009/01/in-praise-of-slowness (accessed 18 April 2010).

10 Sasha Anawalt, 'The Slow Journalism Movement -- heard of it?'. ARTicles, 7 September 2008, http://www.najp.org/articles/2008/09/the-slow-journalism-movement-h.html (accessed 19 April 2010).

11 Roland Barthes, *A Lover's Discourse: Fragments*, London: Penguin Books, 1990, fp 1979, 198-199.

12 In response, I assailed those bollards with scavenged and found knitting. Others have joined in by wrapping streamers around the bollards.

13 Robin Boyd, *The Australian Ugliness*, Sydney: Penguin Books, 1980, c. 1960.

14 See also Tony Fry, *Design Futuring: Sustainability, Ethics and New Practice*, Sydney: UNSW Press, 2009.

15 This text was written before the flooding that struck 75 percent of Queensland in 2011. In Brisbane, 28,000 homes were affected by flooding. This was followed in February by a Category 5 tropical cyclone in Far North Queensland – the worst in the state's history – also resulting in widespread devastation of homes and communities.

Writing as Architecture: Theorist practitioners and DIY architecture 1917/1974

ERIK GHENOIU

Charles Moore's *The Place of Houses* of 1974 (with Gerald Allen and Donlyn Lyndon) and Hermann Muthesius's *Wie baue ich mein Haus?* of 1917 together occupy an unusual place in architectural literature: books showing a lay reader how to assume control of the design of their own house through the characteristic method of the architect/author. This approach constitutes a relationship between author/architect and reader/client that is distinct from related versions found in pattern books, prefab, design-build, or non-professional DIY architecture: the distinction lies in the fact that for Moore and Muthesius, the act of design could be located in the text itself. Moore and Muthesius were both writing as prominent architects past their first fame, reaching out to a wide readership as they began to be unfashionable as models for younger architects. They each fell upon the strategy of entrusting the execution of

design to the client – a position that might at first be taken to undermine the role of the architect – because of key sympathies between their architectural philosophies: both believed that architecture should be closely tailored to the ordinary lives of its inhabitants, and both located design primarily in the elaboration of the relationship between a human and an environment, and not in the formal built result of that relationship. These books functioned by establishing this elaboration in textual form, so that what was in the eyes of Moore and Muthesius the relatively unimportant work of form could be left in the hands of the individual client, or in this case, the reader.

This essay is a game. The purpose of the game is to determine when writing, text, is most directly the act of architecture in itself: not writing *about* buildings or about architecture – not criticism – but writing as the primary vessel of the architect's intervention in the design of actual buildings. I say 'the design of actual buildings' to exclude most of the range of architectural theory, which might otherwise serve as an answer to this question, uselessly too general to consider the writing as itself the architectural act. This requirement would also exclude literature that generates something like an architecture or a story of an architecture within its text. Consider for instance Georges Perec's *Life: A User's Manual*, a novel the many chapters of which are descriptions of the rooms in a Parisian apartment building, imagined frozen in time and with its facade peeled away.[1] Such a book starts with a real building or at least a real building type, then recreates and analyses it in the writing. In trying to find an example of written work that might directly qualify as an act of architecture, we must look for the opposite process, which would start with the writing of an architect and then analyse and recreate this writing in an actual building, or many buildings.

To pursue this, one might turn to a consideration of the relationship between client and architect, asking whether there is a version of this relationship in which the architect's role is confined largely to the writing of a text and not to the direct rendering of an actual plan for a building, but which nevertheless constitutes an act of design more precise than the abstraction of theory and more concrete than imaginary description. The two books currently in question, *Wie baue ich mein Haus? (How Do I Build My Own House?)* and *The Place of Houses*, share an unusual framing of the relationship between architect and client in precisely this way. These books address nearly the same theme: an architect advising his reader how to attend to the design of his or her *own house*. In both cases, the text rehearses an architect's personal way to conceive of the active designing of a house, any house, but both also encourage that the particular design of the individual house largely occurs directly in the hands of the client. Essentially, these books operate not by simply

telling the reader how to be his or her own architect, but by instructing this reader on how to act as a rough facsimile of Muthesius or Moore for as long as it takes to carry out the design of their own house. This isn't to say that either of them rule out the idea that an architect would be involved at all – Muthesius seems to assume that at least the external form of the house will still be entrusted to a professional designer[3] – but in both cases the developing of the brief and the devising of its basic solution is entrusted to the reader, who is also the owner-builder and who, if he or she reads the book correctly, is also effectively an extension of Muthesius or Moore. Note that these are not books about how to *construct* a house, and neither assumes that the reader/client will act as contractor. The subject of these books is designing the scheme of the house, for Muthesius also making this scheme economically practical, and nothing more.

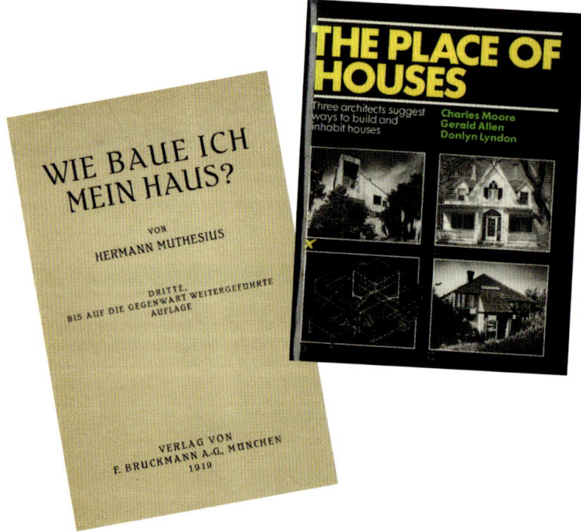

Title page of *Wie baue ich mein Haus?* (third expanded edition), 1919. Cover of *The Place of Houses,* (first Holt Paperbacks edition), 1979.

One might immediately counter that a similar sense of writing architecture would apply to many of the foundation texts of the field, from Vitruvius to Alberti to Durand and so forth; really any textbook meant to outline what architecture is (from one viewpoint or another) and how it is actually done. It's easy to identify books like this at least up until the style wars of the 19th century created enough doubt about the nature of architecture that defining it and telling how to do it could no longer fit comfortably in a single treatise. However, these books share a key trait in that they are all meant not to produce designs, but to produce designers. Muthesius and Moore on the other hand did not mean in these books to train designers per se, but only to help clients satisfy their own needs in a one-time act: not to teach them how to play the role of designer, but to teach them how, for the span of a single project, to play the role of Muthesius or Moore alongside their original role of client.

Before situating these two books in closer detail, it will be useful to delineate how they differ from other possible relationships between client and architect beside the assumed architectural standard of bespoke work executed personally project by project. First, these are adamantly not pattern books. 'We started out to write a pattern book,' Moore and his collaborators tell us, but after some discussion they conclude that 'our experience as architects leads us to believe that houses can and should be more completely suited to the lives of their inhabitants and to the specific places where they are built. No simple or even complex set of house patterns, however ingenious and skilful, would do.'[4] Before writing his book Muthesius had edited several substantial volumes, illustrating exemplary single-storey family houses with plans, more sample books than pattern books (overleaf), but in *Wie baue ich mein Haus?*, he scarcely includes any illustrated examples over four hundred pages.[5] Of course there is a reason for this. Consider the relationship of the client to the architect in the classic pattern book[6] (this page): the design is done

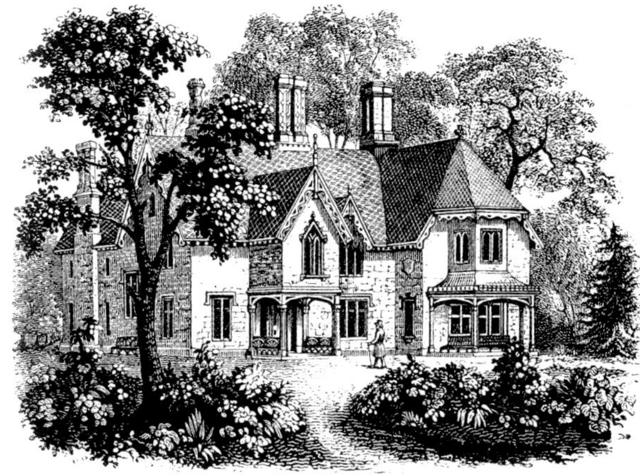

Fig. 54.

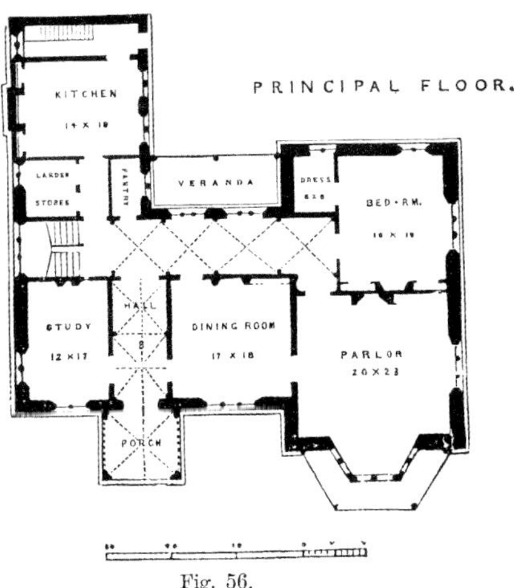

Fig. 56.

Plate from Andrew Jackson Downing, *Cottage Residences*, 1873.

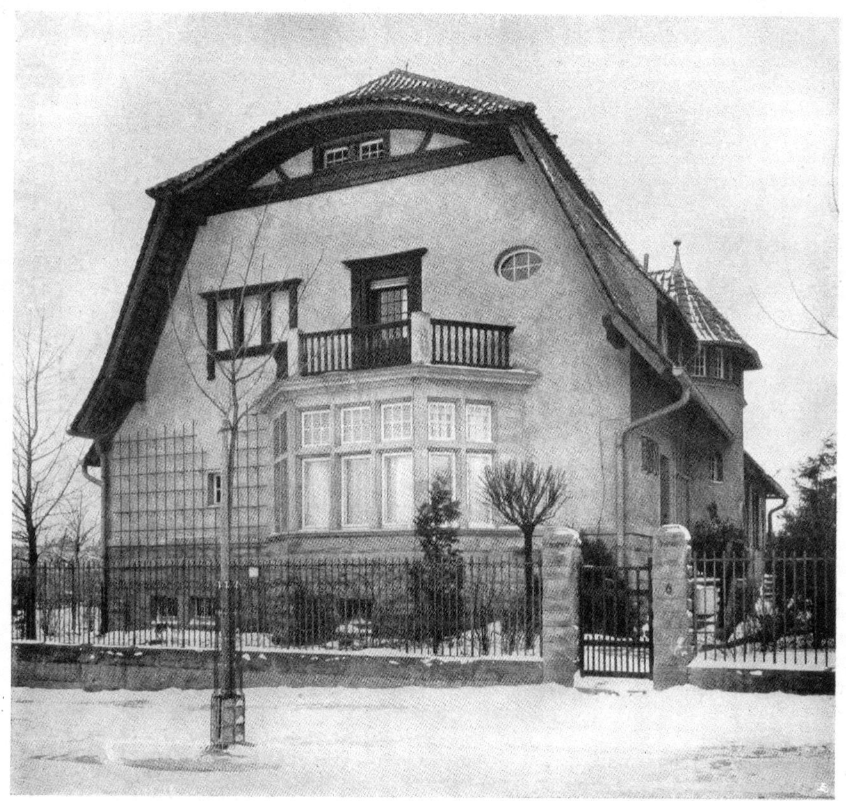

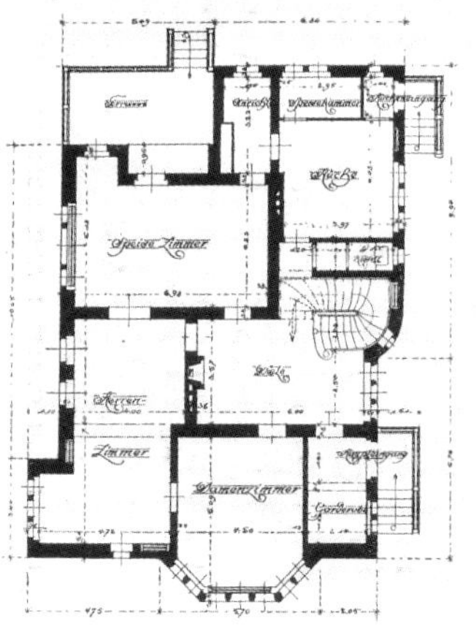

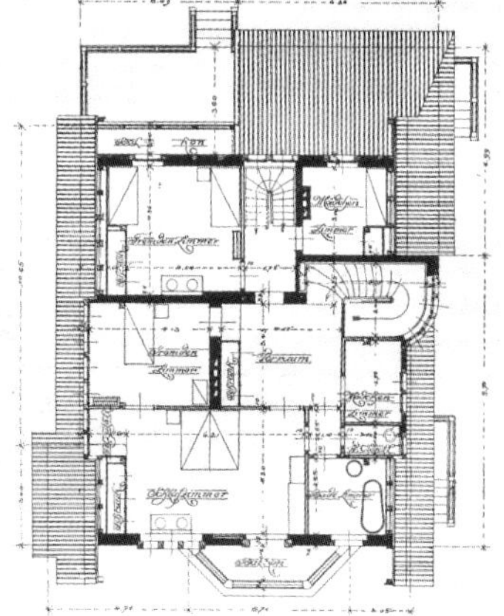

Plate from Muthesius, *Landhaus und Garten*, 1907.

ahead of time with a typical client envisioned, ready cut rather than tailor-made, and with little or no text necessary. There is some room for adaptation during the execution of the pattern, but this is seldom accounted for in the original design. The same temporal relationship of the design to the reader/builder attains in the kind of exemplary sample book that Muthesius had previously written: the work of design seemed already finished and ready for the taking. This bothered Muthesius enough that he warned the reader against drawing solutions directly from the examples in these books: 'A good [architectural] plan is suitable only in the single case for which it was designed.'[7]

This same problem of formal design coming before a particular building commission can become programmatically ossified in what might be taken as the ideological opposite of the two books we're discussing, namely prefab architecture.[8] Although prefab can be done in such a way as to be very malleable for any individual executed building, the danger perpetually looming within it is that mass production will ignore differences of place or identity in the client or commission, particularly in the case of prefab housing. The period between the publication of Muthesius's book and that of Moore's saw an explosion of interest in prefab housing, both in high examples like Moshe Safdie's Habitat 67 and common ones like the camping trailers first mass-produced just before WWI that evolved into the Airstream Trailers and Winnebago 'Motorhomes' of Moore's day. If the high examples tend to seek strategies to establish variety in repetition, the common examples make no such apologies and rather exult in standardisation, and in the case of trailers and motorhomes inherently emphasise emancipation from rootedness in site.

Beyond the pattern book and prefab, there are two other possible relationships between architect and client that I'd like to bring into this discussion, neither of which was much in evidence in Muthesius's day, but both of

which had become hot trends by the time Moore and company were writing, and both of which were associated with the kind of leftist-progressive cultural politics Moore espoused. The first of these is the design-build movement established on the American east coast in 1965 by some disaffected new graduates of the Yale School of Architecture, David Sellers and Bill Rienecke,[9] and more gradually around the same time by early 'green' architects on the west coast like Sim Van der Ryn. Sellers and Rienecke had rebelled against the second-generation modernist leadership at Yale under Paul Rudolph, and this same political energy in the school led to Rudolph's replacement in the fall of that year by Charles Moore. In the few years directly before this, while Moore was serving as chair of architecture at the College of Environmental Design at the University of California at Berkeley, he co-wrote an article with Sim Van der Ryn, and beyond these connections, the similarity of form and material choice would suffice to show that the design-build movement was closely tied to the new postmodernism espoused by Moore.

Separated from its style and rhetoric, design-build is fundamentally defined by the principle that the architect is also the building contractor, and that the whole process is carried out in close collaboration with the client. Here it should be clear that in comparison to the two books presently under discussion, design-build fails to reproduce their relationship of the architect to the client because the architect is always personally present – in fact more so than in almost any other mode of architectural practice. They also manifest a different relationship between architecture and text in that design-build often did away with texts or even drawings altogether. Muthesius and Moore each had many ideas in sympathy with those of the design-build architects, but for the purposes of this essay, one could say that the absence of the intermediary text takes away the critical tension of identification between architect and client.

The opposite problem attains in the stylistically similar hippie craftsman DIY movement of the same time, tied to many of the same people including Van der Ryn.[10] Here, the architect is not present at all in the design process and although both Moore and, in the context of his own time, Muthesius, want their readers to some degree to design their own houses, they want them to do it properly, namely in the way that they themselves would do it. For this, there is only one requirement, the thing that sets in place the whole constellation of forces I've been discussing: the text.

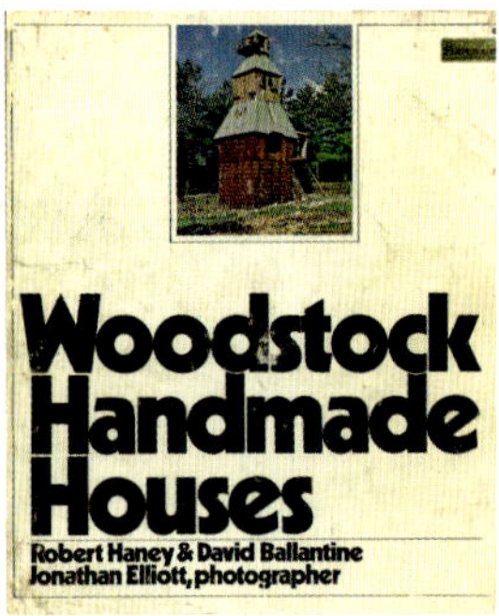

Cover of Robert Haney and David Ballantine, *Woodstock Handmade Houses*, 1974.

And now we can take a look at the two books themselves. First, it is possible to identify a number of additional parallels between them. Though it is hardly read now, *Wie baue ich mein Haus?* was Muthesius's bestselling book, going into three editions within two years (1917–1919) and spawning a companion volume, *Kann ich auch jetzt noch mein Haus bauen?* in 1920.[11] This amounted to tens of thousands of copies, which is to say about 10 times higher than the audience for a successful book aimed at a primarily professional audience within German architecture at that time. Similarly, *The Place of Houses* was the most widely read of the many publications of Moore and his circle, simplifying and systematising many of their articles and shorter works of the preceding decade, and it is still available in print over

35 years later. So not only were the authors serious about their intention of reaching a popular audience, but they were demonstrably successful in this effort.

Second, both books were written by architects at the top of their field, beyond their first fame but occupying and having occupied high positions in architectural education and as icons of new movements. Muthesius[12] had served as the state-appointed apostle of English modernism to Germany (at the time, this meant second generation Arts and Crafts movement), he espoused a new suburban country house ideal that had found broad acceptance in central Europe, he had taken a position of authority over design and craft education for the Prussian Ministry of Commerce, and he had been the principal figure behind the foundation of the influential *Deutsche Werkbund*. Between around 1906 and the battles of the Werkbund Streit of 1914, he was perhaps the single-most powerful architect in the German-speaking world. By 1917, however, with the war winding down and his governmental position and exclusive clientele about to disappear with the establishment of the Weimar Republic, and with his design ideology under attack by prominent members of the new generation like Walter Gropius and Bruno Taut, it was becoming clear that Muthesius's importance within the field was at an end. As a popular writer, however, he was only just hitting his stride.

Similarly, Moore was writing at the moment when the 15 years of his finest works and most senior academic positions was coming to a close, and his reputation as one of the two pillars of early American postmodern architecture (along with Robert Venturi) was firmly established. His firm's Sea Ranch Condominiums of 1965 (opposite) had become canonical in American postmodernism, a status reflected in *Place of Houses*, where it had the third chapter to itself, placing it on a level with the famously beautiful 18th century seaside village of Edgartown and the entire city of Santa Barbara, subjects of the first two chapters. Moore had never achieved the degree of importance that

Muthesius had held, but he had also not suffered from the same setbacks and drying up of prominent commissions, and so he was not writing with the same sense of personal urgency as Muthesius. Even so, it seems clear that both architects were attempting not only to reach a wider audience with these books than they had previously done, but that they were also both interested in using this broadening as a chance to summarise the positions they had been developing over the preceding years.

At this point, however, a problem arises that calls into question the motivation behind both books: why would a prominent architect write a theoretical treatise advising a non-professional reader how to judge and even carry out the design of his own house? That an aesthetic and critical understanding of design might be entrusted to and cultivated in the residential client himself implies both a self-limiting of the authority of the designer in determining the formal solution, and a new role for the architect as educator and guide for the potential self-builder. It seems almost counter-intuitive for someone deeply invested in the professional status of the designer to undermine this status by needlessly disrupting the settled relationship between client and architect. (Consider, for instance, that Muthesius and his circle had not only laid the theoretical groundwork for modern industrial design, but also helped make it professionally feasible by paving the way for the copyright laws that would give designers intellectual property rights over their own work.) This question becomes all the more troubling when we consider that almost no books with a similar mission and by practitioners at a comparable level can be identified in the almost 60 years between the appearance of *Wie baue ich mein Haus?* and *The Place of Houses*, essentially the whole period of the preeminence of international modernism.

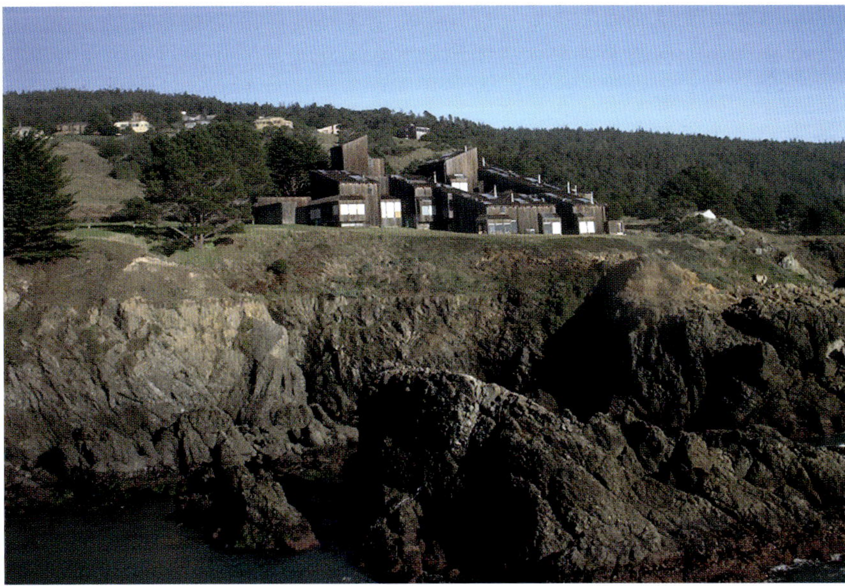

MLTW, Sea Ranch Condominium, California, 1965. Photograph John Spelman.

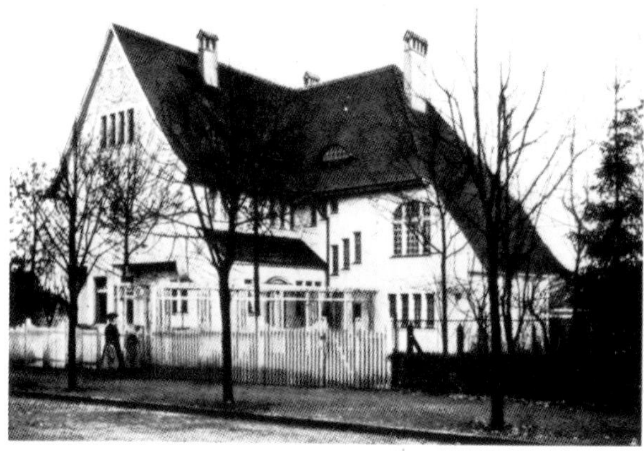

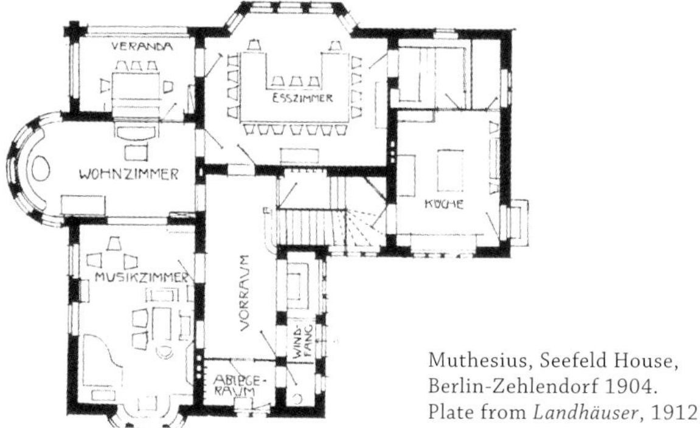

Muthesius, Seefeld House,
Berlin-Zehlendorf 1904.
Plate from *Landhäuser*, 1912.

The beginning of an answer may be found in the fact that both Muthesius and Moore believed in a craft-based architecture generated out of a close adaptation of form and particularly plan to the social life of the buildings' inhabitants, and that both were suspicious of an architecture that emphasises artistic expression. But other writer-architects also felt this way without making similar gestures, and even Muthesius and Moore didn't push the matter this far earlier in their careers. A closer chronology will help cast a better light on this issue.

By 1917 Hermann Muthesius was, as already mentioned, in a difficult professional position. Architectural truths he had once held to be self-evident were now under attack, as were once-canonical buildings like his Seefeld House of 1904, the first of his country houses built after his return from years on assignment studying English architecture and design as a diplomatic attache. More recent buildings like his Mittelhof of 1914–15 (opposite), though more technically accomplished than his earlier work were not receiving the positive attention within the profession that he had once enjoyed. In short, I believe that with the changing professional climate he no longer trusted architects to carry out commissions in the manner in which he was convinced they ought to be done. Ten years earlier, half the young architects in Germany tried to imitate some aspect of Muthesius's houses in their work, but now the fresh young faces at the design schools he had helped to reform, were more likely to regard him as the symbol of an obsolete order. Against this, another tenet Muthesius had long argued came into play: he believed that it was the duty of the designer not only to create exceptional works, but also to educate the taste of the public, particularly of the lower middle-class (*Kleinbuergerlich*) public, so that they would understand how to identify quality and seriousness in design. In this sense, writing directly to the builder-client was an entirely sensible design decision. He writes, 'the house builder is generally of the opinion that the exterior design of the building is a matter for the architect, which he himself could scarcely understand,' [13] and he sets about to correct this situation.

The expanded 1919 edition of *Wie baue ich mein Haus?* comprises 48 short chapters in 424 pages. It begins with a simple proposition.

How do I build my own house? Today this question moves thousands who want to escape the urban ocean of buildings and who believe they can no longer cope with the nerve-shattering stress of the bustling metropolis. It's an alluring thought to have your own little house out and away from this instead of a rented apartment. [...] But an inquiry of this sort is not so easy for beginners.'[14]

From these first lines, the target audience is clear: potential first-time homeowners from the emerging urban lower middle class, a group that Muthesius had long held to be the critical class for modern Germany, both architecturally and from the viewpoint of his social-democratic politics, and whose workingclass forebears had not had the means or opportunity to consider owning their own residence. The book poses itself as a more or less impartial introduction to the many basic questions involved with the process of building a house for oneself, but it is of course never impartial. Beyond the initial promotion of the idea of an English-style small suburban single-family owner-occupied residence, Muthesius manages to weave all of the

stages of his own housing design philosophy in with the more prosaic considerations of his readers: for every chapter like 'Questions of Cost' or 'Heating', there are three on themes such as 'The Placement of the House on the Plot' or the arrangement of every single room of the house as an architectural solution to the use-function of that room and the particular lifestyle of the client. In effect, this is an applied version of the analysis Muthesius first laid out in *Das Englische Haus* and elaborated many times later: analysing everyday life and the cultural history of how architecture accommodates it, carrying out the design on its site and room by room as a fine-grained execution of this accommodation, and regarding the external appearance of the building as a relatively minor consideration. The reader may never before have thought of a dwelling as something that should be tailored to personal preferences and lifestyle as precisely as the contents of a wardrobe

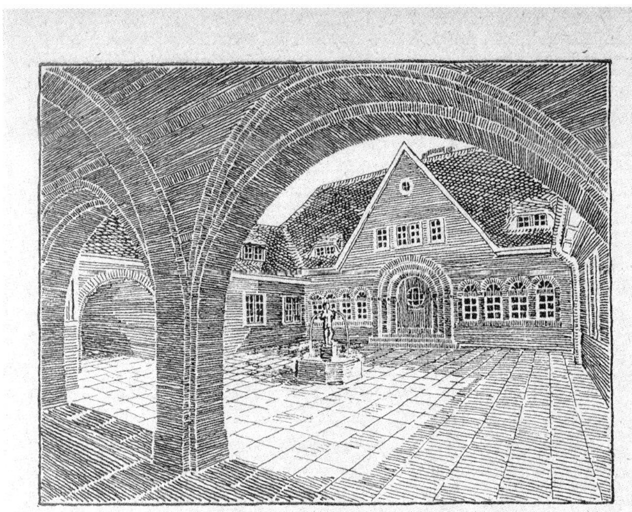

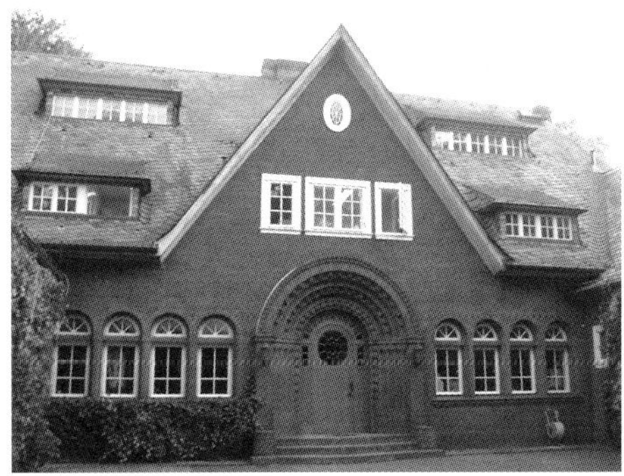

Muthesius, Mittelhof, Berlin-Nikolassee 1914–1915. Plate from *Wie baue ich mein Haus?*, 1919.

Muthesius, Mittelhof. Photograph Erik Ghenoiu.

might be, but Muthesius does his best to convince the reader to insist on nothing less.

This kind of education of public taste to regard design objects and built environments as inherently tied to the way people live their lives may be seen clearly in the writing of Paul Schultze-Naumburg, a colleague of Muthesius, who was famous for reaching a wide popular audience. In his nine-book series, the *Kulturarbeiten* (Works of Culture), published between 1900 and 1917, Schultze-Naumburg worked to consolidate public taste through an extended matrix of plain-speaking essays and rhetorical site photography, playing on popular taste for pre-industrial environments to construct simple contrasts that led the reader through a long series of ethical-aesthetic conclusions (opposite).[15] If we were to translate his conservative everyman tone into the new-age style of the 1970s, we might arrive at a very similarly motivated and similarly successful work of popular taste-making, Christopher Alexander's *A Pattern Language* of 1977. Alexander and his co-authors write: 'What exactly is the status of this published language? (…) The fact is, that we have written this book as a first step in the society-wide process by which people will gradually become conscious of their own pattern languages, and work to improve them.'[16] In this way and a few years after Moore's book, Alexander too wants to guide people in designing their own environments, as long as they design them in a version of his language. Here then, the bridge of public taste can serve as the transition from Muthesius to Moore.

If it is clear why Muthesius takes on this peculiar strategy of reforming the reader's tastes, the question remains why Charles W. Moore does the same thing 60 years later. Although as I've mentioned there are a number of similarities between the two, as a champion of client participation in design and of both public and stylistic inclusiveness, Moore is not comfortable with the idea of telling his readers what to think. *The Place of Houses* begins with the idea of taste.

Good taste, we are told, is a singularly important factor in the design of a house. We are usually told this by someone who is assumed to possess it, and who generally makes a considerable point of the rest of the assumption: that there are people who don't have it, and that includes you, and that you will have to pay dearly to be suitably worked over.[17]

Recall that Moore was walking a fine line between two irreconcilable audiences: professional architects for whom he was a symbol of craftsmanship and community participation, and the group we've seen represented by the design-build dissidents and the craft DIY builders, who were universally leery of the mainstream of architectural discourse. In a way, by choosing an even more extreme version of the approach taken by Muthesius, he does not undermine the role of the architect, but reinjects it into a branch of building that was at the time tending to leave it behind.

Taking this into account, it is interesting that *The Place of Houses* begins not with the crazy-looking new architecture of postmodernism or design-build, but at the same place in time from which Muthesius and Schultze-Naumburg also choose to depart: in vernacular architecture of around 1800, that is to say in the time immediately before industrialisation. Although Moore and his collaborators used the book to showcase their own designs much more than Muthesius, they also describe ordinary places and the works of other architects more than Muthesius does. After examining a series of exemplary places and architectural projects (mostly their own), Moore, Allen, and Lyndon proceed to identify what they call the three 'orders', or realms of consideration around which a house should be designed: rooms, machines and dreams, and then go on to describe in the same sequence how the reader might work out a scheme according to these orders. The order of rooms is very similar to Muthesius's more exhaustive consideration of the house room by

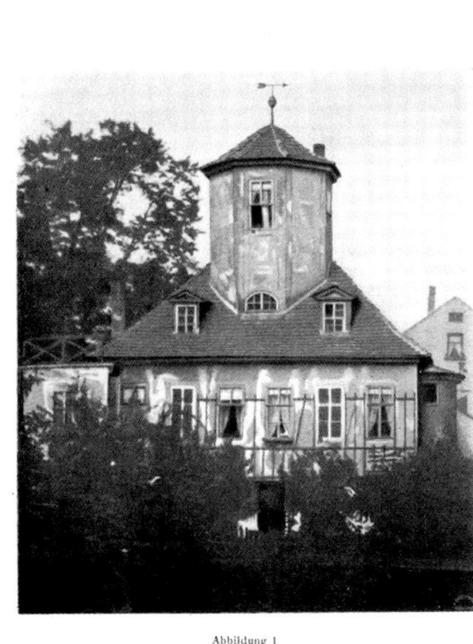

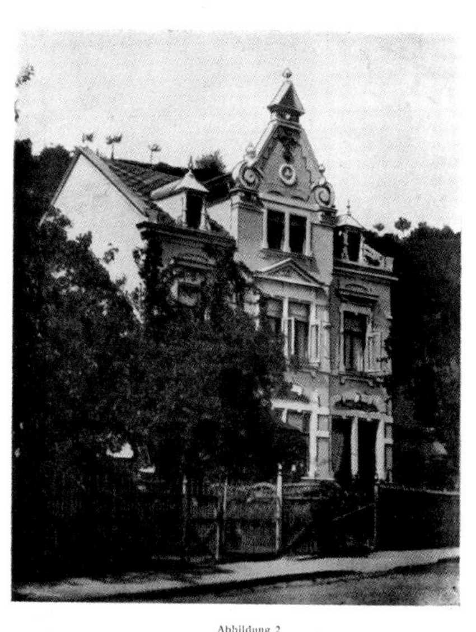

Plate from Paul Schultze-Naumburg,
Kulturarbeiten, 1900.

room, and with the same focus on the ordinary life of the inhabitant. The order of machines is comparable to Muthesius's more technical chapters, but the order of dreams deals with territory Muthesius does not explicitly cover, playing on the often subconscious associations of poetic phenomenology as the means to make the house more closely fit the identity of the person who dwells there, in this case the owner/designer.[18] Where Muthesius begins the design aspect of his book with the situation of the house on the site, Moore, Allen and Lyndon address this near the end of the main part of *The Place of Houses*, as the chapter on the application of the order of dreams.

Finally, where Muthesius began his book with the new possibility for people to build their own houses in the inner-suburbs, Moore and his collaborators conclude on the opposite note: 'The prospects for building single houses are, of course, diminishing. Land which can be afforded for a single house tends now to be far from any recognisable communal centre – on the fringes of previous suburbs or in once remote areas now available to interstate highway weekends.'[19] No longer motivated by Muthesius's desire to promote and control a massive wave of new construction, Moore could hold on to the old suburban single-family house ideal not as a means for reforming society, but for reforming people's idea of their relationship to architecture. Muthesius, having fallen out of fashion within the field but being well known outside of it, turned to a book as an instrument to make the client capable of overseeing every aspect of house design because he could no longer trust his fellow architects to do this in the way he thought right. Moore, also a public figure by the time he wrote his book, was trying to bring a new architectural ideology to people who in the contemporary climate might not have thought they had any personal access to the field of architecture at all. But despite these differences, the fact that both architects turned their hands to creating a text to inform the individual owner/builder about the act of design was rooted in a conviction they held in common: that the purpose of residential architecture is to make the design object a closely adapted formal solution to facilitate and encapsulate the ordinary life of the inhabitant. For them, the transition of design from form to text is made possible because from their position, design was in the elaboration of the relationship between man and his or her environment, and not in this relationship's built result.

1   Georges Perec, *Life: A User's Manual*, translated from the French by David Bellos, London: Vintage, 2003.

2   Charles Moore, Gerald Allen, and Donlyn Lyndon, *The Place of Houses*, New York: Holt, Rinehart, and Winston, 1974; Hermann Muthesius, *Wie baue ich mein Haus?* Munich: F. Bruckmann, 1917; here I use the third, expanded edition of 1919. Each of these books went into several editions. The latter was followed by the volume *Kann ich auch jetzt noch mein Haus bauen?* (Can I still build my own house now?), Munich: F. Bruckmann, 1920, updating the questions it covered for the fundamentally different situation that attained at the end of WWI.

3   In discussing the relationship of client to builder, as early as page 2, Muthesius argues that 'the house must be the result of the collaborative work of both,' and goes on at length here and elsewhere in the book. Although Muthesius had a vested interest in promoting the professional status of the architect because of his prominent role in the reform of design education, much the same could be said of Moore. However, Muthesius had also long taken a stand against the new style movements of around 1900 that were widely associated with artists, predominantly painters, who became amateur architects, whereas Moore's interest in community participation created no such problems with an embrace of amateur design. Note: all translations from the German are by the present author.

4   Moore et al., *The Place of Houses*, viii

5   These books included *Das Englische Haus: Entwicklung, Bedingungen, Anlage, Aufbau, Einrichtung und Innenraum*, 3 Vols. Wasmuth: Berlin, 1904-05; English edition: *The English House*, Dennis Sharp, ed. Rizzoli: New York, 1979; *Landhaus und Garten*, München, Bruckmann, 1907; and *Landhäuser*, München, Bruckmann, 1912, Reprint, Berlin: Gebr. Mann, 2001. All of these books were extremely popular and influential and went into multiple editions, though only much later for the massive and lavishly produced *Das Englische Haus*.

6   For example, Andrew Jackson Downing, *Cottage Residences*, New York: Wiley and Sons, 1873.

7   Muthesius, *Landhaus und Garten*, i.

8   On prefab housing, see Barry Bergdoll and Peter Christensen, *Home Delivery: Fabricating the Modern Dwelling*, New York: Museum of Modern Art, 2008.

9   See Janie Cohen, *Architectural Improvisation: A History of Vermont's Design-Build Movement 1964-1977*, Vermont: Robert Hull Fleming Museum, 2009.

10   See for instance Art Boericke and Barry Shapiro, *Handmade Houses: A Guide to the Woodbutcher's Art*, San Francisco: Scrimshaw Press, 1973, or Robert Haney and David Ballantine, *Woodstock Handmade Houses*, New York: Random House, 1974.

11   See footnote 2 above.

12   The best recent work on Muthesius's writings is Roth, Fedor, *Hermann Muthesius und die Idee der Harmonischen Kultur: Kultur als Einheit des künstlerischen Stils in allen Lebensäusserungen eines Volkes*, Berlin: Gebr. Mann, 2001.

13   Muthesius, *Wie baue ich mein Haus?* ,120.

14   Muthesius, *Wie baue ich mein Haus?*, 1.

15   Paul Schultze-Naumburg, *Kulturarbeiten*, Munich: Callwey and Kunstwart Verlag, 1900-1917. 9 vols. The theme of influencing public taste was a common topic in discussions among and around members of the Werkbund at this time, for example see Joseph August Lux, *Das Geschmack im Alltag* (Everyday Taste), Munich, 1910.

16   Christopher Alexander et al., A *Pattern Language: Towns, Buildings, Construction*, New York: Oxford University Press, 1977, xvi.

17   Moore et al., *The Place of Houses*, vii.

18   On the influence of poetic phenomenology on Moore's thought, see Erik Ghenoiu, 'Charles W. Moore and the Idea of Place,' *Fabrications* 18, no. 2 (Dec. 2008), 90-119.

19   Moore et al., *The Place of Houses*, 269.

The Invisible House:
David Malouf's
12 Edmondstone Street and
a colonial rhetoric of space

DEIRDRE GILFEDDER

David Malouf's autobiographical work *12 Edmondstone Street* is structured like the plan of a house, its subject is a house, and its title is a street address. It writes architecture: we open the cover of the book like a door, and step into virtual rooms of memory. As such the work invites enquiry into the spatial nature of autobiography. If, according to Philippe Lejeune, the main concern of autobiography is the analysis of the constitution of the enunciative subject – the 'I' of the text – then Malouf's work is original in that it traces the movement of the narrating subject through architectural space.[1] This subject is a body in surroundings, rather than a disembodied I. Malouf's self-narration through space also traces his own self-discovery – constituted through the invisible and indivisible boundaries of the tropical Queensland house.

This essay will first discuss *12 Edmondstone Street*

in terms of memory and the phenomenology of space, and then expand upon the architectural frontiers and limits that are, in the narrative, formative for Malouf as the book's subject. Furthermore, I will examine how the narrator imagines his place in a postcolonial society through his experience of the house. Malouf's text, which is almost a prose poem, has been widely studied as both a testimony to regional Queensland architecture and a 'universal narrative', where readers are invited to imagine their own 'first houses'.

The focus of much of the literature on Malouf has been on psychological questions of self and identity, yet more recent criticism has touched on gender, postcolonial issues and a renewed interest in space. Malouf scholar, Amanda Nettlebeck, for example, has concentrated on the theme of space and the body across several of the author's works.[2] Her analysis of *12 Edmondstone Street* is largely concerned with the exploration myth, a colonial approach to space, which she argues to be central to Malouf's imagination. For Nettlebeck, the expanding and contracting child's body marks the explorable space of the house in *Edmondstone Street*, and her text evokes Paul Carter's approach to marking colonial space to discuss the dream of 'returning to beginnings'. Nettlebeck holds that Malouf's spatial imagination is 'postcolonial', looking always for resolution, reconciliation and wholeness. Gillian Whitlock has also examined the exploration theme in *Edmondstone Street* but this time in terms of gender, tracing the male child's penetration of the spaces of the house.[3] Whitlock compares this with the work of another Queensland author, Jessica Anderson, whose *Stories from the Warm Zone* depicts the tropical Queensland house as largely a feminine world of housework and maternal attention.[4]

This paper undertakes a phenomenological analysis of Malouf's narrative, intersected with a postcolonial mode of questioning. Questions of identity are understood in the context of regional variations to an imperial order, which is both hegemonic and sub-conscious. *Edmondstone Street* poses an interesting and specific dilemma through its architectural optic – what did it mean to be a 'white Queenslander', a middle-class Brisbanite growing up in an ethnically mixed subtropical neighbourhood in the middle of the 20th century?

The first phenomenological point to make about *12 Edmondstone Street* is that it addresses an invisible house. The author's first house – a large cream and ochre Victorian colonial Queenslander on stumps with three-quarter wrap-around verandas – had already disappeared at the time of Malouf's writing in 1979. '[N]othing much remains of Edmondstone street now' writes Malouf; 'Like most of South Brisbane it has been torn down and a factory built on its site.'[5] Yet through the process of writing he is able to reconstruct the house of

his past through memory. He introduces his description with closed eyes: 'I can feel my way in the dark through every room' (4).

It is precisely the lack, the loss of the house that stimulates memory – Malouf is able to describe in detail the 'nest of rooms', as well as the garden and neighbourhood of the Brisbane suburb of West End in the 1940s, though it had by the time of writing been greatly transformed. The text renders the building present, hence the title that marks its street address. In many ways memory itself is the subject of the book. Malouf's writing is Bergsonian, exploring memory by invoking the role of imagination and the difficulty of consciously seizing the past, however Malouf's thoughts on memory focus on discontinuity rather than continuity. Like Michel de Certeau in *The Practice of Everday Life*, he notes that, paradoxically, memory is more powerful when something has disappeared. De Certeau explains that memory is mobilised through alteration: 'Like those birds who lay eggs in other birds' nests, memory produces in a place that is not its own.'[6] Unlike Marcel Proust's metonymical Madeleine, the childhood house is here summoned out of disjuncture. Malouf's memory is of invisible structures, enclosed in a series of invisible Chinese boxes: there is not one remembered house in the text but two – the earlier house built at the turn of the 20th century and the mid-century renovated house. In Malouf's imagination they co-exist and super-impose on each other simultaneously; '12 Edmondstone Street as I remember it was really two houses: an earlier, almost unchanged from the beginning of the century, and a later one that was 'done up "during the War"' (10).

It is the loss of the first house that moves Malouf to rebuild, through writing, the primordial, undivided space. The house – at once unified and complex – is a metaphor for early childhood. This point had been made earlier by Gaston Bachelard – in *The Poetics of Space*.[7] The first house, for Bachelard, is our 'first world before being cast out into the world'.[8] Malouf's childhood house can be compared with Bachelard's nest (note Malouf uses the term 'nest of rooms') – a warm refuge, a perfect whole that surrounds the child. For Malouf, the primacy of this originary world means that memory – moved as it is by passion – fails him. He cannot or does not want to remember the door to the new house – he wants the old house to remain whole: 'So long as that door remains blank and our handyman Old Jack has not yet taken his hammer to the wall, I can keep that house undivided' (11). Invisible spaces are conjured through reminiscence and a desire for the whole, and the human subject is constituted through memory's passionate duration.

Through memory and focalisation *12 Edmondstone Street* equally explores the phenomenology and poetics of lived-in space. In architectural studies in Brisbane there has long been an interest in *The Poetics of Space* of Bachelard, and discussion on its applicability to sub-tropical architecture. The breezy system of the house on stumps has been seen as an interesting counter-example to the French phenomenologist's Normandy houses and bourgeois European manors; the architectural setting of his 'oneiric' spaces.

Through literature, Bachelard studied the metaphorical and psychoanalytical significance of the spaces of the house – from the cellar (representing the past) to the attic (representing aspiration). These spaces gather meaning through lived experience and use. Malouf poses many of the same questions as Bachelard: what does it mean to live in a house? What is attachment to place? Who lives in the house? Whom do we let in? Whom do we keep out? What are the complexities, corners, nooks and crannies of a place? 'The house is our corner of the world,' wrote Bachelard, 'and that of our childhood a primary cosmos whether it is a chateau or a hut.'[9] Primary, protective intimacy however is not restricted to the archetypes of Bachelard's world – the chateau or the hut – but extends to other forms of dwelling. The question thus becomes

one of how the colonial house might construct relations and deconstruct European codes of intimacy.

One could argue that the rules of the colonial Queenslander and values attributed to its spaces are organised around a series of binary oppositions. The dominant oppositions suggested by Malouf's *Edmondstone Street* text are nature and civilisation; the permanent and the temporary; the local and the universal; the air and the ground. These values, as Malouf shows, are also socially determined. 'Weatherboard was too close to beginnings,' he writes, 'too dependent on what was merely local and near to hand rather than expensively imported. It was native, provincial, poverty-stricken – poor white' (10). The oppositions that Malouf exemplifies in building materials, can thus be listed in table form:

Weatherboard	Brick
native	British
air	ground
tree	house
vegetable	mineral
'poverty-stricken'	rich
poor white	upper middle-class
local	imported
nomad	fixed
provincial	metropolitan
South Brisbane	Hamilton

Malouf's Brisbane is a city with a postcolonial population living in Southeast Asian spaces. In the mid-century there was a self-consciousness about homes, as if the colonial settler understood his or her place in the scheme of the British Empire via materials. The timber dwelling signified inferiority, and Malouf's father was ashamed of their weatherboard house and would have preferred a solid brick home. 'Like most people in those days, my father was ashamed of our house.'[10] He eventually moved away from South Brisbane to a brick home in the more prestigious suburb of Hamilton. Raised on stilts, the Queenslander houses are described by Malouf as 'floating' or even as 'tree houses' – closer thus to nature than culture, to air than ground. Brisbane is described as 'a floating town, not a real city'.

Malouf thereby suggests a concentric colonial order: the settler is an anomalous sub-species 'somewhere between Bushie and Brick and mortar man' (10). The inhabitant of the weatherboard house is placed in a hierarchy between the metropolitan and the indigenous. Malouf observes of Brisbane settlers, 'You are just one step up from the nomads' (11). In the dwindling years of the British Empire, the years when Malouf was growing up, brick was still superior. Malouf thus traces an ironic hierarchy of imperial 'species': from 'Native Nomad' to 'Bushie' to 'Brisbanite' to 'Brick and Mortar Man'.

The weatherboard dwelling hovers on the Eurocentric frontier between what was then conceived as 'civilisation' and as 'savagery'. Imported from South and Southeast Asia, the tropical house created a hybrid life – barefoot and bare boarded in Brisbane; one was both far from British standards and condemned to preserve their memory. The lush garden was exotic, but the music and literature of the household was English and dinner was always at six o'clock; 'What we are feeding when, at fixed hours … we assemble behind serviette rings initialled with our names, are the spirits of the fathers' (55).

Yet, the places of memory in *12 Edmondstone Street* have their own geography and their own dynamic – the home is not delimited by rational geometry but by the crossing over of movements. Bachelard explained that the house is never about simple geometric form; the lived-in house is not an inert box, and habited space transcends geometric space. This is clear in Malouf's famous description of the space under-the-house. The undercroft of the tropical house is a Bachelardian ultra-cellar – a forgotten space of secrets that proves the subjectivity of measurement. The unchartered space of under-the-house does not match that of upstairs – the lived space of the every day, '[t]hey belong to different dimensions' (44).

The subject of narration perceives space through the tricks of light and perspective, 'as a room filled with sunlight has different dimensions as the same room in the dark' (43). The narrator takes multiple perspectives in focusing on the forest-like under-the-house.

> Seen from the washtubs it slopes steeply upwards to the Front Veranda; but you can also see it another way as existing in a perspective in which the distance from first stump to last isn't at all commensurate with the house above but is to be judged by the tallness of the stumps behind you and the littleness far off (43).

It is an undivided, irrational space: 'the forest under the house is measured by the expanding darkness in your lungs that is partly fear' (43). Bachelard's cellars are said to be irrational, and here in Malouf's description is a space ruled by passion 'because reason has nothing do with it' (44). The under-the-house breaks the generic rules of the upstairs plan: 'You crawl down here when the ordinary feet and inches of the house, its fixed times and rules, will not fit. Or when you won't…' (44).

The other eloquent tropical space Malouf addresses is the large Queensland veranda. Unlike the English home the colonial house mediates between inside and outside through the rhetoric of its open veranda. The veranda deconstructs the codes of in and out, throwing domestic space out into the wilderness. The vernacular architectural language articulates the narrative of colonial settlement, a movement from wandering to settlement: 'As for verandas. Well, their evocation of the raised tent flap gives the game away completely. They are a formal confession that you are just one step up from the nomads' (11).

Verandas set the Brisbanite further away from 'brick-and-mortar man'. Yet, the veranda is an important boundary – it grades the movement away from the 'civilisation' and the warm intimacy of the house. The children were put to sleep there.

Being taken out of the house each night and set
to sleep by the fernery is like being put down at the
edge of the rainforest… I have the strong feeling we
are being abandoned, shut out from the house itself
that secure enclosure (19).

In Malouf's schema, the Queensland veranda is closer
to vegetable than mineral. Conversely, the veranda can
also grade inward to the space of hospitality, for it is like
an extended threshold; 'Visitors are entertained on the
veranda and family and close friends in the kitchen' (18).
The veranda delineates public from private, it is a no-mans
land that serves as a sorting place for who belongs and
who does not. Brisbane verandas for Malouf are 'border
zones that keep contact with the house and its activities on
one face but are open to the other on the street, the night
and the vast unknown areas beyond' (20).

Jacques Derrida has undertaken scholarly work on the
spaces of hospitality and their delimitation, the understanding of 'home' and its borders.[11] The Queensland
veranda is a flexible border. It can be an invitation – in
Malouf's world the veranda's lattice door is never locked,
and he remembers an incident when an ailing stranger
was helped onto the veranda until she had recovered.
It can also be the home's margin – as shown by Malouf's
memory of being 'cast out' of the house to sleep on the
veranda. The poetics of vernacular space also speak of
the boundaries of hospitality.

There are a whole series of invisible boundaries in
Malouf's first house, and their indivisibility is manifest
at the moment of their violation. The veranda itself is
an anomalous border, marked by divisions; 'The front
veranda ends at an invisible barrier which we children
are forbidden to pass' (18). This is the line from which
it is possible to see into the room of the home-helper
– Cassie, part of the family but not in the family. The
law of belonging is invisible but clear, and the child is
tempted to transgress the law – the four-year-old Malouf

pushes his toy car across the notional barrier: 'I cross it.'[12]
There is an initiation process within the house, learnt
precisely through the transgression of unspoken family
law. As Derrida writes: 'Crossing borders always starts with
a step – a step that crosses an indivisible line.'[13]

There are many other invisible borders – the parents'
bedroom is also protected by a notional boundary. There
is no door to the room but, 'we have learned early my
sister and I that this room is not to be trespassed on. Its
thresholds are magic barriers' (24). The young Malouf is
shocked when a burglar breaks into the parents' bedroom,
'impervious it seems to the magic of thresholds' and steals
a box. The burglar gets in but the child cannot.

The front room also has a border. 'The Front Room is
a dead room. Nothing ever happens there: we never enter
it' (48). A paradoxical space of hospitality, this room is
not for entertaining valued friends or family but merely
'business acquaintances'. It constitutes what Derrida would
call a space of 'conditional hospitality'. It is protected
by a double bind – the room is unused but is the most
visible and accessible room in the house. Furthermore, it
is a showcase of interdictions – whisky sets and ashtrays
are on display in a home where nobody smokes or drinks.
'Our Front Room is a warning richly put, against the easy
pleasures of the "social life"' (50). An English protestant
middle-class morality is taught through the home's
distinctions. Despite the seeming openness of tropical
space, there is a fixed set of rules that govern the house
and the code is to be internalised by its inhabitants.
While 'air circulates from room to room through a maze
of interconnecting spaces' (22), the children's circulation
is regulated by clear borders and interdictions. There is
an insistence on self-discipline and self-governance,
coming largely from Malouf's English mother.

Interestingly the Lebanese grandmother, who is
supposedly a strong presence in Malouf's South Brisbane
years, does not enter the house. She sends up Mediterranean
dishes to the father, or sends her daughters to check on

him, and has given the parents an image of 'Jesus, the Sorrowful Watcher', which dominates their bedroom, yet she herself never enters the house. There is a battle between differing 'laws' in the household, which the mother seems to have won.

Meanwhile, there is an unwritten rule that doors in Malouf's house must be open, 'It being a convention in these houses that nothing is seen or heard that is not meant to be' (22). The children have been trained to distinguish between what is socially visible or audible and what should be unspoken and invisible: 'You see what you are meant to see, you hear when you are called' (22). Thus, while the Queensland house seems to deconstruct traditional European codes, it still conceals an internalised civic law. The reason there is no need for doors or locks is revealed in Malouf's statement towards the end of the text: 'The door was in us' (66).

The notion of internalising boundaries is also extended beyond the house. Just as there is a selective visibility in the home ('you see what you are meant to see'), there are parts of society the family will not see. Malouf is painfully honest about the social and racial distinctions of that time. 'If there are those among us whose freedom has been lost, who have been dispossessed, we do not see them. They are invisible' (37).

The statement is rather extraordinary considering the indigenous Murri people ('those who have been dispossessed') gathered in Musgrave Park, also located directly on Edmondstone Street. Yet, they are totally invisible to the family. They are said to have 'not yet established themselves in our consciousness' (37). The Malouf family lives in the ethnically diverse area of South Brisbane – 'close to the half-criminal life of Stanley Street' but they are trained as much to not see as to see. As Malouf puts it: 'A training in perception has as much to do with what is ignored and passed over as with what is observed' (22). Just as his family are trained to overlook the Brisbane heat and challenging conditions ('In a properly

British way we ignore them …'(55)) they are also trained to ignore difference. Thus, indivisible boundaries are set up between the occupants of West End.

The migrants and refugees who at that time often settled in South Brisbane were also seen, but not heard, 'Like the migrants, whose sorrows we do not hear because we have not yet opened our ears to receive them' (37). While Malouf's father's family live nearby and his grandfather represents 'the old country' in his dignified manner, any stories of troubled or dramatic immigration have been censored out. Selective distinction, like the classical oppositions discussed previously, is ruled by the consensual hegemony of the White Australia of the 1940s. Interestingly the 'I' of the text soon becomes replaced with this 'we', though it's not clear whether it refers to an expression of the family or a larger 'imagined community'. Malouf the narrator is circumspect about this anonymous, self-conscious and complacent community. 'The easy life we have grown up in, white for the most part, British almost entirely, in spirit Protestant, has never been under threat.' Indeed, it is from this comfort zone that selectivity has set up a hierarchy of invisibility – ranging from notional borders in a home to the negated other in the community.

While English writer Walter Pater spoke in the late 19th century of first houses as shaping the development of a child's aesthetic sensibilities, Malouf's narrative seems to suggest something further. [14] Learning the law of space and perception means that the first house is not only an aesthetic education, but also an ideological one.

1   Philippe Lejeune, *Je est un autre, L'autobiographie de la littérature aux médias*, Paris: Seuil, 1980.

2   Amanda Nettlebeck, 'Edges of the Self: Topographies of the Body in the Writing of David Malouf' in Amanda Nettlebeck (ed), *Provisional Maps*, Crawley, WA: Westerly Centre, 1994.

3   Gillian Whitlock, 'The child in the (Queensland) house: David Malouf and regional writing' in *Provisional Maps*.

4   Jessica Anderson, *Stories from the Warm Zone and Sydney Stories*, Sydney: Penguin, 1987.

5   All quotes are taken from the Penguin edition. David Malouf, *12 Edmondstone Street*, Ringwood, Victoria: Penguin, 1985. This quotation from page 4, hereafter page numbers of quotations will be marked in brackets in the body text.

6   Michel de Certeau, *The Practice of Everyday Life*, trans. Stephen Rendall, Berkeley: University of California Press, 1984, 86.

7   Gaston Bachelard, *The Poetics of Space*, New York, NY: Orion Press, 1964.

8   Bachelard, *The Poetics of Space*, 7.

9   Bachelard, *The Poetics of Space*, 4.

10   Malouf, *12 Edmondstone Street*, 10.

11   Jacques Derrida, *Of Hospitality: Cultural Memory in the Present*, Palo Alto, CA: Stanford University Press, 2000.

12   Malouf, *12 Edmondstone Street*, 18.

13   Jacques Derrida, *La Dissémination*, Paris: Seuil, 1972, 70.

14   Walter Pater, 'The Child in the House', in *Miscellaneous Studies: A Series of Essays*, London: Macmillan, 1899.

Ekphrasis and the Writing of Architecture

STEPHEN FRITH

What is *ekphrasis*? It is a term that literally means 'bringing to visibility before the eyes'. Ekphrasis brings us to the boundaries of language through verbal description of visual and architectural phenomena. With reliance on the traditions established by the rhetorical handbooks of ancient Greece and Rome, ekphrasis gives licence to the orator to weave an illusion. Its distinguishing quality is the *thauma* or wonder associated with the vividness of description. Aphthonius of Antioch wrote: 'The beauty is greater than one could express. If it is passed over, it comes about in an aside of wonder.'[1] Ekphrasis draws attention to the rhetorical underpinnings of the way a western mind interprets architecture, which assumes that buildings 'speak', and have something to say to us. Ekphrasis extends to descriptions of tents, to imagined cities (such as those of the Heavenly Jerusalem), to accounts of Roman villas by Pliny and Statius.

Modern and ancient conceptions of ekphrasis differ primarily in relation to the location of a descriptive narrative in a live work of oratory, rather than a description of a work of art read in a text: the ancient focus was on the listener, the audience. The task was *enargeia*, vividness, the bringing to visibility before the eyes of the matter under discussion.[2] The notion burdens ekphrasis in the context of ancient Roman rhetoric with the notion of giving voice, of speaking out, or of a telling. It is closely related to *prosopopoeia*, or the granting of voice to a silent object. They related especially to genealogical inscription on ancient sepulchral objects, such as coffins and memorial columns: 'I am the tomb of the famous Glauca' (3rd century BCE), or 'I am the column of Xenvares, son of Meixis, upon his grave' (600 BCE).[3] It is not hard to imagine the telling of stories in the past to a largely non-literate audience being coloured by descriptions of architectural wonders. The task of the storyteller is to create an image of the object in the minds of the audience in such a way that it is as if they were really witnessing the work or place.

Nineteenth century interest in ekphrasis as a genre, paralleled developments in art historical scholarship and art criticism in France. This had the effect of limiting ekphrasis to the description in a text of a painting, even while the origin of ekphrasis is usually seen in Homer's description of the Shield of Achilles from the *Odyssey*.[4] The focus on literary descriptions of paintings was also reinforced by the privileging of some ancient texts over others, such as stories about the origins of painting from Pliny the Elder's *Natural Histories*. The narrowing of the practice to descriptions of painting is also evident in the late 20th century's 'linguistic turn', seen in the writings on the genre of ekphrasis of Roland Barthes. However, in its ancient Greek and Roman versions, the uses of ekphrasis in the handbook exercises used for training rhetoricians to speak in public, called *progymnasmata*, is much broader. Their subject matter includes objects, sculpture, weapons, buildings and cities.

James Heffernan describes ekphrasis as a 'verbal representation of a visual representation'.[5] The many uses of the term are evident in rhetorical training manuals, such as those by Aristotle, Quintilian and Cicero, and the author of *Rhetorica ad Herennium* and Pseudo-Longinus, as well as the *progymnasmata* of Greece and Rome in the first to the fifth centuries. Teachers such as Theon, Nikolaos, Aphthonius, and Pseudo-Hermogenes wrote these handbooks for students of oratory. Students would undergo exercises to teach them skills of ekphrasis useful to oratory. The *progymnasmata* provided a curriculum or framework for understanding the *topoi,* places or *kephalaia* – the 'heads' of various arguments necessary to make a case for either praise or blame.[6] The desired experience of ekphrasis promoted in the handbooks is akin to being a spectator losing oneself in the action of a theatrical performance, like the pathos of absorption into a tragedy. So in the history of the literature of the west, the first important role for ekphrasis is likened to the act of painting a scene in the mind, to 'bring to visibility' to the matter at hand. The second key term is *enargeia,* or 'vividness', which with clarity acts powerfully to 'enslave' an audience, to turn listeners into spectators and participants.[7]

The uses of ekphrasis in oratory also provides a vehicle for a demonstration of the skill of the orator or poet, for ekphrasis attracts attention to the author as much as to the object being described, and sustains a self-reflexive view of the piece of oratory or poem as its own monument. Quintilian, who wrote a major guide to speechmaking, states:

> It is a great gift to be able to set forth the facts on which we are speaking clearly and vividly. For oratory fails of its full effect, and does not assert itself as it should, if its appeal is merely to the hearing, and if the judge merely feels that the facts on which he has to give his decision are being narrated to him, and not displayed in their living truth to the eyes of the mind.[8]

Architecture and *phantasiai*

The stress on *enargeia,* 'vividness', underlies the performative nature of the poetry or oratory. Quintilian in Books 6 and 8 of the *Institutio Oratoria* articulates what he means by *enargeia,* writing that while a simple statement of the matter might be truthful, that forming an image brings vividly and more persuasively the matter to the 'mind's eye' with some emotional force. Leading the audience to imagine in their own minds the scene of a crime, or the destruction of a city enlists the *phantasiai,* those mental images already residing in the minds of others.[9]

What the Greeks call *phantasiai* (we shall call them [in Latin] 'visiones', if you will,) are the means by which images of absent things are represented to the mind in such a way that we seem to see them with our eyes and to be in their presence. Whoever has mastery of them will have a powerful effect on the emotions. Some people say that this type of man who can imagine in himself things, words and deeds well and in accordance with truth is 'good at imagining' (*euphantasiōtos*).[10]

There is an underlying structure to ekphrasis that relies on *phantasiai*, on the building of visual images in the mind and memory, and drawing upon them for any interpretation. In the process a necessary distance of belief is created, between knowing something as real, and perceiving something that is possible. There appears an awareness in the poetry of the 'as if', regarding the difference between truthful representation and *phantasmata*, of imaginings of the possible. The reliance on truth-saying, and truthful representation, of verisimilitude, even in regard to *phantasiai,* is maintained in the rhetorical tradition, especially in regard to judicial settings.

Various forms of ekphrasis articulate a reality that does not exist, and ekphrasis walks a knife-edge with fantasy. This is famously exemplified in the account of a dream in the *Hypnerotomachia Poliphili* attributed to Francesco Colonna during the Renaissance of the 15th century. The title means something close to *Poliphilo's Strife of Love in a Dream*, first published in Venice in 1499. It is an allegory about a young man, Poliphilo, who has a dream that includes the comings and goings of his true love Polia. The action takes place in a series of fantastic descriptions of buildings, architecture being as much the object of desire as the lovely Polia. The author is anonymous, possibly Leon Battista Alberti, but the work is attributed to Francesco Colonna. Its writer probably took inspiration from Lucian of Samosata (125 CE–after

180 CE), a rhetorician from the 2nd century, whose writing we know was read by Alberti. Lucian came under the auspices of the Roman Empire, but wrote in a high-styled Greek for an educated audience. Lucian plays on the ambiguities between the real and the fantastic in his *True Lies*, which takes the form of a travelogue to wondrous places, such as the *Isle of the Blessed*, whose walls of emerald and whose crystal gates have their parallel in the heavenly city of St John of Patmos's *Apocalypse*. Lucian's voyage is in a tradition established in Greek by Homer, whose *Iliad* also takes us to fantastic places. These accounts are within the *periplus* tradition, as is Apollonius's *The Voyage of the Argo* and Pytheas's *Ultima Thule*.[11] The latter was written around 325 BCE, and gives an account of the Britains, whose authenticity the geographer Strabo doubted: '[. . .] however, any man who has told such great falsehoods about the known regions would hardly, I imagine, be able to tell the truth about places that are not known to anybody.'[12]

True Lies also has resonance with the true lies of Pliny the Elder's accounts of the origins of painting in Greece. These ekphrastic stories keep emerging in the history of painting, as in David Allan's *The Origins of Painting* (1773), showing Dibutades tracing the outline of her departing lover on the wall. Pliny in the *Historia Naturalis*[13] tells stories about origins, or aetiologies, about the invention of painting images. A significant underlying theme of his narratives is faithfulness: faithful in love, but also faithful imitation or *mimesis*.

In the Socratic tradition the main vehicle of truth is human conversation, of the too-ing and fro-ing of an argument such as we see in the *Symposium*, where the truth emerges, as it were, amongst the participants. In Aristotle's writings, metaphor is key to this enterprise, which sets the scene or 'puts the subject before our eyes'.[14] The ekphrastic accounts draw attention to the relation between images and their use in that memory-theatre the mind, where imagination in Greek and Roman rhetorical and poetic context was seen as a construction.[15] Ekphrastic writings about architecture become a species of truth-saying, especially when that literature is thought to be revealed by divine authority.

Ekphrases of order: the Shield of Achilles to the heavenly city

Scholars generally attribute the first ekphrasis in literature to Homer, who in his *Iliad* describes the shield that the gods made for Achilles, Book 18, lines 478–608. The decoration on the shield is a statement of unfolding order, with the earth, sky, sea, sun and constellations arranged in the centre. In subsequent rings, the too-ing and fro-ing of various human activities take place, signs of peace and of war. They include a wedding and a field being ploughed and another a king's fields being harvested, and towards the outer edge, a scene of youths and maidens dancing, followed by an encompassing world ocean, Oceanus. The Shield is analogous to order as such, or at least that world order thought appropriate by Homer.

A similar representation of order, a world-encompassing ekphrasis of architecture, is found in the Ancient Near East in the biblical descriptions of the Hebrew Tabernacle, a layered series of tents. The material coverings appear to be substitutions for the 'gathering' of the people into a shrine. It is described in the *Book of Exodus* as being made of four layers of skins stretched over a wooden skeleton (*qerasim*), with a lattice framework of acacia wood (*shittim*). The layers suggest the various produce of a farming and herding people. The one closest to the ark is the Tabernacle proper, the *miskan*, made of linen, decorated with the guardians of the throne from Canaanite culture, the cherubim, coloured using 'blue and purple and scarlet stuff'.[16] The next three layers are the outer coverings of the *miskan*, the one next to it made of goat hair, the typical material for tent making of the people. Two other layers are

applied: sheepskin died red, which has a long history with portable Arabic shrines, and the outer layer *tahas* skins, a word that applies to species of whales and dolphins, and was probably made of dugong skins, plentiful in ancient times in the Red Sea. The attributes and dwelling of the god Yahweh has close affinities with those of the Canaanite god El, whose abode in the Ugaritic texts is mostly referred to as being in 'the midst of the sea', and said to be located at the 'springs of the two rivers, midst the source of the two deeps, *themabbike naharemi*, as well as in a mountain setting, where he presides over the divine council' (Isaiah 14.13). The dugong or dolphin skins can be best understood in the aquatic setting of the El's abode. As for the Shield of Achilles, the architecture of the Tabernacle embraces the representation of a whole world beyond its functional purposes, magnifying architecture's role as a vehicle of symbolic order.

The symbolic capacity of ekphrasis also extends to descriptions of a heavenly city, such as that revealed by an angel to the prophet Ezekiel. This account is indicative of the tension between the real and ideal that we find in descriptions of the Heavenly Temple or city, such as those of the heavenly Jerusalem from both scriptural and non-scriptural sources, of which the vivid descriptions of the *Book of Enoch* is well known. The primary scriptural account is found in the *Book of Ezekiel*,[17] upon which other accounts have been heavily dependent. With the background of Babylonian captivity in exile beginning around the year 587 BCE, Ezekiel dreams of a new temple under instructions from an angelic guide, who like his Sumerian and Akkadian counterparts,[18] is standing in the gateway pictured 'with a line of flax and a measuring reed in his hand'.[19] Ezekiel is 'set down on a very high mountain, on which was a structure like a city opposite me'.[20] Ezekiel then goes on to describe the city in some detail.

Many centuries later, probably in the first quarter of the second century, the writer of the *Temple Scroll 11QT* found at Qumran in the Dead Sea caves, draws upon

Ezekiel's account with innovations added to the architecture. The author of the *Temple Scroll* gives a new name to the city, the 'City of the Sanctuary'. These stories of a heavenly Jerusalem share a reliance on architecture to represent a bounded domain that establishes the necessary conditions where the divine can be made present, or 'shine forth' to a righteous or holy community. The architecture of the Heavenly Temple provides a model (or *tabnit*), which is anticipated, will be built either with human hands or by the hand of the divine at the last day, the eschaton. Here, ordinary space and time are ruptured at the founding of a new order.

The apocalyptic nature of this event is well captured in several accounts of the founding of the heavenly city, such as that in the *Book of Enoch* found in the caves of Qumran (Cave 4):

> And I went in till I drew near to a wall, built of hailstones, with tongues of fire surrounding it on all sides; and it began to terrify me. And I entered into the tongues of fire and drew near to a large house built of hailstones; and the walls of the house were like tessellated paving stones, all of snow, and its floor was of snow. Its upper storeys were, as it were, fireballs and lightnings, and in the midst of them (were) fiery Cherubim, celestial watchers. And a flaming fire was all around its walls, and its doors were ablaze with fire. And I entered into that house, and it was hot as fire and cold as snow; and there were no delights in it; horror overwhelmed me, and trembling took hold of me, and shaking and trembling I fell onto my face, and I saw a vision, and behold! Another house greater than the one and its door was completely opened opposite me; and it (the second house) was all constructed of tongues of fire. In every respect it excelled in glory and honour and grandeur that I am unable to describe to you its glory and grandeur. And its floor

was of fire, and its upper chambers were lightnings and fire-balls, and its roof was of blazing fire.[21]

This apocalyptic narrative is very different in feeling from that we find in the *Book of Ezekiel*. These themes enter Christian accounts of the heavenly city, such as found in the last book of the Christian bible, the *Apocalypse* or *Book of Revelation* of John the Divine. For the Christian era, the most immediately accessible literary description written in the late first or early second century by John on Patmos Island:

> The angel who spoke to me carried a gold measuring-rod, to measure the city, its wall, its gates. The city was built as a square, and was as wide as it was long. [...] The wall was built of jasper, while the city itself was as of pure gold, bright as clear glass. The foundations of the city wall were adorned with jewels of every kind, the first of the foundation stones being jasper, the second lapis lazuli, the third chalcedony, the fourth emerald, the fifth sardonyx, the sixth cornelian, the seventh chrysolite, the eight beryl, the ninth topaz, the tenth chrysoprase, the eleventh turquoise, and the twelfth amethyst. The twelve gates were twelve pearls, each gate being made from a single pearl. The streets of the city were of pure gold, like translucent glass.[22]

The setting of this kind of apocalyptic literature is never outside a community context.[23] The relation between the seven cities of Asia Minor, to whom John was writing, and the heavenly city is a reciprocal one, suggestive of a dialogue between real cities and an ideal one. The communities of Christians in the seven cities are represented as the real sacred centre of urban life, as they are able to embody within their midst the sacred centre itself, the promise of the saviour and the heavenly city descending. The ancient Near Eastern symbol of sacred centre is the temple and its sacred enclosure, even if as at Ephesus the temple is outside the city. John's city is presenting a new sacred centre for the seven cities. The world of apocalyptic is not solely oriented to an historical expression of time, but to a cosmological time providing a 'sacred canopy'[24] where the New Jerusalem is as it was for Tertullian, just out of reach, waiting to break through from eternity into the present. The reciprocity of eternal and temporal order is disclosed in the mythic and symbolic world of the heavenly city, which at the eschaton is able to gather origins in an end time, *Urzeit* and *Endzeit*.

Ekphrasis of the house

The precious marbled mansions of apocalyptic literature have their echo in Roman descriptions around the first century of lavish villas and imperial palaces. The stories of the house or villa, those praising a special place, has its own genre in the history of ekphrastic literature. For example, there are several eye-witness descriptions of the imperial villas at Constantinople, the Great Palace of Constantinople or the Palace of Daphne.[25] Another famous example comes from the letters of Pliny the Younger, where he describes for his readers the architecture of his own villas, such as the one at Laurentum, and at Lake Como where he grew up. Pliny was at one time Governor of Bithynia Pontus under the Emperor Trajan. He describes villas that have been emulated over the centuries, and whose reconstructions has been a staple in the diet of architecture schools since the 1800s.[26] Historian Pierre de la Ruffinière Du Prey argues that the rhetorical form of Pliny's descriptions is really a separate architectural category of ekphrasis, characterised by an elaborate eulogising of artwork of various kinds.[27]

Pliny owned at least six large houses, the most valuable probably being the house on the Esquiline Hill in Rome.[28] He was particularly fond of his house at

Laurentum, on the coast 17 miles from Rome, and not far from Ostia. Due to inheritances from his mother and father, he owned three villas on Lake Como,[29] as well as a villa at Tifernum Tiberinum, which he used for relaxation in summer.[30]

Pliny called his two villas at Comum (Como) 'Comedy' and 'Tragedy'. His account is in a letter to Voconius Romanus, who built a house by the sea, not unlike those of Pliny by Lake Como: 'One is built on the rocks with a view over the lake, like the houses at Baiae, the other stands on the very edge of the water in the same style, and so I have named one Tragedy, because it seems to be raised on actor's boots, and the other Comedy, because it wears low shoes.'[31] Pliny writes that each has its own attractions, as in the following:

> One is untouched by the water and you can look
> down from its height to the fishermen below, while
> the waves break against the other and you can
> fish from it yourself, casting your line from your
> bedroom window and practically from your bed
> as if you were in a boat.[32]

The striking aspect of Pliny's accounts of his houses is the relation to the natural world. Villas become a place for the appreciation of their setting, whether it be the Tuscan villa being described as looking 'more like a beautiful landscape painting than the real thing', or the Laurentum villa mediating the scenery on the shores of the Mediterranean. The villa is to receive the elements and magnify the landscape, with rooms that receive 'the rising and the setting of the sun, and [which] also [have] a view of sea below'.[33] His own quarters at Laurentum – slightly separated from the main part of the house – were particularly carefully set in its landscape next to the water:

> At the end of the terrace beyond the gallery is my
> garden suite, my favourite because I planned it to
> please myself. It contains a solarium which on one

side looks out from the doors upon the terrace, one of the rooms and the gallery, and on the other upon the sea from the window, and receives sunlight from both.

Opposite the central part is my den, a bay window which can be shut off from the rest of the room by drawing the curtains or made a part of its by leaving them open. It contains two chairs and a couch, the sea is below, the woods above, the rest of the house behind. There is a panoramic view from the windows. […]

Another room with an anteroom juts out and catches the first rays of the rising sun and even in the afternoon is sunny.[34]

Pliny's writing about architecture and landscape is lyric in quality, especially when he is writing about his estates. Even though lyrical, the letters are generally concise and measured, in Quintilian's terms, a '*pressus*' style that sought to avoid excessive ornamentation.[35]

Architectural *ekphrasis* of the house in poetry

Ekphrasis permits a reflection, not just on the object or painting being praised, but representation itself.[36] The oldest description of villas that we have in poetic form relate to houses in the *Silvae* by the Roman poet Statius. They all testify to the power of the representation of the house as a sign, firstly of the virtue (*virtus*) of their owners, and secondly of their wealth and social status. In the *Silvae* 1.2, the palatial house of the charming widow Violentilla is chosen for praise over that of her new husband, the wealthy Aruntius Stella, the bride's house a subject presented by Venus herself.[37] The theme of faithfulness is established in an *epithalamium*, or wedding speech, for Violentilla, which includes praise of her house. This is placed immediately

before the chapter of fulsome praise of the villa of Manilius Vobiscus at Tibur (*Silvae* 1.3). To praise the house is also to praise the household, the household ancestors whose portraits might look down from an entrance vestibule, or even the household gods, the *lares* and *penates*, protecting the house in their domesticated shrine.

Similar to descriptions of the Heavenly Jerusalem, Violentilla's house is described as being lined with precious stones, mainly marble of various kinds (148–54), a luxury equal to that of the imperial house:

Here is Libyan stone and Phrygian, here hard Laconian rock shows green, here are versatile alabaster and the vein that matches the deep sea, here marble oft envied by Oebalian purple and the blender of the Tyrian cauldron. Airy gables rest on countless columns, beams glitter allied with Dalmatian ore.[38]

Marble was a relatively new addition to the Roman *domus*. Its only function is representational, and so provided an easy target for the moralists. Pliny the Elder saw marble as a sign of decadence.[39] The sale of marble came under imperial control in the first century, such was its desirability, and indicative of its potential to be a threat to imperial privilege. Carole Newlands has observed the gendered language applied to Violentilla's marbles, an erotic combination of sexual desirability when made to appear like human flesh, possessed by a woman of wealth and beauty, property and letters.[40] Statius describes her as being an object worthy of Jupiter's desire (133–6). The brief description of the house builds on this image of the 'protégé of Venus',[41] a character whose virtue is seen in her care of the household gods, the *penates*, and whose desirability is metonymically associated with the beauty of her house. Inevitably, however, she is also defined as a woman who is worthy of being accepted into her new husband's aristocratic family, her identity subsumed into the patriarchal traditions of Rome.[42]

Palace of Domitian

A newly renovated palace on the Palatine Hill in Rome is described by Statius in the *Silvae* Book 4.2 as a fitting abode for the divine Domitian, '[. . .] embracing much of heaven within its shelter; he fills the household and weighs it down with his mighty being.'[43] Domitian rebuilt the Palatine palaces, greatly expanding the Augustan foundation. The complex was made up of two major palaces, the Domus Augustana, the more private quarters of the palace, and the Domus Flaviana, where public rituals were maintained. As in Violentilla's villa, the palace contains exotic stones, although the use of Luna, a white marble, suggests some modesty: '[h]ere contend the mountains of Libya and the gleaming stone of Ilium, dark Syene too and Chios, and rocks to rival the grey-green sea, and Luna, substituted only to support the columns.'[44] Further reference is made to the 'gilded ceiling of heaven',[45] further supporting Domitian's claim to divine status: 'for him, only him – calm of visage softening its radiance with serene majesty, modestly lowering the banner of his fortune; yet the hidden splendour shone in his face.'[46] The poet Martial in his *Epigrams* similarly describes the palace as analogous to Mount Olympus.[47]

Domitian was the last of the Flavian emperors, his only child, a son, dying in infancy. His failure to adopt and plan a succession created speculation and anxiety. His critics tend to overlook his architectural achievements, his efforts in Rome exceeding those of Augustus. These included the spectacular rebuilding of the Palatine and large sections of Rome.[48] Domitian's imperial propaganda became increasingly focused on his divine invincibility, in part overcoming the concern for lack of sons and heirs, establishing Minerva as his special guardian.[49] Any literature of praise was dangerous in the period, because of the shifting alliances between the emperor and his subjects. An encomium for someone written today might be used as evidence against its author tomorrow. Tacitus in the

Agricola commented that in Domitian's Rome, panegyric was the most dangerous kind of literature, as the political conditions were so unstable. His own account of his father-in-law Agricola he only felt able to publish during the reigns of Nerva and Trajan.[50] Poetry was left with two options, either straightforward description without irony or underlying meaning, or heavily masked literature that plays the dangerous game of reading between the lines.[51]

Statius and the pastoral

In Statius's ekphrasis of villas, he adapts and transforms the pastoral tradition. The poetry of Statius's in the *Silvae* consistently alludes to other poetry, to Rome's past, always present in the work, even while what is described is ever new. The past poetic tradition associated with the pastoral poetry of Horace and Ovid, or the epic traditions of Virgil and Homer, are creatively engaged and transformed in Statius's work, in accordance with contemporary rhetorical and poetic practice. Words and poetic form are reworked for their emotional impact.[52] Statius's poetic audacity lies in his transformation of the pastoral idiom from one where the moralised luxury of a Campanian Villa is turned on its head. The villas of Manilius Vopiscus and of Pollius Felix come with allusions to the poetry of Virgil and Horace, but are eulogised as a model of state and social order.[53] Carole Newlands writes that Statius uses architecture to define his relationship to both his society and to his audience, in *Silvae 3.1* evidence of being an 'audacious, innovative poet who seeks out challenges both in architecture and in literary tradition'.[54] *Silvae* 2.2, describing the villa of Pollius Felix, is overtly an ekphrasis of a sumptuous *Villa Maritima* at Surrentum (Sorrento) on the coast looking over the Bay of Naples, called by Cicero 'The Bay of Luxury', *cratera illum delicatum*.[55] The defining character of the pastoral landscape resides in the notion of *otium*, of idle even if sometimes creative leisure.[56]

Horace suggested that:

Our cares are removed by reason and
prudence, not by a house commanding
a wide sea view. We change our sky, not
our minds by running across the sea.
We are engaged in a strenuous idleness.[57]

Characteristic of Statius's account of villas is the
universalising of the importance of the villas. He uses the
comparison of a villa with a city to describe Pollius Felix's
colonnade, in the same way that Strabo and Pliny compare
collections of villas to cities.[58] The play of macrocosm
and microcosm enhances Pollius's status, and supports
Statius's view of the villa, even in private hands, as an
emblem of civic order. The villa in this sense can be seen
as metaphorically a substitute for the patron, as well as for
the well-ordered state. The old *topos* of comparison of the
self to the city can also be seen in this light, as in Plato's
Republic, where the soul and its relation to the body is
compared to that of a house in relation to a city.[59]

Influenced by Epicurean philosophy, the transformation of nature through Pollius's assertive building program
is for Statius a virtue: nature is ordered, even magnified
in its numinous setting, and peace and tranquillity is
established in Pollius's safe harbour:

But now the fog of things is shaken apart and
you see the truth. Others in their turn are tossed
upon that ocean, but your bark has made safe
harbour and tranquil rest, unshaken. So continue,
nor even send your ship into our storms: her
voyaging is over.[60]

Statius alludes to imagery found in Lucretius's *De Rerum
Natura* (1–4, 7–14) of the self as a soul in a storm-tossed
boat, subject to the too-ing and fro-ing of passions and
desires, and of the wise looking down on the sea of error
from 'the serene temple of the mind', *sapientum templa
serena* (8). Pollius looks down from his *speculatrix*, his

high lookout, over the sea of passion and error with an
Epicurean calm. His villa is metaphorically standing in for
the 'high citadel' of his mind (*Silvae* 2.2. 129–32):

We, worthless crew, ever ready to serve perishable
blessings, ever hoping for more, are scattered to the
winds of chance; whereas you from your mind's
high citadel look down upon our wanderings and
laugh at human joys. [61]

Pollius's soul described as one that has reached the safety
of his calm harbour (*Silvae* 2.2,139–41) is emblematic of
the state of *quies*, freedom from passion, that tranquillity
equivalent to the Greek *ataraxis*.[62] This is echoed by the
word *voluptas*, the pleasure that the Epicurean experiences,
in this case referring to the view from the villa (73). In these
lines Statius owes something to a Roman understanding of
sublime experience, articulated in Longinus's *Peri Hypsous*,
and set against a mythologically charged landscape.

Ekphrasis, through an energetic and vivid description,
inevitably reveals something of this mystery of architecture,
and the recovery of the magic of place. In the early 20th
century Rudolf Otto in his book *Das Heilige (The Holy)*
coined the term 'numinous' to describe a place's *mysterium
tremendum et fasciotum*.[63] While Otto would seek to locate
mystery beyond human culture, language is necessarily
the vehicle of its articulation. Our interpretation of stories
about place – about architecture – seem inescapably to
return to their rhetorical setting. As stories of place are
embedded in language, they take on the character of
rhetoric, that is, something to be persuaded, argued,
interrogated. In this interrogation, rhetoric about architecture in the rhetorical manuals of Greece and Rome
take on a dialectical character. The principal dialectic,
as we see clearly in Statius's ekphrasis of villas, or in the
description of a heavenly city, is a conversation between
this particular place, and all places as such, between local
and global, particular and universal. Dreams of a perfect
place in ancient literature about architecture, in dreams

of villas of fire and ice, contrasting universals are brought into the supreme harmony of the irenic city.[64]

1   Apthonius of Antioch, Spegel II.49, translated by Sprague Becker, 1995: 30.

2   Ruth Webb has observed that it is the *idea* of the visual that is important. Ruth Webb, *Ekphrasis, Imagination and Persuasion in Ancient Rhetorical Theory and Practice*, Burlington, VT: Ashgate, 2009, 8–9.

3   James A. W. Heffernan, 'Ekphrasis and Representation', *New Literary History*, 22, 2, 1991, 302. 'Traditionally, I have argued, *ekphrasis* is narrational and *prosopopoeial*; it releases the narrative impulse that graphical art typically checks, and it enables the silent figures of graphic art to speak.' 304.

4   Webb, *Ekphrasis, Imagination and Persuasion in Ancient Rhetorical Theory and Practice*, 30–34.

5   James A. W. Heffernan, *Museum of Words, The Poetics of Ekphrasis from Homer to Ashbery*, Chicago: University of Chicago Press, 1993, 3. See also Carole Newlands, *Statius' Silvae and the Poetics of Empire*, Cambridge: Cambridge University Press, 2002, 42.

6   Aristotle, *Rhetoric*, III, XI, 2, or, 1411 b24–5, translated by J. H. Freese, Cambridge, MA and London: Heinemann, 1926, Loeb Edition, 1982, 404–5: 'I mean that things are set before the eyes by words that signify actuality.'

7   Nikolaos, *Progymnasmata*, 68. 11. 11–12. Cited by Webb, 52, fn. 54.

8   Quintilian, *Institutio oratoria*, 8. 3. 62, translated by H. E. Butler, Cambridge, MA: Harvard University Press, London: William Heinemann, 1921, Loeb edition, 1986, 244–245.

9   Quintilian, *Institutio oratoria*, 8. 3. 64–65, Loeb edition 1986, 247.

10   Quintilian, *Institutio oratoria* 6. 2. 29–30, translated by Webb.

11   On wonder in the writings of Lucian of Samosata in the Second Sophistic period, see Jennifer Harvey, 'The Ekphrasic Imagination: Architecture and Effect', *Imagining*, edited by Michael Chapman, Society of Architectural Historians of Australia and New Zealand (SAHANZ) Conference, Newcastle.

12   Strabo, *Geographica* 1.4.3

13   Pliny the Elder, *Natural Histories*, XXXV.151.

14   Aristotle, *The Art of Rhetoric*, 1410b, translated by H. C. Lawson-Tancred, Harmondsworth: Penguin, 1991, 236.

15   Ruth Webb has observed the act of calling up images in the minds of others 'creates a feeling *like* that of perception, a simulacrum of perception itself'. Webb, *Ekphrasis, Imagination and Persuasion*, 127–128.

16   Exodus 25.4, 26.1.

17   Ezekiel, 40.3b.

18   Ezekiel, 40.2 RSV translation. Zimmerli, in *Ezekiel 2, A Commentary on the Book of the Prophet Ezekiel Chapters 25-48*, Philadelphia: Fortress, 1983, 340.

19   1 Enoch 14:9-17.

20   Revelation 21.15-21.

21   Christopher Rowland, *Open Heaven*, 415: 'Rarely, if at all, do we find apocalyptic mysteries, whether eschatological or otherwise, being passed on as material which is of interest in its own right. They function within the framework of the spiritual needs of the community addressed.'

22   See Peter Berger, *The Sacred Canopy. Elements of a Sociological Theory of Religion*, Garden City, N.Y.: Doubleday, 1969, 25; Peter Berger and Thomas Luckmann, *The Social Construction of Reality. A Treatise in the Sociology of Knowledge*, Garden City, N.Y.: Doubleday, 1966, 15. For sacred time as a reflection of social order, see John Gager, *Kingdom and Community, The Social World of Early Christianity*, New Jersey: Prentice Hall, 1975, 9-11.

23   Daphne Palace, *Book of Ceremonies* (Reiske trans.), *De Ceremoniis Aulae Byzantinae*, Bonn, 1829). See Nigel Westbrook, 'The Chalkê: the Bronze Gate of the Byzantine Great Palace', in J. Gatley, *Cultural Crossroads: Proceedings of the 26th International SAHANZ Conference*, The University of Auckland, New Zealand, 2-5 July 2009, 61.

24   For a survey, see Pierre de la Ruffinière du Prey, *The Villas of Pliny from Antiquity to Posterity*, Chicago and London: University of Chicago Press, 1994. See also the catalogue of subsequent re-creations, Montreal Museum of Fine Arts: 'The Villas of Pliny and Classical Architecture in Montreal' October-November 1983.

25   Pierre de la Ruffinière du Prey, *The Villas of Pliny from Antiquity to Posterity*, Chicago and London: University of Chicago Press, 1994, 8: 'Pliny [...] thereby invented architectural description as a separate subcategory of *ekphrasis*.'

26   Martial 10.9, (See also Letters 3.21.5.) Richard Duncan–Jones, *The Economy of the Roman Empire, Quantitative Studies*, Cambridge: Cambridge University Press, 1974, 22.

27   *Ep.* 9.7; 2.17.20; 5.6.41.

28 *Ep.* 5.6; 9.36; 9.40. Richard Duncan–Jones, *The Economy of the Roman Empire*, 1974, 24.

29 Pliny the Younger, *Ep.* 9.7. Translation by Betty Radice, Cambridge, MA: Harvard University Press, and London: Heineman, Loeb Classical Library, 1963, 1969 edition, 91.

30 Pliny the Younger, *Ep.* 9.7 ibid.

31 Pliny the Younger, *Ep*, II, 17.

32 Pliny the Younger, *Ep*, II, 17.

33 Quintilian *Inst.*12.10.16, where *pressus* is connected to the style of an ancient Attic school. Pliny was much emulated, notably by Thomas Jefferson at Monticello in Virginia. Jefferson also owned the illustrated Orrery edition of Pliny of 1751 (John Boyle, Earl of Orrery, Pliny, *Letters*, London, 1751.) See James S Ackerman, *The Villa, Form and Ideology of Country Houses*, Princeton, NJ: Princeton University Press, 1990. See also William B. O'Neal, *Jefferson's Fine Arts Library*, Charlottesville: University of Virginia Press, 1976. See also Du Prey, *The Villas of Pliny from Antiquity to Posterity*, 25. Ackerman (p.55) suggests that the subterranean passages at Monticello used by servants and slaves originates in Pliny's description of his *cryptoporticus* at Laurentum.

34 See Heffernan, 'Ekphrasis and Representation', 304.

35 On Stella, see also Martial, *Ep.* 6.47. On architecture moralised as luxury and decay, see C. Edwards, *The Politics of Immorality in Rome,* Cambridge: Cambridge University Press, 1993, 137–172.

36 Statius, *Silvae* 1.2, 148–154. 'Epithalamium in Honour of Stella and Violentilla', translated by D. R. Shackleton Bailey, London and Cambridge, MA: Harvard University Press, Loeb edition 2003, 50–51.

37 Pliny, *NH.* 36.1, 1–3.

38 Carole Newlands, *Statius' Silvae and the Poetics of Empire,* 97.

39 Statius, *Silvae* 2.2, 12, Loeb edition, 41: 'Aeneas' mother [Venus] with her own hand led the bride.'

40 Statius, *Silvae* 4.2, 25–26.

41 Statius, *Silvae* 4.2, 26–29.

42 Statius, *Silvae* 4.2, 31.

43 Statius, *Silvae* 4.2, 25–31; 42–43. Trans. D. R. Shackleton Bailey, Loeb edition, 249–251.

44 Martial, Ep. 7.56, 8.36, 8.39, 9, 91.

45 Suetonius, *Dom.* 12.5.

46 Suetonius, *Dom.* 12.4, 15.

47 Tacitus, *Agricola,* 1–3.

48 See F. Ahl, 'The Art of Safe Criticism in Greece and Rome', *American Journal of Philology* 105 (1984): 174–208. Cited by Newlands, *Statius' Silvae and the Poetics of Empire,* 17–19.

49 Plutarch, *On Listening to Lectures,* (*Moralia* 37F – 38B). It is not without cause that Plutarch saw words as having the ability to enter the soul, suggesting that the young should have earplugs to guard their minds. See Ann Vasaly, *Representations: Images of the World in Ciceronian Oratory*, Berkeley, CA: University of California Press, 1993, 99. Cited by Ruth Webb, *Ekphrasis, Imagination and Persuasion*, 24–25, fn 34, 35.

50 See L. Montrose, 'Of Gentlemen and Shepherds: The Politics of Elizabethan Pastoral Form', in *ELH* 10, (1983), 415-59, 426–33. Recognising the artificiality of Statius's pastoral, and naming it 'aristocratic pastoral', Montrose argues that in a courtly setting it provides 'an imaginary space' in which 'virtue and privilege coincide'. In comparison, Raymond Williams, *The Country and the City*, London: Chatto and Windus, 1973, 30–47, contains a critique of country house poetry and pastoral literature, arguing that the poetry is elitist and superficial, as the labour that underlies the economy of the country house is made invisible. Carole Newlands, *Statius' Silvae and the Poetics of Empire*, 152, sees a parallel in the political circumstances that Statius faced, preferring to call the form in the period of Domitian an 'imperial pastoral', which she argues embodies the tensions between private and courtly patronage at the heart of Statius's villa poems.

51 Newlands, *Statius's Silvae and the Poetics of Empire*, 153. The precedent for this use of architecture to define the role of the poet in society is in the pastoral poetry of Horace. See L. T. Pearcy Jr., 'Horaces' Architectural Imagery', *Collection Latomus*, 36 (1977): 772–81, 779. Cited by Newlands, *Statius's* Silvae *and the Poetics of Empire*, 153.

52 Cicero, *Att.* 2.8.2. On the typology of the *villa maritimae*, distinguishing both the 'peristyle' and the 'porticus' types, see A. G. McKay, *Houses, Villas and Palaces in the Roman World*, Ithaca, NY: Cornell University Press, 1975, 115–118. Cited by Newlands, *Statius's* Silvae *and the Poetics of Empire*, 156, fn. 9.

53 On *otium* as the defining characteristic of pastoral landscape, see T. G. Rosenmeyer, *The Green Cabinet,* Berkeley, LA: University of California Press, 1969, 65–97, cited by Newlands, *Statius's* Silvae *and the Poetics of Empire*, 144.

54 Horace, *Ep.*1.11.26.

55 Hor. *Carm.* 2.15.16; Strabo 5.4.8; Pliny, *Ep.* 2.17.27, at Laurentum.

56 Plato's *Republic*, 2.2.1.368e, translated by Desmond Lee, Harmondsworth: Penguin, 1955, 1981 edition, 117. Plato proceeds to make the right ordering of the *polis* dependent upon the right ordering of the soul. See Alasdair MacIntyre, *Whose Justice? Which Rationality?* London: Duckworth, 1988: 74-75: 'And justice is the key virtue because both in the *psuche* and the *polis* only justice can provide the order which enables the other virtues to do their work.' See also John Milbank, *Theology and Social Theory, Beyond Secular Reason*, Oxford: Basil Blackwell, 1990: 369.

57 Statius, *Silvae* 2.2, 138–42, translated by D. R. Shackleton Bailey, Loeb edition, 2003, 132–135.

58 Statius, *Silvae* 2.2.129–32, translated by D. R. Shackleton Bailey, Loeb edition, 2003, 132 – 133. On the influence of Lucretius see Newlands. *Silvae and the Poetics of Empire,* 170–171, citing D, Konstan, *Some Aspects of Epicurean Psychology,* Leiden: E. J. Brill, 1973, 9.

59 Newlands, *Silvae and the Poetics of Empire,* 172. See also H. –J. Van Dam, *Papinius Statius, Silvae Book 2: A Commentary, Mnemosyne,* Suppl. 82, Leiden, 1984, 209–11.

60 Rudolf Otto, *The Idea of the Holy, An inquiry into the non-rational factor in the idea of the divine and its relation to the rational,* translated by John H. Harvey, London, Oxford and New York: Oxford University Press, 1923, Paperback edition, 1958.

61 Plato dismissed Parmenides's World of Seeming, and substitutes the sensible world as the bad copy of some 'real' ideal. It is really a dialectic of particular and universal. Plato says that this particular house only exists as separate from other houses because all houses jointly participate in an ideal 'house', which exists absolutely and forever, both abstract and universal, and so immutable. Aristotle rescues houses a little, when in opposition to their dematerialisation, he writes '[w]e should not suppose that "house" exists apart from certain houses'. (Aristotle, *Metaphysics* 3.4.8-9) This particular house cannot be separated from any universal house.

Kurilpa Bridge

ANDREW P. STEEN

The struts draw a diagram of my infatuation: me at one end, her at the other. She's held at a distance by some hollowness. A bar of compression separates her from me. Within a weekday morning the same sequence is enacted. The science takes over. Two bodies on opposite paths pass by one another. Their inertia drags them beyond certain sources of gravity encountered along the way. The gaze, the occasional smile. No deviation is seen in the trajectories. The invisible hollow members maintain a space, a void. But what is in that space? A charge? A latent source of energy? The promise of a connection? The exchange of heat? Oh, to collapse life's spurs and be entangled with her in a cat's cradle! Or like insects in a web, me a dull brown moth, her, a butterfly or brightly coloured beetle, stuck but together.

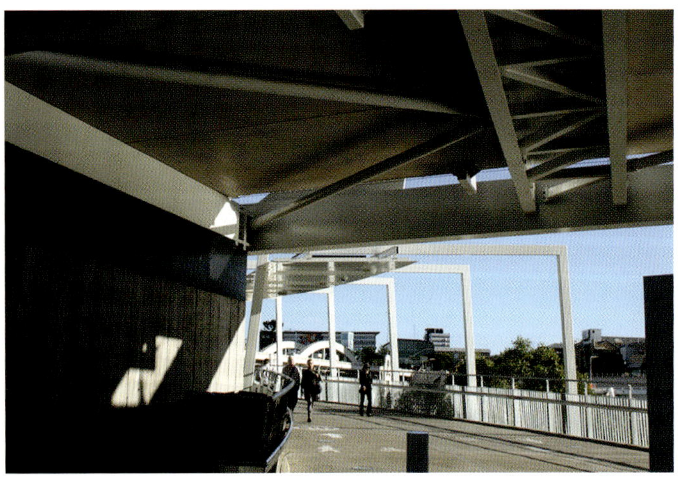

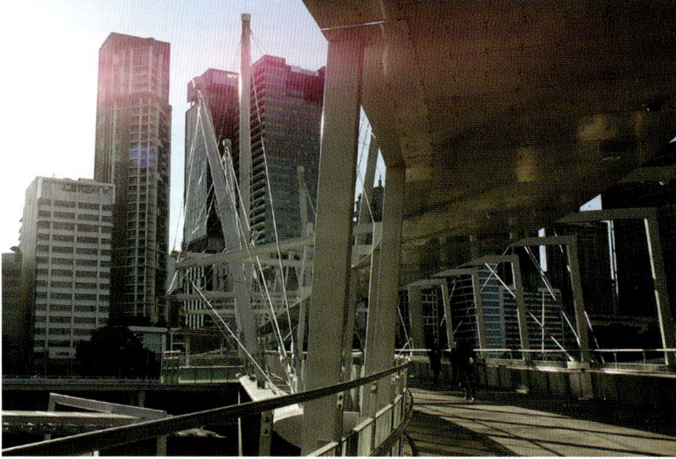

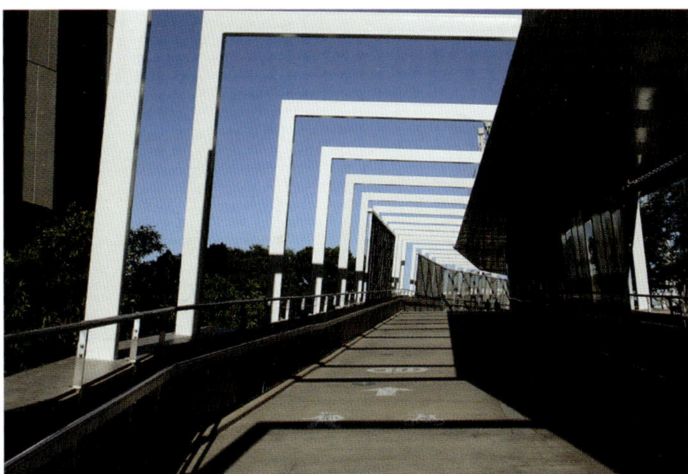 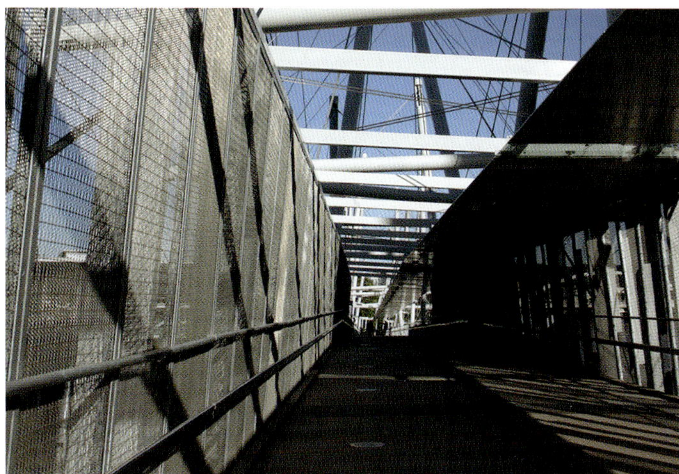

With that step, another bleak day officially begins; my journey to the other side – a journey measured out like mealtimes in a nursing home, something to regularise the incremental passing of hours until the final dreamless sleep. Again – again I find myself on this clichéd journey, barred in a time signature as predictable and orderly as a romance novel. For two bodies to find each other, to touch, to dance, to be entwined – someone's sick idea of a joke, and everyone's complicity in it is just a mere convenience. It's easier to swallow than it is to think, or to taste. The myth of femininity, the slick surfaces, the applications of mistruth; the stocking seamed, slices in half, the promise of something coming from between, something different, something warm and nurturing; the laced corset of obligation one wears to be a version of something else, for another who appreciates, in kind – that is what is done. What an appalling waste.

There! Yes, there, unmistakably! My heart's beat tells me it's her. Her slowness glows within the network of lines, radiant within their pretentious staged chaos. She walks out of time, out of this mess of stresses and pressures. She walks in a radiant bubble of morning sunlight. She walks like her knees are filled with oil. Her head, delicate on her neck, looks as much secured as balanced. The falls of the luxury of her dark hair draw arabesques, graphing some sublime equation with an indeterminate remainder, an ever-fluxing Mandelbrot pattern. Her progress down the incline seems inevitable and wondrous. She is a force of nature. Are Newton's laws of motion true? This energy, this surging rush of energy clogging my throat, it can't be generated out of nothing; it must come from somewhere, mustn't it? Does it have an equal and opposite reaction in her? Our masses passing: do our paths converge, even a little? Am I fighting physics with some desire for propriety? Newton, Newton: where are you when I need you?

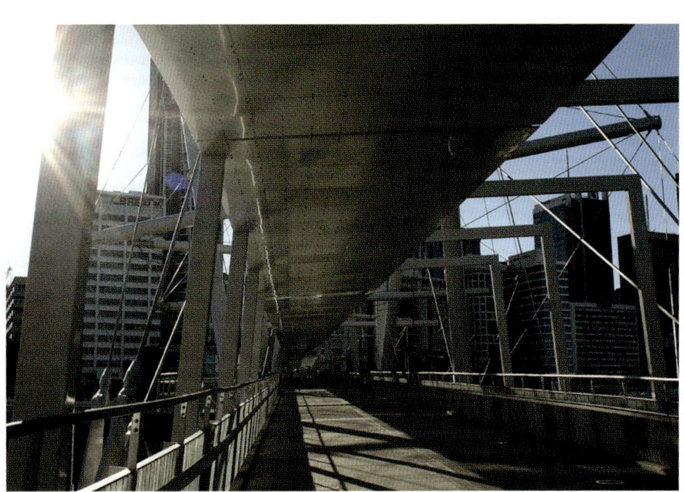

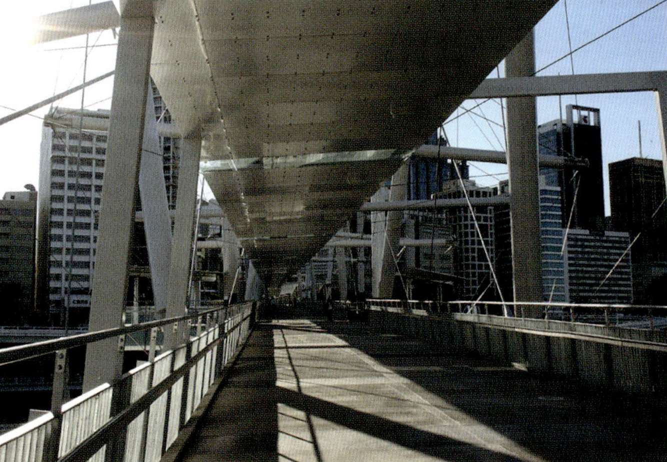

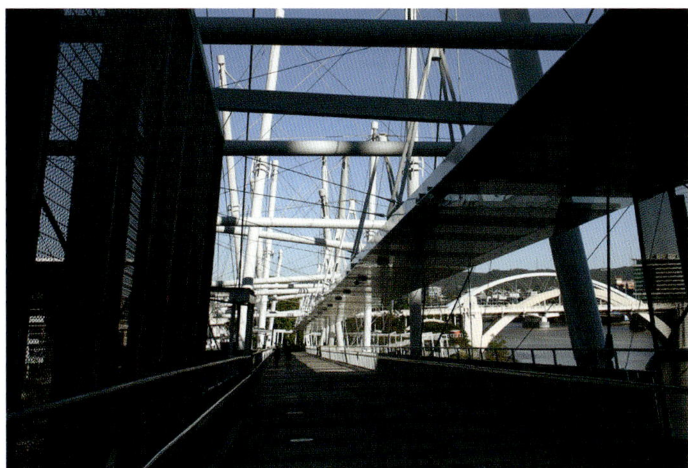 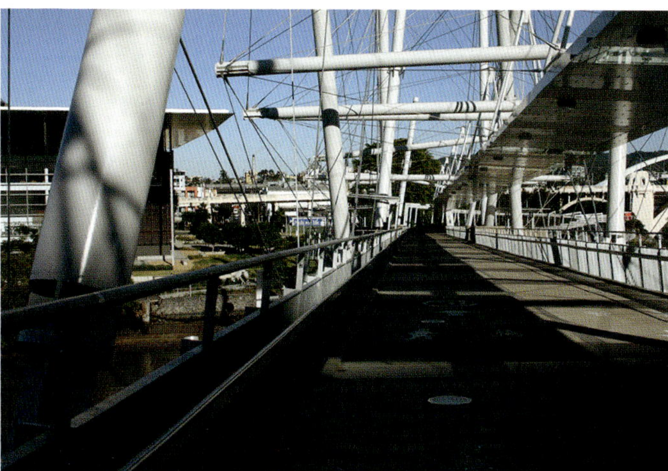

The day has been broken and is making ungodly creaks, crying for help; but here, yet again, the same unchanging walk, the same bridge, over and over again. The nameless faceless figures stream by, ripples of noise; while the conductor, dying in the pit, the pit of hollowed earth, the well, waves on the slow waltz in the spasmodic throes of his death, carrying on as the ship is sinking, the black-blue velvet winter-heavy with promise, certainty; the baton falling from his hand after the final fitful flourish, rolling across the floor, circling, resting there. I can see it in the distance; technical proficiency is a dream. My heels ring out a measured rhythm, me my own metronome, pacing out the seconds of this mournful filling-in of time.

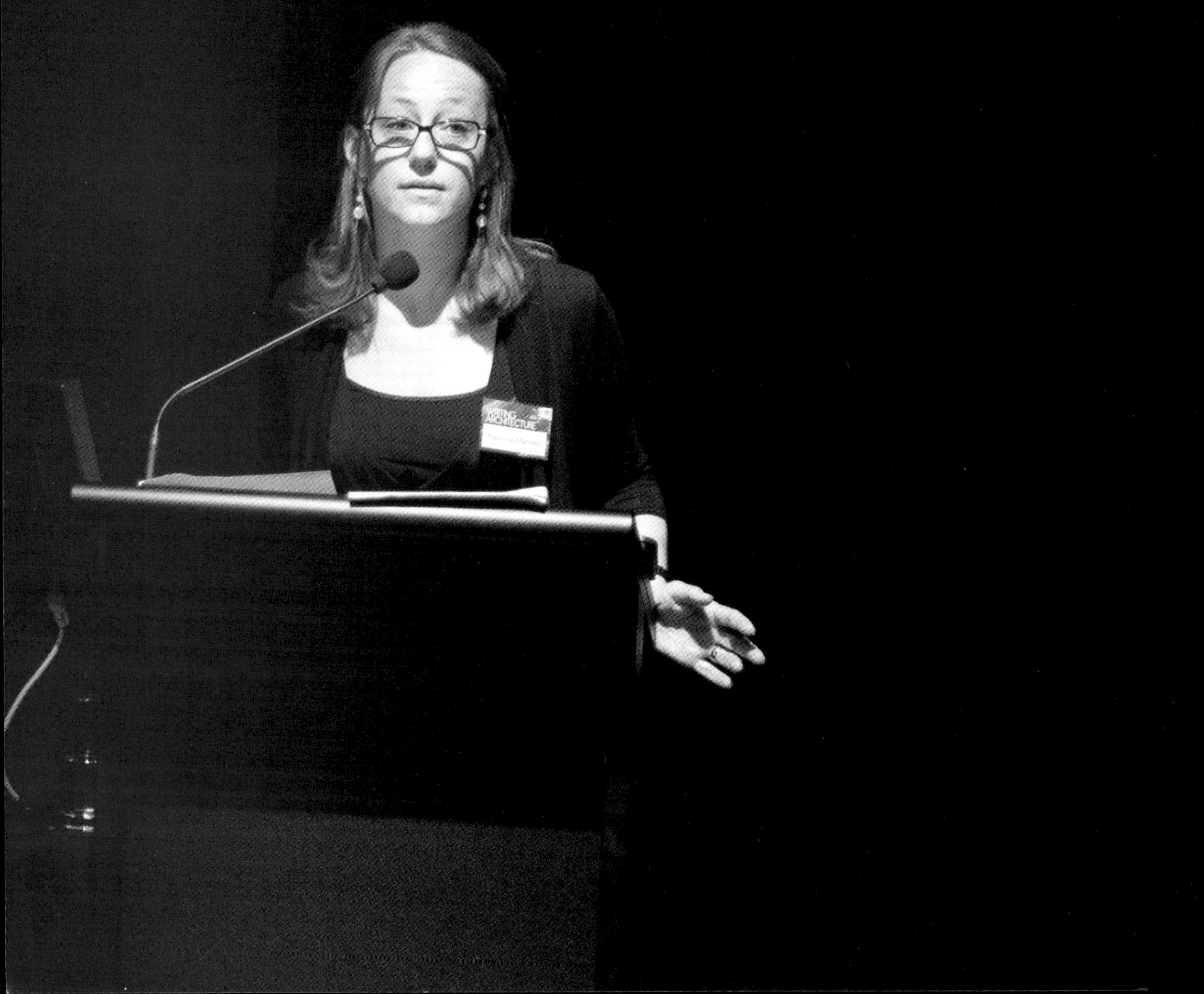

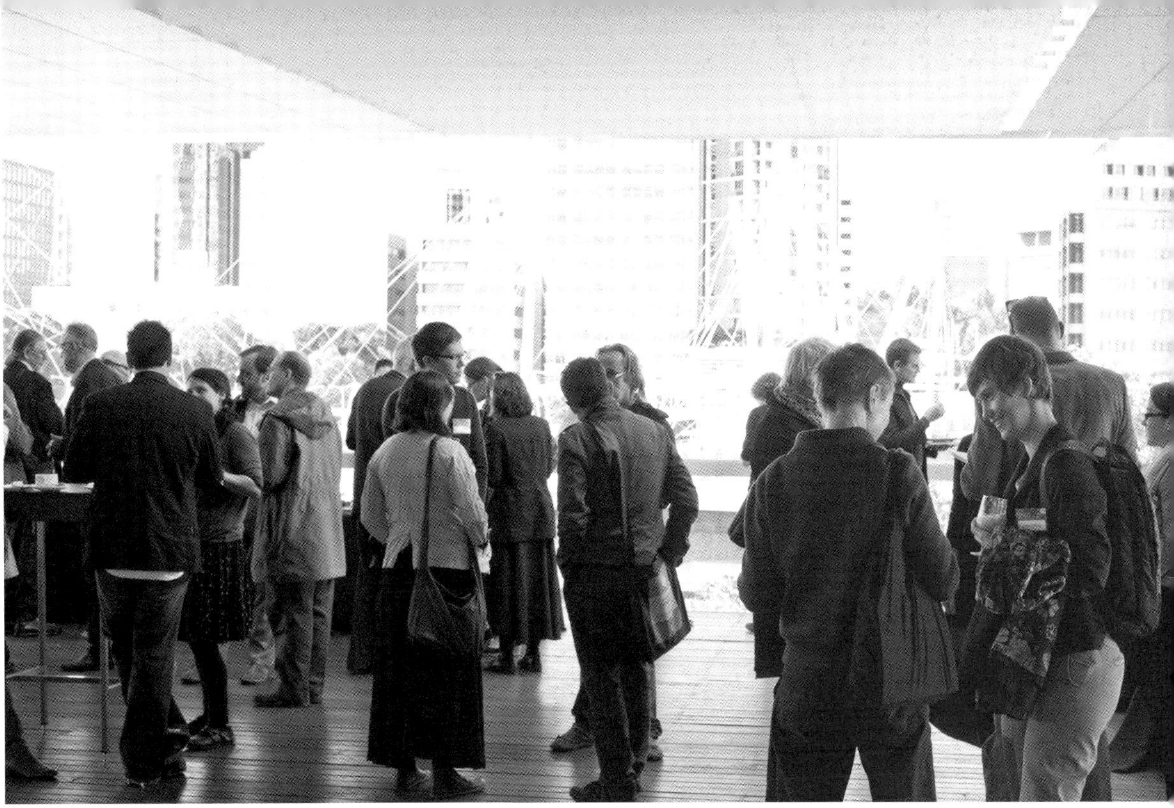

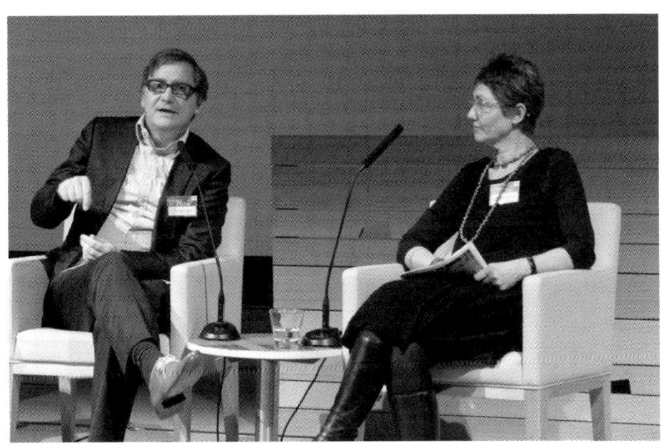
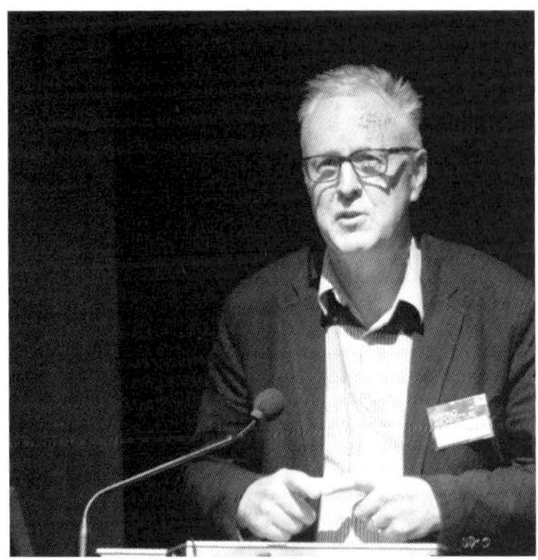

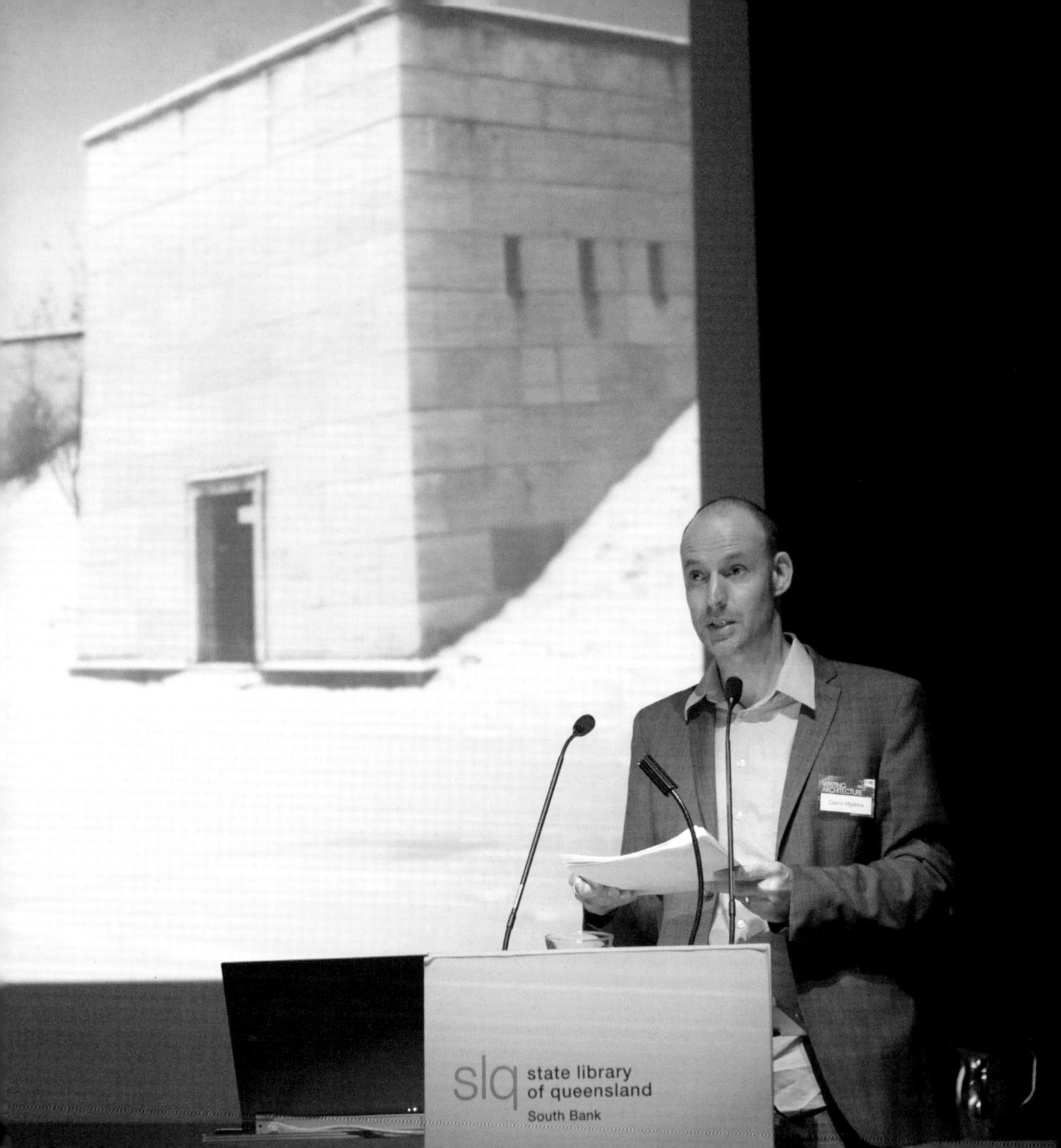

I'm There Right Now: Occupying architectural spaces photographically

GAVIN HIPKINS

The interface between commercial architectural photography and fine arts architectural photography has always been a porous one. Art photographers have enthusiastically turned their cameras to buildings as legitimate subject matter, illustrating edifices as poetic, desirable objects by fragmenting parts of a building or correcting perspectival shifts with precision cameras; making concrete and steel structures beautiful by printing intimate and carefully crafted analogue photographic prints, or today, outputting immaculately groomed digital surfaces as massive glossy inkjet artworks. Commercial photographers have also attempted to make their straighter documents arty when it suited the editorial and art director's premise by calling on and extending a range of devices and aesthetics familiar to fine art circles and histories. Within careerist ambitions, art photographers are regularly and pragmatically commercial editorial

photographers. Typified in history of photography tomes by hallmark figures such as Edward Steichen or Irving Penn, whose practices criss-crossed between popular magazine culture and art museums.

Try and envisage that romanticised moment when Manhattan rose into the New York skyline without recalling iconic photos of this industrial process: a futile exercise. Pictorial markers of modernity, including Alfred Stieglitz and Edward Steichen's exploration of the Flatiron Building circa 1903, or their protégé Paul Strand's harder-edged black and white art documents taken of the same building over a decade later, come to mind. Familiar images such as these define photography's enduring compulsion to simultaneously document a building's functional role while selectively celebrating and enhancing its picturesque attributes. From today's perspective, such 20th century photographic icons conjure up nostalgia for the period-relationship between developing parallel technologies – buildings and film – that is inextricably linked to the avant-garde and high modernism.

My formerly 'innocent' civic relationship to architecture was altered when I started taking photographs of buildings and architectural spaces. At this defining moment, my remnants from the photographic experience – initially snapped as markers of admiration and/or horror for the buildings that I visited as tourist – took on a second status as artwork when hung on a gallery wall or reproduced in an art publication: this contextual shift betraying my position as contemporary artist with a travel-with-camera-in-tow affliction. To photograph buildings within broader publishing contexts is to join an historic model harking back at least to those pioneering photographers of the mid-19th century, who lugged unwieldy gear to foreign sites to record tourist monuments for shrunken contemplation, exhibition display and wider distribution.

In narrowing a focus to this expansive history of travel and architectural photography, and to present an idiosyncratically determined case study, here I want to consider the profile of contemporary architectural photography within fine arts contexts over the last few decades by following a persuasive lineage to the influence of, and key aesthetic strategies fostered by, the husband and wife team of Bernd and Hilla Becher, and the subsequent 'first generation of the Becher circle' as it has been called.[1] Commencing their major project in 1959, the Bechers built an impressive black and white photographic typological study of 19th and 20th century industrial structures, including their infamous water tower collection.

By surveying a developmental moment in my artistic practice when I was looking to established architectural photography methodologies, this paper also introduces my early photographic projects emerging from the mid-1990s on. At the risk of a potentially awkward exegesis structure, I outline a zeitgeist of photographic conventions prevalent

Bernd and Hilla Becher, *Water Towers*, USA, 1974–1983. Copyright Hilla Becher, 2012. Photograph courtesy Die Photographische Sammlung / SK Stiftung Kultur der Sparkasse Köln.

at this time and still popular today within fine arts and popular press context, and simultaneously attempt to position my own projects within an emergent comprehension of these photographic styles (once, somewhat flippantly, I considered myself an unofficial exchange student of the Kunstakademie Düsseldorf). Initially examining the legacies of the Becher school of architectural photography, I identify traditions of representing uninterrupted space emerging from this time, while charting my evolving discontents with these artistic model(s).

Turning back to selected photographic projects within my artistic practice has presented an opportunity to critically reconsider my earlier pictorial engagements with architectural spaces and surrounding landscapes. These projects have visited both well known, and less celebrated, architectural sites, buildings, ruins, monuments, parks, gardens, zoos and amusement parks. A wider question of spectatorship and plausibility through shifting technological developments, underlines an enquiry into projected psychological and bodily occupations of pictures, and this enquiry is no exception. In particular, as my title alludes to, I am compelled by that uncanny projective interplay between representation and imaginative occupation *into* a carefully constructed empty site. This is that magic space that ontologically defines photography and film. In calling on one of David Lynch's darkly surrealist scenes from his 1997 feature film, *Lost Highway,* toward the end of this essay, I chart thresholds of limits between photographic and filmic mediums and their shared requirements of audience wish-fulfilment and imaginative corporeal occupation, and more sinisterly, spatial violation.

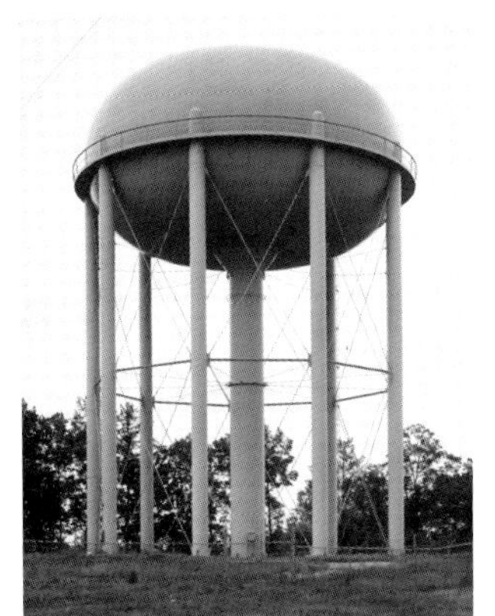
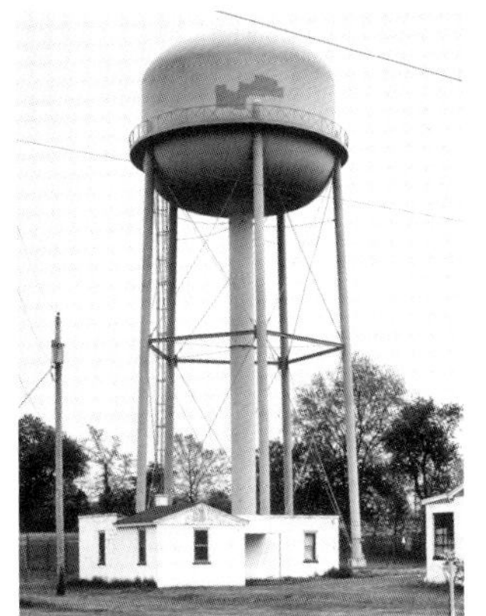
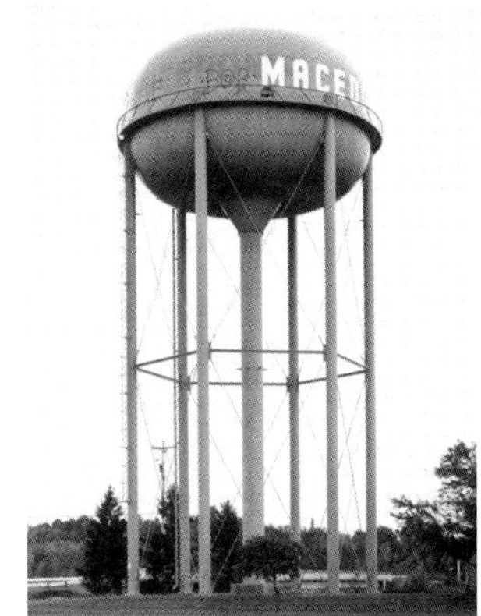
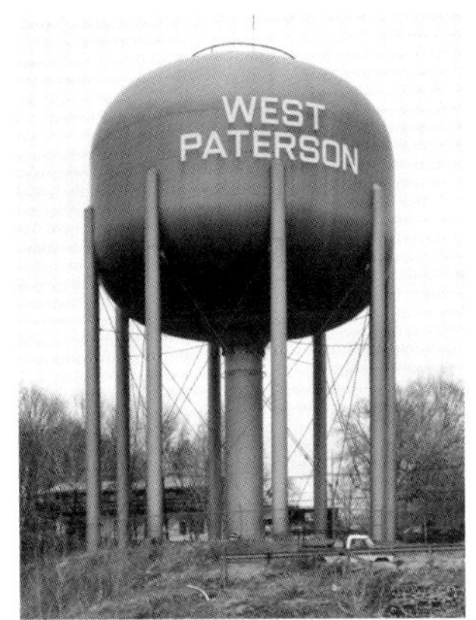
WEST
PATERSON
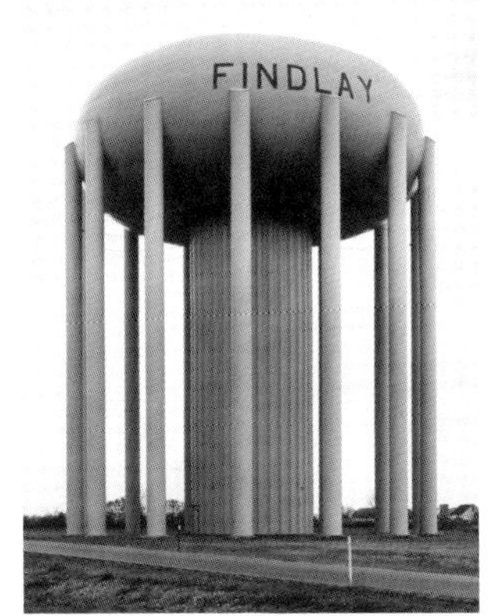
FINDLAY
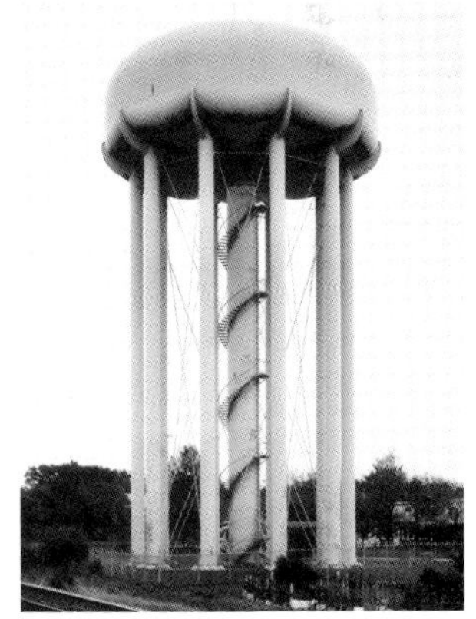
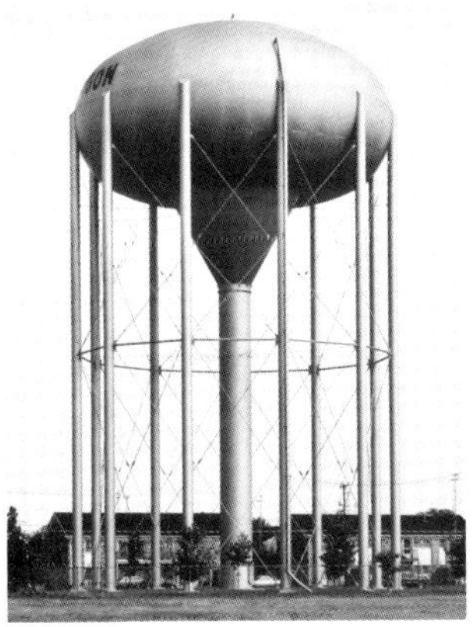
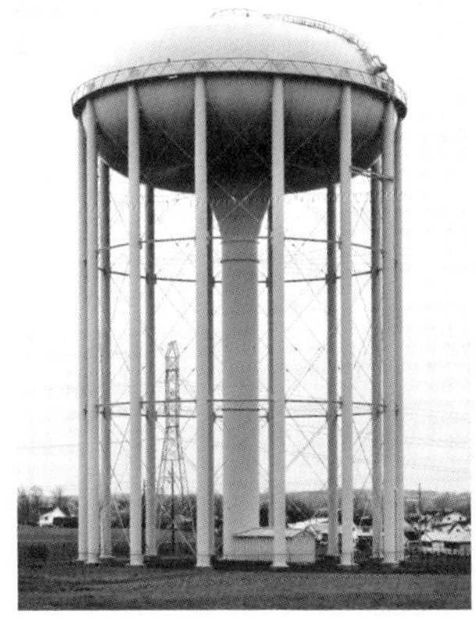
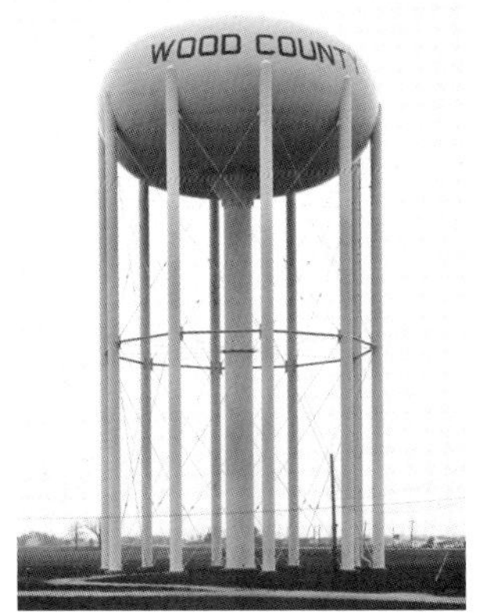
WOOD COUNTY

The Water Tower

As students of Bernd Becher at the Düsseldorf Academy, a generation of high-profile art photographers, including Thomas Struth, Thomas Ruff, Candida Höfer and Andreas Gursky, set about to initially mimic, expand, and then adapt the Bechers's photographic methodologies and disciplined attitude. Viewed from today, these projects have diversified in areas of subject matter, conceptual positioning and stylistic engagement. However, individual series in the 1980s and early 1990s from their respective oeuvres demonstrate a rite of passage via an overlapping photographing of buildings and architectural sites.[2]

A series of European streets by Thomas Struth started in the early 1980s epitomises my love-hate relationship to this architectural photography. As highly detailed photographic prints, this career-making work appears to stylistically mimic 19th century urban photographic landscapes emerging from the 1840s onward. Mid-19th century topographical landscapes revealed what was literally *out there* in a documentary realism that defied claims of falsification. Admittedly, celebrated practitioners including Oscar Rejlander and Henry Peach Robinson had tampered with their photographic negatives and prints, cutting them up and bringing a montage of scenes they hoped would seamlessly come together as a unified work of art – to push photography-as-medium a step closer to its disputed entrance and gradual tolerance into the Salon. Yet such attempts to bravely hack against the grain of a 19th century's photographic ontology were isolated affairs and did little to change the popular consensus that photography rendered life with a curiously unexpressive, yet faithful, optical precision.

In Struth's street photographs of architecture, we locate global *flanerie* at its happy work, such that this shared (generational) project invites some general questions: how does this photographic modus operandi differ from 19th century models of travelling with a camera? As itinerant (and prevalent) poet male walking international streets for new photos of urban architecture and cityscapes, what roles do preservation and stability play in these (anachronistic) technological productions of space and (privileged) locating of place? For those photographers recording European cities within extended series, how are the touristic wanderings marked by gender in a journey that could be argued as a personalised extension of the grand tour? What areas of these cities are represented or absent, and how do discreet neighbourhoods from disparate cities coalesce to form a stylistically unified photographic 'album'?

A closer look at the Düsseldorf way of photographing architecture focuses on methods of camera production. Such visual 'technologies of space', to use Jane M. Jacobs's phrase are signifiers of the branches of 'imperial territori-alisation' at play in a postcolonial age.[3] Frequently then, a soft imperiousness is to be found in these photographs of cities from around a Eurocentric charting of our globe. An authoritative tone is conveyed in the earnestness of this venture, a process of amassing knowledge, of (chemically) fixing the world onto fragile gelatin surfaces of large photographic plates that still turn to analogue technologies in the face of the digital juggernaut.[4]

At first glance with this photography we are invited to see today's world through yesterday's lens. Yet, on closer inspection, the single process of referencing early travel and urban photography is invariably complicated by the inevitable inclusion of contemporary elements: tightly parked cars in European streets, overhead webs of cables in downtown Tokyo, severely gridded facades of late modern housing estates in Geneva. Working with large format view cameras, the professional photographer's pursuit has more purpose than regular tourists, their camera gear heavier. In a search for an idea of 'the authentic', the photographer moves away from favoured city squares and tourist spots towards the suburbs or occasionally an urban unsightly, again, pursuing a notion of 'an actual' distanced from the 'soft-terrain' covered by packaged tours. A notable exception here is the early work of Andreas Gursky, which definitively charted the phenomenon of global tourism at the end of the 20th century via elevation, scale and digital retouching.[5]

Struth's black and white framing of buildings from the 1980s consistently borrows another pictorial strategy from the earlier Bechers's approach: they are all taken on overcast days, seemingly proclaiming a global consistency in weather patterns while referencing the look of 19th century plates when relatively insensitive films could only render blue skies a uniform shade of motley white. This 'look' of an early photography is stylistically pronounced and coincides with a revamped connoisseurship emerging in the 1970s and 1980s when both historic and contemporary photography was bestowed a new exhibition agenda and market appreciation.[6] With architectural photography as stylised methodology, it is comprehensible that Tokyo can look like Düsseldorf, Auckland looks like Vancouver, and that Canberra does indeed look like Brasilia … but only through a tight cropping of a larger social landscape, a highly mediated record that refuses signage in different languages, one that seeks out consistent light qualities regardless of radically different weather seasons, one that ignores a detailed specificity of place, and so on. In short, Canberra looks like Brasilia only when it is photographically constructed so.

Like the Bechers's industrial structures, these streets and buildings share the depopulated status. As Struth has noted on his empty streets, ' … if the scenes are empty, the effect is stronger, that's all and when you look at these empty streets you can more easily imagine yourself in the space.'[7] Imagining yourself in a cityscape is at the core of touristic projective wish-fulfillment: the ubiquitous travel postcard caption 'wish you were here' is inverted in a desirous flip to an heartfelt 'wish I was there': an imaginative projection into that other, represented place, as well as a fanciful nod to escape from the tedium of the every day.

Conceptual justification for a depopulated human landscape also takes on the form of the poetic, even mystical realm. This is the case when Constance Glenn conjures up photographer Candida Hofer's voice:

> [Hofer] preferred her [interior] spaces uncomplicated by the unpredictability of people moving through her rigorously composed frame. She does not, however, think of her spaces as empty. They are animated with light, form, pattern and references to the human presence, which can be felt if not seen.[8]

Such a reading of works sits alongside related artist statements and argues how, for celebrated photographers, apparent empty spaces are not perceived as empty at all, but are considered neutral tableaus to be occupied by their audiences: a literal invitation to spatially occupy the seemingly uninhabited: a pictorial conquest of the empty.

I have identified a number of stylistic traits explored and utilised by the influential 'first generation' of photographers from the Becher school. My intention with this relatively narrow look is not, however, to ignore alternative models of architectural photography practices emerging around this time, but to single out a subscribed disciplined approach – familiar in both art and mainstream architectural magazine culture – to architectural photography. At a personal level, I have charted the Düsseldorf school of thought in light of my own recognition of both its persuasiveness and limitations, and to provide a background for positioning my evolving practice away from its cool shadows: my growing disdain encouraged me to consider how else could I photographically engage buildings and architectural spaces?

Romance: Hinterland

My early forays into photographing architecture shared an appreciation for the significance of the Düsseldorf School and called on related conventions of architectural photography. In the mid-1990s, I travelled extensively in a recently

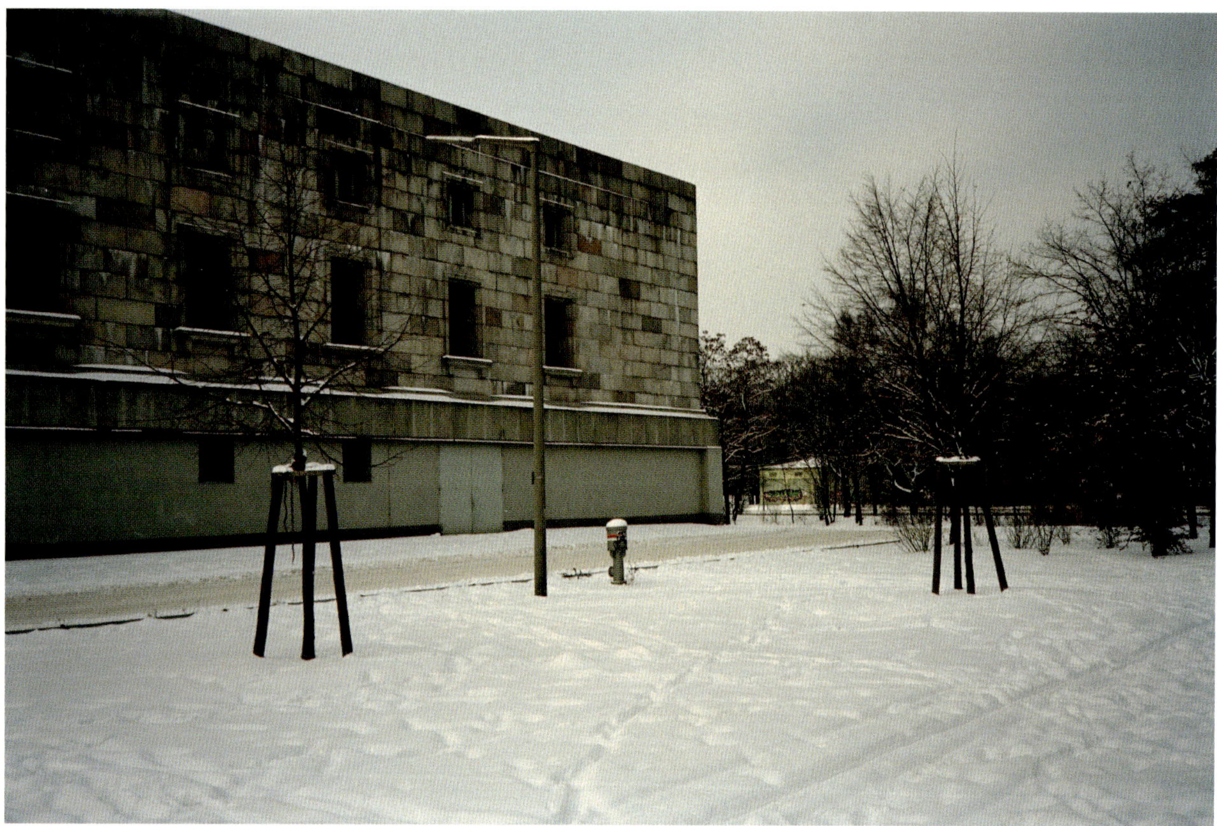

Gavin Hipkins, Nuremberg, Germany, 1996.
All photographs courtesy Gavin Hipkins.

reunified Germany to certify an idea of architecture and architectural photography. Working with a 35mm format camera (a relatively humble camera in scale compared to the large format cameras used by the Becher school[9]), I called on inherited and implicit photographic rules that included: photographing spaces and buildings without people; the removal of extraneous elements through careful framing to avoid markers of the city's function (no street signs, no cars in foreground, no sewers etc.); and perspectival correction, when at all possible.

While the 'first generation' turned their cameras to post-war modern buildings that corresponded to their own childhoods and post-war reconstruction, my interests lay in quite marked (adolescent in another way) architectural categories. Along the lines of Susan Sontag's outline of the legacies of fascism[10], which charted an obsession with the remnants of Nazism, reappraisal of Leni Riefenstahl's photography and films, and associated paraphernalia – for Sontag a *Fascinating Fascism* – I traced neoclassical, fascist and Soviet-inspired edifices of bureaucracy and state bullying; my tidy yet modest snaps of historically celebrated and/or notorious state building constituted picture fragments in a never to be completed jigsaw of pseudo-historic connections, formal relationships and fantasised imaginings. Watchtowers were compared to water towers, the Walhalla sat alongside the Haus der Kunst, and Berlin's Olympiastadion was juxtaposed with the Olympic Stadium in Munich. These collated results of isolated monolithic buildings and grim hard-edged details determined that – in a Barthean nod to authentication – indeed, I was there, and I had been intimidated. The phenomenology of this cold lineage of architecture had both affected my engagement, and at the same time, shaped my photographic recordings of these touristic experiences.

These wanderings in the snow during the brutal winter of 1996–97 (so cold, my shutter would intermittently stutter, capturing only a vertical slit of its whole frame and exposure) inevitably became resource albums for referencing and storing on the shelf marked 'archive of photographs of European architecture and architectural spaces', and never really found their way into the gallery – in unaffected form at least.[11] What was the purpose of these intensive wanderings? On my map of Germany was a list of primarily civic buildings and ruins that consti-tuted potential photogenic sites. Remnants of ruins and recolonised spaces were neatly arranged in my viewfinder — pictorially clear cut by the snow and leaden sky. At a certain point, I had caught myself becoming the photog-rapher I did not want to become: that ubiquitous global student, who marked this moment and the Düsseldorf way of photographically engaging the world. A positioning of the Düsseldorf 'approach' needed to reconsider that the typological school of indexing heralded by the Bechers and their disciples including Struth, Hofer and a contem-porary architectural photography orthodoxy had, by this stage, entered the realm of trope: a refined mimicry of 19th century models of photographing architectural

spaces (buildings, streets and public squares). A tidying up of the Bechers's uncompromising serial approach had, with the first Düsseldorf generation, gradually let go of links to minimalism, and a conceptual underpinning that had previously established 'the treatment of the photograph as a document'.[12]

The Trench

Returning from Germany at the start of 1997, later that year I set about to extend my touristic and linked photographic experiences by visiting Le Corbusier's Chandigarh. Like an architect on a pilgrimage, I repeatedly travelled through the gridded streets north from my hotel to Sector 1 and the Capitol Complex of the Radiant City with cameras in day bag to reflect on, and document, Le Corbusier's famous structures and monuments set against the landscape backdrop of the Himalayas. Like my trip to Germany a year earlier, these recordings were planned to function as visual note-taking, to influence later works and photo-installations, and at the time, constitute research with no particular exhibition output in mind.

In his compelling book *Chandigarh's Le Corbusier: The Struggle for Modernity in Postcolonial India*, Vikramāditya Prakāsh recalls how as architect and architectural critic, he regularly guides visiting architects through Sector 1.[13] Desiring clean shots of The Secretariat, of The Assembly, of the Palace of Justice, of the Open Hand, Prakāsh observes that:

The innumerable architects who pass through Chandigarh … generally prefer to wait patiently until the village people pass on through, so that they can get a 'clean shot' of the buildings. They try to edit out the laundry of their picture frame, usually unsuccessfully, and then complain about the callous Indian government's disrespect for the great French/Swiss architect's creations.[14]

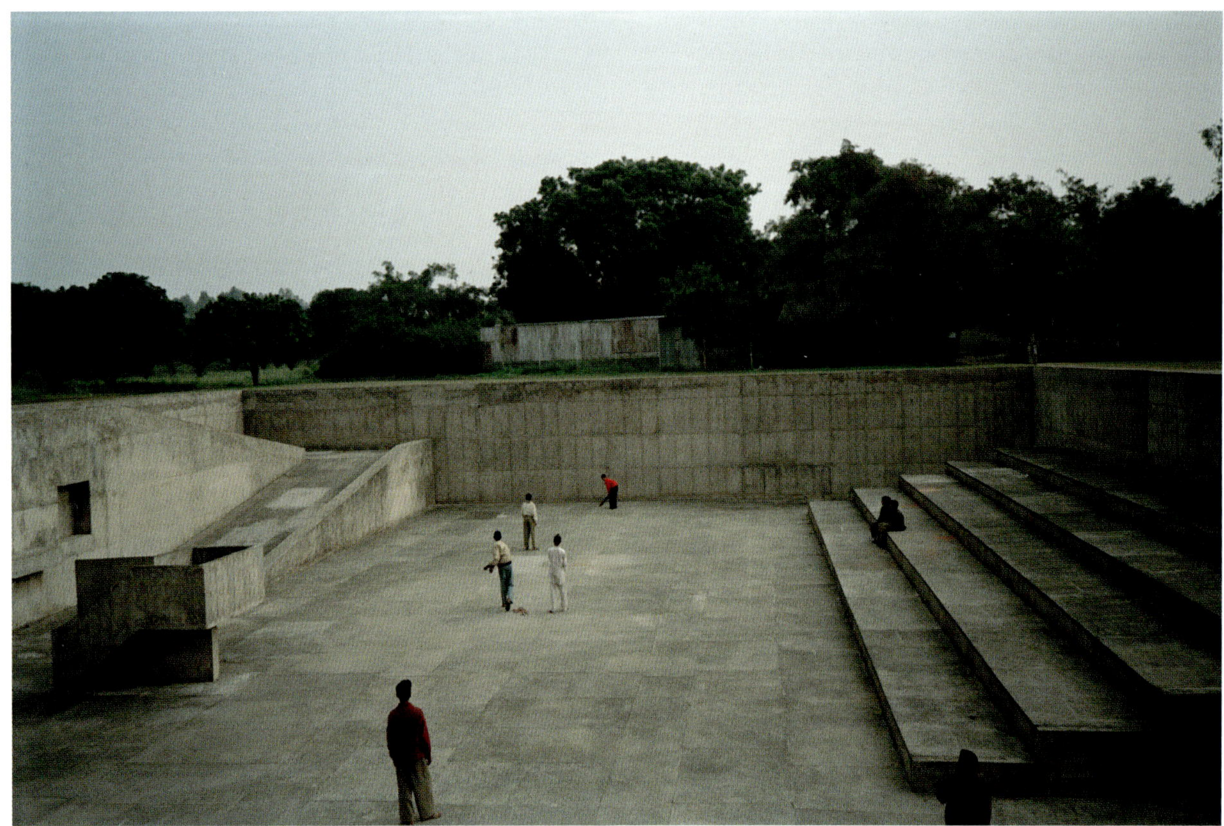

Gavin Hipkins, Chandigarh, India, 1997.

This desire to 'edit out the laundry' for photographers/ architects connotes the drive to replicate reproductions of a de-politicised Chandigarh – a space held in limbo by a perception of its modernist aspirations, and associated wrenching of labourers and villagers away from the background of celebrated architectural features: an empty city that connotes retro-science fiction filmic backdrop or apocalyptic stage set, or, it would seem, architectural and town planning models. For Le Corbusier in his own numerous publications, including *Complete Works,* editorial decisions were made, and a politics of inclusion celebrated and aligned itself with, a mapping of an occupied and fully functioning Chandigarh via the staging and recording of photographs with people, including labourers, in them.

In Sector 1, approaching Le Corbusier's posthumously realised Monument of the Open Hand, a poignant illustration of the complexities of acculturated space and the decolonisation process was to be found. The Trench of Consideration was conceived by the master architect as an amphitheatre for public debate that set about to recall the spirit of the sunken steps from The Parthenon. The architect envisaged those sitting in The Trench would be able to contemplate the adjoining Open Hand, the symbolic crown of Chandigarh as modern capital, a colossal sculpture signalling India's technological embrace for a prosperous and peaceful future. For Le Corbusier, the monument was:

> open to receive the newly created wealth,
> open to distribute it to its people and to others.
> The 'Open Hand' will assert that the second era of
> the machine age has begun: the era of harmony.[15]

At the time of my visit, youthful cricket players had turned The Trench, or The Ditch as it is affectionately known, into the perfect easy-to-field cricket pitch (with adjoining stand). Circling The Hand by walking around The Trench, I took over a hundred colour 35mm slides of the isolated sculptural monument. On a perfectly still day, with a stilted pedestrian's circumnavigation, I emulated the 'wind vane'-like attributes of the monument's ability to rotate in the wind on its massive centred pole. My dismembered photographs of The Monument constituted the first layer of collected material (albeit unknowingly at this time), to be combined with a second layer of pictorial

Gavin Hipkins, *The Trench*, 1998 (detail),
1 of 80 projected slides, install dimensions variable.

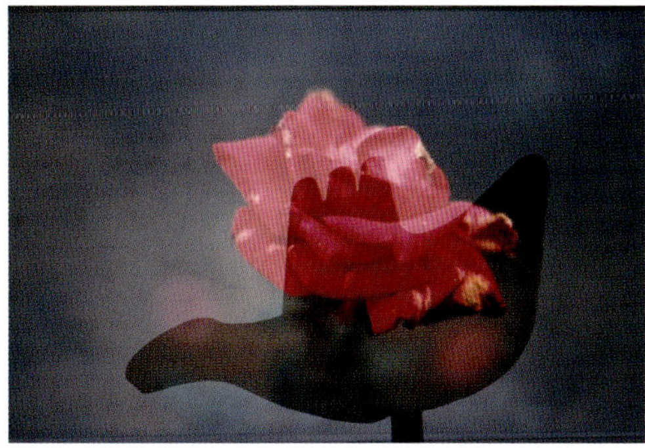

elements also sourced from Chandigarh. In Sector 17 I visited Chandigarh's Rose Garden, where I was drawn to the garden for its colonial associations and potential for later poetic play. Here I photographed centrally composed close-ups of isolated rose heads and noted their poignantly exotic titles: new tower, gold medal, tapestry, Arabian nights, happiness.

Resembling a farewell wave to modernism, my completed work *The Trench* (1997–98) comprises a full 80-slide carousel of projected double-exposed images of metallic hand and blooming roses, advanced every few seconds by electronic timer. A sensual yet mechanical clunking akin to dismembered animatronics display, or neurotic stop-motion sequence demonstrating a twitching hand or bird-like shape in perpetual cycle. When displayed, it is important that the projected work be anti-monumental; brought back down to life size, framed at the scale of a 1950s chocolate box with rose-pictures on the cover, alluding, I hoped, to the portentous nature of the lofty ideals framed by Le Corbusier's late and over-sized gesture, as well as an attempt to foster a legitimate nostalgia for this compelling city and ambitious modern project. For as Prakāsh has noted, '… If modernism failed in India, it was not because it was '"western", or because it relied on universal ideals. It failed because it relied on the ideological conviction that an enlightened elite could lead the rest of the populace simply by relying on the strength of symbolic demonstration.'[16]

The Habitat

If in Chandigarh I had felt a deep sense of familiarity, of being in a zoned city, and of passing by and staying in standardised neighbourhood units, then this familiarity owed itself to my undergraduate days at the University of Auckland (a campus I have now returned to as an academic), and my then daily teaching environment at Massey University, Wellington. The shared primary

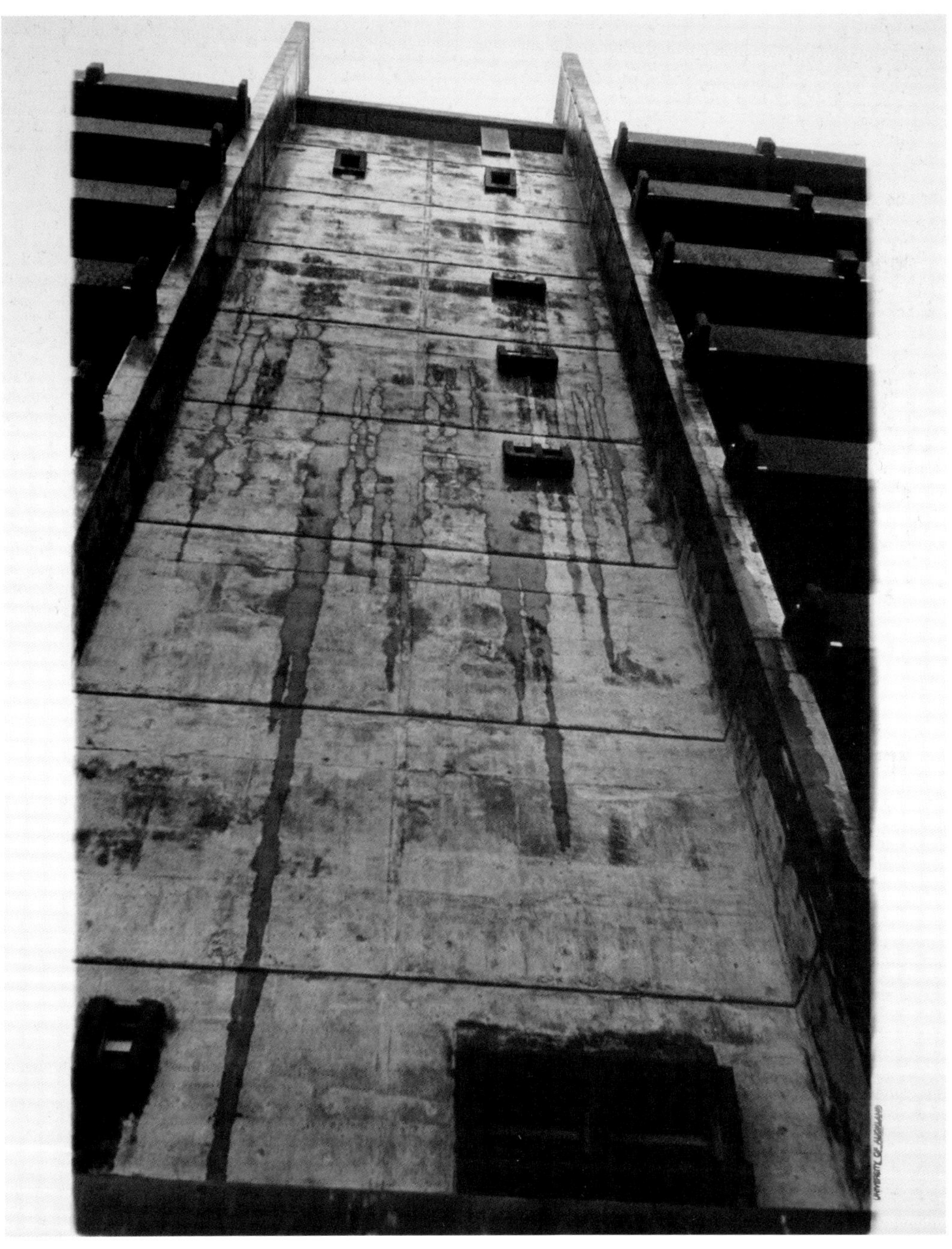

Gavin Hipkins, *The Habitat*, 2000 (detail). 72 silver-gelatin prints each 510mm x 600mm, install dimensions variable.

(Opposite) Gavin Hipkins, *The Habitat*, 2000 (details). 72 silver-gelatin prints each 510mm x 600mm, install dimensions variable.

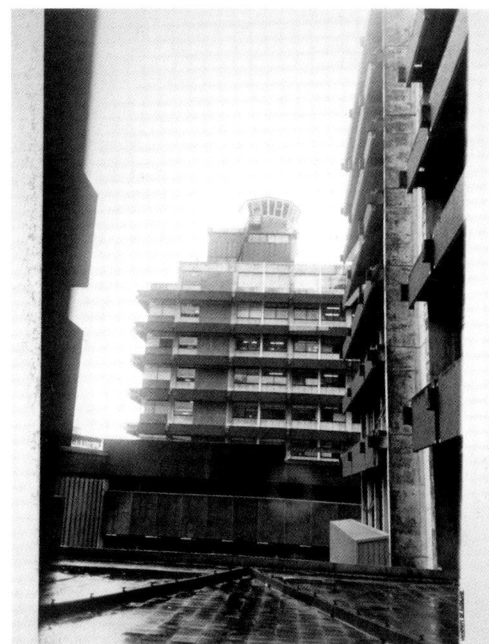
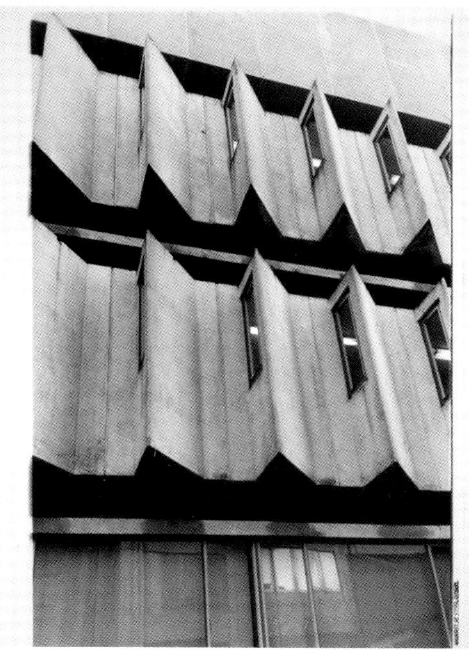

element between Chandigarh and these New Zealand tertiary institutions is, naturally, concrete work. My project *The Habitat* (1999-2000), set out to document late modernist, or more precisely, the stylistic influence of the New Brutalism as found in, and on, New Zealand university campuses: the University of Auckland; the University of Waikato; Massey University, Palmerston North and Wellington; Victoria University of Wellington; the University of Canterbury; and the University of Otago.

The timing of my access to these campuses (during study break or over the summer period) when the buildings were virtually empty represents a photographic exaggeration of the institutionalised feeling of raw concrete and socially abandoned complexes. My decision of when to photograph near empty campuses embodies the images and establishes a mood akin to occupation via photographic prowling. Such that, the title of this multi-part frieze project, *The Habitat,* alludes to the apparent very 'uninhabitable' nature of these overtly functional, yet at times, inhospitable campuses. For Reyner Banham writing on the movement's relationship to habitat in 1966:

> The preoccupation with habitat, the total building environment, that shelters man and directs his movements, is a confirming theme that connects together many diverse Brutalist buildings, and connects Brutalism with other progressive thinking (and action) outside the field of architecture.[17]

Prioritising the raw materiality of this movement, the influential British architects, Alison and Peter Smithson, attempted to link the New Brutalism to Japanese architecture and its apparent spiritual synthesis of form, the natural world and materials:[18]

> It is this reverence for material – a realisation of the affinity, which can be established between buildings and man – which is at the root of the so-called New Brutalism.[19]

If the monolithic history of photography had an equivalent endearment for *a* materiality for, and of, itself – an equal to the Smithson's aestheticised ideal of Japanese architecture and their reading of its relationship to functionality – then this moment would lie in a modernist photography of related hard lines and aesthetic functionality: a movement which would later inform the Düsseldorf School. The Neue Sachlichkeit, or new objectivity movement, emerged in Germany between the wars, and included the arch-modernist photographer, Albert Renger-Patzsch, whose major book project *Die Welt ist Schon* (*The World is Beautiful*) was notoriously attacked by Walter Benjamin's pen for its fetishisation of content – the photographic look more important than subject:

> The world is beautiful — that is its watchword. Therein is unmasked the posture of a photograph that can endow any soup can with cosmic significance but cannot grasp a single one of the human connexions in which it exists …[20]

How then, to dirty earlier and purer aesthetic qualities in a Brutalist manner? How could a photographic medium be true to itself, and constitute a 'rough poetry'. We are familiar with the rhetoric of the New Brutalism as revolutionary spirit: 'Ethic or Aesthetic' as Banham would posit the subtitle of his book on the movement. In this light, how to photograph New Zealand university buildings from this period with stylistic influence, and at the same time, reference the revolutionary zeal of the Brutalist movement,

or at least Brutalist's manifesto(s), as well as identify New Zealand's shifting priorities from a once-taken-for-granted utopian service, government-backed free education, to one of a user-pays education economy?[21]

The New Brutalist movement attempted to make buildings as straightforward and comprehensible as possible. It took an anti-romantic position and applauded functionality. In the New Brutalist spirit, I wrote a manifesto for the production of my 72-part *The Habitat*, evidencing a commitment to a considered materiality required that I:

1   Photograph in colour negative film on an instamatic camera.
2   Print on black and white paper thereby grossly exaggerating tonal contrast from the colour negative projections.
3   Print on expired black and white photo paper to decrease tonal differences (in a contradictory manner to point 2).
4   Make only one print per negative and include overexposed, underexposed or stained and scratched prints in the series.
5   Estimate enlarger exposure and developmental times without testing.
6   Mount the photographic prints on cardboard.
7   Piece holes through the prints and cardboard.
8   Hang the prints with thumbtacks.
9   Display all prints in the exhibition.
10   Sequence prints by idiosyncratic formal considerations and not location.
11   Stamp all prints with a location ink stamp in the bottom right hand corner to label and identify originating campus.
12   Hang as a frieze to ensure a democratisation of aesthetic evaluation of individual pictures from audiences.
13   Exhibit *The Habitat* in modernist or modernist-inspired art galleries.

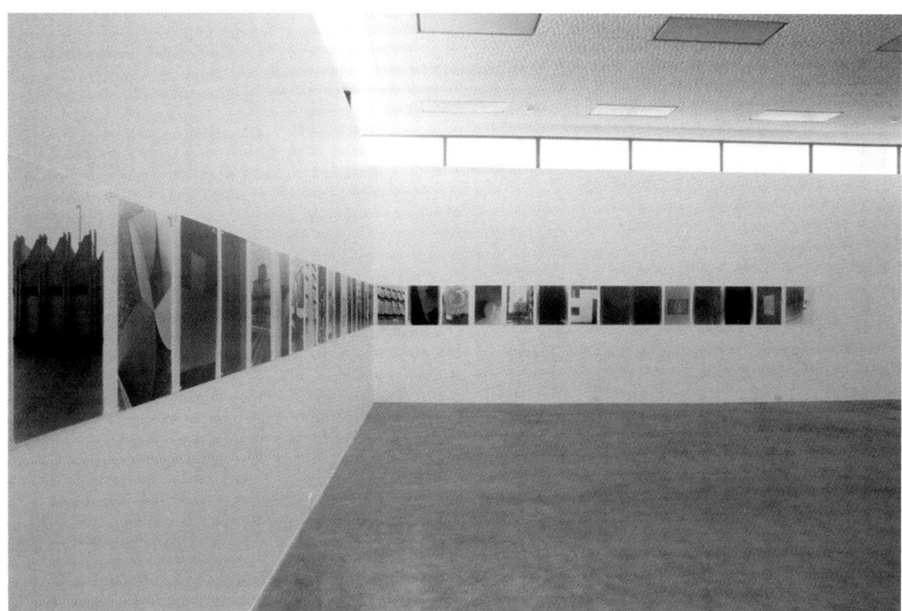

The Habitat (detail) installed
at Artspace, Auckland,
New Zealand, 2000.

Launched at Artspace Auckland in 2000, that same year
the series returned to the Adam Art Gallery at Victoria
University of Wellington, one of the campuses where a
number of the images had originated.[22] Tautologically,
the look of the photographs in *The Habitat* also reference
the patina of illustrations from well-worn books on the
New Brutalism movement borrowed from the university's
architecture library, a building which also looks very
much like it references the very period of architecture
photographed for my series. The works constitute coarse
and grainy black and white and grey photographic prints
that become the medium of abstraction, the rough poetry
of this architectural period: a tribute to the last vestiges of
toxic darkrooms, dusty films and student-photography-
scratches in the advent of a contemporary digital input
to output workflow: a homage to wet and dry processing.

The Sanctuary

In 2003, some years after my earlier travels, I returned
to my negatives from Germany and India in an attempt
to, somewhat literally, fill those apparent unoccupied
spaces. This series started as an exercise in darkroom
experimentation and referenced both pioneering photographic stencilling techniques (William Henry Fox Talbot's
sun drawings, or photogenic drawings, as he called them),
and the avant-garde rediscovery and renaming of this
process (Man Ray's rayographs, for example), by combining the traditional black and white darkroom exposure and
printing technique, with the photogram technique, to
form a hybrid of technical consideration and chance in
the series, *New Age* (2003–ongoing).

Earlier architectural backdrops could now be entered

into via the drawing of shapes by placing beads and craft-scale plastic and metal chains, onto unexposed light sensitive photographic paper before making an exposure above and through the translucent and opaque photogramed objects. Resembling animated character or mutant form, other obvious references include chronophotography and spirit photography, both emerging from the end of the 19th century. My considered selection of overtly gendered materials, including lace and jewellery, identified the translucent qualities of these objects and a suitability for photogenic tracing, and at the same time, mimicked the choice of objects by photo-pioneers, including Talbot and Hippolyte Bayard, who independently selected articles of female garb such as lace snippets and silk gloves, along

Gavin Hipkins, *New Age: Berlin (Airport III)*, 1996/2003. Unique silver-gelatin print, 200 x 250mm.

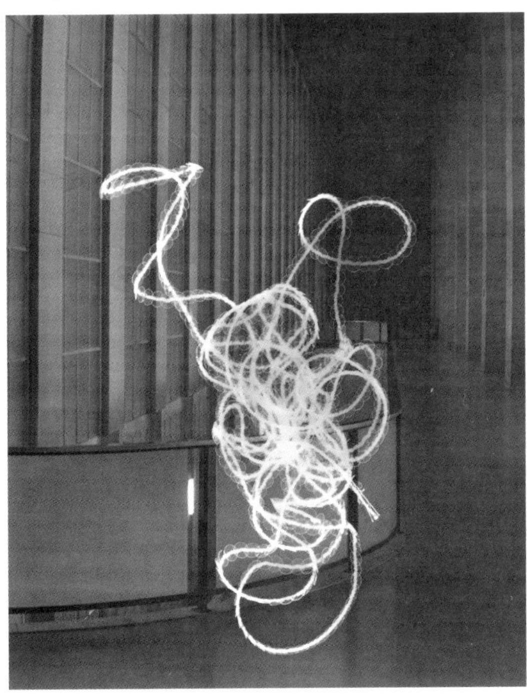

with translucent leaves, as appropriate subject matter to carefully lay on their light sensitive emulsions for prolonged exposure to the sun.

This hybrid photo-tracing darkroom technique was further honed in my series, *The Sanctuary* (2004–ongoing),[23] which specifically set out to collect landscape backdrops as the first stage of this process: a photographing of spaces as explicitly incomplete sites. Starting on the southeast steps of The Albert Memorial in Kensington Gardens, London in 2004, *The Sanctuary* takes as its backdrop scenes from gardens, parks and zoos, and attempts to forge a global relationship between these portals of institutionalised recreational sites. To date these sites have been sourced from cities including London, Hong Kong, Melbourne, Sydney, Auckland, Rotorua, Wellington, Shanghai, Suzhou, New York, Chicago, Rochester, Los Angeles and most recently The Australia Zoo, Queensland. Once again, black and white negatives were brought into the darkroom, where gendered and fetishised markers including beads, lace, jewellery and doilies are laid onto the paper before exposure as amalgam of photogram and photograph.

The abstract figures in *The Sanctuary* recolonise idyllic garden scenes, realigning the sites as contested spaces, or at least, allude to spaces with figurative and lived histories. The gardens and parks look and feel uncannily like each other: the greenhouses and temperate houses mirroring another place, building connections between once-imperial economic sites and 19th century recreational spots; hybridised spaces made picturesque by the qualities of black and white pictorial photography. For James Duncan, the picturesque itself is 'a way of seeing that fosters hybridity, creates it, values it'.[24] The picturesque becomes a method of representing landscape and ruins that homogenises differences and builds connections between distant places, between former colonies and European capitals.

In this imported atmosphere, to enter a European

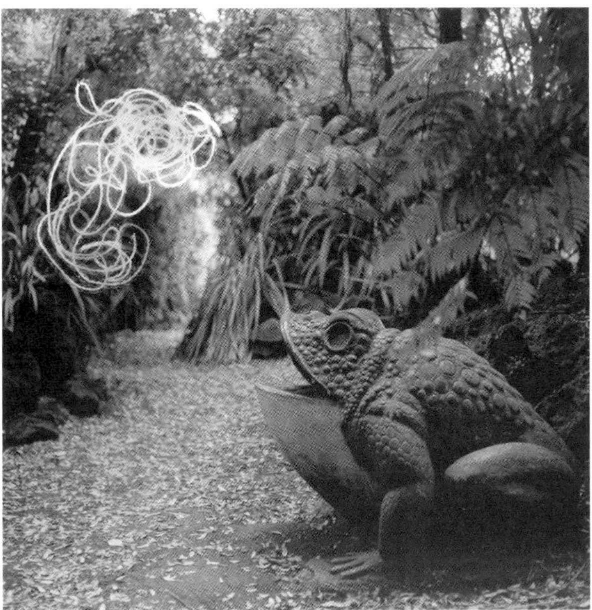

Gavin Hipkins, *The Sanctuary: Auckland
(Path)*, 2004. Unique silver-gelatin print,
375 x 375mm.

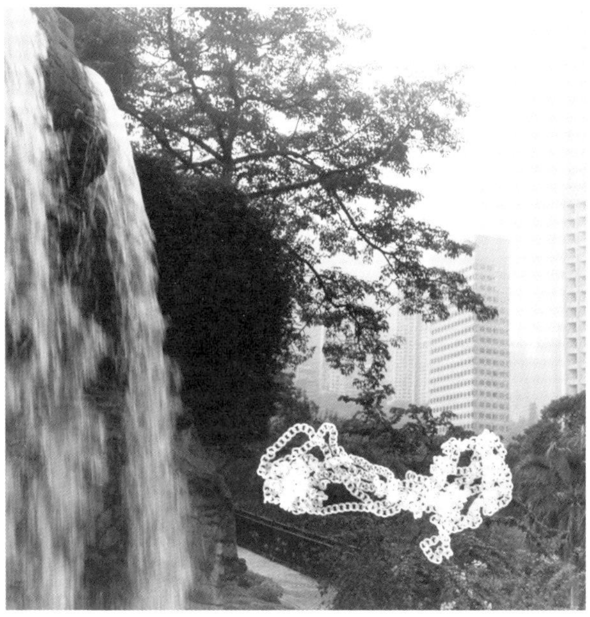

Gavin Hipkins, *The Sanctuary:
Hong Kong (Falls)*, 2004. Unique
silver-gelatin print, 375 x 375mm.

glass house, is to cross a threshold into controlled climates of differences that leave behind the crisp winter air and other domestic botanical familiarities. Photographing in the Temperate House at Kew Gardens, London, for example, I am both uncannily at home, back in my New Zealand Titirangi garden among the ferns and palms, and so consciously away from home. My touristic yearnings have taken me full circle to a place of strangeness, and aestheticised uncanny. The glasshouses, like the museums and zoological parks of the same era of colonial expansion, are sites of preservation for a perceived environmental extinction, or at least once-European transformation of the foreign specimen's names and native lands.

In 2006 this exploration of primarily 19th century established parks and leisure sites was extended in *The Sanctuary* to post-war tourist destinations, including California's Disneyland. Upon the Jungle Cruise attraction, a colonisation of space means a recreation of an idea of tropical jungle, complete with ancient ruins and mechanical wild beasts. In this ultra-controlled terrain, leisure-seeking crowds visit a natural space of palms and waterfall on a tamed yet dangerous river. Twice tamed. Firstly by its man-made properties, and a second taming, by its quaintness today: the ride a remnant from the original Disneyland planning and 1955 opening. With *The Sanctuary* works derived from Disneyland and other theme park sites, doilies and lace feature and play obtuse homage to this domestication of foreign landscape.

On occupation

Connecting these projects is an engagement in the avant-garde model of pictorial fragmentation and pastiche. Recent research, including *New Age* and *The Sanctuary* series, has explored the disruption of pictorial space and the formation of a hybridity by building montages from discreet elements. The sites I have chosen to visit across these bodies of work are linked in their institutional status: parliamentary monuments, educational facilities, recreational parks, gardens and zoos … spaces which ultimately allude to an invitation to the habitable, yet really only put out the welcome mat during opening daylight hours. These sites are not dwellings, nor are they spaces encouraging overnight visits, but are consistently emptied of their respective visitors and clients come closing time or lock out, testament to mechanisms of civic ordering and state disciplines.

The projective occupation of architectural site as photographic remnant (and ruin) reminds us of the intrinsic muteness of the photographic medium. For Walter Benjamin and his legacy on postmodernist thought, the caption accompanying the image would satisfy this voice, becoming as crucial as the photograph itself in establishing the context for a textural reading and assigned decoded meaning of a photograph. In the wake of totalising image exhaustion, coupled with the ease of ubiquitous digital manipulation today, a realignment of the use-value of the caption as contextualising referent places this once resolute bond between image and text on shaky ground.

Moving outside of the exclusively photographic realm in order to illustrate a profound state of technological, psychological, and shifting plausibility of projected corporeal occupation, while alluding to the limits of the still image, it is appropriate to slyly shift beyond the parameters of the photographic medium by specifically recalling the extraordinary 'party scene' from David Lynch's 1997 feature film *Lost Highway*. At Andy's party, protagonist jazz-musician Fred encounters his embodied schizoid personification in the form of The Mystery Man. Duplicitous medium incarnate, The Mystery Man persuasively informs Fred how they have met before 'at your house, don't you remember? … As a matter of fact, I'm there right now'.

To eradicate any doubt that the two had indeed met before, Fred is encouraged by The Mystery Man to call *him* at Fred's house on his mobile phone. During the phone conversation, a horribly telling moment unfolds when a line of acceptance is crossed. When Fred finally gives himself over, and indeed, believes that this 'crazy' meeting is no longer a well-conceived trick, but that The Mystery Man is, in fact, both in front of him at the party in the present, and at the same time, in Fred's own house: a dialogue transition for Fred from a readjusted 'how did you do that?' to a wholly destabilised 'how did you get inside my house?' In which The Mystery Man responds: 'You invited me, it is not my custom to go where I am not wanted.' A polite retort akin to the commissioned photographer on architectural assignment being asked, 'what are they doing on the premises of a tenanted building'.

Noteworthy is a shift from the plausibility of an imagining, to that of feasibility: a change in tune from the dismissal of trickery via the technological medium (in this instance, the mobile phone) to that of a dreaded acceptance of invaded private architectural and psychological space. For audiences, photography has historically played this role of technological and spatial trickery, plausibility, and finally, acceptance. For mid-19th century European audiences, Maxime du Camp's celebrated photographs of the pyramids required such a process of shifting faith: the desert and its magnificent ruins looked just so. Spirit photography and phantasmagorical recordings at the turn of the century, similarly required this leap of faith for viewers into that unimaginably deep and black backdrop of a technological and pictorial sublime, out of which sprang webbed ectoplasm and convulsing mediums. Now a distant past, early photographs of the earth taken from the moon similarly asked us to view ourselves as split, contained, and othered, and to have faith that this spatial adjustment was both feasible and really happening (no studio fabrications). Acceptance of photographic and filmic plausibility has always been based on faith.

In today's digital age, consideration of the documentation of actual occupation in a photo refers not only to the obvious decision to include or exclude figures, people, locals, workers, peasants, and so on, at the time of photographing. But the need to also face a perpetual decision: that reoccurring question of occupation at postproduction stage. Easy enough in our electronic times to seamlessly suture two backgrounds together, to eradicate any signs of lived occupation, or to clone textured backgrounds to ensure the removal of – a clinical inversion of ghost photography – entities disappearing into external walls and interior architectural spaces. Ultimately, then, every photograph of an empty space provides the template for an invitation of occupation and spatial projection. Like The Mystery Man with his oversized phone, the photographer with his camera is the medium, inviting us to enter their miniaturised places and presumably, vacant spaces.

1   Constance W. Glenn, 'Candida Hofer: Absence in Context', in *Candida Hofer: Architecture of Absence,* New York: Aperture, 2004, 15.

2   This German generation's impact on international architectural photography remains solid today. As a localised example, while acknowledging idiosyncrasies and developmental nuances, a number of my generational New Zealand peers and a younger generation of student and emerging photographers can be identified as having absorbed the ripple affect from Düsseldorf. Consider the photography of interior spaces and buildings, including the use of Thomas Ruff's doubling and mirroring device in the work of Ann Shelton; the interior indexing of New Zealand's museum and gallery collection stores recalling

Candida Hofer's subject matter and methods in Neil Pardington's practice; or Fiona Amundsen's large-format representations of New Zealand and Asian capital's public spaces recalling Thomas Struth's earlier documents of civic meeting places.

3   Jane M. Jacobs, *Edge of Empire: Postcolonialism and the City,* London: Routledge, 1996, 21.

4   The use of analogue photography by professional photographers is predominately justified via technical considerations including the increased exposure latitude that (negative) film offers, as well as the amount of information stored on a large exposed negative compared to digital capture devices. These technical considerations explain why feature films are still (primarily) shot on 35mm film.

5   A survey of Gursky's work launched by the Museum of Modern Art, New York in late 2000 brought critical attention to the prevalence of recent pictorial photography in contemporary landscape art. See Alex Alberro's 'Blind Ambition', in *Artforum,* (January 2001), 104–114.

6   See Rosalind Krauss, 'Photography's Discursive Spaces', in Richard Bolton (ed), *The Contest of Meaning: Critical Histories of Photography,* Massachusetts: MIT Press, 1989, 286–301.

7   Quoted in Marc Freidus, *Typologies* in *Typologies: Nine Photographers,* California: Newport Harbor Art Museum, 1991, 18.

8   Glenn, *Candida Hofer: Architecture of Absence,* 17.

9   An exception here is Hofer's early documents of interior spaces that remain idiosyncratically noticeable for their film graininess.

10   Susan Sontag, 'Fascinating Fascism,' in *Under the Sign of Saturn,* New York: Farrar, Straus and Giroux, 1980, 73–105.

11   Issues of fascism, aesthetics, and tourisms were explored in my exhibition *The Blue Light,* Hamish McKay Gallery, Wellington, August 19–September 13, 1997. See Robert Leonard's review of this exhibition in Art/Text no. 60, (February–April 1998), 87–88.

12   Anne Rorimer, *New Art in the 60s and 70s: Redefining Reality,* London: Thames and Hudson, 2001, 119.

13   Vikramaditya Prakash, *Chandigarh's Le Corbusier: The Struggle for Modernity in Postcolonial India,* Seattle: University of Washington Press, 2002.

14   Prakash, *Chandigarh's Le Corbusier: The Struggle for Modernity in Postcolonial India,* 146.

15   Quoted in Stanislaus von Moos, 'The Politics of the Open
     Hand: Notes on Le Corbusier and Nehru at Chandigarh,' in
     Russell Walden (ed), *The Open Hand: Essays on Le Corbusier*,
     Massachusetts: MIT Press, 1977, 447.

16   Prakāsh, *Chandigarh's Le Corbusier: The Struggle for Modernity
     in Postcolonial India*, 153.

17   Reyner Banham, *The New Brutalism: Ethic or Aesthetic?*, London:
     The Architectural Press, 1966, 130.

18   Banham, *The New Brutalism: Ethic or Aesthetic?*, 45.

19   Banham, *The New Brutalism: Ethic or Aesthetic?*, 4.

20   Solomon-Godeau, 'The Armed Vision Disarmed: Radical
     Formalism from Weapon to Style,' 93. Extract originally taken
     from Walter Benjamin's 'A Short History of Photography,'
     originally published in 1931. In defense of Renger-Patzsch's
     book Timothy Martin notes: 'Notwithstanding the shameless
     aestheticism of photographic abstraction, Benjamin's critique
     has stuck specifically and indelibly to *Die Welt ist Schon*,
     permanently staining it with the scarlet suspicion of having
     a wrongheaded view of the world. This, along with the
     reactionary, bourgeois aestheticism attributed to it, was
     particularly untimely, given the rise of fascism that followed.
     Political history has made it easy to dismiss the book as a
     popular cultural palliative to the darkening world-view of
     depression-era Weimar Republic, and to position it unfavorably
     within the ideological extremes of the day: the contest
     between bolshevism and National Socialism.' Timothy Martin,
     'Undressing the Institutional Wound' in Catherine Gudis (ed),
     Oehlen Williams 95, Columbus, Ohio: Wexner Center for the
     Arts, 1995, 123.

21   'By proposing that we look again at the buildings of New
     Zealand universities, *The Habitat* points at the bitter irony
     of the market's occupancy of an architecture of education
     constructed on very different conceptions of cultural capital
     during the 'free education' period of socialism.' Paul Walker,
     'Rough Poetry,' in Robert Leonard and Kelly Carmichael (eds),
     Gavin Hipkins: The Habitat, Auckland: Artspace, 2000, 20.

22   *Gavin Hipkins: The Habitat*, Artspace, Auckland, 8 March–1 April
     2000; Adam Art Galley, Victoria University of Wellington,
     13 May–11 June 2000.

23   *Gavin Hipkins: The Sanctuary*, Auckland: Rim Books, 2006.

24   James Duncan, 'Dis-Orientation: On the shock of the familiar
     in a far-away place,' in James Duncan and Derek Gregory
     (eds), *Writes of Passage: Reading Travel Writing*, London:
     Routledge, 1999, 161.

Dilettantes, Amateurs and Eccentrics:

The Architectural Review's Townscape campaign

MATHEW AITCHISON

The 50th anniversary edition of the *Architectural Review* (*AR*), in January 1947, was part retrospective and part manifesto, marking a departure from the war years and signalling the beginning of a new era of campaigning. The eccentric owner and directing editor of the *AR*, Hubert de Cronin Hastings, wrote of his journal:

> The REVIEW differs from most [other magazines]; it is an architectural paper, but it does not deal only with architecture; and when it deals with architecture, it does not always deal with the right sort of architecture […] herein exists evidence of deliberate policy […] the REVIEW flouts good taste.[1]

Hastings further described this policy as 'visual re-education', one that sought to promote an understanding of architecture and planning as a visual art and part of a wider visual culture. In challenging the good taste of his day, Hastings rethought the form and content of the magazine – a process that had already been under way since the 1930s – and wrote of his numerous contributing authors:

> One of the aspects of the English cultural tradition most worth preserving is the practice of dilettante journalism by experts who are also amateurs […] But the urbane habit of literary dilettantism, of scholar's table talk conducted in public, is not one that can be indulged without a medium.[2]

The publications that resulted from this campaign of 'dilettante journalism' are today aligned with the Townscape movement, and arguably constitute one of the most innovative, eclectic and visually exciting periods

Contents page of the
50th anniversary edition
of the *Architectural Review*,
January 1947.

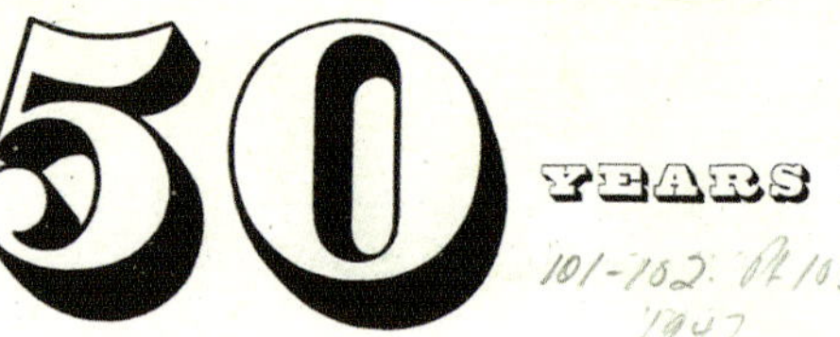

The Architectural Review

50 YEARS

This number of the REVIEW marks
the beginning of its fifty-first year of
architectural journalism. To celebrate
the event it breaks a rule of fifty
years' standing and discloses the
ever-present thread of policy which has
linked what may sometimes super-
ficially have appeared to be a series
of isolated enthusiasms. Following an
editorial foreword (pp. 21-26) a retrospective survey (pp. 27-36) picks out
the REVIEW's architectural landmarks
of fifty years, from the neo-Georgian
revival through the first signs of
upheaval to the revolution, and on to
the establishment of a new architecture. But what is of even greater
augury for the future is the endeavour,
running throughout the story, to
re-establish the supremacy of the eye.

EDITORS
J. M. Richards
Nikolaus Pevsner
Osbert Lancaster
H. de C. Hastings

ASSISTANT EDITOR
Ian McCallum

Vol. CI *No. 601*
THREE SHILLINGS AND SIXPENCE

CONTENTS *for January 1947*

2 A PIONEER IN ST. JAMES'S PALACE

3 THE ARCHITECTURE OF BUREAUCRACY AND THE
ARCHITECTURE OF GENIUS. By Henry-Russell Hitchcock

BUILDING FOR AIR TRANSPORT

7 DUBLIN AIRPORT. Architect: Desmond Fitzgerald

9 AIR TRANSPORT COMMAND AIRPORT, WASHINGTON.
Architect: Charles M. Goodman

11 WIND TUNNEL U.S.A. Engineer: W. D. Henderson

13 ACADEMICAL ELYSIUM. The Landscaping of the Cambridge
Backs. By Marcus Whiffen

19 HOUSE ON ZURICHBERG. Architect: Alfred Roth

21 THE SECOND HALF CENTURY

27 THE FIRST HALF CENTURY

37 WILLIAM MORRIS AT ST. JAMES'S PALACE. By Charles
Mitchell

BOOKS

40 THE AGE OF TASTE. By Henry-Russell Hitchcock. Review of
'Georgian London,' by John Summerson

40 CAST IRON. By George Fairweather. Review of 'Cast Iron in
Building,' by Richard Sheppard

40 SHORTER NOTICES

ANTHOLOGY

41 A VICTORIAN DISSENTS. From 'The Setting Sun,' by James
Hurnard

41 MARGINALIA

THE COVER THE ARCHITECTURAL REVIEW is fifty years
old this month. The painted panel which is reproduced as this
month's cover is just about thirty years older. At first sight there
may seem to be little connection between these two statements.
But a connection there is. For among the REVIEW's contents
this month is an article (*William Morris at St. James's Palace*,
by Charles Mitchell), in which, practically for the first time, work
of the firm founded by
William Morris is treated
as a subject for detailed
historical research. In
other words, the era
immediately preceding
that which saw the found-
ing of the REVIEW is now
far enough off to be seen
as History. The panel on
the cover is from the
Armoury at St. James's
Palace, and was designed
for Morris, Marshall
and Faulkner by Philip
Webb; its colour scheme
is olive green and gold.
All the photographs of
these decorations were
taken by Helmut Gerns-
heim for the Warburg
Institute, and are re-
produced by gracious
permission of His
Majesty the King.

*SUBSCRIPTION RATE: £2 per annum, post free. An index is issued
every six months, covering the period January to June and July to December,
and can be obtained without charge on application to the publishers:*

THE ARCHITECTURAL REVIEW
13 Queen Anne's Gate, Westminster, SW1 · Whitehall 0611

of architectural publishing of the 20th century. Research has revealed around 1400 Townscape-related articles published in the *AR* from the 1930s until the 1970s.[3] These publications document an editorial policy masterminded by Hastings and his team of prominent editors, a policy encouraging novel and popularly accessible approaches to architecture and urban design, through a mixture of critical and creative means.

These publications took on a wide range of formats, including conventional magazine articles, editorials, projects (both real and imaginary), project reviews, book reviews, captioned illustrations, photo essays, how-to design studies, monthly columns and journal correspondence; in summary, *all* the formats at an editor's disposal. They were contributed by numerous authors, around 200 in total, comprised of journalists, poets, cartoonists, graphic artists, painters, photographers and draftspeople, along with more customary contributions from architects and academics, many of whom are rarely associated with the Townscape movement. Some notable personalities in this circle are the poet John Betjeman; painters Paul Nash, John Piper and Kenneth Rowntree; cartoonist Osbert Lancaster; draftsmen and graphic artists Gordon Cullen and Kenneth Browne; architectural photographer Eric de Maré; town planner Thomas Sharp, landscape architect Sylvia Crowe; architectural journalists J.M. Richards and Ian Nairn; leading architects Hugh Casson and Frederick Gibberd; and two of the leading British architectural historians of the day, Nikolaus Pevsner and John Summerson.

Surprisingly, very little has been written about this intense period of publishing activity, and the story of its impact on the post-war discourse and practice of architecture remains largely untold. By illustrating the work by this group and showing how the *AR*'s editorial policy resulted in a very particular mode of writing and illustrating architecture, this article attempts to draw attention to an influential but often overlooked body of architectural publishing.

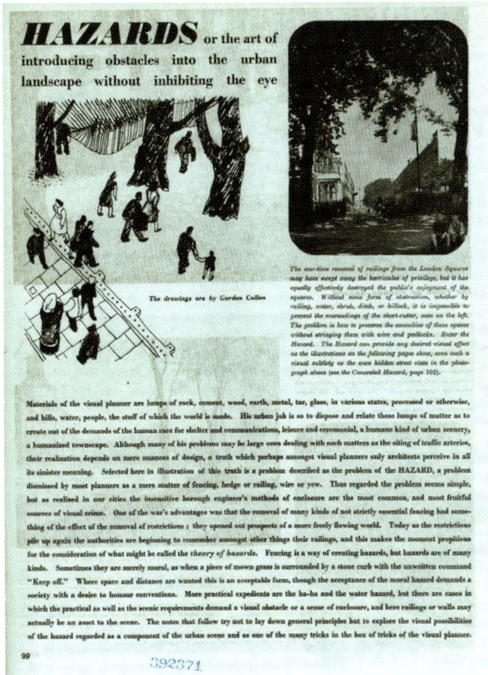

Hazards. Illustrated by Gordon Cullen.
AR, March 1948.

Popular, middlebrow

In their search for new approaches to the problems of post-war reconstruction and modernisation, Hastings and his team of editors proposed a reform of architectural modernism and the implementation of a more picturesque version of urban planning. Accompanying these practical aims, Townscape's initiators tried to resist the views of the 'establishment' in architecture and urban planning of their day with strong yet popularly accessible criticism. They also resisted highbrow discourses by essentially inventing a mainstream discourse of their own, a task for which they were exceptionally well placed, both professionally and strategically. Above all else, Townscape was intended as a popular editorial campaign, to be broadly applicable to all quarters of the architectural world. It aimed at giving the often-invoked 'man in the street' a practical picture of how a city could, or should, look.

In a seminal article of January 1944, Hastings's tone – writing under the title of 'The Editor' – was as critical as it was condescending. Of 'garden city' planning, he wrote:

> Much of what they did was to help Billy Brown,
> the Little Man, and Bill Brown, the working man,
> to live a decent life in decent surroundings. […]
> Just as all good Americans when they die are
> supposed to go to Paris, so Englishmen if they
> were clean might be deemed fit for Letchworth.[4]

In referring to its legacy, many commentators still think of Townscape as a chapter between the Garden City and New Towns movements. But Hastings was clear in his denunciations of these, stating with typical verve that '[a]s a physical solution to the problems arising out of the Industrial Revolution, [the Garden City] is about as efficient as the pikes handed out to the home guard early in the war to stop Hitler's Panzers.'[5] What Billy Brown really wanted, Hastings thought, was 'a picture of the kind of world the physical planner will make', a picture that he and his circle tried to reveal with their Townscape campaign.

A large part of the criticism of Townscape has focused on exactly this popular outlook, with claims that it was intended less for architects (who should have understood its principles already) and more for administrators and council officials. In retrospect this appears to be a major aspect of Townscape's legacy: it did a great deal to influ-ence the values of local and municipal planning authorities. But in this it still relied on an intensely nuanced and highly synthetic approach to design problems – an approach most certainly not attainable by the bulk of practitioners, or, indeed, much of the *AR*'s readership.[6]

Townscape's campaign represented a particular type of publishing activism. The editors of the *AR* were clear and unabashed in their advocacy of projects they thought to be exemplars of Townscape, or of using 'Townscape' techniques to repair real problems in cities. From today's standpoint, what is significant in this advocacy is the mixture of critical *and* creative means, and the complete abandonment of the impartial journalistic voice, or the suspension of judgement customary for a journal of record.

An early example comes in an article by John Piper from March 1945, which focused on the visual qualities of high street shops. The article was richly illustrated with original drawings and paintings and opened with a question:

> The rich-looking marble and chromium of
> Marks and Spencer, or the warm red and gold of
> Woolworth's? Well, neither. Because both are over-
> done, and neither considers enough its setting […].

> The obvious commercial advantage of the multiple
> store, bald-headedly ignoring its surroundings, and
> looking alike everywhere, is part of our present
> undoing; it tends to make every shopping-street
> look like every other shopping-street.[7]

The criticism is clear, but like so many articles from the period Piper is not content to stop there, continuing with recommendations for improvements: 'Let [the shopkeeper] look to the Victorians, not for a copy-book but for an example: an example that in matters of colour it is better to be too vulgar than too nice; too fussy than too simple.'[8]

Moving further afield from the high streets of Britain's towns and cities, something of this same manner – if on a very different scale – can also be identified in a later polemic by Kenneth Browne on the adaptation of a nuclear power plant in the Lea Valley of June 1964.[9] Besides a certain bizarreness, this project shows how seriously the *AR* circle took their comprehensive approach to urban design, demonstrating that there were few situations or objects unworthy of consideration.

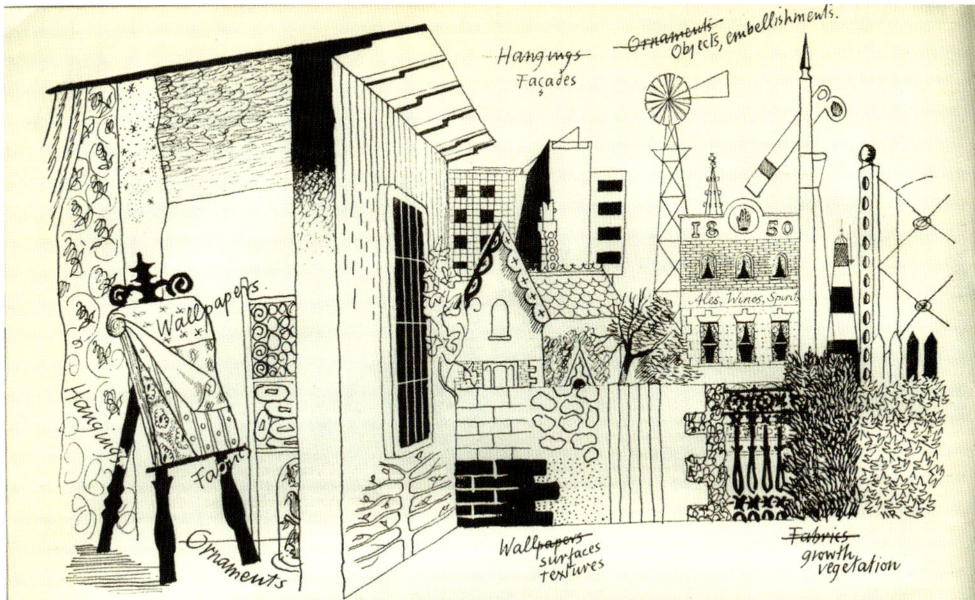

Not an architect, but a painter, Kenneth Rowntree, who contributes the drawings to this article, here paraphrases THE ARCHI-TECTURAL REVIEW'S *programme : the variety of shape, pattern and texture in the ornaments, wallpapers, fabrics, etc., which you buy in the interior furnisher's shop, should be matched by an equally generous variety of shape, pattern, texture and vegetation in our urban exteriors. Make Highpoint lie down with the Victorian pub and the barge-boarded villa. Enjoy the railway signal and the rough stone wall and the pylon by the church. Don't be afraid of adding a twentieth-century wing to a Regency house. All the freedom of the interior furnisher should also be the urban planner's, provided his contrasts and seeming accidents are sensitively devised.*

Billy Brown of London Town, and all the other strap-hangers have proved themselves fertile in devices for exploiting in other ways. In this respect indeed The Man in the Street is often far ahead of the architects. He uses Price's arguments—subconsciously

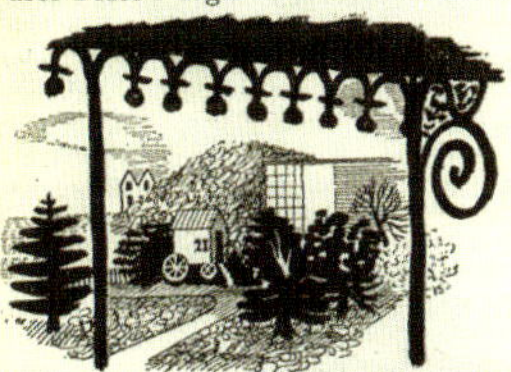

of course—in furnishing and gradually re-modelling the house in which he lives, In his own rooms the planned-for behaves often as independently and as imaginatively as in his back-garden. His ideal of Interior Furnishing is just the opposite of that of his wealthy fellow citizen who goes to Partridge's, or Maple's, or Gordon Russell's and buys suites of genuine antique, imitation antique, or good contemporary furniture, complete with lamps, mirrors, vases and a few odd pieces of sculpture. And he is right in this. An interior to be successful should be the result of growth, of attachments formed over years to things old and new. The fear of one's modern cupboard clashing with the Victorian atmosphere of a room, or one's

Victorian chandelier looking out of place in an Aalto environment is wholly unjustified. Even more undesirable is the fear that any object, in itself not up to a discriminating contemporary æsthetic standard, would be a blot on a whole interior. The æsthetic qualities of the individual items are quite irrelevant. Let them be ugly, let them be incongruous. What matters alone is the unity and congruity of the pattern. A frankly vulgar little bronze poodle on an Italian marble pedestal might even hold a place of honour on the mantel-shelf, either because of its value as an accent in a picturesque whole, or—and here is a new argument—because of some equally legiti-mate sentimental value.

Now all this can perhaps be taken for granted in the interior pattern. When it comes to the urban pattern, its legitimacy has yet to be established. It has yet to be said and recognized that the urban planner's job is one of Exterior Furnishing. We have good planners on whose care in surveying and drawing up socially sound and techni-cally satisfactory schemes we can rely. But many of them—not all—tend to the suite idea, the spick-and-span plan straight from the desk. In the recent past that has quite often meant the unnecessary destruction of old buildings of value, especially buildings of the eighteenth century. Respect for that particular century is perhaps safe-guarding them to-day. But when it comes to the Victorian villa, of the *Summer Inter-*

lude type (see THE ARCHITECTURAL REVIEW, August, 1943) only the conception of ex-terior furnishing can rescue them. And if seen in a larger, more generous context, how well worth rescuing they may be.

It is here not possible to go beyond stating and recommending the exterior fur-nishing principle as being nothing less than the application of Picturesque theory to the urban scene. Pictures would do more than words to convey the truth and charm of a twentieth-century Sharawaggi. But a few reasons may be added why this should have every chance to be applied with human and æsthetic success in England. Planning theory at the moment might be described as

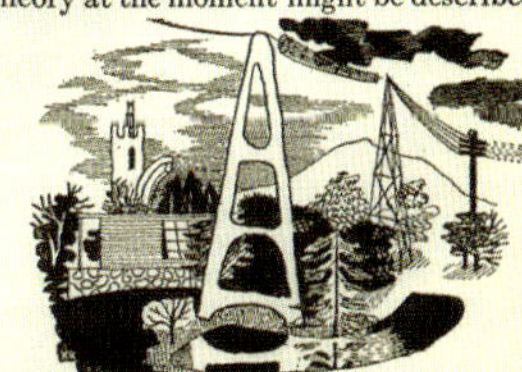

a fight between three groups : the garden city people, the Bauhausians, and the County Councils. The garden city people, as has been said before, have on the credit side a keen sense of the cosy life, but they have little understanding of the metro-politan scene or of the intricacy of social

Exterior Furnishing or Sharawaggi. Text by Hubert de Cronin Hastings [Anon.], illustrated by Kenneth Rowntree. *AR*, January 1944.

In addition to such studies, the journal also carried a steady stream of monthly columns aimed at opinion bending. For several years a column simply titled 'Townscape' appeared, with star contributions by the likes of Robert Venturi, Peter Reyner Banham and later David Watkin. These were followed throughout the 1950s and 60s by monthly sections subsequent to the launch of Ian Nairn's special editions of 'Outrage' and its sequel, 'Counter Attack', which focused on the decay of Britain's built environment through bad design, sprawl, dereliction and exploitation.[10] In the 1960s the 'Look Out' and 'Stop Press' columns eventually supplanted their predecessors, and began to focus on the preservation of old buildings, many of which were under threat by the wrecking ball.[11]

This branch of the *AR*'s activism reached a pinnacle of peculiarity with an unnamed column from the 1970s known only by an image of a human eye, which presumably was intended to draw attention to the visual qualities of an urban scene or building.[12] What all of these columns have in common, and what made them a part of the wider Townscape campaign, was their particular mode of activism and their oscillation between criticism *and* creativity.

In this context it is significant that Townscape did not set out to be an avant-garde movement, but rather to take up the mantle of a middlebrow van-garde. It has thus been the movement's reception in recent years, or the lack thereof, which has shown its paradoxical 'success' to the fullest extent. Townscape is hardly acknowledged in most of the major 20th century historical treatments of architecture and urban design, which is strange for a campaign of such longevity and exposure, the reach of which extended into all quarters of the architectural world: from the academy, to the architect's office, to the halls of government. By the 1970s many architects appear to have forgotten what Townscape was and begun proposing similar ideas, apparently not connecting their work with that of the *AR* and Townscape at all.[13] Arguably, the campaign was so successful within its own popular

terms that many of its innovations, both conceptual and polemical, were hardly seen as such: they had simply become commonplace. They constituted the mainstream of architectural and urban design discourses, as though they were authorless and without a history of their own.

Pseudonyms and anonymous articles

Perhaps the most unusual feature of the Townscape campaign and its literary style is that many of its most important articles were published anonymously or pseudonymously. Presumably this was undertaken to allow sharper criticism and a variety of 'voices' to develop, particularly in light of pressures exerted by the British publishing and architectural establishment. The most famous pseudonym from the period was that of Ivor de Wolfe, the pen name of Hubert de Cronin Hastings, which he used to write most of the articles on Townscape from the late 1940s onwards. Later, Hastings was briefly known as Ivor de Wofle, a printing error that Hastings allowed to stand, and all this was part of a longer history of pseudonymous and anonymous writing spanning back to the 1920s when he also called himself Herman Georg Sheffauer. It appears that Hastings treated this aspect of his persona with relative consistency throughout his professional life.[14] Aside from Hastings, Pevsner was also known as Peter F.R. Donner, John Summerson was John Coolmore, Jim Richards was James MacQuedy, and Hugh Casson wrote the pseudonymous Astragal column for several years at the *AR*'s sister publication, the *Architects' Journal*.

It is not completely clear why such a culture of anonymity developed, but it undoubtedly follows the lead of the reclusive Hastings, reinforced by a school-boyish penchant for the games of wartime secrecy and public school tomfoolery. In any case it clearly resulted in a particularly playful mode of writing and one that was certainly less guarded in its opinions than would have normally been the case for journalism, or other professional magazines, and imbued the Townscape campaign with a more informal tone than might otherwise have been the case.

In an early article using his pen name of Peter F.R. Donner, Pevsner had the courage to attack the very emblem of the English architectural establishment, opening with the question: 'What quality is it in Sir Herbert Baker's extension of the Bank of England that makes it seem to so many people – myself included – so aesthetically unsatisfactory an example of the art of adding to an existing building?'[15] Without shying away from his own criticism, he added: 'Courage and tact are the two qualities needed in the architect who has had to add to an existing building. Courage to hold up the ideal of his own age, tact to blend it with the past.' As in many other Townscape publications, Pevsner felt free enough to provocatively suggest that: 'A surrealist might place two contrasting statements side by side, enjoying the shock of the contrast …'[16]

Visual

That Townscape and its circle of authors developed and relied on a highly visual mode of journalism is not surprising, considering it was a campaign almost exclusively played out on the pages of a professional magazine, which was by its very nature visual. Townscape's publications rely on a richly illustrated mode of writing. The photography drew on the major architectural photographers of the day, such as Dell and Wainwright, Helmut Gernsheim, and Eric de Maré, used in equal measure to striking graphic illustrations by superb architects and draftspeople such as Hugh Casson, Gordon Cullen, Richard Reid or Kenneth Browne. What is novel in Townscape, and paradoxically the aspect which has led to the most telling criticism of the movement, is its insistence on the visual as the 'chief' consideration in urban design. This led the movement's

critics to the label of 'superficiality': a concern for surface rather than structure, form more than content.[17]

The recent publication, by John Macarthur and the present author, of Nikolaus Pevsner's *Visual Planning and the Picturesque* (2010), has demonstrated – in word and deed – that Townscape was intrinsically and single-mindedly conceived in visual terms. Its authors had concocted an intricate historical lineage for this, beginning with picturesque aesthetics and English landscape gardening and leading to their own day. However fanciful this intellectual manoeuvre may appear today, it did result in an architecture and urban design that was striking and unique. It was a mode of design squarely aimed at being eclectic, synthetic and based on compromise. It was also somewhat eccentric, privileging the messy vitality of the present day over the utopia of some future condition, or nostalgia for the past.

Equally as remarkable as Townscape's recommendations in the fields of architecture and urban design, was their corollary in the graphic and visual presentation of the magazine itself. Floral Victorian typefaces were juxtaposed with sans serif scripts, black and white photographs collaged into line drawings, lime green highlights contrasted with the smooth cream of thick paper, or richly textured, romantically inspired prints from original paintings were contrasted with superb professional architectural photography. If Townscape proposed a mixture of a humanised modernism, set within a more outspoken antiquarian or picturesque mode of planning, the journal's visual style provided a clear example of how this might graphically appear.

Dilettante journalism

Hastings's editorial choices reveal that there was more at stake in the journal than simply employing his professional friends and others who amused him such as Betjeman, Piper, Nash, Lancaster, Cullen or even

Pevsner. These choices appear to have developed from his deeply felt belief in the over-specialisation of modern society, a feature of Hastings's psyche illuminated in research by Erdem Erten.[18] On numerous occasions, these beliefs asserted their presence within Townscape, and the only book Hastings ever published in his own name focused on such issues, invoking the fields of cultural theory, politics and economics, and titled *The Alternative Society: Software for the Nineteen Eighties* (1980).[19]

The opening address of a special edition of the *AR* from June 1971, *Civilia*, which illustrated Hastings's project for an imaginary 'new town' set in a reused quarry, unceremoniously directed the reader to 'Stick It'! Continuing in a style which must have been familiar to the *AR*'s regular readers:

> Professional town planners can safely disregard this article, which takes the heat out of planning in an effort to deflate the science to a level at which it can be kicked around by ordinary people in the course of intelligent lay discussion. No real purpose is served by keeping it as a mystique available only to specialists whose policies (which affect everyone) are made behind locked doors.[20]

It is likely that Hastings felt confined within the fields of architecture and urban design, a large part of the interest generated by Townscape and the *AR* more generally can be traced to Hastings's insistence in a broader range of topics for the AR. During his reign as owner and chief editor of the *AR* he did everything possible to open the discourse to as many intellectual influences as possible, such that variety at the *AR* became a deliberate policy. Continuing the quotation introduced in the *AR*'s 50th anniversary edition, Hastings wrote:

> For any art in England there is a public so long as it lends itself to being written about well; indeed the reason why architecture, during the Edwardian

interval, lost so much prestige lies to quite an appreciable extent in the fact that no one had been found, between John Ruskin and John Betjeman, to write about it quite well enough.[21]

When thinking of writing style, there are few texts that surpass in eccentricity those contributed by Betjeman in the 1930s and 40s. A fine example is *The Passing of the Village* from September 1932. Betjeman begins casually with the line, 'Last Saturday I was driving in a dogcart through a remote part of Hampshire …',[22] but despite the flippancy of the lead-in, he goes on to address a more serious concern, namely the losing battle being played out between the 'modern age' and English patrimony. In a tone similar to an earlier article where he announced the 'Death' of modernism, he concluded this account of his weekend drive with a combination of insight and poetic wit, writing:

> We have created a machine age and we should not be afraid of it, but rather become accustomed to it and control it. The machine age may be a roaring lion in the land, but the lamb of agriculture can lie down beside it. It is such a shorn and shivering lamb that it is hardly worth eating. […] Two hundred years ago England was a park dotted here and there with mellow towns; now it is a town dotted here and there with derelict parks. After all, I am not very brave to exchange my dogcart for a motor-car.[23]

With the war barely over, Hastings and Pevsner had laid the foundations for the further development of the Townscape campaign. It has often been overlooked how consistent their opinions on matters of architecture and urban design remained in the following three decades. They were staunch in their plea for an English mode of planning that would be irregular, informal and picturesque, and absolutely not monumental, grand or in any way associated with the French or Beaux Arts

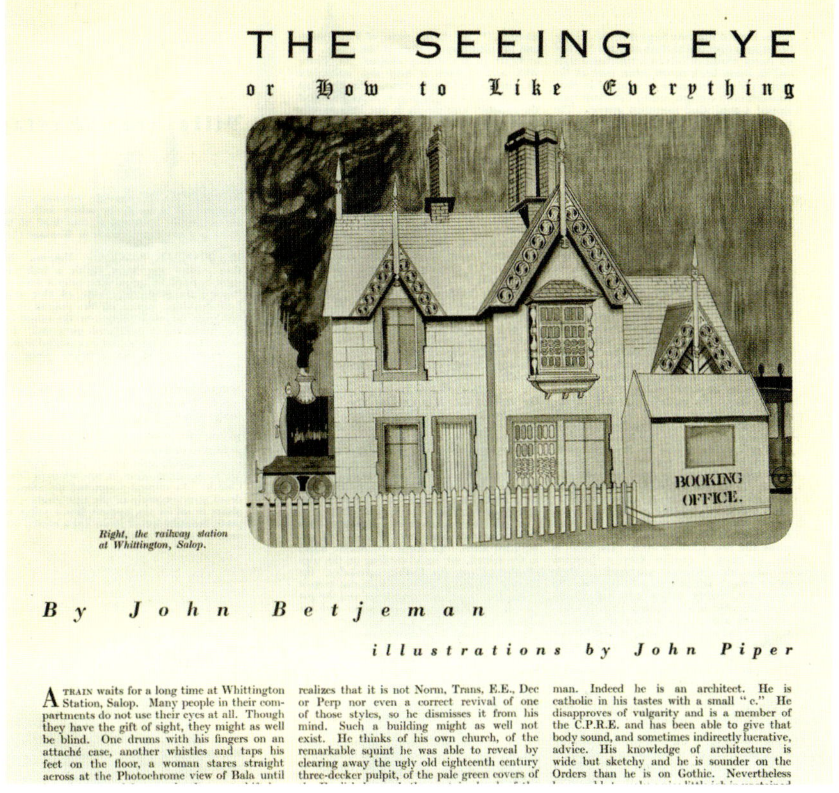

The Seeing Eye.
Text by John Betjeman, illustrated by John Piper. *AR*, 1939.

style of planning. In one of many outbursts of nonsensical prose to this end, Pevsner and Hastings wrote:

> Paris has hypnotised the planning professionals for something like a century. All over the world cities have risen (or had their faces lifted) in the image of Paris – mid-nineteenth century Paris. From Paris has come … a great official system of education in the monumental, the Beaux Arts system, and a massive army of symmetrical planners, each with a future World-Centre in his knapsack. The English Channel proved no tank trap to these mechanised divisions, nor for that matter did the Atlantic Ocean. Slow to give way to the little Corsican on the battlefield, the British who not long after Waterloo were giving birth, under the happy-go-lucky midwifery of John Nash to their own technique, an entirely original one, of town-planning, surrendered in [the] course of the century on the cultural front to another Bonaparte and his Prefect, Haussmann. And no sooner were the English architectural schools started than they were

turning out Beaux Arts planners in frantic imitation of far-from-gay-Paree. Garden City technique was fit only for the suburbs. It was Paris of the second Empire … that came to be identified in the mind of every matriculating architect with the science of town-planning.[24]

It is difficult today to take such an incitement seriously, but underlying the eccentric language and unusual references, there was a very simple message: England deserved a form of planning and urban design as different from French planning as possible, as it would inevitably be if developed from an English tradition. This resulted in a recommendation for architecture and planning that was not symmetrical, formal and austere, but informal, varied, incongruous and slightly eccentric: all qualities both Hastings and Pevsner thought to be inherent to the English themselves. Indeed, it would have been this message that Pevsner's *Visual Planning* book – had it been published in the 1940s or 1950s – would have set out, albeit with less confrontational language.

Conclusion

From today's standpoint, it seems almost inconceivable that an internationally respected journal such as the *AR* not only carried out such radical campaigns, but that their traces have largely vanished. Which architectural publication today could afford to be so stark and unabashed in its criticism of its very own professional readership? Which commissioning editor would be able to fill decades of a magazine with such a prodigious publishing hobby? But having here praised the *AR* and its editors, it is also worth remembering that Hastings almost bankrupted the magazine with his 'Manplan' series, a series that began in the late 1960s and saw an almost complete departure from architectural issues, most likely resulting in the disbandment of the powerful editorial board of Pevsner, Richards and

Casson soon thereafter.[25] Apparently, much of what seemed possible in the 1940s and 50s had become difficult to achieve by the 1970s, and Townscape's decline within the *AR* parallels that of the magazine itself, faced with an exceedingly competitive market for architectural publishing.

Townscape is thus uniformly absent from most histories of post-war architecture and urban design, and awaits a more thorough treatment, which would go some way to illustrating the role played by the *AR* and its circle of editors. On the one hand, the campaign's lessons are only present in the popular consciousness as guidelines for urban beautification, or in relation to their unfashionable cousin in the shape of Prince Charles and the new urbanists. On the other hand, the 'collective amnesia' regarding Townscape's lessons in the second half of the 20th century was perhaps only made possible by the complete saturation and assimilation of Townscape's popular ideas by its audience, emerging from the hands and minds of its unseemly band of dilettantes, amateurs and eccentrics.

1 Hubert de Cronin Hastings (Anon.), 'The Second Half Century', *The Architectural Review*, 101, no. 601 (Jan 1947): 21.

2 Hastings, 'The Second Half Century', 22.

3 Mathew Aitchison, 'Visual Planning and Exterior Furnishing: A Critical History of the Early Townscape Movement, 1930 to 1949', Ph.D Dissertation, University of Queensland, 2009. See also, Nikolaus Pevsner and Mathew Aitchison (eds), *Visual Planning and the Picturesque*, Los Angeles: Getty Research Institute, 2010.

4 Hubert de Cronin Hastings (Anon.), 'Exterior Furnishing or Sharawaggi: The Art of Making Urban Landscape', *The Architectural Review* 95, no. 565 (Jan 1944): 3.

5 Hastings, 'Exterior Furnishing or Sharawaggi', 3.

6 This is the case with an insightful article by Robert Maxwell, 'An Eye for an I: The Failure of the Townscape Tradition', *Architectural Design*, 46, no. 9 (Sep 1976): 534-36.

7 John Piper, 'Shops,' *The Architectural Review*, 97, no. 579 (Mar 1945): 89.

8 Piper, 'Shops', 89.

9   Kenneth Browne, 'Lea Valley Reclaimed. Proposals for a Linear Park for East London', *The Architectural Review*, 135, no. 808 (Jun 1964): 413-21.

10   Ian Nairn (ed.), 'Outrage', *The Architectural Review*, 117, no. 702 (Jun 1955): 361-460; and, 'Counter Attack', *The Architectural Review*, 120, no. 719, Dec (1956): 351-440.

11   The 'Look Out' column feature ran from June to September 1963. 'Stop Press' ran from March 1964 until August 1969.

12   See for example: Kenneth Browne, '[Figure of Eye]', *The Architectural Review*, 160, no. 953 (Jul 1976): 55-8. This series ran from July 1976 to August 1977.

13   A summary list of authors and well-known publications which display some relation or reaction to Townscape's message might include: Kevin Lynch, *The Image of the City*, Cambridge, Mass.: The MIT Press, 1960; Jane Jacobs, *The Death and Life of Great American Cities*, New York: Random House, 1961; Peter Blake, *God's Own Junkyard: The Planned Deterioration of America's Landscape*, New York: Holt, Rinehart & Winston, 1964; Bernard Rudofsky, *Architecture without Architects: An Introduction to Non-Pedigreed Architecture*, Garden City, New York: Doubleday Inc., 1964; Robert Venturi, *Complexity and Contradiction in Architecture*, New York: The Museum of Modern Art, 1966; Robert Venturi, Denise Scott Brown, and Steven Izenour, *Learning from Las Vegas*, Cambridge, Mass.,: MIT Press, 1972; Charles Jencks and Nathan Silver, *Adhocism: The Case for Improvisation*, London: Secker & Warburg, 1972; and Colin Rowe and Fred Koetter, *Collage City*, Cambridge, Mass.: MIT Press, 1978.

14   Using 'Scheffauer' as his title in January 1928, he informed his readers that the author was an American-German journalist, supposedly descended from the von Scheffauers and whose father had gone to school with Schiller. Hastings went on to tell his readers that Sheffauer would no longer be publishing in the *AR*, as he had died aged 50!

15   Peter F.R. Donner [Pevsner], 'Criticism', *The Architectural Review*, 90 (Jul-Dec 1941): 92.

16   Donner [Pevsner], 'Criticism,' 92.

17   See Joseph Rykwert, 'Review of a Review', *Zodiac*, 4 (1959): 13-5; and, Maxwell, 'An Eye for an I'.

18   Erdem Erten, 'Shaping the Second Half Century', The *Architectural Review 1947–1971*, Ph.D Dissertation M.I.T., 2004.

19   Hubert de Cronin Hastings, *The Alternative Society: Software for the Nineteen Eighties*, London, David and Charles, 1980.

20   Ivor de Wolfe [Hastings], 'Civilia. The End of the Sub Urban Man. Towards a Philosophy of the Environment,' *The Architectural Review*, 149, no. 892 (Jun 1971): 327.

21   Hastings, 'The Second Half Century', 22.

22   John Betjeman, 'The Passing of the Village', *The Architectural Review,* 72 (Sep 1932): 89.

23   Betjeman, 'The Passing of the Village', 93.

24   Hubert de Cronin Hastings and Nikolaus Pevsner [Anon.], 'A Programme for the City of London. Part One. The English Planning Tradition and the City', *The Architectural Review*, 97, no. 582 (Jun 1945): 166-67.

25   The 'Manplan' series of special editions ran from September 1969 to September 1970.

Reading and Writing the Seattle Public Library,

New regimes of architectural (re)presentation

ARI SELIGMANN

Upon its completion in May of 2004 the Seattle Public Library by Rem Koolhaas's firm, OMA, and local partner firm, LMN Architects, garnered attention across the international architectural press: as might be expected from a project of its revolutionary stature. The project challenges the simple stacked floor typology of the surrounding generic office buildings with a three-dimensional offset stacking of programmed volumes that are wrapped in a glass facade to create an iconic crystalline building. The new building also reinterprets standard library facilities. For example, the non-fiction collection is distributed in numeric order along a continuous sloped floor 'book spiral', resembling a parking structure. Reference librarians are consolidated in a 'mixing chamber' and connected via wireless communication technologies to aid patrons and facilitate the dissemination of information. The Seattle Public Library also expands notions of public building. Sheltered from the weather and exposed to the dynamism of the city, the ground floor provides a vitrine like a grand 'living room' shared by patrons, citizens and tourists. The project provocatively raises the bar for 21st century libraries, with its innovations across the realms of form, function, structure and program. But more than this, the project precipitated new approaches to writing about architecture. Despite Victor Hugo's famous concern that the printed book would kill cathedral architecture, the information age cathedral of the Seattle Public Library has succeeded in invigorating architectural publication and expanding regimes of architectural (re)presentations.

On its opening the library was showered with accolades in the media. The *New York Times* architecture critic, Herbert Muschamp, gushed: 'In more than 30 years of

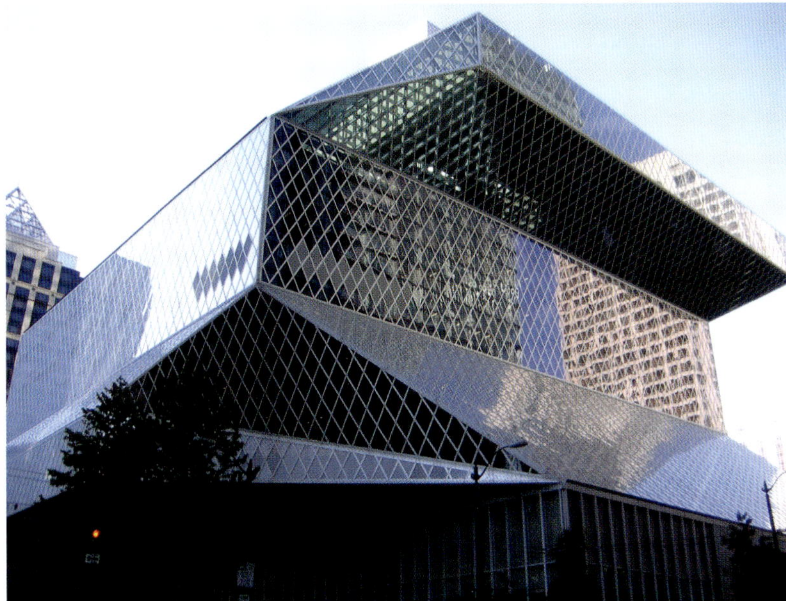

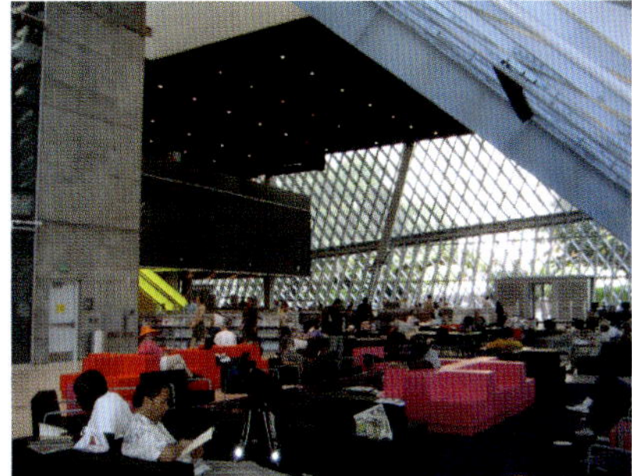

Exterior and interior photographs of the Seattle Public Library. Photographs Ari Seligmann.

writing about architecture, this is the most exciting new building it has been my honor to review. I could go on piling up superlatives like cars in a multiple collision'.[1] *New Yorker Magazine* architecture critic, Paul Goldberger, proclaimed it 'the most important new library to be built in a generation, and the most exhilarating… The Seattle building is thrilling from top to bottom'.[2] While *Library Journal* noted that 'what Bilbao has become for museums, Seattle is becoming for libraries'.[3] In addition to receiving a strong reception across media outlets, the library provoked alternative approaches to capturing and conveying architecture, in print and beyond.

Although Rem Koolhaas has previously engaged in provocative experiments in writing and architecture, from *Delirious New York* to *S,M,L,XL* and *Content*, more than any of his built projects the Seattle Public Library

engendered new (re)presentations of architecture.[4] This essay compares three novel accounts of the completed project to assess the expanding terrain of architectural representations among popular and professional audiences. Firstly, coverage in the US *Metropolis* magazine conveys the collaborative nature of architecture's production and consumption. Secondly, the *Verb Monograph* on the library, by Barcelona-based architectural publisher Actar, draws on their experiments with 'boogazines' and challenges typical monographic presentations by attempting to capture impressions and experiences of the building. Thirdly, *Post-Occupancy*, the inaugural multimedia special issue of the Italian magazine *Domus*, guest edited by Koolhaas and his office's research branch AMO, represents a novel attempt to curate the reactions to and inhabitation of several recent OMA projects, including the Seattle

Public Library. In general, the high degree of community involvement in the library's design process – as part of an unusually broad-ranging design process generally – along with the building's function as a public information nexus, made this project an ideal candidate for exploring alternatives in writing architecture. The three accounts will be examined here in terms of their expressed intentions, organisation, content and implications. Together these portrayals identify alternative practices in writing architecture, they illuminate exploratory configurations of text, image and media, and they intimate new relations with popular audiences for architecture.

'We Built It': the ecstasy of collaboration

In the months after its completion the Seattle Public Library filled the pages of architecture and design magazines around the world.[5] Yet rather than simply document the project in a conventional manner, *Metropolis* magazine used the library to explore alternative modes of representation. *Metropolis* has a 30-year history of covering a broad range of design developments, at a range of scales from urban to object. The magazine continues to pursue the goal of explaining why buildings and objects look the way they do, locating design within broader economic, environmental, social, cultural, political and technological contexts.[6] The library provided *Metropolis* with a means to reaffirm and represent its editorial ambitions.

In the introductory notes to the October 2004 issue, editor-in-chief, Susan Szenasy, explains the intentions behind their cover story on the library titled 'We Built It'. She frames their efforts in 'contrast to the many pieces that would be written about the heroic Mr. Koolhaas as the architect of the library'.[7] She admits that 'through the years we have produced our share of single-focus stories ourselves, but have been unhappy with the approach for some time. We feel that such stories are one-dimensional – a kind of white lie about what makes design great.'[8]

Instead, the *Metropolis* issue attempts to create 'a full-bodied, layered narrative and commentary about the relationships, discoveries, obstacles and triumphs behind a breakthrough project'.[9] Szenasy believes that expanding ways of portraying architecture can help advance a general dialogue on the built environment, but she also acknowledges the challenges of such an endeavour.

The editors borrow from the arrangement of the library for the organisation of their piece. Szenasy explains that the coverage is 'laid out like the library's book spiral, which organizes books as one continuous ribbon of information', and thus 'our story sprawls across 20 pages in a continuous flow of reportage, critique, photographs, diagrams and illustrations'.[10] While the story sprawls to the boundaries of legibility, its multifaceted presentation stresses the collaborative nature of producing, occupying and writing architecture, for a popular audience.

In her introduction to the cover story, Karen Steen echoes Szenasy's expressed intentions to create alternative portrayals of architecture. Steen contends that 'most writing on architecture treats the profession as a realm of sole authorship. Where One Big Name is heaped with praise, quoted extensively and ultimately held responsible for whether a building succeeds or fails. The truth, of course, is so much more complex.'[11] Steen reinforces efforts to present a more complex portrayal of architecture but acknowledges 'we haven't the space to tell the whole story … in this issue we gesture at it – and by scratching the surface hope to reveal both the enormity and the importance that collaboration plays in projects large and small.'[12] Similarly, the 'We Built It' cover story is a collaborative piece combining input from multiple authors and sources. [13] The story they tell is a non-linear, diverse narrative conveying multiple dimensions of the project from its research phase to the selection of furniture and finishes.

Collaboration is both a theme and the underlying message of the feature. The tone is set from the outset

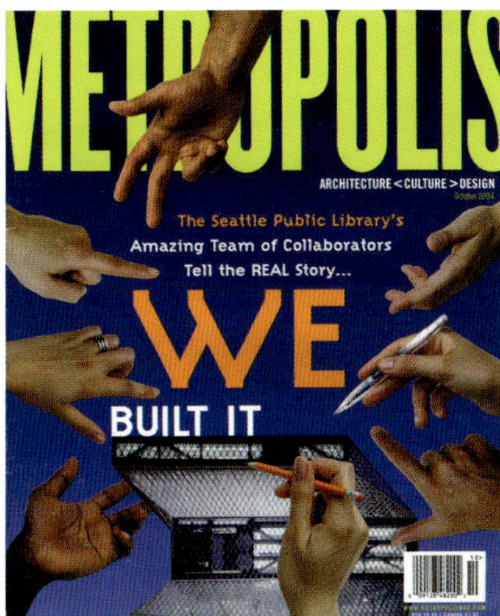

Cover of *Metropolis*,
'We Built It', October 2004.

with the title, 'We Built It', and the cover image illustrating the hands of multiple participants contributing to the project. This image of architectural production stands in marked contrast to the famous image of Le Corbusier's hand authorising his Plan Voisin project. Collaboration is further reinforced in the first page of the feature with Steen's introduction flanked by a list of people involved in the project. Bolstering the emphasis on collaboration, the first spread of the story begins with a column listing all the collaborators, from architects through to vertical transport consultants. This list, typically found at the end of an exposé or relegated to the back of a volume, is prominently foregrounded here at the outset.

Teamwork is further reinforced with quotes from key collaborators woven throughout the layout of the whole exposé, beginning with Tim MacFarlane, one of the facade consultants, explaining in the first spread that 'the number of consultants that work on a project of this complexity are legion. And they have to be, because collaboration is about using the knowledge of as many people as possible'.[14] Though placed at the top of the list of collaborators, quotes from the architectural team, represented by OMA project architect, Joshua Ramus, Rem Koolhaas, and LNM project director, Sam Miller, are interspersed and do not appear until the middle of the feature. This distribution further contributes to a shift of emphasis from an authorial to a collaborative role for the architects.

Along with collaboration, the *Metropolis* feature attempts to convey the complexities of making and using architecture. The narrative starts at the beginning of the library's design process with a description of the atypically detailed research phase that characterised the project, and concludes with a section on the interior furnishings and finishes.[15] The editors adopt a simple colour-coding system to create continuity of information across the series of multi-authored essays. Sections covering the research (orange), the facade (blue), the spiral (green) and the interiors (purple) are interspersed across the feature, deliberately avoiding a linear presentation of process and product. Each section includes an essay and numerous associated images and diagrams. The main topic areas are further augmented by magenta-coloured accounts of how to find books, technological devices used in the library, and even a section recounting fundraising efforts. Moreover, to convey the daily life of the library, snapshots and interviews with library patrons are interspersed throughout the essay, and they include several criticisms of aspects of the building. While it is uncommon for architectural journalism to incorporate a user's impressions and opinions, firsthand accounts of occupying the building highlight its life beyond the intentions of the architects.

In the *Metropolis* feature, efforts to coordinate vast amounts of diverse information created both challenges and opportunities. The textual narrative is quickly diffused among the multiple streams of information, assembled to present the complexities of the project. Like firsthand navigation of the library itself, way-finding in the feature

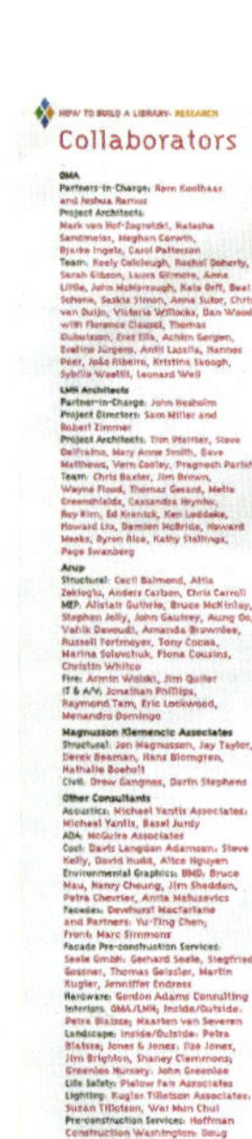

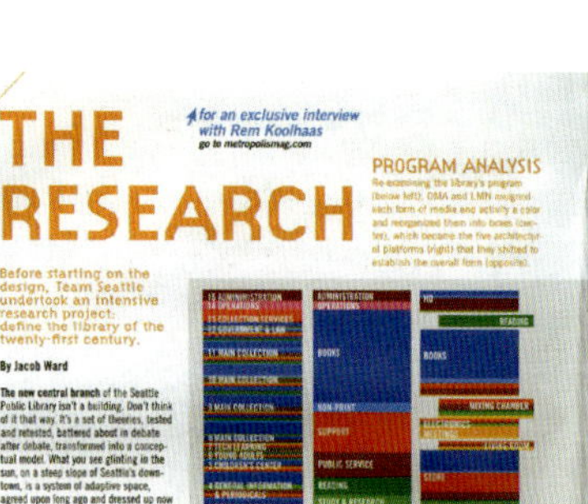

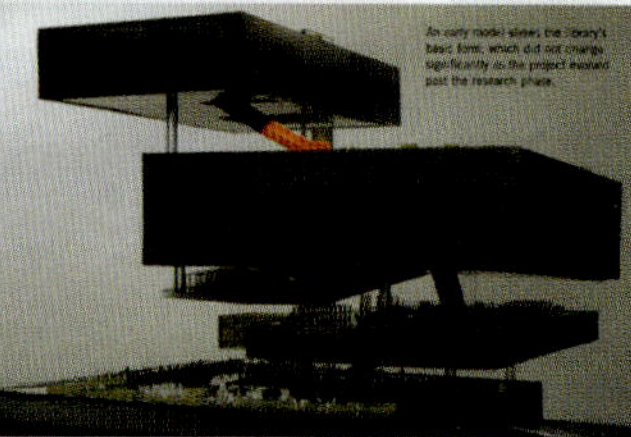

"THE NUMBER OF CONSULTANTS THAT WORK ON A PROJECT OF THIS COMPLEXITY ARE LEGION. AND THEY HAVE TO BE, BECAUSE COLLABORATION IS ABOUT USING THE KNOWLEDGE OF AS MANY PEOPLE AS POSSIBLE."
—TIM MACFARLANE / DEWHURST MACFARLANE AND PARTNERS

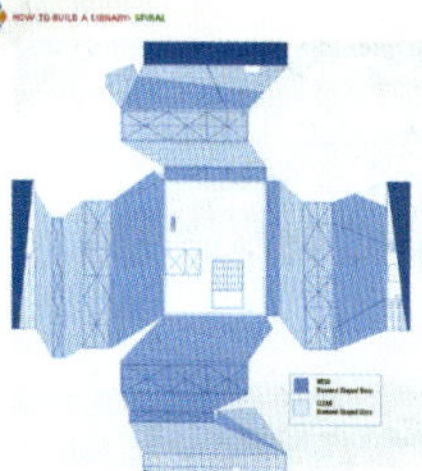

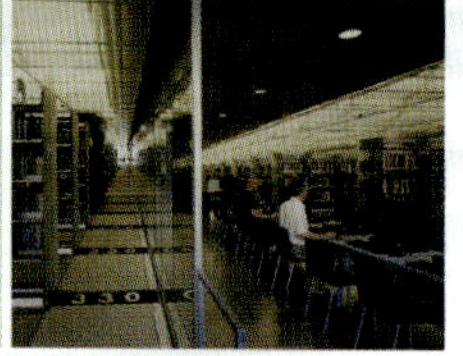

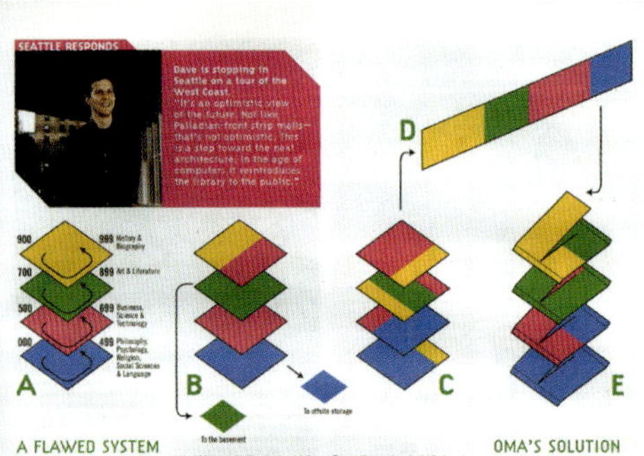

"THE DEVELOPMENT OF THE STACK MATS SYSTEM WAS THE MOST SATISFYING PART OF THE PROJECT. WE WERE ABLE TO COMPLETELY INTEGRATE THE SIGNAGE INTO THE ARCHITECTURE, SINCE EVERYONE WAS COMMITTED TO THE IDEA."
—HENRY HONG-WUI CHEUNG / BRUCE MAU DESIGN

Page spreads from *Metropolis*, 'We Built It', October 2004.

is challenged by the variety of stimuli and information provided. Even though the organisation of the feature is loosely modelled on the library's book spiral, the information overload in the piece conveys the diversity and complexity of stimuli felt when experiencing the library firsthand. Seemingly inadvertently, the feature manages to evoke the experience of the library rather than simply representing the building.

The *Metropolis* feature diversifies both architectural accounts and representational strategies. As a magazine dedicated to 'Architecture <Culture> Design', *Metropolis* does not celebrate buildings as objects in the same ways as many professional architecture magazines.[16] Likewise, *Metropolis* does not always subscribe to standard representational conventions that emphasise objective and sculptural characteristics through photographs without people in them, or through technical drawings – plans, sections, details, etc. In the library feature photographs never present pristine spatial configurations, but instead capture the dynamics of inhabitation. Diagrams rather than plans are used to explain the organisation of the building, and the only technical drawing included is a detail of the facade system.

Geared towards a more popular than professional audience the *Metropolis* piece expands representations of architecture by impressing upon readers the collaborative nature of contemporary design processes, and celebrating the inhabitation of the project. The *Metropolis* coverage of the Seattle Public Library provides a kaleidoscopic view of architectural production, challenging readers to navigate and absorb a diverse range of information. It could also be argued that it challenges readers to get involved and collaborate in their own built environments.

Verb Monograph: impressionistic montage

For *Metropolis* the Seattle Public Library represented an opportunity to explore alternative modes of critical coverage

of a building. For Actar the library offered appropriate content for their existing series of *Verb* publications, explicitly established to challenge representational conventions of architecture in print media. Actar, named as a concatenation of ACTivity and ARchitecture, is a Spanish publisher specialising in contemporary architectural production and in 'exploring open relationships between the creative mediums of the visual arts, between producers and users, between publisher and reader'.[17] Reflecting an active engagement with architecture, the inaugural *Verb* publication, *Processing* (2001), acknowledged that 'as our environments evolve, so do the professions that shape them, and the media that register, recreate and reflect on them'.[18] In response, Actar developed two types of *Verb* publications: *Verb Boogazine* is 'a hybrid, thematic publication that combines the heterogeneity and topicality of a magazine with the referential and comprehensive approach of a book', while *Verb Monograph* is intended as 'a user manual that presents an extensive analysis of a compelling building or situation first examined in the boogazine'.[19] The Seattle Public Library first appeared in *Verb Boogazine, Connection* (2004), and subsequently as a *Verb Monograph* in May 2005.

The *Seattle Public Library Monograph* follows earlier monographs on the Yokohama International Port Terminal (2002) by Foreign Office Architects and the Sendai Mediatheque (2000) by Toyo Ito. All of the monographs reflect the idea 'that publishing architectures is much more than displaying a recently finished product in which the architect is the unique author' and that 'to make architecture is a real undertaking … in which numerous authors participate and which is based on the processing of information before, during and after the materialization of the work.'[20] Though the aspirations of the *Verb* editors echo those of Szenasy at *Metropolis*, the resulting publications employ very different strategies.

The *Seattle Public Library Monograph* is explicitly described as 'the result of the impressions and experiences of Michael Kubo and Ramon Prat after visiting the Seattle Public Library'.[21] The book opens with a series of exterior photographs leading up to the title page. Instead of beginning with the overall building from a photogenic vantage point, the lead-in images are taken from the roofs of surrounding buildings. These curiously un-heroic images set a context for the building before it is fully revealed in the subsequent spreads featuring street level images of the shiny prismatic building.

Without introduction or explanation the first section of the book alternates between spreads that reproduce text and images from the original OMA project proposal, and full bleed interior photographs. The photographs oscillate between populated and unpopulated images, celebrating the spatial and material character of the building. The publication then shifts abruptly to a compilation of newspaper articles documenting the design process. The articles represent a cross-section of local media coverage, beginning with reporting on the local proposition that enabled funding for the project, continuing through the competition process, reactions to public presentations, ensuing debates, with the account culminating in reports of the opening day.

The next section, which represents the bulk of the publication, alternates between three types of representation. The first are time-stamped images, as if stills from a video, suggesting inhabitation. The second are collages of interior photographs, with brief explanations of aspects of the building. The third are black and white technical drawings, augmenting the photographs and providing explanations of the key levels of the building. The publication is bookended with another series of exterior photographs, mostly evening views of the illuminated building. Concluding with evening images may be an allusion to representing a day in the life of the building, but this is never explicitly expressed.

Though *Verb* publications generally strive to be unconventional, arguably the library monograph editors default to conventions in representation, as described above, as well as in attribution. For example, in *Metropolis* the extensive list of collaborators is placed at the beginning. In the *Verb Monograph* this list is relegated to the back of the book prior to the colophon. While the editors acknowledge the wide range of contributors, like the governing logic of the monograph itself, these vital pieces of information are treated as if footnotes.

In contrast to the comprehensiveness of the *Metropolis* feature, the *Verb Monograph* is an undisciplined montage filled with fleeting impressions. While *Metropolis* uses colour coding to coordinate complex information, the monograph offers a fragmentary presentation, wherein parts never resolve into a whole. The text offers no way-finding or clues for navigation from the outset and the explanation of intention, quoted above, only appears in the colophon at the end.

The monograph purports to be an impressionistic account and is decidedly not didactic, but following the *Verb* mandate the authors trace before, during and after the materialisation of the building. In general, the monograph is a montage of existing materials and the editor's photographs without pretension to being comprehensive, or the compulsion to divulge curatorial intentions. Rather than an explanatory text or 'user manual' with extensive analyses, this monograph is more like a Situationist dérive. Similarly, with the editorial position(s) and ambition(s) left unarticulated and the body of the monograph being a jump cut montage of information, the book is more like a music video than the documentary film that the time-stamped photos and narrative descriptions suggest. The volume challenges the conventions of monographic representation with an unmoored impressionistic alternative. Overall, the *Verb Monograph* on the library relies on montages of standard photographic documentation, as well as architectural drawings and diagrams, expanded with a video diary and diverse local newspaper accounts. The uncommon addition of newspaper coverage echoes the populism surrounding the project, but also identifies an often-overlooked

Page spreads from *OMA / LMN: Seattle Public Library, Verb Monograph* (Barcelona: Actar, 2005), courtesy of Actar.

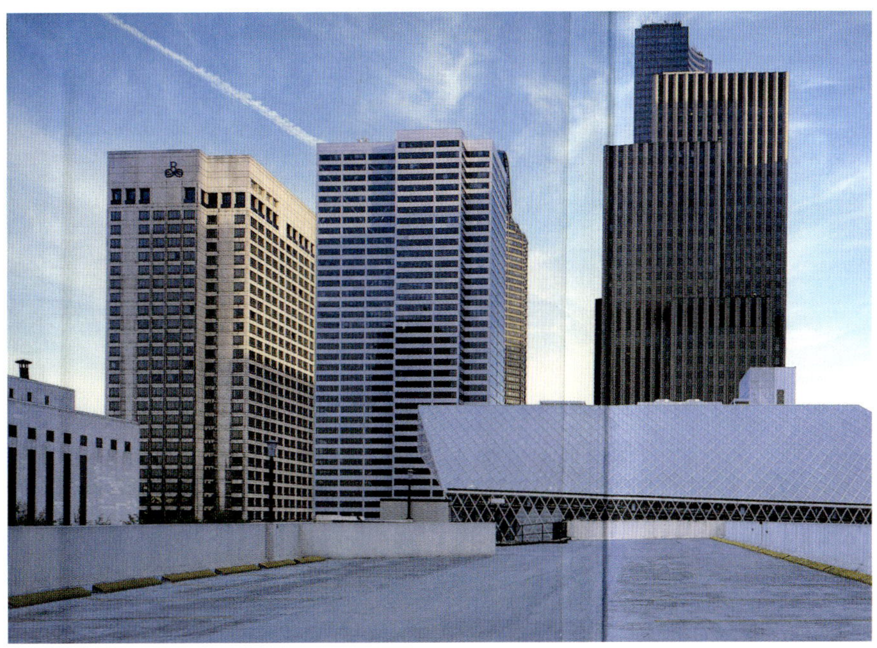

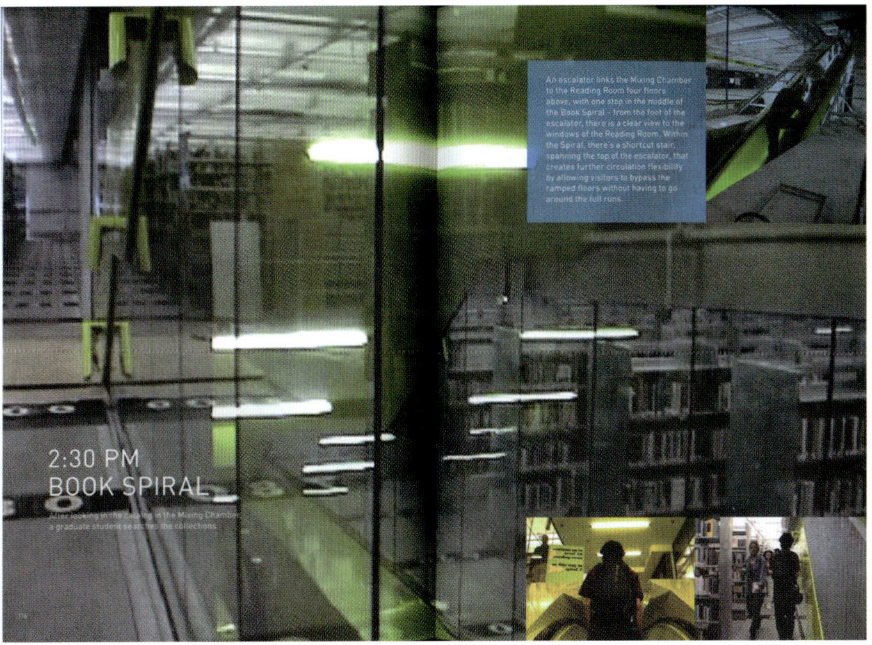

domain of architectural representation and negotiation. The inclusion of alternative architectural media coverage in the *Verb Monograph* is subsequently expanded in the *Domus Post-Occupancy* portrayal of the library.

Post-Occupancy: multimedia mediation

The library provided further stimulus for experimentation in architectural representation, serving as a key example in the inaugural issue of Domus d'Autore, *Post-Occupancy* (2006) edited by Koolhaas and AMO. The publisher, Giovanna Mazzocchi, is explicit about the curatorial ambitions of the journal and the desire to challenge conventions, describing Domus d'Autore as 'a special issue of *Domus*, entrusted to an Editor-Architect of worldwide renown who illustrates Architecture according to its own original codes of communication'.[22] In response, Koolhaas outlines his intentions in the preface, explaining:

> With this issue we try to (re)present four recent buildings in a fresh, more complex way. We don't insist on the buildings' qualities, but monitored [*sic*] their effects on their respective hosts and users. There are no 'critics' – usually, best friends in drag – no intimidation. We have assembled myriad anonymous voices and collected snapshots. We documented how (our) buildings take their place in a primordial sea of influences and predecessors on which their existence depends and to whose existence they contribute. We looked through the eyes of tourists and artists, trusted others to record. Away from the triumphalist or miserablist glare of media, we wanted to see what happens in the absence of the author, to represent the realities we were complicit in creating, post-occupancy, as facts not feats.[23]

As evident in his earlier *S,M,L,XL* and *Content* monographs, Koolhaas has consistently attempted to reinvent conventions and expand the possibilities of architectural

publication. *Post-Occupancy* reflects further efforts to explore alternatives in architectural representation, this time drawing primarily on popular source materials.

Post-Occupancy covers four recent projects by Koolhaas and OMA: the Embassy of the Netherlands in Berlin (2004), McCormick Tribune Campus Centre (2003), Casa da Musica (2005), and the Seattle Public Library (2004). Each project is presented through multiple lenses, including local TV coverage, international newspaper headlines, a survey of internet chat and blog commentary, quotations from critics, and images captured from surveillance cameras. *Post-Occupancy* documents projects through a multimedia mediation of sources beyond the typical architectural media repositories.

While each project in *Post-Occupancy* is treated similarly, this examination focuses only on the section dedicated to the library, which begins with an aerial photograph locating the project. Geographic description is followed by contextualisation, with a spread featuring the key newspaper headlines that occurred on the project's opening day. These headlines help suggest that architecture is related to broader global events and developments rather than an autonomous object.

Further context for the project is provided with a data sheet that covers time, scale, program and equivalences. The timeline identifies the duration of the design and construction of the project while also noting important concurrent world events. The scale section notes the relative size of the project. The program section illustrates the floor area and range of facilities provided. For added context, in a twist of absurdist data collection, *Post-Occupancy* reports that the library is equal to '0.01 of Amazon.com's 2005 revenues, 0.04 of porn downloads in the US in 2005, 0.55 of J.K. Rowling's *Harry Potter* book sales in 2005 and 1.82 of e-books delivered to Japanese mobile phones in 2005'.[24] While the relevance of most of these measures is doubtful, they still contribute to creating a larger context for the project.

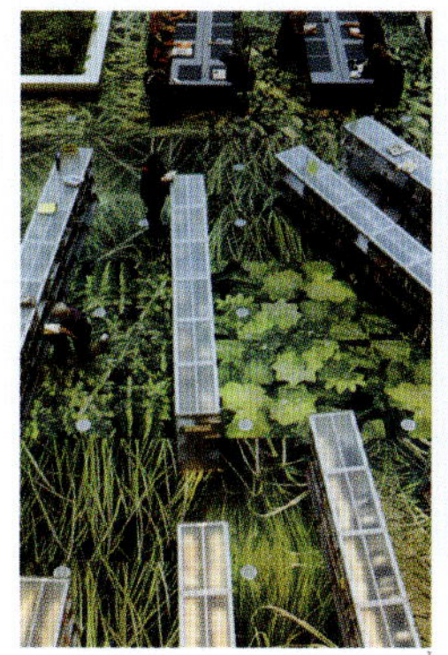
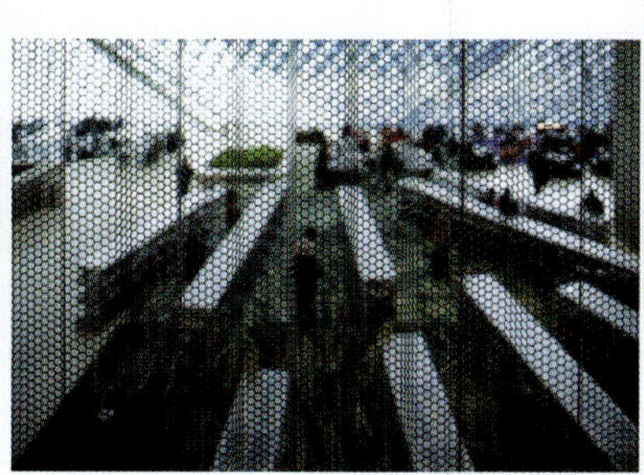
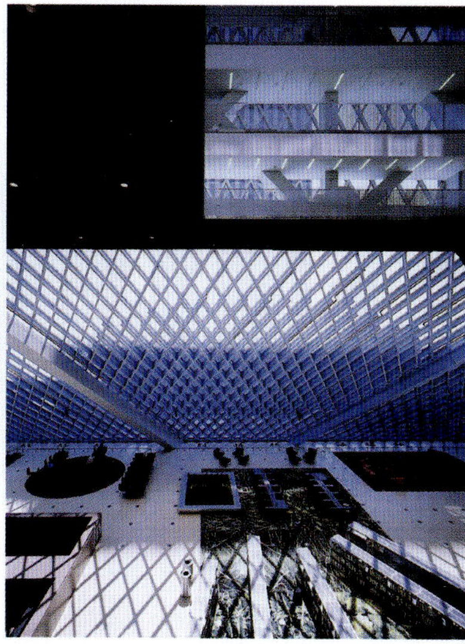

In addition to setting a broader context for the project, *Post-Occupancy* broadens the types and intellectual context for architectural representation. For example, the use of images in the *Post-Occupancy* section on the library challenges conventions of photographic representation. To begin with, the library is presented through a series of photographs of reflections in the exterior facade of the library, and of the library reflected in the facades of neighbouring buildings. These photos celebrate the prismatic effects of the building blending into its environment more than the conventional treatment of a building as an object. The library is subsequently presented through a collection

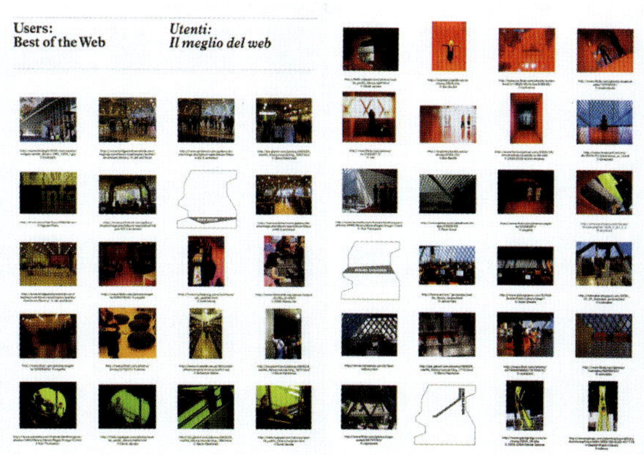

Page spreads from Seattle Public Library section of *Domus d'Autore, Post-Occupancy*. Images courtesy *Editoriale Domus S.p.A.*, all rights reserved.

of interior photographs culled from websites. These images downplay the pedigree and perspective of professional architectural photographs, echoing the populism embedded in the library's conception and reception, and recognising the proliferation of architectural representations across the internet. The web photographs are followed by a series of professional photographs, set in parallel with a critical discussion on architectural photography extracted from a roundtable discussion between Claude Parent, Bruno Latour, Hans Ulrich Obrist, Jean-Luc Moulene, Valerie Pihet and Clotilde Viannay. The accompanying photographs do not comprehensively document the project, but rather provide illustrative content resonating with the parallel debate around photographic representations.

With a further challenge to still images, *Post-Occupancy* breaks the boundaries of the printed page. In an effort to expand the multimedia presentation of the four projects, the publication is accompanied by a CD-ROM, which includes Quicktime VR sequences taken throughout the library. These panoramic sequences extend the reader's ability to experience the project beyond the static single point of view provided by still photography. Quicktime VR brings readers as close as possible to the experience of being a building occupant, without travelling to Seattle.

Post-Occupancy refuses to comply with conventional representational strategies. Technical drawings and sketches are avoided. Playing on the term and representation of medical CAT scans, the only drawing presented is a composite of all the floor plans labelled 'CAD-Scan: Layered Floors'. However, if technical drawings are generally difficult for non-professionals to read, the x-ray composite drawing is an illegible representation for both public and professional audiences alike.

Though expanding modes of architectural representation, the Quicktime VR sequences and the 'CAD-Scan' are counter to Koolhaas the editor's expressed intention to represent realities in the absence of the author. The CAD-Scans do not represent reality and are both unintelligible and uninhabitable. The Quicktime VR sequences expand understanding and perceptual inhabitation, but the planned points of view produce a highly curated reality of their own. The VR representations are supplements that enable virtual occupancy of a pristine project rather than documenting post-occupancy.

Post-Occupancy traces and curates the mediated life of the library in a clinically un-heroic manner, raising questions about the channels and ways in which architecture is received, beyond the controlled dissemination of architectural writing. As *Metropolis* uses the library to expand conceptions of collaborative production, *Domus* challenges domains of architectural representation. Beyond the architectural critic and opening day coverage in television and newspapers, architectural stories proliferate unabated through blogs, photo archives, YouTube, and other online platforms. While *Post-Occupancy* selectively edits these materials, the volume validates the roles of such media for expanding the construction and production of architecture. *Post-Occupancy* acknowledges architects inability to control the media and contents of architectural representation, just as it demands awareness of multiple media and venues for reading and writing architecture.

Intimating new regimes

The *Metropolis* cover story, *Verb Monograph* and special issue of *Domus* mobilise the Seattle Public Library to explore new regimes of architectural (re)presentation. Together these three portrayals of an innovative library building help diversify modes of architectural communication. They expand notions of authorship, broaden standards and media of dissemination, and widen audience and engagement. The three pieces incite a shift from the figure of the heroic authorial architect to acknowledge collaborative production. They offer varied modes of information delivery, ranging from didactic comprehensive documentation to impressionistic montage to the curation of proliferating media. They also represent a reconfigured conception of architectural producers and architectural audiences.

Metropolis, *Domus* and, to a lesser degree, the *Verb Monograph*, each reject the celebration of a singular heroic architect, and the spatial and material compositions of iconic buildings. All three offer thicker descriptions of both architectural object and process. In form and content 'We Built It' explicitly presents the complexity and multi-facetedness of architectural production, consumption and representation. The *Seattle Public Library Monograph* tries to convey the diversity of experience offered by the building, combining documentation of the design and public engagement process with the editor's personal tour of the project. In contrast to the colour-coded linear presentation in *Metropolis*, *Verb* stiches together a fragmented narrative, highlighting varied interactions with architecture over aesthetic appreciation. Even though *Post-Occupancy* is authored by one of the architects it also rejects a primary authorial role yielding to the diversity of multimedia discussions, documentation, and interactions precipitated by architecture. *Post-Occupancy* is less concerned with the multi-vocal collaborative production of the building and more concerned with the cacophony of expert and amateur authors continually reading and re-writing architecture.

Beyond a shift away from the idea of the architect as author all three pieces also expand authorial roles for architectural journalism and publications. The *Metropolis* story is explicitly multi-authored and multi-vocal, reinforcing the collaborative nature of architectural production – both materially and discursively. *Verb* is closest to recognised standards of architectural criticism, but the mode of delivery has morphed from expert commentary to something like travelogue. *Post-Occupancy* begins with a critique of the expert commentary of critics, and then opens the floodgates of discursive production in architecture by validating blogs, websites, and other online platforms as legitimate territories of dissemination and debate.

The three portrayals shift modes of delivery and also of engagement. *Metropolis* offers a didactic overview attempting to comprehensively document both the development and occupation of the building. The *Verb Monograph* provides an impressionistic montage. *Post-Occupancy* broadens the context of building production and the context of the multimedia consumption of architecture through diverse outlets. None of the three default to representational conventions, including pristine vacuous images of spatial compositions, crisp technical drawings or clinical diagrams. Rather than formal prowess, all three focus on active inhabitation, repositioning the building from object of appreciation to armature for engagement.

The three pieces also reflect transforming relationships with audiences. *Metropolis* seeks to explain the library's development, design and occupation to a popular audience. The authors write to help the public read architecture. *Verb Monographs* aspire to provide user manuals, but the *Seattle Public Library Monograph* offers a personalised reading of the project for professionals and architectural enthusiasts. The authors write to offer an alternative reading of the project. *Post-Occupancy* corrals a cross-section of media, accounts and occupations of the project. The authors forgo writing for curating a collection of professional and popular texts. All three portrayals expand territories of author and audience in contemporary architectural (re)presentation.

The three portrayals validate different approaches and venues for disseminating architectural ideas and representing architecture for both professional and popular audiences. The Seattle Public Library challenges typological conventions. The *Metropolis*, *Verb Monograph* and *Domus* exposés on the library demonstrate how documentation of the project subsequently helped challenge and expand conventions for writing and reading architecture.

1   Herbert Muschamp, 'The Library That Puts on Fishnets and Hits the Disco', *New York Times*, May 16 2004, http://www.nytimes.com/.

2   Paul Goldberger, 'High-Tech Bibliophilia', *New Yorker*, May 24 2004, http:// www.newyorker.com/

3   Brian Kenney, 'After Seattle,' *Library Journal* (August 15, 2005).

4   *Delirious New York* (1978) is Koolhaas's 'retroactive manifesto for Manhattan', identifying the historical development of strategies that support the culture of congestion that epitomise urbanism. The book is a canonical urban studies text combining polemical analyses, provocative narratives and projective strategies. *S,M,L,XL* (1995) is a collaboration between Koolhaas and graphic designer Bruce Mau that combines diverse genres – essays, manifestos, diaries, fairy tales, travelogues, meditations and architectural projects – organised across four scales. This book revolutionised the architectural monograph. *Content* (2004) is a reactionary follow-up to *S,M,L,XL* that challenged the conventions of its predecessor while further expanding the boundaries of architectural monographs.

5   International architectural media coverage of the Seattle Public Library included: Sheri Olson, 'Thanks to OMA's Blending of Cool Information Technology and Warm Public Spaces, Seattle's Central Library Kindles Book Lust'. *Architectural Record* 192, no. 7 (2004, July): 88-101; Lawrence W. Cheek, 'Reading Rem', *Architecture* 93, no. 7 (2004, July): 39-47; Barbara Lamprecht, 'The nice and the good: library, Seattle USA', *Architectural Review* 216, no. 1290 (2004, August): 52-7; Shumon Basar, 'Reads Like Teen Spirit', *Blueprint* 221, (2004, July): 54-61; Francesco Dal Co, 'OMA/LMN: Biblioteca Centrale, Seattle', *Casabella* 68, no. 724 (2004): 6-23; Bettina Schurkamp, 'Seattle Central Library', *Bauwelt* 95, no. 23 (2004): 26-35; 'Seattle Central Library'. *Kenchiku Bunka* 59, no. 673 (2004, October): 1-11; 'OMA: Seattle Central Library'. *GA Document* 80 (2004, June): 8-61.

6   For the *Metropolis* magazine mission statement see: http://www.metropolismag.com/story/20061206/who-what-is-metropolis-i

7   *Metropolis*, October 2004, 24.

8   *Metropolis*, October 2004, 24.

9   *Metropolis*, October 2004, 24.

10   *Metropolis*, October 2004, 24.

11   Various, 'We Built It', *Metropolis* (October 2004), 97.

12   'We Built It,' 97.

13   The list of collaborative authors includes: Karen E. Steen, Jacob Ward, Clair Enlow, Christopher Hawthorne, Fred Moody and Paul Makovsky.

14   'We Built It', 98-99.

15   As Joshua Ramus, the OMA partner in charge of the library, recounts they were able to 'suspend the rush to architectural form for three months, making time and space to think'. Joshua Ramus, 'Seattle Central Library', *Architecture and Urbanism*, no. 428 (2006, May), 100. During the research phase the design team and client representatives visited international library precedents, conducted technology seminars, and evaluated the proposed library program. The resulting proposal challenged the formulation of the program and introduced alternative approaches that addressed the drawbacks of current library practices, as well as current and future technological advances. Conducting research was a foundation for the design proposal, but also fortified the project's organisational diagram to withstand the public processes.

16   'Architecture <Culture> Design' is the subtitle of the magazine prominently featured on the cover of *Metropolis*.

17   See Actar website, http://www.actar.com/index.php?option=com_content&task=view&id=18&Itemid=79

18   Salazar, Jaime, *Verb Processing, Architecture Boogazine*. Barcelona: Actar, 2001, 77.

19   See Actar website www.actar.com/index.php?option=com_content&task=view&id=15&lang=en&Itemid=68. In the first Boogazine the editors elaborate on their hybrid, explaining: 'It's a magazine and a book at the same time. It is a magazine because it has a given periodicity and an agile way of dealing with information, but it is also a book because it seeks to show information in such a way that it serves as a point of reference, an essay on a topic that deals with more than just the present moment in time' – *Verb Processing* 2001, 77.

20   *Verb Processing*, 2001, 78.

21   Kubo, Michael, and Ramon Prat (eds.), *Seattle Public Library*. Barcelona: Actar, 2005, 162.

22   'From the Publisher', in AMO/Rem Koolhaas. *Post-Occupancy*. Milan: Editoriale Domus, 2006.

23   'Preface', in *Post-Occupancy*. Milan: Editoriale Domus, 2006.

24   The issue is not paginated. Data appears on the last page of Section II on the Library in Post-Occupancy.

Cinematic Architecture and Subversive Sites: Wong Kar-wai's Hong Kong cityscapes

DANICA VAN DE VELDE

The cinematic work of Hong Kong filmmaker, Wong Kar-wai, has played a significant role in providing global audiences with a visual sense of Hong Kong's urban environment and architectural space. Specifically, his films have provided a variation on the idea of architecture in cinema as mere scenic backdrop, instead creating an intimate geography of the more obscure sites of the region — a topography that is generally overlooked. Parallel to this investment in everyday locations is a reluctance to represent Hong Kong's urban spaces through visual reference to well-known buildings. The monumental architecture of the Central District, the view from The Peak or shots of Victoria Harbour – sights that are constantly used to represent Hong Kong in visual media – are notably absent from Wong's films.

Wong's film camera interacts with both the established and disappearing architecture of the city, most notably in two films that take contemporary Hong Kong as their central setting: *Chungking Express* (1994) and *Fallen Angels* (1995). By fracturing the by-now-accustomed snapshot of Hong Kong, especially by excluding the stunning skyline, which is arguably the most important aspect of its visual identity, Wong refigures views of the city and creates a tension between architectural visibility and invisibility.

Wong's films work to construct an alternative mapping of place, privileging locations that would otherwise remain hidden, to produce a filmic cartography that accords with Marc Augé's theory of the 'non-place'. There are two interpretations of the role of architecture in Wong's films. Firstly, in a city where architectural renewal occurs at a dizzying pace, cinema plays a part in recording buildings, in a preservation project, curating buildings into an urban, cinematic archive. Secondly, specific locations are used to present a local and personal view of the city, a view that is distinct from or critical of touristic perspectives. Conceptually reminiscent of Giuliana Bruno's notion of 'site-seeing', Wong's concern with visually 'writing' a disappearing architecture utilises film as a means to preserve personally significant locations that exist at the margins, before they vanish from the urban topography altogether.

Throughout the history of cinema, the modern cityscape has consistently been woven into the visual texture of celluloid, functioning to provide both context and décor to the film action. Although the charting of architectural spaces has often served as an unconscious or coincidental background to plot development, a number of filmmakers and cinematographers have productively employed the film camera as a tool to engage with built space. Beyond the role of the built environment in providing a setting, cinema and architecture intersect at the nexus of space and image – what Giuliana Bruno refers to as a 'modern cartography' that transforms 'pictures into architecture'.[1] This cartography that mobilises architecture as moving image occurs at a number of different levels. As Mark Lamster argues:

> On a practical level, architecture sets a scene, con-
> veying information about plot and character while
> contributing to the overall feel of a movie. In more
> discreet ways, filmmakers can use their cameras
> to make statements about the built – or unbuilt –
> environment, or use that environment to comment
> metaphorically on any variety of subjects, from the
> lives of the characters in their films to the nature of
> contemporary society.[2]

More evocatively, cinema also serves as an unofficial archive of the urban environment, visually documenting both architectural icons and unassuming sites embedded within the changing cityscape. For Hong Kong filmmaker Wong Kar-wai, the preservation of everyday locations and architecture in the urban fabric is a cinematic imperative, whereby the film camera is utilised to capture and record real locations, setting in motion a unique filmic mapping that turns the choreographed movements of the camera into an architectural journey. Whether the film camera is following dreamily melancholic flâneurs, passing through desolate landscapes via automobile or capturing fleeting views from a train window, Wong's cinematic oeuvre reveals a considered focus on location and place.

Shooting the majority of his films in his home city of Hong Kong, Wong has claimed that this particular spatial setting has consistently provided the starting point for developing the narratives of his films.[3] In *Chungking Express* (1994) and *Fallen Angels* (1995) – two films that form an urban diptych of 1990s Hong Kong – the region's cityscape is not utilised merely for contextual scene setting or backdrop, but as another character, central to the film action. While architectural scholars such as Mitchell Schwarzer have illuminated the capacity for cinema to construct 'architectures that exist only in the mind … composed of sensation … memory and imagination', the role of physical architecture is paramount in Wong's cinema.[4] Specifically, in *Chungking Express* and *Fallen Angels,* Wong and his cinematographer, Christopher Doyle, establish an intimate portrait of Hong Kong – a particular perspective that takes the form of a filmic map.

This intimate cinematic mapping is facilitated by the working habits of Wong's production crew, whereby both films were shot guerrilla-style on the streets of Hong Kong with handheld cameras, available light sources and without the aid of location permits.[5] Importantly, the flexible approach to filming the city by Wong's crew is not merely a reaction to the rhythm of Hong Kong, but can also be read as a critique of touristic representations of the city, which fail to look beyond the surface. In

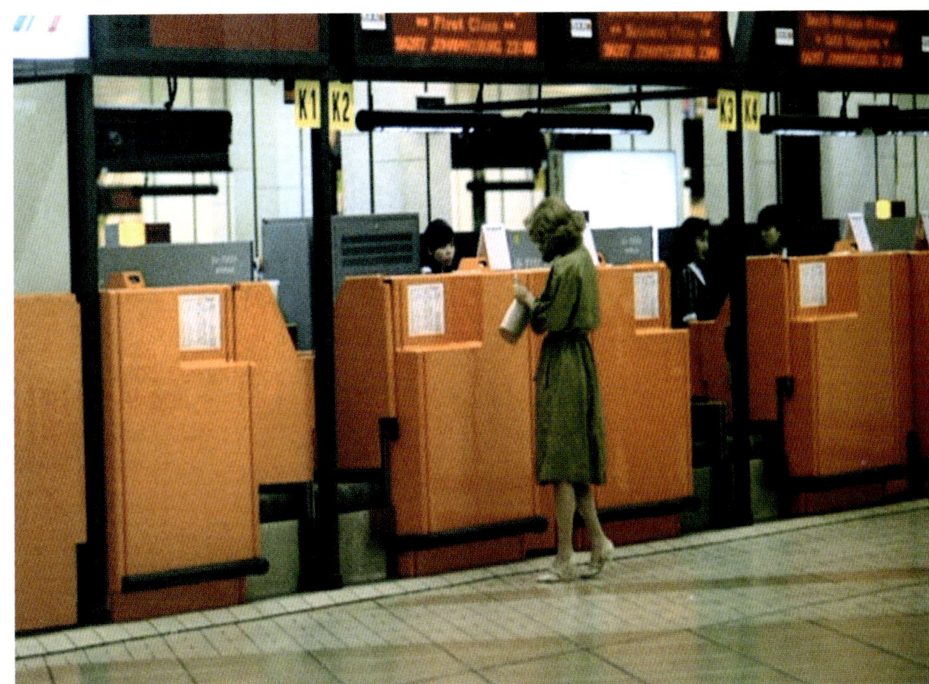

Preserving Kai Tak Airport
in *Chungking Express*.
Image used with permission,
courtesy and copyright of
Jet Tone Productions.

Chungking Express and *Fallen Angels*, Doyle's roaming camerawork traverses streets, decrepit buildings, seedy bars, shops, subway stations, traditional outdoor food stalls called *dai pai dongs*, markets and the tiny apartments that form a part of Hong Kong's architectural topography.

Taking the romantic alienation and the anonymity engendered by city living as their central themes, *Chungking Express* and *Fallen Angels* utilise the changing landscape of the city to symbolically explore the interwoven concepts of memory and forgetting, preservation and amnesia. Blending fictional narrative with an interest in the mnemonics of the physical sites in Hong Kong, both films position cinema as an architectural medium that is particularly attentive to the obsolete. Significantly, both

Chungking Express and *Fallen Angels* were filmed in the mid-1990s; an important period in Hong Kong's socio-political history in the lead-up to the reunification with the People's Republic of China in 1997. At the heart of this historical moment was a sense of cultural anxiety regarding the construction and maintenance of a unique Hong Kong identity and memory. This anxiety was undoubtedly exacerbated by the rapid rate at which Hong Kong continually alters and renews its urban fabric, for bound up with the rapid rise of skyscrapers was the demolition of older architecture embedded with cultural narratives that were sadly left to fade in the rubble. As cultural scholar, Ackbar Abbas has pointed out: '[a] dominant image of Hong Kong is that it is constantly

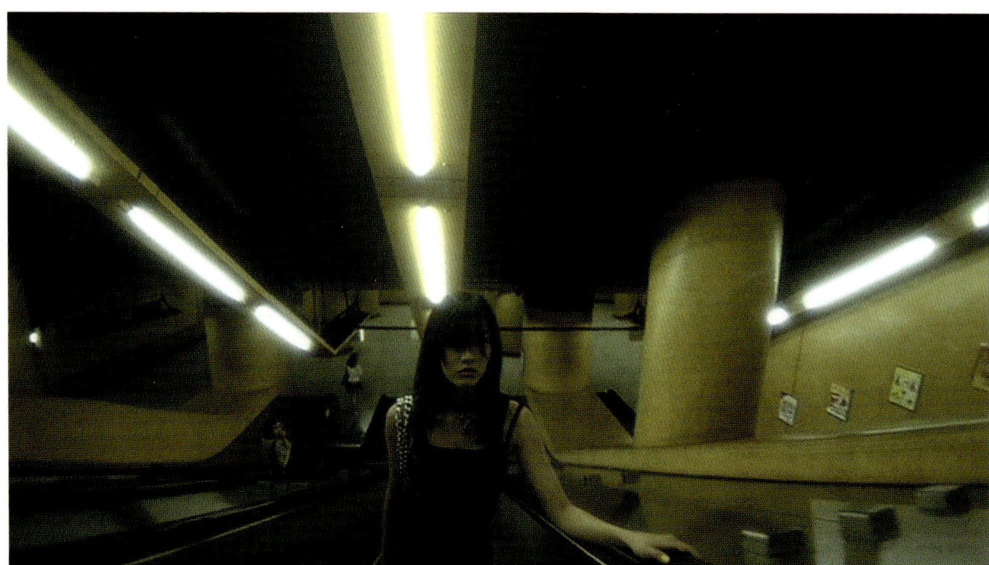

Inside Hong Kong: Travelling on the MTR in *Fallen Angels*. Image used with permission, courtesy and copyright of Jet Tone Productions.

remaking itself, ruthlessly cancelling out the past and moving on, creating a tabula rasa on which to build anew.'[6] The construction of new buildings has resulted in a process of urban renewal, which negates the past, and effaces site-specific narratives and memories.

Clearly concerned with such changes to the physical composition of Hong Kong, Wong consistently represents memory as not only a private concern for his characters, but also inextricably linked to the city's architecture. Discussing his use of the film medium to draw on the tension between architectural presence and absence, Wong made the following statement in an interview in 1995:

> What we are interested in, I think, is the people and Hong Kong. Before *Fallen Angels*, I always chose locations because they were appropriate, and that was it. But things change very fast in Hong Kong. The locations for my first two films have disappeared already. Even in *Chungking Express*, my fourth film, some locations have disappeared, changed into other things … So in *Fallen Angels*, I was trying to include a location which I thought would disappear within a year or two, like the teahouse and restaurants where the killers went, and the place where he lives, things like that. The life-style of Hong Kong in certain periods … I'm trying to preserve it on film.[7]

This conscious decision to seek out particular settings during location scouting certainly indicates a nostalgic desire to embed architectural memories – what Wong has described as: 'an attempt to seal some of the existing images onto the negative, while they are still there.'[8] Wong's commentary on his selection of locations gestures to the relative lack of official heritage listing in Hong Kong, and the absence of formal protections for sites of cultural and historical importance, while also emphasising the capacity for film to record that which would otherwise disappear.[9]

Tracing memory/preserving the city

In Wong's topographic narratives, both public and private memories reside within the folds, layers and contours of his filmic maps. Specifically, the characters in *Chungking Express* and *Fallen Angels* are all obsessed with remembrance and with distilling fleeting moments. As one of the characters in *Chungking Express* laments:

> When did everything start having an expiration date? Swordfish expires. Meat sauce expires. Even plastic wrap expires. I'm starting to wonder: Is there anything in this world that doesn't? … If memories ever come in a can, I hope that can never expires. If it has to have a shelf life, I hope it's 10,000 years.

In both films, the character's desire to retain the past in private mnemonic snapshots are matched by the camera's tracing of the old architecture of the city. As Tony Rayns elucidates in his commentary for the Criterion Collection release of *Chungking Express*: '[t]here is hardly a single glimpse anywhere in this movie of the high-tech, urban, futuristic Hong Kong that is very familiar from tourist brochures…[Wong] has focused almost exclusively on old Hong Kong here and I think that is with a distinct nostalgic bent to it.'[10] The significance of Wong's approach to film setting is proven by the fact that *Chungking Express* and *Fallen Angels* served to capture and archive areas of Hong Kong that have drastically changed over the past 18 years since the films were originally released. In some cases the locations have been relegated to mere memory; some notable examples are the Midnight Express fast food counter in Lan Kwai Fong, Kai Tak Airport and the Bottoms Up Club in Tsim Sha Tsui – three locations that feature in both films. Similarly, other sites have moved to different areas within Hong Kong. Even locations such as

the distinctive dai pai dongs off Central District and the teahouses in Wan Chai District, which are the films most culturally and geographically specific settings, are slowly being removed from Hong Kong's urbanscape.[11]

For a viewer who is unfamiliar with the layout of Hong Kong, these locations may not immediately call to mind specific images of the city or set off a spark of recognition. Indeed, when I showed the opening of *Chungking Express* to the audience of an Asian Studies seminar at The University of Western Australia in 2007, the majority of the viewers were of the opinion that the film's imagery could easily represent any modern Asian city. Wong, on the other hand, has commented that for him, *Chungking Express* 'feels like a diary or a map. All the scenes were shot according to the logic of the place. If you go to Hong Kong after seeing *Chungking Express*, you won't get lost.'[12] This assertion is certainly disputable, whether it is a tourist or a local attempting to navigate the city following a viewing of *Chungking Express*; however, Wong's comment links geography and memory in an interesting way. In the same manner that a diary or an old map records the past through either writing or diagrammatic illustration, *Chungking Express* and *Fallen Angels* visually memorialise the urban environment of Hong Kong at a specific point in its history, and store it for later reflection.

The central reason for Wong's description of *Chungking Express* as a map or diary lies in the film's many visual allusions to the places in the city where he spent his time in the mid-1990s.[13] The repetition of the cinematic journey to these locations in *Fallen Angels* further reinforces their sentimental significance. By mapping Hong Kong through his own personal sites of identification, and thereby constructing an intertwined map and diary, Wong makes accessible a hidden cartography that would otherwise be obscured by Hong Kong's iconic architecture. As Hong Kong exists within a perpetual cycle of architectural alteration and construction, Wong's selective mapping acknowledges that it is almost impossible to cohesively capture what is essentially an unstable topography. His reluctance to represent Hong Kong's urban spaces through reference to well-known buildings has been acknowledged by other scholars; however, my aim here is to examine what effect this has beyond showing a different perspective of Hong Kong from that seen in the mainstream media.[14]

In *Chungking Express* and *Fallen Angels*, as in the majority of Wong's films set in Hong Kong, he does not restrict filming to locations that will instantly evoke the region. Those images that have come to be accepted as representative of Hong Kong, such as the monumental architecture of the Central District, the neon jungles of Mong Kok and Causeway Bay, the view from The Peak or shots of Victoria Harbour – sites that are constantly used to represent Hong Kong in visual media – are notably absent from Wong's mapping. Instead, *Chungking Express* and *Fallen Angels* uncover locations that cannot be accessed through a touristic glance. To quote Lisa Odham Stokes and Michael Hoover: 'Wong circumscribes Hong Kong and shows, as his camera eye sees, what is there.'[15] The manner in which the film camera interacts with architecture produces an anxiety between visibility and invisibility, drawing focus to the cracks in the tourist map and the concealed spaces between buildings.

Behind the Skyscrapers: Seeing Hong Kong

As the Sino-British handover in 1997 was approaching, Ackbar Abbas coined the term 'space of disappearance' to describe the urban mood of Hong Kong as it came to terms with joining mainland China. In his book *Hong Kong: Culture and the Politics of Disappearance*, Abbas defines exactly what he means by disappearance, stating that it 'does not imply nonappearance, absence, or lack of presence. It is not even non-recognition – it is more a question of misrecognition, of recognising a thing as something else.'[16] At the crux of this 'misrecognition' is the city's architecture – the element of the city that has

been used most intensively to visually construct a sense of place. This, as Abbas argues, is particularly evident in Hong Kong cinema. He writes that:

> Hong Kong films made recently, which concern themselves with the city's present historical situation, attempt to identify what is most visible of all, its architecture … But because architecture is seen as a purely photogenic set of objects, we get the same familiar shots of the same well-known buildings, taken from the same angles … It is as if it were necessary to hold on to the familiar for reassurance that the city is real. In any case, no identity emerges … the city is seen but not heard.[17]

Abbas's assertion highlights the tendency of some Hong Kong filmmakers to utilise a 'touristic' mapping of the city, relying on the repetition and recycling of images of significant architectural structures to foreground the film's setting. The desire to delineate Hong Kong as a clearly legible urban space results in an over-determined discourse, attempting to concretise and simplify the city into one image. As Hong Kong-based urban planner and scholar Peter Cookson Smith argues, monumental architecture is inherently problematic, particularly from an urban design point of view, due to the fact that these structures are 'occasionally iconic but inwardly oriented landmarks with ambiguous public identity in relation to social space and the role of the street'.[18] It follows that attempting to ascribe meaning by visually alluding to a city's architecture does not reveal much about what lies beneath a city's surface. What, then, can a viewer take from Wong's lack of focus on the monuments of Hong Kong?

Interdisciplinary film theorist Giuliana Bruno's concept of 'filmic site-seeing' is important in addressing this question. Sightseeing, a phenomenon that generally involves tourists viewing 'sights' chosen for their historical or cultural importance, is amended to highlight the film camera's focus on 'sites'. Bruno claims that this form of

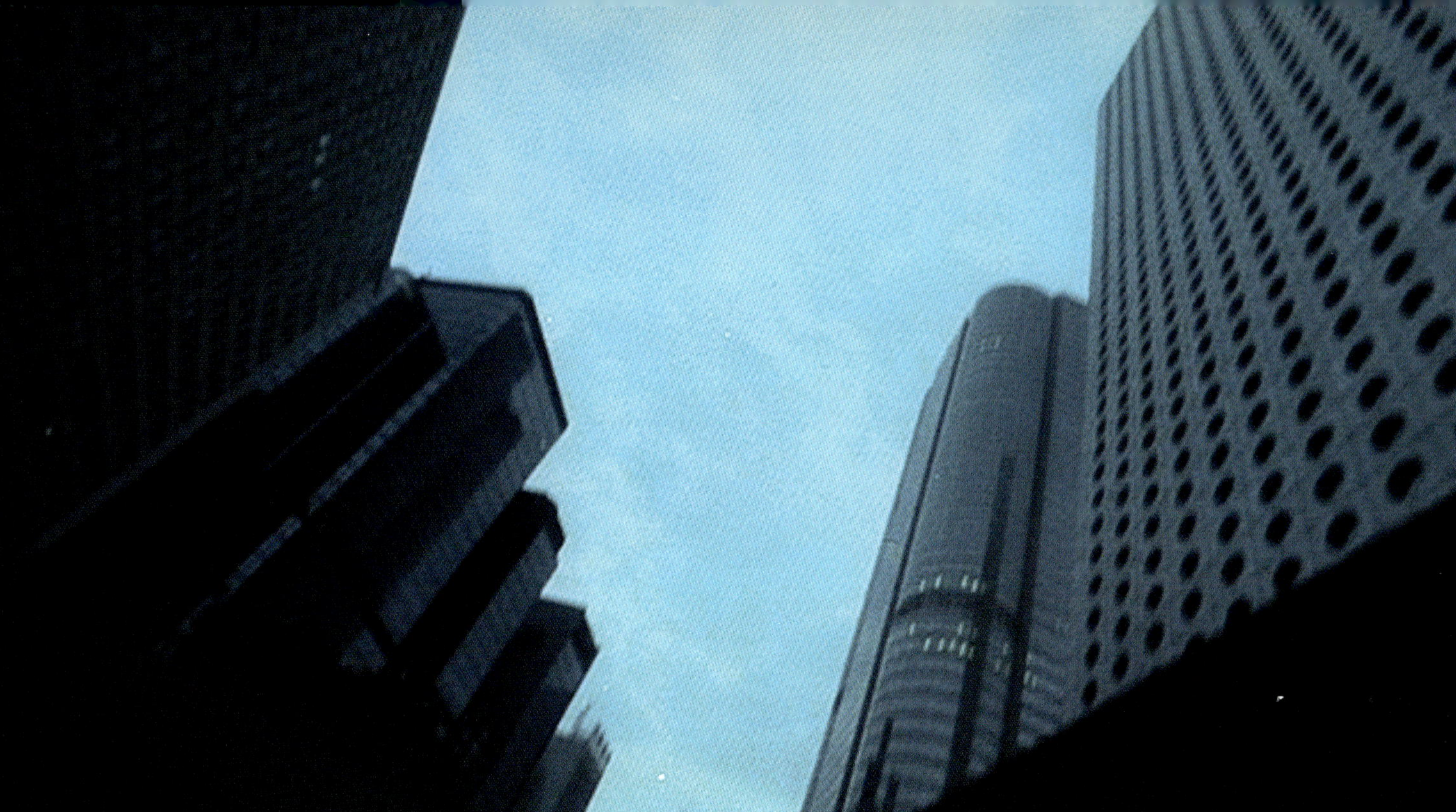

From below: Jardine House in *Fallen Angels*.
Image used with permission, courtesy and
copyright of Jet Tone Productions.

viewing results in 'an *emotional* mapping' that aims to connect 'the local and topographical to the personal'.[19] This distinction draws attention to a shift from places that are integral to establishing a city's identity for the foreign visitor, to locations that form a part of the every day; sites that are mundanely local.

In *Chungking Express* and *Fallen Angels,* Hong Kong's everyday locations are not only presented as environmental settings for film scenes, but also possess great significance to the film narrative. In most scenes, the locations are highlighted through establishing shots that focus on the title of the site or its exterior facade, thereby emphasising the importance of where the

scene occurs. Eschewing postcard perspectives of Hong Kong, both films utilise MTR stations, Circle K (OK) convenience stores, underground bars, fast food and takeout sites, the interiors of hotels and streetscapes to establish place. Moreover, the integration of everyday sites into the film medium moves beyond photographic representations of architecture to reveal the intricacies of lived space. In this regard *Chungking Express* and *Fallen Angels* collectively produce a portrait of how the city is navigated in day-to-day practice, and not merely for the purposes of promotion or place branding. Significantly, Wong consciously inserts these seemingly banal and non-descript spaces into his films, places that were on the cusp of disappearance during shooting, and thus preserves them for posterity.

There are two intertwined ways of interpreting the architecture in Wong's films. First, the locations play a part in Wong's preservation project, as I have outlined: the films collate a selection of sites that form an urban, cinematic archive. Secondly, the use of specific locations aims to present a local and personal view of the city, one that eludes touristic perspectives.

On one of the few occasions where Wong does frame a well-known monument, it is a fleeting travelling shot. In the final moments of *Fallen Angels* the camera pans up from the Cross-Harbour Tunnel to offer a view of Jardine House, with its distinctive facade of porthole windows. The shot belongs to an established pattern of visual and compositional motifs that run through both *Chungking Express* and *Fallen Angels,* where skyscrapers are always filmed from a low camera angle. Using devices such as this, Wong consistently puts forward a subterranean perspective, drawing focus away from the buildings that have come to define Hong Kong as a technologically advanced global city, instead focusing on tenement housing and locations that are commonplace in Hong Kong's urban geography. In Wong's cinema, these are the spaces that are truly representative of life in the city. Indeed, the key location in both films is Chunking Mansions, a tired and antiquated building complex in Tsim Sha Tsui. The building features retail businesses, residential apartments and cheap temporary accommodation, and is best known, in an almost mythic sense, for its illegal housing of immigrants from South Asia and Africa and as a minor crime hub. Although Wong's films have altered the perception of Chungking Mansions and rather ironically transformed the site into a must-see location for Hong Kong film fans and intrepid travellers, in the mid-1990s Chungking Mansions was not a tourist attraction that the Hong Kong Tourism Board were particularly interested in transmitting to a global audience. In this sense, the city perspectives in both

Chungking Express and *Fallen Angels* can be viewed as an alternative urban and architectural history of Hong Kong, existing on the margins of authorised records – a visual mediation of a fading architectural history.

Further, the settings in both *Chungking Express* and *Fallen Angels* are not those that would generally be privileged with inclusion on an official map, and call to mind Marc Augé's concept of a 'non-place'; that is, 'a space which cannot be defined as relational, historical and concerned with identity'.[20] Unlike places that are tied to community, non-places – such as hotels, railway stations and shopping centres – are 'transit points and temporary abodes' that forge a new relationship with space, described by Augé as 'solitary contractuality'.[21]

By filming sites with seemingly little historical or cultural significance, Wong situates his understanding of geography in a state of flux, fluidity and displacement. In so doing, his films expose a web of memory that draws together past and present architecture from Hong Kong's urban landscape and juxtaposes it with the private memories of the film's characters. The locations in *Chungking Express* and *Fallen Angels* are architectural metaphors for the fleeting encounters that take place between the characters and the subtle socio-historical anxieties felt by Hong Kong residents on the eve of the handover. Looking at Wong's films in retrospect, we can see that they have been crucial to theming the passing of time by capturing old buildings that have subsequently disappeared from Hong Kong's cityscape. The viewer is left with the impression that, despite the appearance of supposedly generic locations and non-descript scenery, Wong has actively constructed a form of urban palimpsest. Buried beneath the surface that is commonly portrayed in tourist representations are the layers of memory and architectural history that might be forgotten if not captured on film.

As Abbas proposes in his work on the visual representation of Hong Kong, the 'fascination of … non-places is that they are like the city's reverse image, its negative

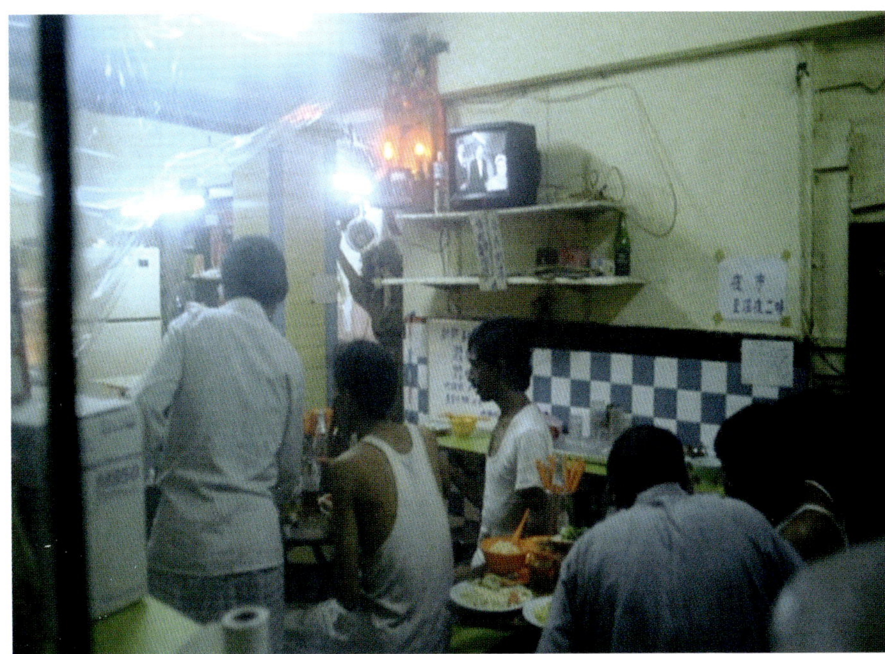

Beyond the skyscraper into the every day: capturing Chungking Mansions in *Chungking Express*. Image used with permission, courtesy and copyright of Jet Tone Productions.

representation'.[22] This negative representation that records the flip-side of the touristic Hong Kong is not only present in the filming of locations that would normally go unnoticed, but also in the investment of these locations with socio-historical import. The architectural narratives of *Chungking Express* and *Fallen Angels* take the filmmaker's central role of storyteller, and reconfigure it to that of urban archivist. In many ways Wong's preservationist approach signals a return to the late 19th century, when the film camera was perceived as 'a sort of memory machine par excellence, which would capture, register, and preserve forever great historical events and the passing moments of the present'.[23] Through shifting away from views of impressive architectural structures, such as the Bank of China or the International Finance Centre, or shots of the now clichéd image of an ancient junk floating on Victoria Harbour, Wong's films suggest that non-places, the subterranean and decrepit structures of the city's urban margins, are the spaces where private memories dwell and intimate histories are made. Wong's films safeguard old buildings by rendering them forever cinematic.

1   Giuliana Bruno, *Atlas of Emotion: Journeys in Art, Architecture, and Film*, London and New York: Verso, 2002, 8-9.

2   Mark Lamster (ed.), 'Introduction', in *Architecture and Film*, New York: Princeton Architectural Press, 2000, 1-2.

3   See Laurent Tirard, *Moviemakers' Master Class: Private Lessons from the World's Foremost Directors*, New York: Faber and Faber, 2002, 197.

4   Mitchell Schwarzer, *Zoomscape: Architecture in Motion and Media*, New York: Princeton Architectural Press, 2004, 230.

5   See Peter Brunette, *Wong Kar-wai*, Urbana and Chicago: University of Illinois Press, 2005, 116. In a 1995 interview with Brunette, Wong revealed his working methodology for *Chungking Express* that was replicated in *Fallen Angels*: 'I sat in the coffee shop writing during the day, and then shooting at night. We didn't have any permits, we didn't have any setups, we just went to places we already knew well. We worked like hell, like thieves, and it was fun. So the working style already dominated the look of the film.'

6   Ackbar Abbas, 'Re-cognising the city', in Anna Koor (ed.), *Mapping Hong Kong*, Hong Kong: Map Book, 2000, 9.

7   Wong quoted in Brunette, *Wong Kar-wai*, 118.

8   Wong quoted in Jimmy Ngai, 'A Dialogue with Wong Kar-wai: Cutting between Time and Space', in Danièle Rivière (ed.), *Wong Kar-wai*, Paris: Dis Voir, 1997, 88.

9   For a list of declared monuments in Hong Kong, see Antiquities and Monuments Office, 'Declared Monuments in Hong Kong', *GovHK Leisure and Cultural Services Department*, http://www.amo.gov.hk/en/monuments.php_(accessed 9 October 2010). See also Ackbar Abbas, 'Cosmopolitan De-scriptions: Shanghai and Hong Kong', *Public Culture*, no. 12.3 (2000): 769-786. In this article, Abbas examines cosmopolitanism in both Shanghai and Hong Kong and briefly looks at the 'ad hoc' process of urban preservation in Hong Kong.

10 Tony Rayns, Audio Commentary, *Chungking Express* (1994), Criterion Collection, 2008.

11 Peter Cookson Smith, *The Urban Design of Impermanence: Streets, Places and Spaces in Hong Kong*, Hong Kong: MCCM Creations, 2006, 190. Cookson Smith writes that in 2006 only 28 licensed *dai pai dongs* were operating in Hong Kong. At that time, the Hong Kong Government desired to close them down permanently; however, this does not appear to have come to fruition.

12 Wong quoted in Michelle Huang, *Walking between slums and skyscrapers: Illusions of open space in Hong Kong, Tokyo and Shanghai*, Hong Kong: Hong Kong University Press, 2004, 50.

13 Olaf Möller, 'Chungking Express', in Jürgen Müller (ed.), *Movies of the 90s*, Köln: Taschen, 2001, 209. According to art director and editor William Chang, 'The scenes in *Chungking Express* […] are set in places that he [Wong Kar-wai] himself frequents, such as the 'Midnight-Express' Fast-Food Stand in the Lan Kwai Fong district.'

14 See Ackbar Abbas, *Hong Kong: Culture and the Politics of Disappearance*, Minneapolis: University of Minnesota Press, 1997, 54; Huang, *Walking between slums and skyscrapers*, 51;

Leung Ping-kwan, 'Urban Cinema and the Cultural Identity of Hong Kong', in Poshek Fu and David Desser (eds), *The Cinema of Hong Kong: History, Arts, Identity*, Cambridge, UK and New York: Cambridge University Press, 2000, 246; Lisa Odham Stokes and Michael Hoover, *City on Fire: Hong Kong Cinema*, London: Verso, 1999, 193-194; Jeremy Tambling, *Wong Kar-wai's Happy Together*, Hong Kong: Hong Kong University Press, 2003, 16; and Janice Tong, 'Chungking Express: Time and its Displacements', in Chris Berry (ed.), *Chinese Films in Focus: 25 New Takes*, London: BFI, 2003, 49.

15 Stokes and Hoover, *City on Fire*, 194.

16 Abbas, *Hong Kong*, 7.

17 Abbas, *Hong Kong*, 77.

18 Smith, *The Urban Design of Impermanence*, 23. For further in-depth critical discussion of the role of architecture in Hong Kong see Ackbar Abbas, 'Building Hong Kong: From Migrancy to Disappearance', in Stephen Cairns (ed.), *Drifting: Architecture and Migrancy*, London and New York: Routledge, 2004, 129-141; Lisa Law, 'Defying Disappearance: Cosmopolitan Public Spaces in Hong Kong', *Urban Studies* 39.9 (2002): 1625-1645; and David Lung, 'Architecture', in Peter Moss (ed.) *The Heritage of Hong Kong: Its History, Architecture & Culture*, Hong Kong: FormAsia, 1999, 30-57.

19 Giuliana Bruno, *Public Intimacy: Architecture and the Visual Arts*, Cambridge, Mass.: MIT Press, 2007, 24.

20 Marc Augé, *Non-Places: Introduction to an Anthropology of Supermodernity*, trans. John Howe, London and New York: Verso, 1995, 78.

21 Augé, *Non-Places*, 78-94.

22 Ackbar Abbas, 'Dialectic of Deception', *Public Culture* 11.2 (1999): 362.

23 Matt K. Matsuda, *The Memory of the Modern*, Oxford and New York: University of Oxford Press, 1996, 13.

Remembering Home

KATARINA WADSTEIN MACLEOD

The home is a topical theme in contemporary art, with endless examples displayed at exhibitions from sweeping surveys to tightly curated themes. The idea of home seems a particularly potent territory for artists dealing with social or political issues, or the staging of psychological scenarios.

During 2010–2011, three events in Stockholm provided a good illustration of the range of current artistic work addressing this theme, as well as the tension between art that represents or examines the home, alongside the popular culture of the home. In the summer of 2010 the National Museum of Arts in Stockholm held an exhibition of art across the centuries, where the common thread was that each painted scene was set in a home or family environment. Later in the year Konsthall C, an artist-run space, hosted an exhibition of contemporary art, uncovering the political aspects of representing the home in art. Simultaneously, two of Sweden's most famous TV comedians were receiving rave reviews for their stage show 'Bright and Fresh' ('Ljust och fräscht'), an ironic and self-reflective take on the current craze of home-staging as an extension of middle class urban identity.

The ambivalent balance between the idea of the home and homemaking as, on the one hand, repressive, and on the other, liberating, as identified by feminist philosopher, Iris Marion Young, seems highly relevant in today's contemporary art and popular culture.[1] The home as a place for artistic creativity or, conversely, as a golden cage, is a long-standing distinction. There is a fine line, sometimes indiscernible, between portraits of family life, scenes set in a home, and representations of the home as an idea, which is important in itself. The idea of the home is essential to architecture, as well as of pressing importance in today's popular culture, global society and political climate, all of which resonates in contemporary art. In her 2011 book *Contemporary Art and the Cosmopolitan Imagination,* Marsha Meskimmon explores how 'being at home' is an experience relating to globalisation and geographical belonging, and which is formative to identity.[2] Jane Rendell points out that although art and architecture tend to be defined separately, they also intersect: 'Unlike architecture, art may not be functional in traditional terms, for example in responding to social needs, giving shelter when it rains or providing a room in which to perform open-heart surgery, but we could say that art is functional in providing certain kinds of tools for self-reflection, critical thinking and social change.'[3]

Installation art is in some ways similar to architecture, requiring weight-bearing structures and engineering techniques. Rendell points to how art can be a critique of architecture, or at least a critical counterpart. Installation pieces may look like architecture, because they are spatial, material and even inhabitable. To a degree they are easy to consider in relation to architecture, but they are built for fundamentally different purposes. One could argue that certain installation art emphasises social, emotional, atmospheric and symbolic aspects – elements that seem to elude discussion in the rational, aesthetic or pragmatic terms, which often characterise architectural discourse.

In this article I will examine works of art that emphasise immaterial aspects of the tension between 'house' and 'home', where the other common denominator is remembering. The art I will address is that which I have encountered in my own home cities: London and Stockholm. Through the notion of memory I explore how installation work by Gregor Schneider, Michael Landy and Meta Isæus-Berlin use the idea of home to visualise horror, mourning and reverie.

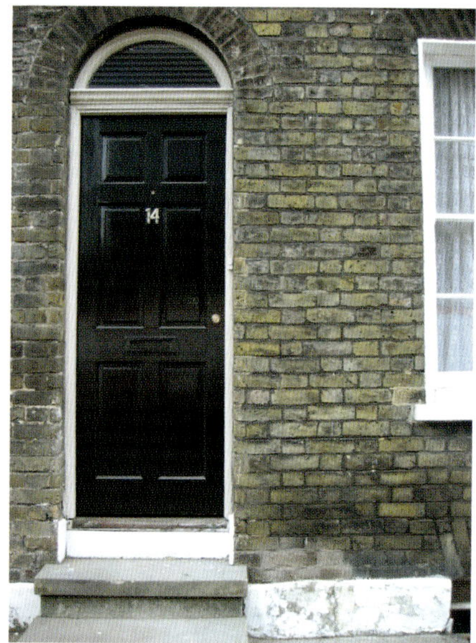

Gregor Schneider, *Die Familie Schneider,* 2004, an Artangel commission. Photograph courtesy Artangel.

Forgetting

In 2004 the German artist Gregor Schneider was invited by the organisation Artangel in London to do a project in the East End – an area with a particularly interesting history as home to successive generations of immigrant groups. Schneider's project, *Die Familie Schneider,* inverted the idea of home as a mnemonic device, playing with intricate webs of illusive memories. Schneider had previously become known for reworking his own family home in the German city of Rheydt, in a project titled *Haus u r.* Rebuilding the house again and again until it became a labyrinth of passageways, soundproof rooms, small dark corridors, trapdoors and dead ends, he exhibited parts of the house around the world.[4]

For the Artangel project Schneider entered someone else's home. Two identical, neighbouring Victorian terraced houses at 14 and 16 Wilton Road were, for a few weeks, inhabited by Schneider's refurbishments and animated by sets of twin actors. This was not an open project that you could walk into at your own leisure. If lucky, pairs of attendees were granted a precious time slot of 20 minutes, handed a key and given 10 minutes in each house. Like *House u r*, Schneider had built and rebuilt the interior, but this time in a more subtle way. It was not visible to the uninformed eye, for example, that the artist had lowered the ceilings, enhancing the effect of creeping discomfort.

Entering each of the two houses alone also meant an uncertainty over whether the viewer shared the same experience with someone else. At my own leisure I could open the fridge or walk around the house while the actors continued their staged activities: a woman endlessly doing the washing up, a child-sized body, placed in a bin bag

Gregor Schneider, *Die Familie Schneider*, 2004, an Artangel commission. Photograph courtesy Artangel.

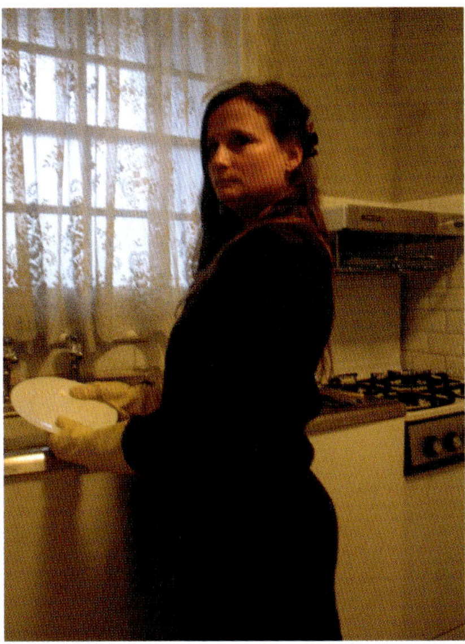

with legs sticking out, was hauntingly moving every now and again; a man masturbating in the shower as if my presence made no difference. I don't know what was most shocking, the actors' ability to completely ignore me, or the private theatrical performance that I was granted. Ten minutes later and time was up, what I'd seen stayed in my memory and nowhere else, no pictures were allowed. It was time to swap keys.[5]

Entering the next house an identical scenario was played out, the actors inhabiting the various roles were all twins, their actions and movements the same. Or were they? Did I actually remember everything I saw and didn't see? Was it a baby's cry from the basement, did I count correctly the number of cigarette butts in the ashtray, the food in the fridge? What on earth had I experienced?

Earlier, in relation to Schneider's exhibit for the German Pavilion at the Venice Biennale in 2001, Elisabeth Bronfen had pointed out the relevance of Freud's concept of the uncanny.[6] In one of his few essays on aesthetics Freud famously interpreted the concept of the 'unheimlich' – the uncanny or unhomely, in its English translation. Both the German heimlich and the English homely are derived from the notion of 'home'. Freud finds that the words homely and unhomely have ambiguous meanings. Heimlich is something known, something familiar and, in its other meaning, also something secret. Unheimlich is unknown, unfamiliar, and its other meaning refers to the moment when what is secret is revealed, uncovered. In Freud's interpretation the unhomely reveals what is private and hidden both from others and from the self. The term rests on the understanding that what is familiar, what we take for granted, is closely related to the idea of the home. The uncanny occurs when the homely is disturbed, and Schneider's project fits within a history of houses where domestic tranquillity has been unsettled.[7] In tracing the uncanny in representations of architecture, Anthony Vidler shows the importance of the haunted house since the early 19th century.[8]

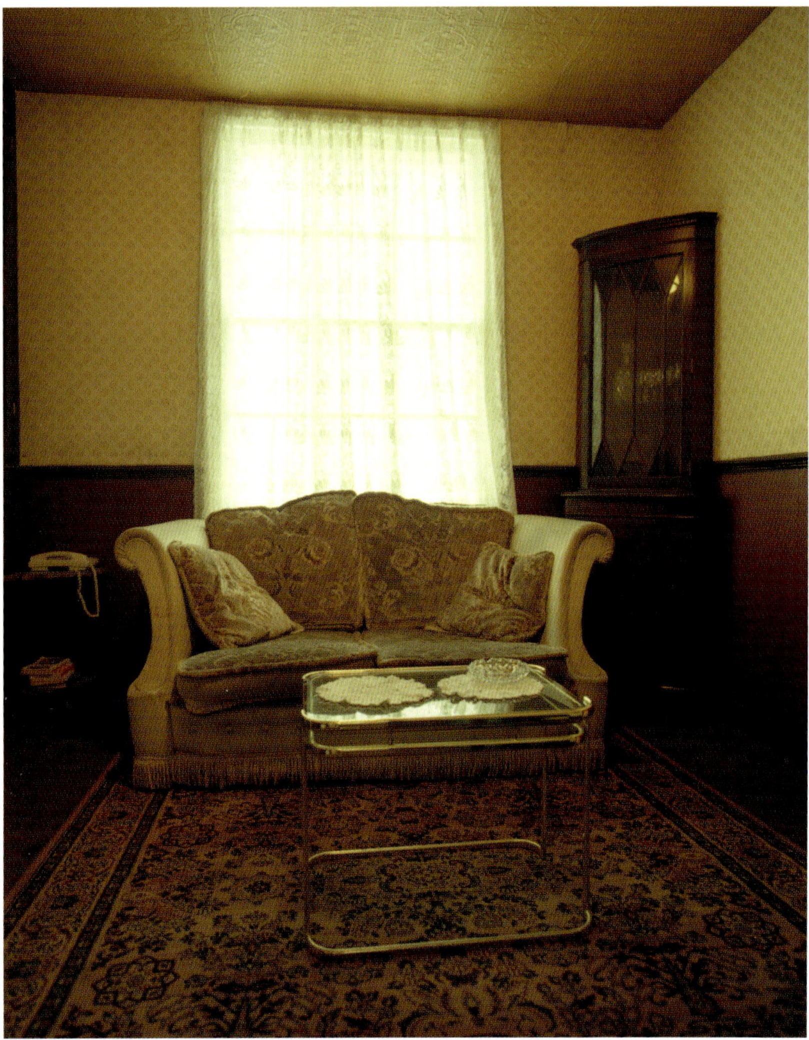

Gregor Schneider, *Die Familie Schneider*, 2004, an Artangel commission. Photograph courtesy Artangel.

For the German Pavilion, Schneider transported and rebuilt the interior of his two-storey house in Rheydt. The first *House u r* was an ongoing, organic project never finished and never fully explored by anyone but the artist. There is a clear echo of Kurt Schwitters's *Merzbau*, his never finished, and later destroyed, home turned into an art project.[9] For the exhibition in Venice, Schneider added the prefix 'dead' to the title: *Dead House u r*. In a statement, he declared an exhibition as something necessarily dead. 'Exhibitions are always the death of the work. We all fail in our endeavours. After the exhibition I will be alone again. Then I will go back to square one and start my work again.' The prefix 'dead' suggests that once removed from its origins, the house and the previous home become inanimate.

Through *Die Familie Schneider* project the artist makes visible the idea that we live everything twice, once in real life, and once (at least) in memory. Every time we look back, our interpretation of what really happened is likely to change, even if only marginally. The installation in the London East End houses evoked a particular memory of foul wallpaper, murky carpets, steeped in a typical English aesthetics of the past. Entering the exhibition was like taking part in a three-dimensional, life-sized memory game; a domestic claustrophobia where the staging and events were ghostlike, scary and evocative. My only recollection of the visits is my own impressions, and those of the art reviews published at the time.[10] Perhaps my own experience is no longer my own at all, but has all to do with the enthusiastic reviews following my visit.[11]

James Westcott writes with insight about how the exhibition at Walden Street was performative in its nature, and a sophisticated display of Schneider's evil sense of humour and control. Westcott aptly captures the feelings, when visiting the exhibition, of curiosity, discomfort and an irritation at being so overtly controlled. He also describes the rooms that I myself didn't have the time or audacity to explore. Behind a bookshelf in the cellar was a child's crib with a stained mattress and a recording playing out a child's scream. It is both theatrical and overwhelming, in situ as well as in hindsight. Westcott argues that the point of Schneider's installation was not what it means, or how it makes you feel, but rather a manipulation of what you feel.[12] In other words, the artist is a masterful puppeteer of memories remembered and forgotten.

In his survey of houses and the uncanny, Vidler talks about remembered houses, in which the house and the memory of a house subsume into one other.[13] The home is of course a fruitful stage on which to evoke memories, as many artists have explored; we are forever linked,

voluntarily or involuntarily, to the home. In the installation, Schneider not only constructed an experience of the uncanny; the set up of the experience, the control of every single detail made an imprint on the psyche that only became clear when revisited in memory. Yet part of what we saw is thereby also, necessarily, hidden by the unavoidable lapses of memory. As if the transgression between art and theatre in this piece was an intricate play on the deeply felt symbolism of revisiting, in memory, the family home. The installation as it exists in the memory of visitors and through the work of critics is a complex elaboration of the afterimage, as steeped in the notion of the unhomely.

Mourning

The British artist Michael Landy's piece *Semi-Detached* was exhibited at Tate Britain in London in 2004.[14] In a replica of Landy's childhood family home, all the faults of the house were carefully redone, every bit of bad DIY, every rusty nail or neglected pipe was copied.[15] This return to the home was Landy's attempt to portray his father, once a muscular miner who defined himself by his manual skills and physical abilities, but who was severely injured with a broken back after an accident at work. Involuntarily bound to the house from the age of 37, his identity, previously defined by what he could achieve and build, shifted to what he could no longer do.[16] The home is portrayed as a site of mourning: a full-scale Victorian two-storey house, built in brick, as a portrait of a man who has lost his masculinity.

The claim that domesticity has been coloured by gender, and specifically the feminine, is anything but controversial. In *The Second Sex,* Simone de Beauvoir published one of the great critiques of women's domestication. She relates how women accept the sexual division of labour: in the home women serve and support their men.[17] At least since the 19th century western bourgeois society, public and private, have been coded and divided

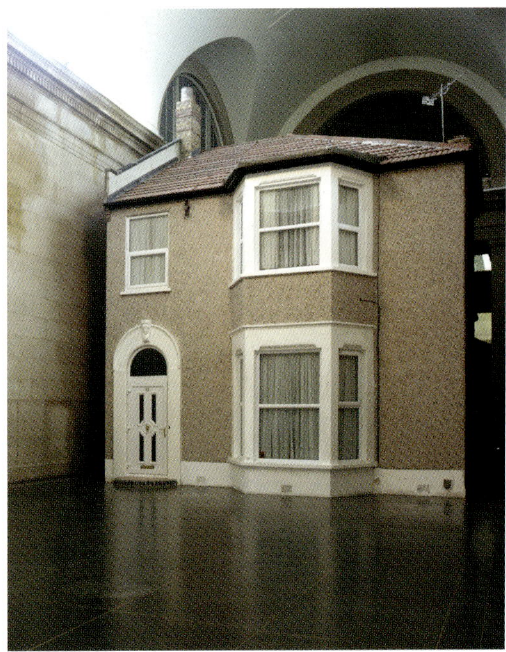

Michael Landy, installation image of *Semi-Detached* (front view), Tate Britain, 2004. © Tate, London 2012. Photograph courtesy Michael Landy and Thomas Dane Gallery.

by gender and this has been particularly evident in the house.[18] Lynne Walker points out, in her discussion of the terms house, dwelling and home, through examples drawn from throughout the modern and postmodern periods that thinking about domestic space has long been structured around gendered binary pairs.[19] Feminist critics and historians have again and again pinpointed the problem of the home for women, and especially women artists. Historically the home has been an enclosure in which wifely duties often caused the woman artist to give up her art, while conversely sometimes providing a space liberating her to pursue art, with scenes set in the home as socially suitable subject matters.[20] The philosopher Iris Marion Young explores the ambivalence of home and homemaking as a negative experience in the work

of other feminist philosophers including de Beauvoir, Luce Irigaray and Teresa de Lauretis.[21]

Landy reproduced his family home as a portrait of his father, although his mother also lived in the house, helping her disabled husband, pursuing compensation for his injuries, sourcing the right medication and also supporting the family financially. As Judith Nesbitt points out, however, her story is not told. The house is entirely a portrait of the involuntarily domesticated father. In Landy's installation the house was sectioned into two parts, where the front and the back were exact replicas of the family home in Essex. The sliced interiors were used as three large screens for projecting films. One of the films, *No. 62,* a video diary of the life of the father, traces his daily movements, from the garden, to the living room; the places where he slept, rested, smoked and sorted his medicines. *Shelf-Life* on the other hand is a slideshow of things from the father's bedroom shelf, holding everything from Vaseline to chainsaw brushes. Another film projected on the back of the facade of the pebbledash house, is a sequence of images from the father's collection of DIY manuals. The artist, and son, sees his father through the house, his 30-year captivity in a building that his disability prevented him from leaving. The home stands in for the failure, and entrapment, of a life where identity is closely bound to the ability to physically work.

It is rare that the home appears in art as a metaphor for the paternal, while the representation of the mother as the symbolic site of home and protection is much more common. In one of his passages on the return to the home of childhood as a way to remember, Gaston Bachelard quotes the 19th century poet Milosz: 'I say Mother. And my thoughts are with you, oh, House. House of the lovely dark summers of my childhood'. The house of childhood is, in this passage, related both to the mother as protective, and childhood as anything but just sunshine.[22] If we view the installation *Semi-Detached* through a historical lens, where the house has often been seen as maternal and protective, then Landy's portrait of his father through his house reinforces the sense of a loss of masculinity. After six months of exhibition, this memorialisation was itself dismantled and removed, adding yet another layer of mourning to the act of remembering.

Longing

The place we call home is charged with feelings, dreams and memories. The poet Rainer Maria Rilke wrote in *The Book of Hours: Love Poems to God* about the pain of searching for a home in a spiritual sense: 'You, the great homesickness we could never shake off, you, the forest that always surrounded us.'[23] Homesickness is in Rilke's poem a profound longing for something, and when the poet longs for home he also longs for God. In this context the home is as ephemeral as

Meta Isæus-Berlin, *I am not at Home,*
1996, 400kg playdough, wood, bulb.
Photograph courtesy KIASMA, Helsinki.

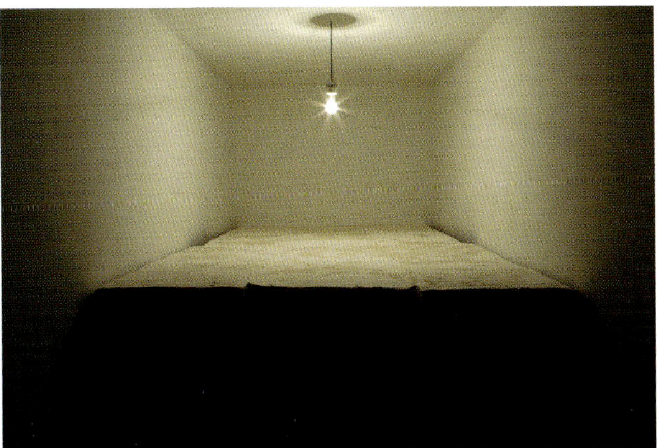

an idea, portrayed as a site of trust, or an internal space related to a belief in God. When Rilke describes 'the great homesickness we could never shake off', he implies that both home and God are impossible to fully recover, and thus are necessarily associated with a sense of loss and longing. In Rilke's poem the home becomes a metaphor for such longing and loss, as well as for love.

In 1996 the Swedish artist Meta Isæus-Berlin explored longing for home in an installation, *I am not at Home,* by experimenting with dough. In the exhibition, 400 kilograms of playdough was placed in a container in Copenhagen, Denmark and over the course of several weeks it acquired a life of its own. The material expands and contracts with heat and humidity. In the end it shrinks, dries and cracks. It is also a material firmly placed in the realm of childhood; thus, when the artist longs for home she does so materially, through dough, and practices of making and baking. If for some, playdough is linked to childhood – either one's own or one's children – the idea of baking as an access to memory is firmly linked with a Proustian sensibility. In his epic novel *In Search of Lost Time,* Proust experienced a flashback of childhood memories the moment he sampled a Madeleine biscuit. Dipping the cookie in his tea released a flood of memories, triggered by that particular taste.[24] Isæus-Berlin's dough is without odour, unpleasant to eat and not bakeable; possibly it is a testimony to memories waiting to be processed.

In other works Isæus-Berlin has used the idea of home as a setting for stories, and explicitly linked the place of the home with memory. The 2001 installation *What Memory Selects* links us to the particular version of domesticity demonstrated in a show home. In a long row, each room of a typical house or flat was lined up after one after the other, as if in a queue. The visitor was obliged to look at the installation by walking around it, but never through it. Each room was emblematic and the structure typical; the bathroom followed the kitchen, sharing (in

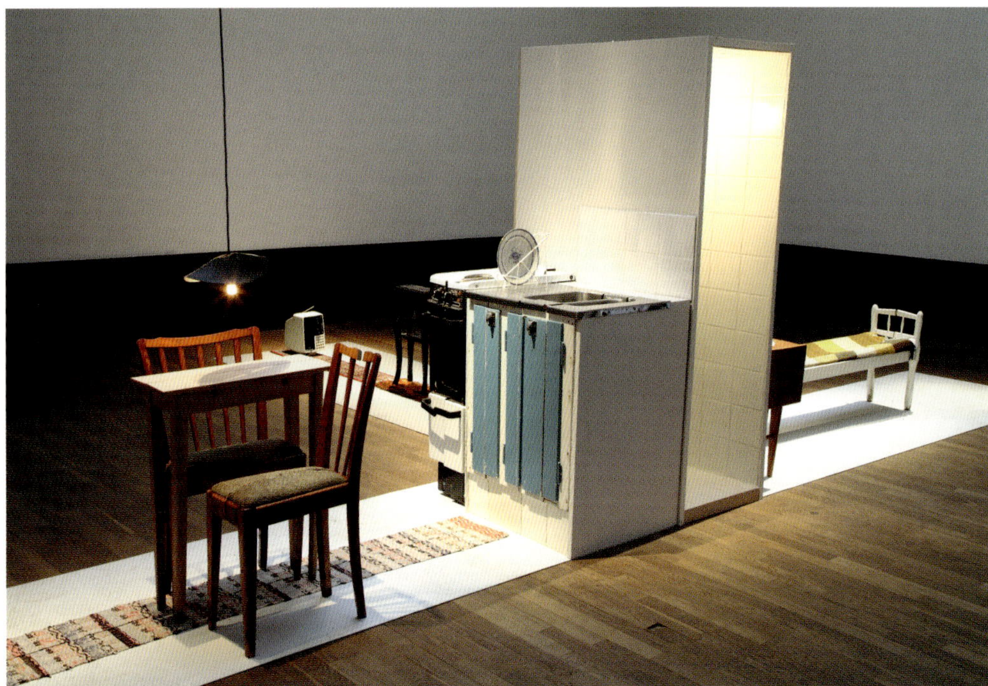

Meta Isæus-Berlin, *What Memory Selects*, 2001, wood, textile, steel, sanitary porcelain, bulb, glass. 180x400x-705cm. Photograph courtesy Norrköpings Konstmuseum.

theory) its plumbing, a bedroom led on from the bathroom. Yet the whole was uninhabitable, only symbolically related to a space we could all recognise.

The way Isæus-Berlin explores the propensities of materials such as water, paint, furniture or textiles can be linked to the work of architecture theorist, Frederick Kiesler. Kiesler described his visionary *Endless House* as a human body with organs. The stairs should be understood as its feet, the ventilation system its nose, a house could even have a digestion system that suffers from constipation. The model of the never realised *Endless House* reveals an organic bulbous structure. Together, image and text suggest the body of the house as a metaphor, perhaps even extension, of the human

body inhabiting it. This is a far cry from Le Corbusier's vision of the house as a machine for living.[25] As much as the psyche cannot be separated from the body, in Kiesler's vision psyche and architecture are inseparable: the material conditions of a house are related to the physical and psychological pleasure experienced in it. The materials of a building and the feeling that these evoke are of course strongly interdependent. Beatriz Colomina discusses Kiesler's concept of 'psycho-function': in which the 'material condition of a building and its mechanical operations' become a form of sensuality, a psychological pleasure.[26] Isæus-Berlin, in turn, uses furniture or room structures to evoke memories. The idea of home is conflated with materials and memories into a similar kind

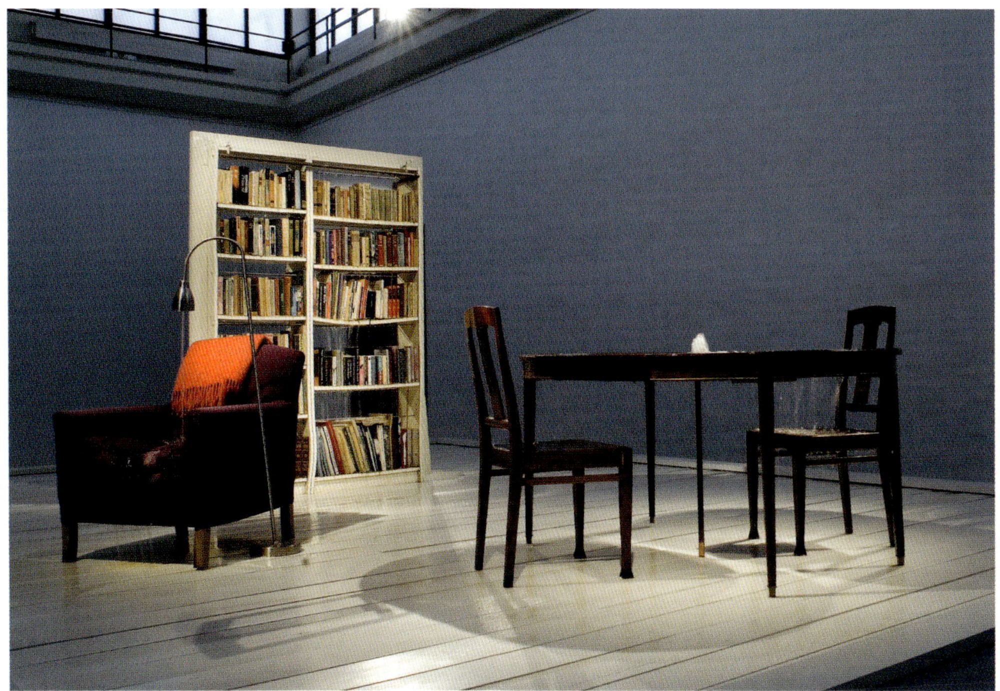

Meta Isæus-Berlin, *I Forgive Nothing*, 2006, water, pumps, paper, wood, textiles, steel. 500x600x310cm. Photograph courtesy Galleri Andersson/ Sandström.

of psycho-function, triggering our psychological, as well as our bodily memories.

The home environment is dependent on the architecture housing it, yet the way that we experience the home is influenced by the objects inhabiting the space, which both Kiesler's projects and Isæus-Berlin's installations make clear. Colomina gives a warning: not to confuse the study of architecture with the study of design objects. Yet, in Isæus-Berlin's work it is precisely the objects, the things that we use for our everyday life, the objects that delineate the space we inhabit, that become so strongly evocative of the symbolic, psychic meanings of the home.

In Isæus-Berlin's *What Memory Selects,* for example, we see a room that is recognisably a bedroom, but which is distorted by a series of cuts. Parts have been removed from the bed, the nightstand, mirror or rug, only to be reassembled again. We have no difficulty recognising the objects but they are of no practical use. The effect of the furniture is inscribed in our bodily memory, the moment we see them we might remember the comfort of our beds, yet in the same instant we also sense being foreshortened, cut apart, even castrated. We are left with fragments pasted together, an end product reflecting our necessarily fragmented memories.[27] The sliced toilet seat for example seems to mock us in its impossibility. It looks ridiculous, and makes us look even more ridiculous, linking the cropped sanitary unit to a failure to carry out our basic needs. In Isæus-Berlin's installation, we see a representation of a home environment that we also understand immediately through a projected physical encounter; the gravity and sadness of her installations cannot fully obscure the comical touch of the fractured lavatory.

In *The Poetics of Space,* Gaston Bachelard's philosophy of daydreaming made possible through the memory of the childhood house, he ascribes significance to the singular objects of the household: 'Wardrobes with their shelves, desks with their drawers, and chests with their false bottoms are veritable organs of the secret psychological life.'[28] Bachelard suggests an alternative space, a 'felicitous space', distinct from the public domestic conflict inherited from bourgeois society and renegotiated by modernist or rationalist architecture.[29] Bachelard's phenomenological account of accessing the deepest layers of the psyche through a return to the childhood home has complications. Several of his critics have pointed out for example the hetero-normativity of his idea of the home, as too firmly grounded in bourgeois culture and as a

Meta Isæus-Berlin, *Everything is Possible*, 2008, oil on canvas. 77x90cm. Photograph courtesy Baukunst Galerie.

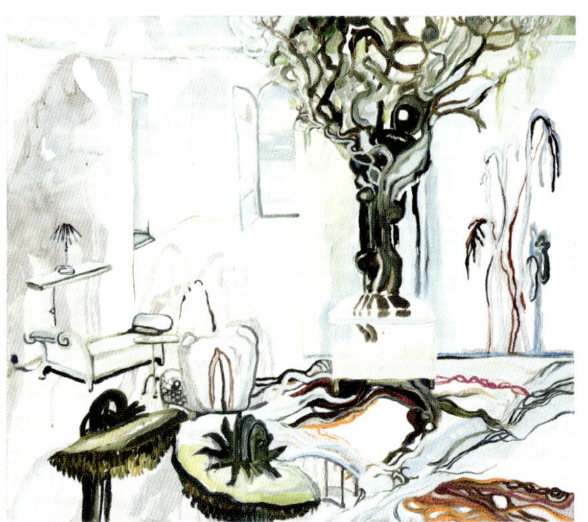

conservative reaction to urbanised society. There is also a critique of the naivety, essentialism and romanticism of his representation of domestic space. Would a woman feel that romantic in this space for reverie, when for her the domestic might be associated with around the clock labour?[30] Or indeed find the home a metaphorically safe space, having been exposed to real life domestic violence or abuse?[31] However, as a poetic text suggestive of the qualities of those nooks and crannies of a house, the potential of a metaphoric attic or cellar in Bachelard's work still has, I would argue, some resonance.[32]

In *I Forgive Nothing*, 2006 – Isæus-Berlin's last installation before the artist returned to painting – the home is represented in the manner of a theatre stage. The pedestal is slightly raised so the visitor is obliged to look up at the furniture, with the perspective of a child. We are physically forced into a dwarfing, which distorts our point of view. The fact that nothing shall ever be forgiven is emphasised through the constant stream of water flooding the furniture. Water spills over everything in a never-ending flood. A moment of hysteria perhaps, over the force majeur of personal history, of childhood trauma. The viewer is free to enter the mined land of personal or collective memory, to dwell, process, and digest without the intercession of historical facts. What then is a memory and can an artwork represent something so ephemeral as a memory? In the *Poetics of Space*, Bachelard describes how the home is something deeply intimate, something that has the capacity to house the influential memories of childhood, and therefore becomes the perfect venue for daydreams, or more precisely poetic daydreaming. If we find a way of reaching these dreams and memories, Bachelard says, we may also have a chance of understanding our own psyche.[33]

After abandoning large-scale installations and material constructions, Isæus-Berlin turned to more subtle experiments, rendering a memory of home through oil on canvas. In several paintings she worked with representing

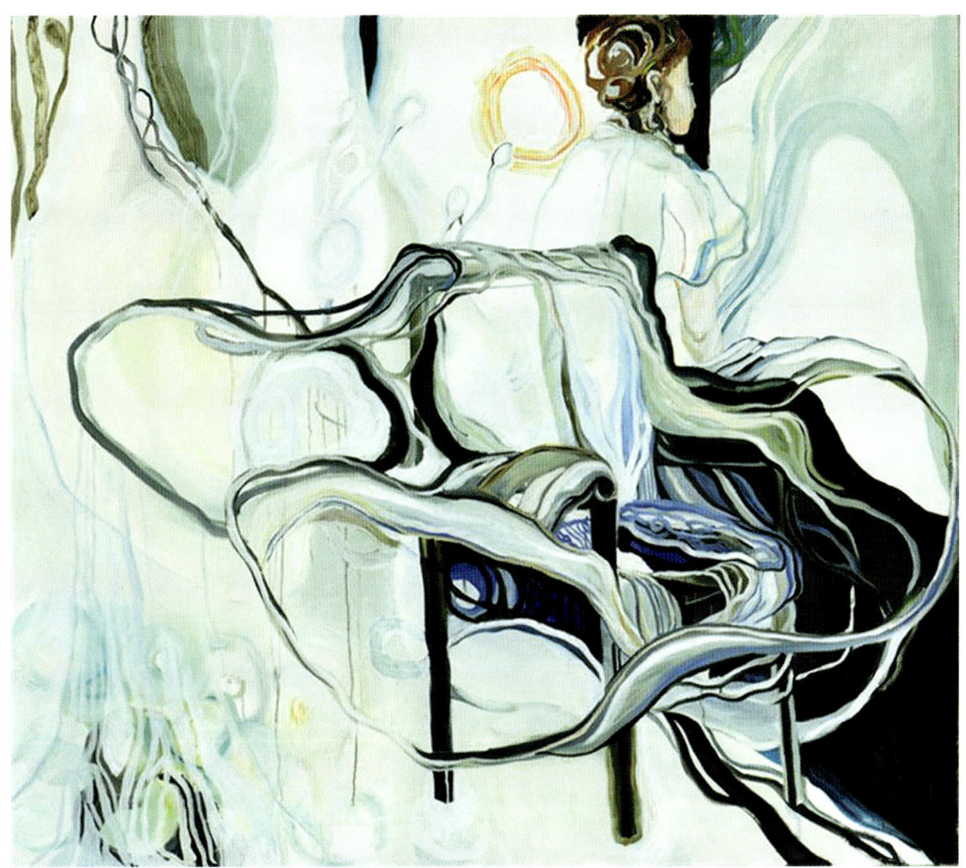

Meta Isæus-Berlin, *Below the Surface*, 2009, oil on canvas. 130x150cm. Photograph courtesy Västerbotten County.

inside and outside within the same frame, scenes from the every day that are both ordinary memories and fragments. In the painting *Everything is Possible* (2008), there is a jumble of things; a chaise-lounge, a set of drawers, a lamp, a tree, underwater plants – all placed in an interior kind of space, a place where night meets day, reverie meets reality. At the back of the painting a door leads to another space. Furniture, plants, textiles and textures are represented to be as fluid as the runny paint itself.

Other paintings, such as *Below the Surface* (2009), reads like a summary of the types of materials Isæus-Berlin has been pre-occupied with throughout her career: furniture, textiles, water, shells, plants and human bodies.

Paint is not only a material with which to paint a picture; I would argue that the paint as such underlines the visual, factual representation of something as ephemeral as memory. The creative act of painting may also be associated with the processing of something, handling something from the past, in a liberating or even cathartic act. But painting as memory may also be about the recalling of events, the preservation of memories and, not least, the creation of new memories.[34] Isæus-Berlin conflates memories and dreams with the space of the home – a visual repartee perhaps of Bachelard's philosophy of the mind. In her work the home features as an outward and inward presence, rather than a place, an oscillating stage between reality and the dreamlike.

In Schneider and Landy's installations the staged homes are very obviously related to real buildings. *Die Familie Schneider* inhabits an actual home for a limited time, subverting the house into a place of dark memories. Michael Landy, by creating a replica of his family home empties it of its function and potential to house a family. The architectural structure of these representations become more than the sum of their parts, capturing that immateriality necessarily bound to family homes. However as in Isæus-Berlin's installation, it is precisely the materiality – the furniture, or water, that throws the viewer into a kind of reverie of the past. A little like Georges Perec, who tempts us to conflate a building we can imagine, recognise or think we know, with a narrative of life, dreams, love and death. The Haussmanian apartment block in Perec's *Life: A User's Manual* is the core of a narrative constructed from lists and systems, where the author links life and memory with a specific place and its objects.[35]

The work of Schneider, Landy and Isæus-Berlin each evoke the familiar dichotomy between reality and representation in which the bricks, mortar, furniture and people are as real as they are fictional. Their installations underline the immateriality of architecture, the social and psychological factors deeply embedded in aesthetic and engineering structures. Most importantly they are evocative reminders of how the notion of home is a complex affair, strongly rooted in our memories.

1   *Home Sweet Home*, ex. cat. Gitte Orskou (ed.), Aarhus: Aarhus Kunstmuseum, 2003, brings together nine contemporary artists working with the home in a wide interpretation of the theme, from representations of families to furniture as a backdrop for a narrative. In Meskimmon *Contemporary Art and the Cosmopolitan Imagination* 2011, several of the artworks explored deal with the idea of the home as a way of belonging. In the exhibition *At Home. Scandinavian Interiors*, National Gallery Stockholm 2010, a large number of the works, historical to modernist ranging from portraits to studies of interiors were grouped under the theme of the 'home'.

2   Marsha Meskimmon, *Contemporary Art and the Cosmopolitan Imagination*, London: Routledge, 2011.

3   Jane Rendell, *Art and Architecture: A Place Between*, London: I.B. Tauris, 2010, 3-4.

4   For the *House u r se* for example, Ulrich Loock, 'The Dead House ur', *Parkett*, no 63, (2001), 138-149; for Schneider's staging of the house as a performance, see for example Philip Auslander, 'Behind the Scenes: Gregor Schneider's "Totes Haus ur"', *PAJ: A Journal of Performance and Art*, 25, no. 3 (2003), 86-90. For an extensive bibliography on Gregor Schneider, see www.gregorschneider.net/media

5   Andrew O'Hagan, 'The Living Rooms', *Gregor Schneider, The Familie Schneider*, Göttingen: Steidl, 2008, article also to be found on www.artangel.org.uk//projects/2004/die_familie_schneider/the_living_rooms_by_andrew_o_hagan/the_living_rooms_by_andrew_o_hagan (accessed 5 November 2011)

6   Elisabeth Bronfen, 'Chryptotopias. Secret Sites / Transmittable Traces' in *Gregor Schneider. Totes Haus ur*, ex. cat., La Biennale di Venezia, Ostfildern: Hatje Cantz Publishers 2001.

7   Sigmund Freud, 'The Uncanny' (1919), *Art and Literature*, vol 14, Harmondsworth: Penguin, 1985. For an extended discussion on a cultural and etymological reading of Freud's unheimlich, see Anthony Vidler, *The Architectural Uncanny: Essays in the Modern Unhomely*, Cambridge Mass.: The MIT Press, 1992, in particular 17-32.

8   Anthony Vidler, 'The Architecture of the Uncanny: The Unhomely Houses of the Romantic Sublime', *Assemblage*, no 3, (1987), 6-29.

9   For a review on the reconstruction of Schwitter's *Merzbau* see for example Cathrine Grant, 'Schwitters and Arp', *The Burlington Magazine*, 146, no. 12 (2004); for the importance of the genealogy of Kurt Schwitters for Gregor Schneider see for example Loock 'The Dead House ur', 2002, p. 141.

10   See for example James Westcott, 'Gregor Schneider and the Flattering Performance Installation', *TDR*, 49, no. 4 (2005), 183-189.

11   Adrian Serle, 'Broken Homes' *The Guardian*, 5 October 2004; Richard Dorment, 'A Very Special Kind of Fear', *The Telegraph*, 6 October 2004; Dan Fox, 'Die Familie Schneider', *Frieze*, 88, 2005, eze.com/issue/article/die_familie_schneider/ (accessed 28 oktober 2011)

12   Westcott, 'Gregor Schneider and the Flattering Performance Installation' 2005.

13   Vidler, 'The architecture of the Uncanny: The Unhomely Houses of the Romantic Sublime', 23.

14   Michael Landy, *Semi-Detached*, exhibition, Tate Britain, 18 May–12 December 2004.

15   See also for example Richard Dorment, 'Moving House', *The Telegraph*, 19 May 2004; Gordon Burn, 'Outdoors indoors', *The Guardian*, 19 May 2011.

16   Judith Nesbitt, 'Everything must go', *Michael Landy Semi-Detached*, Tate Publishing, London, 2004, 19.

17   Simone de Beauvoir, *The Second Sex*, (1949), London: Vintage, 1997.

18   See for example Beatriz Colomina (ed), *Sexuality and Space*, Princeton: Princeton Architectural Press, 1992, for the economy of gendered space see in particular Laura Mulvey, 'Pandora: Topographies of the Mask and Curiosity', and Colomina, 'The Split Wall: Domestic Voyeurism', 73-130.

19   Lynne Walker, 'Home Making: An Architectural Perspective', *Signs*, 27 no. 3 (2002), 823-835.

20   Griselda Pollock's essay is probably one of the earliest and certainly one of the most influential to point out the gender-blindness of art history writing, based on how certain themes were inaccessible to women artists. 'Modernity and the spaces of femininity', *Vision and Difference: Feminism, Femininity and the Histories of Art* (1988) London: Routledge Classics, 2003, 70-127.

21   Iris Marion Young, *Intersecting Voices: Dilemmas of Gender, Political Philosophy and Policy*, Princeton: Princeton University Press, 1997. For a comment on this book see for example Christine Di Stefano, '*Intersecting Voices: Dilemmas of Gender, Political Philosophy, and Policy*', by Iris Marion Young, *Political Theory*, 29, no. 3 (2001), 469-478

22   Gaston Bachelard, *The Poetics of Space*, (1958), Boston: Beacon Press books, 1994, 45. For an account of homemaking and decoration as something feminine, which is largely disregarded within modernist architecture theory, furthermore of making and building as a masculine enterprise, and the family home as a vehicle to portray traditional family values, see further in Walker, 'Home Making: An Architectural Perspective', 2002.

23   Rainer Maria Rilke, *Book of Hours Love Poem to God*, New York: Riverhead, 1996, 70.

24   Marcel Proust's *Swans Way* (1913), London: Penguin Books, 2000, is spun around the two memories of tasting the Madeleine and stepping on a particular paving stone. See also for example, Dana Bettman, 'Marcel Proust Explains Himself', *The Sewanee Review*, 40, no 32, (1932), 129-140. For the ritual of drinking tea as a covert reference to homosexuality in French see Jarrod Hayes, 'Proust in the Tearoom', *PMLA*, 110, no 95, (1995), 992-1005.

25   Le Corbusier, *Towards a new Architecture*, (1923) transl. Frederick Etchells, The Architectural press, New York, 1965.

26   Beatriz Colomina, 'Space House', Iain Borden and Jane Rendell, *Intersections: Architectural Histories and Critical Theories, Routledge*, London 2000, 57.

27   For a visualisation of memory as necessarily fragmented, see for example Chris Marker, *La Jetée*, 1962.

28   Gaston Bachelard, *The Poetics of Space*, (1958), Beacon Press books, Boston, 1994, 78.

29   Ken Worpole, 'Book Of A Lifetime: *The Poetics of Space, By Gaston Bachelard,*' *The Independent*, 29/4 2009.

30   Sharon Haar and Christopher Reed, in Christohper Reed (ed), *Not at Home: The Suppression of Domesticity in Modern Art and Architecture*, London: Thames and Hudson, 257-258.

31   Joshua M. Price, 'The Apotheosis of Home and the Maintenance of Spaces of Violence, *Hypatia*, 17, no. 4, (2002), 39-70.

32   Joan Ockman, 'The poetics of Space', *Harvard Design Magazine*, no 6 (1998), 1-4, for a suggestion that Bachelard's idea of the generic house is best read in relation to artistic and experimental texts.

33   Bachelard, *The Poetics of Space*, 17-36.

34   Katarina Wadstein MacLeod, *Lena Cronqvist, Reflections of Girls*, Malmö: Sekel, 2006, 117-146.

35   Georges Perec, *Life: A User's Manual*, (1978) London: Vintage Books, 2008.

Remembering in Red:
Architectural followings

CATHY SMITH

If, for Gilles Deleuze and Felix Guattari, architecture can be conceived as 'the art of the abode and the territory',[1] then how might this art, this territory, be understood as emerging from an artisanal following of forces and flows? The present text explores the interaction of material flows and intensities at Avebury Street: a project and building, distinct from conventional architectural practice due to the spontaneity of its various constructions, and the lack of architectural drawings. Avebury Street was a decade-long experiment conducted through the occupation and continuous material alteration of a dilapidated house.

Although I have critiqued and analysed Avebury Street in other research contexts, here I focus on flows of matter, artisanal procedures and, in particular, on the 'following'

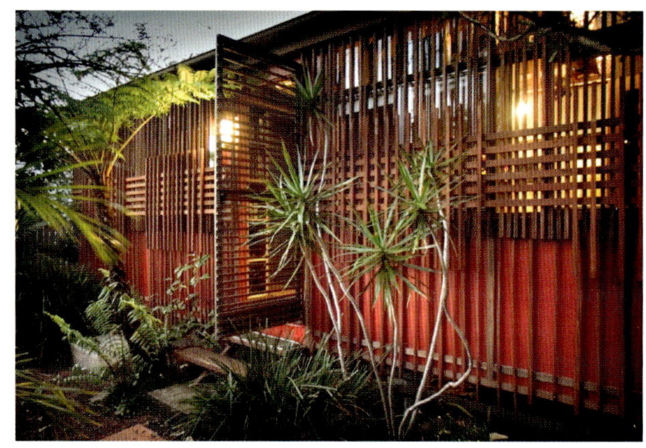

Avebury Street. Photograph Graham Meltzer.

of materials, bodily fluids and neighbourhood. To prompt such considerations, I turn to two notions: that of the artisan, and that of matter-flows, each of which are invoked by philosopher Gilles Deleuze and his collaborator, psychoanalyst Felix Guattari, in their collaborative text *A Thousand Plateaus: Capitalism and Schizophrenia.* Their conception of the artisan suggests a particular way of intuitively engaging, and working with, the flows of materials (organic and inorganic) encountered in real-life sites. This artisanal way of working resonates with the processes and procedures involved in Avebury Street's transformations from the year 1998 – when we initially rented the house, prior to purchasing it from the original owner – to 2010, when we sold it.

Avebury Street was also labelled the Red House by a photographer, because of its colour and also, the photographer's association of the project with another house in England.[2] Avebury Street was made, remade, and in the end, departed from in the manner of Jane Rendell's '[d]oing it, then (un)doing it and finally (over)doing it …'[3] Layers of chipboard and stained carpet were removed, items repaired, walls demolished and rebuilt, functions relocated and reinstated. It was a container for lives, an envelope that was breached and remade along with the bodies that inhabited it. Materials, food, thought, bodies, IKEA furniture, all matter reconfigured in an everyday experiment.

Deleuze and Guattari give a specific definition of the artisan 'as one who is determined in such a way as to follow a flow of matter.'[4] For them, the artisan is distinguished by this characteristic: of following and attending to materials during their various incarnations and transformations. They argue that the artisanal mode 'is no longer a question of imposing a form upon a matter but of elaborating an

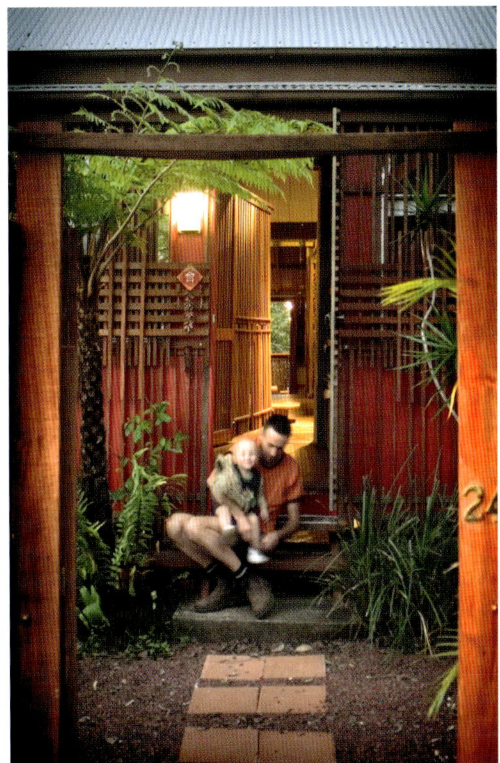

Photograph Graham Meltzer.

increasingly rich and consistent material, the better to tap increasingly intense forces'.[5] This is distinct from other more customary definitions of an artisan, which relate to their status, skill level or expertise. Deleuze and Guattari's definition is used here to invoke the sense of dynamism and indeterminacy associated with Avebury Street.

Avebury Street was always a transitory space, richly in flux. Prior to our inhabitation, it had been a long-standing student household for local design students, who also

(Right, opposite, and overleaf)
The transforming interior,
evolutions of the loft and stair.
Photographs Cathy Smith and
Graham Meltzer.

passed through and beyond its boundaries as a part of
a network of places with cheap rent, staying only long
enough to complete the last assignment. A sense of
flow extends to the site's geographical location. Located
opposite the Brisbane River, the site invokes a sense of
the riparian and the tidal, particularly in light of the
2011 floods that engulfed the backyard.

Other aspects of the site are similarly mobile:
although the property is now in Queensland, it was
originally in New South Wales. In 1851 the title deed
extracted territory from a colonised earth, when 'our
Trusty and Well-beloved Sir Charles Augustus Fitz Roy'
first declared it official land in 'Our Territory of New
South Wales'. Even in the 1930s, after it was already
declared Queensland territory, Avebury Street went by a
different street name: Orleigh Terrace. The surrounding
suburb is similarly fluid, known both as Hill End and
also West End, via the same postcode. A 1990s site
survey declared the property boundaries at odds with
the street grid, an elusive 300mm or so swallowed up
by the neighbours' fences. Even the building itself is
of murky provenance. A former long-term resident of
Avebury Street passed on a myth about the house's watery
birth: that the house was floated on a barge across the
river from the cane fields formerly in St Lucia (now the
University of Queensland). It then became the house of
the ferryman (so legend goes), the one who transported
cane workers back to the fields across the river. The house
belongs to neither one site nor another, but in Deleuze
and Guattari's terms, might be understood as having 'a
vague identity between the two'.[6]

❧

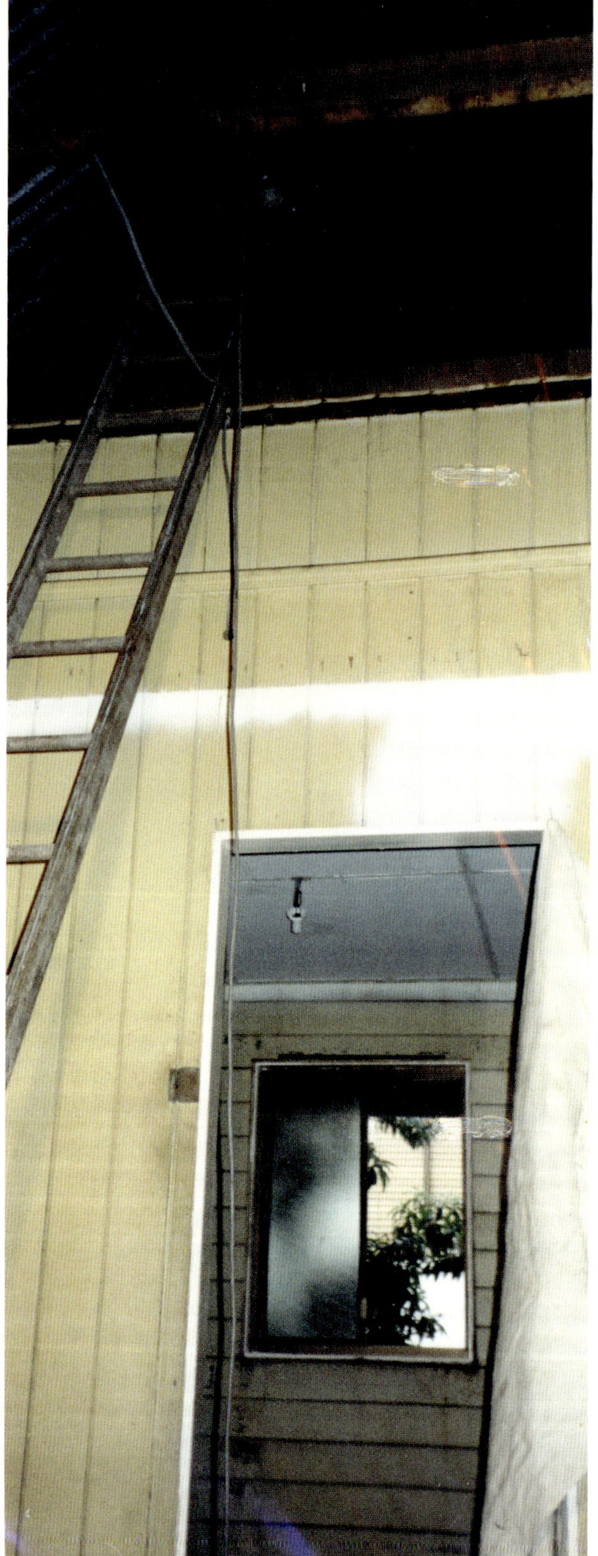

In *A Thousand Plateaus*, during artisanal procedures, materials are encountered in a dynamic state of transformation. This sense of dynamism arises because materials are assumed to exist in a state of flow when they are being 'worked' in the artisanal mode; and because their transformation occurs as part of a series of shifting interactions, between not only 'raw' matter, but makers, tools, project workshops and so forth.[7] For Deleuze and Guattari, artisans are intuits, 'prospectors',[8] coaxing material transformations by working with the self-organisational capacities of wood, clay, metals.[9] Artisans are not simply craftspeople, or labourers, but must always be engaged in a following of some kind of flow.[10] While Deleuze and Guattari suggest woodworkers and metallurgists as examples of artisans in *A Thousand Plateaus*, one could argue that architects could also be artisanal, if they were primarily determined 'to follow a flow of matter'.[11]

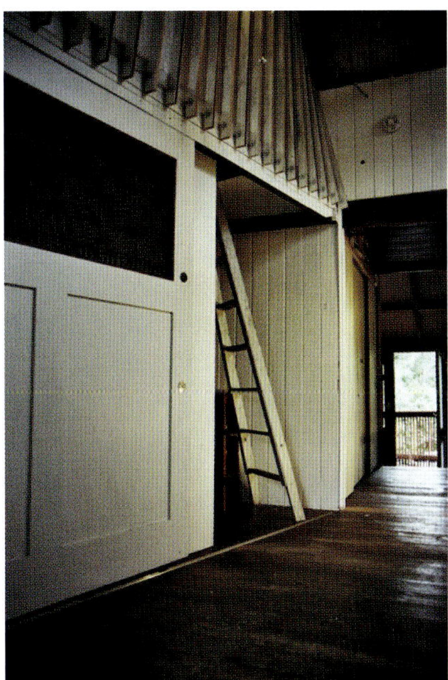

❧

When we first occupied Avebury Street, the building's interiors were configured of layers of cheap vinyl and painted chipboard. As occupants, we looked beneath these layers, peeling away the rental lives, uncovering the termites and the antique mud, the riparian lines of the 1974 Brisbane floods inscribing the underside of the floorboards. Thought and matter intertwined, and as such, alterations and interventions to the interiors, gardens and building envelope were often discarded, dismantled and rebirthed in somewhat spontaneous configurations. First, the old wall and ceiling linings were stripped to their core of timber stud and VJ (a local Queensland acronym standing for vertically jointed tongue and groove timber). Drawings were largely unnecessary as the hands that designed also made, and those same bodies also occupied the resultant space. Then windows, doors and claddings were replaced and refinished, eroding the solidity of the containing envelope. A native garden, planted in the 1990s between a student's landscape assignments,[12] grew and began to starve the grass of sun, but also to shade the house's occupants and provide new orientations for the interiors. The building shell could then be opened to its trees, fibro stripped and replaced with transparent and translucent plastic skins. Garden stake battens were layered in-situ over the building skins with the nail gun, seeking experimental and transitory affects.

❧

Deleuze and Guattari note that artisans are material prospectors: that 'artisans are obliged to follow in another way as well, in other words, to go find the wood where it lies, and to find the wood with the right kind of fibres.'[13] Avebury Street was composed of matter always found or specifically searched out, although sometimes delivered. A door from the old Nestle Chocolate Factory in Fortitude Valley was cast aside from an architectural project in 1998:

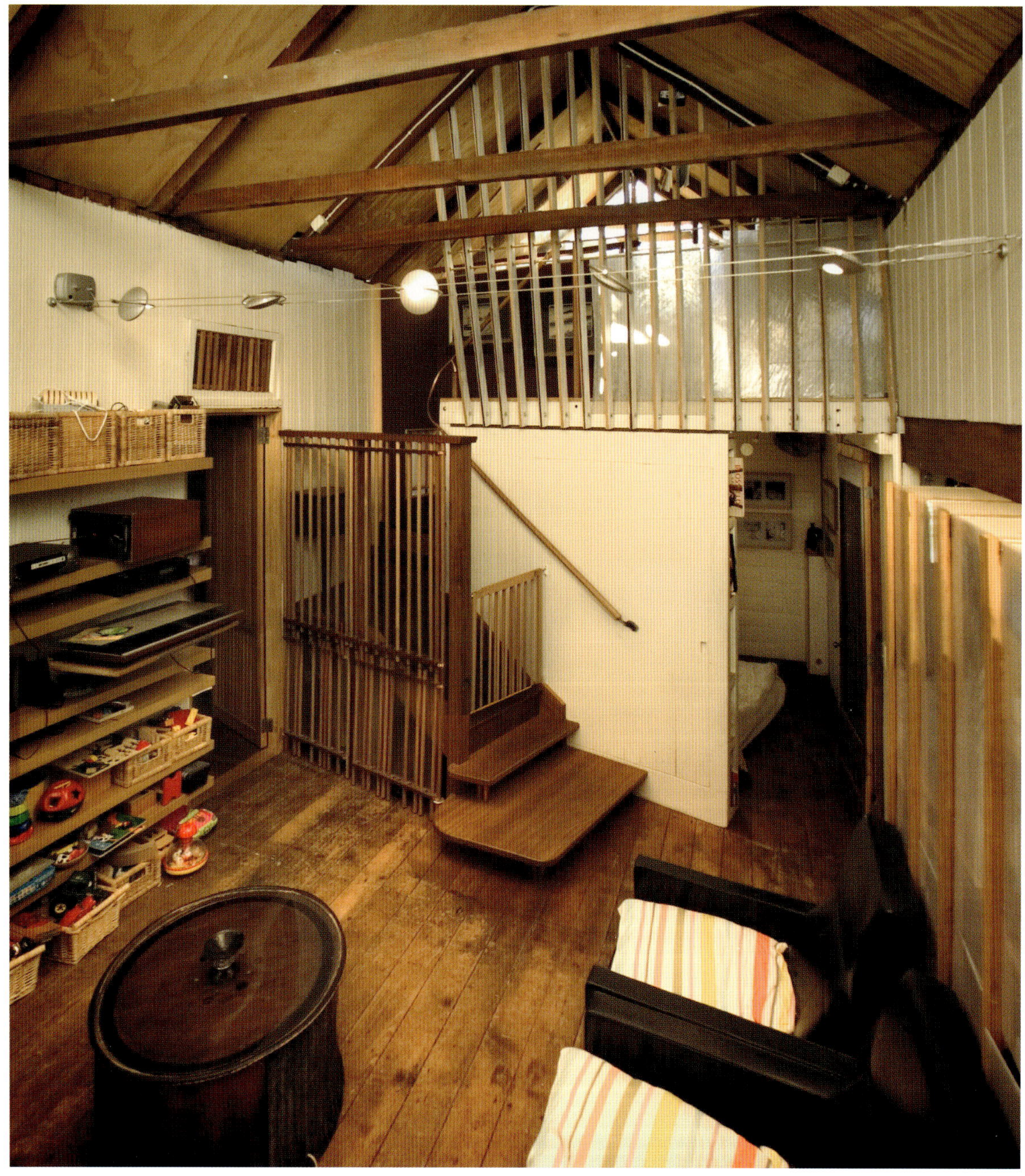

it arrived one night on top of the roof racks of the work four-wheel-drive, and later became a party table, a sliding door and finally, a fixed bedroom partition. Materials were also 'discovered' within the house itself, such as the old VJ pine ripped from the original, concealed ceiling, which was cut and reconfigured into a loft balustrade. Even the loft space itself was discovered hiding amongst the many ceiling layers, waiting to be occupied, and offering a glimpse of that powerful river.

Interior objects and fittings were available for repurposing, hacking, transformation. In the dining room, a larger-than-desired table became a shelf; IKEA shelves became a wall replacing the termite-eaten bathroom partition; the same wall partition was notionally extended into the garden to shield us from the neighbours' domestics; and the wall-becoming-fence, partially made of broomsticks, dissolved gradually into the earth with bacterial assistance. While all these objects and materials already had their own forms and capacities, these forms were never seen to be prescriptive or fixed. Bargain items of furniture, objects by the street curb, all were material with transformative potential. There was the thrill of discovering a discarded air-conditioning duct one night in a CBD skip, a shiny object to be hoisted through the soft-top of the Morris Minor and transported back to the garden, awaiting another transformation. A new form was eventually prompted by a desire for storage: the duct was sliced and reconfigured as shelves fixed to the bathroom walls. The transformations at Avebury Street were also prompted by generous offers of assistance and material supplies. A friend offered some offcut teak that could be remade into a waterproofed bathroom floor assisted by the skilful insights of another friend, a boat-builder and joiner.[14]

❧

The spaces within the interiors and gardens lacked definitive functions and configurations. When Avebury Street transformed into a family home, the new young

'occupants' brought with them all manner of fluids and flux to be followed, if not chased at high speed. At this time, the space became one of colicky vomit dripping onto shoulders and floors, seeking out the cracks between the tongues of the floorboards and returning to the damp clay below. To contain and organise the many bodies that arrived at Avebury Street, the holes in the windows were covered, the loft ladder replaced with a handcrafted stair, the bathroom remade. But any attempts to organise and contain space were always offset by the introduction of new forces: the house's life demanded more and more following, particularly from its young occupants. When older, the children of Avebury Street became spatial prospectors as well, seeking new transformations even when elements of the house were apparently 'finished' – breaking through temporary cupboard linings under the stair, discovering tunnels for trikes and train sets. Avebury Street became a 'field of interaction'[15] between the static and the fluid, the ordered and the indeterminate. The creation of somewhat 'architectural' interventions – the renovation of a bathroom, the reinstatement of internal doors and

The children as dynamic spatial prospectors. Photograph Cathy Smith.

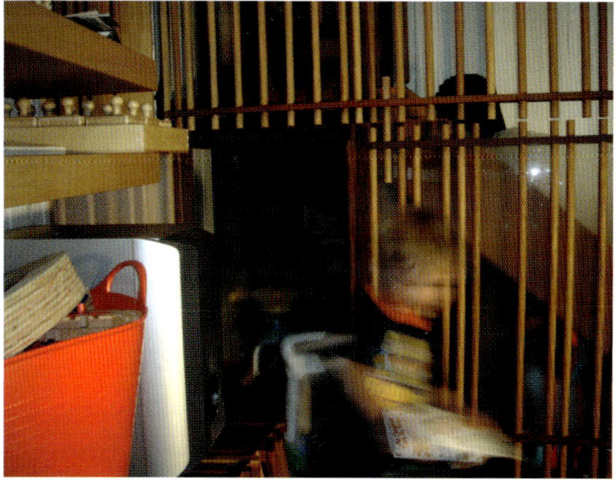

walls, the making of a bespoke stair, and so forth – was inevitably followed by 'resistances'[16] to these interventions, provided by the bodies moving in and through its walls – quite literally in the case of the under-stair tunnel – and the interactions with available materials.

Of the many forces that inflected the Avebury Street project, there were also those of larger markets and economies affecting the rapidly gentrifying suburb of West End, in its planning, cultural mix and affordability. Deleuze and Guattari make the point that within the artisanal mode 'there are second-order itinerancies where it is no longer a flow of matter that one prospects and follows, but, for example, a market.'[17] The real estate desirability of the suburb and the Avebury Street address shifted dramatically over time. The Avebury Street site was first defined in New South Wales, and later adopted by Queensland; in the 1980s, immigrants established eateries in the nearby streets; and in the 1990s, the house was downstream from the drug dealer. In the millennium, Avebury Street became 'funky', as evident in a 2006 article on the house published in a local newspaper under the title 'Tribal Beat'.[18] *The Courier Mail* declared the house was 'creating a niche in the urban jungle'. It became official, named and marketable. The newspaper's deployment of the term 'tribal' differed radically from Deleuze and Guattari's use of the term 'tribal society' in relation to nomadics and following.[19] In *The Courier Mail*, the label 'tribal' was applied to make the project more palatable, clear and communicable to the mass readership, somewhat at odds with the indeterminacy characterising the project's evolution. *The Courier Mail* article became, somewhat ironically, a handy realtor moniker when the interest rates challenged the mortgage and prompted the property's sale. In the end, it was always the ANZ Bank's territory, a hidden and persuasive force that demanded its own following, of sorts.

Avebury Street was continuously composed, decomposed, reconfigured. The DIY sensibility involved site-specific processes, materials and bodies that enacted direct, built transformations. There was a blurring of processes of designing, making and occupying; the materials were found or prospected; and the bodies included not only that of the architect but neighbours, friends, children. Our followings at Avebury Street lasted for over a decade. The house transformed and we transformed. There were human bodies and subjects at Avebury Street; collectively, those bodies were committed to a following of continuously shifting matter. By the end of our occupation, we felt like the house itself: immigrants, and our messy bodies not quite suitable for the dinky new neighbours in the changing demographic of the suburb. 'Please keep your children quiet before 7am weekdays and 9am weekends,' the new neighbours said. 'They scream when they play and it disrupts our sleep.' Avebury Street had grown and connected new bodies, and new occupations, even if uncomfortable ones. The project linked to children, who linked to other bodies, sites, cultures and schools: these connections were more powerful than a single street address. We sold the house and 'floated' back across the river to different intensities, buildings and incarnations, not so much a process of dislocation but rather the making of new connections, new followings.

Avebury Street might be somewhat architectural, emerging from renovations that started with one dilapidated house form and ended with a different, more nuanced form. But between those forms, there were transformations, reversals, demolitions, evolutions, and most of all, followings that existed beyond the will of individual subjects. Perhaps architecture emerges from these flows, sedimenting from the chaos, although the precise moment of its forming and even its demise is unclear. How can one manifest an architectural form from operations that involves a following of the chaos of life and bodies, nappies and milk, tears and mortgages? Avebury Street did not generate environmental

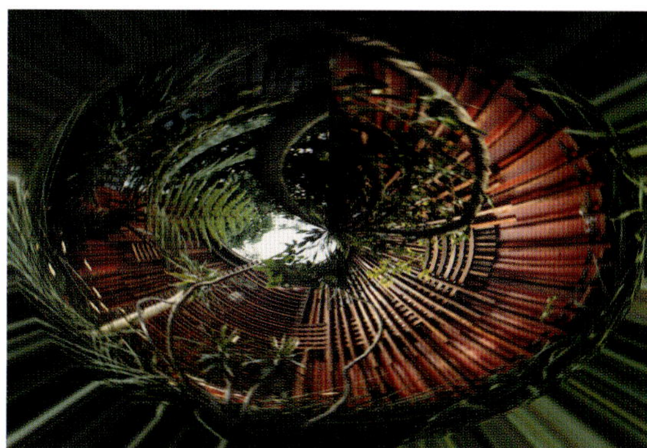

Avebury Street dynamics:
following and prospecting.

'answers' to 'problems' such as a functional brief and resale property values, even if those parameters inevitably inflected its various incarnations and transformations. Rather, each transformation seemed to generate a new set of problems to be negotiated and followed on a daily basis. To borrow from Deleuze and Guattari's own terms, this mode of operation 'is still dependent upon sensitive and sensible evaluations that pose more problems than they solve'.[20] At Avebury Street, it was a following and prospecting of Allen keys and interest rates, milk and timber, and always riparian.

1   Gilles Deleuze and Félix Guattari *A Thousand Plateaus: Capitalism and Schizophrenia*, Brain Massumi (ed./trans.), London: Continuum, 2004, 362.

2   This label was created by Graham Meltzer, an architect and photographer, who photographed the house for the author as a momentary record of its evolution in September 2004. Meltzer drew connections between the processes deployed at *Avebury Street* and the *Red House* in Bexleyheath, England, which belonged to designer William Morris. Morris's Red House – constructed in a distinctive red brick – was created by Morris, his wife and friends.

3   Jane Rendell, '[d]oing it, (un)doing it, (over)doing it: Rhetorics of Architectural Abuse', *Occupying Architecture: Between the Architect and the User*, Jonathan Hill (ed.), London: Routledge, 1998, 246.

4   Deleuze and Guattari, *A Thousand Plateaus*, 452.

5   Deleuze and Guattari, *A Thousand Plateaus*, 363.

6   Deleuze and Guattari, *A Thousand Plateaus*, 450.

7   A point reinforced by Brian Massumi in his text *A User's Guide to Capitalism and Schizophrenia: Deviations From Deleuze and Guattari*. See Brian Massumi, Brian, *A User's Guide to Capitalism and Schizophrenia: Deviations From Deleuze and Guattari*, Cambridge: A Swerve Edition / The MIT Press, 1992, 12.

8   Deleuze and Guattari, *A Thousand Plateaus*, 452.

9   Theorists Mark Bonta and John Protevi refer to the artisan as 'an agent of production who coaxes bodies to thresholds of self-organisation'. See Mark Bonta and John Protevi, *Deleuze and Geophilosophy: A Guide and Glossary*, Edinburgh: Edinburgh University Press, 2004, 53.

10   Deleuze and Guattari, *A Thousand Plateaus*, 452.

11   It is important to note that Bonta and Protevi argue that Deleuze and Guattari do establish a binary between the architect and the artisan in their writings. According to Bonta and Protevi: '[a]rtisans are opposed to the architect.' They argue for this binary on the assumption that architects privilege form over matter, and fail to acknowledge a material's capacities for self-organisation. See Bonta and Protevi, *Deleuze and Geophilosophy*, 53. Nevertheless, Deleuze and Guattari never establish such a clear and direct opposition or dualism between the architect and artisan in *A Thousand Plateaus*. One might thus argue that an architect can be artisanal if deploying an artisanal mode of operation in particular scenarios.

12   As described by Rosamund Woodburn to the author. Roz is a landscape architect and former owner and occupant of *Avebury Street*.

13   Deleuze and Guattari, *A Thousand Plateaus*, 451-452.

14   The timber was sourced through Felix McDonald and the joiner was William McMahon.

15   Deleuze and Guattari, *A Thousand Plateaus*, 413.

16   Deleuze and Guattari, *A Thousand Plateaus*, 411.

17   Deleuze and Guattari, *A Thousand Plateaus*, 452.

18   Cindy Lord, 'Tribal Beat', *The Courier Mail*, Home Magazine, Saturday 30 October 2004, 16-17.

19   Deleuze and Guattari refer to countercultural theorist Marshall McLuhan's use of the term 'tribal', referring to the 'new tribal society as described by Marshall McLuhan'. See Deleuze and Guattari, *A Thousand Plateaus*, 397.

20   Deleuze and Guattari, *A Thousand Plateaus*, 412.

Ancient Modernists: Junction Dam

DIANNE PEACOCK

Junction Dam was the first major structure built in Victoria's Kiewa Hydroelectric Scheme, completed in 1943. It preceded the nation's largest engineering project, the Snowy Mountains Scheme, by several years.

The dam's concrete buttress wall holds and releases water flowing from the Bogong High Plains. It presents as a heroic structure in the landscape. In contrast, and close by, the recently completed Bogong Power Station (2009) lies camouflaged beneath a reconstituted hill of excavated rock; its top and sides planted with indigenous vegetation.

The dam's tall concrete buttresses are roughly triangular in profile. Square section concrete struts hold the spaces between each buttress and its neighbour. Forces necessary to counter the mass of water have shaped the design of the wall and that of its residual internal spaces.

Surface erosion, staining, lichen and growth of the sub-alpine Australian bush around the wall combine to suggest a physical state somewhere between infrastructure and nature.

When photographing the dam in 2008, my camera playback function rotated all vertical format photographs by 90 degrees. These unexpected images describe another building type.

List of Images All photographs by Dianne Peacock. THIS PAGE Junction Dam, completed 1943, Kiewa Hydroelectric Scheme; *Ancient Modernists*: west facade (detail). OVERLEAF *Ancient Modernists*: view from the unfinished 41st floor; *Ancient Modernists*: vertical transport system; *Ancient Modernists*: interior; *Ancient Modernists*: defensive barriers and entry to refuge. LAST SPREAD *Ancient Modernists*: foyer; *Ancient Modernists*: 3rd floor terrace.

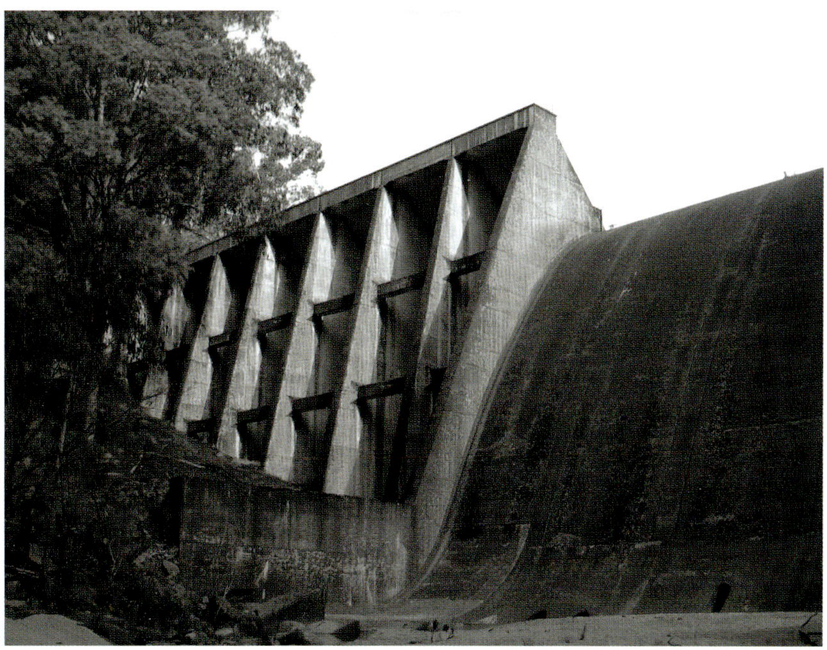

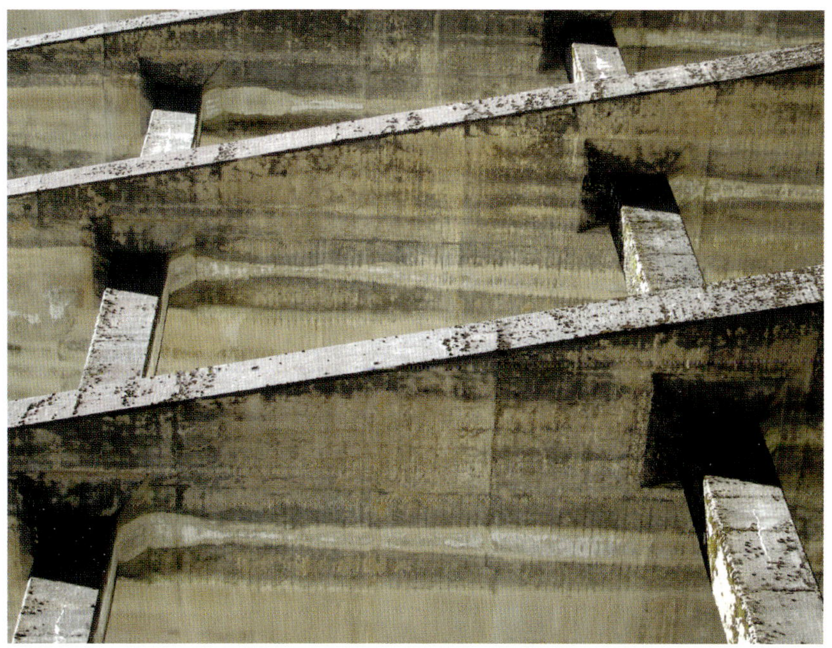

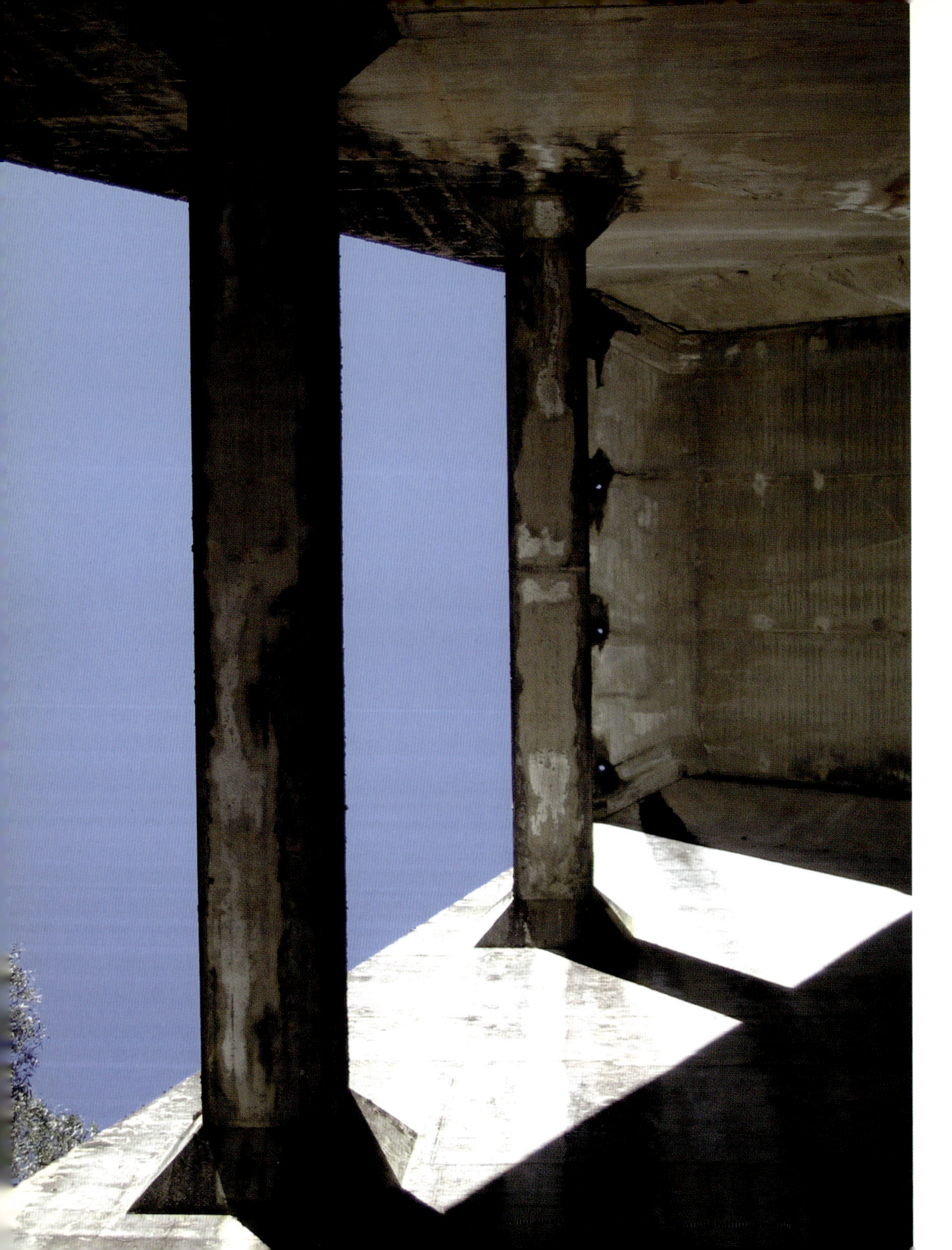

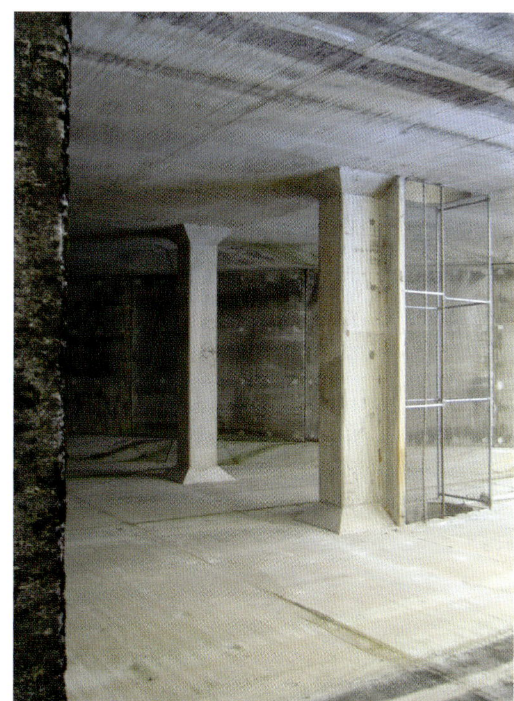
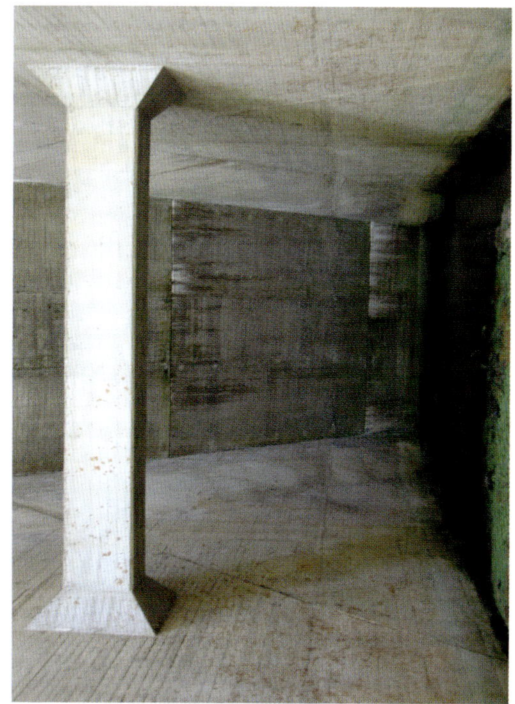
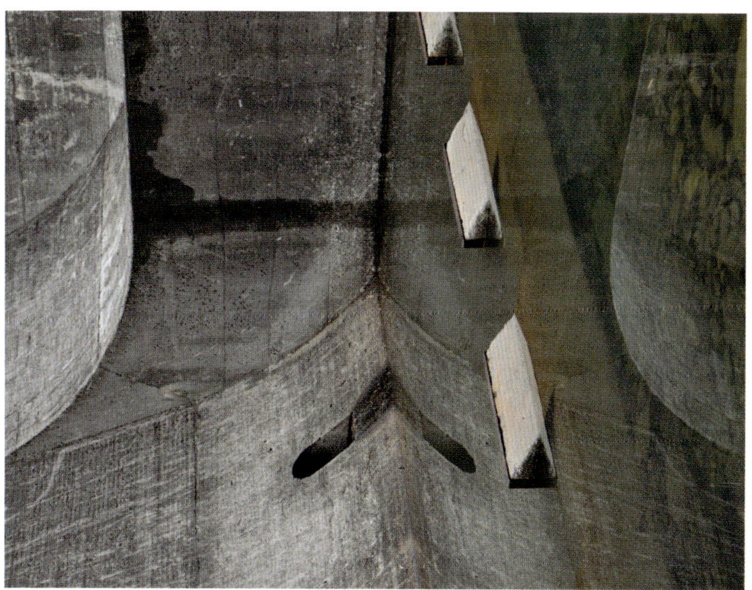

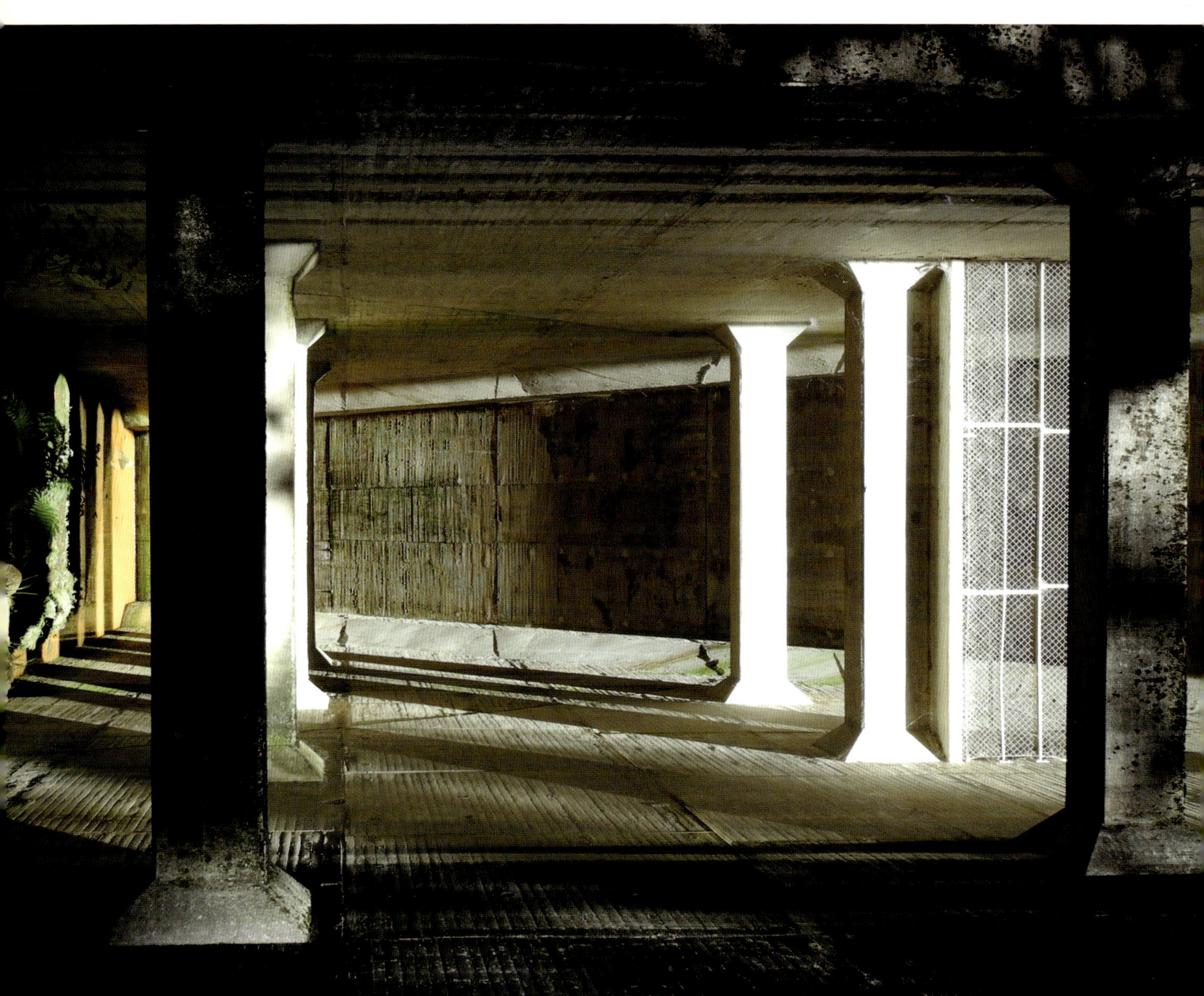

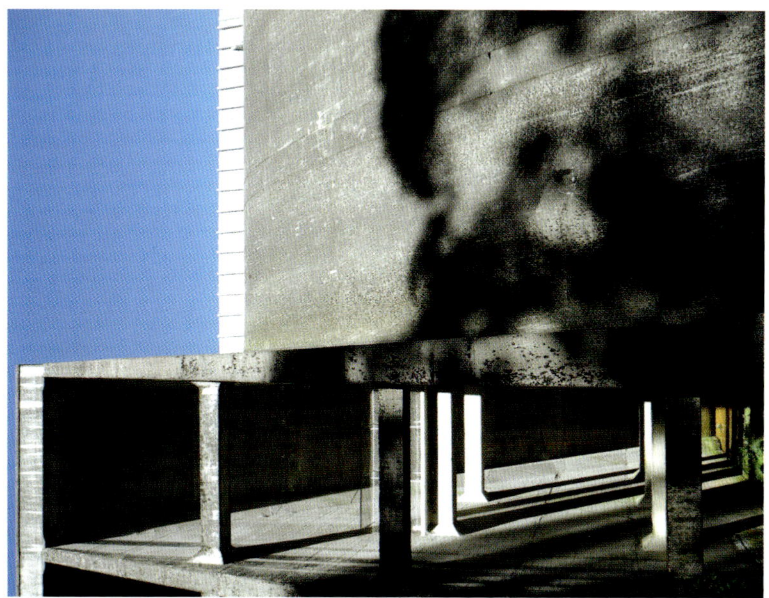

The partially excavated
work of ancient modernists

Ancient Modernists: a project in photography, writing and video is founded on a desire to know a physical structure, its spatial and acoustic qualities; its mysteries, cool air and great mass; its qualities felt by the body. The project is one of a series exploring what I call spatial mystery, where I take time to explore a place that has drawn me in.

Ancient Modernists began in 2008 with photographs of Junction Dam. As certain images were rotated, they appeared to depict an unfinished or abandoned building of columns and floor plates. This encounter established the procedure for a short video, *Ancient Modernists* (2010–11), filmed with the camera on its side. *Ancient Modernists* plays with the vertical and horizontal planes of architectural modernism through the reorientation of Junction Dam's heroic, monumental structure. It seems to work this way because the significant force withstood by the buttress dam is lateral rather than vertical.

An early version of *Ancient Modernists* screened in a presentation at the Writing Architecture Symposium in July 2010. For the Bogong AIR festival 2011, the video was projected onto the surface of its subject's interior within the dark spillway section of the dam. This event took place at the tail end of a torrential storm. The dam filled and water poured over the spillway above. A review of the festival by Bruce Mowson, published in *realtime and onscreen* (issue 102), described the site and festival's specific character and environmental conditions, correctly observing that I reimagined the dam as a type of building, an (open) skyscraper. The photographs and video act as a form of propositional design imagery.

Ancient Modernists was supported by the hospitality provided by my brother, Chris Peacock, at Bogong Village. This body of work forms part of a PhD in Architecture and Design (by project) at RMIT University.

Pillars of a Nation:
A layperson's journey into photographing and writing architecture for the general public

JOAN BEDDOE

I was visiting Rockhampton with my second-hand Olympus camera in 1989 and found myself standing in front of the Rockhampton Customs House, asking the question, 'What is this extraordinary building doing here?' So began a journey that has extended over 20 years. I have been fortunate to travel widely around Australia, and so have been able to photograph the many historic public buildings that form the national heritage of our first century. I concentrated on those buildings that local communities would use every day, the buildings that gave them an identity as well as a sense of pride: commissariat stores, post offices, town halls, court houses, customs houses, railway stations, parliament houses and government offices. I wrote accounts of government services they provided to the growing Australian colonies and so developed a social history.

In 1989 I naively assumed that a couple of hours in a library would answer my questions. How wrong I was. One question led to another and I spent many hours rummaging in state and local libraries, and visiting public works departments, heritage councils, national trusts and the heritage commission in Canberra. I purchased local histories from local newsagencies, and collected tourist information. I needed to discover who our early Australian architects were and what background they came from. I learned that our earliest colonial buildings were the work of military engineers but, as free settlement grew, trained architects were attracted to the colonies. What training did these men bring with them?

By the 19th century most architects were trained in the building industry or as articled clerks with recognised architects. It was a time of popular interest in

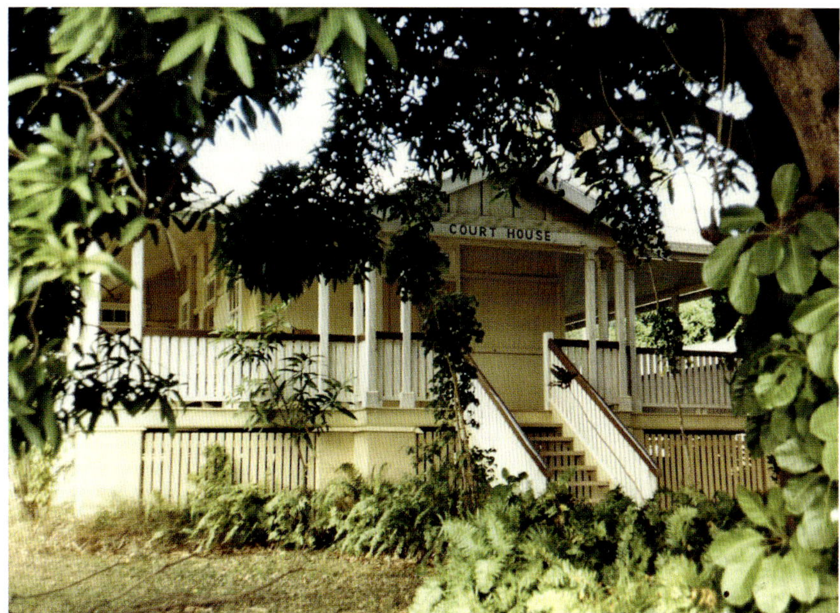
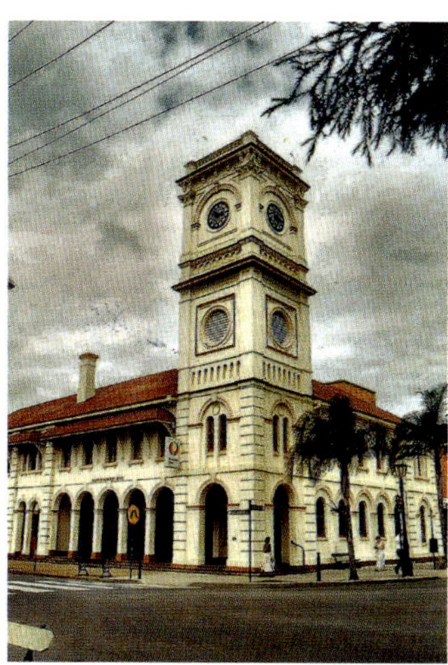

Post Office, Maryborough, Queensland, 1865-66, architect Charles Tiffin. In 1878 architect F.D.G. Stanley extended the tower. Photograph Joan Beddoe, 1995.

Court House, Cooktown, Queensland. Photograph Joan Beddoe, 1991.

architecture, as evidenced by the journals circulated at the time and books such as J. C Loudon's *Encyclopedia of Cottage, Farm and Villa Architecture*. Another popular publication was *The Australasian Builders and Contractors' News* published weekly in the second half of the 19th century. It addressed issues such as an architect's training, the question of an Australian style, current building projects in each of the colonies, as well as international architectural news.

In my journey I read about the development of the public works departments in each of the colonies, and the role of the government architect. I unearthed biographical information on those who served up to the time of federation. I visited exhibitions such as *The Most Useful Art: Architecture in Australia 1788–1985* staged at the State Library of NSW, *Creating the Public Realm* mounted at the State Library of WA, 1994, and *Our Built Heritage,* a display of government buildings designed and erected by the Queensland Department of Public Works mounted in the Queensland State Archives in 2005.

I became aware that there was a wealth of fascinating information about architecture and related arts, which needed to be presented to the general public. What would be the best agency for this task? I approached some of the people who had mounted state exhibitions, but no one was interested in a national presentation. So it looked as if it was going to be up to me! The heritage officer in the Australian Customs Service recommended me to a wonderful editor, Roslyn Russell. I made the acquaintance of architectural historians, and spoke with people such as Miles Lewis in Melbourne and John Kerr in Brisbane. Miles Lewis alerted me to the problems of popularising architectural information: misinformation could circulate, where errors and personal opinions perpetuated through popular accounts were not properly researched and documented. This was a major concern for the discussion of architecture in a popular arena, and I wondered if I should forget my project altogether. I spoke with Henry Reynolds, well-known historian and popular writer. My collection of photographs of schools of arts and mechanics' institutes had just opened for display in his hometown of Launceston. He took an interest in my project and suggested that photographic displays were probably just as effective as written text.

Encouraged by this, I pursued the exhibition of my photographs, with displays of customs houses in the Customs House in Brisbane, town halls in the Adelaide Town Hall (this collection subsequently moved to the Australian Local Government Association, Canberra), court houses in the Supreme Court of the Northern Territory, and Western Australia's court houses in the Supreme Court of Western Australia. In responding to these displays, members of the public often took pride in identifying buildings with which they had been associated. The collection enabled them to make comparisons, consider aspects of architectural design, as well as factors such as climate, building materials, a city's wealth and importance, which helped to determine the status and appearance of the buildings.

Over time, the photographic displays proved to be a success, but the mass of written material still lay there: edited and waiting for an audience, it needed to be

Railway Station, Kuttabul, Queensland. Photograph Joan Beddoe, 1989.

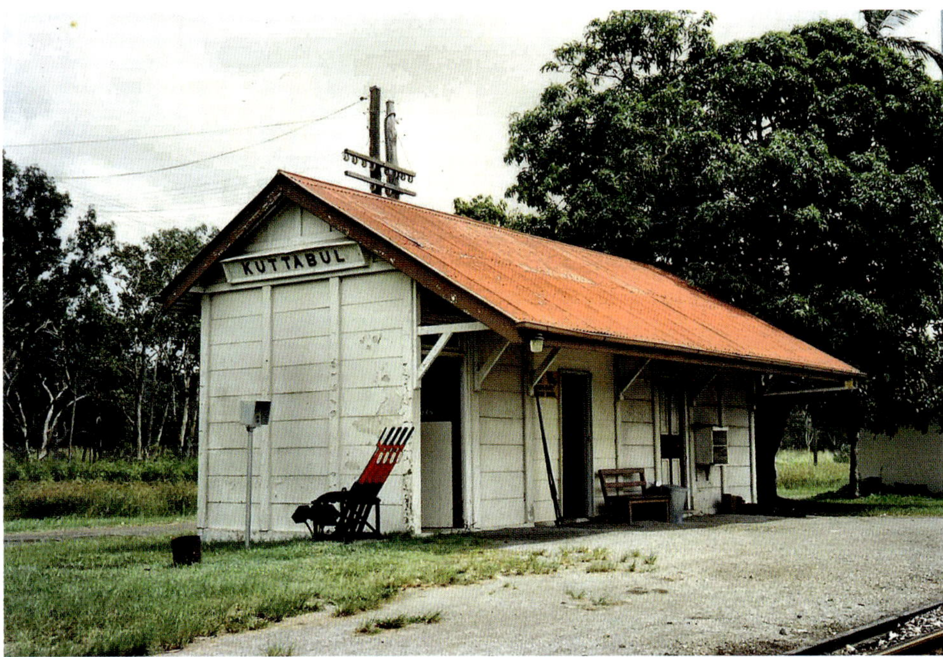

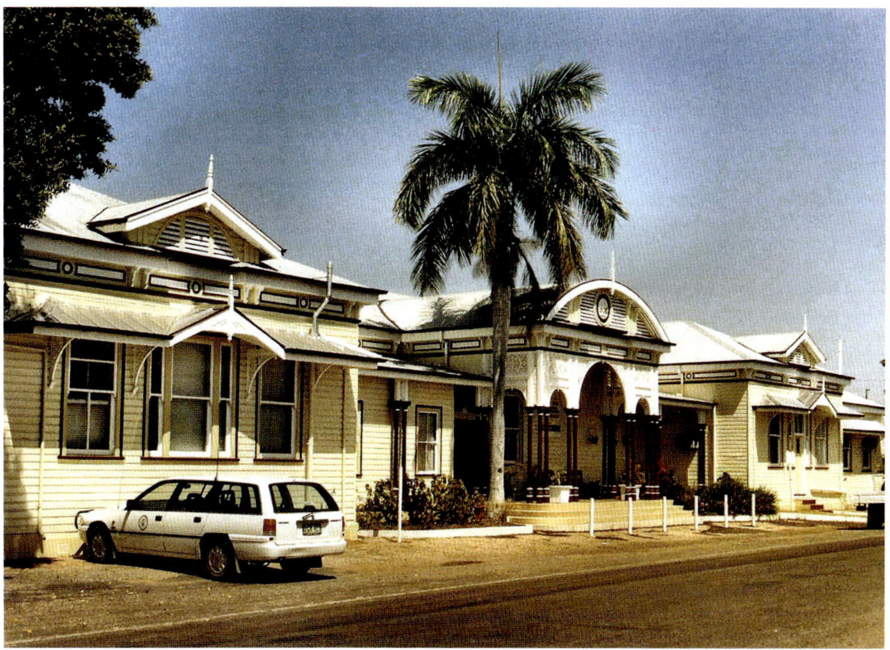

Emerald Historic Railway Station,
Emerald, Queensland, 1900,
architect Henrick Hansen.
Photograph Joan Beddoe, 1992.

made available to the public. I faced numerous problems in this endeavour. No publisher would be interested in the work of an unknown writer without architectural qualifications. Despite all the research, the work was not annotated in accepted academic fashion. I was sure there was a large body of interest out there, but had no way of assessing it. If I self-published then I would need to market the book, with all the difficulties that would entail. The photographs were an integral part of the work, but they would make any publication extraordinarily expensive, and my editor raised further doubts by advising me that a coffee table book would require photographs of extremely high quality. I was not interested in making money. All I wanted to do was share with like-minded people all the fascinating information I had collected. Then digital photograph editing and websites became accessible! My brother kindly spent hours with me producing the website *Pillars of a Nation*.[1]

Technology has changed so much in the 20 odd years I have been working on my project. Initially I needed to visit a major library to read the *Heritage of Australia, the Illustrated Register of the National Estate*.[2] However by the time I was seriously writing architectural criticism on individual buildings, the information was available online in the *Australian Heritage Database* and the *Australian Heritage Places Inventory*. The internet opens a wonderful opportunity to access a popular audience, allowing that audience to also respond. My website needs more than a guest book, it needs a chat facility. This would allow numerous local groups and individuals to contribute information on their local heritage public buildings. In my search for internet sites on Australian architecture, the best so far is Sean Fishlock's 'Walking Melbourne', which is easily navigated, gives reliable information on Melbourne's buildings, and allows readers to respond.[3]

At this point in my project I have been considering architectural criticism, asking myself what the term criticism actually means. I read an article by Ada Louise Huxtable, the doyen of architectural criticism. In an article entitled 'Architecture Criticism Historian' she writes:

> Before I talk about criticism as an art, I would like to talk about the art of criticism as it applies to architecture, for this is like no other criticism. To begin with, and this is not as obvious as it seems, architecture is like no other art. It is the most complex and compromised of the arts, subject to a battery of restraints, controls and conflicts of interest, always striving to find the line where art and utility meet. A building is not a studio work; it is the product of an enormous bag of programs and pressures that go far beyond the unified vision that is possible for the creator, performer, interpreter, or translator of other art forms. It is caught in the endless struggle between the aesthetic and the pragmatic on a battlefield of politics, money and power.[4]

This makes good sense. So do the negatives outweigh the positives, when attempting to provide for a genuine popular interest in architecture? Has the public lost touch with our built environment in an era when large construction companies often build major developments for large corporations? Is the grassroots interest in Australian architecture as alive in the 21st century as it was in the 19th? I believe the public is interested: we read *House and Garden*, we buy books on kitchen design, we watch TV documentaries on famous monuments and Kevin McCloud presenting *Grand Designs*. We troop off on heritage trails and gaze at the homes of the rich

and famous from ferries and bus tours. We watch a film because it portrays particular scenery, architecture or an historic place. We appreciate authors such as Dan Brown for the rich architectural background they offer in their stories. There is a popular audience for architecture, and people do have views and attitudes about buildings.

1   The website can be found at http://www.pillarsofanation.com.au/

2   *The Heritage of Australia: the illustrated register of the National Estate,* Australian Heritage Commission. South Melbourne: Macmillan of Australia in association with the Australian Heritage Commission, 1981.

3   See http://www.walkingmelbourne.com/

4   Ada Louise Huxtable, 'Architecture Criticism Historian', *Proceedings of the American Philosophical Society,* Vol. 134, No. 4 (Dec., 1990), 461-464.

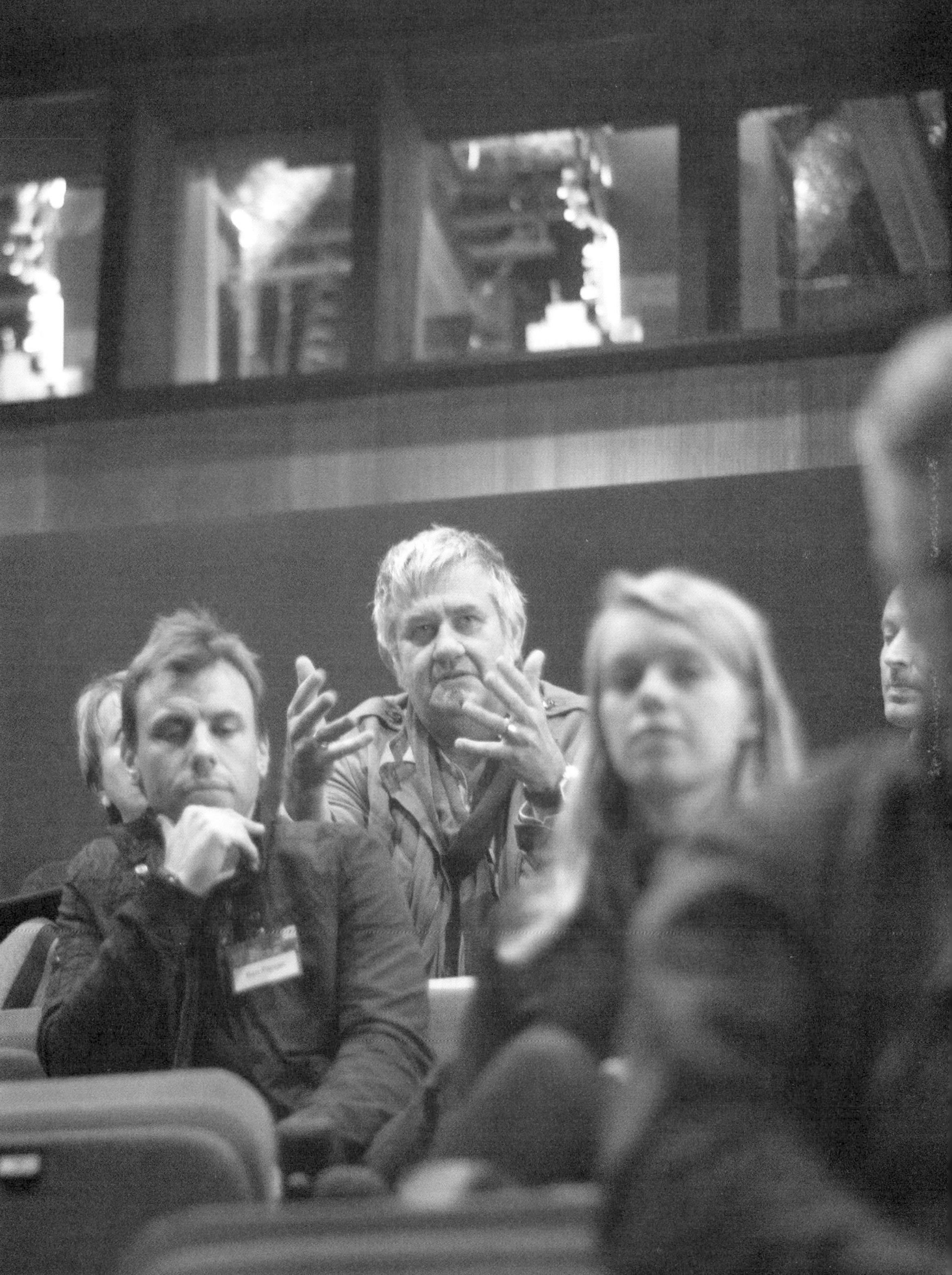

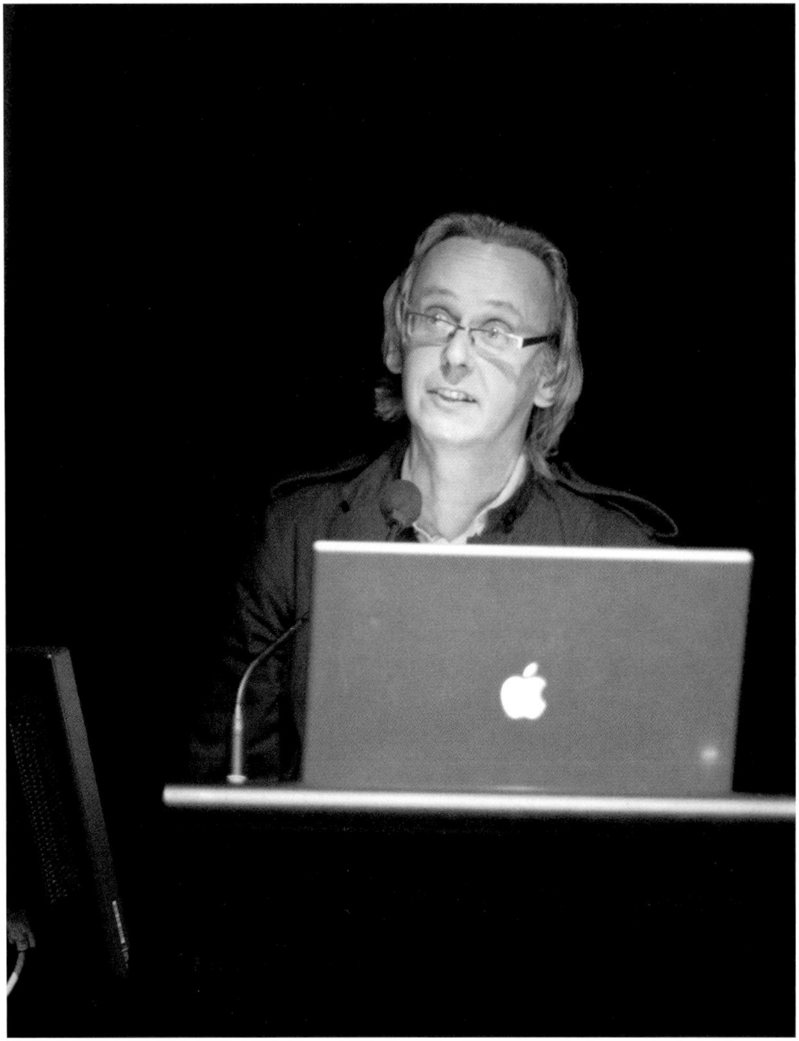

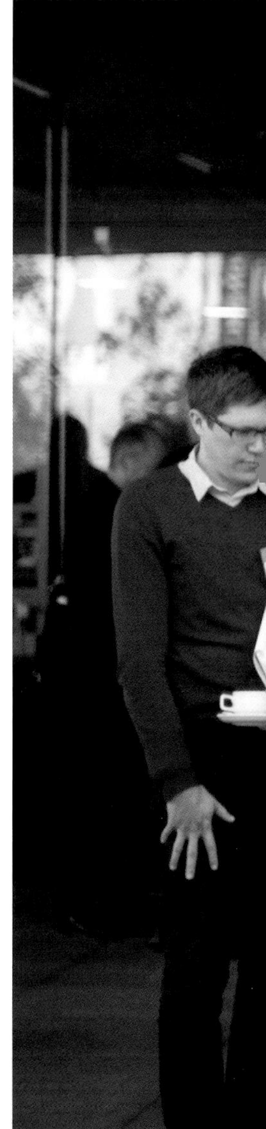

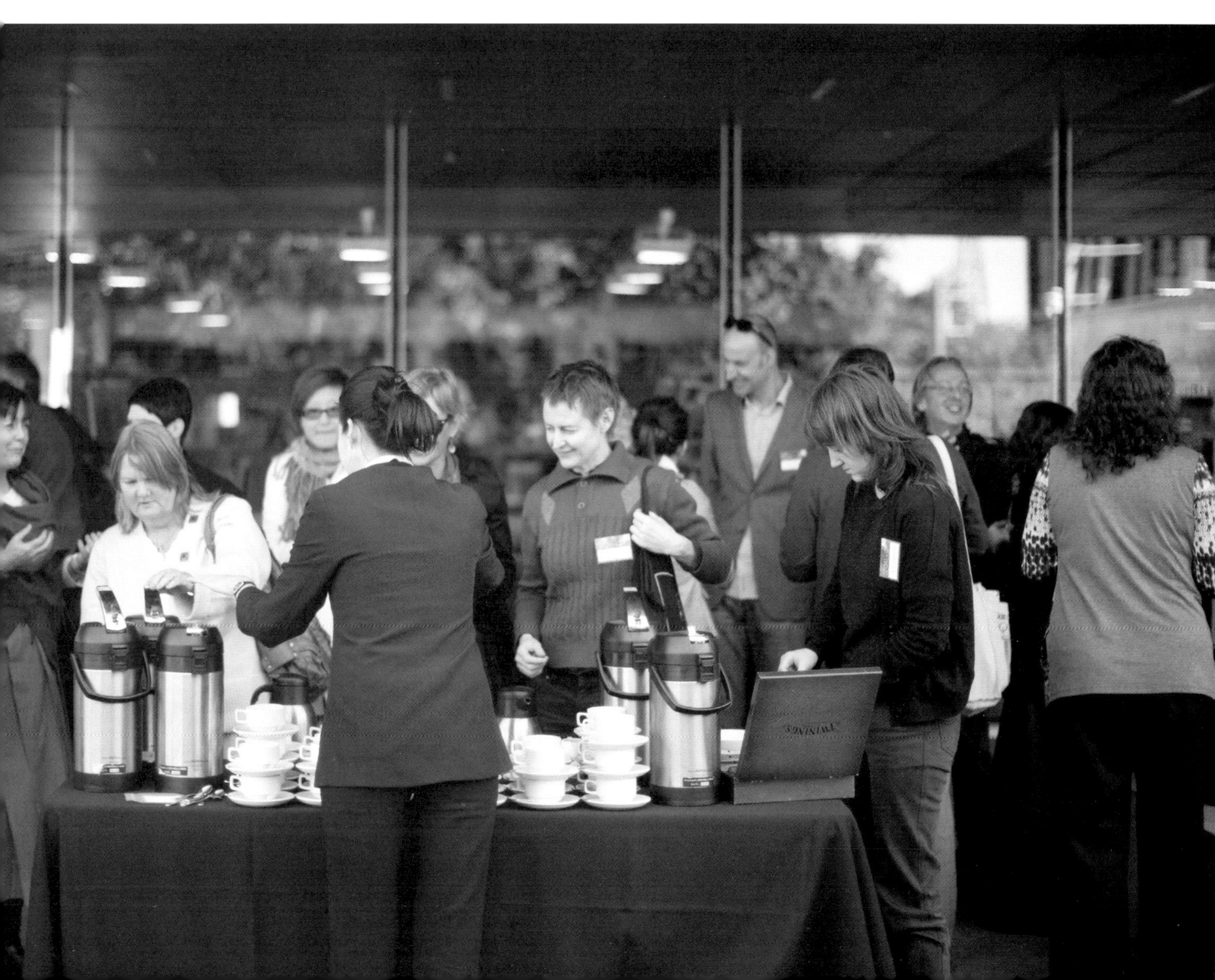

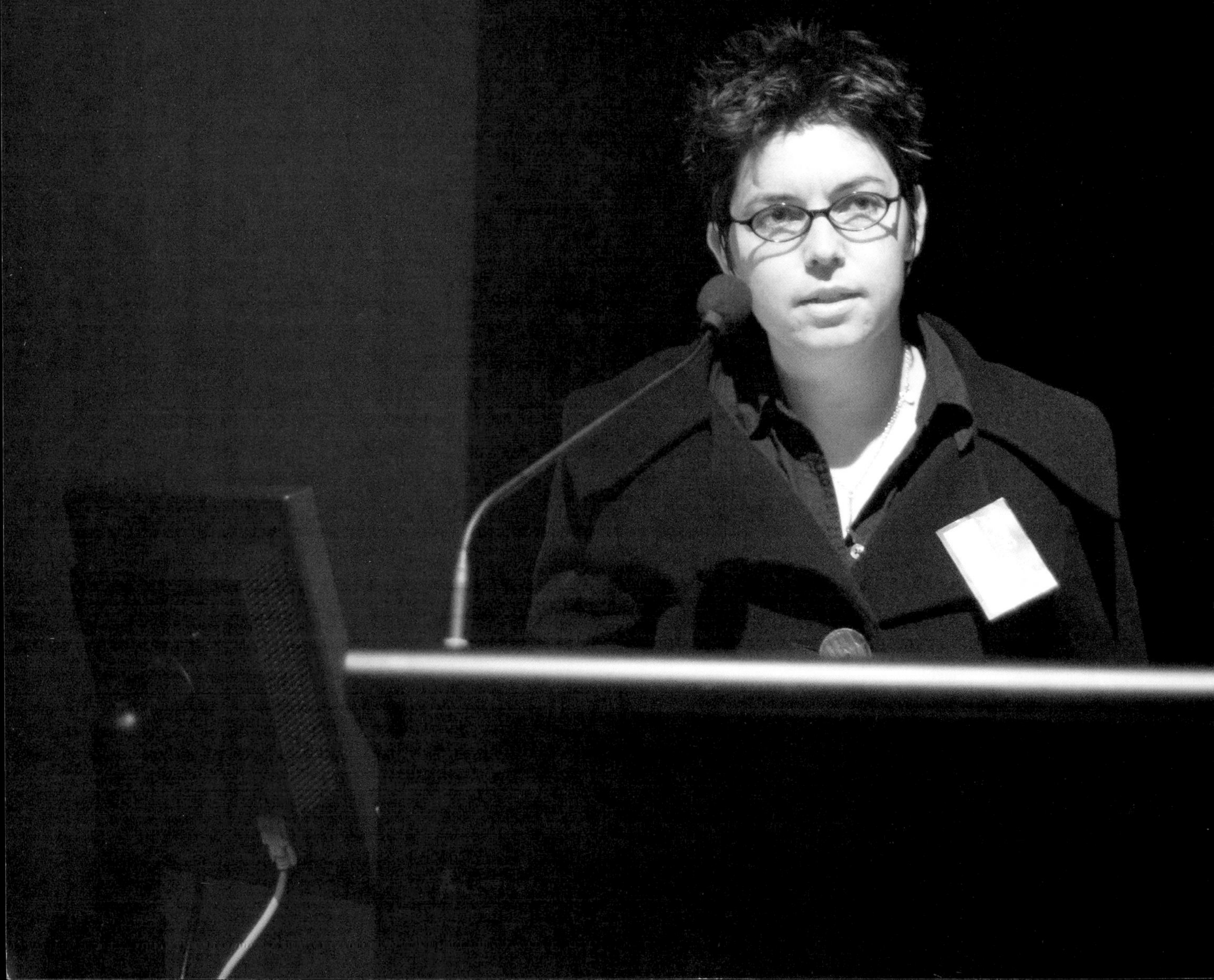

New Belle-Lettrism

NAOMI STEAD

Belles-lettres, in literal translation from the French, means fine or beautiful writing. In the sense of crafted, polished writing, belles-lettres applies to all specifically literary work, including fiction, poetry and drama. But the term is also both more narrow and more nuanced than that. These days it is archaic and rarely used, with the exception that amongst librarians it is the name given to categories of literature that do not fit within other normative genres – for instance in large libraries, humour, essays, volumes of published letters and speeches and literary criticism, will have their own category, but in small libraries they are just as likely to be gathered under the heading of belles-lettre. It could be described as the 'etc.', the excess that refuses to be categorised and thus threatens to explode the system of categorisation, or at least reveal its values and omissions.

In this paper I would like to explore the genre and mode of the belle-lettre as one model for what architectural writing, and architectural criticism, might aspire to. I have written elsewhere about the 'complaints' that are commonly made about written architectural criticism in Australia, complaints which may well be complacent, and under-theorised, but which remain pervasive.[1] Let me caricature them briefly here to get them out of the way, even though they are arguable, sometimes dubious, and not the focus of this paper. They are: that architectural criticism in Australia is not critical enough, that our culture of amiability mitigates against 'real', tough critique and creates a culture of anodyne politeness; that criticism in the professional journals is not adequately objective because tainted by commercial bias, hence it is sycophantic, fixated on glamour photography, unduly attracted by novelty and spectacle, and complicit in the architectural 'star system'; furthermore, that critics are vague or simply incorrect in their criteria for judgement, or that they refuse to be drawn to judgement at all and instead shade into timid, impressionistic and descriptive criticism, which is more about the critic than about the significance or quality of the building and which, therefore, has little role to play in improving the standard of future buildings or the built environment more generally. All of these inter-related ideas have contributed to a wide-spread belief that architectural criticism, in Australia and elsewhere, is in something of a state of crisis.[2] But for me, on this occasion, my primary complaint with architectural criticism is with its conventionality as a specific genre of writing. It is a practice with very strong and well-defined conventions – of tone, of vocabulary, of comportment, of image–text relationship. I wonder how these strong conventions came about, and I especially wonder how they might be bent, or broken.

Much of the most current and lively debate about architectural criticism has occurred online. Part of this has been gathered on the influential *Design Observer* website, for instance Alexandra Lange's essay 'Why Nicolai Ouroussoff Is Not Good Enough', discussing the work of the former *The New York Times* architecture critic and proposing that he might be 'the last architecture critic': that the role might be 'doomed'.[3] This article garnered a huge response of comments and online discussion, including a follow-up article by Nancy Levinson, in which she condemns the notion that architectural criticism is a mode of art criticism, arguing that such ideas promote a dangerous emphasis on formalist critique and 'aesthetics over function, technology, comfort or performance'.[4] In a later essay entitled 'Whatever Happened to Architecture Critique', Lange again speculates on the ongoing viability of the role of the architecture critic, this time on the grounds of the 'uncertainty of the media landscape' in an economic downturn, where new commentators are increasingly

beginning their own publishing ventures online.[5] A good example of this, which began as an independent printed zine and then migrated online, is *Loud Paper* – dedicated to 'increasing the volume of architectural discourse' and written by freelance critic Mimi Zeiger.[6]

So, despite the many and varied predictions of the death of published criticism, of architecture as well as all other forms of culture, it seems to me that a radical rethinking of critical practice might be prompted by the potentials of writing for online media, and to see this as a kind of new belle-lettrism. Surely there are few arts as 'popular' as architecture, in the sense of being widely used and ubiquitous, so why does it not appear in the pages of the pop-culture blogs like Brisbane's *Four Thousand*?[7] The short answer would be that it's not groovy enough, but the longer answer includes the fact that architectural writing is very rarely populist, in the good sense of that word. I am interested in the (small c) writerly culture of the new media, as manifest in the particular tone struck in such writing, a distinctive tone of knowing, hip insouciance, which speaks to a particular sub-culture of savvy and culturally literate people from all over the world, people who are just as much at home in B-grade pop culture as they are in capital A art, and who delight in flitting across this spectrum in a way that collapses traditional boundaries between high and low.

Belles-lettres and the 'gentle reader'

As David Shields writes, belles-lettres has now 'become a vague term, collecting so broad a reference that it now designates the whole of "humane letters" … that is, all imaginative literature or all writing evincing "literariness"',[8] but this was not always the case. He continues:

> [In England,] Prior to the term's semantic expansion in the 1760s, it had a precise employment, naming a mode of writing that subordinated the traditional

tasks of edification, revelation, and memorialization to the work of stimulating social pleasure. Belles lettres was characterized more by its effects than its forms. "Ease" and "agreeableness," qualities adjusted to the taste of the "gentle reader," were the primary belletristic virtues."[9]

As is perhaps anticipated in the refined pleasures described by Shields, by the time we get to the present day, belles-lettres carries some bad associations – of sophisticated elegance but also excessive refinement, of aesthetic aspiration but also aestheticism, of literary pleasure but also trivial flimsiness and lack of substance. Belles-lettre are pieces of writing that emerge from and exist within literary culture, within what might be called the archive of literature – in a self-conscious relationship to other past and present literary work, and in the pursuit of literary art. The *Encyclopædia Britannica* describes belles-lettres as 'the more artistic and imaginative forms of literature, as poetry or romance, as opposed to more pedestrian and exact studies'.[10] The parallel here is clear: Belle-lettrism (as a sub-set of literature in general) is to the majority of writing what architecture is to the majority of buildings. This is a mode of writing that is more than simply practical or informative, rather it is a pleasurable, literary end in itself. One can see how this might have come to seem rather circular and rarefied in the practice of literary criticism – elegant literary texts that describe and discuss other literary texts, for the appreciation of the few people who read and value such things. But it causes me to wonder what might be gained in translation between literary and architectural arts.

So the idea of an architectural belles-lettrism is useful here in several ways. It opens the possibility of a 'fine writing' in architecture that spans across exploratory or descriptive modes, as well as architectural criticism. It also opens the question of subjectivity and affect in both reader and writer. The most influential mode of literary criticism to succeed belle-lettrism was the New Criticism

of the early to mid-20th century, with its radically formalist analytical and objective approach that treated the text 'scientifically', as completely autonomous and isolated from the social and material world. The current rise of subjectivity and affect in all modes of criticism, including that of architecture, is perhaps a late reaction against the New Criticism and a return to the earlier pleasures of belles-lettrism, which included the narration of individual perception, embodiment, eroticism and subjective experience.

Part of the attraction of the idea of belles-lettres lies in its association with actual letters, with the epistolary form, and hence with a particular idea of direct address between author and reader – the idea that a piece of writing travels, as an epistle or emissary between one and the other, with all the immediacy and the imagistic and aphoristic appeal of a postcard. The idea of beautiful letters also suggests that such beauty might not only lie in the text, but in the image of the text – rather in what we might call the para-text, the design and typography. Furthermore, belles-lettres historic association with conversation, wit and the critical cut and thrust of the salon, seems to draw a fascinating parallel with writing in the new media. We could see much of the so-called blogosphere as a contemporary, globalised and dis-located version of the salon. Shields writes that:

> Belles lettres flourished in England in conjunction with the rise of urban sociability in the 1670s. New communities based on shared taste, friendship, or common interest formed in postfire London and in the burgeoning resorts. In the mixed-sex assemblies at the spas and in the male tavern clubs of the metropolis, aspirants to gentility embraced the court's new sociable manner of wit.[11]

Such new communities based on shared taste, friendship, common interest and wit seem to me exactly what we are now seeing online, including in writing on architecture.

Not everyone is happy about this, mind you: Linda Cooper Bowen frets that '[w]ith the introduction of the Internet and its spontaneous, unregulated platforms, people with little or no credentials can invent themselves as critics and comment on design while infiltrating the creative community'.[12] But contrary to Bowen's concerns, it must be said that the internet functions as something like a true meritocracy – someone passing themselves off as an architecture critic but saying silly or ill-informed things will not gather a committed readership, while a self-professed amateur who has an original voice and an engaging and fresh way of seeing designed things, might create a following and hence advance the practice of criticism significantly. Others perhaps more attuned to the democratising possibilities of web 2.0 technologies are more optimistic or philosophical – Robert Campbell and Michael Sorkin, writing in *Architectural Record*, note that 'fledgling new media are generating flabbergasting quantities of content, an ever-present online multiverse of image, information, text and hypertext; and in this illimitable process they are also generating a newer, narrower definition of "public", or rather "publics", as broadcast slivers into narrowcast, and as the old-style, top-down discourse makes way for the looser, more participatory dynamics of online exchange.'[13]

Thus there exists a tension between two types of criticism, associated with print and online media respectively, although this is not a causal link. The traditional, disciplinary critique of the kind that has long appeared in professional architecture journals is written by sanctioned, expert critics and directed at practicing architects, with a view to providing firm judgements and advice on how architects might design better buildings in the future. On the other hand, the cultural commentary of the kind that increasingly appears online tends to be written by enthusiasts, without necessarily any formal training but with a particular interest in and opinions on architecture defined broadly. It seeks to make interpretations of and speculations around architecture, drawing associations with broader formations of both high and popular culture, and appealing to a generalist audience that includes architects amongst a much broader public. Naturally, these two kinds of commentary on architecture have different motivations and objectives. Geoff Manaugh, whose phenomenally popular *BLDGBLOG* falls into the latter speculative and populist category, notes that 'there's an idea that people like myself are treating architectural criticism almost like a tag cloud or a cluster of topics that span related fields, and we're losing sight of the fact that architects are creating buildings and someone needs to critique those architects so that they don't create bad buildings in the future.'[14] Adding that, 'It's a perfectly valid point that we need architecture critics'. Manaugh nevertheless argues that this should not come at the expense of the imaginative commentary that often occurs in the blogosphere, and that draws new audiences to be interested in architecture in the first place.[15]

This polarisation of attitudes towards the value of online and traditional forms of criticism is well exemplified in two recent events, one national and one international, which are unrelated but have remarkably congruent titles. Titled 'Critical Failure' and 'Critical Futures', they chart the wild swings between panic and optimism that attend the new online belletristic writing.

'Critical Futures'

In January 2011 the print journal *Domus* – one of the oldest and most respected of the international professional architecture journals, established in 1928 and published continuously since then in Italian and English – began a series of three public panel discussions on the future of architectural criticism, collectively entitled 'Critical Futures'. The first was held in London, the second in Milan, and the third in New York, with each panel made up of a range of architecture critics from both the print and online media, editors, publishers, bloggers and architectural curators. The panels were filmed and streamed on the web.[16] As introduced by *Domus*, the first event was framed as a somewhat polarised debate between online and print forms of commentary on architecture, whereby under the influence of the internet and its 'free and instantly ubiquitous' flow of images and information, magazines have been forced to 'redefine their purpose and economic model in light of dwindling readerships', whereas 'blogs have given a global audience, potentially of millions, to anyone with an Internet connection'.[17] The introduction closed with the proposition that '[i]n all of this, architecture criticism in the traditional sense appears to have all but vanished – not only from the Internet but from magazines themselves'.[18] The question that this immediately raises, of course, is how architectural criticism is defined here, and for whom it is imagined to be written.

As it transpired, the discussions themselves were more nuanced than this introduction would imply, suggesting that the relationship between print and online writing about architecture is one of mutual influence. Rather than a false dichotomy whereby it appears that we are at a moment of choice between blogs and magazines, the discussions instead positioned all public architectural discourse as currently in a state of transformation: searching for new models and modes of writing, seeking new ways of addressing new audiences, and renegotiating the ethical contract that the architectural critic makes with architects on the one hand, the users of buildings on the other, and with both of these groups as they are readers of the critique. Within this debate lie a whole array of contradictions, afflicting both online and print criticism in architecture, which are integral to architecture as a discipline, but which nevertheless have long been misunderstood, poorly articulated, or simply ignored by architecture critics.

The *Domus* events had been partly inspired by, and framed in relation to, an editorial by Peter Kelly published in the print journal *Blueprint*, in which Kelly had condemned the rise of populist blogs such as Manaugh's *BLDGBLOG*, claiming they had little connection or commitment to actual buildings or building quality.[19] Manaugh retorted that he had never claimed to write 'proper' architectural criticism because his interests lay elsewhere, that there are other ways and means of talking about architecture.[20] What became clear during the course of the 'Critical Futures' discussions is that online vehicles have brought about a 'mutation of the power structures around the formation of architectural cultures', as chair, Joseph Grima, said in the first panel discussion. Online critique might be less sanctioned and legitimated, it might be more opinionated, amateur and passion-based, but it seems to be in the ascendancy. This is, however, a source of concern for some, and this brings us to the second event – 'Critical Failure'.

'Critical Failure'

In September 2010 Melbourne's The Wheeler Centre for Books, Writing and Ideas convened a series of public panel discussions under the collective title 'Critical Failure'. Arguing that 'Australian arts criticism is failing us all',[21] the four panels each addressed a different art form – theatre, film, books and the visual arts – and examined the relationship between artistic production and the critical environment in which it is received, concentrating on the value of criticism for arts producers and audiences alike. Posing questions such as whether the web offers 'a possibility for a new, more democratic environment for the arts in Australia,' and 'what chance does local art have to flourish in an environment where it is too rarely judged on its own terms'.[22] The panels were well-attended and later widely discussed online.

None of the four panels included any discussion on the state of criticism in architecture, which might itself be taken as evidence of the currently marginal place of this practice in the Australian cultural scene. But the panels unanimously agreed upon the value of criticism to cultural production, the integral relationship between critical culture and the liveliness, relevance, quality, and significance of artistic production in any medium. They also reinforced both the challenges and the opportunities presented by the demise of newspaper and print publishing, and the rise of online participatory media – the blogger and the citizen critic.

There was broad disagreement about the significance of online platforms for criticism – the question of whether the new media are merely cheap and accessible instruments for the dissemination of the same old kinds of writing, or whether they are indeed radically new mediums: demanding new ways of seeing, discussing, and evaluating culture. In the former camp is Georgie Williamson who, in an essay entitled 'Bugger the Bloggers: Old-World Critics Still Count'[23] is equivocal about the potentials of the internet for criticism; '[i]t is ridiculously cheap, blisteringly fast and the online community it engenders is one that thrives on argument and constant to-and-fro,' he writes, and '[m]ost significantly, the web breaks the monopoly on criticism once held by analog-era organs and allows everyone to have their say.' Nevertheless, he remains unconvinced: 'However marvellous it may be, the web is no more than a medium: its content is not more virtuous, intelligent or correct for appearing in a novel space.'

On the other hand, many bloggers argue that the shift is far greater than 'old-world critics' recognise; not only because the conventions and canons of online critical writing are still under active negotiation, but also because the tone of online criticism is markedly different – more lively, more irreverent, more steeped in popular culture, more relevant to a younger generation of readers. Rebecca Starford, who was a panelist in the books session of 'Critical Failure', later argued that '[t]raditional forms of literary criticism are failing in this country not because

critical authority is lacking, but because this critical authority is increasingly high-minded and ostentatious; it is criticism that does not reflect the diversity and richness of our national literature.'[24] A similar position was set out by theatre critic, Alison Croggan, who, in discussing the theatre panel, celebrated the return of the 'amateur critic', identifying a 'golden age of criticism' on the internet, a 'surge of quality thinking [made possible] precisely *because* the internet is volatile, democratic, unpredictable and lawless'.[25] Even more pointedly, Croggan proposes that the internet's true challenge to print critics lies in the erosion of institutional authority: '[t]hat so many of these critics mistake institutional authority for critical authority says everything you need to know.'[26]

This idea that criticism has ceased to be a distinct, authorised, expert activity in its own right and that it is instead 'dissolving into the background clutter of ephemeral cultural criticism',[27] might equally be read as a protest at the demise of the specialist critic and the rise of the 'chatter' of the online salon. Furthermore, the retreat from judgement might be seen equally as a return to belletristic modes of criticism, in all their subjectivity, allusiveness and impressionism. What is clear is that architectural criticism finds itself in a state of transition, and the path towards a more pleasurable, 'fine' and entertaining mode of writing about architecture stands open to it. In its breadth and range of association, its aspiration to literary art and pleasure in the text, the new belles-lettrism reveals exciting possibilities for architecture, both online and off.

1   Naomi Stead, 'Three Complaints about Architectural Criticism', *Architecture Australia*, vol 92 no 6, November/December 2003, 50-52.

2   See for example Cathy Lang Ho, 'On Criticism', *The Architect's Newspaper*, 16 November 2005.

3   Alexandra Lange, 'Why Nicolai Ouroussoff Is Not Good Enough', *Design Observer*, 18 February 2010, http://observatory. designobserver.com/entry.html?entry=12708.

4   Nancy Levinson, 'Critical Beats', *Design Observer*, 6 March 2010, http://places.designobserver.com/feature/critical-beats/12948/

5   Alexandra Lange, 'Whatever Happened to Architecture Critique', *Design Observer*, 1 July 2010, http://observatory.designobserver.com/feature/whatever-happened-to-architecture-critique/22808/

6   See http://loudpaper.typepad.com/

7   See http://thethousands.com.au/brisbane/

8   David S. Shields, 'British-American Belles Lettres', *Cambridge Histories Online*, *1590–1820*, eds. Sacvan Bercovitch and Cyrus R. K. Patell, Cambridge: Cambridge University Press, 1994, http://histories.cambridge.org/extract?id=chol9780521301053_CHOL9780521301053A016. DOI:10.1017/CHOL9780521301053.016

9   David S. Shields, 'British-American Belles Lettres'.

10   *Encyclopedia Brittanica*, Eleventh Edition.

11   David S. Shields, 'British-American Belles Lettres'.

12   Linda Cooper Bowen, 'Teaching Design Criticism: Are Design Critics Born or Made?' *Communication Arts*, May/June 2008, vol. 50, issue 2, 26.

13   Robert Campbell and Michael Sorkin, 'Criticism Today: Chasing celebrities, globalization, and the web', *Architectural Record*, vol. 194, issue 3, March 2006, 63-66.

14   Greg Lindsay, an interview with Geoff Manaugh, 'On the Future of Cities', 15 March 2011, in *Work in Progress* presented by Farrar, Strauss and Giroux, http://www.fsgworkinprogress.com/2011/03/greg-lindsay-and-bldgblogs-geoff-manaugh-on-the-future-of-cities/.

15   Greg Lindsay, interview with Geoff Manaugh, 'On the Future of Cities'.

16   See http://www.domusweb.it/en/video/-critical-futures-1/

17   Editoriale *Domus*, 'Critical Futures # 1', January 2011, http://www.domusweb.it/en/video/-critical-futures-1/.

18   Editoriale *Domus*, 'Critical Futures # 1'.

19   Peter Kelly, 'The New Establishment', *Blueprint* http://www.blueprintmagazine.co.uk/index.php/everything-else/the-new-establishment/

20   Geoff Manaugh, 'Critical Condition', http://bldgblog.blogspot.com/2010/11/critical-condition.html.

21   'Critical Failure', website of The Wheeler Centre, http://wheelercentre.com/calendar/program/critical-failure/.

22   'Critical Failure' website.

23   Georgie Williamson, 'Bugger the Bloggers: Old-World Critics Still Count', *The Australian*, online edition, September 1, 2010, http://www.theaustralian.com.au/news/arts/bugger-the-bloggers-old-world-critics-still-count/story-e6frg8nf-1225911745917.

24   Rebecca Starford, 'Failing Critical Failure: The problem with engaging in real conversation about literary criticism', September 10, 2010, in *Kill Your Darlings* Blog, http://www.killyourdarlingsjournal.com/2010/09/failing-critical-failure-the-problem-with-engaging-in-real-conversation-about-literary-criticism/, consulted March 31, 2011.

25   Alison Croggan, 'The Return of the Amateur Critic,' 14 September 2010, in *Unleashed* (Australian Broadcasting Commission), http://www.abc.net.au/unleashed/29938.html.

26   Alison Croggan, 'The Return of the Amateur Critic',

27   James Elkins, *What Happened to Art Criticism*, Prickly Chicago: Paradigm Press, 2003, 2.

Robin Boyd and the Art of Writing Architecture

PHILIP GOAD

Roy Grounds described Australian architect, Robin Boyd (1919–1971), his professional colleague and erstwhile friend, as a 'scribbler'.[1] This was a derogatory remark – a slight against Boyd's career-long passion for writing about architecture. Indeed it was this writing that constitutes – arguably – Boyd's greatest contribution to Australian architecture and Australian social and environmental commentary. Many have argued that this is why Boyd's name is remembered – for his writing. Looking at the complex and diverse nature of Boyd's multiple approaches to architectural writing, reveals how as a practice his work was targeted to particular readerships, ensuring reception at scholarly, professional and popular levels, and within local, regional, national and international spheres. Boyd's ability to cross these boundaries has, in Australia at least, not been equalled since. It can be argued that Boyd's writing, which

made him a public figure in Australia, constituted an architectural practice more persuasive than his own considerable talents as an architect. This paper considers the models, both popular and professional, for Boyd's writings, the unique position internationally that he can claim as a writer on architecture, his use of drawn images to support text and provide polemic, as well as his collaboration with photographer, Mark Strizic, to describe his own designs in *Living in Australia* (1970), a text divided into thematic sections of surface, space, structure and spirit, which also described the style and ornament of his writing art.

Beginnings

Robin Boyd started writing about architecture first in 1938 while a student at the Royal Melbourne Technical

College and then at the Melbourne University Architectural Atelier (MUAA) from 1939 until 1942. Writing was an activity that by all accounts he preferred to the drudgery of the Beaux Arts style esquisses set by Leighton Irwin for the university atelier. One of his first articles was written for the 1938 edition of *Lines*, the annual of the Victorian Architectural Students' Society (VASS). Boyd's article 'Charivari' was based on the regular feature of the same name, which appeared in the English journal of satire, *Punch, or the London Charivari*, and presented a medley of cultural inadequacies across Melbourne's popular appreciation of art, literature, theatre, cinema and photography.[2] Boyd's style of writing was artful, ironic, delighted in caricature and was pointed in its criticism. It struck the perfect pitch for a student readership, was pithy and possessed a dose of humour that had no match in the dour professional journals of the day. The target of criticism was the low-level of and parochial complacency of local cultural appreciation. It was a criticism of culture.

But it was in *Smudges*, the monthly newssheet published by VASS and which folded down to pocket size, that Boyd began to give fuller voice to a way in which Melbourne's student body might develop a lively discourse about contemporary art and architecture. The first issue of May 1939 was the joint production of Boyd and fellow student Roy Simpson (1914-1997). From the second issue, Boyd became editor of *Smudges*, writing most of the contents and continuing in this capacity for three years until issue no. 34 (April 1942) when war enforced temporary cessation of the journal.[3] The first editorial stated clearly the new publication's aim: forthright architectural criticism with the goal of raising standards and promoting modern architecture.

Key features of *Smudges* were its 'Blots' and 'Bouquets' of the month given to works of contemporary Australian architecture, which excited great interest, amusement and even legal action. The most controversial 'Blot' went in June 1941 to Arthur Plaisted's Castle Towers,

Marne Street, South Yarra – a castellated block of apartments, which *Smudges* described as: 'garbage … as bad from a social viewpoint as it is ridiculous from an aesthetic viewpoint.'[4] Plaisted was furious, believing it was not just a smear campaign by VASS against one of his buildings, but part of a plot by the Royal Victorian Institute of Architects (RVIA) to discredit him and his role in Melbourne's architectural scene generally. The case died down but only after Boyd published a retraction, delivered in appropriately Gothic typeface.[5]

Smudges was also political in its criticism, attacking the banning of German architectural journals *Baukunst* and *Bauformen*, criticising prime minister R.G. Menzies for his comment that architecture is the 'lowest form of art in Australia'[6], and castigating both state and federal governments for their inactivity in housing provision[7], while controversially praising the Housing Commission of Victoria's Fishermans Bend housing estate. At the same time, *Smudges* was prepared to comment on the 1939 *Herald Exhibition of French and British Contemporary Art*, to review films such as *Mayerling*, *La Kermesse héroïque* and *Un Carnet de Bal*, and to praise Peter Bellew's editing of *Art in Australia* and R. Haughton (Jimmy) James's article on design in industry in *Australia National Journal*. The vital, pithy format of *Smudges*, distributed nationally and internationally, inspired the establishment of *Angle*, the newssheet of the Modern Architecture Research Society (MARS) in Sydney in May 1941. *Smudges* was also noted in the United States by influential architectural journals, *Pencil Points* and *Architectural Forum*, while students of the Harvard Graduate School of Design in 1941 began *Task*, their own version of *Smudges*.[8]

Boyd's writing as a student was interrupted by the onset of WWII. However he didn't stop writing, producing two articles for *SALT*, the army newsletter, on two subjects that would later become major themes: increasing the design quality of the everyday Australian

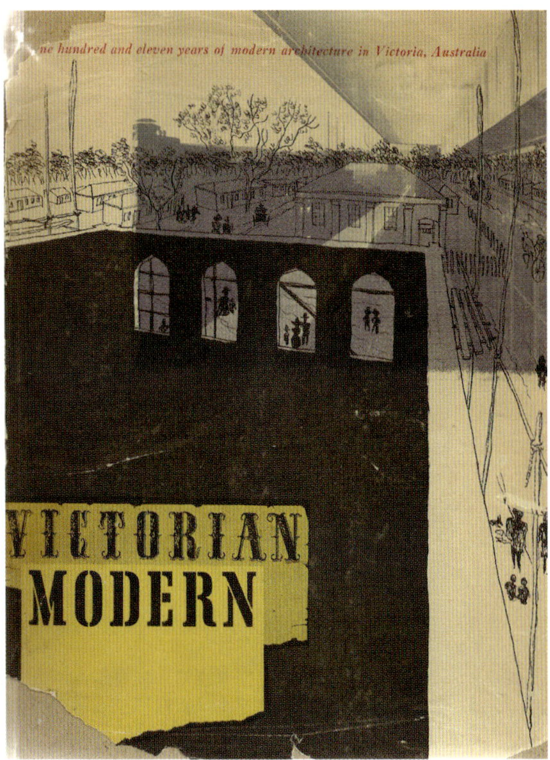

house and encouraging a rethinking of the Australian city.[9] In both articles, Boyd deployed a typical tactic, which would later be used to great effect when writing for *The Age*: architectural polemic matched with an actual architectural design. In this, Boyd reveals himself to be an architect and not a scholar writing in a detached manner, using his skills as a writer and a delineator to forge for himself a way of architectural writing. Drawing was clearly a key aspect of Boyd's persona. His fluency with the pen was matched by a similar fluency with drawing, both serious and satirical. In the immediate post-war years, his drawings for Insulwool advertisements

in *Smudges* already reveal a self-critical position with respect even to the shortcomings of contemporary modern architecture. Drawings such as these recall those of British observers of architecture and popular taste, Osbert Lancaster, Evelyn Waugh and even Boyd's uncle, Martin Boyd (writing under the pseudonym of Martin Mills), whose caricature of the so-called 'Mary Ann Queen Anne' would appear in later Boyd books.[10]

In 1946 VASS commissioned Boyd to write *Victorian Modern: One Hundred and Eleven Years of Modern Architecture in Victoria, Australia*. It was the first attempt by an Australian architect to document an historical pedigree of modernism in Australian architecture. No such book existed and VASS members were keen to document pre-war achievements across a broad spectrum of building types, and critical was Boyd's discovery, through Clerehan's advice, of 'Prophets' like Harold Desbrowe-Annear, Walter Butler and Edward Fielder Billson.[11] Boyd's condensed and carefully edited architectural history from 1834 was outlined as a series of peaks and troughs of architectural progress, with the 19th century delineated as 'Primitives' and 'Pioneers' followed by 'The Opulents' and 'The Decadents' and then rising again with the 'Prophets' of *Victorian Modern*: Walter Burley Griffin and Marion Mahony, Robert Haddon, Harold Desbrowe-Annear, Edward Fielder Billson and Leighton Irwin. Boyd then highlighted the importance of individuals like Best Overend and Roy Grounds (with a special focus on his apartment buildings of the early 1940s), institutions like the Gordon Institute of Technology in Geelong under the leadership of George R. King, and the work of government agencies, in particular the socialised imagination of the State Electricity Commission of Victoria under the direction of A.R. La Gerche and then William Gower from 1937, which sponsored the construction of towns associated with the production of electricity and supply of water at Yallourn, Eildon and the Kiewa Valley. He also showed modernism's breadth across a range of building types, including retail, factories, milk bars, office buildings, flats and kindergartens.

Published in 1947, *Victorian Modern* was not just a landmark piece of selective architectural history, it was also a visual tour-de-force, revealing Boyd's skills as a graphic artist and his love affair with typography.[12] Neil Clerehan had always thought Boyd's subscription to the British journal, *Signature: a Quadrimestria of Typography and Graphic Arts*, arcane and odd, but at the same time quirkily brilliant.[13] Boyd put his interests to full effect from the title page, contents page and throughout the slim volume to reinforce his thesis of peaks and troughs of architectural progress. His cover combines florid type for 'Victorian' and Corbusian stencil for 'Modern'. Boyd then placed a sketch of early Melbourne showing the building of Scots Church in 1841 overlaid onto a Wolfgang Sievers photograph of the rooftop restaurant of Stephenson & Turner's recently completed ES&A Bank in Collins Street (1939–41).[14] This was a calculated palimpsest of past and present and a stronger statement than a comparable book cover and book of just two years before by Sydney architect and planner, Walter Bunning (1912-1977).

While Boyd, Clerehan and others found Bunning's *Homes in the Sun* (1945) crashingly dull, they nevertheless took some cues from its structure and graphic design: a brief potted history of urban planning in Australia followed by spirited advocacy of progressive modern architecture.[15] Bunning's book was far more sober and politically focused, arguing for reform across all aspects of Australian architecture and planning. Boyd's book, by contrast, is decidedly faster and looser, more architectural and focused on a specific place – Victoria – and the book's second half presented a strong thesis for a regionalist approach to the design of the Victorian type. Ironically, Bunning reviewed *Victorian Modern*, and while generally positive, he proffered:

A great critic must of necessity be sufficiently detached from the actual practice of architecture to be able to analyse, compare and draw conclusions without prejudice. He cannot be a distinguished executive.[16]

Boyd would never be able to be fully detached and his writing, throughout his career, reveals an interest or investment in each issue upon which he opens up to his chosen readership. This was, as the years developed, a deliberate strategy. Without a documentary architectural history to fall back upon, his writings, sometimes in the void unfilled by others, became surrogate histories. But in virtually every instance they are really pieces of architectural or cultural criticism. Boyd was in fact writing in the manner of an architect as critic. Like an architect accommodating his clients, Robin Boyd targeted his readers and wrote accordingly. After 1947, two distinct bodies of writing emerged and developed in parallel: the first was that for his Australian readership; the second was international.

In writing on architecture for an Australian readership, Boyd had three principal readerships: popular, professional and what I have called, cultural (as opposed to scholarly), each having a goal of advancing the cause of architecture, of raising public awareness, in effect educating Australians about the significance of the built environment.

An Australian readership: popular

Answering his own 1939 call in *Smudges* for a public voice on architecture, Boyd began writing for a public or popular readership in 1947. Between July 1947 and June 1956, a period of nine years, he was to write at least one article each week on the subject of architecture in the Melbourne-based newspapers *The Age* and then *Herald* newspaper. Between 1964 and 1971, he wrote for the nationally based daily, *The Australian*. The output was prodigious.

In July 1947, he had been appointed director of the RVIA Small Homes Service in Melbourne. Part of this role involved the writing of a regular weekly column, 'Small

Homes Section', in *The Age* newspaper, as well as producing drawings, plan and description of the virtues of a small house being offered by the service for just £5.00, and all the other literature and graphic material required by the service.[17] Just two weeks after resigning as director of the Service in December 1953, he began writing a weekly 'Building and Design' column for the rival Melbourne newspaper, the *Herald*. For both newspapers, Boyd's articles discussed current architectural issues, fashions in materials, colours and form: it was a gentle advocacy for the new modern architecture and incremental cleansing of the taste palette of the average Melburnian. Sometimes it was simple and invaluable advice on how to build in the economically straitened circumstances of the immediate post-war years. In other cases it was about issues being faced by Melbourne such as the funding shortages for the Olympic Village or the new curtain-walled buildings in Melbourne's CBD. As an architect writing for a daily newspaper, Boyd's model would have been another Melbourne architect, Best Overend (1909–1977), who had written regularly in *The Argus* newspaper between 1934 and 1935, where he'd promoted international modernist architecture each week to a general audience, as well as publicising contemporary Melbourne works of progressive architecture.[18] Boyd's presence in the popular press however was longer, more sustained and his writing was lively, witty and succinct journalese. His technique was to excise the over-earnest, and instead appeal to common-sense. In short, he harnessed accessibility and as a result, architecture and Robin Boyd became household names in Victoria in the 1950s.

In 1952 Boyd, aged 33, still at the RVIA Small Homes Service and running a private practice at the same time, consolidated his growing reputation as a critic with another book. This time it was published not by students, but by Melbourne University Press. *Australia's Home* was Boyd's ambitious attempt to delineate an historic survey of the development of the design of the ordinary Australian house from European settlement to the present day.[19] Combining his fluent journalistic writing style with near-caricature drawings of the 'Major Steps of Stylism' in house design, Boyd's history like that of *Victorian Modern* was a powerful polemical tract with the troughs of poor taste contrasted with the pioneering works of selected 'good' architects. The first edition of *Australia's Home* included photographs and these, in medium and in content, were the heroic counters to Boyd's charming drawings. Boyd's front cover was another ironic polemical statement: with a background of Boyd's drawings of houses, all focus was on a red square, normally the sig-natorial stamp of any book by Frank Lloyd Wright. But, instead of Wright's initials, the signature of the Australian house was a homegrown product of dubious taste, a terracotta kangaroo finial atop a terracotta-tiled roof.

While *Australia's Home* was not really a piece of documentary history, because there was little else to match its range in terms of time, architectural knowledge and currency, it did in fact come to be used as a history of Australian domestic architecture, being reprinted again and again for the next 30 years. There was simply nothing to match it. It was far more detailed than the coffee table format of George Beiers's *Houses of Australia* (1948).[20] But it was not the work of a scholar. Indeed the first properly researched work of architectural history, MH Ellis's biography of Francis Greenway, had only appeared in 1949 and Morton Herman's *The Early Australian Architects and Their Work* (1954), arguably Australia's first piece of academic scholarship by an architect/academic, was yet to be published.[21] Building upon the popular success of *Australia's Home*, Boyd capitalised on the educative potential of the focus on the home and 10 years later in 1962, he published *The Walls Around Us*, a history of the Australian house for young people.[22] In a familiar strategy of capturing minds when young, Boyd had now complete coverage of the age-range of the everyday Australian: he'd succeeded in bringing architecture to the people.

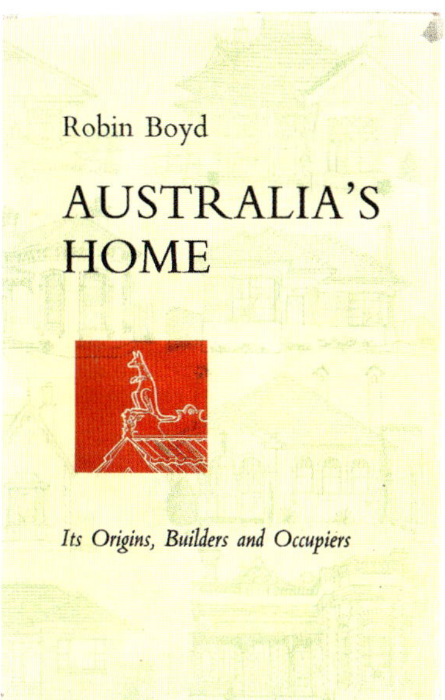
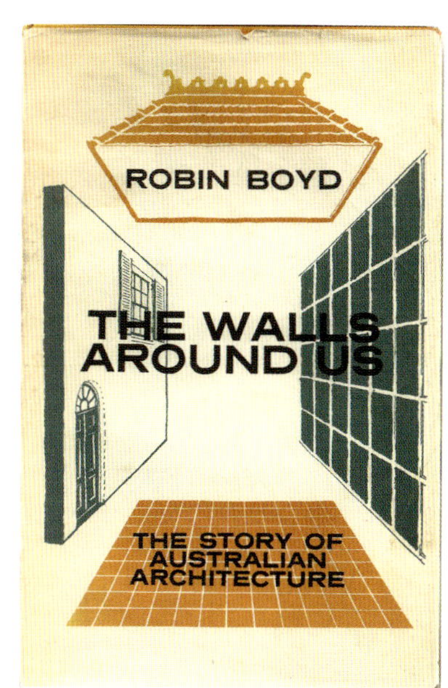

If Boyd by 1962 had reached the minds of many Australians through text, he also had a presence through radio and television. Geoffrey Serle and Helen Stuckey have documented Boyd's long association with television.[23] He had early experience in Boston in 1956 as an interviewee but it was his extended association with TV pioneer, Hector Crawford (1913–1991), and his sister, Dorothy Crawford (1911–1988), founders of Crawford Productions in 1945, that was to prove especially fruitful over a period of about seven years. An adept presenter on screen as well as script writer, Boyd was involved with a segment on the ABC's *Panorama* (1959) on architectural education; two half-hour programs on Channel 9 (1961); three half-hour programs entitled *The First Australian Homes* on the ABC's *University of the Air*; *Architecture*, a 10-part series on 20th century architecture (1962); and an eight-part series *Design in Australia* (1965). In each program Boyd was careful to include contemporary examples of Australian and international modern architecture together, though frequently ascribing a time lag of 10 to 20 years to the arrival of contemporary ideas in Australia. Despite this, in bringing architecture to the Australian public through television Boyd was, like Crawford, without question a pioneer.[24]

In 1964, Boyd resumed regular writing in a daily newspaper, this time it was the nationally based *The Australian*. Amongst the usual dissections of the house, urban issues dominated these articles. The various plights of non-planning and bureaucratic suffocation in Melbourne, Sydney and Canberra were complemented by Boyd's notes from his inveterate bouts of overseas travel. Moscow, Chandigarh, New York and also Brasilia (which Boyd did not visit) were all discussed.[25] Boyd had transferred his focus from the house and the suburb to the city. His last newspaper article was written for *The Australian* on 1 August 1971, just two months before he died.

An Australian readership: professional

If Boyd had been able to bring architecture to the people through the daily media of newspaper, television and radio, he did not neglect his professional peers – far from it. In many respects he was just as active within the professional sphere. The difference was that he pursued architectural ideas with a different tone. It was more serious and engaged. His characteristic caricature drawings played no part here. Between July 1949 and December 1952, Boyd was associate editor of the national magazine, *Architecture*, contributing a regular feature, 'Victorian Scene'. Over the next 20 years, he used the national journal sporadically as a mouthpiece for talking to professional peers and promoting ideas.

With old friend and fellow student, Peter Newell, Boyd wrote the article 'St Lucia: A Housing Revolution is Taking Place in Brisbane' in July 1950.[26] This article extended the idea of regionalism to Queensland, using the same selective historic technique Boyd had used to promote the Victorian Type in *Victorian Modern*. The houses of Robin Dods were touted as exemplars and Boyd and Newell encouraged a new and rational rethinking of the light timber frame, illustrating their pitch with houses by Hayes and Scott, Vitaly Gzell, Karl Langer, and Gordon Banfield amongst others. Three months later, Boyd produced a similar article, entitled 'Mornington Peninsula', a further restatement of his urge to colleagues to think locally and creatively about structure and planning with respect to location and climate.[27] But after his six-month Haddon travelling scholarship tour of Europe in 1950, Boyd brought discussion of international ideas to his Australian readership. He began to shift position, from the New Empiricist stance embedded in his advocacy of regionalism to a more embracing internationalist outlook. Articles like 'More trouble in Ireland' (January–March 1951) and 'The New International' (April–June 1951) indicated for the first time, Boyd's emerging

position of relativism with respect to the intellectual and aesthetic challenges of post-war modern architecture.[28]

His interest in the latest intellectual current was matched by an emerging interest in historic buildings, and he published in 1952 on the centenary of Joseph Reed's arrival in Australia, an article on Reed's buildings.[29] He wrote on design practice in 1957, on motels in 1960, and in June 1967, his article 'The State of Australian architecture' was a perceptive account of the shift in creative energies in Australian architecture from Melbourne in the 1950s to Sydney and Perth in the 1960s.[30] In 1969, his article '1980+' was a transcript of his paper given at the 1969 RAIA Convention in Adelaide.[31] Each of these articles in *Architecture Australia* lent a specific form of authority to Boyd's writings. His preparedness to present broad national overviews, cover a range of issues and indicate direction for the profession was rare.

A more immediate form of 'speaking' to the profession was instigated by Boyd in November 1952 when he and David Saunders (1928–1986), both working at the University of Melbourne, edited the first issue of *Cross-Section*, a four-page pamphlet that published short factual details of current building activity in Australia. An exercise in brevity, *Cross-Section* was aimed exclusively at the architectural and building professions. Themes of production and construction dominated in this matter-of-fact bulletin. Unlike *Architecture Australia*'s current 'Radar' section, which was based on *Cross-Section*, the earlier bulletin combined information and the most condensed form of criticism – in one or two lines. A broad net was cast, and the intention was to awaken interest across the country in what was occurring in all centres: a tactic of criticism by comparison. The mix of brief text and multiple illustrations meant that as a bulletin issued free to architectural practices across Australia, it enjoyed 20 years of unusual success from 1952 until 1971, with editorship being passed onto others including Saunders, Balwant Saini, Neville Quarry and Jeff Turnbull.

Boyd's facility in producing pamphlet-like publications was put to effective use again in early 1969, when as Geoffrey Serle has observed, Boyd returned to the excitement of his *Smudges* days in the production of the RAIA Victorian Chapter magazine, *Architect*.[32] As managing editor, Boyd oversaw the magazine's redesign into a boldly coloured square format with text in marginal 'newsprint' columns and a hole cut out of the cover. Boyd produced nine issues together with Neil Clerehan and Leckie Ord. The journal's visual and writing style was lively, especially in its first editorial lead article entitled 'Architect Power', where Boyd pronounced: 'This is the high season of the underdog, the age of his discovery of strength in unity. Black Power. Student Power. Backbench Power. Teenybop Power.'[33]

Architects, Boyd believed, should embrace discourse, look for some form of architectural consensus (arguing that Sweden, Japan and Canada had done so), and at the same time jettison the idea of a 'Great Australian Style':

> The idea of an Australian National Architectural Style is discredited – economically, ethically, artistically, intellectually and technically – and with it goes the only advantage which our isolation ever gave us. Now that the jet planes and television satellites of the last ten years have drawn us into the world, we cannot pretend to any sensible degree of separate architectural development. Our architecture is part of world architecture and is judged with world architecture – by everyone else, if not yet by ourselves.[34]

Outside the institutional frame of the RAIA, Boyd also contributed for his professional peers a chapter on 'The Neighbourhood' in Ian Mackay's edited volume *Living and Partly Living: Housing in Australia* (1971).[35] Here, Boyd broached the issue of housing choice and the suburbs, raising issues then about density, typology and demographics, issues that were remarkably prescient given Australia's exponential urban growth some 40 years later.

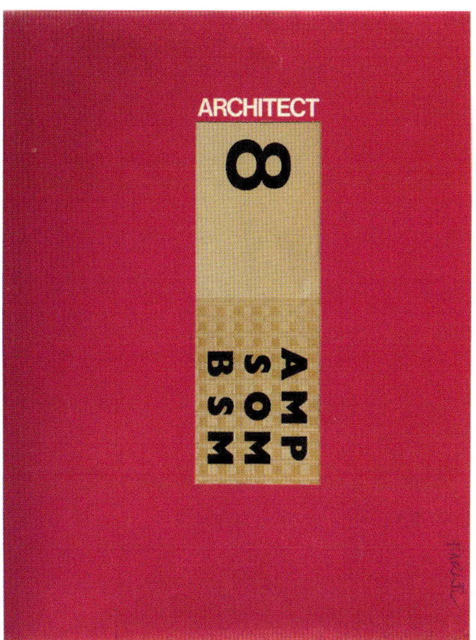

An Australian readership: cultural

If Boyd understood well the mentality of his professional – architectural – readership and wrote accordingly, his public voice, achieved through his constant presence in Australian newspapers, meant that Boyd was often invited to contribute to publications that addressed broad aspects of Australian culture. This was his third form of readership within Australia. Boyd wrote for the literary-cultural journal *Meanjin* in 1952 and 1958; the *Current Affairs Bulletin* in 1954; *The Victorian Historical Magazine* (1955); *The Nation*, *Walkabout*, *The Bulletin*; and for *Hemisphere*, the journal of Australia-Asia cultural exchange.[36] He contributed chapters on Australian towns and cities to W.V. Aughterson's *Taking Stock: Aspects of Mid-Century Life in Australia* (1953); one on 'The Look of Australia', a disquisition on the Australian tendency to amateurism and anti-professionalism in Peter Coleman's *Australian*

Civilization: A Symposium (1962); and even a chapter on 'Mass Communications' in Norman Harper's *Pacific Orbit: Australian-American Relations since 1942* (1968).[37]

However without doubt, his most successful book that addressed Australian visual culture and cemented his position, as Australia's public intellectual in matters of the built environment, was *The Australian Ugliness*, published in 1960. It was a diatribe against the visual impoverishment of the Australian city and a critique of the unthinking acceptance by Australian society of the American commercial and materialist psyche. Here Boyd had free reign. Not only was he able to fashion an entire text but he also designed the cover and executed the illustrations. In this book, Boyd's technique of satirical criticism in drawing and writing reached a new level of sophistication. His cover depicted a white armless Grecian nude atop a Doric column, juxtaposed against similarly brutally pruned trees, a townscape of signs and dustbins and overhead power lines. Covers to later editions illustrated street scenes through cracked spectacles or doubled and upside down images of the commercial strip. He also introduced, tongue-in-cheek, new catchy terms and '–isms', which became part of an Australian cultural lexicon: 'featurism', 'austerica' and 'arboraphobes'. In a familiar strategy, he structured the book with peaks and troughs (mainly troughs) of aesthetic activity. The book was a huge success, probably because of Boyd's by-now familiar preparedness to critique without restraint, and because the style of the writing was accessible, witty and perceptive. *The Australian Ugliness* was reprinted again and again, became required reading across many school syllabi, and was reissued again on its 50th anniversary.[38]

By the early 1960s, Boyd appeared to be everywhere: in the newspaper, on the radio, on television, and in the popular home journals. Significantly, he was a spokesman, a critical voice rather than a documenter of architectural history or academic scholar. In many respects this is a reflection of his position as a practising architect and not as an academic scholar or a full-time journalist or magazine editor, and so his writing is cut to fit – brief, direct and pointed, opinionated but ever present. And this was the goal, to make architecture an everyday point of discussion. His 1967 Boyer Lectures for the Australian Broadcasting Commission were published as the book, *Artificial Australia*.[39] His lecture for the Fabian Society was published with others in John Button's *Look Here!* in 1968.[40] A gifted speaker, he lectured at exhibition openings, conferences, at universities and all manner of professional and cultural gatherings. These speeches were invariably republished as articles in the professional journals or reported in the daily newspapers. People wanted to know what Robin Boyd thought.

An international readership

In Australia, Boyd's hands-on, regular and continual bombardment of the Australian public and the architecture profession with incisive critique, and with his ideas about design and the positive creative skills of the architect, meant that he earned for himself a public reputation as a commentator on architectural affairs few architects any-where in the world could match. It was a rare position. By contrast and at the same time, Boyd was writing for an international market. These articles and books show Boyd to be a writer for a critically literate architectural profession. Their content is discursive. In spite of the lesser need to incite discussion, Boyd now acted as a voice from the frontier: he brought Australian architecture to the world like no other before or since. To the British *Architectural Review*, he brought 'Port Phillip Idiom: recent houses in the Melbourne region', articles on Victorian ironwork, Walter Burley Griffin and Canberra.[41] He was Australian correspondent for the New York-based *Architectural Forum* from 1965 until 1970 and Australia's contributing editor for John Donat's *World Architecture* series, and through these two avenues articles on Harry Seidler, Jørn Utzon

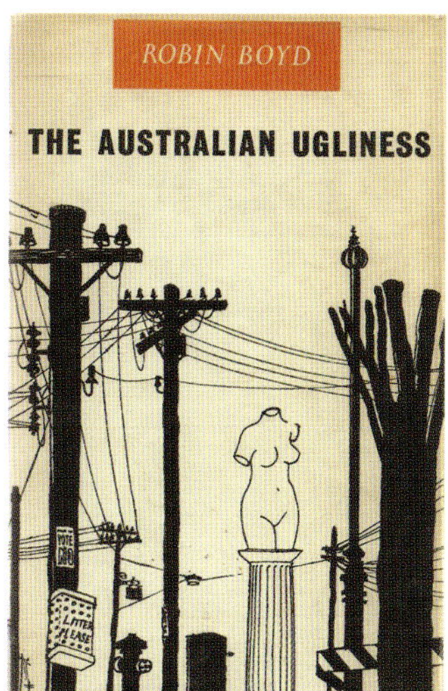
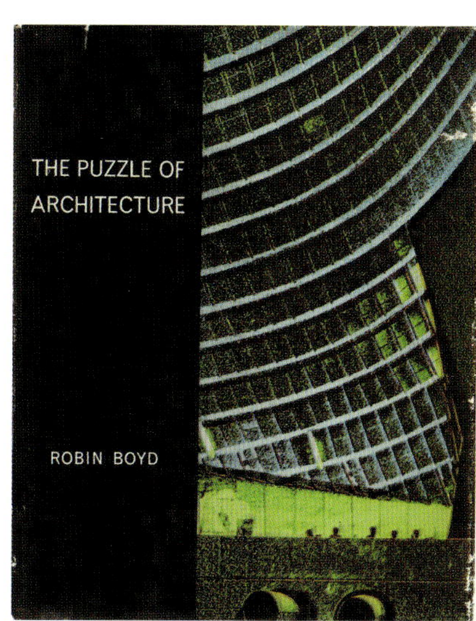

and the Opera House debacle, Yuncken Freeman, Hely, Bell and Horne, and his own firm of Romberg and Boyd, exposed Australian architecture to international eyes.[42]

Importantly, Boyd's international work included theoretical writings. The September 1951 article 'A New Eclecticism?', written for *The Architectural Review*, was one of his most important statements on post-war architectural theory.[43] In arguing for a broader interpretation of functionalism, one that might consider it from multiple viewpoints, Boyd teased readers with another 'ism' just after the *Review*'s dalliance with New Empiricism and before New Brutalism. Supplementing his argument with reference to other important articles in the *Review* by Swiss architectural historian Sigfried Giedion on Alvar Aalto and its editor, JM Richards, both of whom were promoting a more balanced and expanded definition of what functionalism might mean, Boyd's thesis of a 'New Eclecticism', while accurate and internationally relevant, was not widely taken up. Perhaps the examples he used to demonstrate his argument – Harry Seidler's Rose Seidler House, Wahroonga

(1947–50) and Roy Grounds's Goodes House, Frankston (1948) – were not an internationally acceptable basis on which to argue theory. Boyd even prefaced his article with the words, 'Although the subjects are in Australia….' Or perhaps, Boyd's 'New Eclecticism' was too balanced a position. It was almost radically sensible. The irony was that the diversity of form and expression of the post-war work of major architectural figures in modern architecture like Le Corbusier, Walter Gropius and Frank Lloyd Wright would by 1960 demonstrate the veracity of Boyd's thesis.

Importantly, Boyd's writing for overseas magazines placed him on equal terms with internationally renowned critics. Articles for *The Architectural Review* between 1951 and 1970, *Architectural Record*, *Architectural Forum*, *Casabella* and *Progressive Architecture*, as well as *Harper's Magazine* discuss stylism, engineering and the dilemma of modernism in the second half of the 20th century. Titles such as 'The Functional Neurosis', 'Engineering of Excitement', 'Decoration Rides Again', 'Has success spoiled modern architecture?', 'Under Tension', 'The

Search for Pleasingness', and 'The Counter-revolution in Architecture' indicate Boyd's close connections to current international debate.[44]

Some of these articles were reworked and reprinted in *The Australian Ugliness* of 1960 and more importantly in *The Puzzle of Architecture*, published in 1965.[45] This latter book was to have signalled Boyd as a theoretician of world standing. *The Puzzle of Architecture* however suffered from a lack of recognition. As a collection of critical vignettes reflecting on the failure of modern architecture to reach satisfactory results in the post-war years and accompanied by Boyd's relaxed and personable sketches, the book, while stunningly accurate in describing mid-1960s architecture culture, reached no firm conclusion. His identification of the relativism of design practice in the mid-1960s failed to impress an international (largely Anglophone) readership, which was then ready for Robert Venturi's purported academic authority and plethora of tiny but seductive photographs and drawings in *Complexity and Contradiction in Architecture* which appeared in 1966 – one year later – which in layout seemed almost identical to Boyd's, only glossier and with photographic images, and emanating from New York's Museum of Modern Art, a more powerful launderer of discourse than Melbourne University Press.[46]

There was clearly a problem. Boyd's overseas articles and *The Puzzle of Architecture* were themselves at a theoretical frontier – the English end of a fading brutalist discussion just at the moment when English critic, Reyner Banham, published his book on the subject of brutalism and an endpoint which Boyd himself recognised (see for example, 'The Sad End of New Brutalism'[47]) – delving into the work of American formalists such as Paul Rudolph, John Johansen and Edward Durrell Stone, and, at the end of the post-war functionalist debate, which had been perpetuated by Sigfried Giedion, J.M. Richards and extended later by Banham. Boyd's writings, while well aware of the Smithsons, excluded Team 10 and the writings of the Italians. He also excluded Vincent Scully and

Robert Venturi. But like the older generation of critics such as Arthur Drexler and J.M. Richards, he included Japan and, like Giedion, he also included Jørn Utzon. Perhaps chastened by the mixed reviews of *The Puzzle of Architecture*, Boyd in the late 1960s focused his international criticism on expo design, 'anti-architecture' and the debacle of the Opera House: that is, on things closer to home and on areas in which he himself had international design interest, such as his role as exhibits designer for the Australian pavilions at Montreal in 1967 and Osaka in 1970, and in his Fishbowl Takeaway Fish restaurant, South Yarra, Victoria (1969), which bore an uncanny resemblance to the base of the 1958 Brussels Atomium.[48]

If *The Puzzle of Architecture* did not succeed in positioning Boyd as an initiator of ideas on the world architectural scene, the books *Kenzo Tange* (1962) and *New Directions in Japanese Architecture* (1968) placed him firmly in the realm of world commentators on architecture.[49] The Japanese had for many years been on the frontier of western architectural discussion. But in 1962, Kenzo Tange, through Boyd's writing (achieved through the agency of Walter Gropius, who had been tremendously impressed by Boyd's biographical article on Gropius in 1954 for the *Current Affairs Bulletin* and Boyd's subsequent meetings and correspondence with Gropius[50]), was now rightly placed alongside Buckminster Fuller, Philip Johnson, Eero Saarinen and Louis Kahn in the publisher George Braziller's *Makers of Contemporary Architecture* series. This placed Boyd alongside authors such as John McHale, John Jacobus, Allan Temko and Vincent Scully. With *New Directions in Japanese Architecture*, Boyd joined other notable international writers such as Royston Landau, Robert Stern, Vittorio Gregotti and Stanislaus von Moos in another George Braziller series 'New Directions in Architecture'. Boyd was thus an accepted and respected name in world architectural literature, so much so, that in 1973, the American Institute of Architects posthumously awarded him its AIA Architecture Critic's Medal.[51]

Last works

In 1970, Boyd with photographer Mark Strizic published *Living in Australia*.[52] It was Boyd's only book where his own architectural commissions were connected to an idea of a personal theoretical position. Unlike émigré Harry Seidler's *Houses, Interiors, Projects* (1954) or émigré Enrico Taglietti's monograph *Enrico Taglietti: an architect in Australia* (1979), *Living in Australia* was not a documentary catalogue of works. It perhaps best represents the difference between Boyd's unique architectural position and that of his peers.[53] This book is evocative rather than taxonomic and has, as its afterword, an appreciation by David Saunders, one of Australia's first career-based and academically trained architectural historians, something Boyd was not. Boyd's buildings as they are pictured and written about thematically have, like his writings, the engaging presence described elsewhere as the power of the pamphlet at the frontier.[54] With the pamphlet, the reader is as essential as the pamphlet is, by its very nature an article of immediate relevance. The content of a pamphlet has to be strong, persuasive and often has the poetic power of the maxim. This is the quality of Boyd's buildings, an undiscussed quality, which deserves a full study in itself. Boyd's houses fit their clients like a suit of clothes, in much the same way that Boyd knew and accurately gauged his multiple readerships. His architecture never held a definite tectonic course for others to follow. He was a critic in his architecture: his buildings have the requisite relativism of balanced critique.

Conclusion

Robin Boyd died on 16 October 1971, aged 52. In the week that he died the third in his international lecture series, 'The Melbourne Architectural Papers' went ahead. The first two speakers had been critics J.M. Richards and Peter Blake.[55] The third speaker, Italian architect Giancarlo de Carlo, spoke about 'an architecture of participation' on 18 October 1971, just two days after Boyd had died. Boyd's untimely death was a great loss but it also revealed a void in Australian architectural criticism, which few others could fill with the same level of persuasion, accessibility or ubiquitous presence. Certainly there were others who wrote more profoundly and with greater theoretical certitude, such as Peter Kollar in Sydney. And there were real historians such as Morton Herman, James Freeland and David Saunders, who were far more systematic than Boyd but infinitely less colourful and less adaptable to a wider range of public, professional and cultural critique. They were specialists; he was not.

Unlike overseas colleagues such as Reyner Banham and Vincent Scully, Boyd was not a full-time academic nor was he a full-time critic. He was also not a full-time editor of a magazine as were his long-time friends, J.M. Richards (1907-1992) and Peter Blake (1920-2006), editors respectively of *The Architectural Review* (1937-1971) and *The Architectural Forum* (1950-72). He was an architect. But, unlike two architects he admired, Paul Rudolph and Eero Saarinen, Boyd wrote continually throughout his career.

This paper has outlined a structured way of examining a lifetime of writing, specifically as a mechanism to organise a wealth of material. Boyd wrote a great deal. Overlaid onto that structure has been a supposed intent attributed to Boyd, that of being self-aware and consciously targeted in his writing mission. This was because Boyd in his Australian-based publications never discussed his own way of thinking about writing about architecture. However in the course of researching this paper, an article not previously cited in any Boyd study came to light. Entitled 'These Critical Times' and published in the *Journal of Architectural Education* in the summer of 1957, this article is a complete reflection by Boyd on the nature and challenges of writing architectural criticism.[56] Written when he was in Boston as part of his Visiting

Bemis Professorship at MIT in 1956–7, Boyd called for the following: architectural criticism that was actively pursued as a 'pressure for creative design'[57]; popular architectural criticism that was in the tabloids alongside film notes and television reviews; a strict avoidance of the idea that criticism of a building is a criticism of its architect (Boyd believed that the client, society and the apathetic man in the street were all responsible and that the reader was also responsible); that architectural comment should appear in journals like *Time*, where even a text drawing attention to excessive dullness was a valuable contribution; that an expert and comprehensively informed analysis for the professional readership was a valid but different form of criticism from that aimed at a public readership; that courage was required in the professional and public press to make criticism (that films are reviewed without fear, so why not buildings and the city?); that there was room for the specialist detachment of scholars but they have specific readerships of their own; that critics of all kinds should avoid jargon; that architecture needs words to exist and that its language must be maintained as a mechanism of professional and public discourse; that any critic should be able to isolate the conceptual idea, identify the motivating thought – the intention of the work – and then the critic must attempt to judge that intention – whether suitable, sensible, sensitive or shallow; that critics should see how the architect nursed their idea or intention to the end, and check as to whether the intention was lost.

At a moment of reflection on his US sabbatical, Robin Boyd recorded themes that might be followed as a critic, almost all of which he had already put into practice, or would subsequently do so in his own architectural writing over a period of more than 30 years. He had clear writing strategies for his popular, professional and cultural readerships. The 1957 article marks a moment when Boyd realised his own practice of writing architecture was defined by a self-conscious understanding of his own limits and intentions as an architect who not only wanted to make architecture but wanted to write it as well – it was for him a very special form of art.

1 Roy Grounds, quoted in Conrad Hamann, 'Modern architecture in Melbourne: the architecture of Grounds, Romberg and Boyd', PhD thesis, Monash University, 1978, 205.

2 Robin Boyd, 'Charivari', *Lines*, August 1938, 8-9.

3 *Smudges* was revived after World War II in 1946 by new editor Neil Clerehan (1922-).

4 *Smudges*, June 1941.

5 *Smudges*, November 1941.

6 *Smudges*, May 1940.

7 *Smudges*, March 1941.

8 See Robin Boyd, 'Death of the Architect', *Pencil Points*, 23: 4 (April 1942), 182-3; Robin Boyd, 'Voices of the younger men', *Architectural Forum*, 74: 1 (January 1941), 48. *Task: a magazine for the younger generation in architecture* (Summer 1941-c.1948) was published from Robinson Hall by architecture students at Harvard University, Cambridge, Mass., USA.

9 Robin Boyd, 'Houses in the Air', *SALT*, 7: 2 (27 September 1943), 32-5 and Robin Boyd, 'Is this your city? – No, because your city's out of date,' *SALT*, 7: 13 (28 February 1944), 28-31.

10 Martin Mills, 'Domestic architecture in Australia: past mistakes and future possibilities', *The British Australian and New Zealander* (London), July 1927, 18.

11 Conversation with Neil Clerehan, 16 July 2010. See also Harriet Edquist and Richard Black (eds), *The architecture of Neil Clerehan*, Melbourne: RMIT University Press, 2005, 18-19.

12 Robin Boyd, *Victorian Modern: one hundred and eleven years of modern architecture in Victoria, Australia*, Melbourne: Victorian Architectural Students Society, 1947.

13 Conversation with Neil Clerehan, 16 July 2010.

14 A further reason for using this image was that the designer of the rooftop restaurant was German émigré modernist architect Frederick Romberg (1913-1992), who at the time was working in the Stephenson & Turner office.

15 Walter Bunning, *Homes in the sun: the past, present and future of Australian housing*, Sydney: WJ Nesbit, 1945.

16 Walter Bunning, Review of Robin Boyd, *Victorian Modern* (1947), in *Architecture* (October 1947).

17 Philip Goad, Chapter 3 'The RVIA Small Homes Service', in 'The modern house in Melbourne 1945-1975', PhD Thesis, University of Melbourne, 1992, 3/30-3/50.

18 See Philip Goad, 'Best Overend: pioneer modernist in Melbourne', *Fabrications*, 6 (June 1995), 101-24 and Ann Stephen, Andrew McNamara and Philip Goad, *Modernism and Australia: documents on art, design and architecture*, Carlton, Vic.: The Miegunyah Press, 2006, 174-5.

19 Robin Boyd, *Australia's home: its origins, builders and occupiers*, Carlton, Vic.: Melbourne University Press, 1952. Later editions followed in 1968, 1978 and 1987.

20 George Beiers, *Houses of Australia: a survey of domestic archi-tecture*, Sydney: Ure Smith Ptd Ltd, 1948.

21 M.H. Ellis, *Francis Greenway: his life and times*, Sydney: Shepherd Press, 1949. Morton Herman, *The early Australian architects and their work*, Sydney: Angus & Robertson, 1956.

22 Robin Boyd, *The walls around us: the story of Australian architecture*, Melbourne: Cheshire, 1962.

23 Geoffrey Serle, *Robin Boyd: A Life*, Carlton, Vic.: The Miegunyah Press, 1995, 241-5 and Helen Stuckey, 'ABC Television Series: Introduction', *Transition*, 38 (1992), 132-3.

24 Boyd not only brought architecture to the public through television. He also wrote and illustrated *The Flying Dogtor* (1963), an animated cartoon series produced by Crawford Productions and which was set in the Australian outback and starring a dog doctor protecting Australian native animals.

25 See for example, Robin Boyd, 'Two Moscows on the Metro', *The Australian*, 8 August 1964; 'The city of sordid splendour', *The Australian*, 26 August 1964; 'Melbourne: the symbol of Australia's split personality', *The Australian*, 1 September 1964; 'Symbol city: Canberra approaches a new era as a national showpiece', *The Australian*, 28 November 1964; 'Lost chance at Brasilia', *The Australian*, 20 February 1965 and 'Sydney: reluctant patron', *The Australian*, 21 September 1965.

26 Robin Boyd and Peter Newell, 'St. Lucia: A Housing Revolution is Taking Place in Brisbane', *Architecture* (July 1950), 106-9, 114.

27 Robin Boyd, 'Mornington Peninsula', *Architecture*, 38: 4 (October-December 1950), 148-52.

28 Robin Boyd, 'More trouble in Ireland', *Architecture*, 39: 1 (January-March 1951), 27, 36. Robin Boyd, 'The New International', *Architecture* 39: 2 (April-June 1951), 61-2. See also Philip Goad, 'Towards a New International?: Australian houses 1950-1965', in R. Blythe and R. Spence (eds), *Thresholds* (Papers of the Sixteenth Annual Conference of SAHANZ), Launceston and Hobart, 1999, 81-6.

29 Robin Boyd, 'Joseph Reed of Melbourne: Centenary of a Pioneer of the Boom Days', *Architecture*, 40: 4 (December 1952), 132-4, 140.

30 Robin Boyd, 'The Future of Design Practice', *Architecture in Australia*, 46: 3 (July-September 1957), 73-6; Robin Boyd, 'No Vacancy', *Architecture in Australia*, 49: 4 (December 1960), 61-3; Robin Boyd, 'The State of Australian Architecture', *Architecture in Australia*, 56: 3 (June 1967), 454-65.

31 Robin Boyd, '1980+', *Architecture in Australia*, 58: 3 (June 1969), 429-33.

32 Geoffrey Serle, *Robin Boyd: A Life*, 300.

33 Robin Boyd, 'Architect Power', *Architect*, 3: 1 (March-April 1969), 19.

34 Robin Boyd, 'Architect Power', *Architect*, 3: 1 (March-April 1969), 20.

35 Robin Boyd, 'The Neighborhood', in Ian McKay et al, *Living and Partly Living: Housing in Australia*, Melbourne: Thomas Nelson, 1971, 32-43.

36 Robin Boyd, 'The Architect and the Anchor', *Meanjin*, 11 (Summer 1952), 151-3; Robin Boyd, 'Look back in apathy', *Meanjin*, 17: 78 (June 1958), 175-8; Robin Boyd, 'The Modern Mind: Walter Gropius', *Current Affairs Bulletin* (University of Sydney), 14: 1 (26 April 1954); Robin Boyd, 'Walter Burley Griffin in Victoria', *The Victorian Historical Magazine*, 26: 3 (March 1955), 102-15; Robin Boyd articles in *The Nation*, see 'After Greenway' (20 April 1963), 'A I for a Y' (4 May 1963); Robin Boyd, 'Presenting Australia at Expo 70', *Walkabout*, 35 (December 1969), 20-2, 25; Robin Boyd, 'A "fair go" for the artist who doesn't go to far', *The Bulletin*, 89 (2 September 1967), 91-2; Robin Boyd, 'The excitement of world fairs', *Hemisphere*, 10 (September 1966), 8-15.

37 Robin Boyd, 'Australian towns and cities', in W.V. Aughterson (ed.), *Taking Stock: Aspects of Mid-Century Life in Australia*, Melbourne: F.W. Cheshire, 1953, 15-32; Robin Boyd, 'The Look of Australia', in Peter Coleman (ed.), *Australian Civilization*, Melbourne: F.W. Cheshire, 1962, 68-78; Robin Boyd, 'Mass Communication', in Norman Harper (ed.), *Pacific Orbit: Australian-American Relations Since 1942*, Melbourne: F.W. Cheshire, 1968, 144-54.

38 *The Australian Ugliness* was first published with no photo-graphic plates in 1960 by F.W. Cheshire, who quickly produced a second edition in 1961. The book was then republished by

Penguin Books in association with F.W. Cheshire in 1963, with a foreword by John Betjeman and eight pages of photographic plates, with a reprinting in 1968 that included an expanded introduction by Boyd and subsequent reprintings in 1970, 1971, 1979 and again in 1980 with an afterword by Harry Seidler. Then in 2010, on the fiftieth anniversary of its first publication, *The Australian Ugliness* was reissued by Text Publishing, with a new foreword by Melbourne novelist, Christos Tsiolkas, and a further afterword by architects, John Denton, Geoffrey London and Philip Goad.

39   Robin Boyd, *Artificial Australia* (The Boyer Lectures 1967), Sydney: Australian Broadcasting Commission, 1967.

40   Robin Boyd, 'The Nineteen-Sixties in Focus', in John Button (ed.), *Look Here! Considering the Australian Environment*, Melbourne: F.W. Cheshire, 1968, 33-45.

41   Robin Boyd, 'Port Phillip Idiom: recent houses in the Melbourne region', *The Architectural Review*, 112: 671 (November 1952), 309-13; Robin Boyd, 'Victorian Victorian', *The Architectural Review*, 114: 680 (August 1953), 104-8; Robin Boyd, 'Architectural Levee in Canberra', *The Architectural Review*, 116: 692 (August 1954), 115-6; Robin Boyd, 'Melbourne Ironwork', *The Architectural Review*, 120: 716 (September 1956), 192-3; and Robin Boyd, 'Griffin in Melbourne', *The Architectural Review*, 137: 816 (February 1965), 133-6.

42   John Donat (ed.), *World Architecture*, London: Studio Vista, vol. 3 (1966) & vol. 4 (1967).

43   Robin Boyd, 'A New Eclecticism?', *The Architectural Review*, 110: 657 (September 1951), 150-3.

44   Robin Boyd, 'The Functional Neurosis', *The Architectural Review*, 119: 710 (February 1956), 84-8; Robin Boyd, 'Engineering of Excitement', *The Architectural Review*, 124: 742 (November 1958), 294-308; Robin Boyd, 'Decoration Rides Again', *Architectural Record*, 122: 3 (September 1957), 183-6; Robin Boyd, 'Has success spoiled modern architecture?', *Architectural Forum*, 111 (July 1959), 98-103; Robin Boyd, 'Under Tension', *The Architectural Review*, 134: 801 (November 1963), 324-34; Robin Boyd, 'The search for pleasingness', *Progressive Architecture*, 38: 4 (April 1957), 193-205; Robin Boyd, and 'The counter-revolution in architecture', *Harper's Magazine*, 219: 1312 (September 1959), 40-8.

45   Robin Boyd, *The Australian Ugliness*, Melbourne, F.W. Cheshire, 1960 and Robin Boyd, *The Puzzle of Architecture*, Carlton, Vic.: Melbourne University Press, 1965.

46   Robert Venturi, *Complexity and Contradiction in Architecture*, New York: Museum of Modern Art, 1966.

47   Robin Boyd, 'The Sad End of New Brutalism', *The Architectural Review*, 142: 845 (July 1967), 9-11.

48   Robin Boyd, 'Utzon: the end', *Architectural Forum*, 124: 5 (June 1966), 90; Robin Boyd, 'Experimenting with boxes: Habitat's cluster', *Architectural Forum*, 126: 4 (May 1967), 29-41; Robin Boyd, 'Germany', *The Architectural Review*, 142: 846 (August 1967), 129-35; Robin Boyd, 'Antiarchitecture', *Architectural Forum*, 129 (November 1968), 84-5; Robin Boyd, 'Expo and exhibitionism', *The Architectural Review*, 148: 882 (August 1970), 99-100, 109 and posthumously published, Robin Boyd, 'A night at the Opera', *Architecture Plus*, 1: 7 (August 1973), 48-54.

49   Robin Boyd, *Kenzo Tange*, George Braziller, New York, 1962 and Robin Boyd, *New directions in Japanese architecture*, New York: George Braziller, 1968.

50   See Philip Goad, 'Robin Boyd and the Post-war "Japanisation" of Western Ideas', *Architectural Theory Review*. 1:2 (November 1996): 110-120.

51   See 'Architecture Critics' Medal, Citation are awarded for Penetrating Insights', *AIA Journal*, 59: 4 (April 1973), 9-10; 'Facets', *Architectural Forum*, 138: 3 (April 1973), 72; and 'AIA to Present Awards in Architecture and Related Fields at Convention', *Architectural Record*, 153: 4 (April 1973), 36; 'Posthumous award', *Architecture Today*, 15: 4 (May 1973), 7.

52   Robin Boyd, *Living in Australia*, Sydney: Pergamon Press, 1970.

53   Harry Seidler, *Houses, Interiors, Projects*, Sydney: Associated General Publishers, 1954; Enrico Taglietti, *Enrico Taglietti: an architect in Australia*, Milano: Lodigraph, 1979.

54   Philip Goad, 'Pamphlets at the Frontier: Robin Boyd and the will to incite an Australian architectural culture', in Karen Burns and Harriet Edquist (eds.), *Robin Boyd: the architect as critic*, Melbourne: Transition Publishing, 1989.

55   The lectures were published as the 'Melbourne architectural papers: architecture in the seventies'. See J.M. Richards, *A critic's view*, 'Royal Australian Institute of Architects, Victorian Chapter', 1971 and Peter Blake, *The new forces*, Melbourne: Royal Australian Institute of Architects, Victorian Chapter, 1971.

56   Robin Boyd, 'These Critical Times', *Journal of Architectural Education*, 12: 2 (Summer 1957), 33-6.

57   Boyd, 'These Critical Times', 33.

International Comparison as Critical Strategy

PAUL HOGBEN

Some of the most prominent acts of architectural criticism in Australia have been based on international comparison, that is, when speakers and writers have evoked comparisons between architecture in Australia and that overseas, in order to gain leverage in the critical judgement of local buildings. Take, for example, Morton Herman's memorable series of comparisons published in the journal *Architecture* in 1937 and 1938 in which typological contrasts between modern European buildings and their Sydney equivalents were made in order to criticise the state of local architecture and urban pride.[1] Around 20 years later, Robin Boyd described the climate of design in Australia as 'something like an uninhibited California' and 'diametrically opposed to that of Sweden, where the average exhibited taste is cultivated and there are few who rise above or sink below.'[2] This comparison featured in the preface of Boyd's seminal text *The Australian Ugliness*, and in its 1968 edition he proceeded to rank the 'national scores' of America, Britain and Australia 'in the degree of bad conscious design', with Australia 'very high on the list of conspicuous ugliness'.[3] Later, Harry Seidler used international comparisons between Europe, America and Australia to deride the postmodern interests of some of his contemporaries.[4] In each of these examples, international comparison played an important role in the formation of criticism.

In a broad sense, the principal target of the above-named critics was the aesthetic standard of architecture and design current in Australia at their respective times. In many ways they were continuing a tradition of discourse around the values that have underpinned aesthetic production and taste in Australia, and as art historians will testify, this tradition has been derived from complex processes of Australia's cultural formation and position as a recipient of cultural influences from elsewhere. In his study of early art commentary and criticism in Australia, Bernard Smith pointed out that critical activity in the first half of the 19th century showed a close relationship to English thought and taste during the same period.[5] This is to be expected, bringing into focus the historical grounds upon which aesthetic evaluation in Australia has occurred and the manner in which aesthetic standards have been defined and judged. For our colonial forebears, such standards were always relative to developments elsewhere. This suggests that a study of international comparison as a critical strategy, taking into account its conceptual and practical mechanisms, will contribute to a greater understanding of the grounds of aesthetic criticism in Australia and the cultural dynamics of its formation.

To start, it is important to see international comparison as a productive act of assemblage, representation and narration, in which relationships between works and practices from different countries are constituted and drawn into a plane of comparability and evaluation. Critics have an important agency within this. With an understanding of what is happening in other places, they can articulate the horizons through which a work could or should be evaluated, casting that work in a broader field beyond its immediate context of production. Their role is to make an informed, judicious comparison of the work's merits in relation to others, including comment on what the work contributes to the field itself. This can be a source of both insight and anxiety for those involved, since critiquing a work in relation to others from different countries and using an international framework for comparison can enrich an understanding of horizons of possibility, but also of difference. A work can appear in stark relief to others, depending on conditions and contexts of production, but also on the manner in which

comparison is made. It is also important to recognise that international comparison can have a strategic function in relation to the construction, attribution and exercise of critical authority.[6] Depending on the cultural situation, knowledge of other places, whether gained through travel or other means, is generally treated with a degree of deference and respect, and thus can be a valuable currency in discourse and for rhetorical purposes.

In reference to cultural situations, a tendency here might be to evoke the notion of 'cultural cringe' to explain the value attributed to Australian works and practices when compared to works and practices elsewhere. Cultural cringe is defined as an admiration and unquestioning acceptance of the standards of other cultures considered as superior, and where opinions from those cultures are used to define the value of that which is local or home grown. Several publications released at the time of the bicentenary of white settlement in Australia claimed that up until the mid 1960s a cringe culture dominated the literary, artistic, educational, social and economic spheres of Australian life.[7] This view has however been challenged by political scientist Leonard Hume, who exposes the faulty claims and poor research standards of cringe theorists, and finds that when considering the evidence closely, another picture of cultural interest and self-worth emerges.[8] Hume's analysis is persuasive and compels historians to look carefully at the evidence before arriving at conclusions about cringe culture in Australian history. The present study follows Hume's lead and presents three case studies of international comparison in the realm of architectural discourse across 80 years, from the mid-1850s to the late-1930s, in order to pay close attention to the sources and consider them in detail. Even though the argument may appear to manifest cultural cringe, there are dimensions to comparative statements, especially around the construction of critical authority, which would be missed if too great a weight is placed on the analysis of a cringe condition.

The streets of southern Europe and 1850s Melbourne

Among the periodicals that were established in Melbourne during the post-gold rush years was the *Journal of Australasia*, which began publication in July 1856.[9] In its second issue the journal published an article entitled 'Our Buildings', in which its nameless author, realising they might 'stand in a non-conforming minority of one', presented a critical, if somewhat melodramatic, attack on the architecture of Melbourne, claiming it possessed a 'total want of picturesqueness in design, treatment, or otherwise'.[10] Expressing a liking of the urban fabric of cities in southern Spain and northern Italy, its author made this comparison:

> You cannot walk through a street in Cordova, in Verona, in Genoa, in Venice, or in Seville, without experiencing a sense of gratification, as your eye rests – though it be for a moment only – upon some picturesque facade, gateway, arch, window, tower, gable, niche, pinnacle, fragment of tracery or moulding, pillar or perspective; some new grouping of old familiar objects; some accidental adjustment or contrast of light and shade; some fresh tone of colour from an atmospheric variation; or some additional beauty discovered in a mural fresco, or in the mere disposition of the awning in a balcony. You shall diligently pick your way through any street in Melbourne, and experience no other emotions than those of pain and weariness resulting from the ghastly ugliness of the white-faced buildings and the dull and deadly visages of the bluestone structures.[11]

The comparison here is made on the basis of what appears to be first-hand experience of the mentioned cities and a cultivated sense of the picturesque, of delight taken in formal, textural and atmospheric variety, in which aesthetic sensation had an emotional register. The picturesque as an aesthetic theory had its origins in the mid-18th century contemplation of valleys, lakes, ruins and the 'picturesque gardening' of the English countryside and estates as formulated in the writings of William Gilpin and William Shenstone.[12] Uvedale Price was later to extend picturesque aesthetics to the appreciation of rural peasant shelters and landscapes.[13] In the 'Our Buildings' article, the picturesque is evoked in relation to the visual experience of walking along the streets of cities that, within the 18th century, were more readily associated with the 'grand tour', that heady (and hedonistic) custom of the English aristocracy and upper class,[14] which unlike the favoured scenes of picturesque tourism, was oriented towards the classic over the gothic and the regular over the irregular.[15] By the mid-19th century, however, such contradictions had been erased, principally through the writings of John Ruskin who, in *The Poetry of Architecture* (1839), described the picturesque qualities and details of both English and continental cottages and villas, including those of Italy.

The author of the 'Our Buildings' article evoked the image of the dilettante traveller, arriving in present-day Melbourne: 'suppose that I have just landed in the colony – that I am fresh from the continental cities of Europe; and that, with recollections of these still lingering in my mind, and connecting themselves with the powerful impressions of the wealth of Victoria.'[16] The writer claimed that, 'I am neither an architect nor an artist: I simply regard what I see with an eye that has been educated by observation, and a mind that instinctively revolts against ugliness.'[17] This visual and mental capacity was the key distinction the writer considered to separate his own sensitivities from 'those who coolly plan and systematically perpetuate the architectural monstrosities which disfigure the streets and suburbs of this city'.[18] A barb was made against the leaders of the local architectural profession, asking if there was an architect in the colony possessing 'sufficient vigour of mind' and 'genius' to originate a new style of architecture that was picturesque, full of variety, and 'as thoroughly in harmony with the climate and scenery of Australia, as the Gothic was with the climate and scenery of northern, and as the Grecian, the Roman, the Saracenic, the Byzantine and the Romanesque were, with those of southern, Europe?'[19] This question picked up on an earlier section of the article where the author cited Johann Winckelmann's thesis that climatic influences were responsible for 'much that was special' in Greek architecture and sculpture.[20] Asserting the importance of climatic influences on the municipal and domestic architecture of ancient Rome, medieval Italy and Spain, the author rhapsodised over the al fresco life of southern European cities with their shaded arcades and piazzas.[21]

While the 'Our Buildings' article alone can be considered a good example of colonial architectural criticism based on international comparison and a mélange of conceptual ideas and sources, its significance is heightened due to the reaction it received from John George Knight in his first presidential address to the newly formed Institute of Victorian Architects on 9 October 1856.[22] On this important occasion, in front of an audience of fellow architects and members of the institute, as well as guests from the press, the Philosophical Institute and other learned societies, Knight spent a large portion of his one and a half hour speech responding to the 'Our Buildings' article (even reading out a large section of the article). He did not mention the name of its author but stated that he believed the person to be an 'accomplished member of the daily Press', 'a sincere intellectual reformer, with a keen perception of the beautiful', whose talent and ability he acknowledged 'as placing him above the charge of writing a vindictive criticism'.[23] However, Knight recognised the threat that the article posed. The *Journal of Australasia* was aimed at a literary-minded, politically informed readership, and Knight sensed the potential of the article to fuel the profession's 'censors' and critics.[24] In order to disarm and redirect the article's arguments,

Knight struck out at the grounds of its comparison, pointing out the historical differences between European cities and Melbourne, the latter having been only 15 years before 'little more than a gigantic sheep-walk'.[25] He stated that the monuments of antiquity had been designed and built over long periods of time and were rarely completed 'within the life time of their originators'.[26] In addition, unlike the current conditions in Melbourne, 'labour was of nominal value; captives and serfs were employed'.[27]

In destabilising the terms of comparison Knight tried to shift the grounds of judgement, arguing that 'in common fairness' architects and other professionals should judge each other 'by a colonial gauge' and 'not take the greatest men of the greatest eras and grumble at ourselves because we cannot equal them'.[28] 'In common justice let us be tried on no higher scale of merit than we pretend to possess,' Knight proposed.[29] Shifting the grounds of judgement was a strategic move to channel the aesthetic concerns of the 'Our Buildings' article, thus enabling Knight to articulate a political-critical vision of professional agency for the architect, one that was aligned with his own experience and 'common sense view', and one that would underpin the discursive formation of institutional affairs for years to come. Although Knight admitted he did not possess the poetic ability to treat 'the abstract claims of architecture', the occasion of having aesthetic issues placed within the public debate, even with such severity, provided him an opportunity to use these in support of his own arguments about aesthetics in the city of Melbourne. Among other things this included the alignment of buildings, and a revision of the Building Act to allow for colonnades and covered pathways, thus increasing the artistic and compositional scope of building design and construction and giving architects greater influence and control within the realm of urban affairs.[30] This was an instance where public criticism based on an international comparison and a fondness for the picturesque gave added strategic impetus to institutional formation and focus on the terms and mechanisms through which architects could gain critical authority in colonial Melbourne.

The 'American Romanesque' and Sydney

During the late 19th century, most critical currency in architectural discourse in Australia was concerned with theorisation and speculation around the development of a national style of architecture. In Sydney, John Sulman and James Green were active commentators on this topic, each contributing articles to the *Australasian Builder and Contractors' News,* a Sydney-based weekly that circulated widely during the boom period of the late 1880s and early 1890s, and of which Green was an editor.[31]

From 1890 to 1893 Green and the *Australasian Builder and Contractors' News* championed the work of Henry Hobson Richardson, publishing illustrations and descriptions of his designs, in particular the Albany City Hall, New York, constructed between 1880 and 1883 (Figure 1). This building was considered 'a poem in stones', and Richardson was praised for the way he had strengthened and individualised the building through the breadth of the solid masonry in the great angled tower.[32] Buildings that showed the influence of Richardson's work, such as William S. Fraser's design for the Carnegie (Free) Library in Allegheny, Pennsylvania, were also admired.[33] These buildings were considered by Green to be a very good demonstration of the eclectic adaption of older styles to create a distinct modern style of architecture, one that had attracted the name of 'American Romanesque'.[34]

Although Green claimed that the modern Romanesque of the Americans was 'Romanesque in name only', it perfectly fitted his criteria for the development of a national style. He argued that: '[t]he American Romanesque is a genuine attempt to evolve, in the free and independent manner characteristic of the American

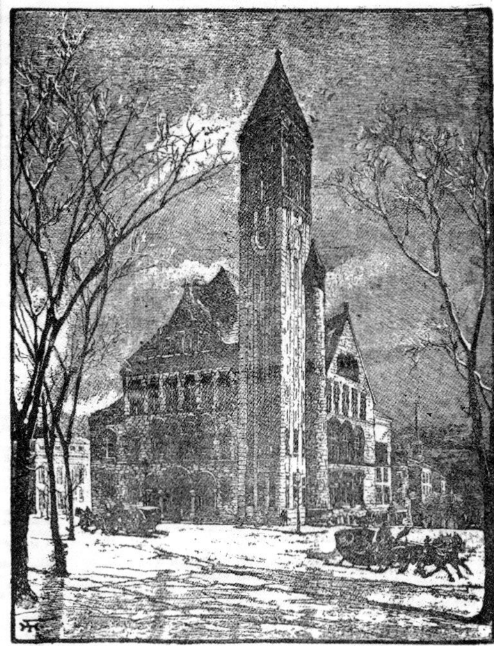

Drawing of City Hall, Albany, New York. Source: *Australasian Builder and Contractors' News,* 7, no. 189 (December 20, 1890): 487.

people, a national style of architecture of their own.'[35] The problem, however, was that the American Romanesque did not fit Green's preference for Grecian architecture as a stylistic model for city buildings in Australia, and this is where the strategic use of international comparison came into play.[36] Green was well aware that architects in Sydney were taking stylistic cues from the American Romanesque for their designs. Two of the largest projects in Sydney at the time displayed this influence – the offices of the Equitable Life Assurance Company of the United States, being constructed on George Street (Figure 2)[37] and the chosen scheme for the new Sydney Markets, to be developed on a site further

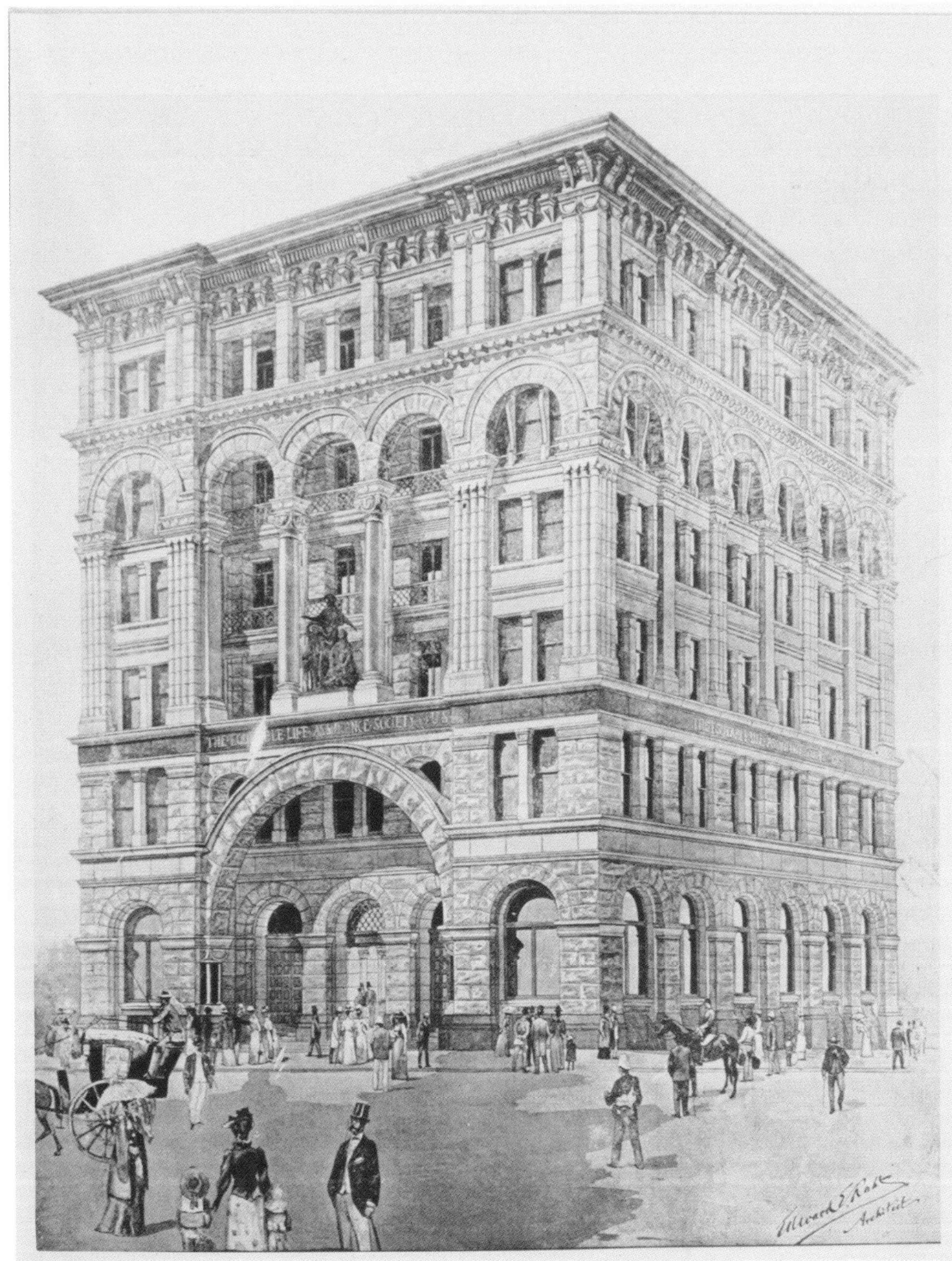

Edward Raht's drawing of the Equitable Life Assurance Building, George Street, Sydney. Source: State Library of New South Wales.

south on the same street, designed by the city architect, George McRae.[38]

For Green, the local importation of the American Romanesque needed to be curtailed and critical measures put in place to stop the trend overshadowing his own stylistic preferences for city architecture. This was the aim of his article 'American Architecture and its Influence', published in the *Australasian Builder and Contractors' News* in August 1893, in which he argued there was a incompatibility between the cities of America and Sydney, which meant the importation of the American Romanesque needed to be handled with 'considerable caution'.[39] Green argued that:

> American cities are planned with the largeness of idea, and on the consequent spacious scale, which characterises everything American; the massiveness of their Romanesque is consequently toned by space and distance; and what, under the conditions of more restricted areas, would be coarseness, becomes, with their surroundings, merely power.[40]

Green felt that Sydney's 'almost criminally narrow streets' did not serve the massiveness of the American Romanesque well, as buildings could not be seen at a sufficient distance to appreciate the impressiveness of composition that was integral to this style of architecture. This was the case with the Equitable Life Assurance Building whose proportions, Green argued, were 'positively overwhelming' to the street viewer standing below. When viewed from a hundred yards or so further south, which was the only possible view, the appearance of the General Post Office, 'on which the city and colony have set such store', was reduced to a 'mere toy erection'.[41] Similarly, there was no angle of view that would allow the imposing effect of the Romanesque facades of the Sydney Markets to be appreciated in their entirety, leaving the various features of the elevations to be viewed as individual installments.[42]

Green's background as a London-based art decorator, music critic and architectural journalist had given him a good grounding in the practice of artistic and architectural criticism. He was well read and his articles drew from a range of literary, philosophic and artistic sources, from Goethe to Nathaniel Parker Willis. His principal source and influence, however, was John Ruskin, 'the great art-critic', and in writing about the aesthetics of Sydney architecture Green took his theoretical cues from Ruskin's *The Seven Lamps of Architecture*.[43] Like Ruskin, Green placed particular significance in composition, and just as it did for Ruskin, this bore consequences for his thinking about the setting and siting of buildings. Composition in architecture, Green argued, was 'the arrangement, proportion and disposition of masses, lines and ornaments, in such a manner as shall express the purposes and uses of the different portions of a building, and shall, at the same time, be completely satisfying to the eye.'[44] Thus issues of building mass, viewing position and the adaptation of detail were crucial, and if a building was designed to have an imposing character, this could only be apparent if it was seen at a sufficient distance so as to 'enable the eye to take in the complete composition at a simple glance'.[45] Green applied this thinking to a critical appraisal of the appropriateness of American Romanesque-styled buildings for Sydney. The limits of siting and viewing the Equitable Life Assurance Building and the new market building, making a clear view of their entire composition difficult, meant that architects needed to compensate by placing greater attention on the details rather than massing and composition. Fortunately, according to Green, the Romanesque 'lends itself to an infinity of beauty in its details', but he also asserted that '[t]he task may be less easy than if a more generally familiar style of architecture had been decided on for the new buildings'.[46]

With this pronouncement Green and the *Australasian Builder and Contractors' News* cooled their interest in the American Romanesque, stopped featuring the work of Richardson and his followers, and directed their attention elsewhere, to something that promised to be more compatible with Green's views of the source of a style of architecture for Australian cities – that of the classically inspired, white-stucco pavilions of the World's Columbian Exposition in Chicago.

Apart from the focus of comparison being on America rather than Europe, what comes to light in this second case is the role played by the media and media-based information. There has been no record found of Green having travelled to the United States and having gained first-hand experience of the work of Richardson and others. It seems his knowledge of American Romanesque buildings was based upon what he had learnt from others, along with images and information published in American journals and magazines, the international circulation of which had grown exponentially in the late 19th century. The *Australasian Builder and Contractors' News* had a reciprocal arrangement with the *American Architect and Building News* and *Architecture and Building*, from which it reprinted images of Richardson's work and other buildings. Mary N. Woods has described the special relationship that existed between Richardson and the *American Architect and Building News*, revealing how Richardson was prepared to pay half of the printing costs of photographic reproductions of his buildings for publication in this journal.[47] Photographic imagery was regarded as having a realism that lithographic renderings lacked, and Woods points out that the journal specifically associated the popularity of Richardson's work and the American Romanesque with the dissemination of these kinds of images.[48]

Green's opinion about the appropriateness of American Romanesque style buildings for Sydney was informed by his access to images of Richardson's work combined with the theoretical precepts that guided his aesthetic criticism. Even though his thinking and interests were an eclectic mix of ideas and positions – he promoted Ruskinian themes yet favoured Greek revival architecture

– the strength of his argument was derived from the sharpness of the international comparison he made of buildings and their urban context.

Flat buildings in Germany and Sydney

One of the main ways in which modern European architecture was described to Australian audiences during the 1920s and 1930s was in reports written by young architects who had been awarded scholarships to travel abroad and document their experiences and new knowledge of European cities and modern buildings.[49] These reports depicted personal encounters with buildings by leading modernists and described the impressions they made, as the young scholars built up an understanding of the material principles involved. This knowledge constituted valuable critical capital for the scholars, especially on their return to Australia when they argued for the adoption of new architectural philosophies, construction techniques and ideas for urban improvement. One such scholar was Morton Herman – author of the series of comparative articles mentioned earlier, who spent six years working and studying in England and travelling throughout the continent.[50] His travels took him to France, Austria and Italy, but it was Germany that made the strongest impression on Herman to the extent that he would later champion modern architecture in Germany more than that of any other country.

Herman travelled through Germany during the summer of 1933, a time when new laws and prohibitions introduced by Adolf Hitler and the Nazi Party were taking effect. Herman's report of this trip registers the impact these prohibitions were having on architecture, claiming that 'architectural thought is arbitrally[sic] deflected from its true course', creating 'the queer paradox that the achievements of German architects, which have made Germany's fame ring throughout the world, are held to be un-German'.[51] This regressive turn did not dampen Herman's keen will to see the architecture of the Weimar period, and his itinerary included visits to the major cities and towns, including Magdeburg, which he considered to be 'one of the cradles of modern architecture'.[52] During his trip, Herman was granted an audience with Paul Bonatz and Martin Wagner, and Hans Poelzig arranged permission for Herman to inspect the Haus des Rundfunks (Radio Building) in Berlin. Herman photographed the buildings he visited, using the images to illustrate his reports and articles. Among these buildings, the housing estates on the outskirts of Frankfurt, Magdeburg and Berlin drew his attention, especially the settlements located in forest and agricultural settings around Berlin designed by Bruno Taut and by Taut in association with Wagner. The skilful use of colour in these buildings impressed Herman immensely.[53] He admired the way garden courts, open space, cafes and restaurants were integrated into the housing settlements and how the settlements had been designed as suburbs rather than individual buildings.[54]

In the late 1930s Germany had lost its popularity as a place for travelling scholars to visit due to Hitler's dictatorship and the rise of extreme fascism.[55] However, local interest in contemporary German architecture remained, fostered by the conservative faction of the Sydney profession. (William) Ronald Richardson visited Germany after attending the Reunion of Architects in Czecho-Slovakia in September 1935,[56] and when back in Sydney gave a lecture to the New South Wales Chapter of the RAIA in which he stated that he had seen 'much of the happy result' that had come from Hitler's decree that architecture in Germany should follow traditional lines.[57] In presenting a vote of thanks to Richardson, Professor Leslie Wilkinson, chair of architecture at the University of Sydney, commented on the 'cleverness with which architectural matters are now being handled in Germany', and that local architects could learn 'a tremendous amount' by studying some of the work

shown in the lecture.[58] This work included brick country houses near Stuttgart and cottages in Hamburg, all with pitched tiled roofs.[59] While high-profile members of the local architectural profession admired Germany's conservative architecture, the political focus was firmly on slum clearance and rehousing, for which European housing schemes, including those in Germany, were being considered as a model to address Sydney's needs.[60] The NSW Housing Improvement Act had been introduced in 1936, creating the Housing Improvement Board whose mandate was to consider schemes for the relief of congested areas and to work in conjunction with local councils in slum clearance planning. Richardson was a member of the board, as well as the chair of the Chapter's Committee on Re-Housing. Soon after his arrival back in Sydney in 1937, Herman started working with Richardson and the board and together the architects were commissioned to design the first housing scheme under the Act, to be located in Erskineville.[61]

The strategy of using international comparison as a mechanism for critical discourse on local architecture was supported by Richardson who, even in citing the old adage that 'comparisons are odious', felt that international comparisons were an effective way to 'jolt' Sydney out of its current 'state'.[62] Herman obviously had no reservations about using this strategy and took it to new levels in composing his eight-piece series in which buildings in Sydney were compared to those from Europe for which solutions had been found for 'identical problems of design'.[63] European buildings were upheld as examples of good and 'intelligent' design that had resulted in coherent and tidy form, whereas in his conception their Sydney equivalents were the haphazard and 'distressing' products of a lack of design. Comparison of flat buildings directed discussion into the area of ideological values in which Herman asserted that the 'architectural spirit' of flat buildings in Europe and Sydney was a reflection of the 'sociological spirit'.[64] He was referring to the way flat buildings were conceived as an amenity for 'man in the mass' and for the benefit of community life. This was seen in flat buildings that had been planned as settings for communal life at the scale of street-defining urban complexes. Herman felt that German architects were leaders in this regard:

> It cannot be repeated too often that the German architects strive to make their buildings happy component parts of the landscape, and the flats in Berlin show what measure of success they so often achieve. Also they consider the *street* as a design as well as the individual buildings, a principle that is followed but rarely, locally.[65]

As illustrations of the German approach, Herman used an image of the Amerikanerblock (1930–31) designed by Otho Orlando Kurz and Eduard Herbert, as part of the Siedlung Neuhausen in Munich, and an image of the Onkel Toms Hütte cooperative housing estate (1926–32) at Berlin Zehlendorf by Bruno Taut. A comparative analysis of urban housing was also the topic of a paper given by Herman to the NSW Chapter in which he presented an extended version of this argument, taking aim at the obsession with land values and financial returns in Sydney that was 'robbing society at large of the amenities of the landscape', and local council by-laws that mitigated against the creation of buildings that enhanced

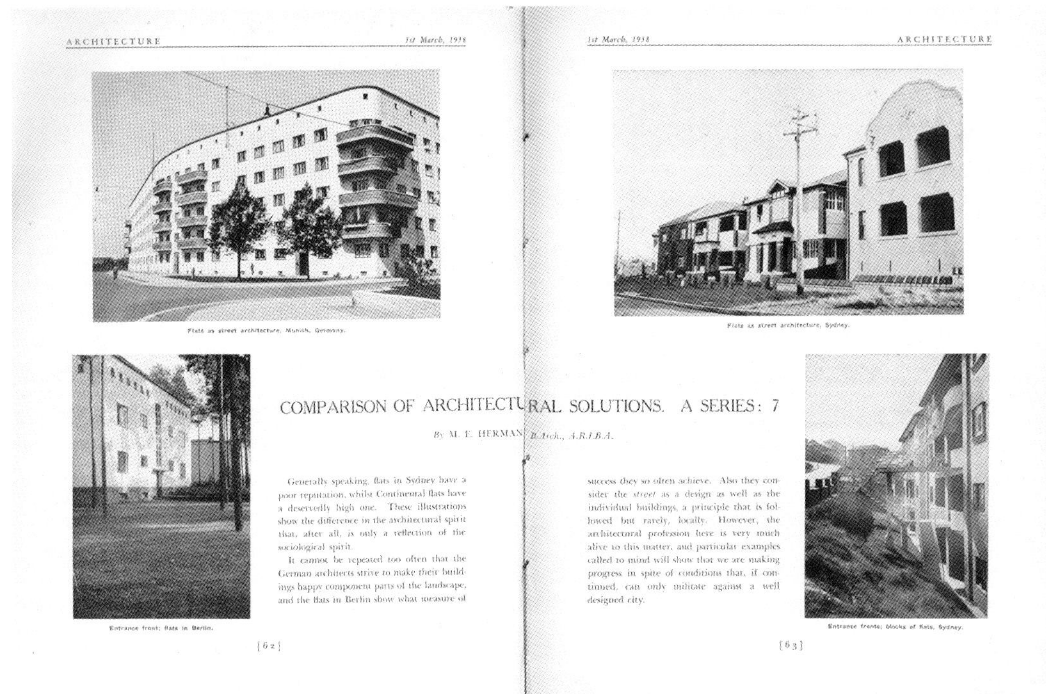

the coherency of the street. Here, too, images of housing estates by Taut, Wagner and Erwin Gutkind were used.[66] Their stark forms and hard lines may have unnerved local conservatives, but Wilkinson and Richardson who expressed their respect for his knowledge on the topic gained through his 'wide' experience nonetheless appreciated Herman's presentation. Experience rather than academic authority, seniority or rank was the basis upon which Herman's critical authority rested, and he was able to heighten this authority by professing knowledge of 'world standards' as the basis of his critical discourse. International comparison was the mechanism through which this authority could be maintained and this served Herman's critical ambitions well, to the point where he was able to make public and critical pronouncements on topics that would have normally been reserved for more senior, learned members of the profession.[67]

Conclusion

These three cases discussed reveal how international comparison has been used for the purposes of architectural criticism in Australia. By drawing on their knowledge of foreign architecture, critics were able to open up the discussion of local architecture and present a comparative assessment of its merit, in aid of particular rhetorical and promotional ends. In recalling the charms of southern European cities, the anonymous author of the 'Our Buildings' article was able to outline a sense of the picturesque for colonial Melbourne and to stir a reaction from the local architectural profession, which he succeeded in doing. For James Green, who was actively editing Sydney's reception of modern American architecture, the aim was to draw attention to an argument about the visual perception

Herman's comparison of flat buildings. Source: *Architecture*, 27, no. 3 (March, 1938): 62-63.

of city architecture that supported his stylistic interests over the importation of the American Romanesque. For Morton Herman, a travelling scholars' experience of modern European architecture allowed him to exploit his knowledge and imagery in an effort to introduce a new paradigm for architectural design in Sydney.

In each case, aesthetic judgement was formed from different theoretical positions and contexts: picturesque tourism, a Ruskin-inspired discussion of architectural composition, and the idea that beauty in modern design was found in its neatness. The theoretical depth of these positions varied, but each case tells a compelling story about the conception of the local in relation to the other and the manner in which this conception was articulated.

Each case might also be considered a part of the larger story of Australia's cultural formation: of the immigration of British artists and professionals to Melbourne during its 'golden era'; of the shift towards models of American business enterprise in the late 19th century; and the Australian introduction to European modernism in the inter-war period. The mechanisms of international comparison within architectural discourse and criticism during these times were conceptually and rhetorically specific, each involving particular constellations of knowledge in which the local and the foreign were pitted against each other. This knowledge might be considered dialectic in nature but it also had strategic dimensions that related to institutional and professional matters around the construction, attribution and exercise of critical authority. The essay has also revealed that the terms and logic of international comparison have themselves been the subjects of critical attention, dating back to George Knight's argument about the unfairness of using European cities and monuments as a measuring stick for the assessment of Melbourne's colonial architecture. In this, and also in Richardson's double take on the value of international comparison, we can detect both the excitements and apprehensions that accompany this activity.

1   Herman's series, entitled 'Comparison of Architectural Solutions', was published in *Architecture* from June 1937 to June 1938.

2   Robin Boyd, *The Australian Ugliness*, Melbourne: F. W. Cheshire, 1960, 2.

3   Robin Boyd, *The Australian Ugliness*, revised edition, Melbourne: Penguin Books in association with F. W. Cheshire, 1968, 15-16.

4   Harry Seidler, 'Principles in the Mainstream of Modern Architecture', *Bulletin*, NSW Chapter, RAIA (August, 1980), 18-19; Harry Seidler, 'Internationalism', *Architecture Australia*, 71, no. 5 (September, 1982), 58-60.

5   Bernard Smith, *Place, Taste and Tradition: A Study of Australian Art since 1788*, Melbourne: Oxford University Press, 1979, 90.

6   The construction of critical authority in architectural discourse is the theme of another research paper of mine entitled, 'Uncovering the Strategic: The Appeal to Nature in Early Twentieth-Century Architectural Discourse in Australia', *Interstices*, 10 (November, 2009), 75-87.

7   See, for instance, Stephen Alomes, *A Nation at Last? The Changing Character of Australian Nationalism, 1880-1988*, Sydney: Angus and Robertson, 1988, and James Walter and Brian Head (eds), *Intellectual Movements and Australian Society*, Melbourne: Oxford University Press, 1988.

8   Leonard John Hume, *Another Look at the Cultural Cringe*, CIS Occasional Paper 45, Sydney: The Centre for Independent Studies, 1993.

9   Founded in July 1856, the *Journal of Australasia* was a monthly literary and current affairs magazine initially edited by William Sydney Gibbons and published by George Slater of Melbourne. Its title was changed in January 1857 to *Illustrated Journal of Australasia: and Monthly Magazine* being handed over to a new proprietor, W. H. Williams, who aimed to popularise the magazine by publishing articles from a wider range of contributors. The magazine ended in 1858 due to financial difficulties.

10   'Our Buildings', *Journal of Australasia*, 2 (July, 1856), 50.

11   'Our Buildings', 51.

12   Malcolm Andrews, *The Search for the Picturesque: Landscape Aesthetics and Tourism in Britain, 1760-1800*, Aldershot: Scolar Press, 1989, 39-56.

13   Andrews, *The Search for the Picturesque*, 58-59.

14   Jeremy Black explains how the physical demands of travel and the amount of time needed to undertake the grand tour tended to make the tour the prerogative of youth and this meant that 'a certain amount of drinking, gaming and wenching was an acceptable cost of the system'. Jeremy Black, *The British Aboard: The Grand Tour in the Eighteenth Century*, New York: St. Martin's Press, 1992, 210.

15   Black, *The British Aboard*, 277.

16   'Our Buildings', 49.

17   'Our Buildings', 49.

18   'Our Buildings', 52.

19   'Our Buildings', 51.

20   'Our Buildings', 50.

21   'Our Buildings', 50.

22   The first Victorian Institute of Architects was formed through a series of meetings in July and August of 1856 and the first general meeting of the Institute was held on 28 August when John George Knight was elected president. This body existed until 1865. A second Victorian Institute of Architects was formed in 1871. Knight arrived in Melbourne in 1852 from England and after a short time in the goldfields he returned to Melbourne and joined the Public Works Department but resigned for private practice in 1854. He formed a partnership with Thomas Kemp and Peter Kerr, with Kemp returning to England in 1855. In 1856 Knight and Kerr were given supervision of the design and construction of the new Victorian Houses of Parliament.

23   'Meeting of the Victorian Institute of Architects', *Australian Builder and Practical Mechanic* (October 16, 1856), 274.

24   One of the Institute's first decisions was to introduce a scale of fees involving payment by builders for drawings and this had drawn disapproval from master builders, the courts and the public. There were also problems with the discrepancy of opinion between architects about the merits of buildings in Melbourne, leaving architects susceptible to disrespect and even legal abuse when serving as witnesses in court.

25   'Meeting of the Victorian Institute of Architects', 274.

26   'Meeting of the Victorian Institute of Architects', 274.

27   'Meeting of the Victorian Institute of Architects', 274.

28   'Meeting of the Victorian Institute of Architects,' 274.

29   'Meeting of the Victorian Institute of Architects', 274.

30   In this regard, Knight proposed the establishment of a Board or Commission of Public Improvement, which would have the power to adjudicate over the design of building elevations for particular localities and to define a general style of

architectural treatment for Melbourne's principal streets. 'Meeting of the Victorian Institute of Architects', 277.

31 John Sulman's articles, entitled 'An Australian Style', were published in the *Australasian Builder and Contractors' News* from May to June 1887. For a study of these articles see John Phillips, 'John Sulman and the Question of an 'Australian Style of Architecture',' *Fabrications*, 8 (July, 1997): 87-116.

32 James Green, 'Architecture in Many Lands: America,' *Australasian Builder and Contractors' New*, 7, no. 191 (December, 1890): 514. Other Richardson designs were featured in 'Our Illustrations: American Architecture', *Australasian Builder and Contractors' News*, 9, no. 222 (August 8, 1891): 108.

33 'Our Illustrations: American Architecture', *Australasian Builder and Contractors' News*, 8, no. 211 (May 23, 1891): 397.

34 Green, 'Architecture in Many Lands: America', 513. Green stated, 'the Americans have set an example to the world (including even India) of eclectically adapting older styles to the requirements of their life and climate, and impressing their modern architecture with a distinctive individuality of its own, which has led to the style being often designated the 'American Romanesque'.'

35 'American Architecture and its Influence', *Australasian Builder and Contractors' News*, 13, no. 327 (August 12, 1893): 78.

36 Green used the terms 'early Classic' and 'Grecian Doric' to indicate what he argued should be the source of a modern style of architecture for public buildings in Australian cities. He claimed that: '[t]he need for roomy porticos or colonnades, well sheltered from the sun, exists upon the shores of the Pacific as fully as on the borders of the Mediterranean, as does equally the tendency towards out-door life, arising out of the temperature and climate.' James Green, 'An Australian Style of Architecture: II', *Australasian Builder and Contractors' News*, 7, no. 181 (October 25, 1890): 302. As a guide, Green cited the 'Neo-Grec' buildings of Leo von Klenze and 'modern Germany', buildings he said that could claim 'parentage from Athens'. Locally, Green commended James Barnet's Australian Museum, saying 'the feeling that inspires it is more completely classic than in the case of any other building of the Colonial Architect's that I am acquainted with'. James Green, 'Sydney Architecture Aesthetically Considered II: Composition', *Australasian Builder and Contractors' News*, 6, no. 142 (January 25, 1890): 691. Later, Green pointed to Barnet's Law Courts and Telegraph Offices in Bathurst where the '[t]he Attic spirit seems to have been translated from Greek into Australian with singular felicity.' James Green, 'An Australian Style of

Architecture: II,' *Australasian Builder and Contractors' News*, 7, no. 181 (October 25, 1890): 302.

37 These offices were designed by the Austrian-American architect, Edward Raht, who arrived in Australia in 1891 to oversee the design and construction of buildings in Sydney and Melbourne for the Equitable Life Assurance Society of the United States.

38 McRae presented four different stylistic proposals for the design of the markets, described at the time as 'scholarly Renaissance', 'picturesque Queen Anne', 'classic Gothic' and 'American Romanesque'.

39 'American Architecture and its Influence', 78.

40 'American Architecture and its Influence', 79.

41 'American Architecture and its Influence', 79.

42 'American Architecture and its Influence', 79.

43 James Green, 'Sydney Architecture Aesthetically Considered I: Sites and Ground-Plans, and Things in General', *Australasian Builder and Contractors' News*, 6, no. 141 (January 18, 1890): 672. For a study of Green's Ruskinian tendencies see Mark Stiles, 'Reading Ruskin: Architecture and Social Reform in Australia, 1889–1908,' PhD thesis, University of New South Wales, 2010, 58-63.

44 Green, 'Sydney Architecture Aesthetically Considered II', 691.

45 Green, 'Sydney Architecture Aesthetically Considered II', 691.

46 'American Architecture and its Influence', 79.

47 Mary N. Woods, 'The Photograph as Tastemaker: The *American Architect* and H. H. Richardson', *History of Photography*, 14, no. 2 (April-June, 1990).

48 Woods, 'The Photograph as Tastemaker', 160.

49 Judith Brine has examined the reports of these travelling scholars in a paper, 'Substance or Form? Early Australian Readings of Modern Architecture', presented at the Reading Architecture conference, Adelaide, September 1989 (unpublished).

50 Herman graduated with first class honours from the University of Sydney in 1930 and left Sydney for England in July that year, having been awarded an Australian Medallion and Travelling Scholarship from the Board of Architects of New South Wales. In London, Herman initially found work in the office of Robert Atkinson who, in association with Harry Stuart Goodhart-Rendel, was engaged in the design of a large office and warehouse building on the south bank of the Thames. After returning from a trip to Austria with the Architectural Association in September 1931, Herman

resumed work with Atkinson and contributed to the design of the Building Centre in London.

51   'Board of Architects of New South Wales: Reports of Travelling Scholars: Morton E. Herman', *Architecture*, 23, no. 4 (April, 1934): 84.

52   'Board of Architects of New South Wales: Reports of Travelling Scholars: Morton E. Herman', 85.

53   Herman declared, 'Taut is something of a genius and his designs in colour are exquisite.' 'Board of Architects of New South Wales: Reports of Travelling Scholars: Morton E. Herman', 86.

54   'Board of Architects of New South Wales: Reports of Travelling Scholars: Morton E. Herman', 87.

55   See Brine, 'Substance or Form? Early Australian Readings of Modern Architecture',

56   See W. R. Richardson, 'Third International Reunion of Architects, Mid-Europe, 1935', *Architecture*, 25, no. 4 (April, 1936), 107-109.

57   'The Royal Australian Institute of Architects: New South Wales Chapter – Ordinary General Meeting', *Architecture*, 26, no. 9 (September, 1937), 190.

58   'The Royal Australian Institute of Architects: New South Wales Chapter – Ordinary General Meeting', 190-191.

59   Wilkinson declared that 'the architectural work owes a great deal to Herr Hitler for the attitude he has adopted' and that Hitler's actions indicated that he possessed a 'knowledge and understanding of architecture, and the traditions upon which it is founded'. This sentiment was reinforced in relation to another lecture by Richardson in October 1938, where the 'very charming homes' being produced in Germany drew the admiration of E. D. Wilson, S. G. Thorp and Wilkinson. It was reported that Wilkinson felt 'the absence of hard lines, the air of softness, and charming proportions carried with them an excellent lesson', See 'The Royal Australian Institute of Architects: New South Wales Chapter – Prescribed General Meeting', *Architecture*, 27, no. 11 (November, 1938): 278-279; 'Domestic Architecture in Germany', *Architecture*, 27, no. 11 (November, 1938), 266.

60   In 1936, Bertram Stevens, the Premier of New South Wales, undertook an overseas study tour of England and a selection of other countries to examine how communities in these countries were addressing the issues of slum clearance and the development of public housing. A report of this trip and its findings was published as *Housing, Slum Clearance and Abatement of Overcrowding in England: with brief mention of similar activities in Germany, Scandinavia and Italy*, Sydney: David Harold Paisley, Government Printer, 1937.

61   For studies of the NSW Housing Improvement Board and the Erskineville Re-housing Scheme see Matthew Conlon, 'Re-Seeing Modernist Fragments: Sydney's Erskineville Re-Housing Scheme, 1938', *Panorama to Paradise: Scopic Regimes in Architectural and Urban History and Theory*, Conference Proceedings of the 24th Conference of the Society of Architectural Historians, Australia and New Zealand, edited by Stephen Loo and Katharine Bartsch, Adelaide, September, 2007, as well as Harvey Volke, 'The Politics of State Rental Housing in New South Wales, 1900-1939: Three Case Studies', M. Phil., Faculty of Architecture, University of Sydney, 2006.

62   'Are We Satisfied With Sydney?' *Architecture*, 25, no. 4 (April, 1936): 89. In a 1936 essay entitled 'Housing Abroad', Richardson coupled images of workers' flats in Berlin, Brno and London with an image entitled 'A Sydney Slum', showing a weathered and cramped scene of back lots along a row of terraces, in an attempt to dramatise the difference between the ordered environments of housing overseas and the 'chaos and dreariness here'. 'Housing Aboard', *Architecture*, 25, no. 5 (May, 1936), 123.

63   M. E. Herman, 'Comparison of Architectural Solutions. Series 1; A', *Architecture*, 26, no. 6 (June, 1937), 121.

64   M. E. Herman, 'Comparison of Architectural Solutions. A Series: 7', *Architecture*, 27, no. 3 (March, 1938), 62.

65   M. E. Herman, 'Comparison of Architectural Solutions. A Series: 7', *Architecture*, 27, no. 3 (March, 1938), 62-63. Herman's italics.

66   The full title of the paper was 'Urban Housing: Continental Achievements and Possibilities in Australia', and was published in *Architecture* as 'Urban Housing' (October, 1937), 221-227.

67   See, for instance, M. E. Herman, 'The Position of the Architect in the Cultural Life of the Community', *Architecture*, 27, no. 8 (August, 1938), 189-191.

Critical [Re]connections: Oscar Wilde's 'The Critic as Artist' (1891)

DEBORAH VAN DER PLAAT

In 1891 the Irish poet, writer and aesthete, Oscar Wilde (1854–1900), identified criticism as an act that was both imaginative and cosmopolitan. In doing so he challenged Victorian conceptions of criticism as judgement (determining whether a work was good or bad) or education (describing to an uninformed market the artist's intent and method) by instead locating the critical within the subjective response of the observer. Allowing him to assert criticism's 'artistic' status, Wilde's thesis also positioned the critical as an alternative mode of artistic accomplishment, one that sat alongside romantic genius, but which, due to a new cosmopolitan focus, could be made accessible to a wider, non-specialist, and middle class audience. Focused on conceptual processes rather than type or form, Wilde also established new equivalencies between criticism and the decorative arts or design. Identifying criticism with art and design with criticism, Wilde's thesis also sought the elevation of late 19th century design to art. Sharing this project with the likes of John Ruskin and William Morris, Wilde countered their idealisation of labour and craftsmanship, with artistic convention and decoration – the very focus of Ruskin and Morris's critique. In doing so, Wilde's thesis reveals the critical ambitions of late 19th century design reform, decoration and its institutions.

In 1891 in a small volume entitled *Intentions,* Oscar Wilde collated a series of essays exploring the role of criticism within the modern world.[1] A significant portion of the volume is taken up with one essay, 'The Critic as Artist'. Consisting of two parts, '…with remarks on the importance of doing nothing' (Part I) and '…the importance of discussing everything' (Part II), and spanning approximately 222 pages, the text recounts 'a dialogue' between two characters: Gilbert and Ernest.[2] The setting for this conversation is a library in a house in Piccadilly, overlooking Green Park in London. The question that occupies much of their conversation is the state and role of English art (more specifically the literary and visual arts), the public's capacity to appreciate these, and the value or influence of modern criticism. The conversation moves between the modern novel, its construction, intent and impact, and the visual arts, specifically painting and the decorative arts. Throughout the conversation Ernest asks the questions and Gilbert responds. As the conversation progresses, a number of claims are put forth by Wilde, through his characters, about the practice of criticism.

Wilde's first claim links criticism to the improvement of the English mind. Arguing that 'self-culture is the true ideal of man'[3] and that the English race is a 'degraded one', sunk under a 'mess of facts'. Wilde also argues that the only possible improvement to the situation would be from the encouragement and 'growth of the critical instinct'.[4] Drawing on Matthew Arnold's (1822–1888) earlier observation that the cultural critic is the one who determines the intellectual atmosphere of an age, Wilde not only positioned criticism as a mechanism for the improvement of the modern mind – elevating it to a 'fine instrument' – but also as offering an alternative to 19th century educational systems focused on the accumulation and recall of 'unconnected facts'. 'It has never occurred to us,' Wilde lamented, 'to try and develop in the mind a more subtle quality of apprehension and discernment.' The need for an elevation of 'public opinion' in English society, a mode of thought 'from which Wisdom has always been hidden,' further stressed the urgency of such a task.[5]

Extending this idea, Wilde argued for a link between criticism and a growing cosmopolitan ethic. Drawing attention to the failure of capitalism, ethics, diplomacy and peace societies in their efforts to realise a 'brotherhood of man', to Wilde criticism offered new opportunities to avoid both nationalism and Imperialism and its associated conflicts. 'It is only by the cultivation of the habit of intellectual criticism,' Wilde suggested, 'that we shall be able to rise superior to race prejudices. … It is criticism that makes us cosmopolitan.'[6]

Wilde's third claim for criticism is for artistic status in its own right. Suggesting that the critic's relationship to the work of art is like of that of the artist to the 'visible world of colour and form', Wilde argued that the role of the critic is not to document or explain the work of art, but rather to reveal the 'impressions' it imposes on the critic himself.[7] Working with material and creating forms that are at once 'new and delightful' criticism is, for Wilde, a creative and imaginative practice. Art is its catalyst.[8]

The aim of the current essay is to examine Wilde's thesis on criticism and to consider its association with artistic agency. Wilde's thesis is significant, it will be argued, as it contributes to our understanding of the historical discourse on criticism at the close of the 19th century, its relationship to the arts – fine or otherwise – and its role within larger social and political projects. Wilde's argument helps us to understanding the late 19th century disassociation of criticism from the roles of judgement (determining whether a work is good or bad) and description (revealing to a non-specialist audience the maker's intentions and methods), and its repositioning as a mode of artistic agency in its own right. Wilde's thesis also contributes to our understanding of the Victorian project of self-improvement and cultivation, by demonstrating expansion of romantic agency beyond the heroic subjectivity of the artistic genius. This is an identification of criticism as an alternative mode of making, one that can be made available to new, non-specialist and middle class audiences. Finally, in discussing criticism's 'cosmopolitan' character, Wilde's thesis begins to reveal the analogical intent of Victorian criticism and its conceptual bonds with the literary and decorative arts. In arguing this, Wilde asserted not only the artistic status of criticism and its ability to represent an original and inventive idea, but also the artistic status of design, a discipline rendered mute by the Ruskinian critique of the machine and the decorative practices of artistic convention.[9]

The critic as artist

The critic occupies the same relation to the work of art he critiques as the artist does to the visible world of form and colour, Wilde argued. Thus the aim of the critic is not to explain the intent of the artist or determine the truth of the work, but simply to represent the 'impressions' the work has produced on the critic himself.[10] Labelling criticism as the 'only civilised form of autobiography', as it chronicles the 'spiritual moods and imaginative passions of the [critic's] mind', for Wilde it is for the critic that 'pictures are painted, books written, and marble hewn into form'.[11]

Paralleling the work of the critic with that of the artist, Wilde linked critical practice to artistic agency while also dissociating criticism from its more traditional roles of judgement and education. 'I am always amused,' he wrote, 'by the silly vanity of those writers and artists of our day who seem to imagine that the primary function of the critic is to chatter about their second-rate work.'[12] Going on to define art as 'imaginative and pleasurable work', that 'invents, imagines and dreams', and which has little relation to 'fact', Wilde also demonstrated his continuation of a romantic ideal of artistic agency, one that is in turn determined by the romantic thesis of the Imagination.[13] It is worth revisiting such ideas briefly here.

The Romantic imagination

Rejecting the empiricist assumption that the mind is a tabula rasa on which external experiences and sense impressions are imprinted, stored, recalled and combined through a process of association, the English poet Samuel Taylor Coleridge (1772–1834) in his *Biographia Literaria* (1817), divided the 'mind' into two distinct faculties. He labelled these the 'Imagination' and 'Fancy'.

The IMAGINATION then, I consider either as primary, or secondary. The primary IMAGINATION I hold to be the living Power and prime Agent of all human Perception, and as a repetition in the finite mind of the eternal act of creation in the infinite I AM. The secondary Imagination I consider as an echo of the former, co-existing with the conscious will, yet still as identical with the primary in the *kind* of its agency, and differing only in *degree,* and in the *mode* of operation. It dissolves, diffuses, dissipates, in order to recreate; or where this process is rendered impossible, yet still at all events it struggles to idealise and unify. It is essentially *vital,* even as all objects (as objects) are essentially fixed and dead.

FANCY, on the contrary, has no other counters to play with, but fixities and definites. The Fancy is indeed no other than a mode of Memory emancipated from the order of time and space; while it is blended with, and modified by that empirical phenomenon of the will, which we express by the word CHOICE. But equally with the ordinary memory the Fancy must receive all its materials ready made from the law of association.[14]

Explaining that the Imagination and Fancy represented two 'very different tools' with which 'a man may work', but that they should be seen as interdependent rather than exclusive or inimical to one another, Coleridge also argued that 'the work' produced by each was quite 'distinct and different'.[15] 'Always the ape', Fancy was for Coleridge 'too often the adulterator and counterfeiter of memory', the passive accumulation and storage of sensory data extracted from the physical world. The Imagination, on the other hand, was 'vital' and transformative, 'a repetition in the finite mind of the eternal act of creation'.[16] Enabling a coalescence of self and nature, the Imagination also asserted the universal and common and established art and nature as the product of a singular organic or moral force.[17] Defining this synthetic ability of the mind as 'ESEMPLASTIC', a term he borrowed from the Greek meaning to 'shape into one' and to 'convey a new sense', Coleridge associated such processes with the production of the higher arts, 'the wider and deeper powers of some poetry' and that which distinguished it from the mediocre or bad.[18] Importantly, it also encouraged the artist's retreat into a subjective idealism. Attempting to 'make the senses out of the mind – not the mind out of the senses', Coleridge's Imagination ensured that thought and reality grow indistinguishable and intelligent self-consciousness becomes inseparable from our perceptions of the world.[19] As Michael Sprinker has argued:

> … the aesthetics of romanticism was an indication of the profoundest dissatisfaction with reality, the sign of a peculiar sort of nihilism in which the wish to integrate the self and nature was merely a disguise for the imperialistic designs of the imagination on the real world.[20]

Distinguishing Imagination from Fancy, Coleridge further divided the Imagination into primary and secondary processes. In doing so, he linked art to a newly liberated subject – a 'superior voluntary control … co-existing with the conscious will.'[21] Free to invent outside the constraints of tradition, convention or even perception, the Secondary Imagination also marked out that which was original and unique. Breaking down what was perceived in order to recreate by an autonomous wilful act of the mind, the Secondary Imagination ensured a product that had no analogue in the natural world.[22] Finally, drawing a distinction between creative acts that are unconscious from those that are intentional and deliberate, Coleridge's Secondary Imagination also identified acts that were exceptional. 'The Primary Imagination' was for Coleridge,

the 'necessary imagination' as it 'automatically balanced and fused the innate capacities and powers of the mind with the external presence of the objective world'. It represented man's ability to learn from nature. The overarching property of the Primary Imagination was that it was common to all people. The Secondary Imagination, on the other hand, represented a superior faculty that could only be associated with artistic genius. Thus the production or judgement of fine art (and the subjectivity represented by a liberated will) was also denied to the ordinary person. The knowledge and insight generated from the Secondary Imagination was confined to an elite and cultivated few.[23]

Three functions of the Victorian critic

Seemingly esemplastic in motive, Wilde's critic appears to partake in the atomistic heroism of romantic agency. 'It is only by intensifying his own personality,' Wilde suggested, 'that the critic can interpret the personality and works of others.' The 'more strongly this personality enters into the interpretation the more real the interpretation becomes, [and] the more satisfying, the more convincing, the more true.'[24] Seeking to 'distil … into finer essence' the 'cumbersome mass of creative works' and to identify the 'thread' that will 'guide' one through such material, the motive of Wilde's critic was also to seek that which is universal.[25]

Wilde however, complicated his position by stressing the necessity for the critic to occupy multiple lives and views points at any one time, be they racial, geographical or temporal. Suggesting that the development of the critical spirit is dependent not only on an understanding of the 19th century, but also of 'every century which preceded it', and that to 'know oneself, one must know about all others', Wilde also stressed the need for the critic to empathise with the art of all ages and places. 'There must be no mood with which one cannot sympathise, no dead mode of life that one cannot make alive.'[26]

Importantly for Wilde, the inability of the 'artist' to escape his own subjectivity – to be many-sided – also disqualified him from the act of criticism.[27] Recalling John Stuart Mill's earlier identification of alternative modes of Victorian accomplishment that sat alongside artistic genius, the artist, unlike the critic, was unable to move interchangeably between these two roles.[28]

In making this distinction, Wilde claimed three important functions for the late-Victorian critic. Firstly, in occupying multiple lives, the critic was positioned as 'absolutely modern' by realising not only 'our own lives but the collective life of the race'.[29] Secondly, the critic could facilitate a process that remained in Wilde's view open-ended and 'incomplete'. Locating the critic's method in 'those modes which suggest reverie and mood' rather than the 'obvious' – 'art forms that have but one message to deliver' – also ensured that all 'interpretations [were] true' and none 'final'.[30] Finally, and perhaps most importantly for Wilde as an aesthete, the critic in tempering the universal by acknowledging the 'incomplete' could also enact a conceptual process (rather than represent) that which would reveal the beautiful in art.

> It is through its very incompleteness that Art becomes complete in beauty, and so addresses itself not to the faculty of recognition nor to the faculty of reason, but to the aesthetic sense alone, which while accepting both reason and recognition as stages of apprehension subordinates them both to a pure synthetic impression of the art as a whole taking whatever alien emotional elements the work may possess, uses their very complexity as a means by which a richer unity may be added to the ultimate impression itself.[31]

Turning to the discipline of late 19th century design, Wilde identified two common decorative tropes as representative of the above intentions. The first was the use of a keynote colour, be it in a painted image or a decorated interior. Unifying a composition into 'a harmonious whole', colour also left the work open to a multitude of readings: 'Mere colour, unspoiled by meaning, and unallied with definite form can speak to the soul in a thousand different ways.'[32] A reliance on 'artistic convention', a practice Wilde labelled 'Orientalist' achieved a similar result. Decorative rather than pictorial in motive, the appeal of Orientalism lay in its 'frank rejection of imitation, its love of artistic convention, [and] its dislike to the actual representation of any object in Nature'. Embodying the 'transmutation of visible things into beautiful and imaginative work', it also offered a counter to the 'imitative spirit' in western art, one focused on life and nature, and one that was ultimately for Wilde, 'vulgar, common and uninteresting'.[33] Associating block colour and artistic convention – practices common to the decorative arts and design – with strategies identified by Wilde as critical rather than artistic (in a romantic sense) he also positioned the decorative as an everyday catalyst for the development of a critical temperament. Such decorative strategies not only prepared the 'soul for the reception of the true imaginative work', in Wilde's view, but they also developed within the viewer a 'sense of form' that was the 'basis of creative no less than of critical achievement'.[34]

> The harmony that resides in the delicate proportions of lines and masses becomes mirrored in the mind. The repetitions of pattern give us rest. The marvels of design stir the imagination. In the mere loveliness of the materials employed there are latent elements of culture.[35]

Analogy, its ancient precedents and modern applications

Linking the decorative with the critical, Wilde goes on to identify Plato as the source of his thinking in this area. Drawing on Plato's observation that the true aim of education is a 'love of beauty', and that the best methods to achieve this are the 'development of temperament, the cultivation of taste, and the creation of a critical spirit', Wilde also repeated Plato's conviction that such objectives are dependent upon the characteristics of an individual's physical surroundings. A beautiful environment would intuitively build within the observer taste, judgement and ultimately critical discernment.

> By slow degrees there is to be engendered in [the student] such a temperament as will lead him naturally and simply to choose the good from the bad, and rejecting what is vulgar and discordant, to follow by fine instinctive taste all that possesses grace and charm and loveliness. Ultimately, in its due course, this taste is to become critical and self-conscious, but at first it is to exist purely as cultivated instinct, and 'he who has received this true culture of the inner man will with clear and certain vision perceive the omissions and faults in art or nature, and with a taste that cannot err, while he praises, and finds his pleasure in what is good, and receives into his soul, and so becomes good and noble, he will rightly blame and hate the bad, now in the days of his youth, even before he is able to know the reason why:' and so, when, later on, the critical spirit and self conscious spirit develops in him, he 'will recognise and salute it as a friend with whom his education has made him long familiar'.[36]

Barbara Maria Stafford in *Visual Analogy, Consciousness as the Art of Connecting* (2001), explains Plato's thesis as one that is determined by the ancient ideal of 'participatory analogy'. Distinguishing participatory from proportional analogy, a method based 'on establishing quantitative proportions using a geometrical language of equality and inequality', the rhetoric of participation relied on 'a mimetic vocabulary of similarity and dissimilarity'.[37]

Identifying the latter 'specifically with Plato' – who 'declared that analogy was the most beautiful bond possible' – Stafford goes on to describe analogy as a 'metaphoric and metamorphic practice for weaving discordant particulars into a partial concordance' that 'spurs the imagination to discover similarities in dissimilarities'. Importantly, analogy, like Wilde's thesis of incompleteness, reverie or mood, continued to acknowledge 'difference' by avoiding the 'subsumption of two inferior, dichotomous terms into a superior third (as in Hegel's principle of *Aufhebung* or Marx's theory of exchange).'[38] Suggesting that participatory analogy is celebrated by Plato in the *Timaeus* (29-30) and the *Republic* (472 b-e), where he developed the notion of an 'image sharing or partaking in a pattern', Stafford goes on to argue that for Plato it represented both a 'metaphysics and a logic, a vision and a form of reasoning' that allow us to infer 'the ontological and phenomenological likenesses binding seemingly unrelated things'.[39]

For Stafford, a revival of analogy offers present day art practice the opportunity to develop a 'language for talking about resemblance' and to counter an 'exaggerated awareness of difference' in contemporary western culture. Significantly, this too was a concern for Wilde and his contemporaries. As already noted, Wilde was critical of English educational systems in the 19th century. His complaint focused on the exaggerated role they gave to memory and the accumulation of information. 'We in our education systems, have burdened the memory with a load of unconnected facts. … We teach people how to think [yet] we never teach them how to grow.'[40] Advocating the reintroduction of 'wisdom' and the development of a critical temperament in education, Wilde also encouraged a return to the critical strategies of the ancient Greeks, the analogical practice of reconnecting unlike things (be they form, media or discipline), as a means of enacting this process:

The Greeks did this, and when we come in contact with the Greek critical intellect, we cannot but be conscious that, while our subject-matter is in every respect larger and more varied than theirs, theirs is the only method by which this subject-matter can be interpreted.[41]

Wilde was not alone in such sentiments. The inability of modern man to develop strategies to accommodate the quantities of data acquired in the modern age, leaving him 'sunk under a mass of facts', was also indentified by the German naturalist, Alexander von Humboldt (1769–1859), as the great problem of the modern age.[42] For the social critic and art theorist, William Morris (1834–1986), the decline of the arts in western society, and its division into the fine and lesser or decorative arts, was a direct result of the progress of the western intellect. 'As the thought of man became more intricate and more difficult to express' both knowledge and the arts were divided into discrete disciplinary units of specialisation.[43] Arguing that in the past 'handicraftsmen were *artists*', and that it was only in 'latter times, and under the most intricate conditions of life that they [had] fallen apart from one another', Morris concluded that it was only when 'the thought of man became more intricate, more difficult to express', that 'art grew a heavier thing to deal with' and 'labour was… divided among great men, lesser men, and little men'. The result, he continued was 'ill for the Arts altogether'. The lesser arts became: 'trivial, mechanical, unintelligent, incapable of resisting the changes pressed down on them by fashion or dishonesty.' The fine or higher arts, on the other hand, while 'practiced for a while by great minds and wonder-making hands, unhelped by the lesser', lost 'the dignity of popular arts and [became] nothing but dull adjuncts to unmeaning pomp, or the ingenious toys for a few rich and idle men'. The sole solution to this decline was to reinvigorate the 'lesser arts' of handicraft and to once again elevate the craftsman to the status of the artist.[44]

Orientalism and modern criticism

Morris's elevation of the decorative arts was achieved by his, and previously Ruskin's, identification of the hand – craftsmanship and the physical labour of making – with the imagination, and in turn, artistic agency.[45] Importantly, the strategies of artistic convention – or Orientalism – valued by Wilde, were openly excluded from this project. In 1858, in a lecture entitled 'The Deteriorative Power of Conventional Art over Nations', the critic John Ruskin rejected the contribution of 'artistic convention' to the reformation of British decorative arts and design.[46] Ruskin's lecture was presented at the opening meeting of the Architectural Collection at the South Kensington Museum in London (the current day V&A), an institution which, following the International Exhibition of 1851, was founded to improve the design, production and appreciation of British decorative arts.[47] The focus of Ruskin's critique was the architect Owen Jones, the author of the *Grammar of Ornament,* first published in 1856, and a strong advocate of artistic convention.[48] For Ruskin, not only was the process of abstraction which convention engendered openly dismissive of the mimetic function of art, it importantly also denied the operation of a liberated and autonomous will on which art proper (according to doctrines of the imagination) was dependent. The practice of artistic convention enslaved the artist and removed 'his' ability to invent, imagine and to poetically create. Rendering the artefact mute by disconnecting it from its motive (the Imagination), it also opened the door to machine production and the complete removal of the craftsman from the art process. Wilde's identification of Orientalism with the critical temperament openly challenged Ruskin's view. By identifying such practices not with artistic agency as it is defined within romantic thought, but rather with a Victorian ideal of criticism, an alternative mode of accomplishment that is different to yet equal with the subjectivity of 'genius', Wilde was able to reassert the 'artistic' credentials not only of criticism but also of artistic convention. Significantly, this link to art proper was now made through a process of analogy – a conceptual process of connecting and contemplation – rather than in the physiological labour of the hand.

Wilde's location of both the critical and the decorative within an analogical function also offers a new reading of the South Kensington project. As noted above, the aim of the institution was to build both the skill of the artisan and the taste of the general public, the future consumers of British design, in an attempt to improve the quality and production of English decorative arts. The museum's success in the former, Wilde argued, was demonstrated each Saturday night, 'by the scene … where artisans are to be seen, notebook in hand, gathering ideas to be used in their next week's work'.[49] The ambitions of the latter, on the other hand, appear to have rested on the instructional display of work. An early demonstration of this principle is the Gallery of 'Decorations on False Principles' first established in Marlborough House in 1853, the initial location of the South Kensington collection. The display was placed in the principal corridor leading to the main exhibition spaces and included 87 items of ornamental art – samples of wallpaper, carpets, glassware, porcelain, garment fabrics, etc.[50] Focused on the bad and 'false', rather than the good or exceptional (the more common focus of institutional displays today), the instructional intent of the exhibition was to demonstrate to the observer the types of ornamentation they should endeavour to avoid both in terms of production and consumption. The critical function of the collection becomes in this instant explicit. Its educational role in the building of taste is one of demonstration and example: in turn, the determination of quality, judgement, is undertaken by informed institutional representatives. Such objectives were not exclusive to the design museum but also characterise much of the art writing that appeared in Victorian newspapers and serials.[51]

Wilde's thesis on criticism, and its visual equivalents such as Orientalism, suggested that his appreciation of the museum and its display of the decorative should not be restricted to the study of institutional judgements of quality. Locating the value of decorative and artistic convention in its ability to trigger an analogical process – the identification of both sameness and difference across artefacts – Wilde locates the critical temperament and its development not in the study of external judgements, or in the traditions (or history) that inform such decisions, but in the observer's direct response to the viewed objects. The role of the displayed artefact within the institution, and of criticism more broadly, was not to determine the good from the bad and then disseminate this knowledge, but rather to initiate a mode of thought within the observer that was in-itself inventive and critical. Wilde's thesis thus promoted a genuinely democratic system of aesthetics that was theoretically accessible to all.

Conclusion

The role of the critic is conventionally framed within the context of a surrounding art practice or culture, one to which the critic responds by either explaining the maker's methods and intent or determining the quality – good or bad – of the work produced. Defining the critic as artist, Wilde not only shifted the location of creative agency – that which should be critiqued – to the critic himself, but also established criticism as the context and rationale for art. Inverting present day assumptions, Wilde claimed the painting of pictures, the writing of books and the carving of sculpture for the aesthetic benefit of the critic alone; and the progression of the 19th century decorative arts – Orientalism – for the advancement of a modern critical temperament. Drawing on Victorian critiques of romantic agency, Wilde's thesis confirms the possibility of alternative modes of accomplishment that are conceived as sitting alongside romantic genius. Binding criticism to an aesthetic sense, one based on incompleteness and continued interpretation rather than a singular truth, taste or ideal, Wilde, in conforming to Victorian ideas, also opens criticism to a larger and non-specialist audience. Finally, in linking criticism to the improvement of the English mind and a growing cosmopolitanism ethic, Wilde tied criticism and the aesthetic to a larger project of educational and political reform.

1   Oscar Wilde, *Intentions,* New York: Promethus Books, 2004 (1891).

2   Oscar Wilde, 'The Critic as Artist, Part I: With some remarks upon the importance of doing nothing', and 'The Critic as Artist, Part I: With some remarks upon the importance of discussing everything', in *Intentions,* New York: Promethus Books, 2004 (1891), 95-149 and 153-217.

3   Wilde attributes this idea to the German polymath Johann Wolfgang von Goethe (1749-1832).

4   Oscar Wilde, 'The Decay of Lying,' in *Intentions,* 19; 'The Critic as Artist', 108, 209.

5   Wilde, 'The Critic as Artist', 209.

6   Wilde, 'The Critic as Artist', 210-212.

7   Wilde, 'The Critic as Artist', 136-7.

8   Wilde, 'The Critic as Artist', 137-8.

9   John Ruskin, *The Deteriorative Power of Conventional Art over Nations: An Inaugural Lecture Delivered at the Opening Meeting of the Architectural Museum*, South Kensington Museum, January 13th, 1858, London: George Allen, 1905 (1878), 1-53.

10 Wilde, 'Critic as Artist', 136-7, 142-143 and 139 respectively.

11 Wilde, 'Critic as Artist', 139.

12 Wilde, 'Critic as Artist', 139.

13 I have written elsewhere on the importance of the romantic imagination to the writings of John Ruskin. Wilde's debt to Ruskin has been noted in the past by a number of scholars. It is suggested that Wilde's definition of art and its continuity of romantic ideals of artistic agency can also be attributed to the influence of Ruskin. See: Deborah van der Plaat, 'The Ambivalence of English Modernism: Matthew Arnold's Theory of Cultural Perfection and the Search for a Modern Architecture'. Paper presented at the *Formulation and Fabrication: The Architecture of History*: Proceedings of the 17th Conference of the Society of Architectural Historians of Australia and New Zealand Wellington, 2000; Michael Sprinker, 'Ruskin on the Imagination', *Studies in Romanticism,* 18, (Spring, 1979): 116-7. Charlotte Gere and Lesley Hoskins. *The House Beautiful: Oscar Wilde and the Aesthetic Interior,* London: Lund Humphries and Geffrye Museum, 2000; Kevin H.F. O'Brien, 'The House Beautiful': A Reconstruction of Oscar Wilde's American Lecture, *Victorian Studies* 17, no. 4 (1974): 395-418.

14 Samuel Taylor Coleridge, *Biographia Literaria,* J. Shawcross (ed), Oxford: Clarendon Press, 1907, vol. I, 202.

15 *Biographia Literaria*, vol. I, 94.

16 *Biographia Literaria*, vol. II, 208 and vol. I, 202

17 *Biographia Literaria*, vol. II, 12. While the objective of the romantic critic was to facilitate such a synthesis of opposites, the 'active' and 'creative' powers given to the Romantic Imagination guaranteed that no such synthesis could take place. Rather the Imagination motivated a situation where the subject subsumed the identity and autonomy of the object. The relationship between the subject and nature, in such an instance, as Paul de Man has demonstrated in 'The Rhetoric of Temporality' (1969) 'is superseded by an inter-subjective, interpersonal relationship that, in the last analysis, is a relation-ship of the subject towards itself. Thus the priority has passed from the outside world entirely within the subject, and we end up with something that resembles radical idealism.' Paul de Man, 'The Rhetoric of Temporality', in Charles S. Singleton (ed), *Interpretation: Theory and Practice,* Baltimore: John Hopkins University Press, 1969, 180.

18 Coleridge in the tenth chapter of *Biographia Literaria* described this ability of the imagination as 'Esemplastic'. Noting that esemplastic was a word he borrowed from the Greek 'to shape', Coleridge explained that it referred to the imagination's ability to 'shape into one, having to convey a new sense'. He felt such a term was necessary as 'it would aid the recollection of my meaning and prevent it being confounded with the usual import of the word imagination'. Coleridge, *Biographia Literaria,* vol. I, p. 86. See also I. A. Richards, *Coleridge on Imagination* (London: Routledge & Kegan Paul Ltd, 1962), 96 and 84.

19 As Coleridge was himself to point out, 'the identity of thesis and antithesis is the substance of all being'. Coleridge, 'The Friend', in *The Complete Works of Samuel Taylor Coleridge,* vol. II, p. 91n.

20 Michael Sprinker, 'Ruskin on the Imagination', *Studies in Romanticism,* 18 (Spring 1979): 116-7.

21   Coleridge, *Biographia Literaria*, vol. I, 193, 202.

22   Richards, *Coleridge on Imagination*, 96 and 84.

23   James Engell, *The Creative Imagination: Enlightenment to Romanticism,* Cambridge: Harvard University Press, 1981, 344.

24   Wilde, 'Critic as Artist', 155-156.

25   Wilde, 'Critic as Artist', 210.

26   Wilde, 'Critic as Artist', 172-3.

27   Wilde, 'Critic as Artist', 185-6.

28   John Stuart Mill, *On Liberty*, London: John W. Parker & Son, 1859 cited by David Wayne Thomas, *Cultivating Victorians: Liberal Culture and the Aesthetic*, Philadelphia: University of Pennsylvania Press, 2004, 47.

29   Wilde, 'Critic as Artist', 172-3.

30   Wilde, 'Critic as Artist', 147-8.

31   Wilde, 'Critic as Artist', 147-8.

32   Wilde, 'Critic as Artist', 147-8.

33   Oscar Wilde, 'Decay of Lying', in *Intentions,* 25.

34   Wilde, 'Critic as Artist', 199-200. Kevin H.F. O'Brien, 'The House Beautiful': A Reconstruction of Oscar Wilde's American Lecture, *Victorian Studies* 17, no. 4 (1974): 396.

35   Wilde, 'Critic as Artist', 199-200.

36   Wilde, 'The Critic as Artist', 194-5.

37   Barbara Maria Stafford, *Visual Analogy: Consciousness as the Art of Connecting*, Cambridge (Mass.) and London: MIT Press, 2011, 2-3.

38   Stafford, *Visual Analogy,* 8-9.

39   Stafford, *Visual Analogy,* 89.

40   Wilde, 'Critic as Artist', 209.

41   Wilde, 'Critic as Artist', 209.

42   Alexander von Humboldt, *Cosmos: A Sketch of the Physical Description of the Universe,* trans. E.C. Otté. London: Henry G Bohn, 1849 (1845), vol. 2, 370-71.

43   William Morris, 'The Lesser Arts', a lecture given to the Trades' Guild of Learning in 1877, reprinted in Christine Poulson (ed), *Morris on Art and Design,* Sheffield: Sheffield Academic Press, 1996, 157.

44   Morris, 'The Lesser Arts', 157. Morris's lectures appear to be a response to the thesis developed by James Ferguson who argued that architecture was the result of three distinct types of labour; the mechanical or 'technic', the 'aesthetic', and the 'phonetic'. James Fergusson, *An Historical Enquiry in the True Principles of Beauty in Art, More Especially with Reference to Architecture,* Longman, London, 1849, p. 104. For a discussion of Fergusson see Peter Kohane, 'Architecture, Labor and the Human Body: Fergusson, Cockerell and Ruskin', PhD thesis, University of Pennsylvania, 1993, chapter 5.

45   John Ruskin, 'The Nature of Gothic', (1853) in E.T. Cook and A. Wedderburn, eds., *The Works of John Ruskin,* London: George Allen, 1903-12, vol. 10, 180-269 and especially 180-189.

46   John Ruskin, 'The Deteriorative Power of Conventional Art over Nations: An Inaugural Lecture Delivered at the Opening Meeting of the Architectural Museum', South Kensington Museum, January 13th, 1858, London: George Allen, 1905 (1878), 1-53.

47   Hermione Hobhouse, *The Crystal Palace and the Great Exhibition. Art, Science and Productive History. A History of the Royal Commission for the Exhibition of 1851,* London and New York: Continuum, 2002; Elizabeth Bonython and Anthony Burton, *The Great Exhibitor. The Life and Work of Henry Cole,* London: V&A Publications, 2003.

48   Owen Jones, *The Grammar of Ornament,* London: Day & Son, 1856.

49   Wilde, House Beautiful Lecture, 410-411.

50   Christopher Frayling, *Henry Cole and the Chamber of Horrors: The Curious Origins of the Victoria and Albert Museum,* London: V&A Publishing, 2010.

51   Kate Flint, *The Victorians and the Visual Imagination,* Cambridge: Cambridge University Press, 2000, 167-196; Racheal Teukolsky, *The Literate Eye: Victorian Art Writing and Modernist Aesthetics,* Oxford & New York: Oxford University Press, 2009.

Interpretation, Intention and the Work of Architecture

JUSTINE CLARK AND PAUL WALKER

… every act of reading is a difficult transaction between the competence of the reader (the reader's world knowledge) and the kind of competence that a given text postulates in order to be read in an economic way.

Umberto Eco, *Interpretation and Overinterpretation*[1]

We would like to open up the question of intention in architectural criticism – the intention of the architect, the intention of the writer, and even the intention of the editor. In doing so we will also address questions of interpretation, authorship and authority.

'Intention' is a complex and problematic idea. It brings in its wake the spectre of the architect as a singular (male)

genius, which despite having been deconstructed over and over again for many decades, and regardless of all the contemporary avowals of collaborative practice, remains strong in much of the architectural community. Of course, the privileging of the 'author' is not limited to architecture, and nor is its disavowal. It is 40 years since Barthes proclaimed the death of the author, Foucault asked 'What is an Author?' and Benjamin's essay, 'The Author as Producer', was dug from its previous obscurity.[2] These works analysed the privilege hitherto conceded to interpretation as the unveiling of authorial intention in the reception of a creative work – be it book, painting or building. They detailed the cultural construction and historical contingency of this situation, and Barthes in particular emphasised instead the inventive and productive role of the reader. But despite the wide influence of these propositions, the 'author' continues to have significant traction in most fields of creative endeavour. Within architecture, the idea of the author prevails, despite sophisticated attempts to undo or complicate it. *Architecture and Authorship,* a collection of essays edited by Tim Anstey, Katja Grillner and Rolf Hughes, provides the most recent account of the ways in which the author has been constructed and challenged within architecture.[3] Yet, the attempts to unsettle authorship in architecture seem quite tame compared to the dizzying possibilities for undisciplined semiosis that the death of the author heralded in literature, where it seemed both far more radical and far more evasive. For the vanquishing of authorship, and the concomitant birth of the reader and of the critic, also brought with it another spectre: that of over-interpretation, authorial intention's unruly other.

These various problems around intention, authorship and interpretation are well known, yet we do not seem to have developed ways of thinking about intention in architecture that operate beyond these two paradigms – one, the privileging of the intention of the architect, the other, the privileging of the interpretation of the critic. Indeed, everyday understandings of and responses to architectural writing reflect these tacit constructions. On the one hand, architectural criticism in the popular and professional press is often denigrated as little more than 'puff' – captive writers telling happy stories of what the architect wanted to do and how they did it (always successfully). This entails the proposition that architectural criticism remains in thrall to the author function of the architect. On the other hand, critique that disregards the intention of the architect to pursue other agendas is frequently derided as arcane, jargon-ridden showing off that has little role beyond the confines of academia. This formulation – of criticism untethered from its ostensible subject – sees criticism as entirely disregarding the architect's authority and authorial prerogative, and

imposing over it that of the critic: critics, after all, are authors too. Writing at each of these extremes does exist, but in general these descriptions are clichés, straw men that avoid the complexities of writing about architecture, and the difficulties inherent in the idea of intentionality itself. Developing a more complex account of architectural intention might enable us to step outside such clichés and develop more nuanced modes of interpretation and architectural criticism.

Intention is interesting partly because it is always to some extent in doubt – one can never entirely know (or explain) the intent of either architect or writer/critic, even if one *is* the architect or the writer. But this does not mean we should abandon intention altogether. Indeed, more nuanced understandings of intention may offer richer accounts of architecture, and the potential of architectural writing, than either the cliché of criticism as the pursuit of authorial intent or the cliché of criticism as autonomous invention. As such, they might also open up opportunities for alternative writing practices. Raising intention also allows us to consider related questions such as the place of judgement in architectural criticism – which in turn links to another common complaint: that architectural writing is not critical enough.

To work our way through the complexity of 'intention' we want to turn to another post-structuralist and semiotician, Umberto Eco. As a theorist, critic and novelist, Eco writes compellingly about the ongoing life of one of his own creative works in *Reflections on the Name of the Rose*.[4] There he reflects on his famous first novel's reception, commenting that, 'A narrator should not supply interpretations of his work, otherwise he would not have written a novel, which is a machine for interpretation', and – alluding to the title of Barthes's famous essay – that 'The author should die once he has finished, so as not to trouble the path of the text'.[5] So far, so death of the author. But Eco goes on to write with great joy about the making of the novel: he allows himself this, arguing that 'The author must not interpret, but he may say how and why he wrote his book.'[6] He discusses his intentions, and the contexts for them, in some detail, making it clear that these should not limit or define the book's reception. He delights in the various subsequent interpretations made of the novel, some of which identify meanings that he intended, and many others that found meanings he had not consciously included but which he nevertheless decides may be legitimate.

Nonetheless, in a later series of talks, published as *Interpretation and Overinterpretation*, Eco expresses discomfort with 'overinterpretation', which he describes as readings that represent an 'uneconomic' response to the text at hand – or, even worse, an uninteresting one.[7] For Eco an uneconomic reading is one that, although it draws on pertinent aspects of a work, puts them together in farfetched ways that are not supported by the cultural context. For example: 'The Titanic bumped into an iceberg and Freud lived in Berggasse, but such a pseudo-etymological analogy cannot justify a psychoanalytic explanation of the Titanic case.' He points out that, 'To say that a text potentially has no end does not mean that every act of interpretation can have a happy end.'[8] Is there, he asks, anything that should limit our interpretation of a text? His answer is that the text itself might provide such limits. 'Between the intention of the author (very difficult to find out and frequently irrelevant for the interpretation of the text) and the intention of the interpreter who, (to quote Richard Rorty) simply "beats the text into a shape that will serve for his purpose", there is a third possibility. There is an *intention of the text*.'[9]

Eco's *intentio operis* is translated from Latin variously as the intention of the work and as the intention of the text. Given this, we use the terms 'work' and 'text' alternately here; we do so knowingly to avoid the dichotomy between work and text set up by Barthes, most famously in his 1971 essay, 'From Work to Text', as Eco's intention of the text seems to offer a way out of this dichotomy.[10]

The intention of the text reflects the sociocultural context(s) in which the work is produced and disseminated. Eco writes that:

> When a text is produced not for a single addressee but for a community of readers, the author knows [or should know] that he or she will be interpreted not according to his or her intentions but according to a complex strategy of interactions which also involves the readers, along with their competence in language as a social treasury. … Thus, every act of reading is a difficult transaction between the competence of the reader (the reader's world knowledge) and the kind of competence that a given text postulates in order to be read in an economic way.[11]

The intention of the text thus describes the way in which a reasonable interpretation of a text is caught between the volition of the author and the competence of the reader. This occurs on ground where both the social and the formal are at stake, for the protocols for packing and unpacking relationships between form and meaning are maintained and mutate in social contracts. Eco's formula, then, is particularly useful in that it enables a discussion of intention, while also locating a work in a cultural context.

Now, to make it clear, the intention of the text is not some transcendent quality in the text as a material or formal system. Eco emphasises the role of the reader in locating intention through conjecture. 'The text's intention is not displayed by the textual surface. Or, if it is displayed, it is so in the sense of the purloined letter. One has to decide to "see" it. Thus it is possible to speak of the text's intention only as the result of a conjecture on the part of the reader. The initiative of the reader basically consists in making a conjecture about the text's intention.'[12] That is, for Eco, the *intentio operis* interacts with the *intentio auctoris* and the *intentio lecturis* (the intentions of the author and the reader). This locates interpretation as a site of interaction and exchange – the intention of the work can only come about through an active encounter with the work.

In this formulation, interpretation has a relationship to the intention of the text – or more broadly, of the work – which entails some regard for what we might call cultural fidelity. But this does not preclude other kinds of uses to which texts or works might be put, to delirious, inventive, and provocative readings; Eco comments that while a text might be used in many and varying ways, what distinguishes interpretation is that it respects the cultural circumstances of the text's production. This places some responsibility on interpretation to attend to the specificity of each work it addresses; in this sense, Eco's retrieval of interpretation is not a return to the application to literature of the grand interpretative strategies of, say, Marxism and psychoanalysis, which is the object of Susan Sontag's attack in her famous essay 'Against Interpretation'.[13] Eco's theory of the 'intention of the work' is not a conservative call to literary order; rather, it particularises interpretation and interpretative criticism as specific kinds of reading, of apprehension.

So, what might this all mean for architecture? Eco mostly discusses written texts, but the approach he sets out seems to hold great potential for thinking about the interpretation of works of architecture, where authorship and intention are already very complicated.

The challenges to the authority of the author posed by Barthes, Foucault, Benjamin et al, have, of course, already been taken up in architecture in a number of ways. These are thoroughly surveyed in Anstey, Grillner and Hughes's collection, *Architecture and Authorship*. Barthes in particular seems to have had architectural influence. Diana Agrest and Mario Gandelsonas's design work and critical writing, for example, self-consciously adopted lessons from Barthes, and they described their work as 'design-as-reading – a reading-transformation of existent architectural texts'.[14] Because they proposed

architectural design as a continuation of this process into the future, their work is not always easy and familiar: it is caught, they say, between memory and amnesia, between convention and invention. But their work cannot assume the condition of what Agrest has called non-design – it remains within architecture, remains marked by Agrest and Gandelsonas as authorial subjects.

Bernard Tschumi was also directly influenced by Barthes, and although his theoretical and his design work suggest opening architecture to contingency and the incidental, and at Parc de la Villette, to multiple designer-auteurs, we agree with Carola Ebert's assessment in her contribution to the *Architecture and Authorship* volume – Tschumi does not so much dispense with authorial intention as 'translate the site in which creative intention is seen to act, from the composition of forms in space to the creation of design methodologies and systems of architecture.'[15]

More recently, Jonathan Hill has explicitly adopted Barthes's position in *The Death of the Author* as a paradigm to think of architecture beyond the institutional boundaries that define it both as profession and as discipline. Hill transposes literature's readers to architecture's users.[16] He is critical of the way much architectural discourse positions questions of habitation and consumption – for example, the scientist functionalism of the 1920s, the theatrical metaphor of inhabitants as 'actors' that he finds in Beatriz Colomina's work on Le Corbusier and Loos (which implicitly leaves the architect as director, Hill points out), or the connoisseurship apparent in formalist writing on architecture that treats it as if it were art. Nonetheless, he accompanies his critique with propositions that seem, like Agrest and Gandelsonas, to constantly return to architectural form. Hill's books are illustrated with design proposals (including his own Institute of Illegal Architects) that, while incorporating interactive relationships beyond those usual between buildings and users, are orchestrated in such a way that authorship still prevails.

Agrest and Gandelsonas, Tschumi and Hill all, in different ways, use poststructuralist accounts of the author to rethink their own practices and the practices of other architects in the 'production' of architecture. Our interest, instead, is in considering how complex accounts of intention, interpretation and authority, might be at play in the 'reception' of architecture – in the critical writing about and around buildings once they make their way into the world.

We would like to briefly describe one architectural example where such complexity is overtly at stake. This specifically raises a question of cultural appropriateness, or possibly appropriation. The Melbourne architectural practice, McBride Charles Ryan, recently completed a project in which they deployed patterns that appeared, to a critic writing interpretatively about the project, to relate to the geometric forms of Islamic tile decoration. On being asked about this, the partners in the firm said that although they were generally aware of these origins, they chose the pattern because they liked it, and it suited their purpose. They also commented that it was already found in Melbourne, in the décor of an early twentieth-century 'atmospheric' theatre, the Forum. This troubled the critic – in contemporary Melbourne, it is hard to construe such patterns simply in formal terms: the experiences of multiculturalism have made this untenable. This is a case where the intention of the architectural text does not reflect the intentions of its authors. In pointing this out, we are not necessarily implying that further responsibility should be laid at the feet of the already over-burdened architect: in our cultural context, such misprision as in this case will be inevitable. Rather, responsibility is laid on interpretation.

Literary criticism has, of course, sustained and sophisticated models for thinking about the role of the reader, and the relationship of any one work to those that come before and after it. We are not suggesting that these are directly transferable to architecture.

Indeed, there have been many criticisms of architecture importing theoretical frameworks from other disciplines and 'plastering' them on to architecture, rather than understanding and exploring architecture as a discipline and mode of knowledge in its own right. We do not want to repeat these mistakes. However, this does not mean there is nothing to learn from other disciplines. Indeed, we would also argue that one of architecture's faults is its ability to forget the cross-disciplinary encounters in its recent history: as soon as an idea is no longer fashionable, out it goes, regardless of whether there are things still to learn. And many useful lessons are abandoned in the rush to turn yet another set of ideas into form. And so it was with Eco's semiotic theories.

We would like to speculate on various ways the intention of the work might be brought to bear on architecture. For Eco the text projects a model reader. But who are architecture's readers? Under what conditions do their interpretative encounters with architecture take place?

Four issues arise out of this for us. Firstly, the intention of the work unfolds in a worldly space. What we have in mind here are the comments made by K. Michael Hays in his article 'Critical Architecture: Between Culture and Form'.[17] In this piece, Hays rejects two contrasting positions that he claims subtend much architectural thinking: on the one hand, a conception of architecture as an index of a more profound sociocultural nexus, and on the other of architecture as autonomous form. As Eco proposes his intention of the work as a third term between the intention of the author and unconstrained textual play, Hays proposes a third stance for architecture between socio-economic index and autonomy: 'An alternative interpretative position which cuts across this dichotomy would bear not only a more robust description of the artifacts [of architecture], but also the more intricate analysis demanded by artifacts situated explicitly and critically *in the world* – in culture, in theories of culture, in theories of interpretation itself.'[18] Hays argues that both the architect and the critic use their authorial agency – sometimes self-consciously, sometimes not – to negotiate the worldly space *between* sociocultural imperatives and form. In this space, he suggests, interpretation of the architectural object 'has already commenced but is never complete'.[19] The intention of the text, in this regard, is always provisional, but nevertheless it is the responsibility of criticism to decide meaning even when it is provisional.

This brings us to our second point. Any work of architecture is made by many hands in complex circumstances, some of which are within the influence of the architectural team, and some of which are beyond it – procurement and delivery processes; regulation, budgets, briefs; the particular interests of clients; the knowledge, ability and experience of the architect and of other consultants, and so on. Much of this is the subject of serious and considered development of ideas and strategies. Indeed, one of the architect's skills is to synthesise and negotiate their way through the many different modes of knowledge that bear on any one project, to simultaneously juggle diverse kinds of information, to be nimble and fleet of foot through the often protracted conditions of production. It is this contingent quality of architecture that Jeremy Till explores in his recent book *Architecture Depends*.[20]

But as any act of making takes place in the messy everydayness of the world; serendipity and incident are always involved, to some extent. The work itself carries traces, overt and subtle, of this – indices of the activities, both intentional and accidental, that made it. One of the appealing things about Eco's 'intention of the work' is that it makes space for these traces in the construction of an interpretation. It allows the reader/interpreter to contemplate the conditions of production and the role of contingency and happenstance, to work in the space between serendipity and authority, between economics and the ideal, between messiness and order.

Worldliness and contingency are of course not only a condition of architecture's production and its critical reception, but also more broadly of its apprehension by the users, visitors and inhabitants of buildings. This brings us to our third point: distraction. The stuff that is the foreground for the architectural discipline is everyone else's background: most people who encounter architectural objects and spaces do so in a distracted frame of mind. In 'The Work of Art in the Age of Mechanical Reproduction', Walter Benjamin famously made a comparison between cinema and architecture on the grounds that both were characterised by the distracted state of their audiences.[21] For Manfredo Tafuri, an important aspect of Benjamin's comparison is that it situates architecture, in its likeness to cinema, as a mass medium: distraction characterises not so much the individual as it does community, or communities we might now rather say.[22] Architecture and cinema are therefore politically potent in a way that painting for example is not: the focus entailed in apprehending the conventional fine arts is individual and contemplative, and in this sense averse to action. What writing practices could further unpack this issue? Possibly the radical post-occupancy evaluation being pursued by *Post* magazine in Melbourne; Jonathan Hill's work; long, narrow, densely described histories of buildings or sites, projecting both into the past and into the future.

The worldliness of the context through which architecture's texts and works move entails historical and cultural complexity. This is a fourth point: the world in which the intention of the text is encountered and determined is not homogenous but rather characterised by its multiplicity of cultures, competencies, evolving communities of readership and interpretation. This is a condition of architecture described clearly by Gianni Vattimo's essay, 'The End of Modernity, The End of the

Project?'. [23] The particular configuration of these pertaining in any place at any time is, again, a matter of contingency rather than coherence: Vattimo refers to the contemporary condition as 'the conflict of interpretations in which we live', and suggests that the role of the architect in this context is not that of the genius but instead the rather more provisional one of 'symbolic operator'. [24]

The intention of the work does not limit the possible readings or uses to which an architectural work might be subjected – an architectural work, like a work of literature, can be put to multiple uses, some sanctioned by the text itself, others not. Nor does it preclude critical attention to the architect. Eco writes:

> I have scarcely been generous to the empirical author. Still there is at least one case in which the witness of the empirical author acquires an important function, not so much in order to understand his text better, but to understand the creative process. To understand the creative process is also to understand how certain textual solutions come into being by serendipity or as the result of unconscious mechanisms. [25]

But the idea of the intention of the work offers much opportunity for thinking about how architecture is received and written about, precisely because it locates the significance of the architectural work in its negotiation between various kinds of readerly competencies and architectural commitments. This suggests that one role for architectural critic might be in the 'construction' of the intention of the work. The intention of the work might also be something that can be construed to be produced collectively, over time, through the histories that bear on the conventions and competencies through which objects are read and the histories that bear on architectural works/texts themselves.

To locate the intention of the work as the outcome of negotiation and interaction implies that architecture is neither subordinate to its worldly context nor autonomous of it (Hays). The intention of work is a third term, between Barthes's characterisations of 'work' and 'text' or – to use the terms employed by Agrest and Gandelsonas – between memory and amnesia, convention and invention. Thinking about architecture from this position does not so much vanquish the architect as authorial subject as allow a complication of what the architect might be. It acknowledges that architecture is always the outcome of multiple authors, and is produced through multiple, sometimes competing, systems for multiple 'readers'. The intention of the work is produced through the interaction between all these things: the challenge for the architectural critic or historian as reader/interpreter is to do justice to this complexity.

1   Umberto Eco, *Interpretation and Overinterpretation*, ed Stefan Collini, Cambridge, New York: Cambridge University Press, 1992, 68.

2   Roland Barthes, 'The Death of the Author' in Stephen Heath (ed & trans) *Image-Music-Text*, London: Fontana, 1977; Michel Foucault 'What is an Author?' (1969) in *Language, Counter-Memory, Practice: Selected Essays and Interviews by Michel Foucault*, ed. Donald F. Bouchard, trans. Donald F. Bouchard and Sherry Simon, New York: Cornell University Press, 1977; Walter Benjamin, 'The Author as Producer,' (1936) in *New Left Review*, 1, 62 (1970).

3   Tim Anstey, Katja Grillner & Rolf Hughes (eds), *Architecture and Authorship*, London: Black Dog Publishing, 2007. For a helpful summary, see the editor's introduction.

4   Umberto Eco, *Reflections on the Name of the Rose*, London: Secker & Warburg, 1985.

5   Eco, *Reflections on the Name of the Rose*, 1, xx

6   Eco, *Reflections on the Name of the Rose*, 8.

7   Umberto Eco, *Interpretation and Overinterpretation*, ed Stefan Collini, Cambridge, New York: Cambridge University Press, 1992.

8   Eco, *Interpretation and Overinterpretation*, 24.

9   Eco, *Interpretation and Overinterpretation*, 25.

10   Barthes, 'From Work to Text', in Stephen Heath (ed & trans), *Image Music Text*, London: Fontana, 1977.

11   Eco, *Interpretation and Overinterpretation*, 68.

12   Eco, *Interpretation and Overinterpretation*, 64.

13   Susan Sontag, 'Against Interpretation', in *Against Interpretation*, London: Vintage, 1994. The essay was first published in 1964.

14   Diana Agrest and Mario Gandelsonas, 'On Practice', *International Architect*, 1, no. 1 (1979): 50.

15   Carola Ebert, 'Post-mortem: Architectural Postmodernism and the Death of the Author', in Tim Anstey, Katja Grillner and Rolf Hughes (eds), *Architecture and Authorship*, London: Black Dog Publishing, 2007, 46.

16   Jonathan Hill, *The Illegal Architect*, London: Black Dog Publishing, 2001; and *Actions of Architecture: Architects and Creative Users*, London: Routledge, 2003.

17   K. Michael Hays, 'Critical Architecture: Between Culture and Form', *Perspecta*, 21, 1984.

18   Hays 'Critical Architecture: Between Culture and Form', 17.

19   Hays 'Critical Architecture: Between Culture and Form', 27.

20   Jeremy Till, *Architecture Depends*, Cambridge, Mass.: MIT Press, 2009.

21   Walter Benjamin, 'The Work of Art in the Age of Mechanical Reproduction', in *Illuminations: Essays and Reflections*, New York: Harcourt, Brace & World, 1968.

22   Manfredo Tafuri, *Theories and History of Architecture*, New York: Harper & Row, 1980, 86.

23   Gianni Vattimo, 'The End of Modernity, The End of the Project?' in Neil Leach (ed), *Rethinking Architecture: A Reader in Cultural Theory*, London: Routledge, 1997.

24   Vattimo, 'The End of Modernity, The End of the Project?' 154.

25   Eco, *Interpretation and Overinterpretation*, 84.

Sense, Meaning and Taste in Architectural Criticism

JOHN MACARTHUR

In architecture the role of criticism is on the rise. There is new interest in all kinds of literary non-fiction, including writing about architecture and places, as the symposium and conference that generated this book demonstrate. What is more, as Naomi Stead and I have attempted to show elsewhere, the recent fall in the status of academic theoretical writing about architecture leaves an intellectual space that the practice of criticism has started to fill.[1] To put it simply, and without regret or celebration, there used to be a lot of architectural theory written that had a secondary function as criticism. Now that such theory is unpopular, perhaps because of its at times rebarbative language, the practical criticism of buildings has become more important, and increasingly has a secondary role of theorising more general relations of architecture, society and history. There is a binary opposition in this situation, of critical theory versus criticism that is theoretically astute: two sides of one coin if we think in terms of genre and modes of writing. Beneath these formal issues, however, lie questions of philosophy and facts of history. The binary I have identified could also include the philosophical question of whether criticism gives primacy to meaning or the sensory experience of the work. This fundamental question is complicated for us by its history in architecture, and by the question of the qualifications needed to be a critic, qualifications that were once called 'taste'.

Architecture has generally been valued for its meaningfulness and only in the last few centuries has this criterion been troubled by interest in its sensory affects. It is arguable that architecture as we know it today began when Leon Battista Alberti reformulated it as a humanistic discipline in the Italian Renaissance.[2] Then architecture was a kind of rhetoric, it had the task of explaining and connecting meanings emblematically, and its beauty was a matter of propriety in the same sense as the graces of a literary figure are proper to their meaning. Thus, for most of the past, judging buildings was a matter of how properly and eloquently they were what they were intended to be. Criticism, understood as a detailed accounting for preferences and judgements, only comes about in modern times with the rise of aesthetics in the 18th century. Aesthetics supposes that we can examine our perceptions and directly experience ideas of form that are the equivalent of conceptual rational ideas. An aesthetic understanding of culture rises from British Empiricism from the 17th century before its modern formulation by Immanuel Kant at the end of the 18th century. The focus on sensory experience meant a radical change in the concept of architecture. Where once it was a kind of language in a culture where all the arts were rhetorical, architecture became a visual and spatial form. Picturesque aesthetics was the first attempt to describe what is common and different to our experience of the natural world and cultural constructs like buildings and gardens, by comparing these with the purely visual form of paintings.[3] From the 18th century aesthetics grew as a general account of our pleasure and displeasure at sensory experience. Much of aesthetics tended towards naturalism in the sense that it sought to discover basic human orientations, for example, to a forest and a gothic cathedral, without a priori distinctions of kind, such as those between nature and architecture, forests and woods, cathedrals and bicycle sheds. Aesthetics tended to merge with psychology from gestalt and empathy theory at the beginning of the 20th century to later neurological accounts of the recognition of colour, symmetry and so on. The effect of aesthetics in architecture tended to be normative. Depending on the model of the mind supposed architects might survey groups to find common preferences in forms, or suppose archetypes of space that could be observed across cultures at the evolutionary scale of human history.

By the late 1960s, such normative accounts of architectural experience were attacked by poststructuralists, who held that the human subject is to a degree constructed. What we see might be optically straightforward, but how we look, what we look for and how we represent visual and spatial experience is constructed socially and culturally. This was the time of postmodernism and the critical values of sense and meaning flipped once again. In the mid-20th century one might have written that a building was good or bad because it felt satisfying or pleasing: perhaps it was proportioned in a way that made the brain hum, or, alternatively because it employed some primordial spatial category that was like a secure cave looking out across a plain in which there were no enemies and lots of tasty antelope. By the 1970s we would tend not to discuss whether a building was pleasing or displeasing, but rather how it manipulated and deployed existing cultural schemas. Buildings would be insightful or eloquent if they opened old signifying systems such as classicism to new signifieds.

Suffice to say that in the last years we have flipped once more. Postmodernism is almost forgotten and many architects are in a phase so neo-modernist that they do not want to recognise, let alone refer to, the precedents they employ, but rather simply aim to feel modern. Consumerism has encouraged us to have preferences and to display them. People speak with few cautions of the beauty of buildings and how they make them feel. It is rare to hear discussion of architecture as a whole-of-culture enterprise to which a building contributes or not, because this kind of meaning has been pushed into the background by the question of whether an individual building pleases. Perhaps it is clear from my rapid characterisation that I find our current critical culture in architecture unsatisfactory, and I am concerned at what the rise of a consumerist 'design culture' might mean for architecture. I want a culture that is evaluative, but socially so, not some hyper-consumerism of individuating preferences. I know that culture actually works at the level of acuities and dispositions that are learned, but there must be a role for discussion of the facts of sense perception without erecting a biological determinism. I want a discussion of architecture that accounts for sense *and* for cultural meaning.

The 18th century Scottish philosopher, David Hume, provides such a model in his famous essay, 'On the Standard of Taste' of 1757.[4] Hume's account of critical judgement pre-dates many of the delimitations of the aesthetic that have been commonly accepted since Kant's *Critique of Judgement* at the end of the 18th century.[5] Kant, and other thinkers and practitioners of culture since, have sharply distinguished our moral and aesthetic faculties. Unlike them, Hume is unconcerned that our appreciation of the goodness or truth of a work might prejudice us to find it beautiful against the evidence of our senses. With this more commonsense attitude, Hume also has no problem in simultaneously judging the sensual pleasing and the meaning of a work. He is not concerned that we might judge an object for its fit to a cultural concept; a situation that Kant thought prejudiced aesthetic judgement by confusing it with reason. What does concern Hume is 'taste', and it is a concept like this that I argue that we need today.

'Taste' is now a word used pejoratively, as when we say that a work is 'tasteful' and mean that it is anodyne, conforms to societal expectations and shows no true aesthetic discernment. Similarly, a person who claims to have a facility for taste, we think of as foolishly presuming that their individual preferences will be a model to others. Such pejorative understandings of taste result from the later rise of romantic individualism. Central to romanticism is concept of genius, of spirit imminent in places and people, and if we understand the capacity to make art in this way, then taste seems to be a category

mistake – an instructed form of genius. But this is not how 18th century thinkers saw it. The concept of taste in art is an analogy to the taste of the mouth, thus it strongly emphasises sensation over rules and norms, and in its original usage helped to explain the new theories of aesthetics. A taste for architecture implied that one could oneself determine the pleasing-ness of a building as directly and indubitably as tasting an unfamiliar fruit, and without reference to canons of form or concepts. But this emphasis on sense was not entirely a refutation of the value of meaning, prior experience and the culture of art. For Hume and his contemporaries, the point was not only to better know one's own taste, but also to display one's preferences to others, to compare and to form standards of taste, which would then confirm or overthrow the top-down rules for beauty that had been propounded in an earlier rhetorical culture. We can see the freshness that this idea once had by looking at 18th century uses of the word 'disgust', which meant something more like 'distasteful' than the stronger usage that it has since acquired.[6] Eighteenth century writers were busily discussing what disgusted them as a matter of useful information to be shared. Were we to act like this today the conversation might go something like this: Imagine that I disliked (I hesitate to employ the 18th century usage) the works of contemporary American architect Greg Lynn.[7] If I wish to claim my role as an active constituent in the world of architecture, I cannot be unsure of this, nor can I keep this judgement to myself. Therefore, I have to say his work does not meet the standard of taste, and if you think that it does, then we need to resolve this because not to do so would imply that we are accusing one another of a lack of aesthetic sensibility and a paucity of judgement. Nowadays we might just accept that my architecture community is not your architecture community, but this kind of relativism is what a standard of taste opposes, and which I suggest that we accede to too easily in modern times. If we are committed to a community of thought on architecture, then our different responses to Lynn are an interesting and valuable occasion to progress the taste of the whole of that community. You might say that Lynn's work interests you, but doesn't strongly compel your attention. I might say that it is boring rather than distasteful, and thus we might move closer to a boundary of taste across which we could continue the discussion, that boundary might move as a result and we might find that we agree about Lynn, but disagree about the shape and edges of architectural culture. One of the main issues introduced by the graduations assumed in taste is that there are two measures by which we might gauge the extent of our differences. I could put it to you that Lynn's buildings are plain ugly in the sense that they give me no sensuous pleasure in beholding them. Here my argument relies on persuading you of the accuracy of my perceptions and my astuteness in identifying and understanding what affects me and how. Or I could tell you that Lynn's buildings are instances of a pernicious naturalism that has troubled architecture for centuries and which defers the questions of architects' responsibility for form-making by giving this over to organic nature, or even worse, to technological change mystified as nature. This second explanation of my preference supposes an authority of judgement that is founded on knowledge of architecture and my ability to see Lynn's work in relation to larger trends and movements in architectural culture.

The qualifications that a critic of architecture should have are notoriously difficult to agree on, and there is nothing particular to architecture in this. Whether architects have some superiority in judging buildings over non-architects is merely a case of the more general problem of comparing any opinion with that of an expert in any field. Some would argue that expertise in criticism shows that it is simply normative: that those with the power and position to publish their criticisms are simply applying rules, the existence of which justifies their roles.

While this might be true in some, or even many, circumstances, it does not account for the commonly occurring shifts in taste in clothing, car design or building and the ability of some critics, and not others, to describe and explain what many individuals feel in common. The question is rather where this critical expertise lies, in acuity of sensory perception, or in ability to adduce the meaning of such experiences. The concept of taste, even though it was riding the pendulum rapidly towards sense in the 18th century, still at that time supposed a balance of the values of sense and meaning.

Several iterations of this dialectic later, in the architectural culture of the latter 20th century, criticism has been largely about meaning. Critics have tended to be exegetes who give written expression to the implicit architectural workings of a building. The assumption here is that the building has some kind of meaning internal to itself, a logic of spaces and uses, joints and views, novelty and relations to precedent; and the role of the critic is to put these matters in words, and hence in concepts that are common with how we might make a similar discussion of a musical work, or other artwork, or indeed other designed object or environment. In such a model the critic's expertise in architecture is vital, and their relation to the profession and other architects is clear. But this exegetical criticism puts aside the thorny issue of judgements of value. Typically such critics write of buildings with admirable qualities, but how buildings are chosen for criticism is not discussed. If criticism were purely instrumental, then there would be as much, or more, value in the exegesis of bad buildings. Similarly, this 'architectural criticism' seems narrow and even sophistic in moving so far from the question of the preferences of the public and individuals who commission and pay for buildings. Thus, in our dispute over Lynn, if I were a professor of architecture, who could make a long exegesis of the internal logic and the precedents and references in Lynn's work, and you were, say a professor of music, equally used to making fine aesthetic discriminations, then my authority in the matter should persuade you. But equally, you might still find Lynn's buildings unbearably attractive, and then we reach a serious impasse, because then either your taste is perverse, or the architectural discourse, which I claim my judgement represents, is unanchored from aesthetic experience and untrue. The values of sense and meaning ought to converge: this is the promise of art.

If exegesis tends to be the dominant mode of writing criticism in architecture, no one actually thinks that evaluation is not at stake. In the broader culture of criticism we give numerical ratings to movies, restaurants and music, while critics of literature and the visual arts tend to be very forthright in praise and condemnation. Architectural criticism has tended to have less 'amplitude', perhaps because of the financial interests involved in building and an increasingly litigious civil culture. But despite its smaller, vaguer range of approbation and opprobrium, even the most descriptive architectural criticism is read for faintness of praise, degrees of conceptual sophistication said to be in the building, and any other hints that a reader might have about how their own evaluation measures against that of the expert critic. For ultimately, one might follow all the points of an analytical account of a building chosen for our approbation by a critic, and still not like it. The meaning of a building might be lucidly explained, and even self-evident in the experience of it, and still one's sensory experience of the building might be unsatisfying. Is it then the case that the expertise of the architectural critic must not only consist of the knowledge of architecture and the literary ability to communicating that knowledge with concrete cases, but also a higher, finer sensory acuity than those who simply like or dislike?

Hume claims that this is the case and that it is self-evident. He writes: 'It seldom, or never happens, that a man of sense, who has experience in any art, cannot judge of its beauty; and it is no less rare to meet with a man who has a just taste without a sound understanding.'[8] It would surprise Hume if I merely told him that Lynn's work was ugly, but could not give a reason based on a wider understanding of what architecture is and should be. Conversely, if I had no opinion on the beauty of Lynn's buildings, who would credit me with understanding – what would the purpose and value of architectural knowledge be?

If we accept that sense and meaning, perception and cognition are simply interdependent in critical judgement the problem of degrees of expertise still remains, but in this case it is not knowledge of architecture, but rather the cumulative experience of reflecting on sensuous experience. Hume thought that a good critic has through practice learned to sort and organise sensory experience, and this process is guided by understanding the debates and history of the art in question. Hume calls this attribute 'delicacy of taste'.[9] Some people possess this greater delicacy, and that is evidenced in that what they notice and write about in a work has a wider agreement and seems true to a larger group of people. Taste and its degree of refinement and delicacy are thus matters of fact for Hume, despite their also being contestable, and there being little prospect of finding evidence that my taste is more delicate than yours. Hume explains this with a story from Cervantes.[10] Sancho tells the anecdote of two of his ancestors famous for their taste in wine. They sample a cask and agree its merit, but one finds fault in an underlying hint of leather, the other in a metallic finish. They proceed to argue about the characteristics that such a wine should or should not have. When they have drained the cask they find at the bottom an old key tied with a leather thong. Thus, for Hume, good critics use their informed experience to sort and order sense impressions not commonly susceptible to consciousness. The fact that critics differ and may not understand why they differ does not mean that the higher aesthetic discernment he called delicacy of taste does not exist. Nor does it mean that critical judgements that differ cannot both be based on evidence of sensory experience. Later thinkers, particularly Joshua Reynolds, founder of the Royal Academy of Arts in Britain, thought that understanding the standard of taste could lead to its improvement, that taste would become progressively more objective, and that ultimately artists would know what to make and the public what to like.[11] This did not happen largely because of the rise of romantic individualism, and the interest in aesthetic feeling beyond pleasing-ness that emerges in the concepts of the sublime and picturesque. I think that Hume's idea of a standard of taste is useful to us today despite the serious reservation that taste and its standards have been a rationalisation of aristocracy.

In the 18th century critical judgements about cultural works were analogues of political judgements. A republic of taste was the mirror of the political republic and the disinterestedness with which the good critic approached judgement was analogous to the members of parliament having no pecuniary interest in matters they were legislating.[12] The standard of taste was thus an analogue of franchise. The critic whose judgements fell within the standard of taste had established a right, just as qualifications of landed property and gender qualified a man to vote or be elected. This is an ideology of the kind where the good taste of those with the leisure and education to practise it, seem to belong naturally to those with wealth and power. Some of the narrative and structure of aristocracy continued as capitalism and parliamentary democracy grew, and as Pierre Bourdieu has shown, nowhere is this clearer than in the way that the displays of taste in contemporary societies function to produce an aristocracy of culture.[13] It is the proper debunking of these pretentions that leads us today to use 'tasteful' as a pejorative term, the opposite of what it meant for Hume, and which also says something of the dangers in reviving a concept of taste.

Nevertheless, I argue that it is something like a standard of taste in architecture that we need today. Of course Greg Lynn would fall within it; even though I have no great fondness for his work, I understand it, and I also understand the appreciation of Lynn by those I recognise as my peers. My dislike of Lynn's work is thus different in kind to my dismissal of much banal and clichéd building and those who promote and discuss it beyond the standard of taste. Criticism should have a project of its own parallel to architecture – beyond assessing individual works and their tendencies. Good criticism should tell us not only if a building succeeded or failed, and more than whether this meant that architectural culture should follow path A or B. It would also build a capacity for discernment in the critic and the reader, which would be of value in itself and useful in future circumstances unknown – it would be a standard of taste as much as of architecture.

Even if this modern standard grew through the organic consensus of many good judges of architecture, there would of course be the problem how this constituency of good judges would be formed. Suffice to say if it is to avoid being an aristocracy it could not be formed from university schools, professional institutes, development councils and planning agencies. Equally it could not be 'the market': the supposedly self-evident expression of an aggregate of individual preferences of consumers of architecture where the moment of judgement is reduced to the decision whether to buy. The real estate pages of the weekend newspapers and magazines of the beautiful home offer the opportunity to practise one's taste, but this is not by itself enough to develop what Hume called the 'delicacy of taste'. It is not directed, as it should be, beyond personal desire, experience and self-knowing, toward a public matter – architecture. It is sometimes claimed that architects write for architects and not for the public because expertise leads them to elitism and chauvinism. I am not sure if this is the correct way to put the problem. Criticism, no matter who makes it, is a claim to expertise and authority, it is, by its nature, a claim that all should feel towards the work as the critic does, and a differentiated naming of those feelings by reference to issues and ideas larger than the work at hand. It is also a claim that is to be contested: not by anyone through reference merely to their own preferences, but by anyone willing to test the claim and progress our mutual understanding. What is missing in architectural culture today is a sense of a mutual project of criticism that concerns the whole community.

Until recently architects writing criticism rarely admitted that their preference was at stake and sometimes wrote of buildings as mere illustrations of architectural theory. Today with the fetishisation of design as the marker of success in the creative economy I fear the pendulum of sense and meaning is swinging rapidly in the other direction. Criticism risks becoming a commentary on star architects and the preferences of those with the resources to express themselves through their choice of cars, handbags and buildings. We need critics who are prepared to admit their preferences and allow that their sensible feelings for a building have the power to recalibrate their knowledge of architecture. At the same time we should recognise that proposing a personal feeling of preference as critical judgement asserts an expertise and a consequent obligation to engage the wider knowledge of a cultural community. Perhaps such a criticism might read not like a legal judgement, nor like celebrity gossip, but rather like the project that taste once was.

1   John Macarthur and Naomi Stead, 'The Judge is not an Operator: Historiography, Criticality and Architectural Criticism / De betekenis van kritiek in post-kritische tijden: architectuur, historiografie en oordeel,' *Oase*, 26, (2006), 116-139.

2   Leon Battista Alberti, *On the Art of Building in Ten Books*, Cambridge, Mass. & London: MIT Press, 1988.

3   John Macarthur, *The Picturesque: architecture, disgust and other irregularities*, London, Routledge, 2007.

4   David Hume, 'Of the Standard of Taste', In *Four Dissertations*, London: A. Millar, 1757. Available online at http://www.csulb.edu/~jvancamp/361r15.html. In my reading of Hume I have relied on: Ted Gracyk, 'Hume's Aesthetics,' in *The Stanford Encyclopedia of Philosophy* (Winter 2011 Edition), Edward N. Zalta (ed.), forthcoming URL <http://plato.stanford.edu/archives/win2011/entries/hume-aesthetics/>; Carolyn W. Korsmeyer, 'Hume and the Foundations of Taste', *The Journal of Aesthetics and Art Criticism*, 35, No. 2 (Winter, 1976), 201- 215; Jerrold Levinson, 'Hume's Standard of Taste: The Real Problem', *The Journal of Aesthetics and Art Criticism*, 60, No. 3 (Summer, 2002), 227- 238; Jens Kulenkampff, 'The Objectivity of Taste: Hume and Kant', *Noûs*, 24, 1, On the Bicentenary of Immanuel Kant's Critique of Judgement (Mar., 1990), pp. 93-110.

5   Immanuel Kant, *Kant's Critique of Aesthetic Judgement*, Translated by James Creed Meredith, Oxford: Clarendon Press, 1911.

6   Winfried Menninghaus, *Disgust: Theory and History of a Strong Sensation*. Translated by Howard Eiland and Joel Golb, Albany: State University of New York Press, 2003. Also see Macarthur, *The Picturesque: architecture, disgust and other irregularities*, in particular chapter 3 "Disgust".

7   The work of Greg Lynn is only an example and the opinions that I state are nothing more than a pretext for this argument, which does not require the reader to have an opinion. Thus I have not sought permission to illustrate his work.

8   Hume, 'Of the Standard of Taste', 22.

9   Hume, 'Of the Standard of Taste', 16.

10   Hume, 'Of the Standard of Taste', 16.

11   Sir Joshua Reynolds, *Discourses on Art*. Edited by Robert R. Wark, New Haven and London: Published for the Paul Mellon Centre for Studies in British Art (London) Ltd. by Yale University Press, 1975.

12   On this idea see John Barrell, *The Political Theory of Painting from Reynolds to Hazlit: the Body of the Public*, New Haven and London: Yale University Press, 1986. Among other sources Barrell draws on J. G. A. Pocock, *The Machiavellian Moment: Florentine political thought and the Atlantic republican tradition*, Princeton, N.J.: Princeton University Press, 1975.

13   Pierre Bourdieu, 'The Aristocracy of Culture', *Media, Culture and Society*, 2: (1980), 225-254; and *Distinction: A Social Critique of the Judgement of Taste*. Cambridge: Harvard University Press, 1984.

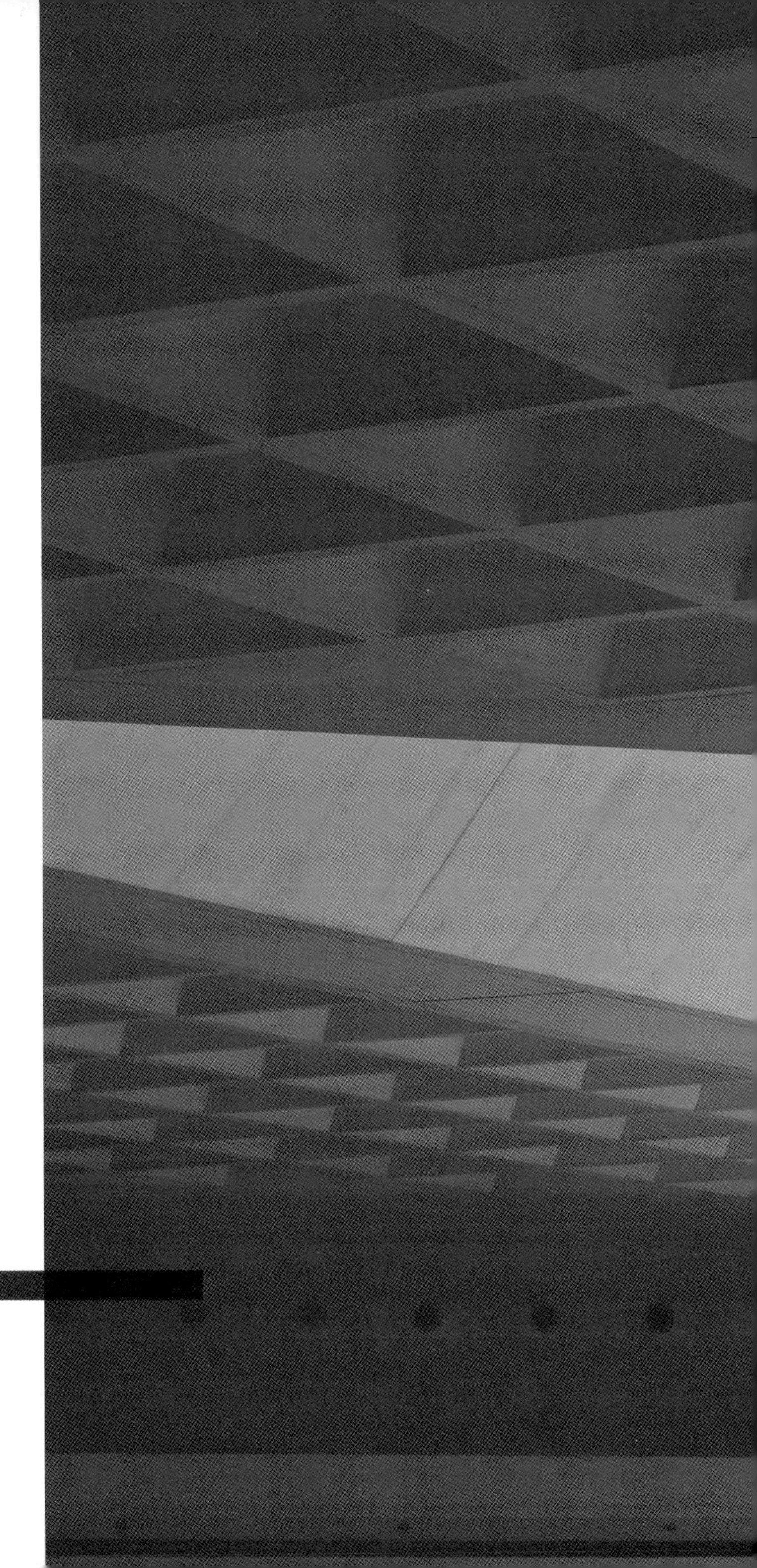

PRACTICE

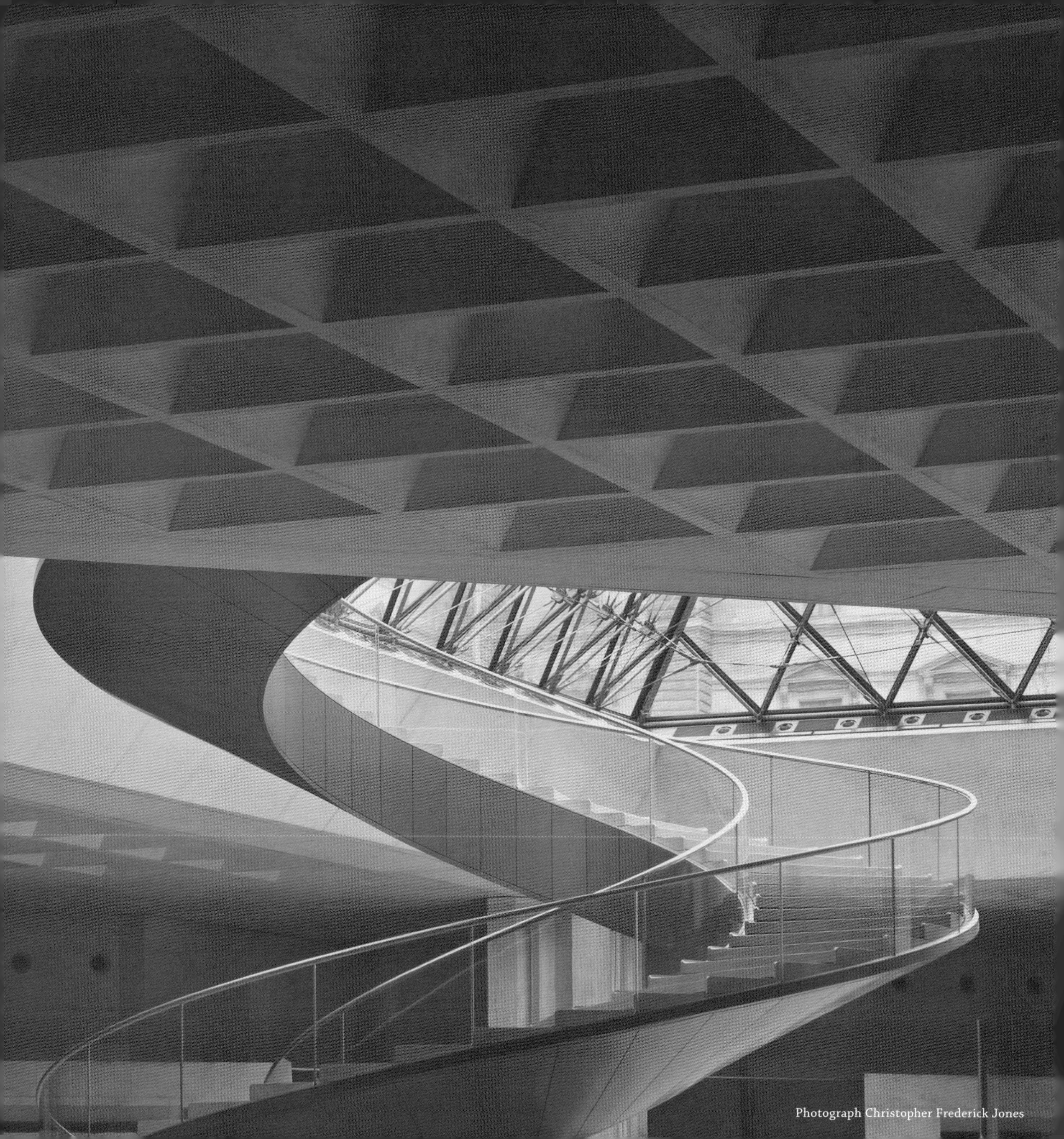

Photograph Christopher Frederick Jones

Words and Pictures: Communication in architectural practice

NAOMI STEAD

In a review of Adrian Forty's *Words and Buildings*, published in the *London Review of Books*, the architectural theorist and historian Andrew Saint writes wittily of the role of verbal communication in architecture.

> Architects spend little of their time at the drawing board and the various devices that have half-succeeded it. To get anything built they must organise, cajole and present the big picture: all of which needs good words. Many famous modern architects have been charismatic wordsmiths, at least orally; and it is arguable that the profession maintains its high status in the pecking order of the construction industry only because most architects are better rhetoricians than their fellow professionals.[1]

One might add to this that architects are also better at using photography to communicate their work, they have excellent photographers to collaborate with, and they often have close and symbiotic relationships with the architectural media. This section examines the three-way relationship between practicing architects, professional architectural photographers and architectural editors – an intense and intertwined relationship between three sets of professionals who each make a living from words and pictures about architecture.

It is a truism that architects don't make buildings – they make elaborate sets of instructions that enable others to make buildings. These instructions are set out in drawings, yes, but crucially also in texts and spoken words – the telephone is as vital an architectural tool as the pen, perhaps even more so today. Communication is thus a crucial skill for architects, as much before and during as after construction – it is communication that catches the imagination of the client and allows a particular design idea to proceed; communication instructs and negotiates with the builder and other collaborators; and communication allows the architect to explain and share his or her ideas about the completed work with the world. More than this, most architects are also architectural commentators and critics in their own right, whether formally or informally, and many also engage in teaching and advocacy, requiring rhetorical skills all of their own. The relationship between these various modes and methods of communication, and their respective voices and tones, is captured in this section of the book through conversations. Each of the contributors has complex roles in the communication of architecture, both within and outside the profession.

From Sydney, Olivia Hyde, a senior practice director at BVN Architecture, spoke with Marcus Trimble, a director of Bennett and Trimble, who also runs the blog *Super Colossal*, and started the Pecha Kucha night in Sydney. Both Olivia and Marcus teach design at several Sydney universities, and between them contribute as critics to various architectural magazines. From Brisbane, Paul Owen, a director of the Brisbane architectural practice Owen and Vokes, spoke with Elizabeth Watson Brown, who has practiced architecture for more than 30 years, most recently as design director at Architectus. Both are actively involved in architectural culture, education and discourse in Queensland. From Melbourne, Jill Garner, co-founder of Garner Davis Architects and current Associate Victorian Government Architect, spoke with Jan van Schaik, a lecturer at RMIT University, and a director of Minifie van Schaik Architects, whose work has been awarded, published and exhibited both locally and internationally.

The section is opened by a conversation (via email) between two former editors, both highly influential figures in Australian architecture for the best part of the last decade. Justine Clark was editor of *Architecture Australia* from 2003 to 2011, and is now an independent architectural writer, researcher and critic, while Andrew Mackenzie was for nine years the Editor-In-Chief of *Architectural Review Australia* (now known as *Architectural Review Asia Pacific*) and *(Inside) Australia Design Review*, before leaving to set up URO media, the publisher of this book.

Communication is obviously also a crucial skill for photographers. And while their primary medium is visual, it would be a poor photographer (and a commercially unsuccessful one), who could not talk to architects about buildings, write to editors about image selection, and discuss their methods and ideas with other photographers. But it is fair to say that while most architectural photographers, like architects themselves, are engaged with verbal and visual communication about buildings every day, they don't often have time to pause and reflect on this as a practice. This section of the book offered just that opportunity to some of Australia's most prominent architectural photographers – Shannon McGrath, Dianna Snape, Peter Bennetts, Christopher Frederick Jones and Brett Boardman (in the order in which they appear). Here they reflect on their practice, and the way that architectural photography serves to mediate architecture and publicise it – to literally make it public. Peter Bennetts, in particular, must be acknowledged for his significant role in the conference and workshop from which much of the rest of the book sprang – as one of the leaders of the workshop, Peter also photographed that event and the conference, and his photographs throughout the book are a testament to his ability to capture people equally as well as buildings.

<hr>

1   Andrew Saint, 'What architects said before they said "space"', *London Review of Books*, vol 22, no 23, 30 November 2000, 28-29. The review refers to Adrian Forty, *Words and Buildings: A Vocabulary of Modern Architecture*, London: Thames and Hudson, 2004.

'It may be that the image outlives the project itself'

SHANNON MCGRATH

What key principles do you bring to your work as a photographer?
The photographer wears three hats:
The documenter: to record architecture in time and create an historic record.
The artist: to make an interpretation of the subject, transforming it from three-dimensional form into two-dimensional plane in the best light.
The businessperson: to consider the commercial viability of translating the project into published form, on behalf of the architect.

Do these principles engage with architectural criticism and, if so, how?
By making a record of a project in published form: these images may be the only occasion in which people encounter that project, or the only occasion that is true to the architect's intention of that time. So it does become an important part of the critical process. This is where it is important that the photographer interprets the project in the documentary sense, as well as with an understanding of the architect's vision and brief, such that we portray it in its best form. Once the brief has been met, the photographer can then allow his/her artistic license to come through and the project can be taken to another level of visualisation. This cues an emotional interpretation of the project.

How does photographic convention support or subvert these principles?
Some architects only draw and think in elevations, so by knowing this the photographer can record the project in elevation. Meanwhile, other architects may visualise their project with dramatic distortion, so we can also push this idea in how we approach photographing it. We look to approach a project in many ways, from the full context to the abstract detail, it all depends on how it is to be represented, and this is elaborated through the dialogue between architect and photographer, which informs our understanding of the intent of the project.

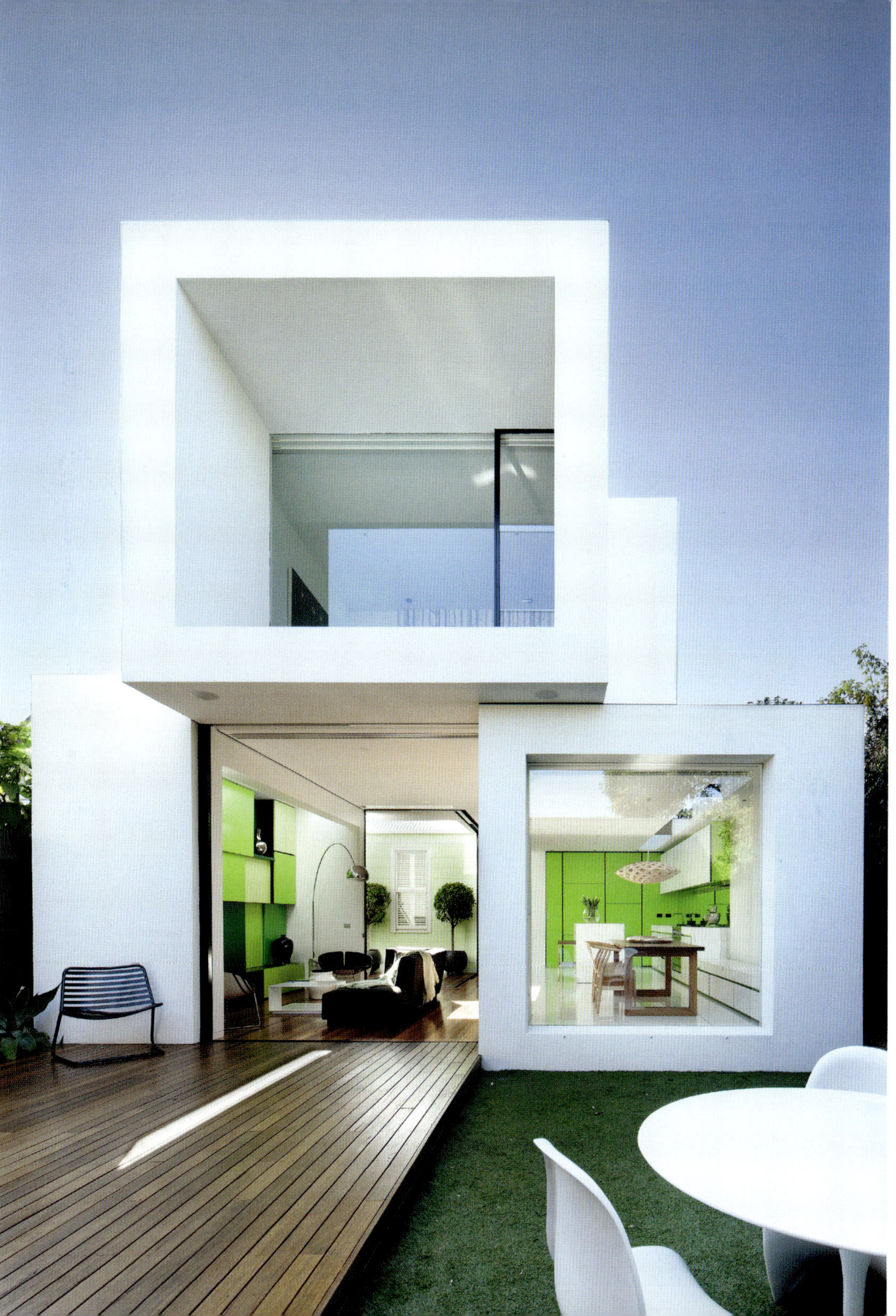

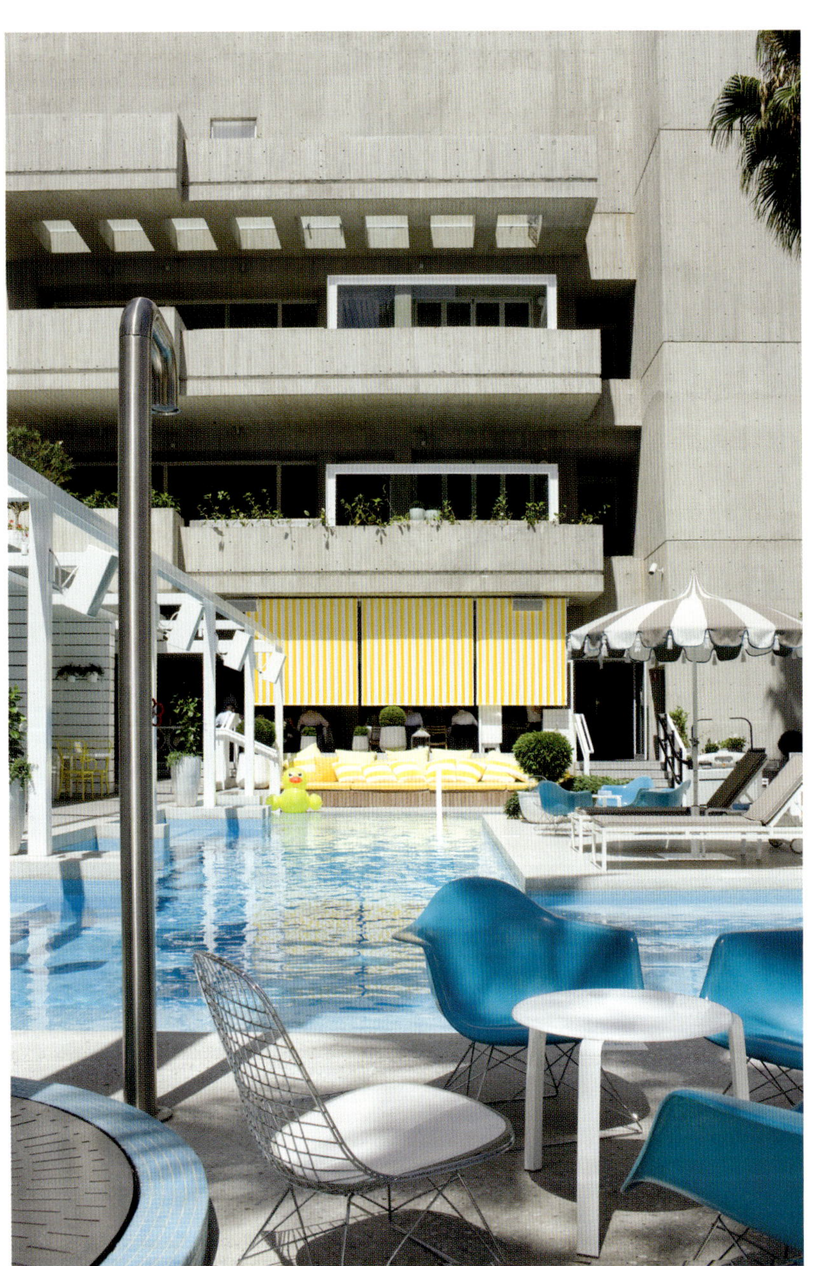

Can photography be used to form an independent visual architectural critique?

Absolutely, this is where the relationship between the architect and the photographer is paramount, since, at the end of the day, it is the photographer who is visually representing the project for now and the future. It may be that eventually the image outlives the project itself.

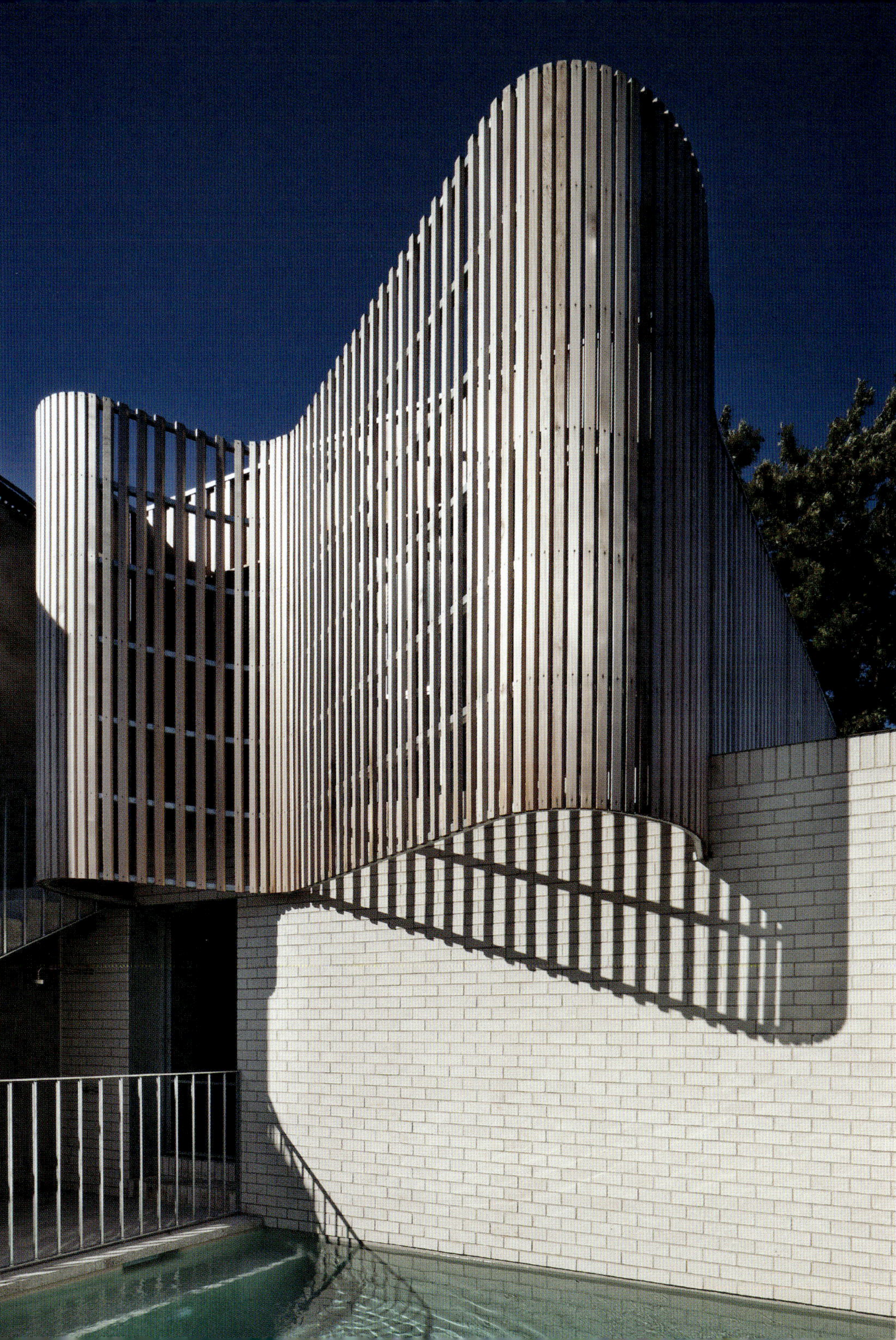

Justine Clark and Andrew Mackenzie

IN CONVERSATION

AM I would like to start by challenging a common cliché of architecture's relationship to architecture media. In my time as editor of *Architecture Review Australia* I was often struck by the conflicted relationship that architects had to the magazine. On the one hand it is to be courted and used almost like a professional support service. On the other hand it is to be resisted, as an enervating influence on architecture's higher principles. In either case, media is cast as an affect that is 'done' to architecture, with good or bad outcomes. Common codes of representation, such as the missing human presence, the tendency towards perspectival distortion, the partiality of reviewer to subject reviewed, are seen as codes owned by media and perniciously imposed on architecture.

This is a convenient story, as it offshores the agency of mediation outside the territory of professional practice. However, if we consider other art forms, such as theatre, film or literature, the critical review of architecture appears conspicuously constrained. There are many reasons for this, but to a large extent those constraints seemed, as an editor, to be exerted in some part from without. This is not to deny media's agency, but to suggest that its effects are the results of an interaction that you could call collaborative, or perhaps more accurately collusive.

Is this something you recognise from your experiences at *Architecture Australia*?

JC Yes, I recognise the cliché – in fact, one of the things that irritated me most was when an architect treated me as if I was their PR agent. It rarely ended well. And yes, the courting and resisting you describe are flip sides of the same condition – a fairly simplistic understanding of what are, in fact, complex relationships. Architecture and media have been intimately entwined for centuries and the representational codes you outline are deeply entrenched. This entanglement has been well documented, analysed and critiqued. I found this work crucial to my ability to do my job as editor of *AA*; it allowed me to think my way through the more prosaic day-to-day activities of making a magazine within bigger frames of reference. The conventions are very hard to shift, which is the nature of conventions, but I nudged them wherever and whenever I could, usually in small ways.

I agree that any publication is the outcome of a collaborative, or possibly collusive, interaction. This can be problematic, but I am not sure it is necessarily something to bemoan. Like any 'work', a magazine is a product of the culture that we operate within, and we – editors, authors and architects – are all cultural agents, even as we attempt to shift that culture. This is not to deny the agency of the editor, but it is to acknowledge that deploying that agency is a constant act of negotiation rather than a straightforward expression of singular intention (it's rather like making a building). I always liked the idea that this 'authoritative' magazine was always slightly beyond my (or any one person's control) – that all those involved, including the reader, brought something to it that could never quite be predicted.

I am interested in the way that architectural culture is constructed through communal activity and engagement – between and among us all. This is another reason why the publishing-as-marketing paradigm is impoverished – one can never quite predict how a work will be received. This means that, for the architect, publishing a project is more risky and more generous than the self-aggrandisement of self-promotion (whether or not the architect recognised the risk or the generosity). In publishing a project you are both contributing to the building of architectural culture, and exposing one's work in ways that are outside your control.

AM Perhaps I should be more specific in my use of the word collusive. It is rather weighted. As you say, the project review involves both generosity and risk, and there is often a high degree of integrity in the relationship between participants. But participation is the issue. The specific proximity between reviewer and reviewed, which is uniquely framed within architectural criticism, places limits on what is said and what is not said. The conventional project review is in fact a form of embedded criticism, as the reviewer generally needs the architect's permission to do the review. This makes the architect a participant of sorts.

There are strategies one can put in place to more or less mitigate this, but it nevertheless impacts critical independence. I'm not saying independence is only exercised when we condemn something, but there is a problem when punches are pulled and criticism that might rightly be levelled at a specific piece of architecture, is self-censured or gets displaced to an 'issue'.

Why is this? It might sound counter-intuitive for an art form that exists theoretically in the public realm, but the business of reviewing architecture is tightly bound to privacy of access and ownership – of property, photography, plans and sections. I know that in nearly a decade, I never commissioned a single review of a project where the permission of the project's architect was withheld. So while those parts of the magazine that covered book and conference reviews and general industry news were sometimes positive and sometimes very not positive, when it came to the project reviews there was polite decorum at play, as a consequence of the internal conflict of participants.

JC It is important to distinguish between the magazine having 'permission' to publish a project and the reviewer having 'permission' to write about it – ideally, the reviewer gains permission through the commission, not through the architect. I agree that it is very difficult to publish a project in a magazine like *Architecture Australia* without the input of the architect – they almost always supply the drawings and pay for the photography, for one thing, which is certainly collusive. But I was also very clear that it was my job to commission the reviewer – and my job to decide who that was. Only rarely did an architect try to exert undue influence, and if they did I didn't commissioned that writer. I don't respond well to being pushed around. We also had a strict policy of not showing reviews to architects prior to publication (although sometimes the writer would prior to sending it to us).

But I think you are really referring to a much more subtle and pervasive kind of 'collusion'. Architectural publications are not outside architecture, but are an integral part of the dissemination and development of ideas – so, to a degree they are always collusive. I certainly consider myself part of architecture – it is my discipline.

Nonetheless I hope that if one operates with integrity, some of its more disturbing aspects of 'collusion' might be mitigated. This sounds a bit pompous and Pollyanna-ish, but what else can we do? There is no 'pure' situation; we operate in the world. You have to find ways to work as effectively as possible in the situations you find yourself in – while also trying to improve/shift those situations. You have to resist being 'played'. But yes, it can all get a bit cosy sometimes. Maybe that is when it is time to change jobs!

I do think we should be careful not to romanticise the critical cultures of other disciplines – most of which also complain about a lack of criticality. I agree that the circumstances under which new buildings are reviewed in professional magazines are quite particular, but other disciplines also have elaborate, if different, conditions of access. For example, in the art world the gallery system has a huge amount of influence and control about what gets seen, before the reviewer ever walks in the door.

AM Different disciplines have different cultures, and we do sometimes look outside our communities to 'farther fields'. But to take an example, you mention the critical constraints of the art world. As a long time reader and occasional contributor to various art magazines, I would say that it is rare for an art magazine not to include one or more highly critical exhibition reviews. Sometimes

good artists produce bad art. Instead of demurring, the art reviewer will often hold the exhibition and the artist to account, robustly. It just happens. On the other hand, it is rare to find the same level of unambiguous criticism expressed on the pages of an architecture magazine. It happens in the newspapers, but not in the profession's journals. So my point is simply that, despite the undoubted constraints of the gallery system, my experience of the art review in say, *Artforum* or *Frieze*, is that it is more candid than architecture review. This I believe is fundamentally conditioned by the mechanics of different publication regimes.

JC There are bigger cultural forces at work. To put another spin on it, I am interested in the collegial and the communal aspect of architectural culture. In this I am very influenced by Juan Pablo Bonta's teasing out of the mechanisms through which buildings enter the canon. He emphasises that that is a consensual, communal process happening over time and through the input of many and varied voices (and that publication and photography are crucial to it). These are important points. Again it doesn't deny us individual agency, but it points out that we also act within larger contexts, and in relation to many others. A key issue though is who gets to have a voice in such cultures, who is listened to and who isn't. Another is that the contemporary Australian architectural community is effective at policing itself, particularly in relation to what people are prepared to say in print (in my experience it is not the editors limiting what is said). And the new building review is the most policed section. But good writers are also very accomplished at saying what needs to be said.

On the other hand, sometimes closeness can be very productive – some of the best reviews I ever published were by writers who were personally very close to the architect, but where there was integrity and professional respect on both sides. These writers didn't let the architects off the hook over any aspect of the project, and the intimacy lent a very special quality to the writing.

Critical distance is, of course, the default position, and it is a good default position. But it is a construct, which brings with it its own complications. It is both desired and problematic. Other kinds of relationships can also lead to effective and productive work.

AM   I agree that there are writers who can work around it. You call it policed. I call it embedded criticism.

The question of who gets to have a voice is an interesting one, although in my experience I'd have said it was relatively simple to answer. At *AR* I published the opinions of anyone in the profession who wanted a voice, had something to say and who could write reasonably well. Even the last condition was optional. I have in the past, engineered significant rewrites of terribly written prose, because I thought the content was worth publishing and expressed an opinion that was important to be heard.

I'm not saying we had an open door policy regarding writers and content, but it would be fair to say that I hunted down people who had an architectural opinion and crucially, were willing to share it. There is not what I would call a surplus of those kinds of people around. As you say, the profession can be highly self-censoring. If I could have published half of the dinner table debates I have had with architects, *AR* would have had twice the readership!

JC   I had a similar approach to writers – it was always exciting to find someone new who could think and write well and was prepared to say what they thought. In fact, one of the things I am most proud of from my tenure at *AA* is the group of very fine writers I built up. But, I am referring to the way cultures give voice to some groups over than others, and who puts themselves forward to speak 'authoritatively' and who needs to be coaxed. There are lessons here from history, from feminism, from postcolonial studies, which I hope we learn from and bring to bear in some way.

There are many other constraints in a print magazine aimed at the profession, funded through advertising, and in the established format of the project review in these publications – 6–10 pages, 1200 words. There are also severe limitations on the kind of work that gets published in this context. Two gaps I always felt existed are: a forum to recognise good solid projects, which are not 'star' buildings, but make a decent contribution, and a forum in which to call out the real shockers (I was told that Australian libel laws make the latter impossible).

Perhaps the online environment has potential here. There is a lot of opportunity with changing media in terms of how architectural writing, criticism and representation might shift and develop. (But no one yet knows how to pay for it – this isn't specific to architecture). Perhaps we can talk about 'new' media.

AM   As you say, we don't yet seem to have reached a sustainable paid content model for online. Free is the benchmark, except of course for the advertisers, who are steadily reallocating print spend to online. So we seem to be in a hiatus, where print is bleeding ad revenue so it's cutting editorial costs (one of the few non-fixed costs). Meanwhile online is still building its base, and not yet able to support editorial costs in a conventional sense. I'm not sure it ever will, because there is an interesting paradigm shift happening in the relationship between advertising and editorial.

Print architecture titles traditionally rely heavily on advertising to keep the lights on. In many cases it's 75 percent of total revenue. The promise to advertisers is simple; the magazine's high-quality content delivers high quality readers (decision-makers). Advertisers then place ads next to the content to build brand awareness within the right audience. The promise is of course thoroughly unaccountable. Who reads what page, when and for how long, is unknowable.

Online brings a whole new world of data gathering, so the advertisers are happy because they know how many eyeballs looked at what pages and then where they clicked through to. Beyond page impressions, the next phase means more complex data capture, which Google are infamously trailblazing. In no time, consumer profiling will be standard in the online media environment. Advertisers obsess over such details, yet don't care at all how long the reader spent on the page. *ADR's* average two minutes per page was pretty great compared to industry standards. But those advertising online don't care about whether you spent 20 seconds or 20 minutes reading something. They want to harvest and interpret traffic and visitors.

So here's the rub. Why invest in long form essays or even short well-read reviews, if a well-timed piece of churnism can do the same amount of work, in advertising terms? In my own experience, it was a little scary to see a popular three line news item outstrip the monthly traffic to the entire book review section, in four hours. If traffic pays to keep the lights on, who cares if it's 50 words or 5000 words.

That said, the online space is a highly differentiated space. It's not a piece of cloth. The difference between Dan Hill's *City of Sound* and the amebic vitriol that passes for comment is the difference between *The Times Literary Supplement* and *New Idea*. I don't believe, as some would-be gurus argue, that there are any universal truths about where it's going or what it's doing. But I'm happy for it to give old media a run for its money, quite literally.

JC Yes, of course. Like any medium there is a wide variety and different economic structures play a big part in what's possible. The issue of the future of the long form piece is interesting – and there is some useful analysis going on about this journalism, which gives me hope. I am sure that news has always had more 'hits' – Radar Headlines was always the most-read section of *AA* – but the implications of being able to measure this are indeed alarming if that is the only way impact and value are measured. The issue of funding models is enormous – I think many readers underestimate the role that this plays – and we are in the midst of big paradigm shifts.

There is a huge amount of 'collusive' publishing online – but, in addition to great blogs like Dan's, there are also some excellent 'journals' reaching big audiences with serious content. I am thinking, for example, of 'Places', now part of *Design Observer*. I particularly like the Lunch with the Critics' series, which transcribes conversations between Alexandra Lange and Mark Lamster immediately after they have visited a building. The discussion is rougher and rawer, and often quite self-reflexive about the process of review and critique. Of course you could do this in print, but it seems that *Design Observer*, and Nancy Levinson as editor of 'Places', provides a particular context that enables a particular approach.

I am not giving up on print either – although magazines can sometimes feel both ossified and hidebound, they do offer particular opportunities, and they can be shifted and changed incrementally. But I am also interested in how different media might work together in inventive ways.

Something else I'm interested in is the rise of the architectural 'advocate', a term that seems to be being bandied around a lot of late. A few years ago budding architectural writers aspired to be critics, now it seems that the thing to be is an advocate. At first glance this seems to jettison 'critical distance', and replace it with cheerleading for a profession in decline. Yet, at it best, it relates to the idea of the public intellectual (such as Robin Boyd), to the tradition of the advocate/activist historian (Gideon, Pevsner etc.), and to an optimism about what the profession might become.

I have yet to get my head around the current enthusiasm for this fully. The most articulate account that I know is Barry Bergdoll's essay on *Design Observer* 'The Art of Advocacy'. Here he redefines the role of the architect and designer as advocates. 'The most pertinent stance young … designers can take is to translate the wealth of research emerging from design schools into

further activist engagement and new research opportunities
– and to advocate for that central role for designers
in solving the profound dilemmas that define our time.
This will require us, individually and as a discipline, to
calibrate our ethical compass, to set a standard for what
it means to act as a designer.'

Do you have thoughts on the rise of the advocate here?

AM It seems largely a defensive construct. We have moved
beyond defending good design against bad, and instead
find ourselves defending design. This is hardly surprising,
given the common perception of architecture as defined by
the iconic or the lifestyle. Caught between the profligate
and the banal. I can't say the profession has tried too hard
to resist that perception.

So my concern is both the cheerleading, and the
profession in decline. There's a lot of stress placed on the
need for the profession to communicate better. I think
this has the potential to be displacement therapy. What
the profession needs to do is look in the mirror and
undertake a profound reassessment of its place in the world,
and determine a means to re-engage more meaningfully.
To engage big questions of authorship, agency, value and
meaning, not little questions of how to doctor the spin.
If I were a design advocate I'd spend my time campaigning
within the profession, not to the rest of the world.

JC That is why I think Bergdoll's position is a strong
one – it moves beyond the defensive 'cheerleading' stance
to a much more complex exploration of the possibilities
of the discipline and the contributions it can make. It is
about those big issues, not the spin. It is both hopeful
and critical – it demands an active rethinking of and by
the profession, but it expects this to happen through an
engagement with the world. In the end we all share the
responsibility to act in large and small ways to move the
discipline along. There is some good work going on in
this regard, so despite all the problems we have canvassed
I am still optimistic.

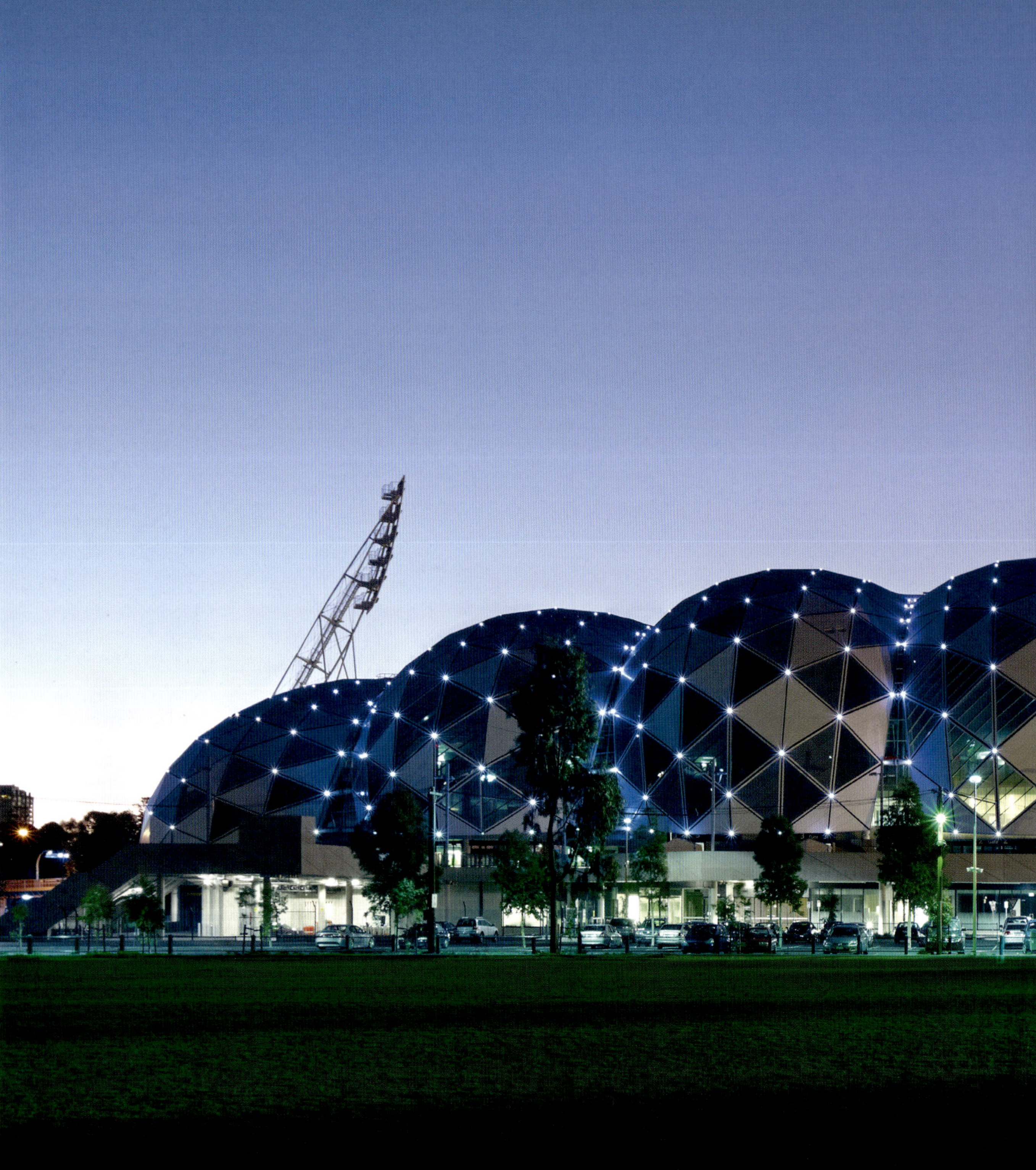

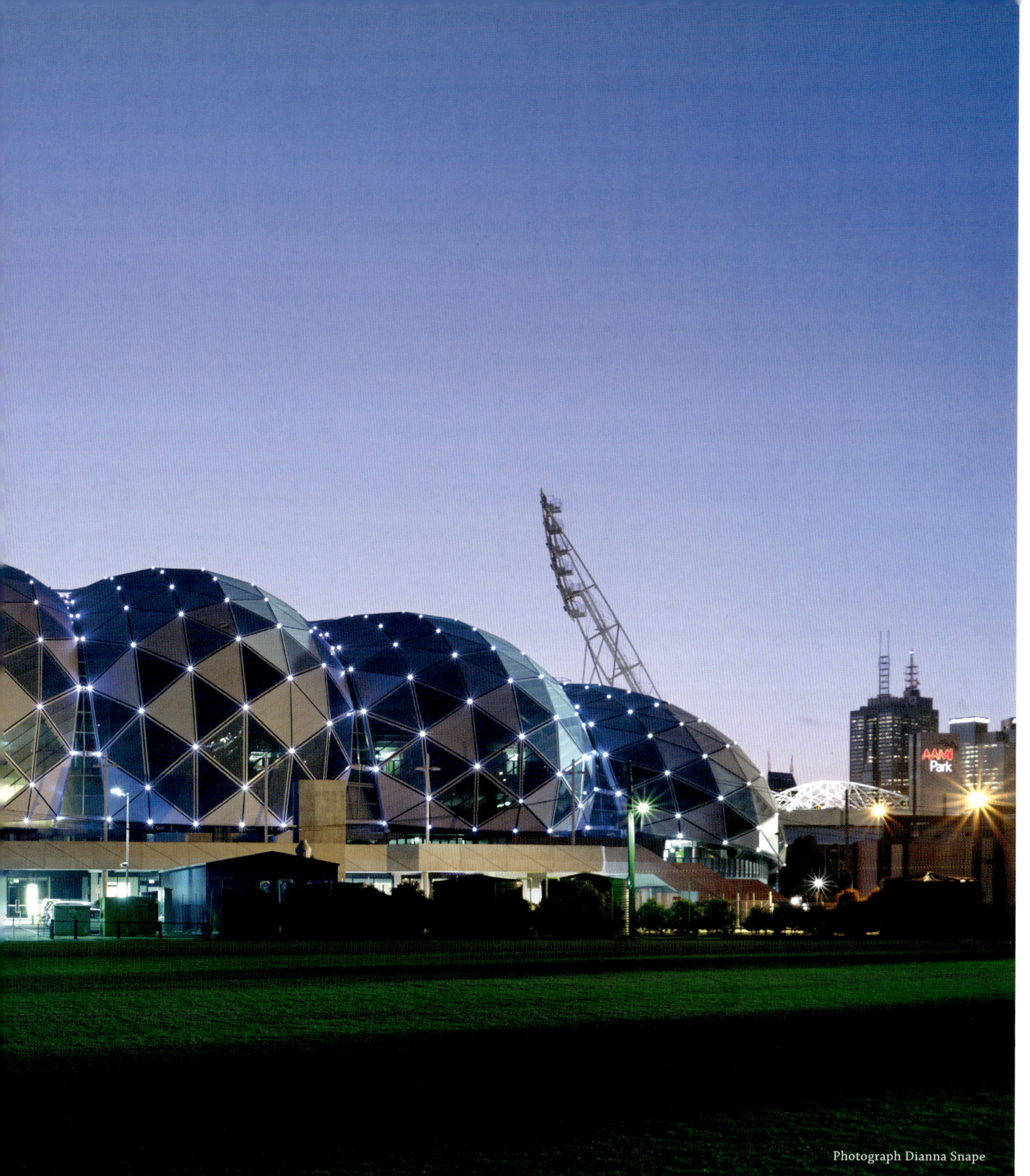

Photograph Dianna Snape

'The architect's involvement must be considered as an influence'

DIANNA SNAPE

What key principles do you bring to your work as a photographer?
A responsibility to realise the architect's vision and a desire to produce my own interpretation of the work I photograph. I'm about what's best for the work and what pleases the architect; this differs from client to client and from building to building. I adapt my vision accordingly. I consider the briefing and discussion preceding the shoot equally as important as the execution of the photography itself.

With interiors specifically, often the literal reading of the subject is contrary to what the architect wishes to express in the images. Architects are often looking for glimpses, spatial relationships, connections and dissections of the subject, as opposed to a record of the entirety of the spaces or what photographers perceive as simply great images. It is a process to establish an intellectual understanding of this, and it often involves excluding the objects or components of the projects that architects wish to avoid.

In the commercial arena we are paid to produce a satisfactory outcome for our clients and this is what I consider my foremost responsibility. The skill is to establish from client to client how this is best managed. It's a juggling act, shifting from one client to another and getting into the thought processes that differentiate how they see the relationship of the photographic record and the architecture. On some occasions you have complete freedom, on others absolute supervision and direction, and generally it is somewhere in between these two.

There is often a short window and limited budget to create what is essentially the historic record of a building or space so you need to work efficiently to achieve this, often with many obstacles.

The postproduction side of the images is where a large portion of the aesthetic is resolved, with density, mood and colour choices generally made and applied independently by the photographer. This is a very time-consuming and important part of the final outcome.

Do these principles engage with architectural criticism and, if so, how? How does photographic convention support or subvert these principles?

Architectural criticism in Australia is expressed mainly in the realm of a few boutique publishing houses in printed and online form. These publishing houses rely primarily on the submission of images by the architect themselves. So with this in mind, the criticism is already swayed or informed by the manner in which the architect chooses to provide the visual story. Despite the writer visiting the building, one must give some thought to the fact that the visual collateral available to run with the words will in some way direct the writing. The architect's involvement must also be considered as an influence on the published outcome.

The digital era and the widespread access to digital cameras means that there is a much broader visual story available, with architects themselves and amateur photographers posting documentation of buildings on websites such as Flickr. In the current climate it is not unusual to be given an entire record of a project as documented by the architect's office prior to shooting that same project. One might look at this as informative, but for the photographer it is a juggling act to work out how much emphasis to place on these images – as a guide to what the architect is seeking from the shoot, balanced with providing a fresh and interpretive approach. Sometimes, too much emphasis on one or the other can set you up for failure.

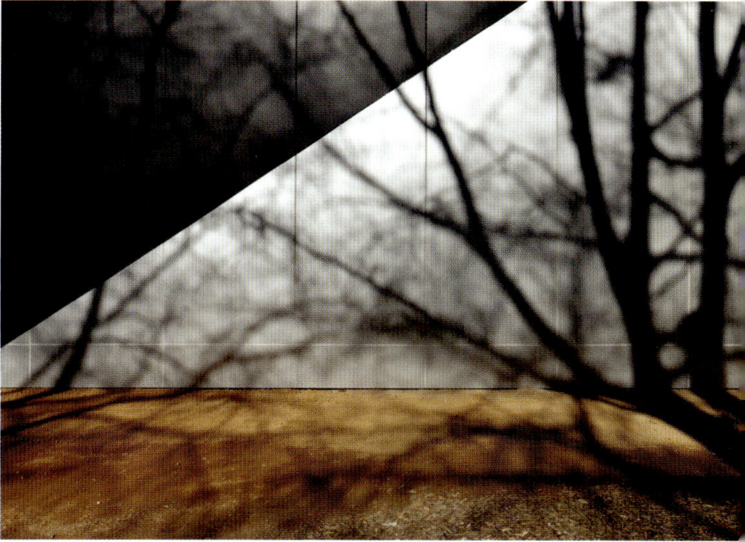

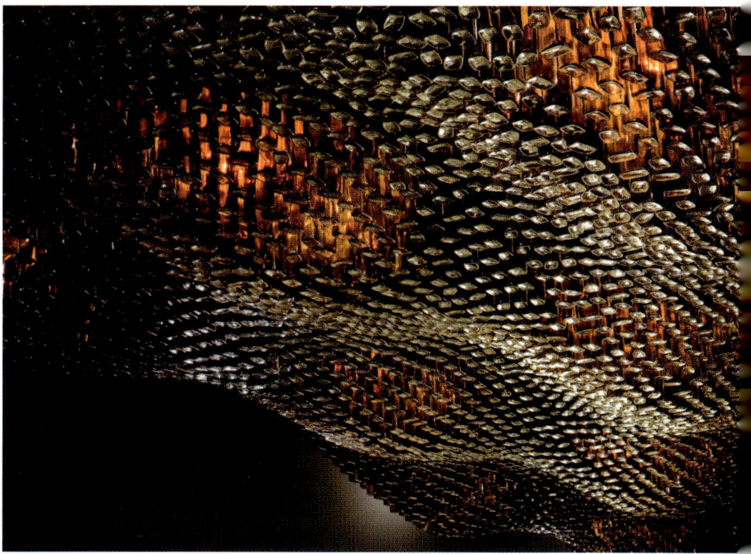

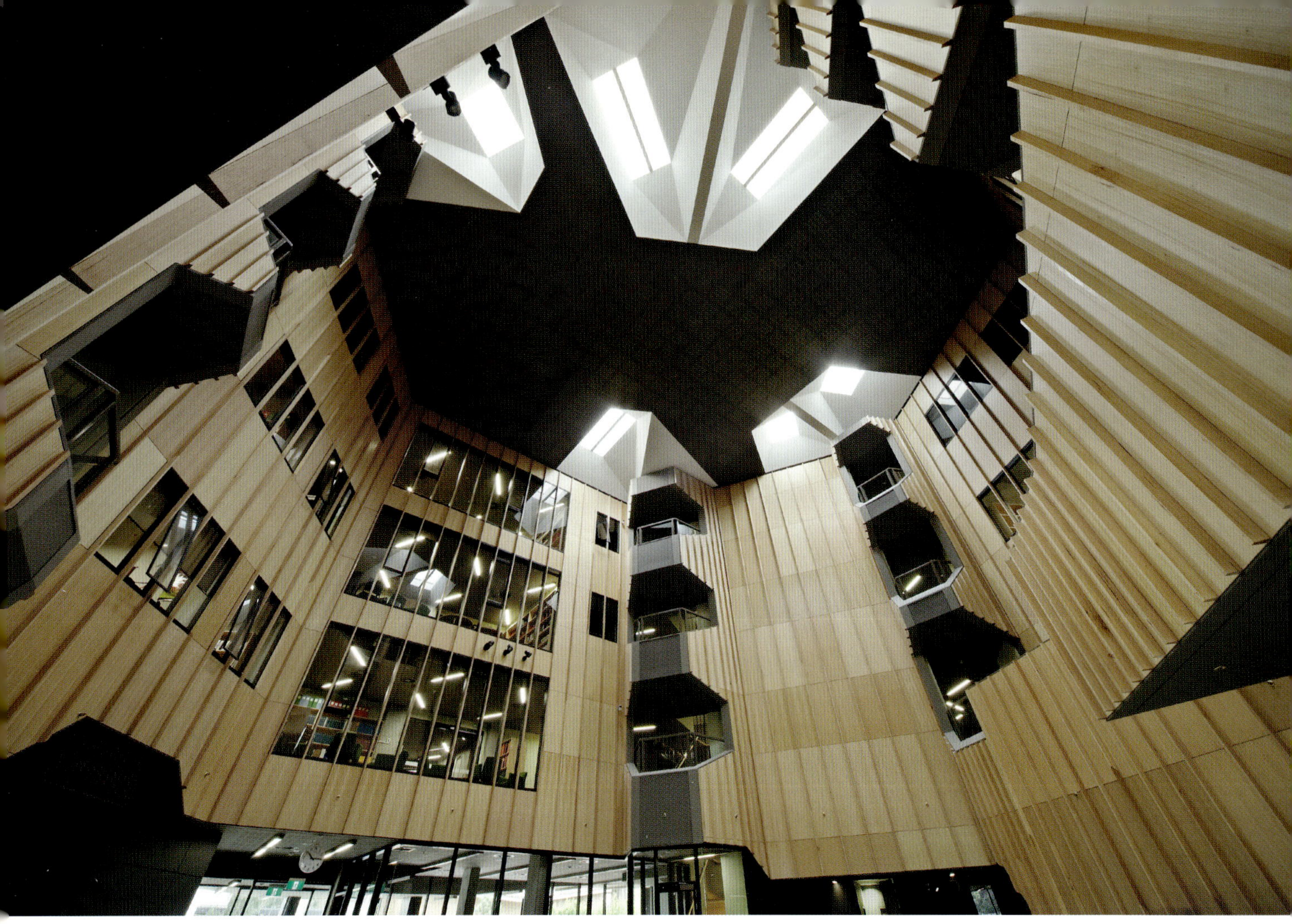

Can photography form an independent visual architectural critique?
Images are often the only experience many people will have of a building. Globally this is how we are seeing the world unless we have the opportunity to travel to visit these buildings. Most awards programs, both nationally and internationally, are judged and awarded based primarily on images, without the judges necessarily having seen the work in person. This isn't the best way to judge architecture and design, but it is the reality, so photography often becomes the only visual architectural critique. This enables us, as image-makers, to edit, distort and direct the impression of the work, one could argue perhaps not honourably and perhaps with trickery, but certainly under the guidance and ultimate approval of the architect.

While I believe the best way to understand architecture is to experience it in person, the camera gives us the ability to exploit line and form in a composition that may never be seen even when visiting the space. It allows us to be interpretive; it allows everyone to see like a photographer does.

Olivia Hyde and Marcus Trimble

IN CONVERSATION

MT Maybe if we start by defining the types of writing that we do …

OH Well I guess there are two types of writing. There's the writing that both of us try to do, which is for the architectural media. And then, there's the writing that I do on a day-to-day basis, which is often written under enormous time pressure, often half-cooked and full of typos and really quite second rate.

MT It's interesting you say that because I find I am almost the opposite. The writing I do for magazines and particularly for the blog is increasingly half-baked. Finding the time to write the blog means that it's becoming a much faster, looser process.

The practice is becoming more focused and more measured in its writing. Matthew Bennett and I write collaboratively, which aids the process. Also, as we're starting a practice we're writing all the standard things you have to put in proposals, defining our practice in a way, and we're trying to get that right first time.

OH Do you think the experience of writing on the blog and writing elsewhere has helped you in terms of how to craft that?

MT Yeah maybe, though I think reading is the best thing for learning to write.

OH It's interesting you mention the process of setting up a new practice and so everything you write is being crafted for the first time. Working in a big practice that's long established, most of those big statements are probably regularly reviewed in BVN but not by myself.

A lot of the time I'm putting together documents, cutting and pasting, trying to use a combination of texts that already exist, adding new material for a specific project. We have been talking recently about the fact we need a dedicated staff writer, because of the pressures of projects and timelines…

MT I think that cut and pasting is quite interesting… You grab this line from here or maybe a consultant has a really good paragraph on ESD so you take a sentence and change a few words around. It's a kind of conglomerate of content.

OH When you are writing on projects on a daily basis, it is difficult to avoid the same trite clichés and standard turns of phrase, keeping it fresh.

MT Do you think in a large practice, with many directors, that falling back on turns of phrase might be a good way of representing five unique voices, coming from one focus, like a party line?

OH It's a conversation we are having a lot between ourselves at the moment. What are the organisational structures that ensure that it happens? Writing has a part to play in that.

MT So that's practice writing and you also write for journals, magazines?

OH Yes, I write pretty much entirely within Australia. There's also Urban Islands, an annual student workshop that I'm a part of, on Cockatoo Island in Sydney. And there's teaching. Actually, one of the things I really enjoy is formulating a brief for students.

MT Let's come back to the idea of reading and how that relates to your writing. How much architectural critical reading do you do?

OH I must say it ebbs and flows. In retrospect one of the most important things I did in my career was to head off to the US. After I finished graduation I worked for just under 10 years, I then headed off overseas and got a teaching fellowship at the University of Michigan. It was this really fantastic opportunity to just re-engage with the life of the mind.

There are a few journals that I adore such as *Log*. Playfulness was my big discovery when I was teaching

in the US – just how immensely playful writing about architecture can be.

MT So as your reading patterns changed, did your writings change also?

OH Yes, definitely.

MT It's the same for myself. I read a lot – comic books and science fiction novels, as well as essays, general articles – but a lot of it is peripheral to architecture. I also follow a lot of architectural blogs, where the writings are very different to academic text.

There are far more people practicing architecture than there are reading about architecture. I suspect that if you were able to measure the actual number of people who read peer reviewed, journaled, architectural writing the number would be very low. I'm not putting any value judgement on that, but how does that writing get transferred into practice?

OH In other words, why bother?

MT Engagement is a key word in terms of why I do the writing I do. I don't think I'm a very good writer, and it doesn't come easily at all but I run the blog. I write the articles because it's a way of maintaining an active engagement with the profession. It's quite interesting in that I don't think it's a particularly good blog, but it has had great efficacy in terms of reaching an audience and also in terms of how it has benefited my practice, which I find quite surprising.

OH But I wonder, is it also about being there at the right time and place, I wonder how many blogs there would be now?

MT Yeah. It was the right time. I started it when there were only a couple of reasonably well-known ones.

OH Was Geoff Manaugh [*BLDGBLOG*] already up and running then? Because he's almost like the symbol of the successful blogger isn't he?

MT He wasn't, but he's very interesting in that his position on architecture isn't something that's really about buildings. It's the broader discussion. The profession is starting to respond to that wider field and it's reflected in the evolving nature of the profession.

OH Do you have any sense of how many readers you have that are architects?

MT No, not really. The comments that you get are often from people who aren't architects, but you have no real way of knowing. *Super Colossal* has very little straight architecture content on there. It's almost a scrapbook of what I was interested in at the time.

Changing the subject, there's one other point to discuss here, about popular architectural writing in mainstream media, and the question is, 'Why is there not more?'

OH Another aligned question would be, why is so much of the writing that happens in the architectural press so polite. I don't think you ever get the scathing review in the architectural press.

MT I don't think that architecture is different from any other profession, save maybe investment banking, in terms of the coverage it gets. Who writes about graphic design in the popular media? There's very rarely stuff about medicine and the medical profession. It may hit the papers if there's a scandal but it's not written about in the daily papers.

Even film, which is the primary form of popular entertainment globally, yet they get a page every week in the paper and then maybe there's some gossip about a film star. There are three or four renovation shows and there are not 'high brow' or serious, critical, architectural discussions taking place on those shows, but they are talking about architecture, in some form.

OH And then you've got *Domain*.

MT Yeah. That's one of my crusades at the moment; that *Domain* should get more recognition by architects. Not so much the writing about architecture, but that, on the *Domain* website, every single real estate listing has a floor plan. They're educating people.

OH The standard comparison seems to be architecture and film. So you read a film review and sometimes they're scathing, sometimes they're glowing. Why isn't there that? Why doesn't the daily newspaper have an article about architecture or, not so much architecture as the built fabric around us, the urban environment?

MT When people write about film, they write the reviews of it so that the audience can make a judgement about whether they want to go out and see a film. You're using it to help you make a decision. Whereas an architectural review isn't helping anybody to make a decision. It's telling people about this thing that's been built, and why it's interesting, or not.

OH The context is different. Also the audience is completely different, because if you write about film in *Variety* magazine, I'm sure that everyone is being very nice to everyone else. That tends to be the medium for architectural writing as well, when you do get an architect writing about architecture in the newspaper. In Sydney, we've got Elizabeth Farrelly and I think she's, by and large, good as a voice to have there. Her writing is very broad, not about architecture actually.

MT Infrequently about architecture.

OH In the British press now, if you read *The Guardian*, you will find a weekly column on the built environment. Then you've got *The Village Voice*, which has been covering urban design issues for years and years. It's not so much about choosing a building and giving it a spin. It's more about a topic that is relevant and is about the built environment.

MT Jonathan Glancey at *The Guardian* and *The New York Times* guy, Nicolai Ouroussoff, they've almost become star architect critics. And they get flown around the world for their typical review, Zaha's Opera House in Beijing, and so on. But increasingly you start to question their independence…

OH Presumably they bring their critical faculties to bear. It's all about wanting people to think about the public realm at all.

MT That's a question of discovery: how does someone

chance upon reading something that they otherwise would not have thought about, and then are intrigued by it and drawn in, and then want to find out more? That's where social media is very useful, where you have a high degree of serendipity in terms of discovering new things. And maybe that's a way of architectural writing finding new avenues.

OH   The place of architectural writing in popular media is an interesting question. A lot of the time in practice you have one conversation within the practice, about the project, what you're doing and why you're doing it. Somehow you have to bundle this up, and explain it to an audience, often in a completely different way using a completely different language.

MT   You generally have to explain a project in terms that someone with no architectural vocabulary can understand.

OH   Which brings us back to our architectural vocabulary at work, where you become so adept at doing the internal meta-conversation that you forget how to do that external presentation of the architectural ideas.

MT   But I also think that you can explain a building in quite simple terms. I think there's often a lot of mystery to what is behind the building, and what moves are being made, and what the intentions of the architect are.

OH   That's true, though often with clients those things may well be simple, but they're not justifiable. There's the narrative of the architecture that you're trying to create, which you have to explore with the client to a certain degree, but the narrative you have to take them on is often very much one of cost-effectiveness and functionality. You put one hat on and you take the other off, and the important thing to always remember is to switch your hats. It's quite enjoyable in a way. Architecture by stealth.

MT   The other thing I wanted to mention, in relation to the typical project review for a magazine, is that often you're friends with a colleague of the person you're writing about. And we'd all like to be hard-core critics that aren't influenced by friendships in life, but I know I am. And this is another point where the film analogy breaks down, because you don't have someone like Steven Spielberg reviewing the latest Martin Scorsese film and giving two stars.

OH   That's a very good point. We need critics that are genuinely impartial and outside the realm in a sense.

MT   Is it even possible for an independent architecture critic to make a living professionally?

OH   And the question is how do you generate your expertise? Ultimately anyone writing is going to have to come into quite close contact with the professional, in a country like Australia where everyone knows each other. Impartiality is almost impossible I would say. And is that really a problem?

But is that because good writing is there but it's not being published broadly enough? When I was in the States, I'd walk into a bookshop or be online and find hundreds of books being published by my peers.

MT   What might an experimental writing in architecture be like? This is my bias, but I think the most interesting speculation on architecture and the city is taking place outside of architectural writing. It's taking place among science fiction authors and game designers as they speculate and present pretty forward positions for what the city of the near future might be.

I'm in the middle of playing my way through Modern Warfare 3, which has an incredible representation of urban environments in the future. There are alternate conversations happening outside of critical writing that I think are very relevant and have an incredibly broad audience. Modern Warfare 3 is the number one entertainment thing ever circa 2012. In its opening weekend it sold more than any other film in terms of revenue. This is a very broad, popular audience.

OH   It's broad and it isn't. I would say that it's majority men in a certain age group.

MT   Probably, aged 15 to 40; they all grow up to become people that either design cities or live in cities or pay for cities to be built. That said, science fiction has a very wide female readership. Science fiction and fantasy outsell any other fiction genre and have a very broad demographic readership.

OH But what is the relevance actually? What is the difference between a novel, constructing a city through words, or a game, where it's visually created for you?

MT The importance lies in the fact that very few people understand that the city can shape people's actions. The city or a building can have some agency in shaping people's lives. That's made quite evident in some fiction.

OH I guess *Blade Runner* is a classic film exemplar. It's difficult for me to discuss this, as I'm not a gamer. I have read some science fiction, but it's not a genre that I gravitate towards. I do actually think of it, especially the computer game environment, as so incredibly masculine that I find it quite exclusionary.

MT There's a lot of testosterone.

OH What are the texts that women are reading? Maybe it doesn't matter, because in the end there's not that many women who are making big decisions about the city.

MT But that's changing. We are working on a very large project in Queensland at the moment that is worth a lot of money. It's about making a lot of money and it's a significant state project. Of the client group, the top three positions are women.

OH They wouldn't have played Game Warfare 3, or most probably not!

MT Who knows? I don't know. But it's probably a safe bet that they haven't.

OH We had a guy in here just a few weeks ago who is doing his PhD and he's looking at the interface between gaming engines and architectural models, and so on. He set up a surround screen and we loaded one of the 3D models from one of the projects. It's potentially an incredibly useful tool.

MT Actually, I'm just remembering why I brought up the science fiction stuff. It was just in terms of what an experimental form of writing architecture might be.

OH It would be nice to write a piece of speculative fiction about a real project. But actually, all pieces of architecture are speculative. I don't just mean economically. They all exist as a representation of why they're happening.

'Clarity, to distil a moment'

PETER BENNETTS

What key principles do you bring to your work as a photographer?

My work is fundamentally about my responsiveness to the environment I find myself in. That environment is usually a building, sometimes not. Whatever it is I look for clarity, to distil a moment and to ground it in a consideration of where that moment sits within history. I want to know all that there is to be known about whatever it is in front of the camera, and I want to try to capture that within an image. I want to find a deeper under- standing of the work and represent that.

Do these principles engage with architectural criticism and, if so, how?

I'm forging my own path through the noise. I seek to comment on architecture through photography, by looking at how a building responds to the environment … I want to see how a building works at a fundamental environmental level. For me, the photography is a form of visual architectural criticism, which can cement, create or effect positive change. And I photograph bad architecture well, because that's equally an effective critique. But I avoid neo-anything, and I eschew artificial light wherever possible.

How do photographic conventions support or subvert these principles?

I came to architectural photography via reportage photography and the convention of that 'decisive moment' has been for me converted into the 'distilled moment', extracting a moment that places the image within a broader context. I don't subscribe to evident distortions.

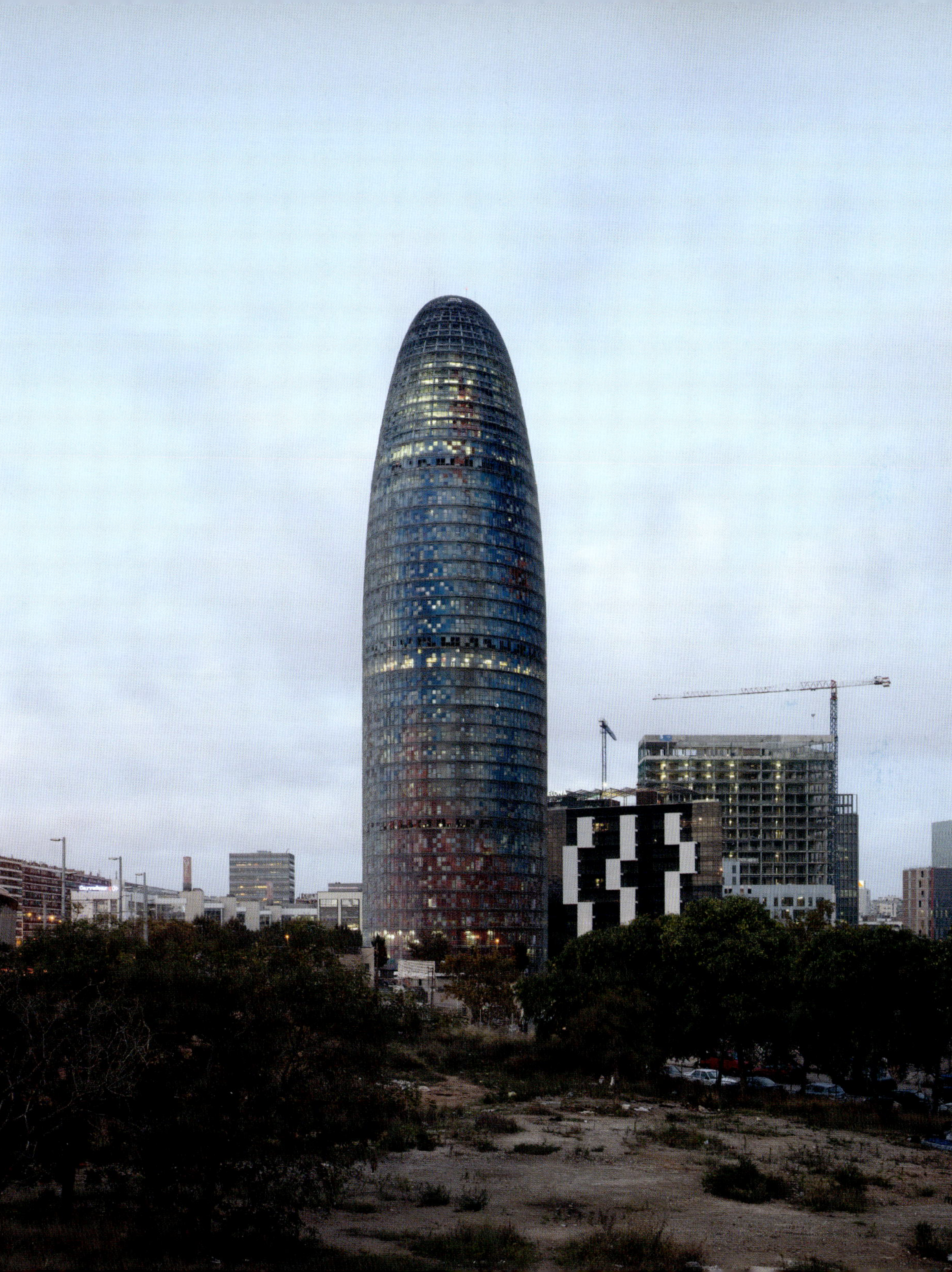

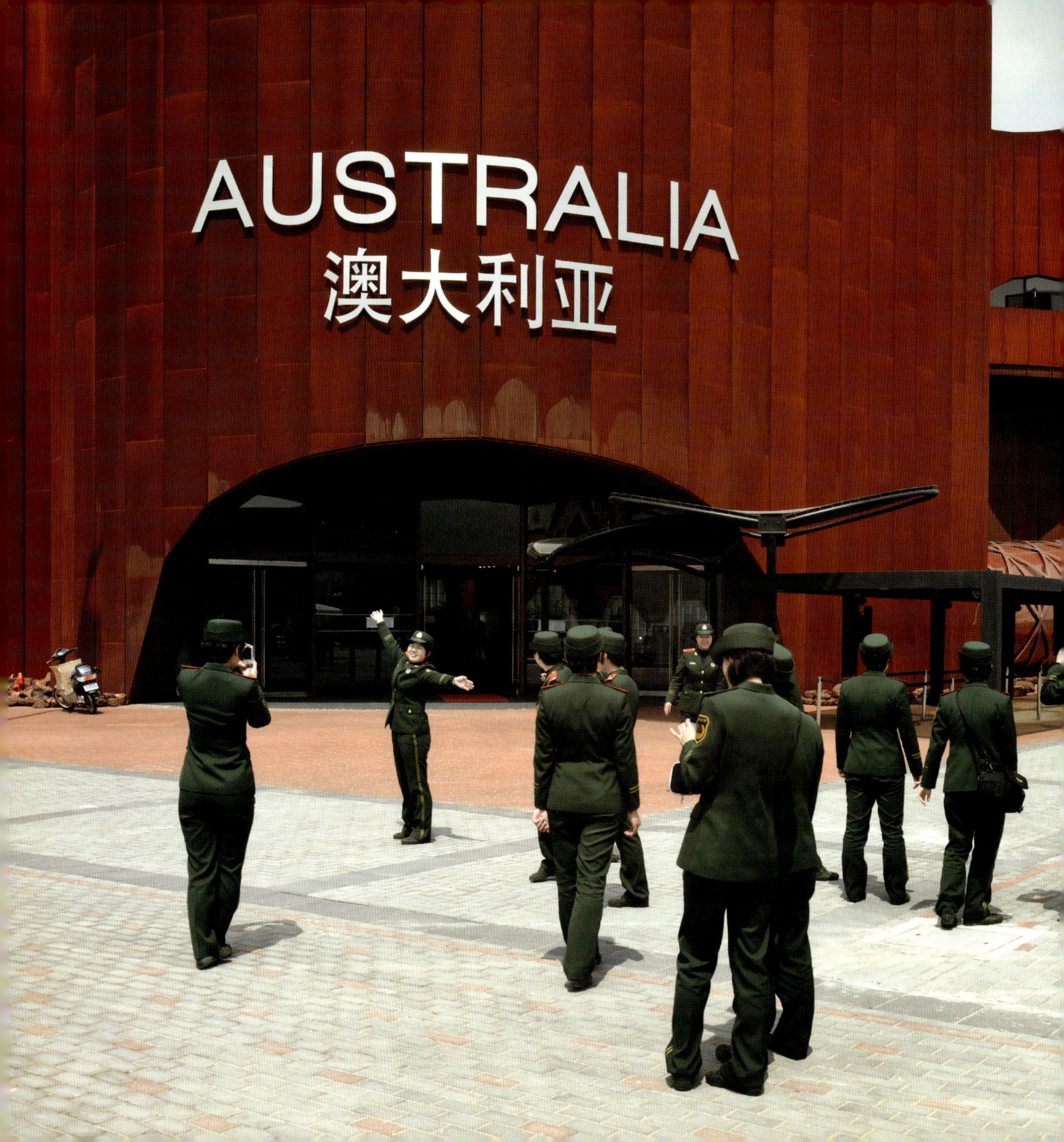
AUSTRALIA
澳大利亚

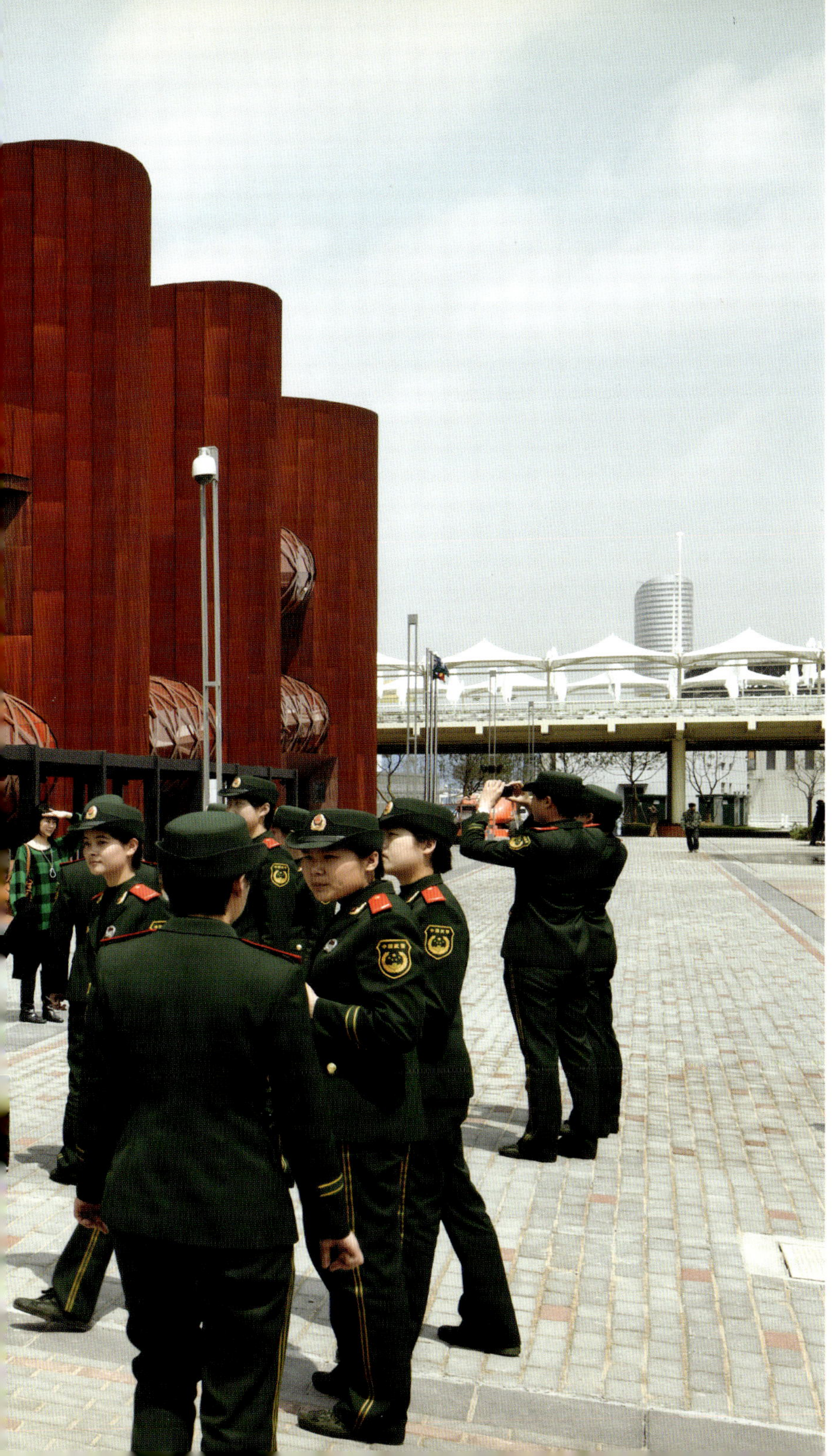

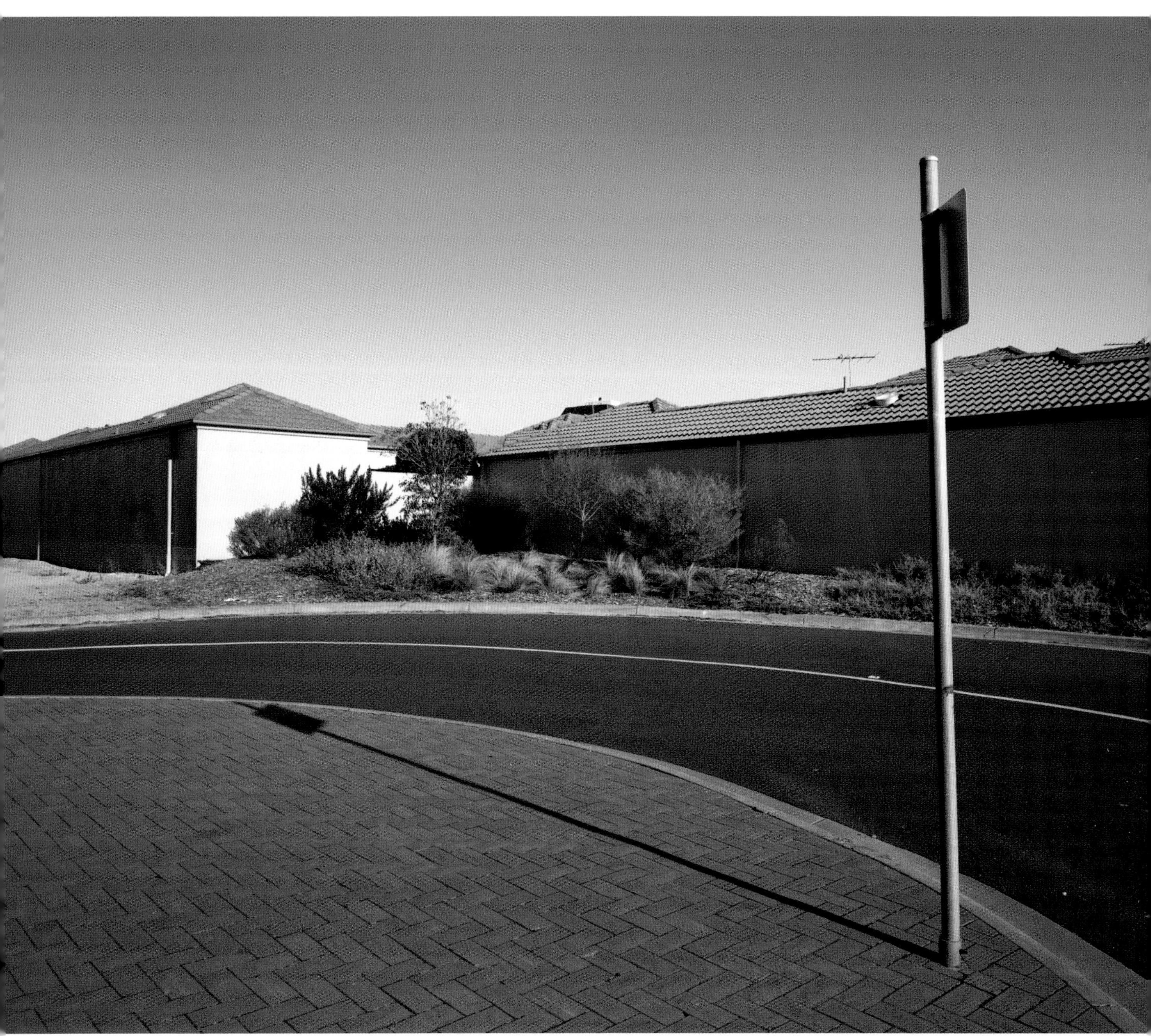

Paul Owen and Elizabeth Watson-Brown

IN CONVERSATION

EW One of the questions that has been occupying me recently is the idea of how an architect can re-inspire to overcome a possible staleness that can set in after decades of being in a groove. I'm certainly revisiting some of the language that I use in conversing about architecture. Clarity is important and to achieve that you need to confront what you think, which is a good discipline. Otherwise, you can retreat to using the buildings that you do as a way of saying, 'that kind of explains what I'm about'. As soon as you have to be really clear about explaining it to somebody else, you'd better bloody well work out what it is you think. It can be clouded a lot of the time – don't you think?

PO I agree. Writing is an opportunity to think clearly about the work. In our practice we've always written about projects, not so much for outside the office, but to understand it ourselves. We also have conversations, which may sound obvious, but it is possible when your practice is small and contained in one room. Operating together in a single room is important to us and it's one of the standard headings on our business plan. I have always thought that within our current practice structure, we should be in one room, so that everyone can hear conversations. This way you generate an implicit and tacit knowledge that belongs to the practice.

EW There's an automatic sharing that happens. Then, when you're having all these intramural conversations, like a family talking in code, the big trick is how you externalise that. How do you extend that conversation to the client or a consultant? How do you put into words or drawings this kind of intimate and personal conversation that you have in a practice. Writing becomes the window into the internal conversation. To return to our theme, the best critics and writers are the ones who pick that up and interpret that, reframe it and relate it to others.

PO In a way, this is about storytelling, and this relates back to practice and more specifically, the design brief. I think that a lot of architects would consider a design brief to be a room list. We do often start with a list of rooms, and even a wish list of other things that a client might aspire to. But really, the true way we collect a design brief is by getting them to tell stories. It gets you to think about the building not as a commodity, not as a wish list, a list of rooms, but as a genuinely human thing. For example, a client of ours loves cooking and her fiancé loves watching TV. But she hates the idea of having TVs in the house. If they write a room list, they wouldn't necessarily represent that properly. They would say they need a media room and they need a big kitchen, because she likes cooking and he likes watching TV. But through her writing it out properly as a story, just like writing a letter to me as the architect, this yields a diagram for their house that genuinely does work, and without the extra rooms that people might ask for.

EW What we often say to clients is, 'How do you want to talk about it? Tell us about your place, in the most comfortable way that you want to tell that story.' Some people are writers; other people collect, they make a scrapbook of images and things. This turns the architect into an interpreter. It's your job to interpret, to sift and to understand through their way of having a conversation what it is that they're after. They might have a different way of expressing it to you, but you're the interpreter. It comes into the processing plant, at one end there are these different ways to communicate: conversation, narrative, scribbles, scrapbooks, and then it comes out the other end as an interpretation? In the meantime, you've made a building.

PO A lot of editors and writers are searching for that stuff from us. There are always questions about what was the client's brief, trying to search for that aspect of the story.

EW Again, this is where the best writers and critics are, because they're like representatives of the inhabitants. They are the ones who can actually understand no matter what the architect tells them! It's so often packaged in the desired way to represent the practice. So often, architecture is presented as a commodity, as a thing. Yet it's also so much about a conversation, a process, being together, and producing this thing. Then the end thing is not a thing. It's an experience.

❧

PO OK, so I have this story, I don't know if I was a student or a graduate, but I was working in a practice that wasn't being dissolved, but it was going through change. There were directors leaving, and a new director was coming on board. The directors who were leaving were experienced practitioners, and the director who was coming on board was a younger architect from another city. I was sitting in the office drawing and one of the outgoing directors came to collect some stuff. And on the other side of the partition, he asked the new director if he could take some slides and negatives and some large-format negatives of images of the buildings that had been produced by the original practice. The director who was leaving asked, 'Do you mind if I take these?', and the young guy said, 'Yes, sure, take them. Yes. No problem.' And I'm sitting there and it occurred to me, holy shit. That's the whole practice right there in those images. That is everything.

Because everything that's happened over the time the practice had existed: all the work that had been made, all the drawings, all the conversations, all the fees, all the commissions, everything. It's embodied by those archival quality images.

When I started I worked on my own for two years at home the practice was called Paul Owen Architect. The first thing I did, even when I was working on private jobs, was to make sure that I had things professionally photographed. The photographer was David Sanderson at the time.

It was the case then, and it's still the case now, that the way I see the photographs that we have taken of our buildings is as archival records of what we did and what happened. It's a snapshot of the building when it was finished.

EW One framed moment that was not necessarily meant to be the representation yet it is in an instant.

PO Going back to the recording of practice, photographs are in fact the most important record of the building, because that's all we get. That's all we can walk away with – images of our building. For our practice, and I'm sure it's the same for yours and lots of others, they're the images that end up being published in magazines.

EW It's interesting, because then you start remembering. And it's weird when you possess real memories of the whole process, but the images become the thing. The images actually become your memory. So you construct this kind of narrative about whatever number of images you've got of the thing. And they're not actually the reality, but they become your memory of it.

PO That's what we were talking about yesterday, when along the process that occurs, to arrive at the finished product, the building, none of that's recorded. None of that's really discussed very much. But it's all to do with data. It's to do with values, your take on the cultural condition, geographical considerations, topographical and climatic considerations. But it's all the stuff that nobody really wants to talk about, because it's not interesting to mass market.

I think there are three reasons why architects, including us, publish work. One reason is for ego and career satisfaction. I don't think that's being cynical, just being honest. Another reason is to engage in profession. The third is as a form of advertising. At least for us, most of our jobs are private house commissions, so that's the only way people can find out about us, and that's the commodity aspect. And yet whenever we talk about our work within the practice or amongst ourselves as architects, we talk about anything but that.

EW We talk about all the messy things in life and not the commodity, yet that's how it's represented. And you know, I think deep down this is what people who read magazines are after.

PO They're searching for it.

EW It's actually a conversation about making a good place to live with other people. It's about relating to other people. Meanwhile there's a danger of the hyper-intellectualisation of this pretty direct and importantly basic and kind of elemental craft that we're doing. There is nothing wrong with doing that in a powerfully engaging and emotional way. And it's fine to also think about it intellectually, obviously, and connected with intellectual and philosophical rapport down throughout the ages. I think that if you want to have a conversation with everyone, not just with other architects or philosophers or theoreticians or whatever, the language that you have to use is about experience. It's about how in good commerce human beings engage with what we make.

PO To return to the theme of this book, it appears as though architects have very little to say. But I think they've got a lot to say but they're not saying much in a genuine way. It's either highly academic or it's highly commercial. And the middle ground of practice, of the actual making of things, where you establish a one-on-one relationship with the client or patron… none of that's discussed or recorded. And that's where the true information about architecture lies.

EW That's how it happens. You're right. You know, that is the territory in which all of that happens. So we seem to be able to talk in the language of theory and the language of the commodity, but not about the in between, which is probably what most humans would engage with very well.

PO Think about Atelier Bow-Wow from Japan, who communicate their work through every medium – data, images, diagrams, text. So there are photos that are aren't professionally taken. Beautiful little diagrams that have been made by students, and simple words that aren't academic and they're not poetic and they're not decorative. They're kind of just plain descriptions. And then the last thing they have is simple raw data. How many square metres is the building and what does it do?

EW Yes, then it's up to who's looking at it to interpret. That is what Atelier Bow-Wow does. They put it down in an unglamorous and straightforward way, then whoever's looking at that, they can do the work.

PO They don't make any conclusions. Another thing that I've been contemplating lately is that as a student in the late 80s, early 90s, any sort of architectural inspiration was pretty thin on the ground. The magazines were full of postmodernism and Brutalist-looking architecture.

EW And postmodernism curiously was just as unsatisfactory as pure modernism.

PO Yes. So, there was very little to be inspired by. So I reverted back to being inspired by the modernists … Corbusier and Kahn. Anyway, so now the things we talk about in our practice are architects from the past, not the present. There are certainly architects from the present that we admire a great deal, and we read what they have to say. Take an architect such as Aalto, for example. He was highly ambitious, a genius, who could make work that was very particular to his region. It's exactly what architecture should be. So, he makes his work, he understands his place, he understands technology, and he's a maker of things, he's someone who sits and draws, and he does what an architect, any architect is supposed to do, he was just doing his job well. So then he has a whole career and makes all these wonderful things, and these buildings are revered, and they're written about, and they're written about again, and they're written about again and again, and they're photographed over and over.

EW People construct whole academic careers around an architect like Aalto.

PO So then if you flip back to imagine you're not me, you're a third-year student, who loves architecture and is

discovering it. And what you read, not only about Aalto, but about everyone else, is way beyond the final product, and so you think that's what architecture is. You think it is making a heroic building, and that it's so poetic, and that there's so much meaning in it, which there is. But what's not communicated and what a young student won't learn is that it started with the basics, with drawing, and thinking about the basic things, about climate, about topography, about the local culture. And architects like Aalto and Scarpa, they all started from these humble beginnings – of the simple making of things.

EW There's a dangerous tendency for heroism and hero worship, and it's quite possible that none of them – and they're all blokes, aren't they – would have set out to be heroes or considered themselves as that.

PO That wasn't their origins. But the moment you see them in an interview or magazine, that's the moment of their fame. That's the fruition of their whole career. This leads me to think that the way architecture is published promotes ego in architects. It elevates our egos. This is a cyclical thing, so then the work needs to be ego-based. What if there was no publishing?

EW What if there was no author mentioned? Would people be interested in it?

PO How will that change design?

EW What if you didn't? What if you actually explained something or represented it or divulged what experience you had in a space or something like that without actually mentioning the author?

PO That would completely change everything.

EW It would upend everything. It's the same as if you went into a designer dress shop and there were no labels on anything, and you just selected what appealed to you on the basis of this honest, elemental appeal, without being clouded by the whole history of what a brand means.

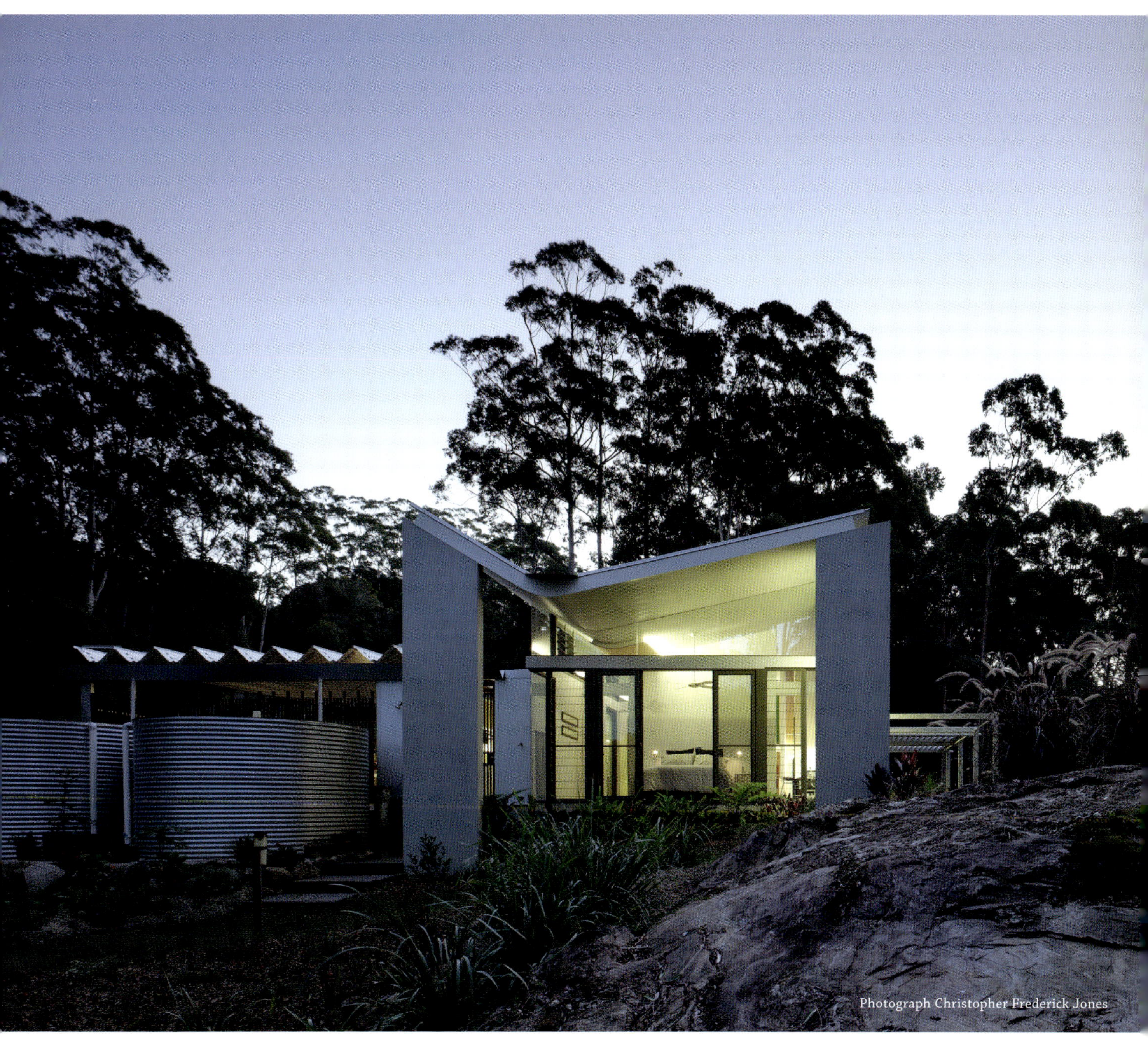

Photograph Christopher Frederick Jones

'The photographer applies a mask to the building'

CHRISTOPHER FREDERICK JONES

Can photography form an independent visual architectural critique?
Yes. Photography is a form of 'death of the architect', with the images taking on a life of their own. There is always a mask applied to a building to further my own species of critique. The photographer creates the recognised or known image of a building, just as much as a piece of writing does. The photographer determines what they perceive as important and includes this in the images that the public will see, influencing how a building is read. The photographer applies a mask to the building…

What key principles do you bring to your work as a photographer?
Where possible I always try to shoot clean considered elevations with one point perspective to best represent the building as the architect conceived it. I avoid uncomfortable angles, which can sometimes create distortions in the building, misleading the viewer in their interpretation of the architecture. Positioning the building in its surroundings and determining the right time of day for best illuminating its elevations is paramount in describing its relationship with the environment and controlling light values for a more naturalistic appearance.

I try to capture moments within the architecture that people otherwise would never experience by making a picture within the subject. I also like to maintain some sort of human scale to the images, either by including people or human elements, such as a carefully placed chair within an interior.

Do these principles engage with architectural criticism, and if so how?
I think by remaining truthful to the building and recording the environmental relationships and function, informing the design, photography can be a very useful tool for architectural criticism. Allowing the viewer to experience the building through images that are a reflection on architectural ideas, as well as also seeing with fresh eyes parts of the building that they would

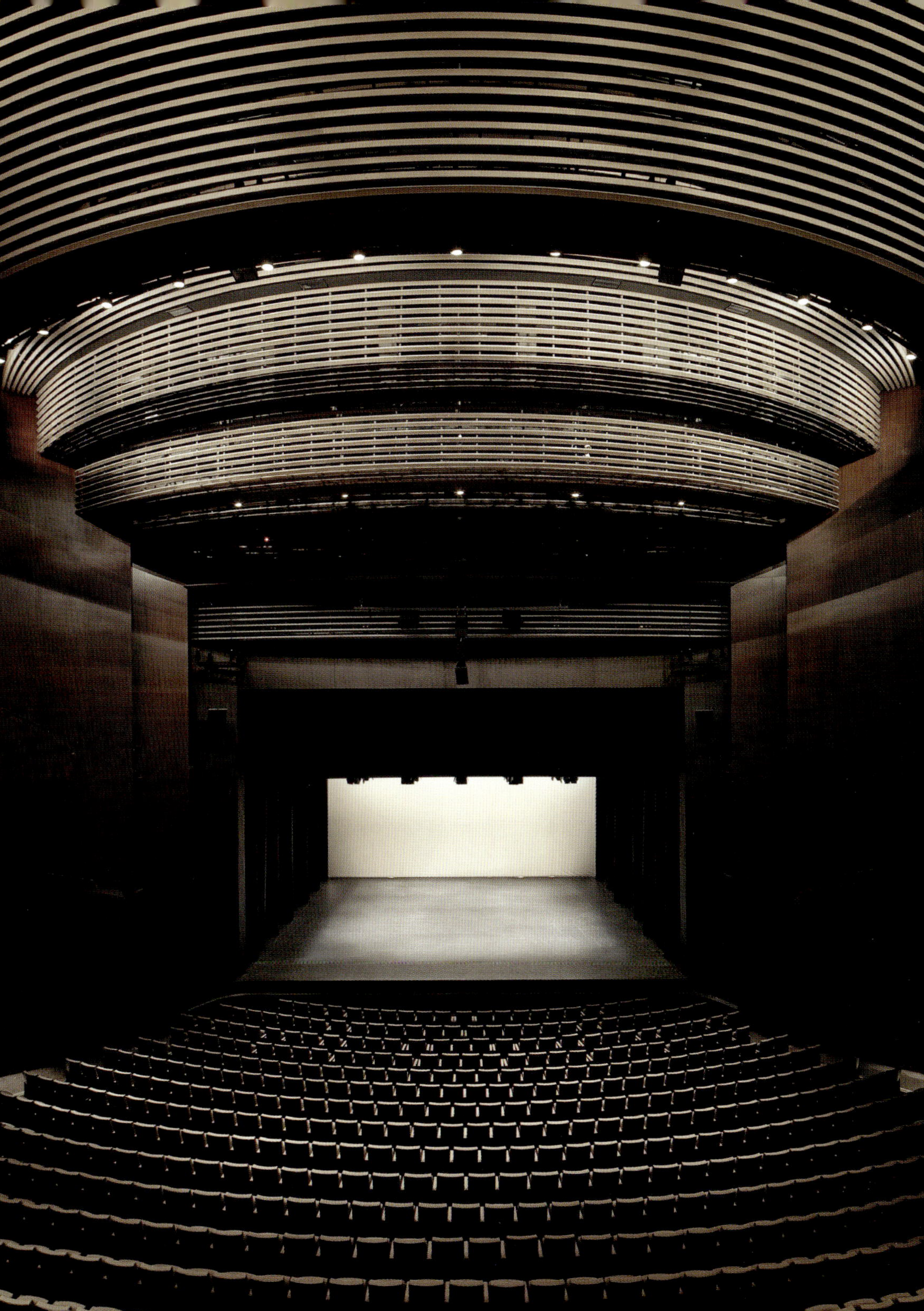

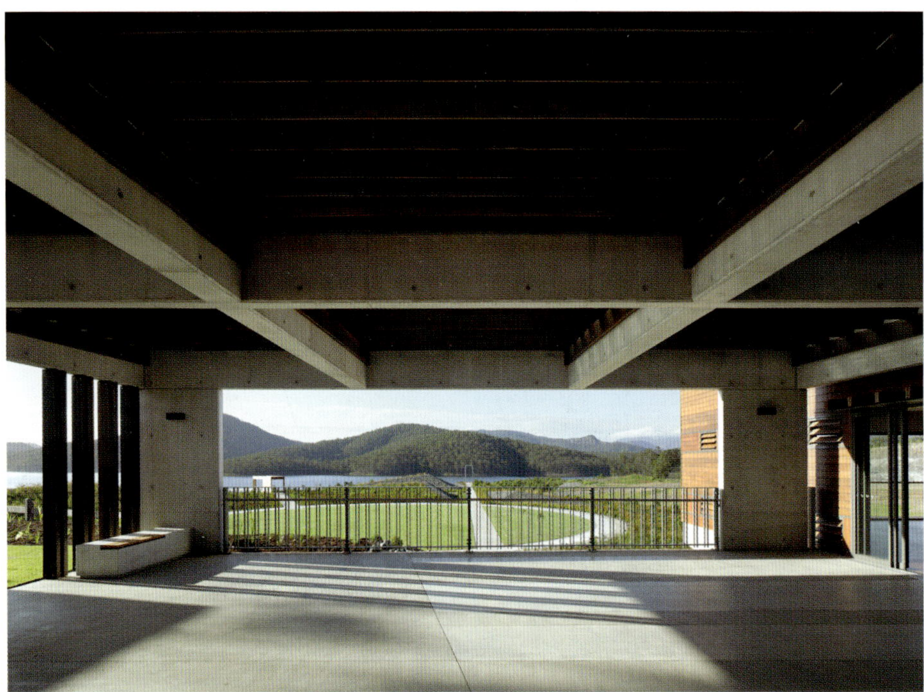

never normally experience makes for a connection with the building and can open up discussion.

How does photographic convention support or subvert these principles?
Architectural photography requires the use of specialised technical equipment to accurately capture a building and volumetric space. New digital techniques are starting to challenge these principles in ways that are, in my opinion, not truthful in recording architecture. This is done in part through distortion by super wide-angle lenses and high ranges in light values that even the human eye cannot calculate. The recent trend in architectural photography to

include people within the image has a positive impact on how we read the photography of a building. Images containing people or human elements can help describe how spaces are used and provide a measure of scale within the image. This is important when photographing commercial interiors, public buildings and spaces.

Can photography form an independent visual architectural critique?
I think so but when you are told by the architect 'you have made the building look better than it is', the images are probably protecting it from comments that might otherwise be different if you were to visit the actual building. Other

times people may feel that the image doesn't do the building justice and the true sense of architecture can only be realised when actually visiting the building or site. The first impressions of architecture however are often from the photograph and sometimes this is the only way people will get to experience a building. It allows the viewer to see the building in ways other than they would normally perceive. If an image captures the design intent and opens up new experiences then photography can be used as an independent architectural critique. I believe it does this subliminally every time you open a book or magazine and look at an image.

Jill Garner and Jan van Schaik

JG Writing is a good discipline, because every project has an idea, some premise that you started from? None of them are purely about answering the client's brief. They've always got something else wound into them, even if it's your own architectural history, which I think with some projects, that's all you end up doing, winding in your own interests.

JvS Writing is very powerful in its suggestive capacity, while visuals tend to lack that suggestive power – they're more explicit.

JG One of the things that I find really interesting is that there are those that are very skilful with words, and then you check their design against their words, and …

JvS They often don't match.

JG You can talk all you like about the beauty of a surface, but the capacity to actually build three dimensionally what you're talking about is an extraordinary skill.

JvS So, writing can get you into a lot of trouble.

JG If you are a better writer than you are an architect then there's the sort of writing that might be called post-rationalisation…

JvS Often when we start piecing a design together our motivations are broad. We arrive at something we really like, which is an architectural representation through drawing of spatial quality. Expressing its qualities in words follows.

JG Agreed. But also the built result that you end up with is subjected to so many manipulations along the way, which I imagine any author would go through.

JvS Yeah, chopping and changing, editing, cutting and pasting…

JG And every word is highly considered, and editing the relationship between words is an arduous process…

And to me, that's kind of the same as the arduous process of detailing a building. What's really different is that the decisions that you make when you write are your own, and the outcome or the output is framed by you, whereas a piece of architecture is a constant work of compromise, and a constant collaborative result through everybody having needs and inputs and structural requirements, mechanical requirements or the reality of climate or whatever it happens to be, shaping the final product.

JvS   You mentioned manifestos and the concept of the architect as someone that states on a piece of paper before anyone talks to them about what it is they may want to do, what it is they stand for, and then delivers that manifesto unwaveringly through his entire career. Do you think that still exists?

JG   I'm not sure. Perhaps architecture can no longer be unwavering. With the end of the manifesto and the beginning of architects seeking legitimation through literary theory, art theory, architects tended to struggle translating such academic theories into architecture. I think it became a very busy time for writing about architecture as it became accepted that you tore things to pieces and put them back together, discussing things in detail. As opposed to what you had in the era of the manifestos.

JvS   The modernists.

JG   Yeah, the modernists.

JvS   And that's true of the modernists in literature as well.

JG   We're probably being a little bit more focused on the real now, which is not a bad thing.

JvS   Recently I was asked at a dinner party about the difference between architecture and drafting? I quipped that to design a house in which people live, you had to have an opinion about what living was, and therefore architecture was a philosophical dispute. The theory and philosophies of life and spirituality have been communicated for centuries through writing and through the telling of stories and songs.

JG   I think you would find that the best architects in the world would represent their philosophy of occupation or space through their architectural work…

JvS   We often write on a giant whiteboard, which we resisted for a long time because of the corporate implications, but writing on them, standing up and talking and writing, is actually a really powerful thinking tool.

JG   Yes, I agree with that.

JvS   … and then that word, on its own, can be quite esoteric, and then we start to work out how it fits into a series of other things. So it becomes like a diagram with writing in it. For example, we often write the word 'ugly' on the board, and that's an interesting thing.

JG   Because you like it?

JvS   Things that are ugly for us represent something beautiful in a way that is not yet known. If you recognise something as beautiful instantly, it's probably already understood why it's beautiful by…

JG   By everybody.

JvS   A lot of our buildings do have a poetic awkwardness to them … we quite often approach new creative works through ugliness. So we often start with that word.

JG   It's a really ugly word.

JvS   And it's difficult to communicate to a client why you are deliberately trying to make their project ugly. So then you start to try to extrapolate from that how to translate that word ugly into…

JG   It's your interpretation of ugly… I don't think my perception of beauty is necessarily everybody's perception of beauty. If I walk into a space that has got something perfect about it, in terms of volume, scale, details, nothingness, emptiness, materiality, I'd call that beauty. Other people would walk in and say, 'There is nothing here. It's empty'. Whereas I would just say, 'No, this is a really beautiful space'. I think there is a tradition in Melbourne…

JvS   Yes, there is.

JG   … of what you're talking about, and a perception of that being beautiful, if you know what I mean?

JvS   It's a lineage in Melbourne.

JG Your interpretation is based on your own judgement. I had a conversation years ago with Howard Raggatt – he was talking about their work on the Howard Kronberg Medical Clinic and how they would just accept the distortions of the photocopier. I disagreed suggesting that at some point the author makes a conscious decision about when to stop.

JvS That's a really beautiful example of post-rationalisation, that the setting up of a process in order to be able to say that the process designed the building, not the author; that's a constructive and written argument. It's not actually what happened.

JG But what I love about it is that I completely admire the process, but I also admire the capacity of the eye to say that's where I stop, and this is the building. And I think in some ways, the dishonesty of the post-rationalisation argument is interesting.

JvS It was interesting to say that at that point, to say that this is a design process in which there is no author, and in this process – we're not making any aesthetic decisions.

JG And that's what we've written about, which, at the end of the day, is impossible, really. Because you actually choose a point in the system where you stop or you exit it or whatever. I think it's just another part of the design process, and that in itself is fascinating.

JvS What do you think about the sorts of writing that we often receive as architects … I know you have a lot of exposure to that through your work as a government architect?

JG You mean procurement documents… there is work being done at the government architect's office on procurement, and an effort to rationalise it, because it's extraordinarily diverse, and is currently guided by everything other than a design outcome. So the philosophy is to try to have an impact on these documents, to introduce, from a very early stage, some of the language that we use in attempting to get a really highly considered design outcome to a context, which can be very difficult to embed in these documents.

JvS Design is an interesting word, isn't it, because so many people use it, and it can mean so many different things.

JG I feel like we are not out there enough in the written world, though we write to each other, we write in our own journals, we write our own responses to briefs … I believe that an environment or a culture where people understand that a city is designed, or an urban space has been designed, the community and culture is better for it, and the outcome is better.

JvS In Sydney, for example, while real estate is a really important part of the city, often it's the location of the site and its view that brings in the most value. But Melbourne doesn't have such a landscape or prized view, so when design does bring value to something, it has a greater impact than when you do something in Sydney.

Let's get back to writing: Is there a relationship between what's written and the experience of the built project?

JG A wealth of knowledge is brought to the interpretation of any built project enriching the capacity to enjoy that work. I do think that having something written about a piece of architecture affects your experience.

JvS Maybe we can say that if we're constantly interpreting things, then anything that expands our ability to interpret is actually allowing us to build better connections.

JG Definitely. We were working on the St Kilda Library for a little while with Lovell Chen, and we organised for the original architect, Enrico Taglietti, to come to Melbourne and talk to us about the building. We were across the road looking at ARM's addition to the original library, and he wouldn't walk in, because it was so different to his interpretation of what the library was intended to be. I wonder had ARM had access to a piece of writing that discussed the architectural journey into the building, the kind of architectural experience of the building, and the architectural intent of the building, might they have designed something quite different. I wonder the same thing about the addition to the National Gallery of Victoria.

JvS It's almost as though the way that all people who have lived in Melbourne for a while understood the original NGV to be, and the way that they understood it to operate is not allowed for in the new design. Did the architect of the addition have access to a written version of that collective understanding?

JG I guess that's my point, particularly in this environment where we have adaptive reuse and other architects brought in over the top, there needs to be an understanding of the actual original intent – in writing.

JvS I wonder if that's an interesting test for a building, whether it can be written about poetically? The devil's advocate in me then asks, I wonder if it's possible to write poetically about a bad building?

JG I suspect that, in a way, what might happen with a bad building, is that any words that go with it, in the analysis of it, is the building doing what the writing is portraying it to do.

JvS Well, it's the thing you were talking about before where you write something aspirational about your design, and then your ability to deliver is tested. If something is written about a building by anybody, a critic or an architect, they should be able to stand together.

JG And one should actually strengthen the other.

Think about a project in Melbourne such as Federation Square, which is a project that was hugely controversial, people got involved in a public debate, and that was seen to some degree to ignore those untrained as architects. Years later, however, everyone loves it.

JvS It is a loved building, which is interesting: it's a manifesto building.

JG But that once again, it could be post-rationalised into a whole lot of successful architectural spaces.

JvS There is a story about the piece of that building that the Bracks Government took out of the design – there was supposed to be a piece of zinc and stone building on the corner – it was called 'The Shard' – which was removed and replaced by the much smaller information kiosk.

At the time, the architects articulated through the press how terrible it was that the design had been edited the way that it was. I can't help thinking that if it had been called something other than 'The Shard' perhaps it wouldn't have been removed. If it had been called 'The Cornerstone of Federation' for example, then no government would say, 'We're cutting out the Cornerstone of Federation'.

'We shoot, stuff and exhibit the game'

BRETT BOARDMAN

What key principles do you bring to your work as a photographer?

Harry Stuart Goodhart-Rendel observed somewhat tongue-in-cheek in the 1930s: 'The modern architectural drawing is interesting, the photograph is magnificent, the building is an unfortunate but necessary stage between the two.'

First there is the 'idea', or in architectural terms, the conceptual framework. The 'job' as I see it is to return the architect their idea or drawing. I see myself as a translator and/or narrator of architecture to an ever-widening audience. The spectrum of this audience ranges from the architectural academic to the casual occupant of a building, to the internet surfer – so

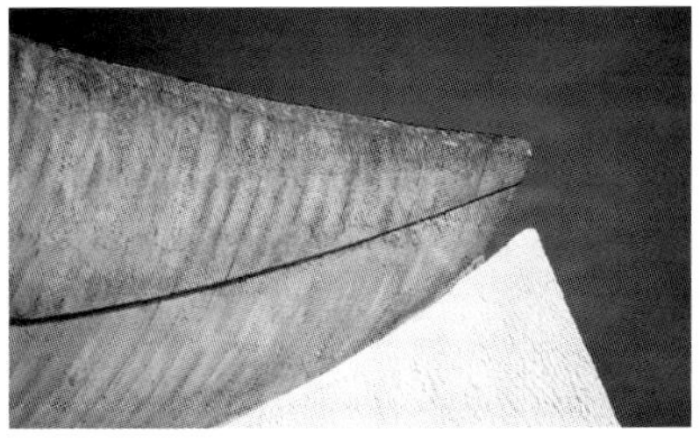
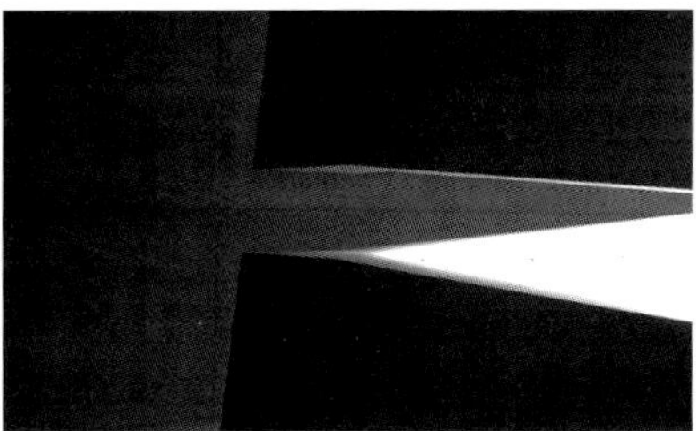

really it can be anyone. The process for me is a conversation with the architect about the project that results in images.

Second there is the 'story' of the building. The story consists of the project's context, both historical and environmental. Its origins – the economic or political aspect of the building's how and why. The making of the architecture,

spatially, tectonically and materially, and finally the user experience. These issues are just as true of the toilet block, as they are of domestic space, corporate headquarters, church or house of parliament.

So I suppose the key principle deployed would be that of narrative told through sequence. There are of course standalone images or punctuation marks within

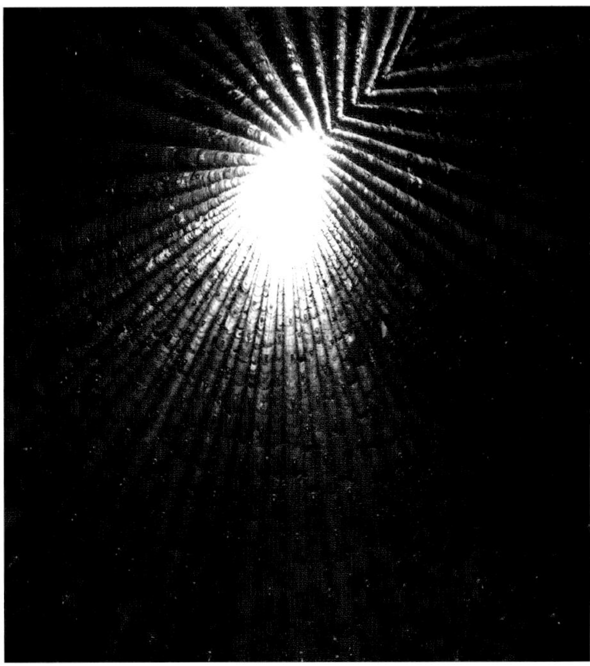

the chapters, I think of these as 'architectural moments' (the wall and roof separating at Ronchamp, the space left between walls to make a handrail at Chichu Art Museum in Naoshima) – but they exist within a larger story (previous page).

The 'hero' or 'money shot' that has defined architectural photography and its published form over the last 60 years reduces architecture to a singular moment of pleasure – archiporn if you will. There is of course a commercial necessity to deliver these images but I always attempt to have them fit within a wider narrative. Every architectural image exists on a scale between distance and sensation or more accurately between description and emotion. The images on these two pages illustrate this point – the first describes the building's setting, the second attempts to define the sensation: description and emotion. To just show one image tells only half the story – the vast difference between the exterior or communal symbol and the interior personal and spiritual experience.

Critic and historian, Janet Abrams, described the life of the architectural photographer as a 'wildlife observer, permanently on safari', which I think is accurate. We shoot stuff and exhibit the game and as in all adventures it is the idea and story that makes for something memorable.

Do these principles engage with architectural criticism, and if so how?
Commercial architectural photography refers to the photography of architecture commissioned by architects or magazines for the purpose of documentation, publication, marketing and promotion of specific projects. The intention of this photography is sometimes aligned to, but more often opposed to photography that exploits architecture as a photographic subject for the purpose of reflecting or criticising the economic and cultural history of society.

The question of criticism arises primarily, I think, from the commission. Who has commissioned the work and for what purpose? The story that I present to the architect in the set of images becomes re-contextualised by the art directors and editors of the magazine or journal. I'm not saying it's bad – it just is. Each publication has its own agenda, politics and prejudices. When an architects engages you as a commercial photographer there is an implicit understanding that you will amplify the strong aspects of the project and minimise problem areas. I tend to shoot the whole building and leave it to the architect to determine the use of the images. Images of defects can prove useful for future design decisions, material performance and for examining practice – they may also be needed for future litigation. It might be instructive to show an example of direct critical engagement (below).

Let's ignore the title for a moment. On a basic reading of the image (or to an audience unfamiliar with the building), we can describe two buildings of similar proportions – not scale. Because of centuries of perspectival representation we can also reasonably say that the building on the right (being further away) is probably bigger than the one in the foreground. One is partially obscured by vegetation, the other standing clear in a field. They appear to be made of different materials. The weather looks rather pleasant also. All this is inference and may or may not be true. It may all be untrue as it could be computer-generated.

With a bit more knowledge of say, a foreign language, we could deduce that the foreground building is a portable toilet. With more knowledge of the scene – you may have been there or you've read the title, you could say that

it's the Bruder Klaus Kapelle designed by Peter Zumthor and a portable toilet. Meaning is really only given in photography by the title. To someone who has intimate knowledge of the project, the image works on a critical level – criticism achieved by the photographic principles of framing and juxtaposition. This was the solution to the bodily functions of the countless hordes of arch-tourists and pilgrims. Rather than incorporating toilets into the brief (which would have compromised the purity of the idea), to paraphrase Frank Lloyd Wright, the architect has advised his client to plant vines.

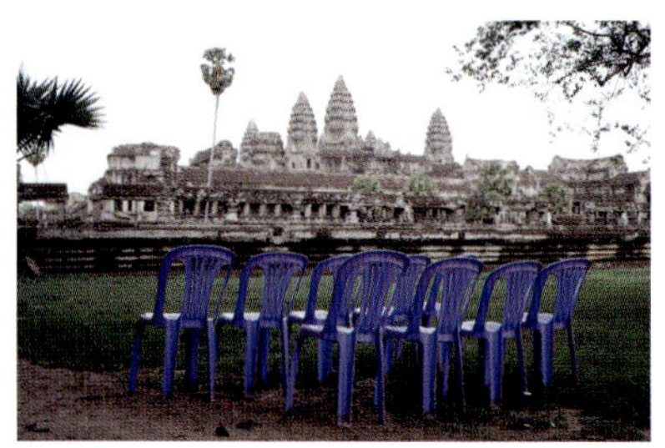

How does photographic convention support or subvert these principles?
The two photographic conventions that I believe are the most important with regard to the question of criticism are time and the frame. I think (to revisit Abrams's safari analogy) the architectural photograph's greatest problem and its

strongest attribute is that it presents architecture as taxidermy – it divorces architecture from its time. Who hasn't been disappointed / shocked / amazed / bewildered or pleasantly surprised upon arriving at a building, expecting to see the photograph only to see the effect of time on the building through weathering, context or change of use? Architecture exists through and in time and the photograph disrupts this continuum. Of interest to me are the ways that this temporal disruption can be reinstated through juxtaposition (above).

The other photographic convention that I think engages most often with criticism is the frame. It really is the antithesis of architectural experience, which is generally unbounded. So now we have the stuffed animal and we add the display case. We put a frame around something and say, 'Hey look at this!' or 'This is worth looking at – not the other bits outside the frame'. Yet images of the bits outside the frame often inform the politics of the images we present.

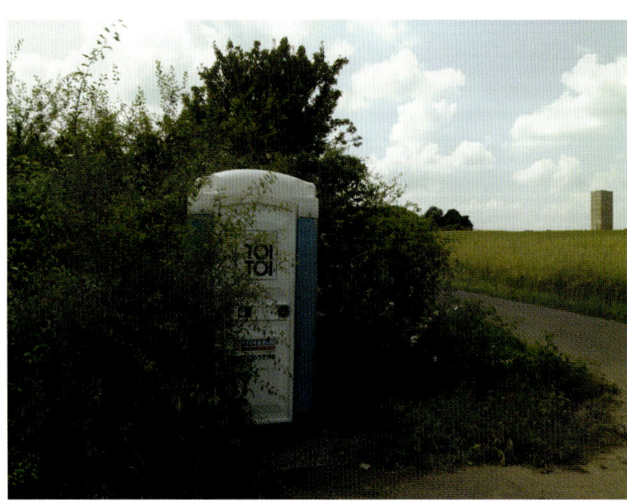

Can photography be used to form an independent visual architectural critique?

Yes I think it can, particularly when freed from commercial obligation. I suspect this is why there are a large number of artists who use architecture, and more specifically photography of architecture, for their investigations and politics. Citing Levin, Pallasmaa describes two modes of vision: the assertoric gaze and the aletheic gaze: 'The assertoric gaze is narrow, dogmatic, intolerant, rigid, fixed, inflexible, exclusionary and unmoved, whereas the aletheic gaze, associated with the hermeneutic theory of truth, tends to see from a multiplicity of standpoints and perspectives, and is multiple, pluralistic, democratic, contextual, inclusionary, horizontal and caring.'[1]

While architectural photography traditionally has favoured the former mode, Pallasmaa is optimistic that a photographic rethinking – particularly in view of emergent technologies and modes of imaging – could generate a shift towards an aletheic mode of architectural reproduction.

Photography's greatest ability lies in its power of providing new ways of seeing – the liberation of the image from both the printed and analogue realm into the screen and digital space allows for greater possibilities of architectural critique.

1   Juhani Pallasmaa The Eyes of the Skin, London: Academy Editions, 1996, 25.

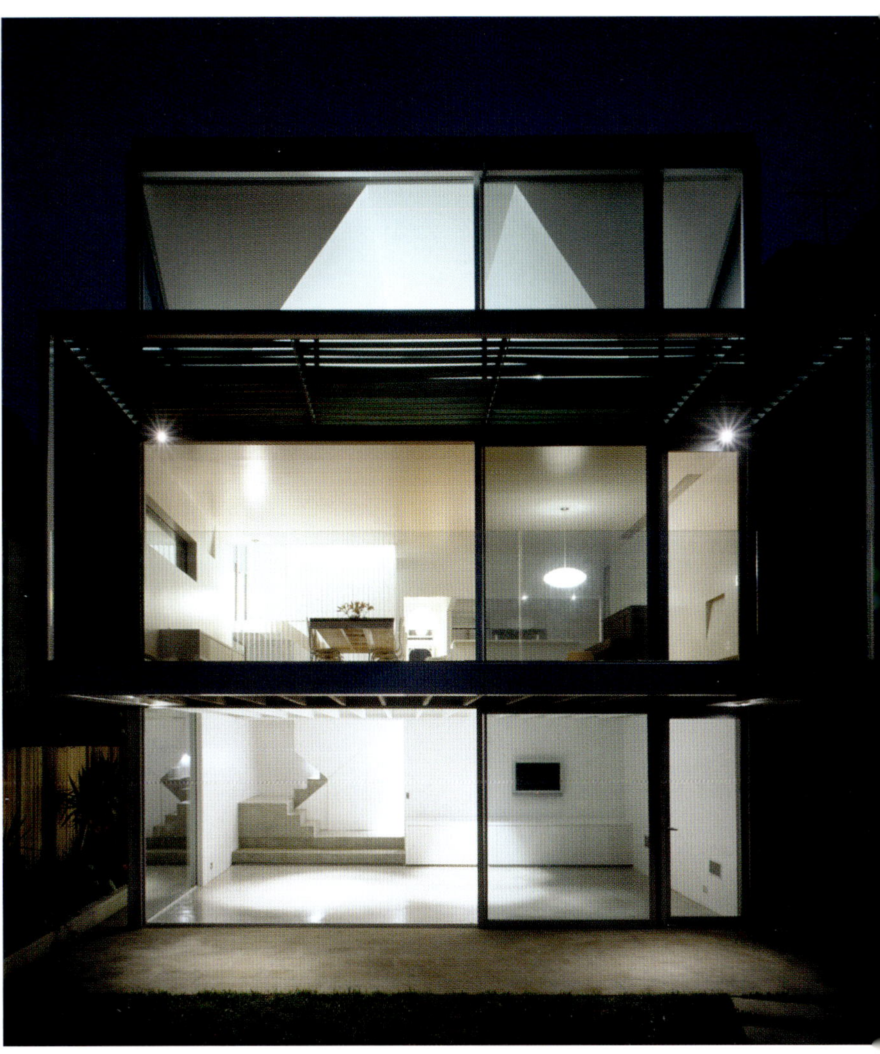

WORKSHOP

...through it now. The danger has passed.

It was the beginning of that project
... become aware of ...

... beam has ... volume attached ...

... the wall from which the beam springs
from the ...

The sun is a ... point of light but
we can... light but it was
that

... says that ... things about an open space.
It appears inaccessible
complex movements

The danger has passed

Take a camel when ...

The library
I want to sleep here
for 300 years
+ see it later

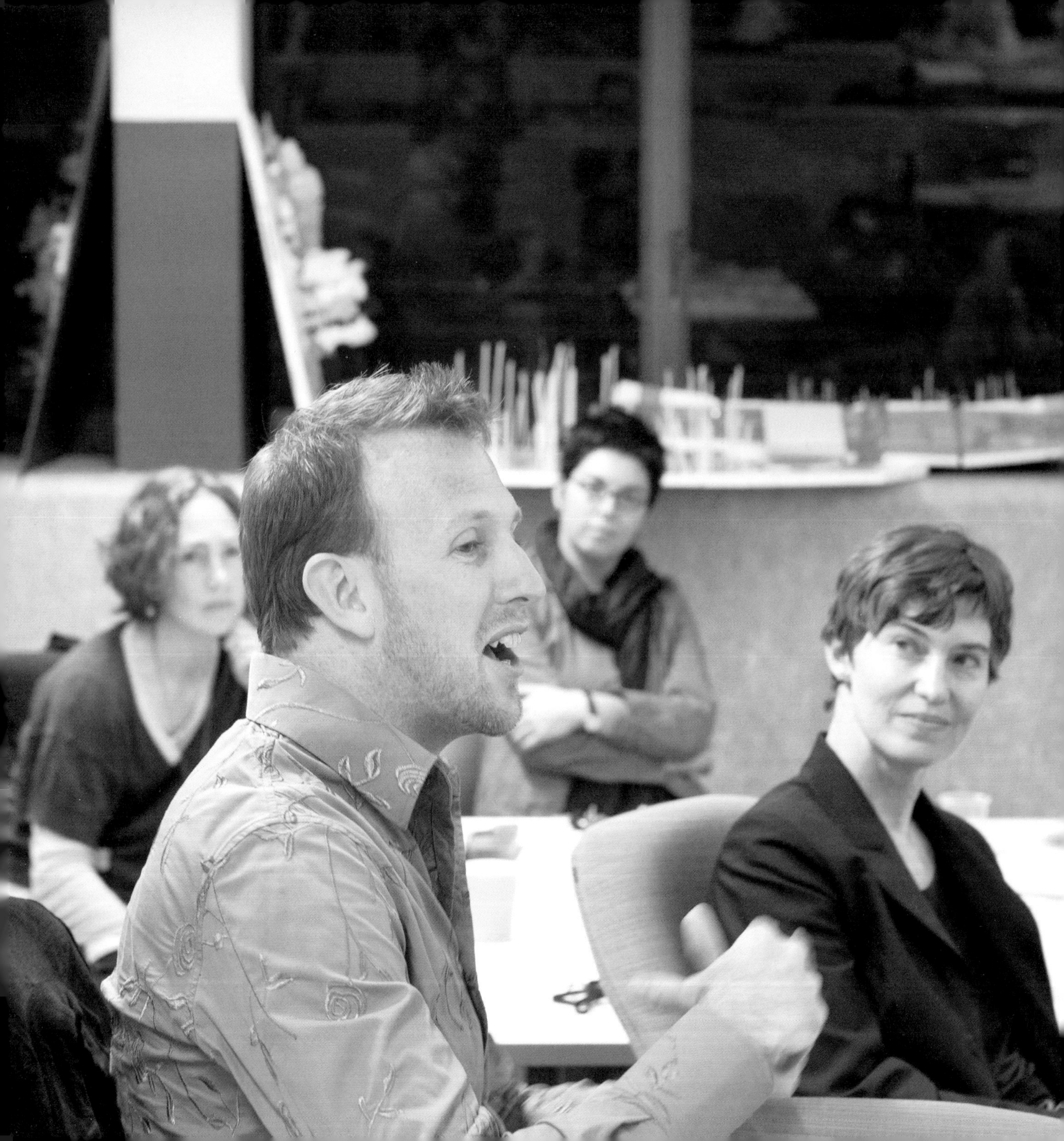

Messages of the Wind

LINDA MARIE WALKER

In July 2010 I was invited to lead the first day of a workshop on *Writing Architecture*, a two-day intensive experiment with 'innovations in the textual and visual critique of buildings', held at the University of Queensland School of Architecture. The workshop was part of a suite of events associated with a conference, also on *Writing Architecture*, and this workshop brought together diverse writers and photographers engaged in critical and creative practices related to the built environment. My focus for participants was to consider writing as an art/craft that in itself is a built environment; not one premised on representation (or one in service to a three-dimensional materiality), but one 'composed', 'made', networked, object-like; a kind of living thing or substance, whose work is to construct (by various physical and emotional means) a space (like a sculpture or a piece of music) for the time and action of reading – including rewriting, quoting, editing, collaging, assembling. And, as part of 'making', an attending to language that asks (from the inside of the endeavour): what is it then/now, what has it (not) become, what does it do, and so on. The following text is put together from parts of a longer text of the same name (unpublished); 'content' was the subject of that writing, whereas here 'content' gives way to the essay-as-subject, a small room, a tiny insect-like cosmos, rearranged; a makeshift space that is more likely to be in the process of being dismantled, or abandoned.

The title, *Messages of the Wind,* comes from a talk Kev Carmody gave on ABC Radio National about music and messages; he mentioned his grandfather who told him to '… listen and read the messages of the wind … there's music all around …'.[1] Sound, as content, as world; rain and leaves and animals and birds and us.

'Content' then as ecstasy, or as apparitional or unintelligible (maddening) movement/matter, beyond structure. Georges Bataille wrote: 'Ecstasy explains nothing, does not shed light on anything, and neither does it justify anything. It is nothing but a flower, being necessarily as unfinished and as perishable as a flower. The only way to approach the lack of an exit is to take the flower and to look at it to the point of harmony in such a way that it can explain, enlighten and justify, *being [étant]* itself unaccomplished, *being* perishable.'[2]

Writing becomes memory with an 'as if' method, or a 'no' method; a collage writing[3] for itself (as if a flower); a writing in the midst of disaster, and from an interminable situation (as one *is*, within the space of *this* life) – with diffused substances (love affairs of every kind); a made thing without drama, without a voice whispering the word 'whisper' or a body performing 'mourning'; content that is birdsongs or breezes or 'words', a friendliness, an alliance – a sense of failing/falling, a mutable process of confusion.

Whatever *is* (being) constructed 'bursts its banks' suddenly (trouble right *there;* perhaps where there's a swamp or a tributary or debris), and resists the good intentions of 'control'; that is, one's vain hope is shattered by all that's 'in the atmosphere' (flashing lights in the night sky) – whether exterior to my interior or interior to my exterior.

A making (like walking) open to another, for another, with another – distinct, and willing to pass into unknown states – is 'alive'. Bataille wrote: 'The different beings distinct from one another *communicate* because it is possible to talk about incompletion, animal nudity, wound, and it is in the *communication* from one to the other that they come alive through losing themselves.'[4]

Inside 'the work' (of writing) several states (or moods) of thought remain (curtailed trajectories, stalled conversations, ruined projects) gathered like friends (strangers too); this is not an 'unresolved' or 'wanting' state, but is, rather, a 'poem' state; Hélène Cixous writes: 'She had tried to figure out how to call this unwritten book. This object of restraint … and, lacking a name for designating a thing that was not of this world, our own, the visible, had proposed to herself the word *poem.* This was not entirely unfitting … its starry wandering … the presence of an order other than our own … seemed to her to relate this book to the species of the poem. Poems, too, are of this astral nature, sparks as they are of a dead or distantly imminent fire.'[5]

For one thing to 'communicate' with another – writing with writing, being with being, writing with being – the flaw, fault, or wound must be on show or welcome (to make an appearance), handled with thought, aired (so as to dry), (ad)dressed, given the freedom to transform (the wound, (w)hole in the work, carries itself like a dancer, placing its feet on the hard ground momentarily; the wound and the ground together '… composed in equal parts of physical motion, subtle rhythms, and their corresponding images or words …').[6]

The activity (the endeavour, the undertaking) of producing, of making, in the face of 'profound reality', is one of (perhaps) listening to 'the messages of the wind' or engaging with complex processes – with oblique strategies, chance operations, deliberate tactics (with the massive system of flawed appearances[7] and so on;[8] an engagement that sets in train a composition of various tensions and temporalities.[9]

In Jacques Derrida's discussion of Maurice Blanchot's *The Instant of my Death,* the movement in the text between fiction and testimony makes 'appearance' shimmer, proof is no more true (when) in one form or the other – content is woven: 'On the one hand, non-literary testimony is no more proof than is testimony in the form of a literary fiction. On the other hand, the author of the two, always the sole witness to that of which he speaks, may speak truly or falsely, speak truly here and falsely there, interweaving a series of interpretations, implications, reflections, unverifiable effects around a woof or a warp objectively recognized and beyond suspicion. We will study [he says of his own writing in relation to the matter] the meshes of the net formed by the limits *between* fiction and testimony, which are also *interior* each to the other. The net's texture remains loose, unstable, permeable. Historical through and through, this texture is the texture of literature and all of the passions it suffers and sustains, to which it testifies as its truth without truth, all of the passions with which it is swollen or which catch themselves in it.'[10]

Blanchot is, wrote Derrida, '… the witness who reminds us that the testimonial act is poetic or it is not, from the moment it must invent its language and form itself in an incommensurable performative.'[11]

Work/writing is a tiny fold or the unfurling of a deep crease (on the surface of other creases) – not a battle-ground,[12] a gesture of tact toward another's body or habitat.

Already, at once, or prior to instance, the piece-of-writing (as content) is the scent of another writing; it is real (here) and sur-real (there): finding itself and presenting itself. Something is expressed with each and every move, changing shape, rhythm, with cuts, insertions, digressions, contradictions, doubts, intervals.[13] Deleuze wrote: 'The world exists only in its representatives as long as they are included in each monad [each substance/matter a microcosm of differing quantity]. It is a lapping of waves, a rumour, a fog, or a mass of dancing particles of dust. It is a state of death or catalepsy, of sleep, drowsiness, or of numbness. It is as if the depths of every monad were made from an infinity of tiny folds (inflections) endlessly furling and unfurling in every direction, so that the … [microcosm's] spontaneity resembles that of agitated sleepers who twist and turn on their mattresses."[14]

The writing is made of words – *these* consistencies, bodies, inherences, possessions (substances/matters), each with their own origin and map of travels – that gather as perceptions (as clarity), and also as bundles of disquiet. Words are nomadic potencies: '… [they signify] that there exists minute perceptions that are not integrated into present perception, but also minute perceptions that are not integrated into the preceding one and that nourish the one that comes along ('so it was that!').'[15]

Ross Gibson in his text 'Changescapes' writes of the 'life-work' of a man called 'Muller' and his 'compound' in a forest: '… a superb aesthetic system whose matter, method and thematics were the fragility, mutability and fecundity of the world; Muller had "collections", machinery that worked in make-shift but "beautiful" ways, a particular way of speaking, raked ground, and a shack … a predominantly meditative, albeit laborious construct maintained and evolving in concert with a dynamic environment … Muller produced a complex aesthetic expression of the cohesive energies and the disruptive instabilities that entangle the forest, himself and the clearing.'[16]

The compound (like a chemical) is an exhaustive place (perhaps even healing), a writing of content-without-content (raking, speaking, collecting), and yet an insistence toward the coming into the world of an expression (understood or not). The 'real' is tenderly questioned – the forms and senses of the given (and the meant) – while looking at and appearing with the inexhaustive 'appearances' (all around: the messages); this is force of an indeterminate kind and perhaps, in relation to/with that force, one makes oneself something else (Muller-like).

1   Kev Carmody, Perspective, ABC National Radio, 5.55-6.00pm, 12 July, 2005.

2   Georges Bataille, 'Friendship', in *Parallax*, 7, no. 1 (2001): 7
    (http://www.scribed.com/doc/59509724/bataille-friendship,
    accessed December 1, 2011)

3   See Paul Carter, 'Bridgeheads', in *The Culture of Landscape
    Architecture*, Harriet Edquist & Vanessa Bird (eds.), Melbourne:
    Edge Publishing, 1994: writing, as I am here discussing it,
    could also be named an extract-method: 'The extracts from
    Bridgehead are a textual collage from the following: *The Lie
    of the Land* (quotations from various drafts); a performance
    work called *Introducing Ulysses*; preliminary research for a
    catalogue note on the artist, Victor Litherland; draft concept
    statement commissioned by the Museum of Sydney; draft
    proposals for a sound installation on the theme of Colonel
    William Light intended for the 1996 Adelaide Festival; extract
    from *Ground Sound: a Local History*.' Carter, 52.

4   Bataille, 'Friendship', 6.

5   Hélène Cixous, *Firstdays of the Year*, trans. Catherine
    A.F. MacGillivray, Minneapolis: University of Minnesota Press,
    1998: 5-6.

6   Paul Carter writes: 'In this view [that of the poet Valery
    walking his familiar ground, and being able to think without
    looking where he's putting his feet] the ground forfeits its
    independent existence [here I imagine the wound as feet]; it
    is turned into a road for thoughts. To promote the movement
    of his sensibility as a whole, it is necessary that the road meet
    his feet at every point, as if it were made for them and, apart
    from them, did not exist – did not, say, render movement
    difficult by offering an array of alternative routes. Like a tank
    or a bicycle the poetic mind is wherever it is; it carries its
    'place' with it in the form of a complex equilibrium composed
    in equal part of physical motion, subtle rhythms and their
    corresponding images or words.' Carter, *'Bridgeheads'*, 58.

7   The flaw in the totality: '… a flaw that will itself be borrowed
    from the system of appearances and is also an appearance in
    itself.' Bataille, *'Friendship'*, 8.

8   For example, see: a. oblique strategies, Brian Eno and Peter
    Schmidt; b. the ear, Jacques Derrida; c. chance operations,
    John Cage; d. a-memesis, Merce Cunningham; e. trajectories
    (tactics), Michel de Certeau:

    a.   'The Oblique Strategies' are a deck of cards devised
         by Brian Eno and Peter Schmidt as aids to creative
         work practices. They are instructions that one can use
         when under pressure or in; the card is trusted even if
         its appropriateness is unclear.

    b.   'The ear is uncanny. Uncanny is what it is; double is
         what it can become; large or small is what it can make
         or let happen (as in laisser-faire, since the ear is the most
         tendered and most open organ, the one that, as Freud
         reminds us, the infant cannot close); large or small, as
         well as the manner in which one may offer or lend an ear.'
         Jacques Derrida, 'Otobiographies', in *The Ear of the Other,
         Otobiography, Transference, Translation, Texts and Discussions
         with Jacques Derrida,* trans. Avital Ronell, Christine V. Mc
         Donald (ed.), New York: Schocken Books, 1985: 33.

    c.   John Cage: 'Chance operations … are a means … of
         silencing the ego so that the rest of the world has a
         chance to enter into the ego's own experience …'
         Quoted in Joan Retallack, 'Poethics of a Complex Realism',
         in *John Cage, Composed in America,* Marjorie Perloff &
         Charles Junkerman (eds.), Chicago & London: The
         University of Chicago Press, 1994: 248.

    d.   On Merce Cunningham: 'The idea, for Cunningham,
         was to do away with mimesis in danced movements:
         the mimesis of "figures", the mimesis of a stage space
         that reproduced outside space, and even a kind of mimesis
         of "interiority", since the body was thought to be capable
         of translating the emotions of a subject or group. […]
         Cunningham goes about it by making an empty space
         outside and inside. […]' José Gil, 'The Dancer's Body, in
         A Shock to Thought, Expression After Deleuze and Guattari,
         Brian Massumi (ed.), London & New York: Routledge,
         2002: 117, 121-122.

    e.   Trajectories: 'Unrecognised producers, poets of their
         own affairs, trailblazers in the jungles of functionalist
         rationality, consumers produce something resembling
         the *'lignes d'erre'* [wandering lines/routes] … They trace
         'indeterminate trajectories' that are apparently meaning-
         less, since they do not cohere with the constructed,
         written, and prefabricated space through which they
         move. They are sentences that remain unpredictable
         within the space ordered by the organising techniques
         of systems.' Michel de Certeau, *The Practice of Everyday
         Life,* trans. Steven Rendall, Berkeley: University of
         California Press, 1988: 34.

9   Renaissance music (c.1450-1600) is characterised by polyphonic
    styles of textures, rhythmically flowing lines, equality among
    voice parts, and sonorous harmonies. Renaissance music is
    sometimes termed 'equal-voice polyphony' a complex mix of
    different voices ('voice' does not mean individual singer but

various musical lines – soprano, alto, tenor, bass). Composers focused, in the beginning, on abstract relationships, layered textures and counter/contrapoint rather than on emotions and linear ideas.

10 Jacques Derrida, *Demeure, Fiction and Testimony,* trans. Elizabeth Rottenberg, Stanford: Stanford University Press, 2000: 56.

11 Derrida, *Demeure, Fiction and Testimony,* 83.

12 'Everywhere the subject swirls in the midst of forces[,] they exert stress that defines the individual body, its elasticity, and its bending motions in volumes that produce movement in and of extension. The subject lives and re-enacts its own embryonic development as a play of folds (endo-, meso-, and ectoderm) rather than as a battleground pitting the self against the world. By way of Leibniz's critique of Cartesian space the author pleads for tact of body and environment.' Tom Conley, Translator's Foreword, A Plea for Leibniz, in Gilles Deleuze, *The Fold, Leibniz and the Baroque,* Minneapolis: University of Minnesota Press, 1999, xvii.

13 "… the Baroque universe witnesses the blurring of its melodic lines, but what it appears to lose it also regains in and through harmony. Confronted by the power of dissonance, it discovers a florescence of extraordinary accords, at a distance, that are resolved in a chosen world, even at the cost of damnation. … In its turn harmony goes through a crisis that leads to a broadened chromatic scale, to an emancipation of dissonance or of unresolved accords, accords not brought back to a tonality. The musical model is the most apt to make clear the rise of harmony in the Baroque, and then the dissipation of tonality in the neo-Baroque: from harmonic closure to an opening onto a polytonality or, as Boulez will say, a "polyphony of polyphonies".' Deleuze, *The Fold, Leibniz and the Baroque,* 82.

14 Deleuze, *The Fold, Leibniz and the Baroque,* 86.

15 Deleuze, *The Fold, Leibniz and the Baroque,* 87: 'The theory on minute perceptions is based thus on two causes: a metaphysical cause, according to which every perceptive monad conveys an infinite world that it contains; a psychological cause, according to which every conscious perception implies this infinity of minute perceptions that prepare, compose, or follow it. *From the cosmological to the microscopic, but also from the microscopic to the macroscopic.*

The task of perception entails pulverising the world, but also one of spiritualising its dust. The point is one of knowing how we move from minute perceptions to conscious perceptions, or from molecular perceptions to molar perceptions. Is it through a process of totalisation, when for instance I grasp a whole whose parts are imperceptible to me? Thus I apprehend the sound of the sea, or of an assembly of people, but not the murmur of each wave or person who nonetheless is part of each whole. … We are not dealing with a relation of parts-and-wholes because the totality can be as imperceptible as the parts, as also when I *do not* sense the grinding noise of the water mill to which I am overly accustomed. And a buzzing or a deadening effect are whole without necessarily being perceptions.' Deleuze, The Fold, Leibniz and the Baroque, 87.

16 Ross Gibson, 'Changescape', in *IDEA Journal,* Gini Lee and Suzie Attiwell (eds.), 2005.

They Told us They Would be Checking ~~our~~ Papers (Sic): A text under revision

ISABEL D'AVILA WINTER

We gathered in a room off the landing and waited. For an hour or two, we sat still on our rolling chairs, >and watched each other out of the corner of our eyes<. We were cautious, naturally, knowing we were all there for the same thing and wondering who would get it first. ~~But t~~Then one of us starting>ed< a gentle ~~oscillation by~~ pushing >off< the floor ~~the~~ >with< the ~~soles~~ >heels< of ~~our~~ >his< shoes~~, and~~ After a while we were all doing it. Rolling.

>Swaying.<

Then suddenly, it seemed, it felt colder in the room, and angles in the landing >surfaces<, ~~now shadowed more strongly on one side,~~ appeared sharper. Those of us who >stepped out of the room to investigate the void,< looked up and noted the glass for the ceiling; noted the sky and wondered about the weather. > Was it a white sky ~~outside~~ or just a white glass? <. [~~Also above us, on the ceiling of our landing, we noted a figure 8 clinging onto the ceiling.~~] 'Do you have that expression in your language,' asked the woman next to me. 'Glass ceiling?' We smiled together and watched the opaque glass above us, both of us standing with our arms crossed and neck straining, ~~we could merely speculate on clouds and weather.~~

The building hummed ~~with its own sense >of purpose<~~ and some of us hummed along with it ~~waiting;~~. We sat, back inside the room >,< tapping our feet and listening. Voices >and noises< travelled from beneath us and above us. >Through our glass walls we could see the landing across from ours. We watched doors that occasionally opened to reveal a figure who disappeared further along the landing, into another door. < Sound arrived at our end ~~frayed and~~ dissolved like ink spreading in water. All of us, naturally, wondered about the landing across from ours, about the doors, and where they led.

We {spoke} quietly >each to each and said how we< liked the green cement walls. They were stencilled green, rather than painted, ~~and~~ so there were patches where ~~it~~ they were not green but just cement. It made us think of what had been removed, or else, what >~~the~~< this was leaving room for. "What _is_ it leaving room for?" a woman amongst us asked. There was no telling.

There were many feeling restless among us. A few ~~of us~~ got up to look ~~looked~~ down at the void from our landing. ~~Four levels below, on street level,~~ ~~w~~We watched people walking on the tiled floor four levels below. Their feet looked sharp on the white tiles, like arrows, as if the rest of them knew well where they were heading. > Many of them headed towards the stairs~~, the lift~~ (was it the lift behind that column, the lift we'd taken?). But none of them reappeared on our landing.

By now most of us were wandering around our ~~landing~~ >level< exploring, making private judgements. [We discovered the niches then.]< ~~Some one~~ >One of us< returned from the stairwell and reported on a light fixture that was ~~out of order~~; >unlit, out of order.< Blank, he said, like a sleeping face. ψ ~~And~~ And all around us was disorder, we supposed, if we looked closely enough. Still, these ideas were mostly discounted, in favour of the larger picture, _the bottom line_. We wouldn't all be here, unless we had at one time insisted on the larger picture and made changes, accordingly. ψ The glass ceiling woman

reported on a book she'd discovered in an unlit display case; it was called: _A Curse and its Cure in Two Volumes_. ~~Then~~ We wondered what the curse was, and speculated. 'It's a very old book,' someone else remarked, as if that held the answer. 'I've seen older,' another said.

Silk brocade was not what anyone had expected; the implausible sumptuousness of that silk-lined wall in a corridor off our landing (we touched it and wondered about the cost. 'Why?' said a tall woman – she had wildly wispy hair, which made her look harried). ~~=and,~~ As usual, we had no answer; nor about the niches along ~~along~~ one wall ~~which we could enter~~ like >a< railway carriages. There was the niche of the opium permits issued in 1904. We went in, one at a time, and wondered about permits and what it took then and what it might take now. ~~ander~~ Not that the display provided answers, exactly. This niche was covered by a tin roof, of the corrugated kind. By now so many of us were feeling corrugated – overwhelmed, it could be said. >It had been a long< ~~by the hard day~~ wait already, and there was more to go. They told us they would be checking ~~our~~ papers, and there was no telling how long it would take.

In one of the niches, the enlarged ~~mangrove~~ photograph of a mangrove held a surprise: all those roots seeking air up through the mud; one bright yellow leaf in all that >inhospitable< murkiness. 'I have no sympathy for mangroves,' said the tall woman. Those who heard her nodded, seeing we had sympathy for her. 'They seem so unnatural,' she went on, 'those roots growing upwards, rather than downwards.' It's different, naturally, where she's from. We moved away from her. Down below, the persistent wail of a young child carried upwards through the void, magnified by all that hard green cement~~, the cold >flat< panels of plasterboard~~.

Evident overall, we decided, was a strong faith in straight lines. Which left some of us feeling all the more round. Round pegs in square holes, someone said. ~~Inevitably,~~ Yes, there was laughter amongst us, from time to time. 'Scientifically,' someone began, and we all wondered what could possibly follow, 'there's no such thing as ambient noise. There's no instrument precise enough to analyse its subtleties, to identify its components, to predict it.'

We all thought about this curious pronouncement, quietly, aware that we were hardly providing ambient noise of our own. The ~~young~~ child had stopped wailing by then, but ~~but~~ all of us stopped to listen, nonetheless. One of us said then she could hear a ship, out at sea. A foghorn, someone else suggested. 'That's no sea,' we all said.

But then we heard a seagull ~~(a sound effect we had not noticed before that)~~. 'There's always a sea,' >a< a woman said. Many agreed. But the woman who'd heard the sea suddenly looked doubtful, then pensive, then strained her ~~eyes inside her head~~ >eyes upwards< as though trying to find an answer inside her head. Thankfully, most of us can resort to those great oceans inside our heads. When everything else fails.

Meanwhile, most of us had moved back to our chairs in the room off the landing. We sat down again, having exhausted most available time-killing possibilities, and waited.

Horizontality

JASON HAIGH

After being here so many times, I feel I could make the journey blindfolded. Looking up or down rather than straight ahead lets me find the traces and marks that others pass by. Who made these marks? Were they made on purpose? These pockets of light are beautiful but they don't seem to know it. Accidental. The underbelly above is laid out before me, willing me to try to understand its workings.

Crossing the Brisbane Convention and Exhibition Centre car park while walking between South Brisbane and West End is a journey I make numerous times a week. A horizontal chasm concealed from the jostling of Melbourne Street.

These images explore unseen attributes that only a repeat visitor might notice as their gaze drifts upwards or downwards. Looking up reveals the many intricate mechanisms of the building's use, as well as leftover traces from the construction process. Looking down, one finds the patterns of wear and markings that track the path of vehicles.

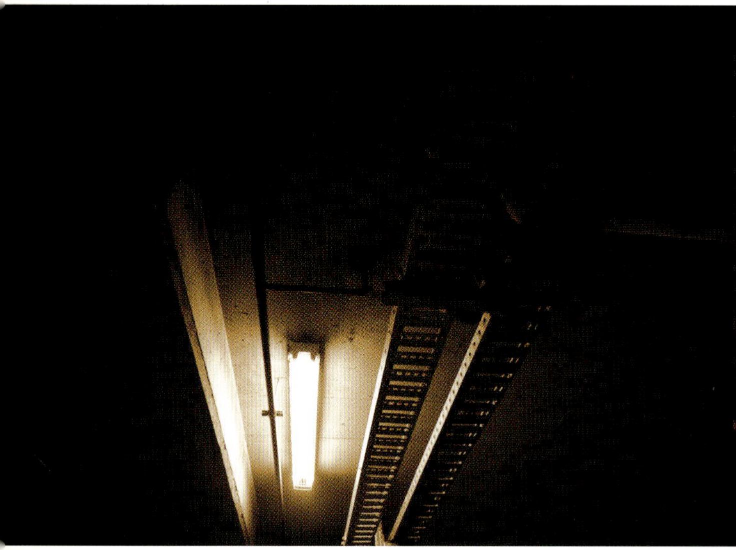

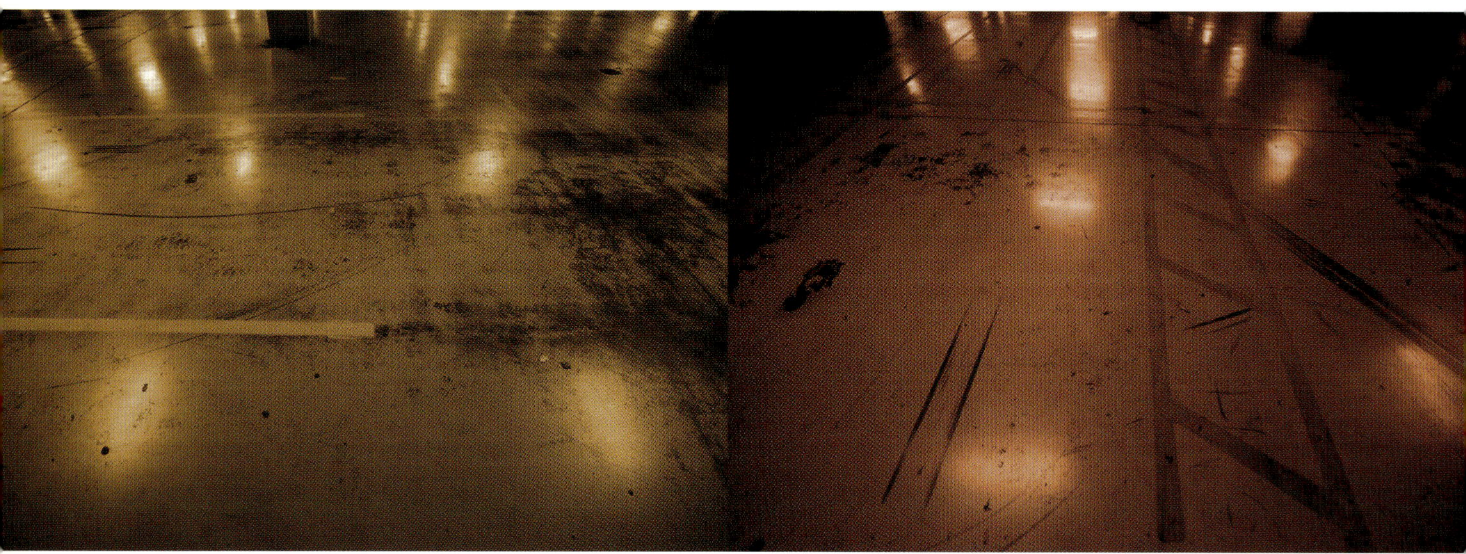

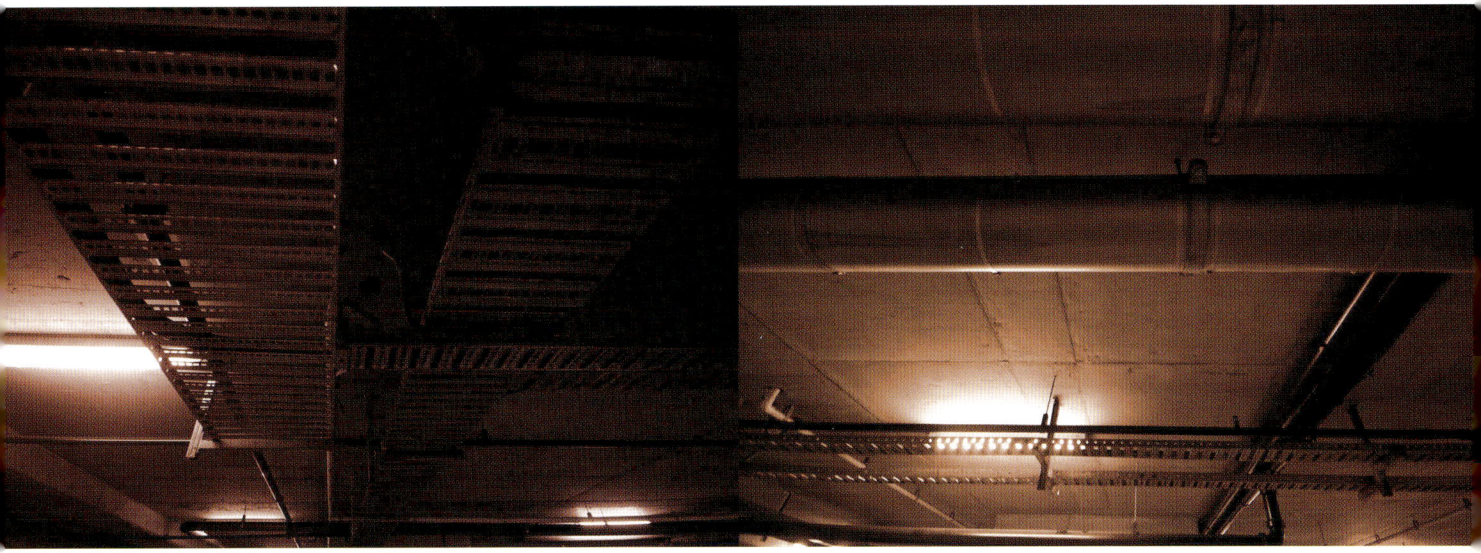

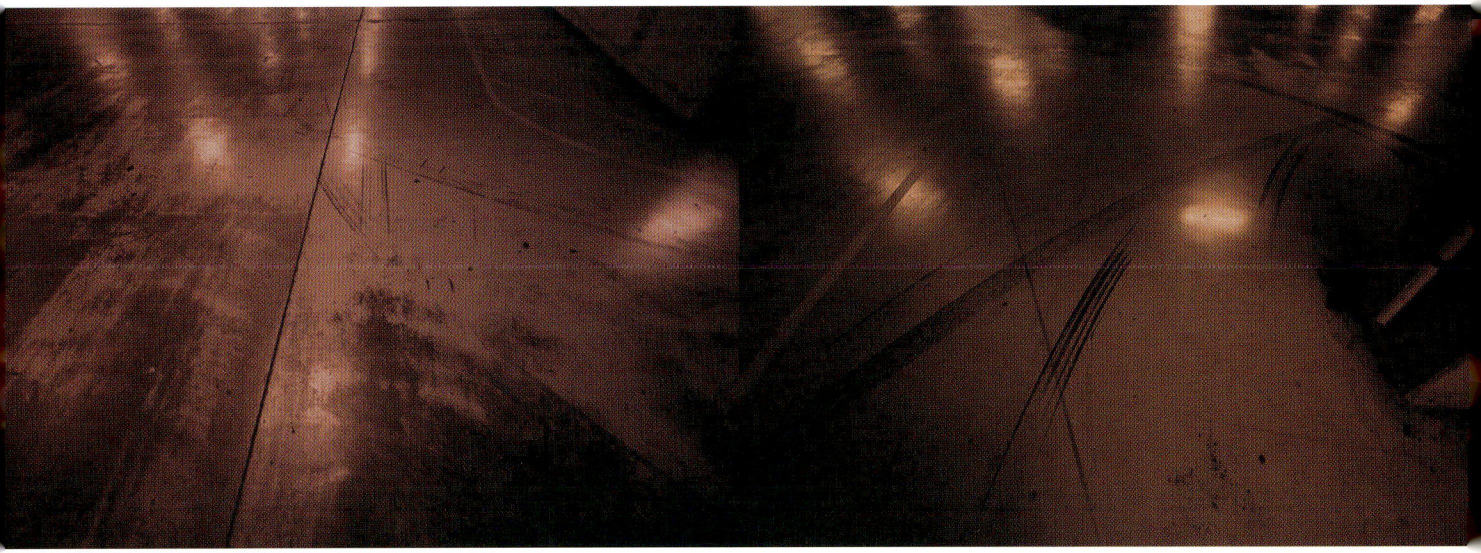

Picture Perfect: The home that wasn't

ANDREW BLYTHE

My house, once my home, exists in at least three splinters of time; three photographs tell me so. It is currently being transformed into a fourth, as you read this; that is someone else's story. A bitter split within the house is what lost it to me. The photos are also lost.

The first picture held promise. A stock real estate agent's photo designed to lure the unsuspecting buyer into the cul-de-sac dream of ownership – a 'renovator's delight'. Grey clouds frame the roof and divine the mood interior.

The wife organises the selling; the husband has already gone, to a mistress and engorging brain tumour. He survives one but the other devours him. I can't remember which. The agent, who drives a battered kombi van and brings her children to inspections, smiles in solidarity with the wife, telling the agent the dog has escaped. It has left behind a groove of discontent where it paced the garden. She wonders how far behind it she'll be.

Yet, on the last day, with settlement complete, the wife still valiantly struggles to complete her interior paint job. She says she needs the closure. At the end of the day she says goodbye, with washcloth and paintbrushes. We say hello to electric blue walls, custard yellow trims and an Indian red ceiling. The unrelenting, visual cacophony screams at me as I sleep, and I dream of sandpaper, industrial stripper and beige, in 80 different shades. Each night, every night.

We press on, owning then conserving. Walls are scraped for paint samples, period fittings hunted down and reinstalled. The house sighs with decorative door jams and authentic acroteria; cedar and silky oak are liberated to feel the sun once more.

This rebirth reveals a second photograph, discovered under tattered 1940s linoleum and attached to a 1973 calendar. The year I was born. The local shopkeeper laughs and tells me the house once belonged to the town flasher, advertising his wares through the cracked louvres to unsuspecting female pensioners passing by. He asks me if I intend to keep up the tradition.

Neighbours add dark layers to this story, hinting at earlier scenes of a cruel father, old Ned, and his over-zealous preoccupation with his daughters. We discover peepholes drilled into the bedroom walls, allowing the percolated air of anguish to circulate freely. The renovations stall as the toxic waste of paint stripper collects around the floor, monument to fading dreams.

The house belches its suppressed rage. Shadows dart out of the corner of my eye, even under the full glare of newly installed cut-glass chandeliers. In the bath, the hot water tap turns itself on unassisted. A visitor, a former tenant, prepares to depart and finds that her shoes – left at the front door – have been moved outside her old bedroom. There are only the two of us there and neither has left the other's sight.

One morning I wake to find a wizened face in the glass of the kitchen door, pressed into life through a collection of smudged finger prints and the soot of the passing traffic. Later, another visitor, who specialises in bridging worlds, says that Ned wants to know what we are doing in his house.

I resolve to cover this reality. Hope decays into violence and shouted words bite into freshly painted walls. The semblance of respectability is spat onto the polished floors, which refuse to gleam like the picture on the tin shows they should.

A new agent, flush with commissions, comes to snap her propaganda. Her artistic pretensions find her lying across the opposite footpath, getting depth and perspective she says. When the picture is developed – the third – it shows a house that hulks in defiance. Only the colours are changed, our colours, its secrets remain obscured.

The buyer is from interstate, and doesn't even visit. But I do, one last time, a few weeks after settlement. My sister, straight from England and unfamiliar with either the Queenslander aesthetic or my experiences, accompanies me. We walk under the wide veranda and a chill settles on her shoulders. She asks to leave, immediately. Her only explanation – that something was not quite right.

Kurilpa Reach and Northbank

JON HENZELL

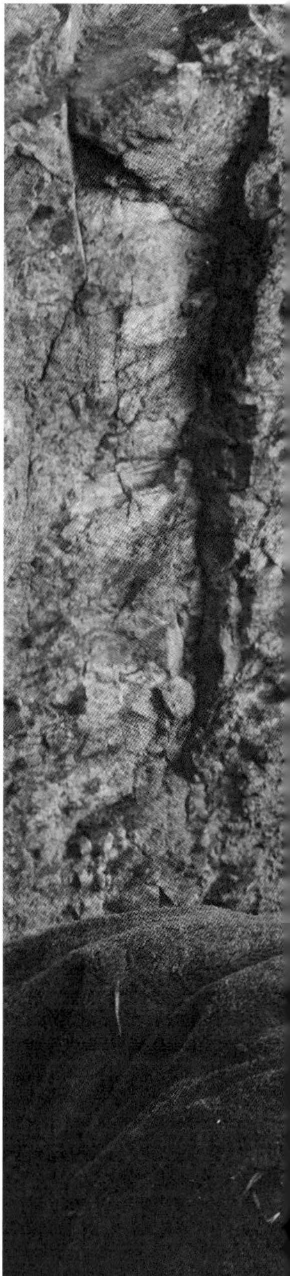

Photography is the art of capturing the light reflected off the surfaces of objects. On the surface, the place in the images is a hard and undesirable place. The smell of rotting river vegetation and exhaust fumes permeate the underbelly region of the concrete centipede that is the 'riverside expressway'. All legs and exo-structure.

In order to see beyond the surface you need to look as though through tears allowing things to blur into eachother. Through unclear eyes a parrallel vision emerges. Alongside the hard objective clarity is another: a vision of the place filtered through distant memories of significant places half recalled. Places where the mark left on the memory is burned in by the qualities of the light and the depth of the shadow. What is revealed is a worthy and remarkable landscape, constructed by light, invisible to all but those who give it pause.

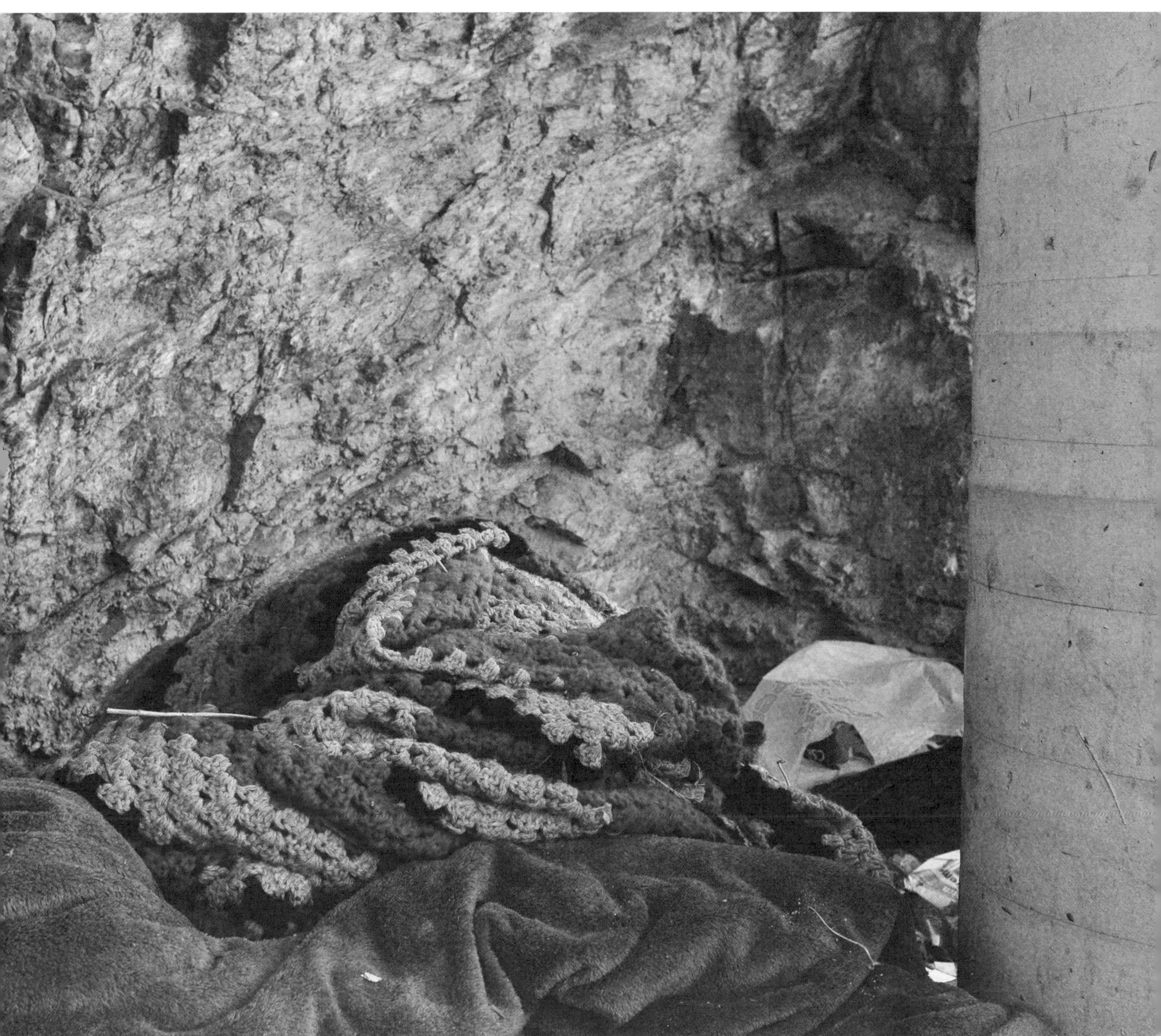

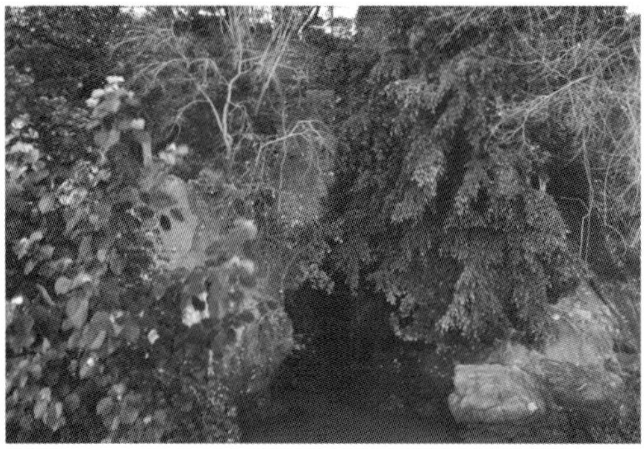

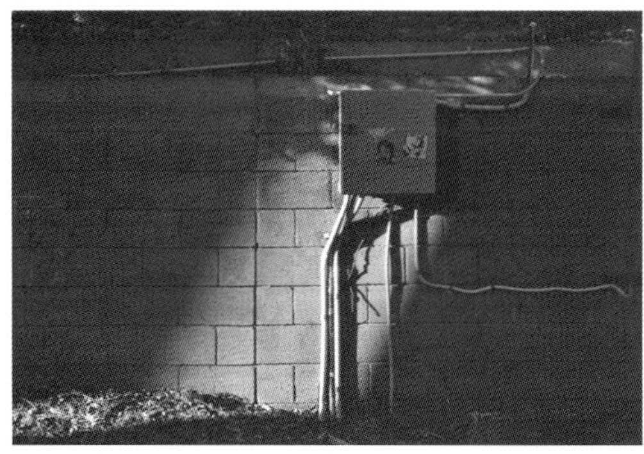

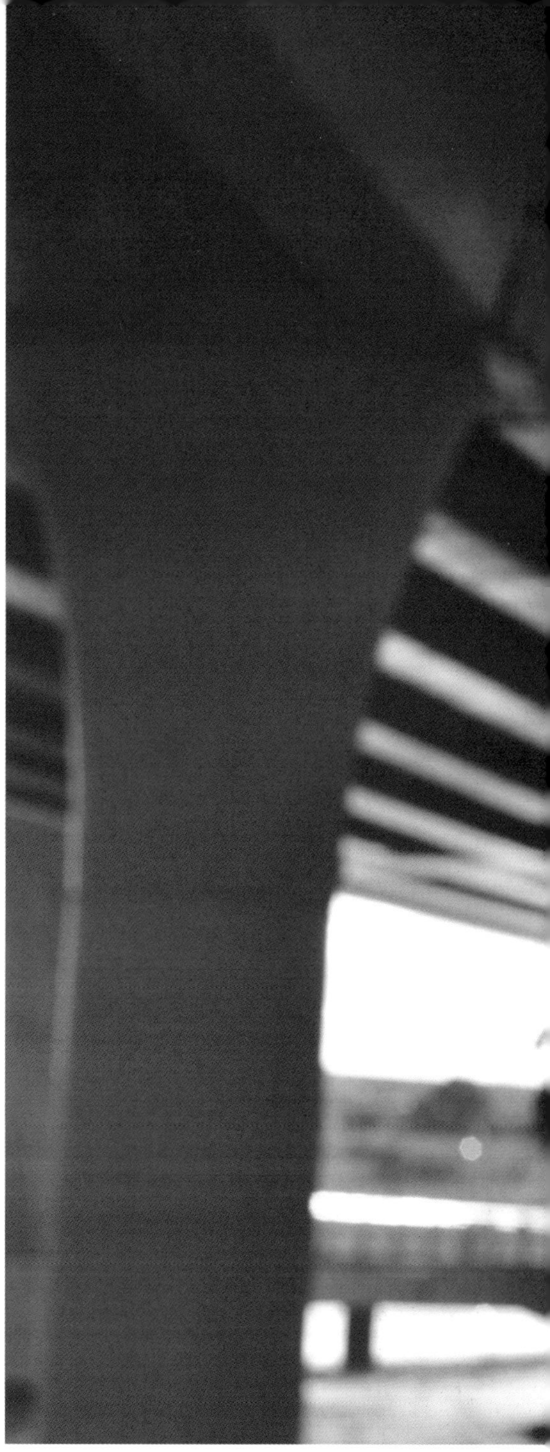

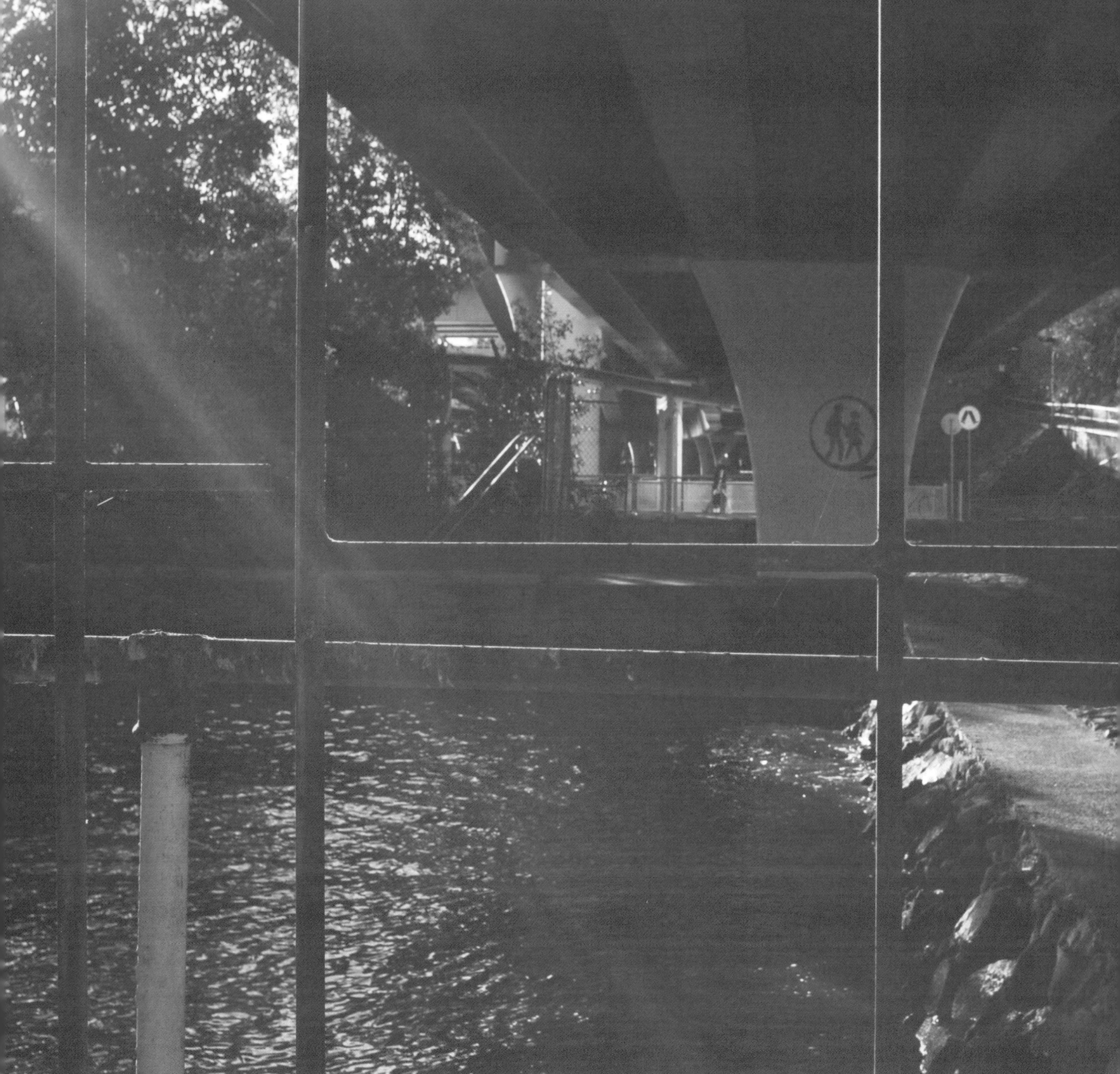

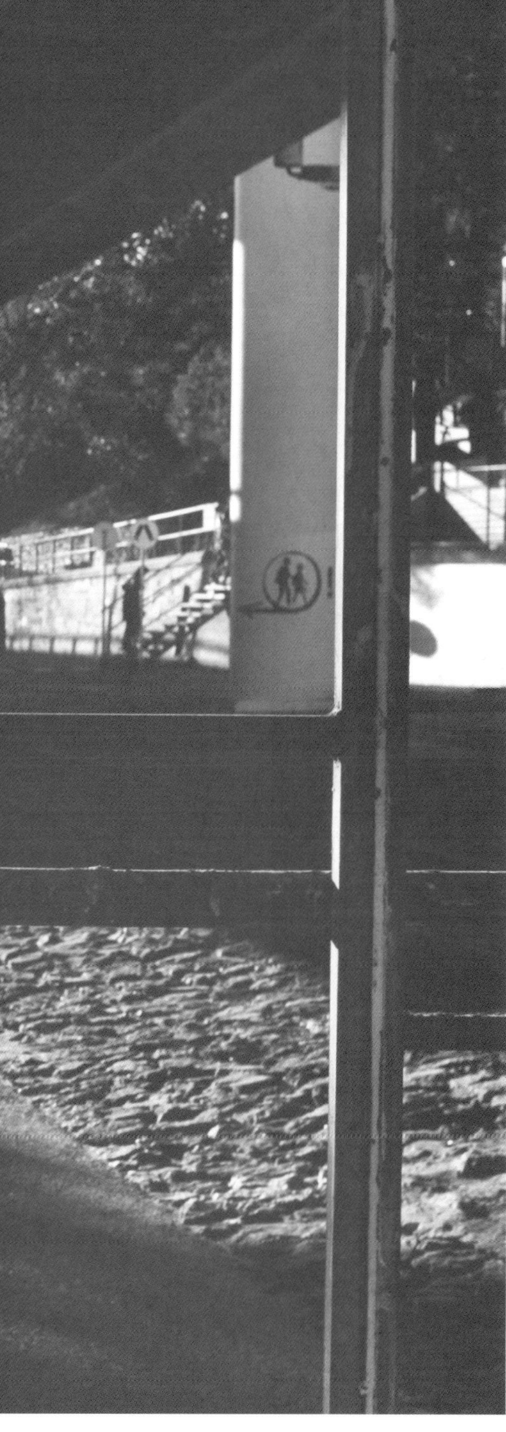

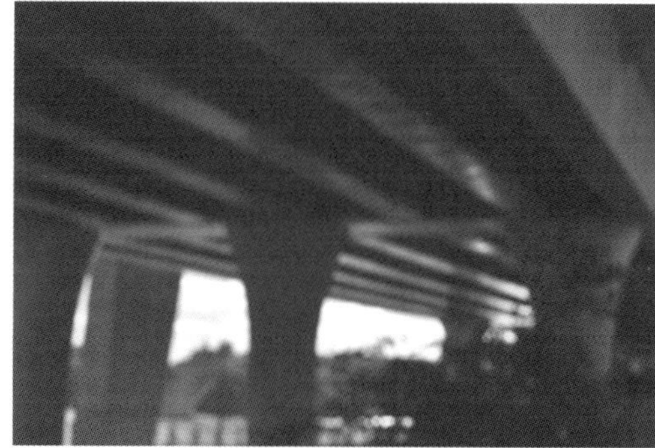

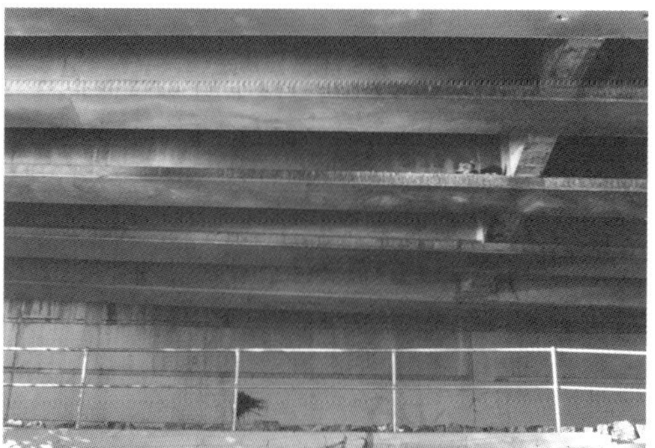

St Lucia House Film Stills

CLAIRE HUMPHREYS

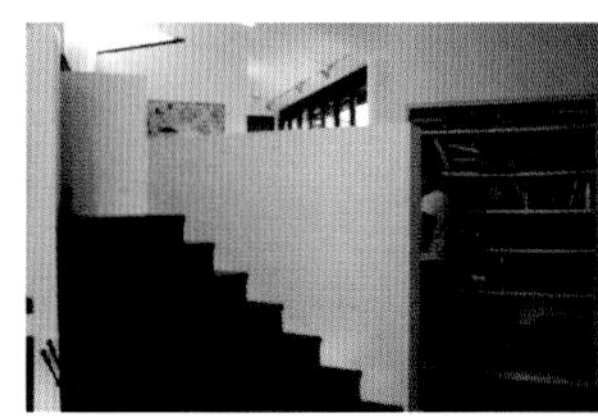

These stills are taken from *Sister Pan*, one of two very short video experiments completed in 2010. Both were made in response to Heinz Emigholz's *Sense of Architecture*, a 168-minute montage of filmed stationary shots that document 42 recently built architectural spaces and their ambient sound. Most of the film's scenes do not contain people, leaving a complex impression of stillness and absence. In *Sister Pan* (00:47 seconds), I was interested in how this filmed stillness might be further nuanced and changed by human presence. It opens with a still shot of my architect-designed childhood home. It shows my sister entering the shot, which mobilises to follow her as she disappears behind a wall and reappears in a different space. It is a variation on a scene in Tarkovsky's film *Solaris*. The timing of *Sister Pan* is heavily weighted towards two types of moment: a still period of time where she is absent and the building is empty; and a long pan where her unseen presence is followed throughout the house. Her footsteps are audible. The second experiment, *Mother Narrative* (00:44), is a series of stationary shots of spaces in the same home, but with a fleeting human presence that turns the context of each shot. It was an attempt to document the subtlest ways a present human body might manifest itself on film. In series, the shots gesture at a narrative as an unseen person is followed through the house.

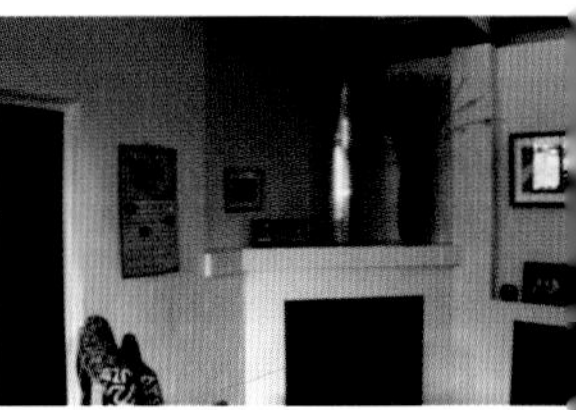

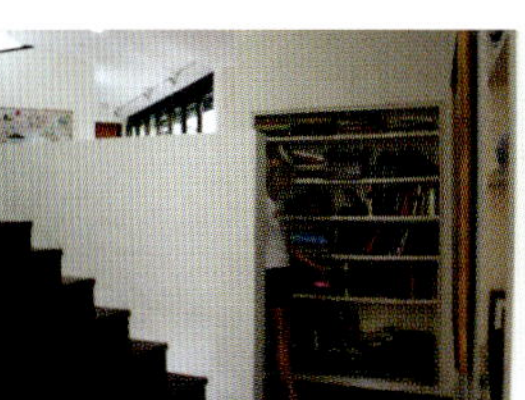
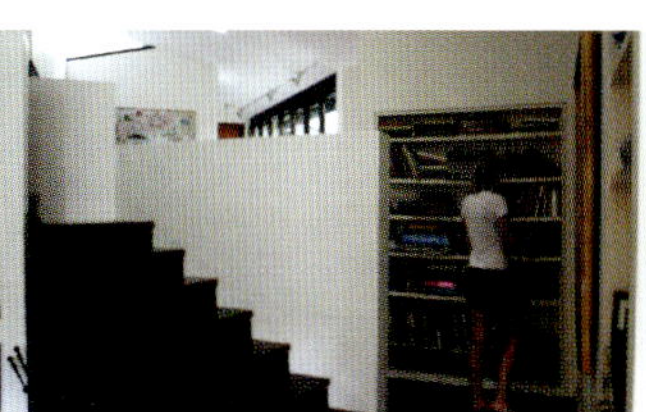
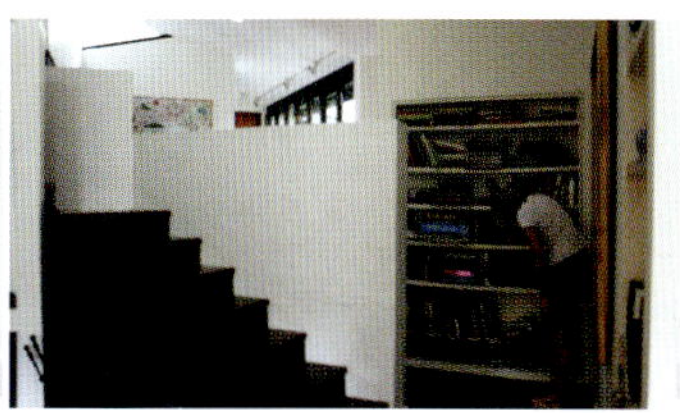
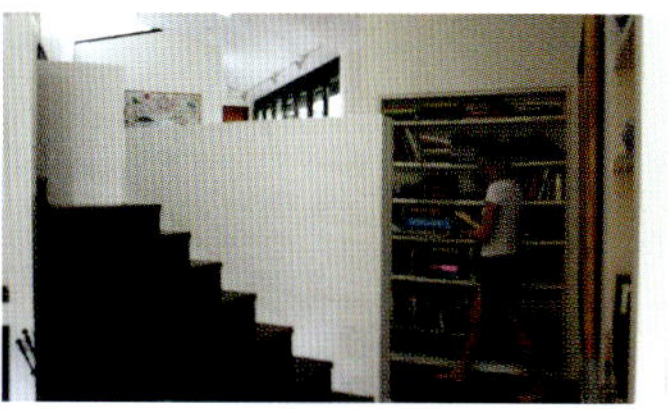
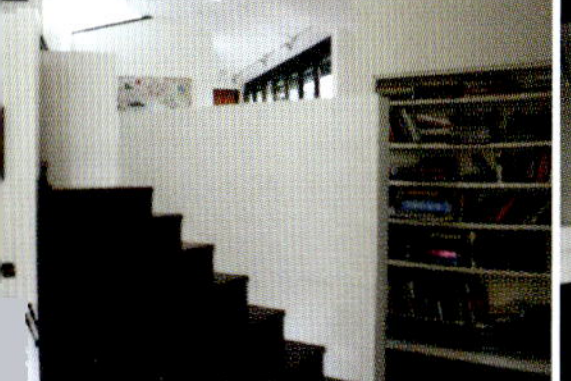
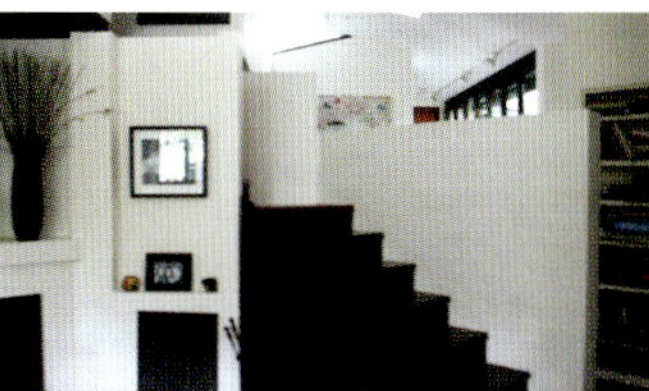
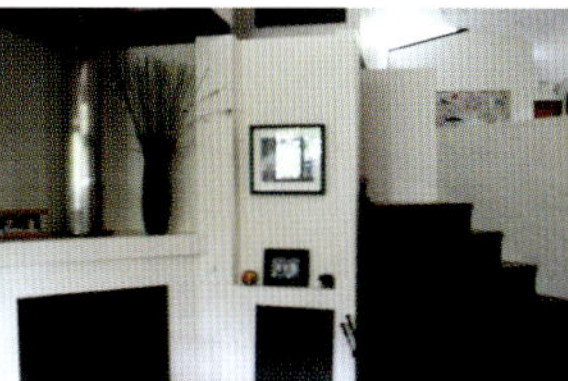
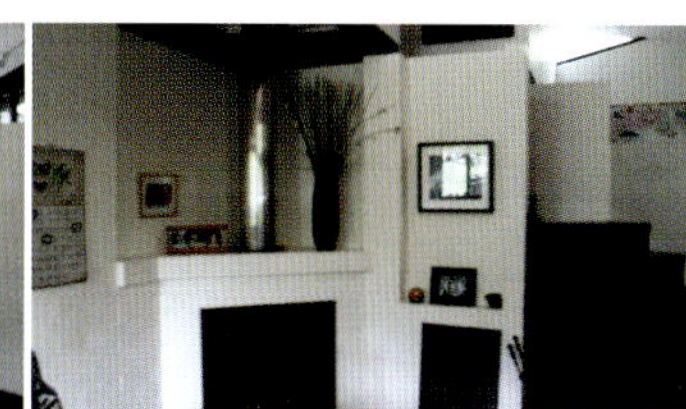
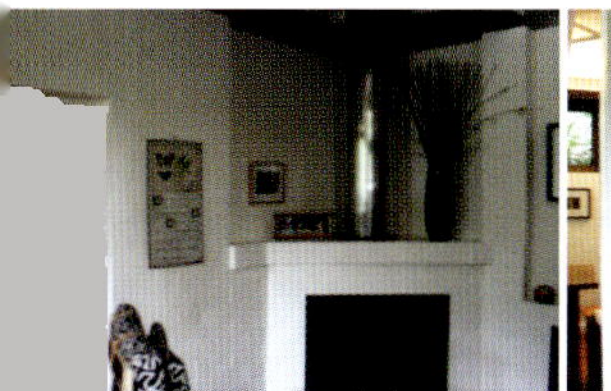
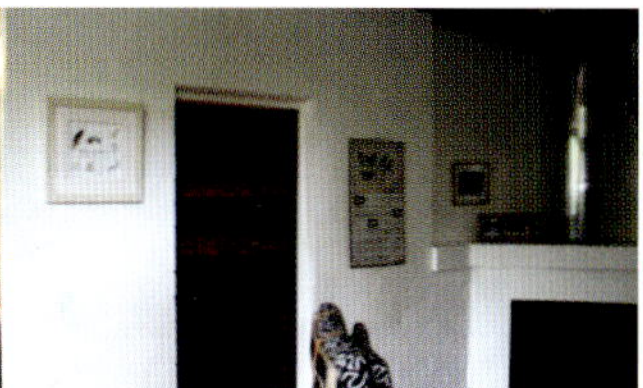
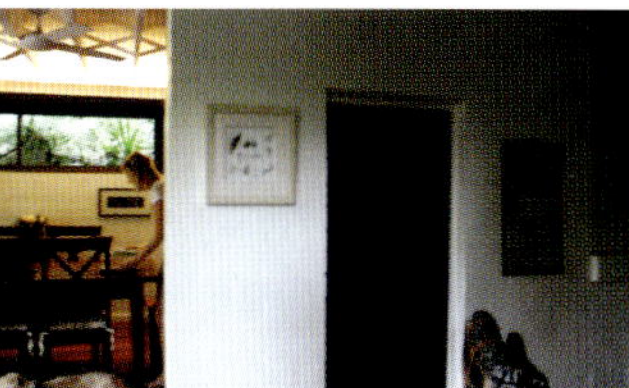
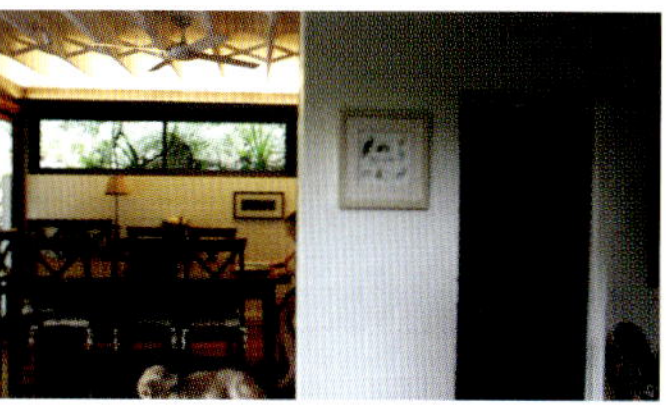

Land Living and Spatiality: My home at The Gap

CHRISTINE DAUBER

Space or the surfeit of space can be a daunting thing. This became evident when we were selling our home at The Gap, a Brisbane suburb close to the heart of the city, acting as a corridor or gap to the D'Aguilar Range west of the city. As people came and went, appraising, evaluating, dismissing, it was always the space that was problematic. How do you tend this space? How do you fence it in? Is it safe for children? The house it seemed was almost irrelevant. Their questions offended me for it seemed that these people were wasting my time, did they have no understanding of just how large an eleven acre block of land was? Why had they come? Certainly they knew that in terms of city expectations, it was expansive, the dimensions told them that. But what they did not understand was the 'it' that was in all their questions.

At the time, these enquiries seemed practical, related to everyday living, but inherent within that questioning was the recognition of something threatening, which stemmed from an inability to comprehend the spatial freedom of an 'urban' acreage. In the city, yet not of the city it was an anomaly, something wild, leftover. These interlopers to my home were used to something different, something more sociable, or to the sense of containment and security that the standard city 'block' or dwelling delivered. Paradoxically, here, they were confronted not by containment, to which they could relate, but by the psychic dimensionality of space, the limitlessness of which posed a threat to their composure. That the land backed on to state forest and was part of a buffering greenbelt to the city's devouring expansion meant that it could not be subdivided. Therefore, to most the land was useless. For me it was different. It was a place to be experienced and felt rather than seen. It offered adventure, an opening out rather than a closing in. It was a space in which to grow. Twenty years of living there had awakened me to the nuances and secrets of the land… To the traces and tracks left by others, to the radical changes of deluging rain, the anxiety of slow burning bushfire, the small animals such as pademelons and the fast disappearing bandicoots. Mine was an experience that could only be attained by long attachment and tending.

The dappled light hits my body. The trees I have planted (schizolobium or giant tree ferns) have grown. This is my place, my gully. I like to walk here in the coolness under the rainforest canopy. The rock steps assist my descent to where that old half burnt-out gum tree – a shell really – lies across the deep basin in which my boys and their friends dug day after day as they searched for lobbies in the dried-out creek bed. With heavy rain the water rushes down the mountain, transforming this same basin into a small lake. This water settles deeply into the ground to sustain the lobbies from year to year. The gardenias are in flower behind the garage and down the steep slope to the flatter ground below. Their scent is sweet and cloying. The native ferns brush my legs as I pass.

The house sits, tucked into the lea of the hill, at the top of a long drive. It steps back across the contours of the land as it faces northeast into the prevailing breezes. The kitchen forms the hub, with the family room and pool close by. It is an extroverted house. Its extensive verandas smilingly extend an invitation to sit and look out across the valley. From inside it is possible to look through the rooms to the vistas beyond. On frosty winter mornings I would stand in the kitchen and gaze at the mist as it hung suspended low across the valley - so low that the mountain on the other side protruded through the mist. At other times I watched the clouds through the high windows…

As my children grew and left, it was I who wanted to sell the land and it was I who grieved for the loss of 'it'.

Mechanics of Materials (or: Mechanics of Deformable Bodies)

AUDREY LAM

This is a project on mechanics of materials. It enacts mechanical and alchemical movement and textures immanent in a vacated, decaying dwelling. Specifically, it investigates the speed and slowness of deforming, reforming and performing bodies – a building's bodies and photographic bodies.

> Mechanics of materials is a branch of applied mechanics that deals with the behaviour of solid bodies subjected to various types of loading. Other names for this field of study are strength of materials and mechanics of deformable bodies. … Statics and dynamics deal primarily with the forces and motions associated with particles and rigid bodies. In mechanics of materials, we go one step further by examining the stresses and strains inside real bodies, that is, bodies of finite dimensions that deform under loads.[1]

1   James Gere, *Mechanics of Materials*, 6th edition, London: Brooks and Cole, 2004.

Series 1 (colour):
Elasticity, plasticity and creep.

Series 2 (black and white):
Viscosity of solids.

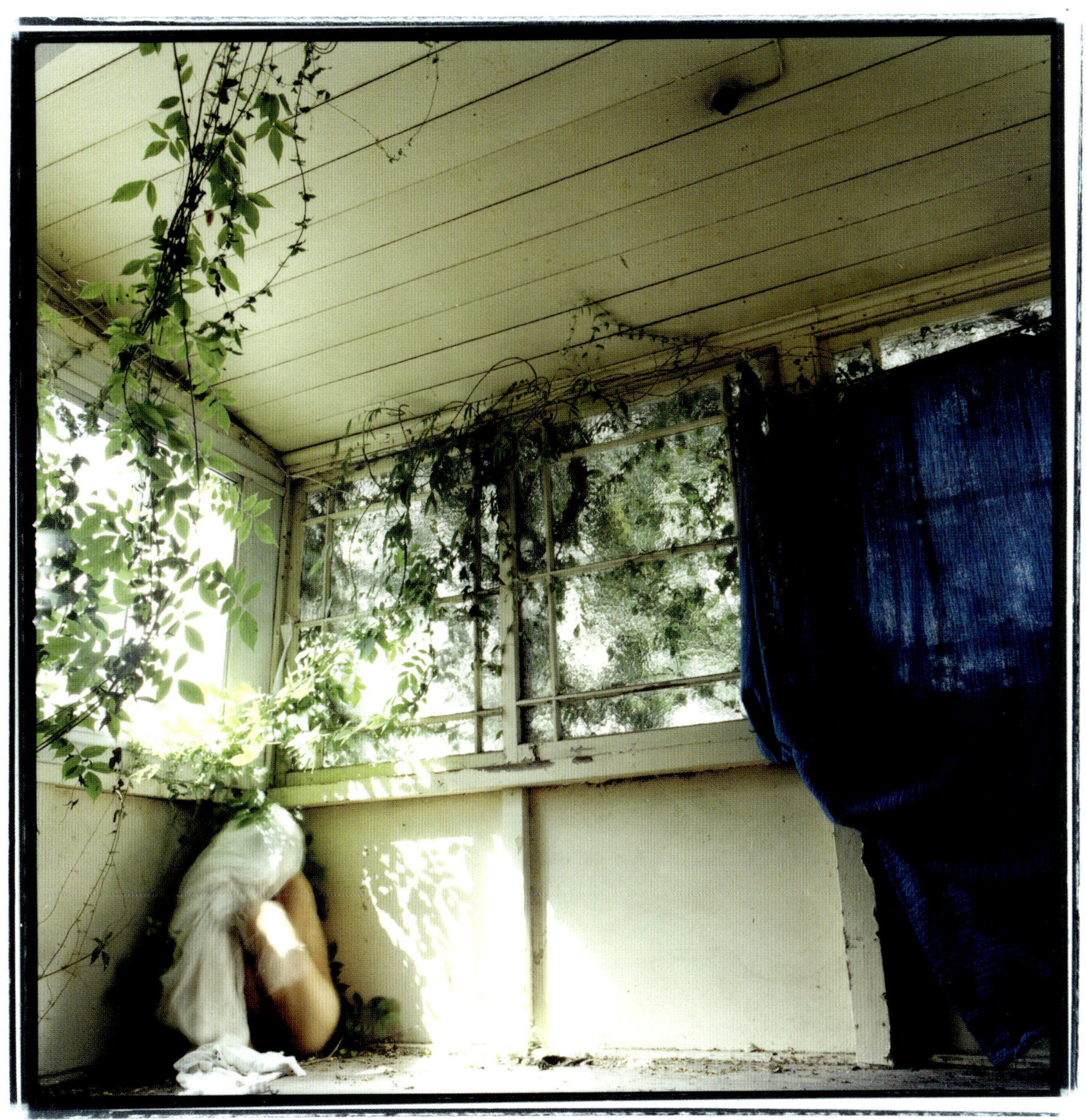

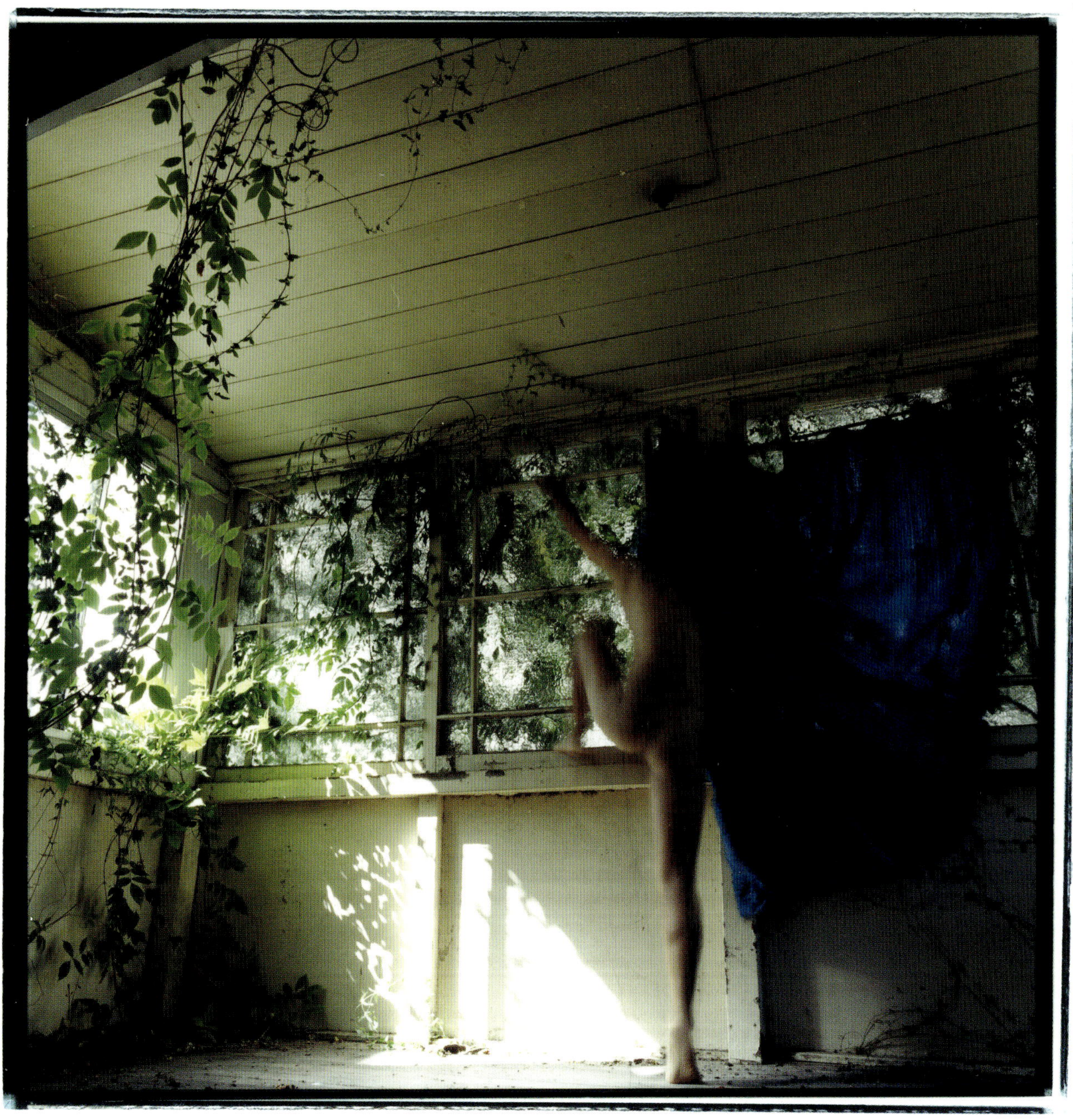

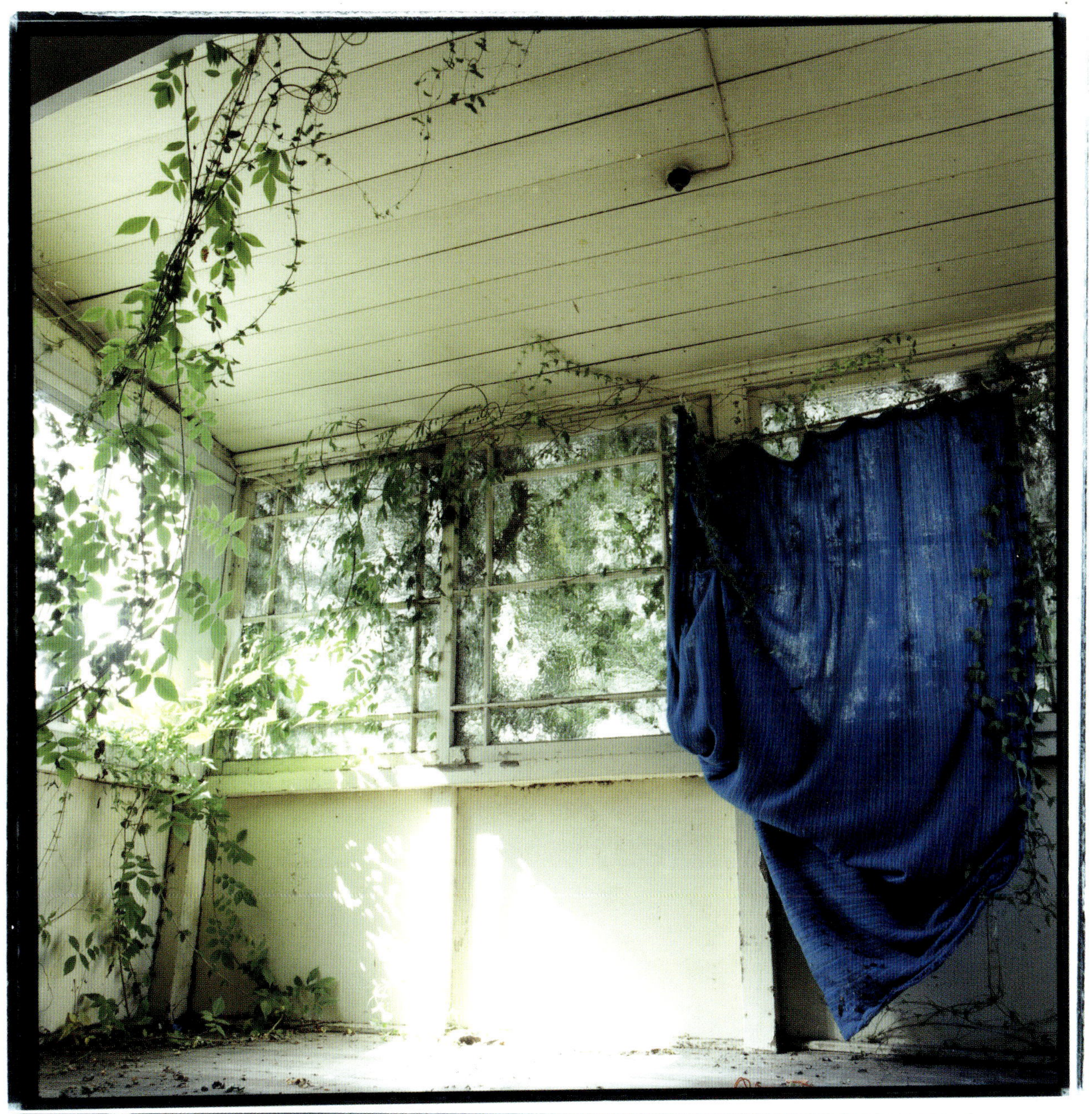

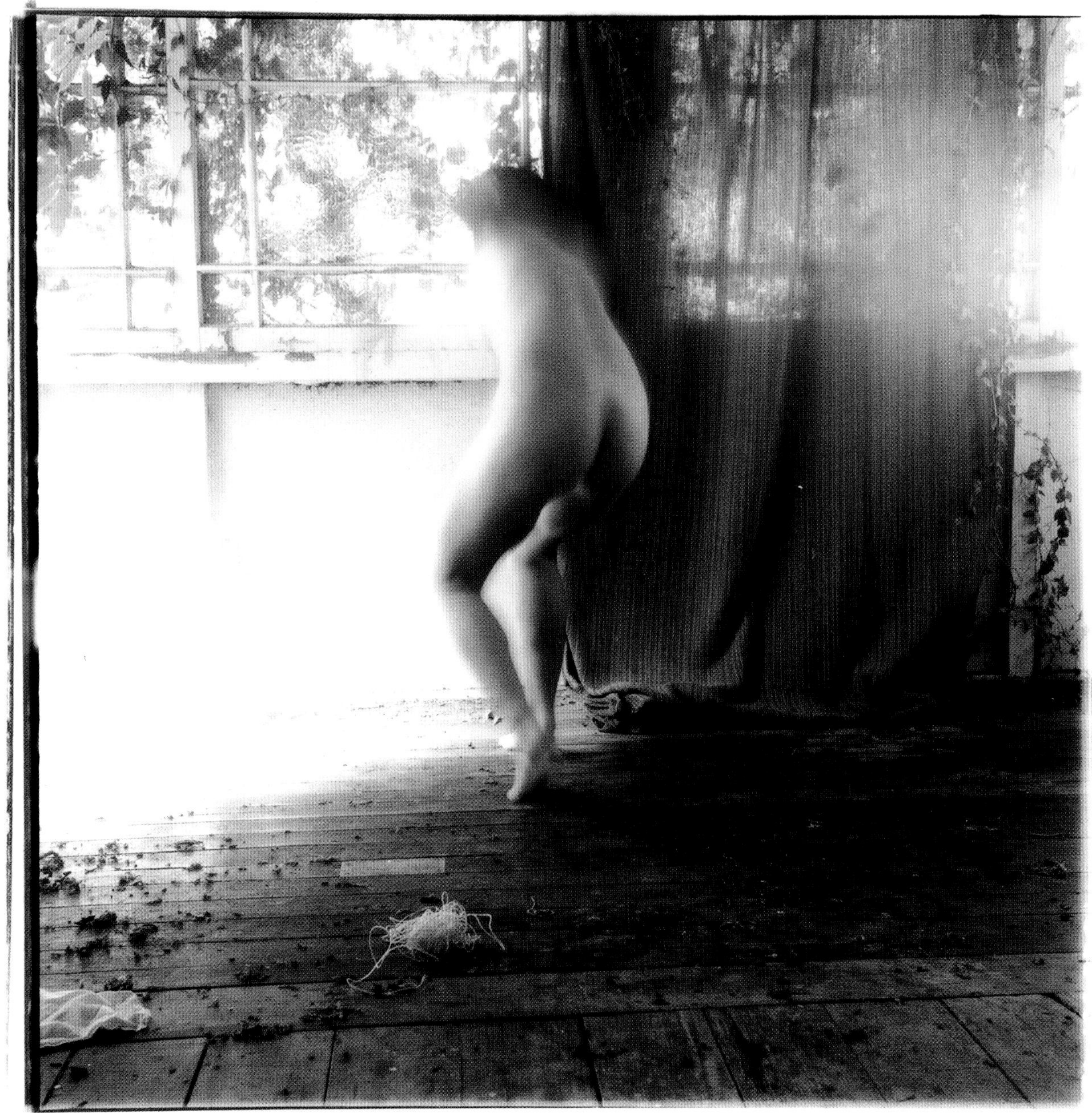

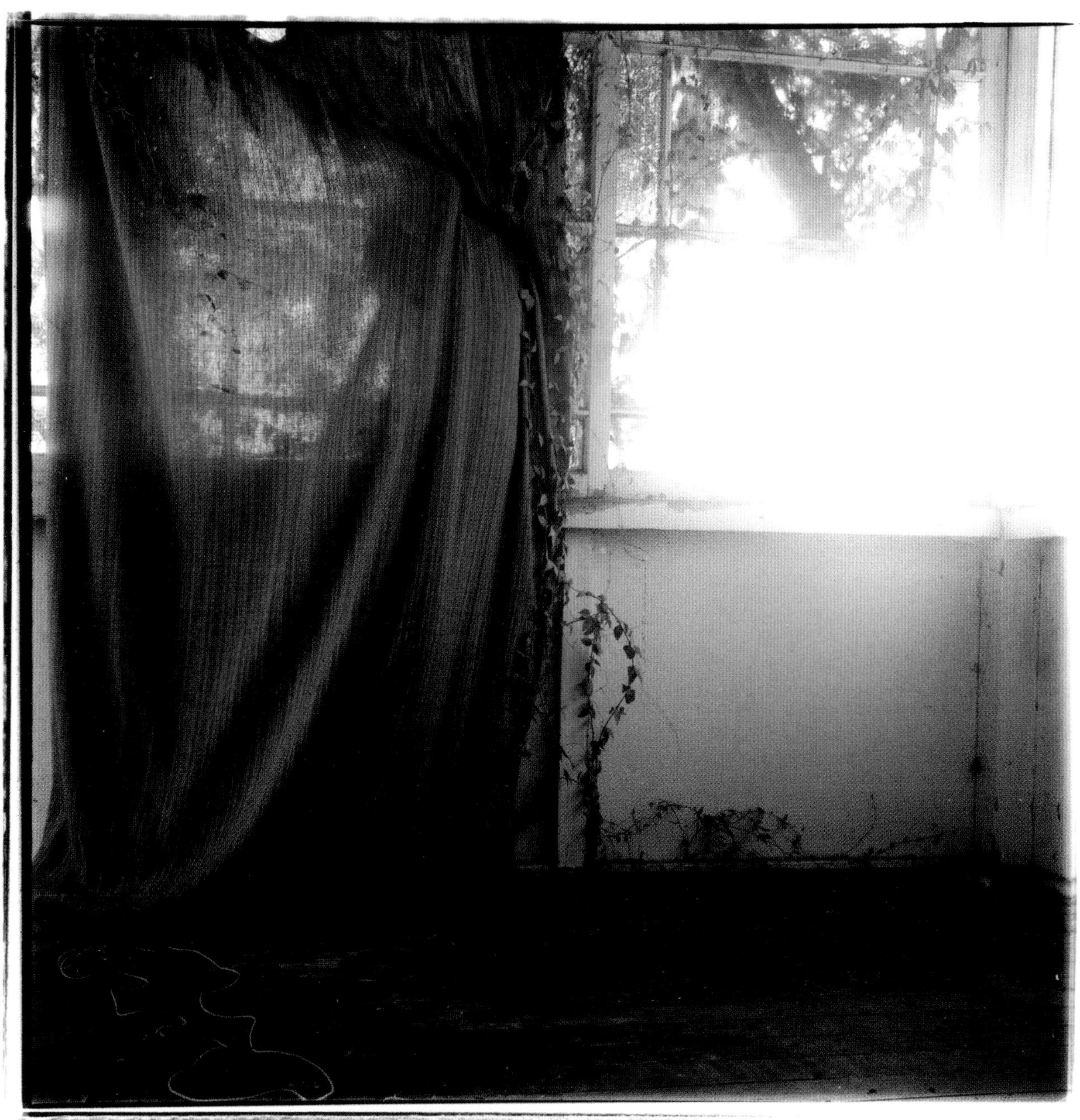

The Queen's Land – 2010

LYNETTE GURR

This short piece was written as part of the Writing Architecture Workshop. The group was asked to investigate the State Library of Queensland building and write a response to that experience. An interest in genealogy and social history led me to the library's family history section. The Hamburg Passenger List was a reminder of my grandfather's migration from Hamburg to Australia in the 1890s. What would it have been like to drop into Australia, into this building, more than a century later? How would he experience the place?

Dreams, fears, fantasies, discoveries and adventures occupy the mind of a migrant heading to a new home. We explore our environment laden with individual values and experiences. "Black Opium", a sculptural artwork by Fiona Foley featuring suspended poppy heads, became a springboard for the notion of micro-environments, alienation and re-settlement – issues relevant to architecture and a sense of place.

Reborn, Christian Bernhard Nawo tumbles from the pages of the *Hamburg Passenger List*, a thin volume in the Family History section of the State Library of Queensland.

Gasping a first breath – acclimatising to surroundings that no longer sway with the seas – Christian picks himself up from an expanse of carpet and wipes the sea-spray from his face. A moment ago, at 2.45pm on Friday the 23rd of August 1894, he had been staggering along the deck of the passenger ship *Adele*, looking out across choppy grey ocean. The vessel was on the final leg of its journey from Hamburg to Melbourne, via Port Adelaide, assisted by the Roaring Forties. Christian was travelling with his brother, Amandus Heinrich, to a new home in a new land.

Twenty five years old, tall, with blonde hair and blue eyes, Christian was happy to escape the pomposity of the new German Empire. There, he felt misplaced. He shuddered at the thought of where that fervour might lead the united country. Just weeks before they left Berlin, Christian and Amandus had witnessed the opening of the Reichstag, a temple to German nationalistic imperialism. The Neo-Baroque building with its monumental dome and ornate statuary simultaneously oppressed and impressed him. Christian had bought a postcard of the Reichstag – it was in his cabin propped up beside his bunk. He had sketched several details of the building in his journal. They lay alongside his other sketches – a collection of memories to be carried forth from the old world to the new.

Amandus and Christian were searching for a life of peace and rural tranquility. Both apiarists, they yearned for a land where native red gum trees produced aromatic honey collected by exotic bee species. Amandus had read about the *Megachile pluto*, the world's largest bee, discovered by the naturalist, Alfred Russell Wallace, on Indonesia's island of Bacan. Now he dreamed of discovering his own bee species and producing extraordinary honey and mead.

For the moment, however, ferocious waves and howling winds are replaced by the buzz of mechanical air. Around him, studious folk sit in rows, at benches, poring over books. Used to the glare of the sun and the vast

tumultuous ocean, it seems dark and strange to be inside. The studious ones stare at shiny windows. Wordless, transfixed, they play with buttons, but no music emerges. A mute harpsichord? Books surrounding him on shelves give a monastic feel. The reverential atmosphere is lit by magical flames on the ceiling and desks, unflickering candles – silence, mystical lights. This is a very strange place. Could it be a monastery?

By way of greeting, Christian tips his hat to a beardless youth. 'Guten tag', he mutters. The man smiles nervously before looking away. 'Guten tag', he nods to a second person, dressed in tight breeches but looking strangely female-like with breasts and hips. A third person glares disapprovingly. They seem unfriendly.

Walking to one of the shelves, Christian sees a thin bound volume with 'Shostakovich' on the spine. The rest of the text he does not understand - he examines the music inside, filled with crazy notation. This is not music to his ear. 'Amadeus Mozart' stands next to it. He fingers the musical score. Ah yes, a fine composer – this is music to play on his violin. But what is this sacred place with its accumulation of knowledge? Do they compose music in this deafening silence?

He looks towards the windows, the dazzling sunlight outside. In the distance is a meandering river and the tall, crystal glass walls of buildings that rise higher than any cathedral spire he has seen. The ground seems to drop away for miles, a mix of burnt golden grass, unfamiliar, thin-leafed trees and paving. He has a strong urge to move outside, to smell the air. Despite these vast panes of glass there appear to be no open windows.

Turning around, the apiarist is shocked to see a long, clear, moving wall slide open. A tall gentleman walks into this vast chamber. What madness is this? He needs to escape. As he approaches the sheer wall, the closed gap opens again. This could be his door of opportunity, and he charges through the wall only to find himself on a deck, like the bow of a ship. But the deck travels around an internal space. He is confused, is it possible to ever find his way to the outside? People sit as though familiar with the place, talking quietly, laughing, muttering as they gaze, smiling at those shiny screens.

As he looks upwards, his keen eye and ear are drawn to something in the heavens – is it on the ceiling, or the roof, he wonders? Purposefully he climbs the stairs to take a closer look. Rooms jut out into the courtyard as he ascends, climbing and weaving his way towards what he instinctively knows to be bees hiding in a nest, humming their beautiful music. Hundreds of giant metallic flowers suspend from the ceiling, planted in a number "eight" formation. As he moves closer to inspect the flowers, he recognises them – poppies. His eye is caught by the golden glow from a room where leaves fall like magic from the sky. What is Black Opium? Christian does not understand.

But, there, hiding amid the poppies… giant bees, long, glossy and metallic: the yellow and black carpenter bee, *Xylocopa*. He recognises them from his encyclopaedia of apiculture. He longs to take the bees back on board *Adele*, to show his brother. They have so much work to do to establish and settle their bee collection – new hives, queen and her drones, all settling into their new home.

He is intrigued by the strange building he is exploring, with its glass walls and layers of balconies looking into the courtyard. Christian wants to move outside, be back on board *Adele*, but he wants to takes this new bee and drones with him.

Christian reaches into his pocket and pulls out his veil to cover his face. He always travels with it. Covered and secure, he expertly scoops up the queen bee and larvae from within the poppy. If he takes the queen, the others will follow. He cups the queen in the palms of his hands and prays. He must find his brother.

Slowly and carefully he travels out into the intense sunlight. Swarming behind him the bee colony trails. Christian heads towards the river and like the Pied Piper, the worker bees follow their fertile queen. He will take his new colony back to his brother on board the *Adele*. To their cabin, and the bees that have accompanied them from Germany, protected in a wire covered hive. The river, he hopes, should lead him back. He will walk along the banks and catch a lift on one of the vessels gliding along. How long will the drones follow their queen? He is in a strange land and there is much to learn. He steps into a small boat and starts to row, searching for Amandus and the *Adele,* nearing the end of the journey from Hamburg.

Fantasy Island: Suburban dreams on the Isle of Capri

VIRGINIA RIGNEY AND ALEX CHOMICZ

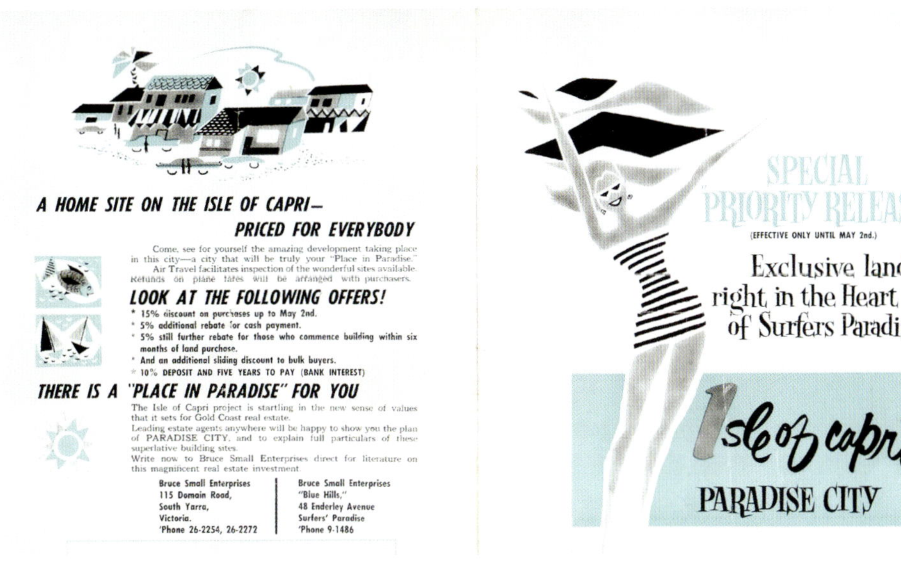

Isle of Capri promotional brochure, c. 1960. Bruce Small Enterprises. Photograph courtesy Gold Coast City Council Local Studies Library.

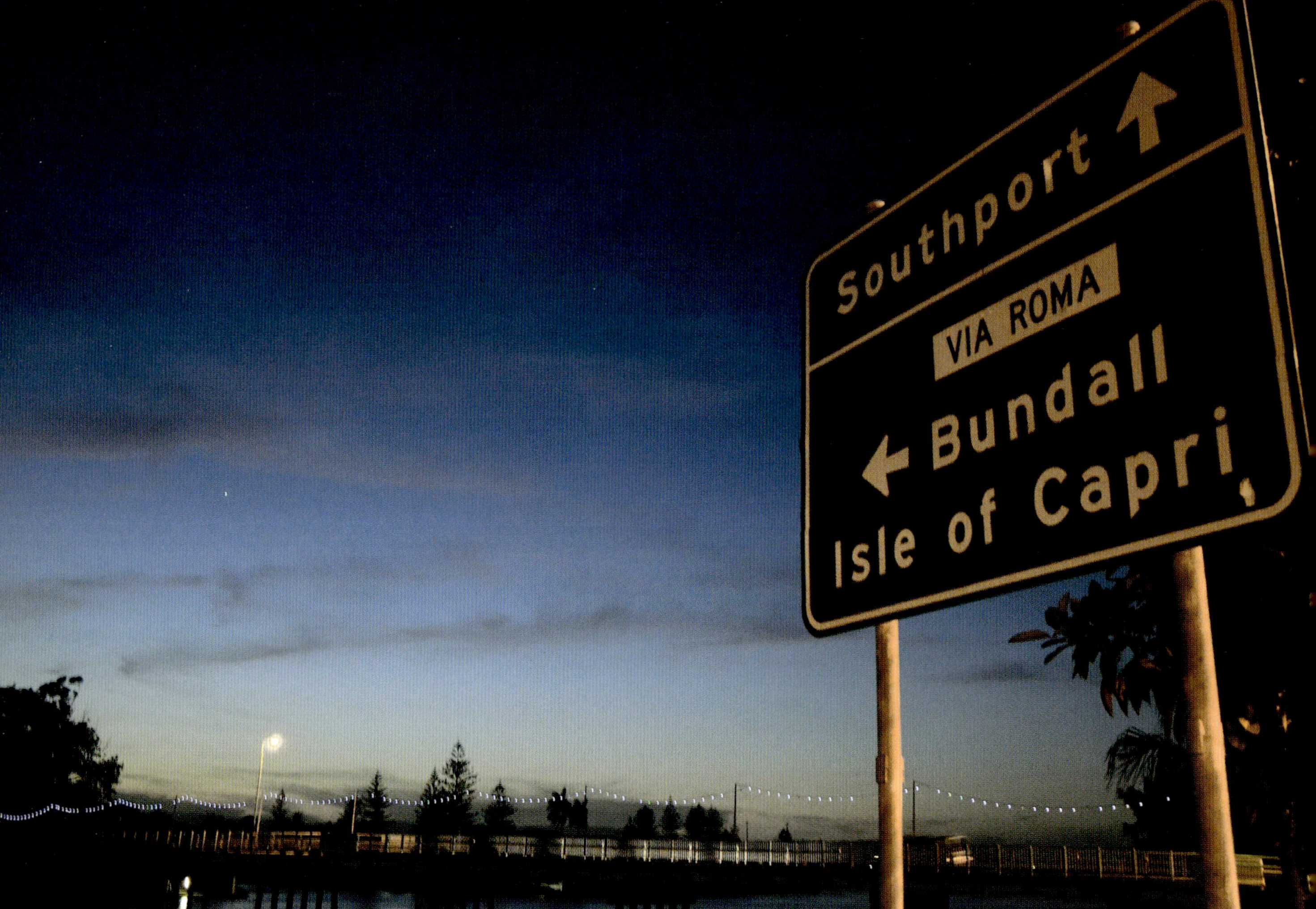

Isle of Capri Bridge, Via Roma, 2011.
Photograph Alex Chomicz

A gently arching bridge over an expanse of water gives architectural form to an idea of transformation. Coloured lights, strung in swags across the length of the bridge, change their tone almost imperceptibly from purple to blue, to pink and citrine. Their soft glow at night is the immediate clue that this bridge signals the entry to a place outside the ordinary. Of course the Road Transport Authority directional signage – turn left, Isle of Capri – might startle the visitor into wondering whether by some teasing fault of their satellite navigation system, they have been transported to the famed Isola Di Capri just off the Italian Amalfi Coast. But this is the Gold Coast, in Queensland, in Australia.

The Isle of Capri, Surfers Paradise, is the urban invention of Sir Bruce Small. It is a little-known canal estate defined by the sweeping curve of the Nerang River, sitting just across the water from the concentrated precinct of high-rise towers that make up the signature image of the Gold Coast.

If our driver makes that turn onto the island, along the Via Roma, they might recognise that they have come ashore to an island suburb that can be regarded as the embodiment of 1960s aspirational Australian living in the architectural details of street names, house design and urban layout.

Sir Bruce Private Estate, Naples Avenue, Isle of Capri, 2011. Photograph Alex Chomicz

Sir Bruce was himself a man accustomed to reinvention. He had begun business life with a bicycle shop and his flair for promotion was sharpened as sponsor and manager travelling with the legendary Australian road cyclist, Hubert Opperman, who wowed cycle-mad French audiences in the late 1920s with his long distance prowess. Small's real wealth expanded from the Malvern Star trade name and his diversification into electronics retail in the immediate post-war period.

Sir Bruce moved his major business interests to the Gold Coast in 1960, sensing the opportunities in Surfers Paradise, as described by architect and critic Robin Boyd in 1957.

There is a feeling, rare enough in Australia, of adventure and enterprise... a feeling that Australia's heavy shroud of conservatism is here burst open, providing an outlet for the type of entrepreneur who is stifled by the plodding restrictive ways of southern cities'

Sir Bruce inherited the name of the estate from Efim Zola, the developer who originally consolidated the land, but he embraced the Italianate pleasure isle concept with characteristic enthusiasm, confidently naming the bare streets of his unbuilt paradise with a lexicon of allure: Amalfi Drive, The Promenade, The Corso, The Lido, La Scala Court, Verona Avenue, Margarita Place, Castile Circuit.

He built his own low-set modern home on a private island at the end of Naples Avenue. A little bridge, flanked by imposing bulbous street lamps, marks the entry to this inner-sanctum of his suburban imagining.

The audacity of such wholehearted romantic appropriation of place names from the other side of the world, from an era loaded with historical associations, now seems faintly absurd. But where other towns might name their streets after scarcely notable local worthies, this was a city yet to be made, so anything was possible.

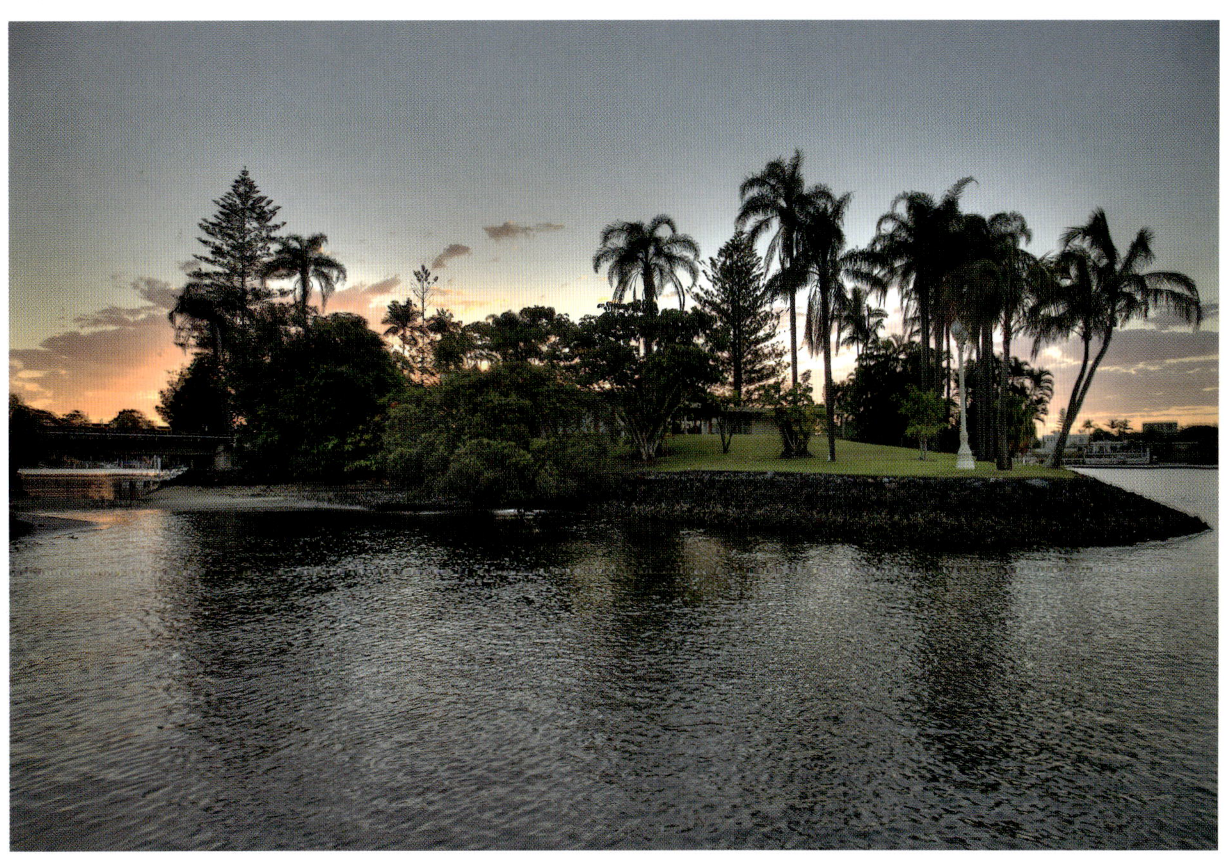

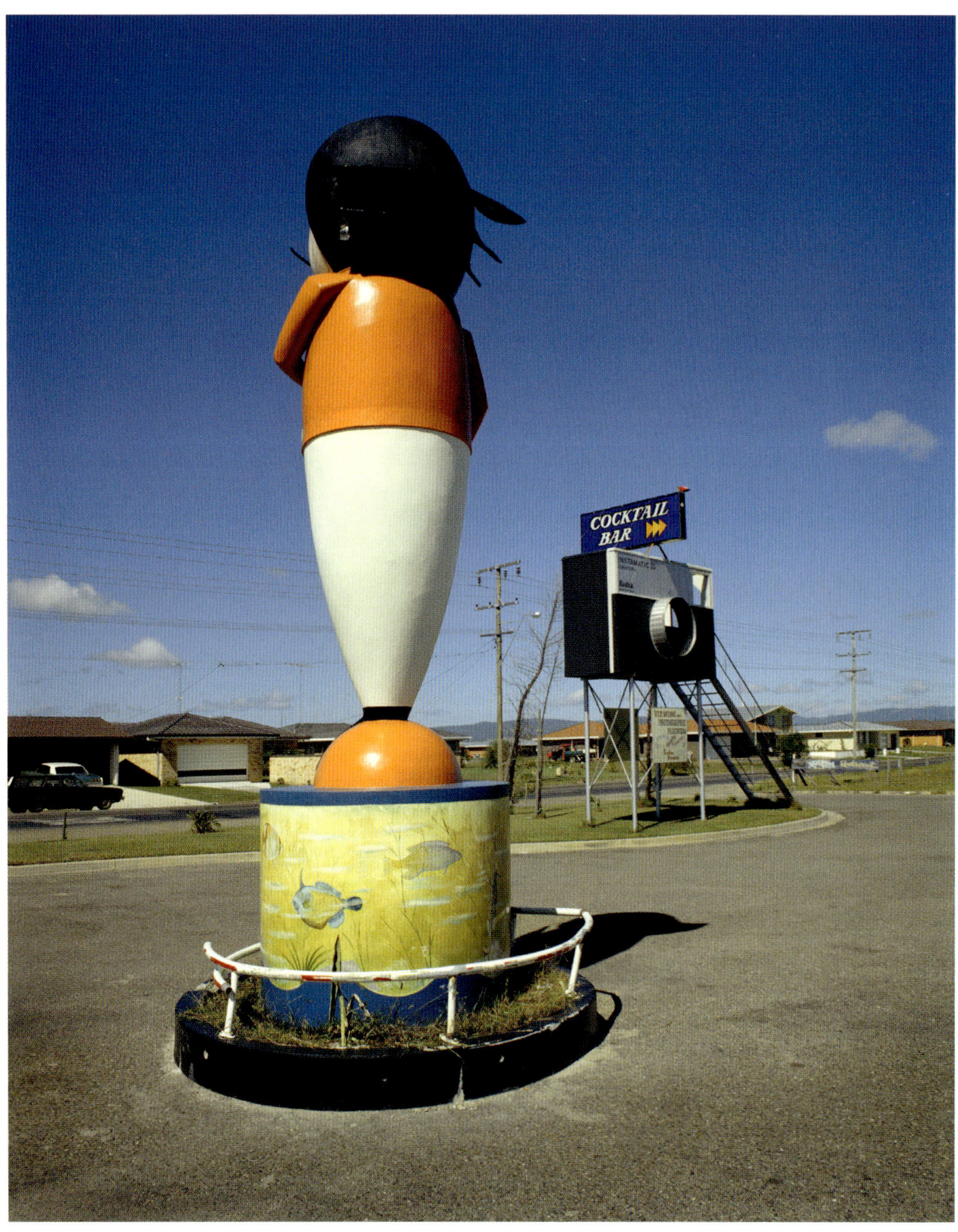
COCKTAIL
BAR
INSTAMATIC
Kodak

Sign for Revolving Aquarium Restaurant, Salerno Street, Isle of Capri, 1973. Photograph John Gollings

Up from Melbourne on Gold Coast family holidays in the 1960s, the photographer John Gollings recalls his father's interest in seeing the progress of Small's developing canal estate. He took the family across the bridge to see the houses that were beginning to dot the streets.

A few years later, close to finishing architectural studies at Melbourne University and prompted by the just-published Learning from Las Vegas, which was to become a seminal architectural text, Gollings came to Surfers Paradise with fellow students to make their own investigations of the signage and urban forms of the Strip City.

They found the friendly fish sign welcoming guests to the improbable Revolving Aquarium Restaurant. Cannily, the sign itself doubled as

an attraction, with the adjacent photo viewing platform allowing the tourist to gain an elevated vantage point to look back north over the prestige streets of the Promenade and the Lido towards a view of burgeoning high-rises, and to capture this unfolding spectacle in a photograph of their own.

The restaurant is now an Anglican church. It does not revolve.

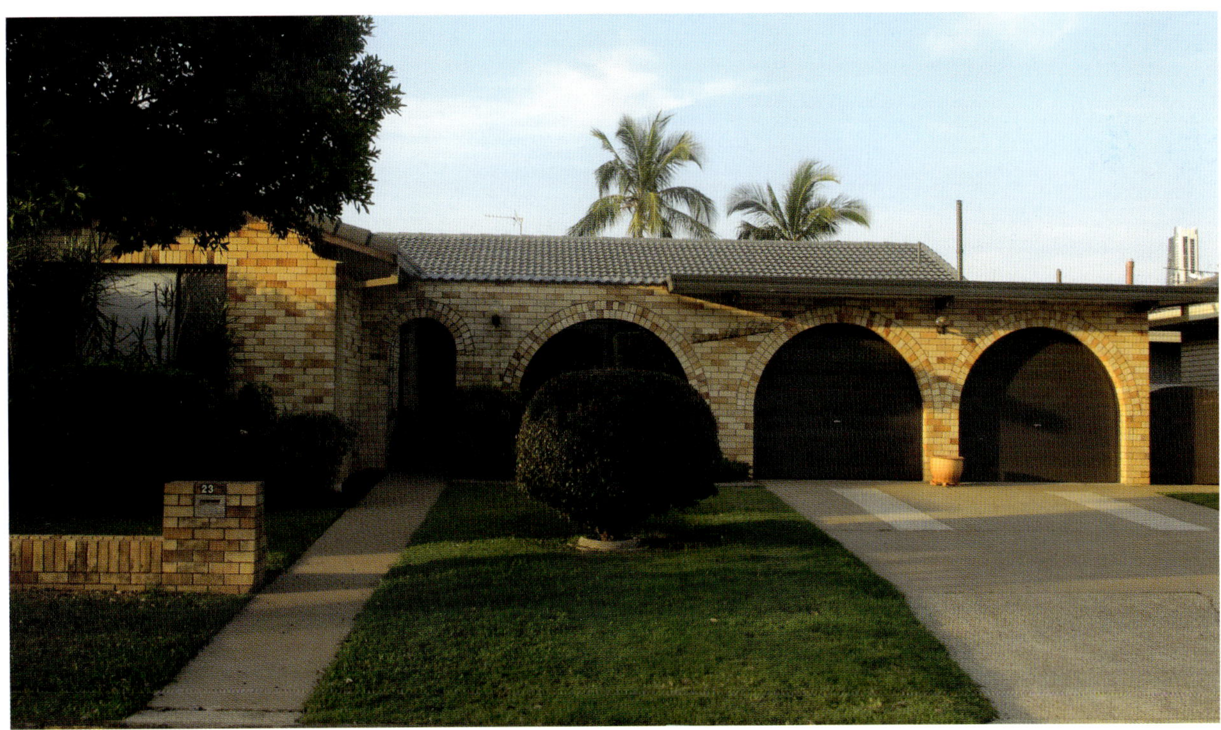

Villa Roma, Isle of Capri, 2011. Photograph Virginia Rigney

Private homebuilders embraced Small's vision of suburban exotica, and built homes detailed with a mélange of Spanish hacienda archways, Italianate statuary, and gardens with formal French topiary. Decorative metal grills and block work are common features, asserting security and

privacy, but also giving a sense of architectural permeability and a tantalising glimpse into an entry courtyard or to the water beyond.

The traditional Australian suburban backyard on its quarter acre block is something of a private ambling indeterminate space, with hills hoist, shed and perhaps a vegetable patch forming a triumvirate of utilitarian features. On the Isle of

Capri however, the backyard was also the front of the house, for your neighbour across the water or passing boat traffic, treating this as your public view.

The water frontage needed a jetty, tiered gardens, perhaps a pool and what has now become ubiquitous in Australian living – the outdoor entertainment area, perfect for sunset cocktails.

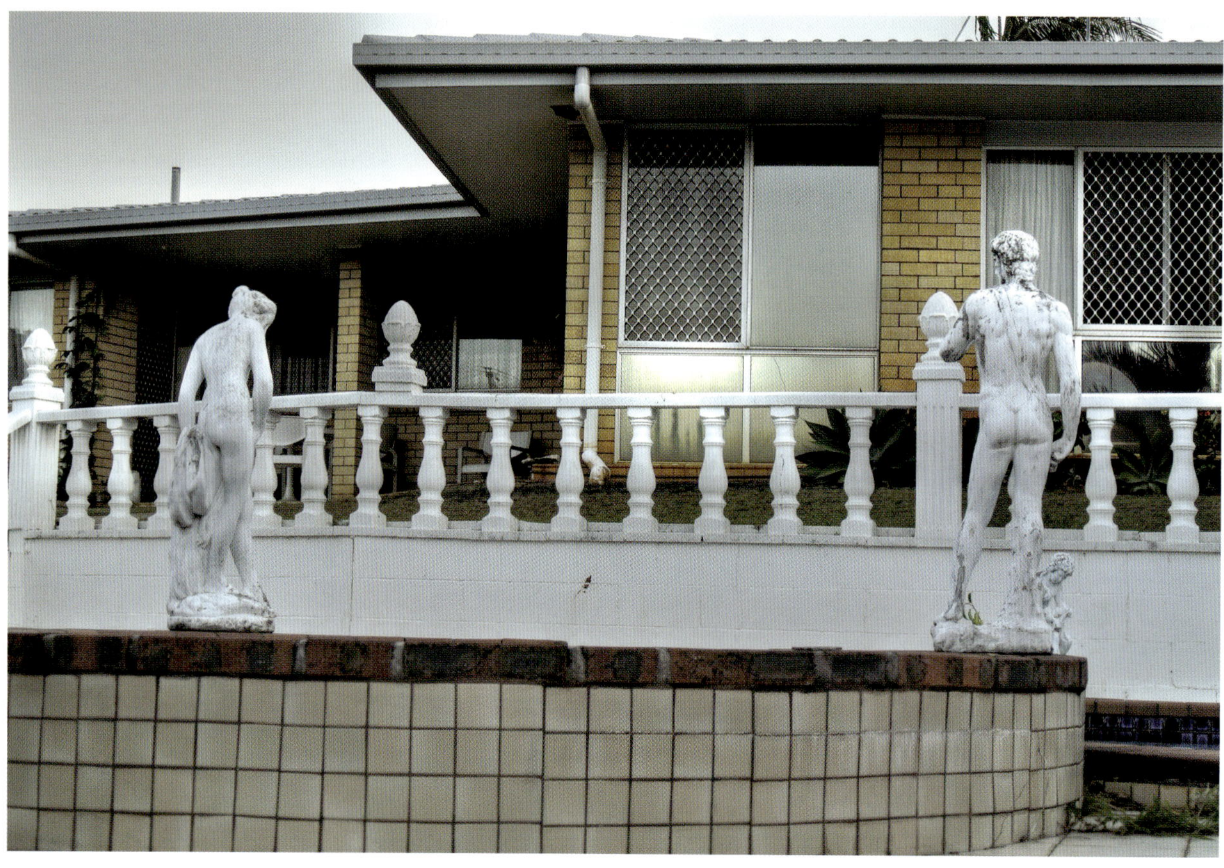

David and Diana, private residence, Rapallo Avenue,
Isle of Capri, 2011. Photograph Alex Chomicz

David and Diana are a couple joined forever in style
despite their age difference. Here in their canal-side
incarnation on Rapallo Avenue, they gaze across the
pool in frozen longing for better days.

The cycles of Gold Coast property booms and busts
have left their marks through the streets. Quite
a few houses remain with original owners tenderly
maintaining their blocks, for others the illusion
has worn away.

Many more have been renovated or rebuilt; the
suburb now a varied patchwork of styles – stately
Tuscan, Bali resort and, more recently, sharp-lined
shimmering glass structures.

Capri on Via Roma construction site, 2011. Photograph Virginia Rigney

Five years ago my family came to live on this Island. Explaining the new address to incredulous friends from outside of the Gold Coast initially carried a slight twinge of embarrassment, at the thought that we too were participants in Small's unabashed European nostalgia.

I might have come much earlier, when my own father, visiting Queensland for a conference in the mid-1970s decided that this was the place for us. Schools were sourced and property values checked, but after consulting with his bank about relocating his business he was roundly discouraged, and so we remained landlocked in Canberra.

In the 50 years since the bridge over the Via Roma was opened, new residents weigh up the vocabulary of real estate agents, who describe properties as wet or dry, north to water, wide water, Main River, renovator or prestige. Large block sizes and close proximity to the beach, as well as tight restrictions on height and subdivision, are the undoubted attractions for families today. Despite the current nervous economic climate, the local shopping centre is currently undergoing redevelopment. Branded Capri on Via Roma, it will preserve Small's vision of having a jetty to enable shoppers to pull up in a boat, tie up and do their shopping.

The Isle of Capri remains a testament to our enduring willingness to suspend disbelief, to imagine another time and place but to live in the present. Just up the road in the burgeoning growth corridor of the northern Gold Coast, a vast new suburban estate is currently in the planning stages. Gainsbourgh Green will soon welcome its first residents, this time imagining England's green and pleasant land.

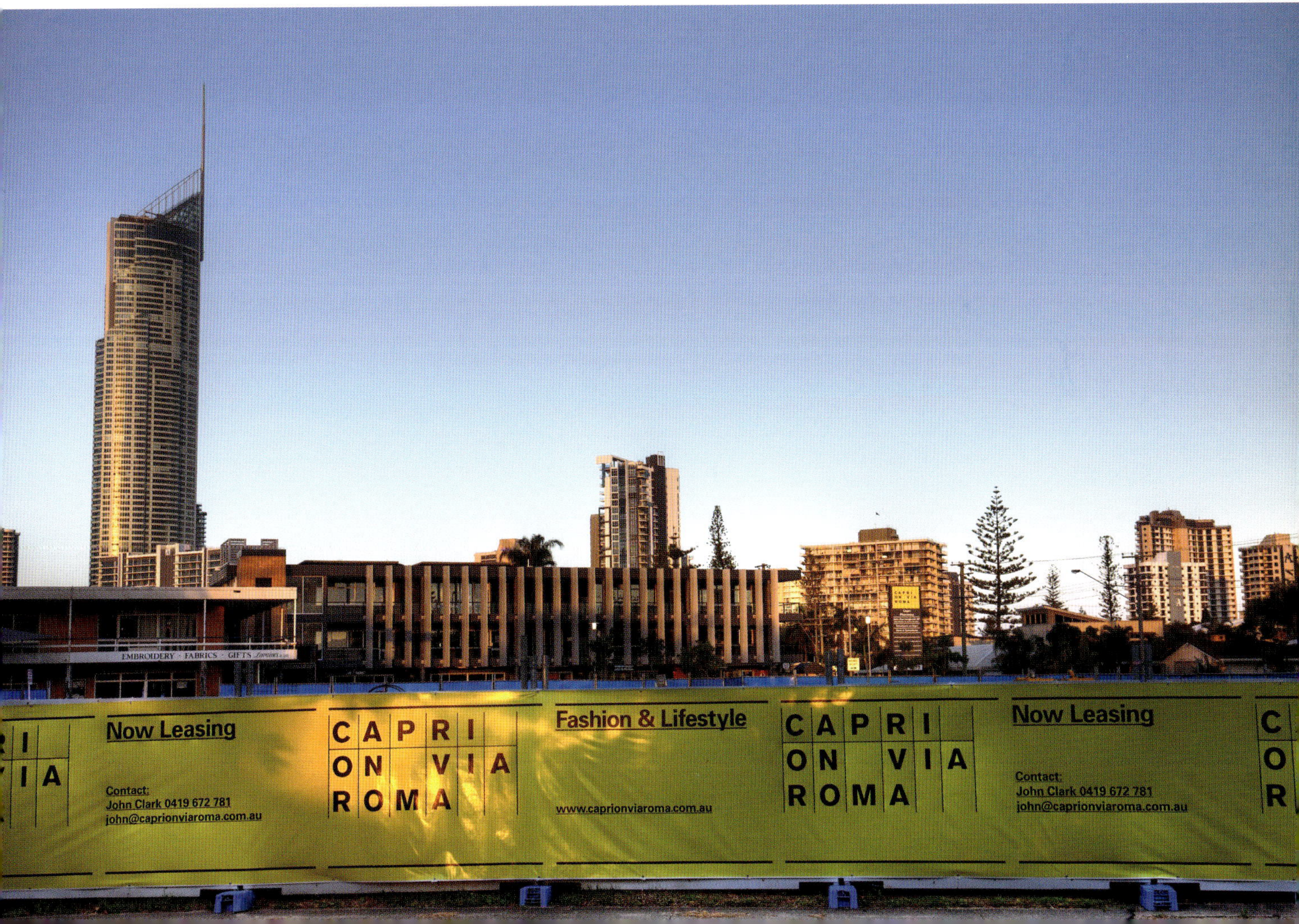

Isle of Capri promotional brochure.
Bruce Small Enterprises. Photograph
courtesy Gold Coast City Council
Local Studies Library.

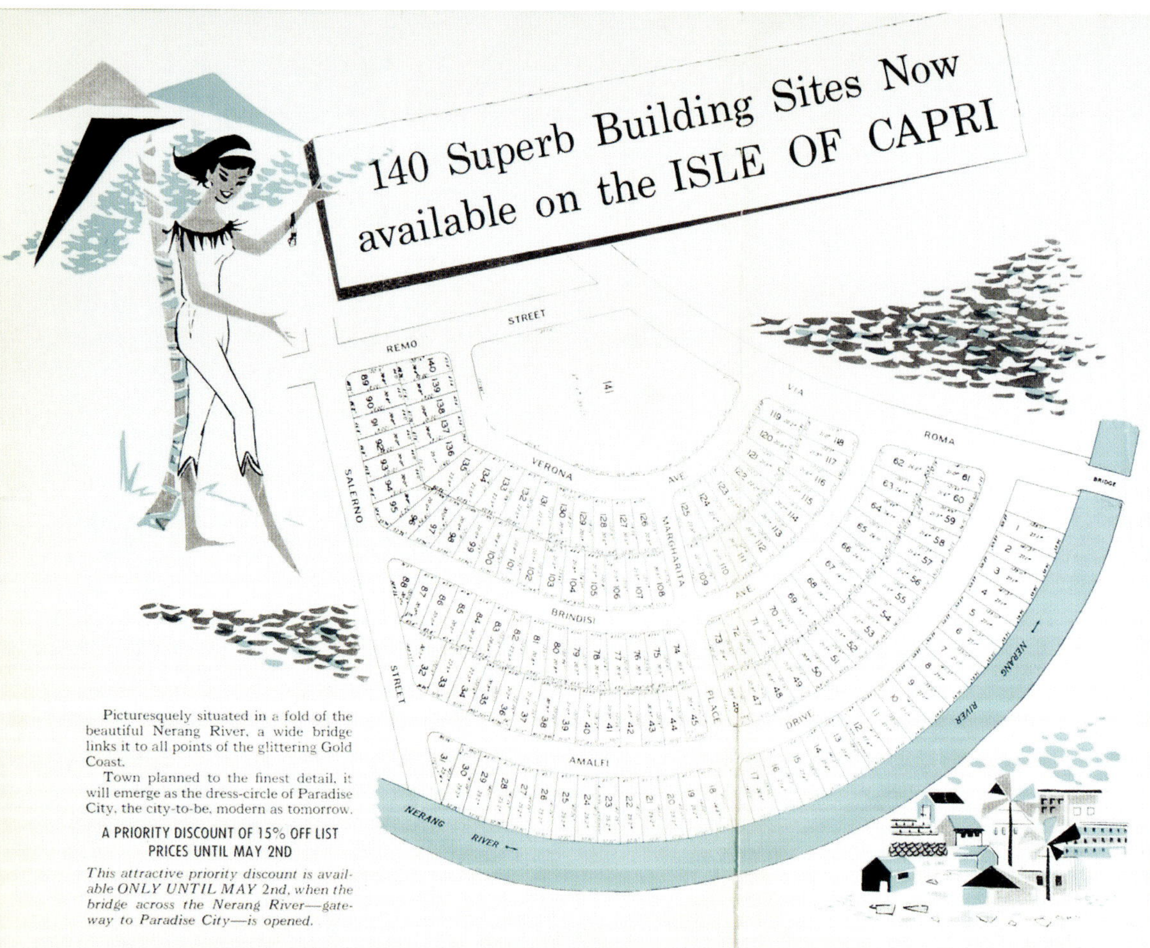

Picturesquely situated in a fold of the beautiful Nerang River, a wide bridge links it to all points of the glittering Gold Coast.

Town planned to the finest detail, it will emerge as the dress-circle of Paradise City, the city-to-be, modern as tomorrow.

A PRIORITY DISCOUNT OF 15% OFF LIST PRICES UNTIL MAY 2ND

This attractive priority discount is available ONLY UNTIL MAY 2nd, when the bridge across the Nerang River—gateway to Paradise City—is opened.

ISLE OF CAPRI In Paradise City

Each of the 140 lots in this release is kerbed and channelled. Concrete footpaths and wide sealed roads are already constructed, water and electricity are being laid to every block and will involve the home builder in no additional expense. Each lot has been raised well above record flood level, and top-dressed with an abundance of rich, loamy soil.

ALL river frontage blocks have a gently grassed slope that runs down to the sun-spun reaches of the Nerang River . . . there is no erosion (Isle of Capri is protected from this because it is situated INSIDE the curve of the river), no sharp drop to the water.

The wide, tree-lined avenues and profusion of tropical shrubs, plus all other amenities, qualify Isle of Capri, Paradise City, as offering the highest standard of city planning found anywhere in Australia.

The Isle of Capri is the lovely front garden of Paradise City . . . Three others — Cannes, Sorrento and Riviera — have been planned to make Paradise City Australia's newest and most exciting creation.

Bridges - commercial centres with supermarkets - religious centres - generous free parking areas - spacious parks and sports grounds with concrete-bedded swimming pools - kiosk and many other amenities have been planned to harmonize with the overall design rhythm of the island. Many of the planned buildings front a wide, tree-rimmed square.

Paradise City offers the home-builder all the luxuries of a modern city, yet provides superb relaxation too, right in the centre of the renowned Surfers' Paradise area.

Unfixed Collage

GEORGINA RUSSELL

The unfixed collage provides a space where words and images combine in an attempt to capture the layers of memories alive in this place.

The pieces of paper are pieces of memory, strung together by one common element, the place they inhabit. These memory fragments overlap, converge, change and merge within the visible or invisible confines of this place, each one capturing a few precious seconds in history.

Memory is unreliable. Words and pictures rearrange and transfigure our memories, and places that now cease to exist in the physical world only do so within these thoughts, so vulnerable to modification. The simple act of writing down such a memory, or speaking it, inevitably transforms it from how it existed in its imaginary state within the mind.

Each time the pieces of the collage are arranged, while they resemble what has been before, it remains impossible to replicate exactly. Pieces may temporarily be misplaced or lost altogether, or fade so that the text printed upon the paper can no longer be read, or understood. Each person will arrange the pieces slightly differently, and draw different meaning from the words that string together to form these fragments of remembered or imagined thought.

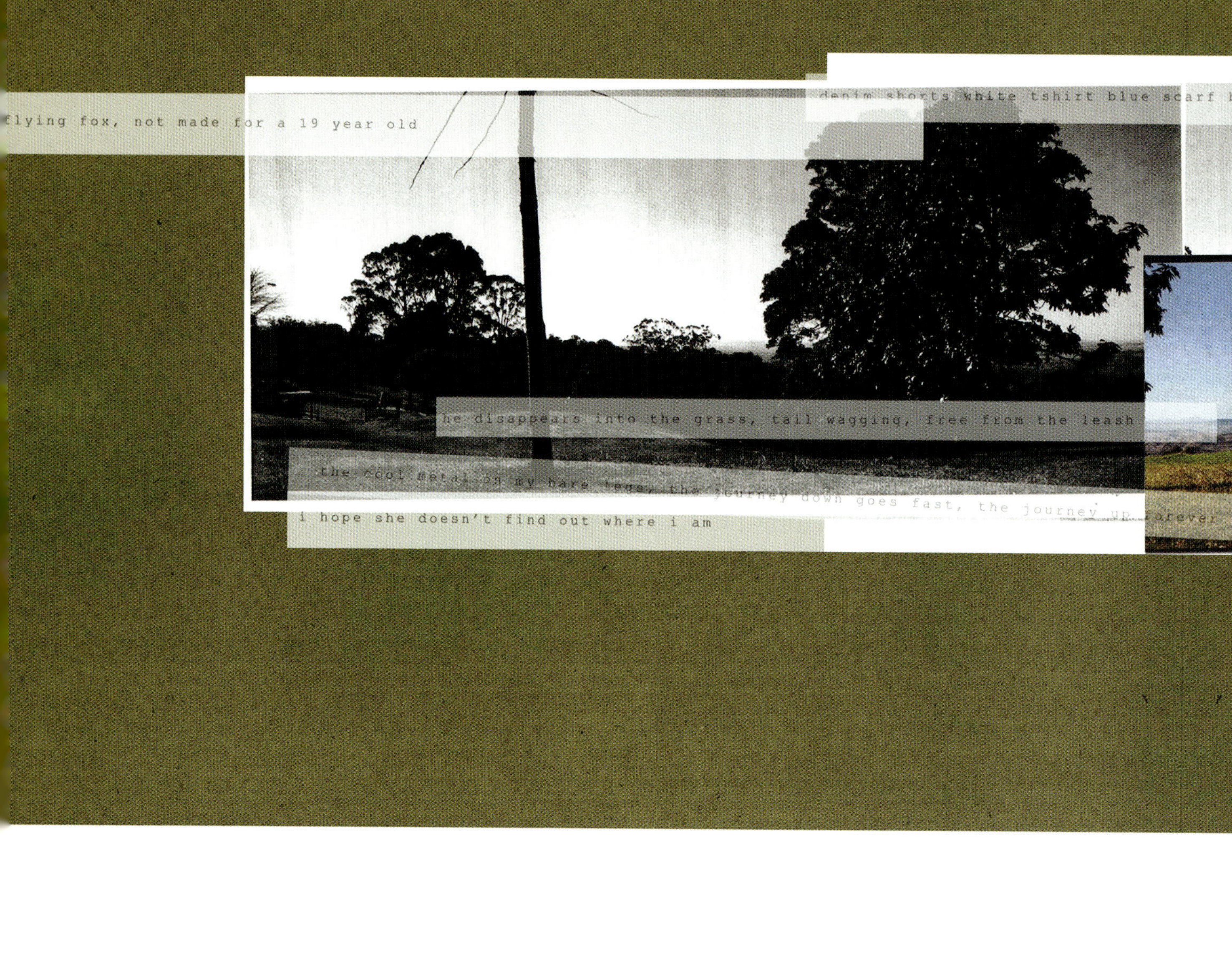
flying fox, not made for a 19 year old
denim shorts white tshirt blue scarf
he disappears into the grass, tail wagging, free from the leash
the cool metal on my bare legs, the journey down goes fast, the journey up forever
i hope she doesn't find out where i am

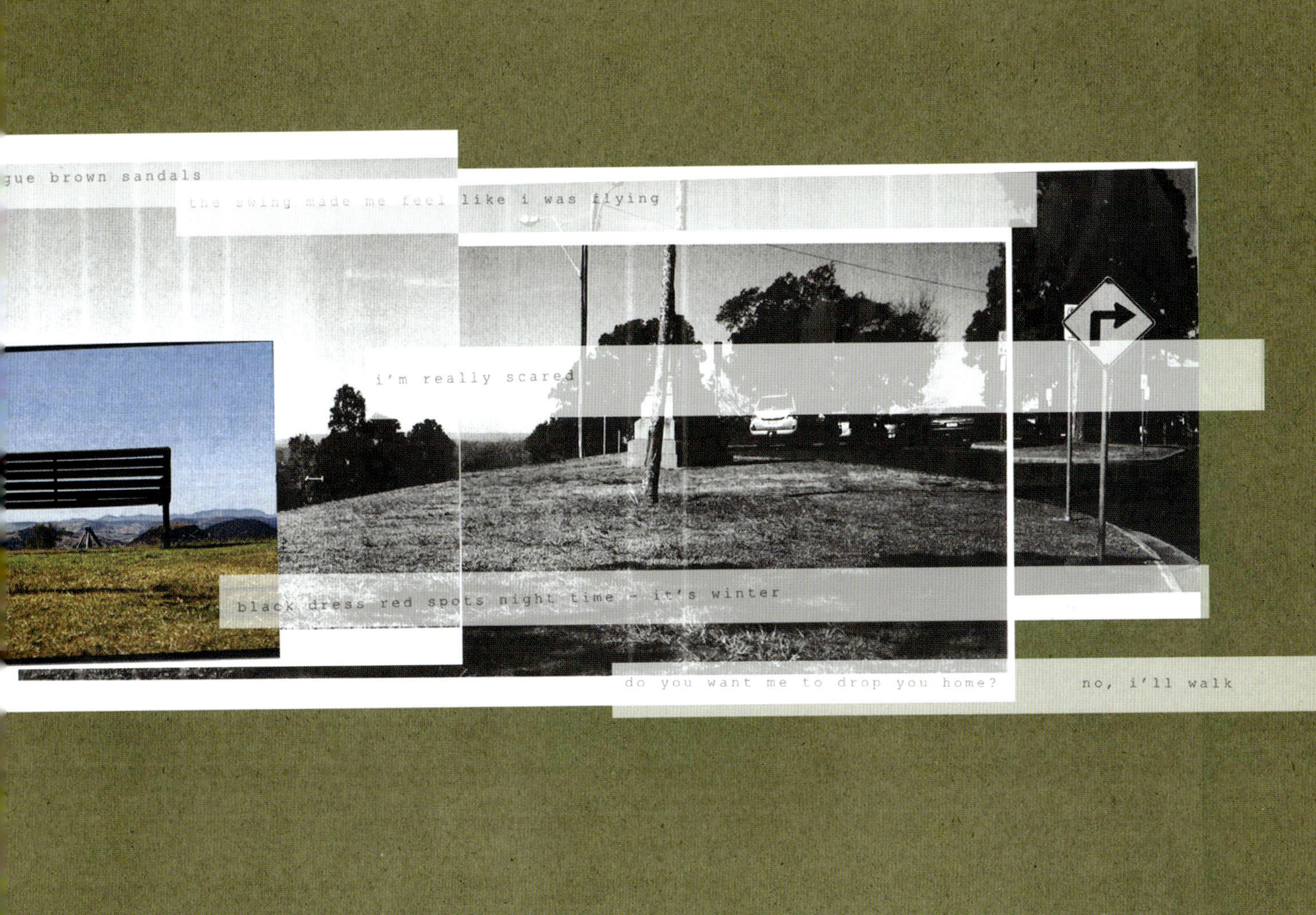

The park bench, with its flaking paint and solid frame so resoundingly attached to its concrete base, anchors so many pieces of thought, discussion and event around it. You are completely exposed on the park bench, yet feel a sense of calm, of safety. The anonymity of the bench inspires honesty, confession and revelation.

Memories from this place do not all belong to me. Some are single lines, or words, of conversation snatched from a conversation as I have wandered by, as I'm sure that fragments of my words and thought exist in another's unfixed collage of memory.

The Effects of Time

SUSAN ROTHNIE

To and from school, we used to walk around this park. Huge trees lined its perimeter, sweeping the ground. In the gloomy space beneath, their seeds caked the footpath in soft granular mush. Rotting, it stuck to our shoes. The park's grassy expanse swept steeply downwards. The only path across was out of bounds for girls. The public toilets were full of perverts. Occasionally a drunk would stagger into view. When we were older, we braved the old bitumen path in noisy groups, edging along the shadowy depths. It was a shortcut.

Of course that was ages ago. Now the old railway yards at the bottom have been reclaimed and the park is much bigger. The transformation can be seen from the Lookout, where the city appears modern and glamorous through the trees. A new suspension bridge soars out from there through the canopy before it spirals down into the rainforest below. Cool and dank. Tree ferns and tropical vines. A gushing stream. Mist jets deliver mist and bird song emanates from a metal post.

The old path remains, but paved. To each side, the sweeping lawns resolve in carefully crafted sites. Each one with a purpose and name, stands ready for an occasion – especially a wedding, when clouds of tulle teeter on heels and puncture the grass. No place is more documented.

The celebration lawn is huge. For clapping, swaying, stamping events. Music and feet. Painted faces. Smells: spiced, wrapped, baked. Flattened grass, crushed cups, never enough bins.

And ceremonies. At the entrance to the park a memorial has been constructed to wars fought in other places. Like an outdoor lounge room, it is flat and furnished with monuments to approved conflicts and shiny buckles and buttons and boots and the boom of cannons. Jets cut the sky.

On Sundays, picnic blankets are tucked into nooks and crannies. Stroll amongst the flowers. In the 'spectacle garden' nothing dies. Fresh plants in full blossom appear miraculously overnight, sitting pot-shaped in grids of bright colour. What a show!

At the end of any day it's quiet. The noise of trains and traffic swirls distantly around. In trees above watery expanses, birds jostle into position. Sometimes there are hijinks under the spotlights on the lawn. Maybe in the future this garden will open its green fingers and reclaim this whole city...

CONTRIBUTOR BIOGRAPHIES

MATHEW AITCHISON is research fellow and manager of the ATCH research centre at the University of Queensland's School of Architecture. He is editor of *Visual Planning and the Picturesque* (Getty Publications, 2010), and is currently working towards publishing a comprehensive monograph of the Townscape movement. He has worked as an architect and teacher internationally.

JOAN BEDDOE was educated at Melbourne University and her teaching career included primary, secondary and special education in three states. Since 1998 she has coordinated community writing groups and indulged her passion for heritage public buildings with photographic displays, presentations at conferences and published articles. She is the originator of the website www.pillarsofanation.com.au.

PETER BENNETTS is an architectural photographer based in Melbourne who works around the world. For more than 20 years Bennetts's work has regularly appeared in internationally acclaimed publications and he has photographed for numerous books, including four monographs. In addition to architectural photography Bennetts delves into environmental concerns; his book *Time and Tide: the islands of Tuvalu* (published by Lonely Planet) documents the country most vulnerable to rising sea levels induced by climate change. Back on dry land the award-winning Bennetts photographs the vanguard of architecture and design.

ANDREW BLYTHE is a freelance writer and current editor of *Queensland Pride*. He has previously won a National Trust award for heritage education and has experience in heritage conservation and promotion. His thesis on the recent history of Ipswich retailing was published last year. He has recently begun teaching life writing to people in mental health wards and is researching the role that storytelling and environment have on promoting health and wellness in institutional settings.

BRETT BOARDMAN is a commercial photographer specialising in architecture, design and industry. Brett works throughout Australia, Asia, Europe, and his images appear in architecture and design journals globally. He holds a degree in architecture from the University of Sydney and has been awarded Australian Professional Photographer of the Year.

SALLY BREEN is lecturer in writing and publishing at Griffith University and fiction editor of Wet Ink the Magazine for New Writing. She was associate editor of the Griffith REVIEW from 2006-2008. Her fiction and non-fiction work have appeared in a variety of publications and collections including *Best Australian Stories 2007* and *The Australian*. In 2011 her memoir, *The Casuals* was published by Harper Collins who will release her novel *Ante Up* in September 2012.

ELIZABETH WATSON BROWN is an award-winning architect who has practiced for more than 30 years and is recognised for high quality residential, institutional, educational and community architecture. Her work has been published and exhibited widely. She is an active participant in architectural and urban design discourse in many roles, including currently as a member of the Queensland Board for Urban Places and as Adjunct Professor of Architecture at the University of Queensland. Elizabeth is a Life Fellow of the Australian Institute of Architects and has been Queensland State Awards Director and National Awards Juror.

LINDA CARROLI is an award-winning writer and consultant. She works on interdisciplinary projects in urban, regional, cultural and social planning. She works with Harbinger Consultants (http://harbingerconsultants.wordpress.com) and publishes several blog projects including *PlaceBlog* and *Changescaping*, as part of the Placing Project, and Enabling Suburbs. lindacarroli@hotmail.com

ALEX CHOMICZ is the son of a builder who grew up following his father's footsteps on the Gold Coast, then made a sudden U-turn to experimental films which led to studies at the AFTRS and an array of award-winning short film drama projects which have screened internationally and on SBS and ABC TV. He also works in Architectural photography, art photography and video art, with a large-scale work recently commissioned for the scoreboard at Metricon Stadium Gold Coast. Alex and Virginia Rigney have previously collaborated on two short films about artists – *Michael Zavros – the Good Son* and *Ian Smith On the Road* which was nominated for Best Queensland Short Film at the 2010 BIFF Awards.

JUSTINE CLARK is an independent architectural editor, writer, researcher and critic. She was the editor of *Architecture Australia*, the national magazine of the

Australian Institute of Architects from 2003 to March 2011. Justine is regularly invited to speak on architectural matters and to serve on juries for prizes and competitions, both nationally and internationally. She has designed and curated architectural exhibitions and published various books and book chapters. She has a BArch (hons) from the University of Auckland and a MArch by research thesis from Victoria University of Wellington.

CHRISTINE DAUBER is a Brisbane-based art historian. Her articles have been published both in Australia and internationally. Her PhD thesis, 'Highjacked Agenda: The National Museum of Australia and the Gallery of the First Australians' (2007), examines concepts of the national in Australian cultural life.

STEPHEN FRITH is Professor of Architecture at the University of Canberra, Australia. He is a registered architect, and taught at Columbia University, New York, in the early 1980s. After completing a PhD at Cambridge, UK, he taught at UNSW, and for 2008-9 was President of the Association of Architecture Schools of Australasia (AASA). stephen.frith@canberra.edu.au

JILL GARNER co-founded Garner Davis Architects after an apprenticeship with several of Melbourne's influential design practices. Garner Davis Architects is a St Kilda-based studio with a highly considered lineage of built works. Jill's appointment as Associate Victorian Government Architect in 2010 formalised her commitment to being a visible architectural advocate for the importance of design in the built environment.

ERIK GHENOIU is Adjunct Associate Professor at Pratt Institute in Brooklyn and holds a PhD in architecture from Harvard University. He writes on German design culture around 1910, on the history of picturesque and visual urbanism, and on current issues in design theory and practice. He is principal organiser of *tarp*, the Pratt architecture journal.

DEIRDRE GILFEDDER is senior lecturer at the University of Paris Dauphine. She has published in Australia, France, the UK, the USA and Italy mostly in the area of Australian studies. She researches and writes about memory and culture; World War I memorials in Australia, the stolen generation narratives, Australian cinema and literature, as well as questions of branding in our culture. She is interested in the link between visual culture and citizenship, in memory and forgetting and other things such as the history of consumption and economic themes in literature. She lives in Paris, France.

PHILIP GOAD is Chair of Architecture and Director of the Melbourne School of Design at the University of Melbourne. He writes on Australian architecture as an architectural historian and as a design critic. With Julie Willis, he was co-editor of *The Encyclopedia of Australian Architecture* (Cambridge University Press, 2011).

KATJA GRILLNER is an architect and critic based in Stockholm, Sweden. She is Professor of Critical Studies in Architecture at the KTH Royal Institute of Technology, School of Architecture, and Director of the Strong Research Environment Architecture in Effect, a collaboration between the four schools of architecture in Sweden. Her research on architecture and landscape combines theoretical, historical and literary strategies for spatial exploration. Among her book publications are her PhD dissertation Ramble, Linger and Gaze – Philosophical Dialogues in the Landscape Garden (Stockholm: KTH 2000), as principal editor 01-AKAD – Experimental Research in Architecture and Design (Stockholm: AxlBooks, 2005), and, as co-editor, Architecture and Authorship (London: Black Dog, 2007). She is co-founder of the feminist architecture teaching and research group FATALE. Katja Grillner was a keynote speaker at the conference *Writing Architecture: On Innovations in the Textual and Visual Critique of Buildings*, upon which this book is based.

LYNETTE GURR, Senior heritage consultant at NBRS+PARTNERS, has a background in architecture, heritage, fine arts, history and archaeology. She has extensive experience in heritage management and enjoys working on a diverse range of projects. While report writing forms part of her professional life, creative writing is a passion and escape.

JASON HAIGH is an architect who graduated from Queensland University of Technology. He is a principal of Brisbane-based practice Cloud Dwellers, undertaking residential and small public projects. Jason is a past winner of the RAIA Queensland Chapter's Architect's Art prize, and has recently written his first published article for *Australian Modern*.

JON HENZELL co-founded architectural photography practice Camera Obscura, with fellow architect and photographer David Hanson, upon completing his architecture degree in 2008. While based in Brisbane, Camera Obscura's commissions have taken them as far afield as Lockhart River, Mt Isa, Woorabinda, Isisford, Tambo and Noosa. Their work has been featured in various local and international publications. jon@cameraobscura.net.au

GAVIN HIPKINS is an Auckland-based artist who works with photography and film. He has exhibited widely in New Zealand and Australia and his works have been included in major curated exhibitions in North America and Europe. He represented New Zealand at the 1998 Sydney Biennale and the 2002 Sao Paulo Biennale. In 2011 his experimental short film *This Fine Island* premiered at Centre Pompidou, Paris. In 2012 his key early architectural works were included in the exhibition *Envisioning Buildings: Reflecting Architecture in Contemporary Art Photography,* Austrian Museum of Applied and Contemporary Art (MAK), Vienna. His work is included in major public collections including The Queensland Art Gallery; Museum of New Zealand Te Papa Tongarewa; and George Eastman Museum of Photography and Film, Rochester, New York. He is Senior Lecturer and Associate Head Research at Elam School of Fine Arts, The University of Auckland. Gavin Hipkins was a keynote speaker at the conference *Writing Architecture: On Innovations in the Textual and Visual Critique of Buildings,* upon which this book is based.

PAUL HOGBEN is a senior lecturer in architecture at the University of New South Wales. His research focuses on promotional politics and the discourse of architecture. This research has been published in *Architectural Theory Review, Interstices* and *Content 5: Skyplane* (UNSW Press, 2009). With Xing Ruan, he co-edited *Topophilia and Topophobia: Reflections on Twentieth-Century Human Habitat* (Routledge, 2007).

CLAIRE HUMPHREYS is currently supervising construction of her first designed and built project, in association with Kevin O'Brien Architects. She has also pursued a number of side projects in recent years including exhibition design, research trips, conference organisation, teaching, zine making, and (now) very very short film-making. In 2009, she graduated with a Master of Architecture from the University of Queensland, receiving a number of awards for her work.

OLIVIA HYDE is a senior practice director at BVN Architecture. She has taught design at Sydney University and UNSW, and is co-coordinator of the Urban Islands independent elective design studio. Olivia has worked in Europe, Asia and the United States where she held a teaching fellowship at the University of Michigan. She is an occasional contributor to *Architecture Australia.*

CHRISTOPHER FREDERICK JONES left England after University eighteen years ago and now lives with his wife Carla in Brisbane. He has been shooting architecture professionally for eight years and works for many of the leading architectural firms in Queensland. During this time he has won many awards for his work and is a regular contributor to architectural media throughout Australia and Europe.

AUDREY LAM was born in Hong Kong and lives in Brisbane. Her art practice spans film, animation and photography, and has been widely exhibited nationally and internationally. In 2008, she participated in an international workshop at Fondazione Ratti, led by artist and architect Yona Friedman.

JOHN MACARTHUR is Professor, Dean and Head of the School of Architecture at the University of Queensland, Australia, where he directs the research group ATCH (Architecture, theory, criticism, history). He writes on the cultural history and aesthetics of architecture and his particular interest has been the picturesque and its relation to modern architecture, urbanism and visual culture. A recent publication is John Macarthur and Naomi Stead 'Introduction: architecture and aesthetics', in Crysler, Cairns & Heynen (eds) *The Sage Handbook of Architectural Theory,* London: Sage, 2012.

ANDREW MACKENZIE is a director at URO media, an architecture publishing company, as well as a director at the architectural consultancy CityLab. For nine years he was Editor-In-Chief of *Architectural Review Australia* and *(Inside) Australia Design Review* and it now a contributing editor to *Architecture Australia.* He has worked across the fields of architecture, art and design for over 20 years as an editor, curator, writer, documentary maker and artist.

KATARINA WADSTEIN MACLEOD is a Stockholm-based freelance art critic and lecturer in art history at Södertörn University, Stockholm. She is currently working on a monograph on the home in 20th century Scandinavian Art, and is researching identity and gender in cultural heritage. Recent publications include articles on identity, femininity and space such as 'Hanna Hirsch Pauli's Friends – A disrupted perspective'. Her PhD on representations of girls in art, *Lena Cronqvist: Reflections of Girls* was published in 2006.

SHANNON MCGRATH is a Melbourne-based architectural photographer. Over the past 12 years she has travelled Australia extensively, photographing for Australia's top architects and designers and contributing to a number of books and publications both locally and internationally. Shannon describes her role: 'My job is to capture the dynamics of a space and to translate the essence of the architect's vision into two dimensional images. My work is based on a dialogue with the architect/interior designer that informs me about the conceptual framework behind the design and the important features of the project.'

PAUL OWEN is a director of the Brisbane architectural practice Owen and Vokes, a small practice undertaking private house commissions, furniture design, specialised commercial work and institutional commissions. The practice seeks appropriateness rather than novelty with each work taking the form of a subtle innovation incrementally building upon a lineage of works. Ideas are generated from sustained observation of the field of practice, appropriate exemplars, and human occupation.

DIANNE PEACOCK is a Melbourne-based architect and artist with an interest in spatial mystery. Her architectural practice, Subplot operates alongside projects in collage, video, installation and zine making. Dianne is a PhD candidate in architecture and design by project at RMIT.

DEBORAH VAN DER PLAAT is a Research Fellow with the Architectural Theory Criticism History research group ATCH at the University of Queensland. Her published research considers ideas on art, the imagination, climate, place and modernity in19th century British and Australian architectural theory and practice. With Paul Walker she is the current editor of *Fabrications*, the journal of the Society of Architectural Historians of Australia and New Zealand.

VIRGINIA RIGNEY has been a curator at Gold Coast City Gallery since 2003. She studied at The ANU and University of Sydney and since 1985 has worked in curatorial roles in the following institutions – The Powerhouse Museum, The Art Gallery of NSW, The Victoria and Albert Museum and Glasgow Museums. She was appointed chair of the curatorial Panel for art+place the Queensland Fund for Public Art administered by Arts Queensland 2007–2010 and reappointed to the panel for 2011.

SUSAN ROTHNIE has completed degrees in art history and visual arts. She works freelance as an arts writer and is currently undertaking her PhD at the University of Queensland, looking at Australian art in the 1970s.

GEORGINA RUSSELL completed a Bachelor of Architectural Design at the University of Queensland in 2010. Through studying and working within research at the School of Architecture, she has developed a strong interest in exploring ideas of architecture and place through theoretical and historical writing and literature, and she looks forward to pursuing this in her Master of Architecture and beyond.

JAN VAN SCHAIK is a director of Minifie van Schaik Architects whose urban, architectural, interior and academic work has been awarded, published and exhibited both locally and internationally. He is a lecturer and PHD candidate at RMIT University and the chair of the Melbourne City Council Creative Spaces Working Group.

ARI SELIGMANN is currently program coordinator overseeing the new architecture program at Monash University, Melbourne. He is also directing innovative history and theory units and the burgeoning design research PhD program. He is a critic and designer engaged in studies of contemporary architecture and urbanism, Japanese architecture, and relations between architecture and media.

CATHY SMITH is a registered architect (Qld), an interior designer and a lecturer in architecture at the University of Queensland, where she teaches design studio and technology. Her current research focus is on developing a theorisation of artisanal, DIY architecture, with reference to DIY in post-war North America to the present.

DIANNA SNAPE is a freelance commercial photographer specialising in architecture, interior and landscape photography. She is an Honours graduate of Melbourne's RMIT BA (Photography) Course and assisted world-renowned architectural photographer John Gollings before establishing her own freelance photography practice in2001. Dianna's works features regularly in leading architectural and design magazines both nationally and internationally. She was voted in the top 10 Architectural Photographers in 'Australia's Top Photographers' competition in 2009 and 2010. Dianna is based in St Kilda, Melbourne.

NAOMI STEAD is a Research Fellow in the ATCH (Architecture | Theory | Criticism | History) Centre at the University of Queensland. She holds a PhD from the University of Queensland and a Bachelor of Architecture from the University of South Australia. Her research interests lie within the cultural studies of architecture, including architectural criticism, and in 2010 she convened the conference and workshop *Writing Architecture: Innovations in the Textual and Visual Critique of Buildings,* which is the subject of this book. Naomi is widely published in Australia as an art and architectural critic, writing for a range of professional journals. She is co-editor of the journal *Architectural Theory Review.* In 2008 she won the Adrian Ashton Prize for architectural writing.

ANDREW P. STEEN focuses on observation and process. He applies film, literature and cultural theory onto the field of architecture. Steen completed his MPhil thesis *Re Made in Tokyo* in 2011, and is currently working on a PhD at the University of Queensland with the working title *Umberto Eco, Semiotics, Architecture, Interpretation.*

MARCUS TRIMBLE is a director of Bennett and Trimble. He runs the blog *Super Colossal,* started the Sydney Pecha Kucha night, teaches design at University of New South Wales and writes for a number of architecture magazines and journals.

DANICA VAN DE VELDE is a doctoral candidate in English and Cultural Studies at The University of Western Australia where she is completing a thesis on select films by Wong Kar-wai. Her areas of specialisation are film studies and visual culture, with a specific focus on the intersections of urban space, architecture, memory and desire. She can be contacted on vanded02@student.uwa.edu.au

LINDA MARIE WALKER is a senior lecturer in the Art Architecture School of the University of South Australia, teaching both undergraduate and postgraduate students. She is a writer, artist and curator. Her research concerns writing as a non-instrumental and improvisational medium that informs and affects on different scales and registers of sense and situation. Her writing is published in academic journals and artist catalogues. Linda Marie Walker was one of the leaders of the workshop *Writing Architecture: On Innovations in the Textual and Visual Critique of Buildings,* upon which this book is based.

PAUL WALKER is Professor of Architecture at the University of Melbourne. He teaches architectural history, theory and design. Walker has published on New Zealand architectural history, contemporary architecture in Australia and New Zealand, and on museum architecture in colonial and post-colonial contexts.

ISABEL D'AVILA WINTER is a Portuguese-Australian writer. Her 2008 novel *Dona Stella and Her Rivals* won two literary prizes in Portugal, where it was translated and published. Isabel lives in Brisbane and is currently working on a novel about a nineteenth-century Portuguese-Australian artist.

ACKNOWLEDGEMENTS

The series of events of which this book is the culmination have involved many people, all of whom deserve thanks. First I would like to thank the participants in the workshop and conference, which lie at the origins of this book, for their time, effort and commitment to a public discussion about architecture and the built environment in Queensland and elsewhere. Thanks also to conference keynote speakers, Katja Grillner, Gavin Hipkins and John Birmingham, whose work has contributed immeasurably to the project and to this book. Thanks also to Linda Marie Walker, Peter Bennetts and Katja Grillner again, for their roles in leading the workshop. I have been blessed with magnificent assistants throughout the life of this project, including Angela Hirst, Andrew Steen, Clair Keleher, Charles Rowe, Sam Charles-Ginn, Cheri Cunningham and Erin Lewis, and I thank them all. For the book in particular, I owe a debt of gratitude to publisher Andrew Mackenzie, designer Rita Reuter, and sub-editor Lisa Starkey, who have all done a magnificent job and with whom it has been a pleasure to work.

This book, and the conference and workshop that preceded it, were all made possible by financial assistance from the Queensland Government through Arts Queensland, and I am delighted to acknowledge this vital support. Assistance was also received from the School of Architecture at the University of Queensland, and I would like to particularly thank the head of school, Professor John Macarthur, and my colleagues in the ATCH Research Centre for their support. This book has received financial assistance from the Faculty of Architecture, Building and Planning at The University of Melbourne, and I thank Professor Philip Goad and Professor Paul Walker for orchestrating this.

The larger project has also been supported by a number of other institutional partners, including ArchitectureMedia, publisher of Architecture Australia, and I especially thank former editor Justine Clark for offering unfailingly good advice and excellent ideas throughout. The Institute of Modern Art has been another stalwart institutional partner, and I warmly thank director Robert Leonard for his support throughout the project. Other institutional partners had roles at various times throughout the longer project: the Creative Industries Unit of the Queensland Government via HEAT; the University of Queensland Art Museum (thanks to Gillian Ridsdale); The Queensland Chapter of the Australian Institute of Architects, and the Queensland Writers Centre (thanks to Julie Beveridge). A warm thanks is due to the two venues for the conference: Queensland Art Gallery Gallery of Modern Art (particularly Margot Robins and Mark Whittaker) and the State Library of Queensland (particularly Susan Kuckuka and Jes Wawrzynski).

Thanks to Annie Hogan for allowing us to use her photograph 'Inward 2006', from the series Seen and Not Heard, for the book cover. This series was commissioned by the Ipswich Art Gallery, and thanks are also due to director Michael Beckmann for permission to use the image. Peter Bennetts was present at both the workshop and the conference, and documented these events in photographs, which appear throughout this book – warmest thanks to him for allowing their use.

This volume is dedicated to Belinda and Tristan Daw.

COLOPHON

Many of the contributions to this book were developed from papers first presented at the conference 'Writing Architecture: A symposium on innovations in the textual and visual critique of buildings', held on Thursday 22 and Friday 23 July 2010 at the Queensland Art Gallery's Gallery of Modern Art, and the State Library of Queensland. Other contributions were presented or developed during a workshop held at The University of Queensland School of Architecture on 19 and 20 July, 2010. All contributions were refereed by the editorial committee at abstract and full paper stage.

ISBN 978-0-9872281-3-0

Published by Uro Media, Melbourne, 2012

Editorial Committee: Dr Naomi Stead, Dr Angela Hirst, Professor John Macarthur

Cover image: Annie Hogan, *Inward 2006*, from the series *Seen and Not Heard,* a commission for the Ipswich Art Gallery. Courtesy of the artist and Michael Beckmann, director, Ipswich Art Gallery.

Katja Grillner's 'A Performative Mode of Writing Place: Out and about the Rosenlund Park, Stockholm, 2008–2010', was originally published in Mona Livholts (ed), *Emergent Writing Methodologies in Feminist Studies,* London: Routledge, 2011, republished with permission and thanks to the editor and to Routledge.

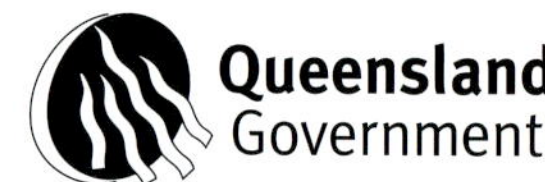

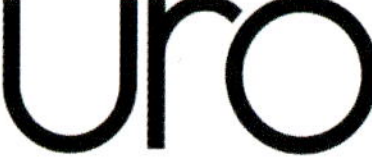

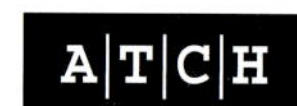 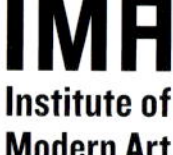 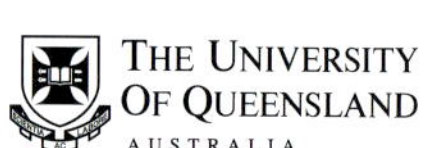 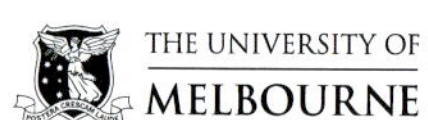

Edited by Naomi Stead
Sub-edited by Lisa Starkey
Designed by Rita Reuter

This project has received financial assistance from the Queensland Government through Arts Queensland. It has also received financial and other assistance from the ATCH (Architecture, Theory, Criticism, History) Research Centre in the School of Architecture at the University of Queensland; the Faculty of Architecture, Building and Planning at the University of Melbourne; and The Institute of Modern Art.